WHO'S WHO IN CANADIAN SPORT

2551

$15-

D1511662

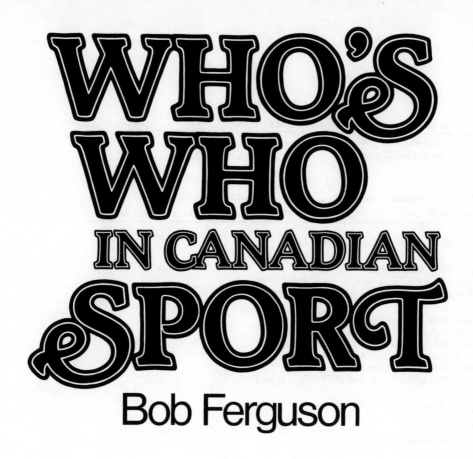

Bob Ferguson

PRENTICE-HALL OF CANADA, LTD. SCARBOROUGH, ONTARIO

Canadian Cataloguing in Publication Data

Ferguson, Bob, 1931-
  Who's who in Canadian sport

Includes index.
ISBN 0-13-958421-8

1. Athletes — Canada — Biography. 2. Sports — Canada — Biography. I. Title.

GV697.A1F47   796'.092'2   C77-001420-8

© 1977 by Prentice-Hall of Canada, Ltd.

ALL RIGHTS RESERVED
No part of this book may be reproduced in any form
without permission in writing from the publishers.

Prentice-Hall, Inc., Englewood Cliffs, New Jersey
Prentice-Hall International, Inc., London
Prentice-Hall of Australia, Pty., Ltd., Sydney
Prentice-Hall of India Pvt., Ltd., New Delhi
Prentice-Hall of Japan, Inc., Tokyo
Prentice-Hall of Southeast Asia (PTE.) Ltd., Singapore

ISBN 0-13-958421-8

Design: Julian Cleva

Printed and bound in Canada

To Scott and Shane
Sons of whom any father would be proud
And Lee
A strong motivating influence

Acknowledgements

Bob Ackles *B.C. Lions*
Ray Alviano *Kitchener-Waterloo Record*
Ron Andrews *National Hockey League*
Len Back *Hamilton Tiger-Cats*
David Berger *Montreal Alouettes*
Miau Betlem *Canadian Table Tennis, Fencing Associations*
Jim Bishop *Canadian Lacrosse Association*
Sheila Bresalier *Canadian Amateur Swimming Association*
Aggie Brockman *Stratford Beacon-Herald*
Tom Casey *Ottawa Citizen*
Martin Cleary *Ottawa Citizen*
Fred Collins *Winnipeg Tribune, Calgary Herald*
Larry Condon *MP Middlesex-London-Lambton*
Paul Condon *U of Waterloo*
Graham Cox *Canadian Press Ottawa*
Guy D'Avignon *Information Canada*
Joan Decarie *CTFA*
Claude Deschamps *Canadian Amateur Softball Association*
Harry Eisen *London Free Press*
Bob Elliott *Ottawa Journal*
Claire Ferguson
Scott Ferguson
Shane Ferguson
Dave Folinsbee *Canadian Badminton Association*
Jack Fulton *Lacrosse Hall of Fame*
Bob Gage *London Free Press*
Doug Gilbert *Montreal Gazette*
Tom Gorman *Connaught Park*
Gord Hammond *Canadian Lacrosse Association*
Doug Hardie *Ottawa Citizen*
Geordie Hilton *RCGA*
John Hurdis *Canadian Speedskating Association*
Peggy King
Jack Koffman *Montreal Sunday Express*
Garth Lee
Tracey Lee
Don Lovegrove *Hamilton Spectator*
Gus MacFarlane *MP Hamilton Mountain*
Ian MacLaine *Canadian Press Toronto*
Brian Mainman *Saskatoon Star-Phoenix*

David Marshall
Leona Marshall
John McConachie *CIAU*
Carol Meek *Canadian Archery Association*
Bob Mellor *Ottawa Citizen*
Hal Middlesworth *Detroit Tigers*
Rollie Miles *Edmonton Eskimos*
Doug Milton *Ottawa Citizen*
Herbert Morell *Senior Intercounty Baseball League*
Earle Morris *Canadian Forces Sports Hall of Fame*
Don Morrison *Charlottetown Guardian-Patriot*
Marv Moss *Montreal Gazette, Golf Digest*
Ken Murray *COA*
John Nooney *Ontario Gymnastics Association*
Stan Obodiak *Toronto Maple Leafs*
Doug Peden *Victoria Times*
Gordon Perry *Canadian Football Hall of Fame*
Frank Polnazek *World Hockey Association*
Lefty Reid *Hockey Hall of Fame*
Dan Shaw *OAFA, Argos Alumni Association*
Jane Shortts *Canadian Ski Association*
Whit Tucker
Ken Twigg *CTFA*
Walter Valentan *BPAO*
Bruce Walker *Ontario Jockey Club*
Gord Walker *Canadian Football League*
Peter Webster *B.C. Sports Hall of Fame*
Kathy Whitty *N.B. Sports Hall of Fame*
Jack Woodward *Winnipeg Blue Bomber Alumni Association*
Dave Zink *CPGA*

National Archives
Ottawa Public Library
Sport Canada
Sport Ontario
Saskatchewan Sports Hall of Fame
Curl Canada
Canadian Sports Hall of Fame
National Sports Administration Centre and all national sports bodies
    therein
Canadian Boxing Hall of Fame

Introduction

During the quarter-century in which I have been involved in chronicling the exploits of Canada's athletes, I have lamented the lack of readily available and accurate information.

This Who's Who is an attempt to fill the gap, but do not expect to find everyone listed who gained laurels in every field of sports activity. Information on some athletes has been impossible to trace, and requests for information from some of those we were able to locate has not always been answered.

Over 1,300 athletes and sports figures, amateur and professional, living and dead, are included. They were selected on the basis of their achievements on the national sports scene. Canadian citizenship has not been a prerequisite.

It is my hope that you, the reader, will submit names and addresses and additional information, in care of the publisher, for inclusion in future editions.

This volume can never be definitive. It is, however, a beginning.

Bob Ferguson

ABBRUZZI, Pat (football); *b*. 29 Aug 1932, Providence, R.I.; *given name:* Pasquale; *m*. Philomena Andreozzi; *children:* Diane, Debra, Michael, Mary, Julie, Jane; Warren HS, Marianapolis Prep, U of Rhode Island, B.S.; phys ed teacher, football coach, restaurateur; all-State honors 1948-49 Warren HS; all-prep Marianapolis 1950; all-Yankee Conference 1951-54; little all-American 1952, 1954; all-New England 1952-54; competed 1954 North-South Shrine Game; turned pro Montreal Alouettes 1955, all-pro 1955-58; established CFL record for TDs single season with 20, 1956; gained 201yds vs Toronto at Montreal 1955; carried 182 times for 1,248yds, 17 TDs 1955; 207 times for 1,062yds, 17 TDs 1956; second only to Gerry James (18 TDs), for TDs rushing single CFL season with 17 twice; led EFC scorers 120 points 1956; traded to Calgary for Veryl Switzer 1958 but retired; 10 all-time R.I., New England records including 306yds single game 1952; 99yd TD run 1951; four-year college rushing record 3,389yds ranks among best; since 1961 Warren HS football coach; won seven titles; team holds State record 32 consecutive victories; pres. Rhode Island Football

Coaches Association 1972-73; R.I. athlete of year 1954; R.I. Italian athlete of year 1953-54; Canadian Schenley outstanding player 1955; R.I. coach of year 1975; mem. U of R.I. Hall of Fame; *res*. Warren, R.I.

ABEL, Sid (hockey); *b*. 22 Feb 1918, Melville, Sask; *given name:* Sidney Gerald; *m*. Gloria Moranday; *children:* Gerry, Linda; Melville HS; retired hockey executive; amateur hockey to Flin Flon Bombers, Manitoba senior league; began NHL career 1938 Detroit Red Wings; nine full seasons with Detroit; team captain at 24; centred Production Line of Gordie Howe and Ted Lindsay; in 13 seasons played 612 regular season games, scored 189 goals, 283 assists for 472 points, 376 penalty minutes; in 97 playoff games scored 28 goals, 30 assists for 58 points, 79 penalty minutes; player-coach Chicago Black Hawks 1952-54 retiring as player 1954; rejoined Red Wings as coach replacing Jimmy Skinner midway through 1957-58 campaign; general manager 1962; coached St. Louis Blues 1971, general manager part way through season through 1972-1973; became general manager of Kansas City Scouts April 1973; in 15 seasons as coach involved in 960 games, won 382, lost 423, tied 155; teams made playoffs in nine seasons involving 76 games, 32 wins, 44 losses but no championships; played on three Stanley Cup winners; Hart Trophy (MVP) 1949; mem. Hockey, Canadian Sports Halls of Fame; *res*. Detroit, Mich.

ABENDSCHAN, Jack (football); *b*. 1943, New Mexico; *m*. Virginia; *children:* two daughters, one son; U of New Mexico; personnel director; college reputation as offensive guard, defensive linebacker, place kicker; honorable mention various all-American teams; turned pro as offensive guard, placement specialist Saskatchewan Rough-riders 1965, played 10 years; kicked 312 converts, 159 field goals, 74 singles for 863 career points 1965-75; sat out 1974 campaign with knee injury; quit Riders 1968 for trial with Denver Broncos (AFL) but when cut rejoined Riders; seven times WFC all-star, five times all-Canadian; *res.* New Mexico.

ACKLES, Bob (football); *b.* 16 Sep 1938, Sarnia, Ont; *given name:* Robert William; *m.* Kay; *children:* Steve, Scott; King Edward HS, Vancouver; general manager B.C. Lions; played for junior Blue Bombers; joined B.C. Lions at inception 1954; served as water boy, equipment manager, director of player personnel, assistant general manager, club historian to general manager 1975; *res.* Vancouver, B.C.

ADAIR, Colin (squash); *b.* 4 Nov 1942, Montreal; *given name:* Colin John; *m.* Margot Jean Lafleur; *children:* Jacquelin, Gregor, Dylan; McGill, B.A.; investment banker; since 1960 has won over 100 major tournaments in Canada and U S; only Canadian to win U S singles title twice, 1968, 1971; twice Canadian singles champion; only Canadian to win U S doubles, 1974; four times Canadian doubles champion; McGill athlete of year 1964; *res.* Montreal, Que.

ADAMS, Dick (football); *b.* 13 Feb 1948, Athens, Ohio; *given name:* Richard Earl; *div.; children:* Timothy Eugene, Anthony William; Athens HS, Northeastern Oklahoma A&M, Miami of Ohio, B.S.; football player, coach; played high school football, basketball, baseball, all-Southeastern Ohio League football honors 1963-66, all-Southern Ohio baseball 1966; with Miami U all-Mid-American Conference 1969-70; best

defensive back two years, MVP two years; UPI all-American second team 1969-70; athlete of year 1970; Mid-American Conference defensive player of year 1970; at one time held 14 Miami school records; Ottawa Rough Riders 1972, defensive halfback, punter; four years EFC, all-Canadian; led EFC in punt returns with 92 for 608yds 1974; mem. 1973 Grey Cup winners; turned to coaching 1976 Carleton U, assistant to Bryan Kealey; *res.* Ottawa, Ont.

ADAMS, Harry (curling); *b.* 7 Dec 1932, D'Arcy, Sask.; *m.* Shirley Goodwin; *children:* Ken, Connie, Debbie, Lisa; D'Arcy HS; owns, operates several businesses; established reputation in mixed curling winning Salls Trophy, Canadian Branch Lady Gilmour competition; represented Division Two OCA in provincial mixed playdowns three times, won title twice; winner Branch Governor-General's once; OCA Silver Tankard 1977; finalist OCA Intermediates; represented Division One Ontario Consols 1975, 1976, Ontario mixed 1976; mem. Carleton Heights, Navy, Lansdowne Curling Clubs; *res.* Ottawa, Ont.

ADAMS, Jack (hockey); *b.* 14 Jun 1895, Ft. William, Ont., *d.* 1 May, 1968, Detroit, Mich.; *given name:* John James; *m.* Helen; Ft. William HS; hockey executive; Ft. William amateur ranks to Peterborough, Sarnia; turned pro as centre Toronto Arenas 1918; Vancouver for three seasons, Pacific Coast League scoring title 1920 with 24 goals, 18 assists in 24 games; Toronto St. Pats 1922-26; Ottawa Senators 1926-27 Stanley Cup winning season; Detroit Red Wings' manager 1927; 18 years as manager and/or coach winning 12 league titles, seven in succession, seven Stanley Cups; coached first and second NHL all-star teams once each;

innovator of hockey farm system; Central Pro League pres. from 1962; mem. Hockey Hall of Fame.

ADAMS, Robert (track and field); *b.* 20 Dec 1924, Alsask, Sask.; *m.* Marjorie Pascoe; *children:* Janice, Murray; U of Saskatchewan, B.A., B.Ed.; supervisor of HS phys ed; represented Canada in decathlon 1952 Helsinki Olympics; fourth pole vault, 12th high jump 1954 British Empire Games Vancouver; captain Canadian track team 1954; awarded Fred Rowell Trophy by AAU of C as outstanding Canadian field event athlete 1954; set Canadian senior native discus record 1949 with 148′ 10″; Canadian senior native decathlon record of 6,636 points in 1952 Olympic trials; coach Canadian T&F team Cardiff Commonwealth Games 1958, Tokyo Olympics 1964, Trinidad Games 1968; coach five years Royal Canadian Legion coaching clinic Guelph; head judge pole vaulting 1976 Montreal Olympics; holds level five T&F official rating; over 30 years of T&F involvement as competitor, administrator, official earned him Centennial medal 1967; mem. Saskatchewan Sports Hall of Fame; *res.* Saskatoon, Sask..

ADELMAN, Louis (football); *b.* 13 Jan 1905, Devil's Lake, N.D.; *m.* Molly Rosenblat; *children:* David, Howard, Robert, Sheila; St. John's HS, Winnipeg; retired; HS football to Tammany Tigers (forerunner Blue Bombers); played centre 1924-38; in four Grey Cup finals, won once; captained 1935 team which brought West first Grey Cup; manager Winnipeg club from retirement through 1945; *res.* Desert Hot Springs, Calif.

AGER, Barry (basketball); *b.* 29 Jan 1938, London, Ont.; *given name:* Barry Laurence; *m.* Catherine Mutsch; *children:* David, Robert, Carolyn; Medway HS, U Western Ontario, B.A., McMaster U, B.P.E., Ithaca College, M.S., HS v.-principal; London and District all-star 1956; helped Western Colts win 1957 junior Intercollegiate title; with UWO Mustangs 1958; joined London Lounge intermediate A team 1959, helped Tillsonburg Livingstons win Canadian senior A title, represented Canada Rome Olympics; with McMaster 1961 senior Intercollegiate all-star; with Ottawa Joe Feller's senior A team 1962, ACT basketballer of year nomination; with Ottawa senior A Lapointes 1963, Bert Marshall Trophy; coached Ridgemont Spartans to Ottawa HS, Ottawa Valley championships 1969; *res.* Ottawa, Ont.

AHEARN, Frank (hockey); *b.* 10 May 1886, Ottawa, Ont., *d.* 17 Nov. 1962, Ottawa, Ont.; promoter of junior, senior hockey; bought Ottawa Senators from Tommy Gorman 1924 and assembled powerful team which included Jack Adams, George Boucher, Alex Connell, Hec Kilrea, Frank Nighbor, Syd Howe and Hooley Smith; won 1927 Stanley Cup; depression years forced him to sell his arena and star players in series of deals considered spectacular at time; mem. Hockey Hall of Fame.

AITCHISON, Gordon (basketball); *b.* 1909, North Bay, Ont.; *m.* Melba Malott; *children:* Andy, Peggy; Windsor CI, U of Detroit, Assumption College, B.A., U of Toronto; retired HS principal; set Canadian Interscholastic pole vault mark in Montreal; played basketball U of D, Windsor Alumni, Canadian finals several times; while at Assumption mem. Canadian senior basketball finalists 1934; with Windsor Fords won 1935 Eastern, Canadian senior men's basketball title and right to represent Canada in 1936 Olympics; mem. Olympic silver medal team; played at U of T 1938 while attending OCE; coached, played with Portage La Prairie Man. while serving as RCAF phys ed officer; coached football, basketball, T&F, in charge of cadet corps Cornwall 1945; *res.* Windsor, Ont.

ALBERT, Herb (archery); *b.* 17 Jan 1905, Germany; *m.* Marjorie Docherty; *children:* Edward, Sonja, Elizabeth, Sandra; retired machine tool manufacturer, engraver; emigrated to Canada as youngster, developed early interest in archery; first official competition 1914, a distance event (flight shooting); won with homemade bow and arrows; best long distance shooter in modern flight archery in Canada; since 1950 held all Canadian flight records, including standard for 50 lb light bow of 613yds; high altitude shooting in California produced higher standard, 702yds, but not considered Canadian record; during heyday also held British Empire flight archery records; helped form Canadian Archery Association 1951; past pres. FCA, mem. AAU of C Hall of Fame; *res.* Clearbrook, B.C.

ALDRIDGE, Dick (football); *b.* 19 Jan 1941, Toronto, Ont.; *given name:* Richard Frederick; *m.* Elisabeth von Haastrecht; *children:* Joni Elisabeth, Richard Todd; Runnymede CI, U of Waterloo, B.A., B.P.H.E.; HS teacher, football coach; played with OFSAA basketball champions 1959-60, MVP Lakeshore Bears junior ORFU 1962; at Waterloo, MVP twice in football, once in basketball, outstanding athlete 1966; since 1966 Dick Aldridge trophy presented annually to Waterloo football MVP; drafted 1964 by B.C. Lions then traded to Hamilton for

Bob Apps, Toronto for Jim Leo; star linebacker with Argos 1965-73; concluded CFL career with Hamilton 1974; led Argos in punts returned 1965, in interceptions with seven 1970; career record CFL 19 interceptions in 127 regular season games; head coach York U 1976; *res.* Tottenham, Ont.

ALLAN, Maurice (weightlifting); *b.* 17 Apr 1927, Montreal, Que.; *m.* Pierrette Laroche; *children:* Michel, Lucie, Jean; Laval U, B.A.; program-marketing manager Air Canada; became involved in weight training, weightlifting 1942; operator of Gymnase Hercule; 1950 won Quebec shot put, hammer throw; coached weightlifting 1950-68, several trainees represented Canada in international competition; pres. Canadian Weightlifting Federation 1960-70; category 1 international weightlifting referee; coached 1964 Olympic weightlifters; pres. British Commonwealth WL Federation 1966-74; manager WL Jamaican Commonwealth Games team 1966; technical advisor first Canadian Winter Games Quebec 1967, WL Winnipeg Pan-Am Games 1967, first Canada Summer Games Halifax 1969; Chef de Mission Mexico Little Olympics 1967; assistant Chef de Mission 1968 Mexico Olympics; bureau mem. International Weightlifting Federation 1968-72; since 1968 v.-pres. COA; since 1972 v.-pres. International Weightlifting Federation; since 1970 honorary life pres. Canadian Weightlifting Federation; pres. AAU of C 1970-71; v.-pres. Canadian Amateur Sports Federation 1970-71; Chef de Mission 1972 Munich, 1976 Montreal Olympics; director Mission Quebec 1974-76; 1967 Centennial medal; gold medal for 25 years in weightlifting; 1969 Foley Award sport administrator of year; 1967 Air Canada Merit award; mem. AAU of C Hall of Fame; *res.* Dorval, Que.

ALLETSON, Kim (figure skating); *b.* 30 Jun 1953, Brockville, Ont.; *given name:* Patricia Kim; Saint Pius X HS; student; mem. Minto Skating Club; test record: gold figures, senior silver, dance; won 1968 Eastern Ontario (EO) pre-juvenile, 1969 EO juvenile, 1970 EO novice; third 1971 EO junior; second 1972 Canadian novice; 1973 won EO junior, second Canadian junior, third Grand Prix International St. Gervais France; 1974 won EO junior, Canadian junior, sixth Nebelhorn Trophy Oberstdorf Germany, fourth St. Gervais Grand Prix, fifth Richmond Trophy Middlesex England; 1975 won EO seniors, second Canadian seniors, seventh Skate Canada, 12th world; 1976 14th Innsbruck Olympics, second Canadian seniors, 12th world, won Skate Canada; 1977 third Canadian seniors; *res.* Ottawa, Ont.

ALLISON, Ian (basketball); *b.* 26 Jul 1909, Greenock, Scotland; *given name:* Ian Alaistair; *m.* Jean Reid; *children:* Heather, Jane; Walkerville CI, Assumption College, UWO, OCE; retired Walkerville CI athletic director; five years with WOSSA soccer champions, four years senior HS basketball winning four WOSSA, Ontario titles, Eastern Canadian championship 1928; held WOSSA 440 track championship in HS; all-conference halfback as Assumption footballer; played with Assumption Ontario basketball champions; while at OCE played ORFU football with St. Michael's, Intercollegiate basketball titlists with U of T; played basketball with Windsor Alumni, Ford V8s winning Canadian senior title; mem. Canadian silver medal basketball team 1936 Berlin Olympics; coached Ontario basketball titlists, WOSSA track, volleyball champions, football at Walkerville CI; Windsor Coaches Association award for outstanding contribution to HS athletics; Alpha Kai Omega fraternity award for service in junior sport; National Basketball Association of Coaches award for outstanding contribution to basketball in Canada; city of Windsor award for outstanding contribution to HS athletics; *res.* Kingsville, Ont.

AMUNDRUD, Gail (swimming); *b.* 6 Apr 1957, Toronto, Ont.; Hillcrest HS, Sentinel HS,; began competitive swimming Ottawa Kingfish 1967; Vancouver Dolphins under Deryk Snelling 1974; 100m national age-group (11-12) backstroke title 1970; first Canadian record, :54.0 in 100yd freestyle (FS) Cincinnati AAU championship 1973; first Canadian girl to swim 100m FS under one minute (:59.8) 1973 world championships Belgrade Yugoslavia; two gold, silver, bronze Commonwealth Games Christchurch N.Z. 1974; two gold, two silver, bronze 1974 Ontario senior finals; bronze AAU finals Dallas Tex. 1974, set Canadian record 100yd FS (:52.04); represented Canada numerous internationals including 1975 Pan-Am Games Mexico, won two silvers, bronze 1976 Olympics; seven firsts Canadian Nationals 1976; Canadian records: 100yd FS (:51.74), 200yd FS (1:51.49), 500yd FS (4:57.98), 100m FS (:58.1 short course), 100m FS (:58.6 long course), 200m FS (2:04.63 long course), 800m FS (8:26.0), 400m FS relay (3:52.98), 200m medley relay (1:59.16); *res.* Vancouver, B.C.

AMYOT, Frank (canoeing); *b.* 14 Sep 1904, Toronto, Ont., *d.* 21 Nov 1962, Ottawa, Ont.; *m.* Mary Kelly; Ottawa HS; civil servant; one of six children of Dr. John Amyot, Canada's first deputy minister of health and pensions; Canadian Canoe Association intermediate singles 1923; six Canadian senior singles, one double-blade title;

captained, managed, coached Canadian canoe team entry in 1936 Berlin Olympics; only Canadian ever to win gold medal in 1000m Canadian singles setting 5:32.1 record; instrumental in saving three lives, including footballer Dave Sprague, in boating mishap; mem. Canadian Sports Hall of Fame.

ANAKIN, Doug (bobsledding); *b.* 6 Nov 1930, Chatham, Ont.; *given name:* Douglas Thomas; *m.* Mary Jean; *children:* Megan, Bridget; Queen's U, B.A., OCE; teacher; Intercollegiate wrestling, skiing, mountaineering; selected by Vic Emery for number two spot on 1964 Olympic bobsled, gold medal Innsbruck; same role 1965 Lake Placid, North American title; *res.* Beaconsfield, Que.

ANDERSEN, Dale (boxing); *b.* 21 May 1953, Yellowknife, N.W.T.; *given name:* Dale Irwin; *m.* Gail Adele; HS graduate; power saw operator; mem. Rocky Legion boxing club under coach Alex Bogusky; Canadian featherweight title three times; mem. Canadian team 1971 Pan-Am Games Cali Colombia, 1971 Scandinavian tour, 1972 Munich Olympics, 1974 Commonwealth Games Christchurch N.Z.; Golden Gloves champion of Alberta four times, B.C. once; bronze medal 1974 Commonwealth Games; silver medal Sixth Tournament of Europeans East Berlin 1973; three times North American championships silver medalist; boxer of year award 1974; runner-up male athlete of year 1974; several provincial achievement awards; *res.* Rocky Mountain House, Alta.

ANDERSON, Don (curling, golf); *b.* 14 Apr 1910, St. Thomas, Ont.; *given name:* Donald Hume; *m.* Mary Morley; *children:*

Katie, Robert, Betsy; U of Toronto, B.Comm.; merchant; captain U of T golf team; St. Thomas Golf and Country Club champion; St. Thomas Early Bird tournament winner; governor, team captain Canadian Seniors Golf Association; in curling won OCA Governor-General's trophy 1961; pres. Ontario Curling Association 1970; *res.* St. Thomas, Ont.

ANDERSON, Gabby (baseball); *b.* 29 Nov 1929, Detroit, Mich.; *given name:* Stanley Robert; *m.* Lorella Talbot; *children:* Jeffrey, Richard, Lisa; H.B. Beal THS; inspector automobile quality control; pro ball in Pony League, 1950 rookie of year with .335 avg. Peoria Ill.; class D with Olean N.Y. 1954-55, hit .355 in 1954; quit pro ball and returned to London 1955 joining London Majors briefly; rejoined Majors in Great Lakes-Niagara League 1957 winning batting title with .403 avg., MVP; returned to Ontario Senior Intercounty League with London Majors 1958; tied for second in batting with .398; followed with second place .420 avg. 1959 and took 1960 title with .391, MVP 1959; twice led league in doubles, once each in home runs, runs batted in; lifetime avg. (12 seasons) .339; managed Majors 1963; v.-pres. Eager Beaver Baseball League (Little League) 1965-66, pres. 1967-68; helped launch Tyke Division (9-10 year olds) 1968; since 1973 minor hockey coach in tyke division for East London Optimists; *res.* London, Ont.

ANDERSON, George (soccer); *b.* 23 Jun 1890, Fraserburgh, Aberdeenshire, Scotland; retired compositor; organized, managed Caledonia junior, juvenile, midget teams; executive Manitoba junior soccer association 10 years, four years secretary-treasurer; executive Manitoba senior soccer association

1936-39; secretary-treasurer Manitoba senior football association prominent in organizing competitions in Manitoba, Saskatchewan; involved in reactivation Dominion Football Association 1946, secretary from 1951-56, secretary-treasurer, tour manager from 1956-68; key figure in first World Cup entry by Canadian team 1957; organized Canadian team tour of Europe 1960; delegate CFA to 1961 Federation Internationale de Football Associations, 100th anniversary FA of England, 1966 World Congress; key role Canadian entry Olympic soccer 1968; organizer, business manager Expo 67 soccer tournament; active in Pan-Am tournament Winnipeg 1967; secretary-treasurer Rockwood unit 303 Army, Navy, Air Force Veterans minor soccer program; mem. Canadian Sports Hall of Fame; *res.* Winnipeg, Man.

ANDERSON, Les (archery); *b.* 31 May 1940, Wells, B.C.; *given name:* Leslie Ernest; *m.* Lorraine Marie DeLong; senior electrical technical assistant; won first of eight Saskatchewan provincial archery championships April 1971; three Alberta provincial titles; winner 16 invitational tournaments; second field events 1973 Canadian championships; winner 1974 FCA Mail match classified, third overall; winner field events 1973 Championships of Americas Orlando Fla., second overall; sixth target competition 1974 San Juan Puerto Rico; third field events Yugoslavia world championships 1974; competed 1975 Western Canada Summer Games; B card athlete under Game Plan 1976; certificate of recognition for outstanding achievement amateur sport from Western Christian College Weyburn Sask. 1976; *res.* North Battleford, Sask.

ANDERSON, Verne (skiing); *b.* 1937, Rossland, B.C.; *given name:* Verne Ralph; *m.* Ardis; *children:* two daughters; ski clothing sales representative; won Junior Western Canadian downhill 1953; Canadian downhill 1958-59; represented Canada 1960 Squaw Valley Olympics placing ninth combined; top Canadian male competitor 1961 European, North American circuits; hampered by injuries competing 1962 FIS championships Chamonix France; coach Canadian men's national team 1962-64, including Innsbruck Olympics; helped coach Nancy Greene; women's national team coach 1966-68, including Grenoble Olympics; *res.* Boulder, Colo.

ANDREOTTI, Jim (football); *b.* 27 Mar 1938, Chicago, Ill., *given name:* James Peter; *m.* Joan Wray; Northwestern U; stockbroker; co-captain Northwestern in junior year, all-American linebacker; pro 1960 with Toronto Argos; to Alouettes 1963 for Billy Shipp, Doug McNichol; returned to Argos 1967 with Ed Learn for Al Ecuyer; sat out 1968 season under suspension for failure to report to Argos; four times EFC all-star, twice all-Canadian; during 1976 Olympics worked with COJO as liaison officer with U S Olympic team; *res.* Montreal, Que.

ANDREWS, Porky (basketball); *b.* 18 Sep 1917, Victoria, B.C.; *given name:* George Lloyd; *m.* Marion; *children:* Wayne Murray, Janet Louise, Scott Alexander; Victoria HS, U of Oregon, B.Sc.; teacher; three times Victoria HS track champion; holder of Canadian high hurdle record; played B.C. rugby, fastball, lacrosse championship teams; held Royal Colwood Golf Club championship; two decades as one of Canada's top basketballers; mem. two national championship teams 1935, 1946; player-coach Victoria

Dominoes; pro Vancouver Hornets and Alberni Athletics, a team he started 1949; captain U of Oregon team two years, all-Coast guard, all-American; coach Victoria Hudson Bay senior A women's team two years, Victoria HS boys to three provincial titles, Victoria HS girls to one provincial title; mem. Sports Hall of Fame; *res.* Victoria, B.C.

ANDRU, John (fencing); *b.* 20 Nov 1933, Toronto, Ont.; U of Toronto; executive director Canadian Fencing Association; best overall competitive record by any native born fencer in Canada; nine times national champion, twice team champion; medalist 32 times; eight times Eastern Ontario, 11 times Ontario champion; represented Canada 1964, 1968 Olympics, four times in Pan-Am Games winning three medals; four times in Commonwealth Games winning six medals; manager, team captain 1968 Olympic, 1970 Commonwealth, 1971 Pan-Am Games, world youth teams; Chef de Mission 1972 world youth team; international director, judge 1972, 1976 Olympics; coach Caribbean tour 1965; first Canadian qualified as class A pres. of jury by Frederation Internationale d'Escrime; six years mem., director AAU of C Central Ontario Branch; Canadian Fencing Association pres. 1967-73, technical, executive director since 1973; director Canadian Olympic Association 1967-72, AAU of C 1967-71; v.-pres. Commonwealth Fencing Federation 1970-74; Centennial medal 1967; Norton Crowe AAU of C medal 1969; three Ontario Achievement Awards; six times Don Collinge OFA award; mem. AAU of C Hall of Fame; *res.* Ottawa, Ont.

APPS, Syl Sr. (hockey); *b.* 18 Jan 1915, Paris, Ont.; *given name:* Charles Joseph Sylvanus; *m.* Mary Josephine Marshall; *children:* Joanne, Robert, Carol, Sylvanus Jr., Janet; McMaster U, B.A.; brick manufacturer, politician; national recognition as pole vaulter winning Canadian and 1934 British Empire Games titles; sixth 1936 Olympics; captained McMaster to Intercollegiate football title; played junior hockey Hamilton Tigers; joined Toronto Maple Leafs 1936-37 season as centre; led NHL in assists that year and 1937-38; Calder Cup as rookie of year; CP poll Canadian male athlete of year 1937; centred line of Busher Jackson, Gordie Drillon, later Drillon, Bob Davidson; retired from hockey as team captain following 1947-48 season with 10-year record of 201 goals, 231 assists for 432 points and only 56 penalty minutes; in eight playoff seasons scored 25 goals, 28 assists for 53 points and six penalty minutes; Lady Byng trophy 1941-42 with no penalty minutes; played on three Stanley Cup winners; Ontario athletic commissioner 1946-48; MLA Ontario for Kingston and the Islands (PC) since 1963. Minister Correctional Services 1971-74; mem. Hockey, Canadian Sports, Canadian Amateur Sports Halls of Fame. *res.* Kingston, Toronto, Ont.

APSIMON, John (fencing); *b.* 5 Aug 1935, England; *sep.* Claire Manning; *children:* Joanne, Paul, Michele; U of Liverpool, B.Sc., Ph.D.; professor of chemistry; captain U of Liverpool fencing team 1957-59; national (U.K.) universities champion 1958; second Liverpool Open foils 1959, fourth 1958; North Western Section champion 1958; emigrated to Canada where ranked as class A fencer in foil, sabre, épée 1960-72; four times winner McFarland three-weapon trophy, runner-up twice, third twice; winner Governor-General's épée 1969, finalist several times; mem. RA Les Spadassins winning two team gold, one silver, one bronze in épée, two silver, four bronze in foil, five silver, two bronze in sabre; Ontario foil champion 1971; winner 1971 Ontario Winter Games foil, second sabre, fifth épée; captain winning Ontario team 1971 Canada Winter Games; won gold individual, team foil, silver team, seventh individual épée 1971 Canada Winter Games; coached fencing since 1960 with Ottawa RA Les Spadassins, Carleton University; Ontario senior amateur coach; guided Carleton to Intercollegiate titles 1967-68; coach individual OUAA champions 1967-69, 1974; FIE class B director in three weapons; Don Collinge Trophy 1971 Ontario Fencing Association; v.-pres. Canadian FA 1968-73, pres. 1973-76; manager 1972 Munich Olympic fencing team, 1974 junior world title teams, 1975 Ontario team Canada Winter Games; 1976 judge Montreal Olympics; *res.* Ottawa, Ont.

ARBOUR, Al (hockey); *b.* 1 Nov 1932, Sudbury, Ont.; *given name:* Alger; *m.* Claire Sabourin; Sudbury HS, Assumption College; hockey coach; Holy Trinity bantams, midgets, Sacred Heart juveniles as forward; sought by Toronto, Detroit scouts, signed with latter and played junior B Windsor Hettches then A with Spitfires as defenceman; joined Edmonton 1952 where he sparked Flyers to league title; joined Detroit 1956; claimed in interleague draft by Chicago 1958, Toronto 1961-66; stint in Rochester (AHL); picked by St. Louis in expansion draft 1967; coach 1970 but after 50 games returned to playing; through 1972 played intermittently, St. Louis assistant general manager and coach and Atlanta Flames scout; NY Islanders coach 1973; during 19 playing seasons never missed playoffs; in 12 NHL campaigns played 626 regular season games, scored 12 goals, 58 assists for 70 points, 617 penalty minutes; 86 playoff games, one goal, eight assists, nine points, 92

penalty minutes; seven seasons as coach (to 1976-77) produced 183 wins, 148 losses, 94 ties in 425 games; four times led team to playoffs; *res.* Long Island, N.Y.

ARMSTRONG, Brian (track); *b.* 9 Sep 1948, Toronto, Ont.; *given name:* Brian Joseph; U of Toronto, B.A., LL.B.; lawyer; since 1969 represented Canada in international cross-country, marathon races; second Canadian marathon, Olympic trials 1972; winner Detroit Motor City, Western Hemisphere (Los Angeles) marathons in 2:18.46 and 2:18.54 respectively 1972; third in 2:13.30 Maxol marathon Manchester Eng. 1973; second 1973 Canadian marathon St. John's Nfld. in 2:13.39; runner-up Fukuoka Japan marathon 1973 in 2:13.43; third in world among marathon runners 1973 by *Track & Field News;* represented Canada 1974 Commonwealth Games Christchurch N.Z.; second Canadian championships 1974 at Waterloo in 2:18.06; *res.* Toronto, Ont.

ARMSTRONG, George (hockey); *b.* 6 Jul 1930, Skead, Ont.; *given name:* George Edward; *m.* Betty Shannon; *children:* Brian, Betty Ann, Fred, Lorne; Sudbury HS; hockey coach; played Toronto Marlboros juniors and seniors, with latter club won Allan Cup; nicknamed Chief; two-game trial with Toronto Maple Leafs 1949-50; played 20 games with them 1951-52, playing interim with Pittsburgh (AHL), before joining Leafs as regular 1952-53; Leafs' captain after Ted Kennedy's retirement, remained as centre through 1970-71 season; played 1,187 regular season games scoring 296 goals, 417 assists for 713 points; in 110 playoff games scored 26 goals, 34 assists for 60 points; played in seven all-star games; following retirement coached Toronto Marlboro juniors winning two Memorial Cups; mem. Hockey Hall of Fame; *res.* Toronto, Ont.

ARMSTRONG, Ken (diving); *b.* 12 Oct. 1953, Ingersoll, Ont.; Ingersoll DHS, student; coached by Marnie Tatham of Woodstock Diving Club, Don Webb at Pointe Claire; silver medal 1m, gold 3m 1973 Canadian winter championships; silver 3m 1974 summer championships; silver 3m 1974 CSSR championships; represented Canada 1973, 1975 Yugoslavia world, 1974 Commonwealth, 1976 Olympics; competed internationally as mem. Canadian diving team since 1973; *res.* Pointe Claire, Que.

ARNOLD, Don (rowing); *b.* 1935, Kelowna, B.C.; *given name:* Donald John; *m.* Gwendolyn Mary Amor; *children:* Malcolm, Graham, Andrew; Rutland HS, UBC, Diploma agriculture, B.P.E., San Francisco State, M.Sc., Indiana U; professor; specialist in four-oared crew with or without coxswain, eight-oared crews and 2000m course; 1955 Pacific Coast sprint title, junior varsity eight-oared crew title; gold medal 1956 four-oared UBC crew without cox Canadian Olympic trials St. Catharines Ont. as stroke; set unofficial world record of 6:05.8 on 2000m course; 1956 gold medal Melbourne Olympics, four-oared UBC crew without coxswain in 6:36.6—.6 off Olympic record; stroke for gold medal UBC eight-oared crew with coxswain Canadian rowing trials St. Catharines 1958; same year won gold eight-oared with cox, silver four-oared with cox Commonwealth Games Cardiff Wales, Grand Challenge Trophy Bedford Regatta four-oared with cox; gold medal eight-oared with cox Canadian rowing championships St. Catharines 1960; silver as fourth eight-oared with cox Rome Olympics; Robert Gaul Memorial Trophy UBC outstanding graduating student 1962; B.C. Sports Federation citation 1976; Ontario Achievement Award 1974; runner-up 1958 Hector Mac-Donald Memorial Award B.C. athlete of year; mem. AAU of C, B.C. Sports, Canadian Sports Halls of Fame; *res.* Vancouver, B.C.

ARUSOO, Toomas (swimming); *b.* 22 Jul 1948, Sweden; *m.* Angela Coughlan; U of Michigan; civil engineer; head coach, manager Oakville Aquatic Club; mem. Canadian swimming team 1965-71; represented Canada Commonwealth Games 1966, 1970, Pan-Am Games 1967, 1971, Olympics 1968; silver medal (second to Mark Spitz of U S) 200m butterfly 1967 Pan-Am Games; 11th 100m, 200m butterfly 1968 Olympics; gold medal 200m, silver 100m butterfly 1970 Commonwealth Games; coach national team English tour, 1975 Pan-Am Games Mexico; *res.* Acton, Ont.

ATHANS, George Jr. (water-skiing); *b.* 6 Jul 1952, Kelowna, B.C.; *m.* Claire Sicotte; *children:* Shawn; Sir George Williams U, B.A., Nikon School of Photography, Concordia U; age 11 mem. Canadian water-ski team competing in first world championship age 13; Canadian senior champion 1965-74, Western Hemisphere 1968, 1970; California World Cup 1970, 1972; Australian masters 1972; U S masters 1974; Tahitian World Cup 1971; Swedish Lida Cup 1974; world championship 1971, 1973; with father George Sr., a former diving standout, holds distinction of being only father-son in AAU of C Hall of Fame; above avg. alpine skier declined 1969 invitation to join Canadian national team; competes on Canadian pro ski tour during winter; B.C. athlete of year 1971; Canadian amateur athlete of year 1972-73; Quebec athlete of year 1973; mem. Order of Canada 1974; mem. Canadian Sports Hall of Fame; *res.* Montreal, Que.

ATHANS, George Sr. (diving); *b.* 4 Jan 1921, Vancouver, B.C.; *given name:* George Demetrie; *m.* Irene Hartzell; *children:* George, Greg, Gary; U of Washington, B.A., McGill, M.D.; physician; won first of 10 Canadian championships and berth on Canadian Olympic team 1936; Pacific Coast diving title 1940-44; British Empire Games title New Zealand 1950; bronze medal 1938 British Empire Games; seventh place 1948 Olympic Games; diving coach 1954 British Empire Games, 1960 Olympics; with son George Jr., mem. AAU of C, B.C., Canadian Aquatic Halls of Fame; *res.* Kelowna, B.C.

ATHANS, Greg (water-skiing, skiing); *b.* 18 Jun 1955; U British Columbia; student; equally proficient on snow or water skis; following in footsteps of prominent athletic family; only Canadian athlete to win gold medals in both summer and winter Canada Games (1971 Winter Games slalom, 1973 Summer Games water-skiing tricks); Canadian water-ski title 1975-76; mem. Canadian water-ski team 1973, 1975 world tournaments; world freestyle alpine pro ski champion 1976, led pro freestyle alpine ski money winners 1976-77; *res.* Kelowna, B.C.

ATHWAL, Nimi (table tennis); *b.* 5 Jul 1960, India; *given name:* Nimrat Kaur; HS student; considered one of Canada's brightest table tennis prospects; under-13 Canadian title 1974, third Canadian junior finals; 10th singles Mapoel Games Israel, second women's doubles 1975; second place team event Canada Winter Games 1975; *res.* Comox, B.C.

AVERY, Frank (curling); *b.* 25 Feb 1902, Austin, Man.; *m.* Freda (*d.*); *children:* Brian; retired; Vancouver's Mr. Curler through work in pioneering and promoting game on B.C. coast; B.C. provincial title 1935; third on first B.C. Brier entry 1936, third two, skip one other Brier; 1943 B.C. title; represented B.C. Canadian senior men's championships 1966-67; hon. mem. Canadian Curling Reporters, life mem. Vancouver Curling Club, Pacific Coast Curling Association, mem. Canadian Curling, B.C. Sports Halls of Fame; *res.* Vancouver, B.C.

AVERY, Jeff (football); *b.* 28 Mar 1953, Ottawa, Ont.; *given name:* Jeffrey Clarke; Woodroffe HS, U of Ottawa, B.A.; in four seasons with U of O amassed 1,973yds on 110 pass receptions (avg. 17.9yds-per-catch) and 15 TDs; three times OUAA all-star, twice all-Canadian; Frank Tindall Award, MVP 1975 Central Bowl; three times U of O's most valuable receiver, once leadership award winner; played on 1975 Yates Cup (OUAA title), Vanier Cup (Canadian College Bowl) champions; placed on Ottawa Rough Rider protected list 1976; turned pro with Riders 1976 helping win Grey Cup; *res.* Ottawa, Ont.

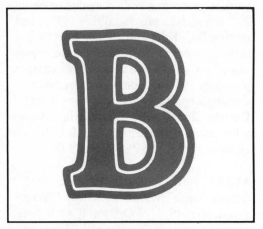

BABBITT, Ethel (tennis); *b.* 13 Jul 1876, Fredericton, N.B., *d.* 20 Aug 1969, Fredericton, N.B.; *given name:* Ethel Mary Hatt; *m.* Harold Babbitt; *children:* Isobel, John David; standout tennis player 1908-27; 14 N.B. championships, three Maritime titles in ladies' singles, mixed doubles; national honors 1910; mem. N.B. Sports Hall of Fame.

BABBITT, John (tennis); *b.* 2 Feb. 1908, Fredericton, N.B.; *given name:* John David; *m.* Dorothy Elizabeth Rooney; *children:* David, Robert, Susan, Cynthia, James, Andrew (*d.*); Fredericton HS, U of New Brunswick, Oxford U; retired NRC physicist; like mother Ethel and sister Isobel, prominent tennis star in Maritimes; N.B. singles titles 1928-29; Maritime championship 1929; Oxford on Rhodes Scholarship, starred in tennis, hockey, English rugger; mem. UNB English rugger team, captain four years; twice on winning McTier Trophy team; *res.* Ottawa, Ont.

BACK, Len (football); *b.* 21 Jul 1900, Hamilton, Ont.; *given name:* Leonard Percival; *m.* Lillian (*d.*); *children:* Beverley; *m.* Grace; Central HS; football executive; played two seasons with Hamilton Tigers juniors 1918-19 before skull fracture ended playing days; team manager 1920; manager Hamilton Tigers intermediates 1921-26; manager Tiger senior ORFU team 1928-40; joined Brian Timmis as manager Hamilton Wildcats, won 1943 Grey Cup; rejoined Tigers following WW2, on hand when Tigers and Wildcats combined; manager Ticats since 1950; honored by Grey Cup dinner committee 1961, City of Hamilton, Ticats football club; mem. Canadian Football Hall of Fame; *res.* Port Dover, Ont.

BACKSTROM, Ralph (hockey); *b.* 18 Sep 1937, Kirkland Lake, Ont.; *given name:* Ralph Gerald; *m.* Fran; *children:* three; minor hockey ranks to Hull-Ottawa Junior Canadiens; in 81 games 1956-57 scored 54 goals, 43 assists for 97 points, 1957-58 with 45 goals, 53 assists for 98 points; captained Junior Canadiens to Memorial Cup; in 28 junior playoff games scored 34 goals, 22 assists; pro with Montreal Canadiens 1958-59; Calder Trophy NHL rookie of year with 18 goals, 40 assists for 58 points; centre with Canadiens 12 seasons; traded to Los Angeles Kings for Gord Labrossiere, Ray Fortin 1971, to Chicago Black Hawks for Dan Maloney 1973; WHA with Chicago Cougars 1973-75, Denver Spurs 1976, New England Whalers 1977; WHA most sportsmanlike player 1974; most popular Cougar award 1973-74; WHA all-star centre once; starred with Team Canada 1974 in losing series vs USSR; in 15 NHL campaigns played 1032 games scoring 278 goals, 361 assists for 639 points, 386 penalty minutes, plus 116 playoff games, 27 goals, 32 assists for 59 points, 68 penalty minutes; WHA record through 1976-77, 304 games, 100 goals, 153 assists, 253 points, 104 penalty minutes; *res.* Connecticut.

BAILEY, By (football); *b.* 12 Oct 1930, Omaha, Neb.; *given name:* Byron *m.* Diana Churchill; *children:* Laura, Lynn; Washington State U, B.Ed.; marketing manager; Seattle HS halfback; all-Pacific Coast honors as WSU running back; Detroit Lions 1952, NFL championship team; to Green Bay Packers 1953 as right halfback; charter mem. B.C. Lions 1954 scoring first TD ever by a Lion and first TD ever by Lion in winning cause; all-Canadian halfback 1957, MVP, WIFU all-star team; first Lion honored by 'night' 1960; mem. B.C. Lions Grey Cup champions 1964, executive mem., trustee, B.C. Sports Hall of Fame, mem. Canadian Football Hall of Fame; *res.* North Vancouver, B.C.

BAILEY, Dave (track); *b.* 17 Mar 1945, Toronto, Ont.; *given name:* David George; *m.* Barbara Gillespie; *children:* Karen Joanne; Northview Heights CI, U of Toronto, B.Sc., M.Sc., Ph.D.; scientific advisor provincial prescription drug plan, university lecturer; joined East York Track Club under Fred Foot, began training 1961; 1962 ran 4:07.5 mile, world record for 17-year-old; vibration fractures halted training; resumed running 1963 and year later back to 4:07 mile; toured Europe with EYTC; by summer 1965 time down to 4:02; 11 June 1966 became first Canadian to crack four-minute mile with 3:59.1 at San Diego; disillusioned with track as man in middle of Bill Crothers-Lloyd Percival pep pill hassle; during mile qualifying round at 1966 Jamaica Empire Games fell with 50m to go; mile in 3:57.7 Toronto Police Games 1967; third Pan-Am Games Winnipeg; won California relays; second World Student Games; fourth pre-Olympic finals; disappointing 1968 Olympic 1500m performance ended career; third California relays 1970 comeback bid; bad reac-

tion to drugs administered after sustaining foot injury again shelved him; trained well in 1972, planned to compete for Olympics but broke ankle and quit T&F, interest in coaching rekindled with 1976 Olympics; *res.* Saskatoon, Sask.

BAILEY, Marjorie (track); *b.* 21 Nov 1947, Lockeport, N.S.; *given name:* Marjorie Evalena; *sep.; children:* Anthony Bobby George; Lockeport HS, Manitoba Institute of Technology; practical nurse; sprint specialist competed internationally for Canada since 1964; competed Commonwealth Games 1966, 1974 placing sixth 100m, fourth 200m 1974; bronze medal 100m (11.42), 4x100m relay, fourth 200m (23.32) 1975 Pan-Am Games; fourth 4x100m relay 1976 Montreal Olympics; Canadian record 200m with 23.13 1974, bettered mark to 23.06 placing fifth 1976 Olympics semifinal; *res.* Vancouver, B.C.

BAIN, Dan (all-around); *b.* 1874, Belleville, Ont., *d.* 15 Aug 1962, Winnipeg, Man.; *given name:* Donald Henderson; wholesale merchant; excelled in hockey, cycling, gymnastics, figure skating, roller skating, golf, trap and skeet shooting; first athletic medal, Manitoba three-mile roller skating title, at 13; last athletic medal figure skating at 56; starred for Winnipeg hockey team winning nine of 11 matches vs East 1893; captain Winnipeg Victorias Stanley Cup champions 1896; retired from top-flight hockey 1901 after team won Stanley Cup; Canadian trapshooting title Toronto 1903; enjoyed wildfowl shooting, owned shoreline of Grant's Lake, one of best geese lakes in Manitoba flyway, turned property over to Ducks Unlimited; at 70 gave skate waltzing exhibitions with partners half century his junior; mem. Canadian Hockey, Sports Halls of Fame.

BAKER, Joann (swimming); *b.* 24 Nov 1960, Moose Jaw, Sask.; *given name:* Joann Elaine; Sir Winston Churchill HS; student; silver medals 200m breast stroke, 400m relay Mexico Pan-Am Games 1975; three gold, two silver East Berlin age-group meet; sixth Cali Colombia world championships; Canadian, Commonwealth Records 100, 200m breast stroke; represented Canada 1976 Olympics; 1976 three seconds, four thirds Canadian Nationals; toured Japan 1976; Paris meet 1977; Manitoba senior champion 1977; *res.* Thunder Bay, Ont.

BAKER, Norm (basketball); *b.* 17 Feb 1923, Victoria, B.C.; *m.* Nancy; *children:* Norman Jr.; Nanaimo HS; retired policeman; began basketball at 10 with Nanaimo Mosquitos; at 15 played with Nanaimo junior finalists; at 16 became regular with Victoria Dominoes Canadian senior champions 1939-40, 1942; on RCAF 1943 Canadian championship team; set scoring record 38 points in one game; began pro career Chicago Stags of newly-formed Basketball Association of America; returned to Vancouver Hornets dominating scoring two years setting record 1,862 points for 70-game schedule; Portland for 1948 pro playoffs; first player to have written pact with Abe Saperstein; toured Europe, North Africa with Stars of World team 1950; played one pro season with Boston; mem. New Westminster Adanacs Mann Cup lacrosse champions 1947; played Victoria Shamrocks through 1954, coached that team 1959-60 before retiring from sport; mild stroke 1971 curtailed activities; CP poll Canadian basketballer of half century 1950; mem. B.C., Canadian Sports Halls of Fame; *res.* Victoria, B.C.

BALDING, Al (golf); *b.* 29 Apr 1924, Toronto, Ont.; *m.* Moreen; *children:* Allan Jr., Erin; golf pro; turned pro 1949 as starter Toronto Oakdale; assistant Burlington Chinery 1950; assistant Islington 1951-53; head pro 1954-57 Credit Valley, Erindale, Markland Woods 1963-66; first tourney win Quebec Open 1952; joined U S pro tour same year; first Canadian to win U S pro tour with 1955 Mayfair Inn Open; 1957 won Miami Beach Open, West Palm Beach Open, Havana Invitational, 1963 Mexican Open; four times CPGA titlist, four times runner-up; four times Millar Trophy winner, CPGA match champion; twice low Canadian pro in Canadian Open, once tied George Knudson; with Knudson won 1968 World Cup team matches in Rome Italy, Balding took low individual honors; Ontario athlete of year 1955, 1957; recurring back ailment curtailed competitive efforts 1975-76; eighth USPGA Seniors 1977; *res.* Toronto, Ont.

BALDWIN, Matt (curling); *b.* 3 May 1926, Blucher, Sask.; *given name:* Mathew Martyn; *m.* Betty Jean Hamilton; *children:* Susan, Sally, Leslie; U of Alta., B.Sc.; retired petroleum engineer; eight times Northern Alberta champion; five times Alberta titlist; three times Canadian Brier champion; winner 1954 Edmonton carspiel; winner numerous major bonspiels; winner Keen Ice singles curling television series seven of 10 years; director Edmonton Eskimos Football Club five years, club pres.; mem. Edmonton Sports, Canadian Sports, Canadian Curling Halls of Fame; *res.* Edmonton, Alta.

BALDWIN, Ralph (harness racing); *b.* 25 Feb 1916, Lloydminster, Sask.; *m.* Jeannette; Lloydminster HS; harness race driver, trainer; apprenticed with father, becoming second trainer for him, later for Harry Fitzpatrick before opening own public stables; began racing in 30s shifting to U S tracks 1946 after serving in U S army; recorded more than 1,100 winners with purses totalling more than $5 million; major victories include two Hambletonians (Speedy Scott 1963, Flirth 1973), five Kentucky Futurities, two Dexter Cups, three American-National four-year-old trots, two Yonkers Futurities, two Westbury Futurities, two Realization Trots, Messenger Stakes; head trainer Castleton Farms Lexington Ky. 1960-69; following year's absence returned to racing as head trainer, sometimes driver, Arden Homestead Stables Goshen N.Y.; mem. Canadian Sports, USTA Living Halls of Fame; *res.* Goshen, N.Y. (summer), Pompano Park, Fla. (winter).

BALES, John (canoeing); *b.* 6 Jul 1950, Lachine, Que.; Brookfield HS, McMaster, B.A., B.P.E.; sports consultant, Sport Canada; Canadian juvenile boys' singles canoe champion 1967; head coach Rideau Canoe Club Ottawa 1970-76, Canadian club title 1973; Canadian Canoe Association national team coach 1973 world, junior European championships, 1974-75 world championships, 1976 Olympics; *res.* Ottawa, Ont.

BALL, James (track); *b.* 7 May 1903, Dauphin, Man.; *m.* Violet Laird Parker; *children:* Jacqueline Allan; U of Manitoba; pharmacist; HS, college track teams winning Manitoba, Western Canadian Intercollegiate titles; 1927 won Canadian quarter-miler title, anchored winning mile relay team; 1928 Olympic trials won 400m in record 48.6 breaking 49.4 standard he had set in a heat one hour earlier; silver medal with 48 seconds Amsterdam Olympics, team bronze mile relay; won Glasgow quarter-mile, Dublin relay, set Irish 200m mark breaking

standard set 20 years earlier by Hamilton's Bobby Kerr; mem. Canadian relay team which beat best U S runners in Melrose Games Madison Square Gardens 1932; qualified for 1932 Olympics winning relay bronze; painful carbuncle slowed him in 400m semifinal and he finished last; Norton Crowe Trophy (AAU of C) 1933; mem. Canadian Sports Hall of Fame; *res.* Victoria, B.C.

BALLANTINE, Bonny (bowling); *b.* 10 Feb 1929, Regina, Sask.; *given name:* Bonny Bonnell; *m.* William Ballantine; *children:* Drew, Grey, Dawne, Jaye, Brad; Scott CI; secretary; began bowling career as five-pinner; mixed championship team 1955; Western Canadian team championship 1961; moved into 10-pin winning Regina mixed doubles; competed on women's championship team 1963, 1965; city, provincial women's doubles titles 1964, 1965, 1966; Regina Sask., Canadian O'Keefe Open singles titles 1966; certified AMF 10-pin bowling instructor, began working with youth leagues 1967; won Regina scratch singles, all-events, ladies' team 1968, city, provincial, national open singles 1969; represented Canada Puerto Rico world championships 1969; won city, provincial all-events, city, provincial open singles, bowling in nationals 1971; Regina Lakeshore Lions sportswoman of year 1966; mem. Saskatchewan Sports Hall of Fame; *res.* Regina Beach, Sask.

BAPTIE, Norval (speedskating); *b.* 1879, Bethany, Ont., *d.* 1966, Baltimore, Md.; *m.* Gladys Lamb; showman; at 14 became North Dakota speed champion, two years later defeated Winnipeg's Jack McCulloch for world title; shattered all speed records and as amateur and pro remained in competition over 25 years winning close to 5,000 races at distances from 220 yds to five miles; turned to stunt and figure skating, setting record for barrel jumping, skating backwards, broad jumping, skating on stilts; after WWI launched touring ice shows; directed first shows featuring Sonja Henie; retired from active skating 1939, became first pro coach Washington D.C. Figure Skating Club; diabetes led to amputation of left leg 1954, right leg 1958; continued to coach in Baltimore and Washington; with Miss Henie became first skaters named to U S Ice Skating Hall of Fame; mem. Canadian Sports Hall of Fame.

BARBER, Sara (swimming); *b.* 25 Jan 1941, Brantford, Ont.; *m.* Donald Jenkins; *children:* David, Robert, Margie; McMaster U, B.A., B.H.E.; teacher; mem. Canadian international swim teams 1954-62 competing British Empire Games, Pan-Am Games, Olympics; 1959 world record 100m backstroke; silver medal 1959 Pan-Am Games; silver, bronze medals in relays 1958, 1962 British Empire Games; finalist backstroke, butterfly 1956 Olympics; *res.* Hawkestone, Ont.

BARNES, Rolph (track); *b.* 16 Jun 1904, Hamilton, Ont.; *given name:* William Rolph; *m.* Charlotte Innes (*d.*); *children:* Bill, Rennie, Peter, Bruce; *m.* Marnie Wilmot Holton; *children:* Gerry, Margot; Princeton U; industrialist; represented Canada 1924 Olympics 1500m; Hamilton and District badminton singles, doubles, mixed doubles champion 1932-34; Savanah Club Barbados, Tennis Club title team 1972; *res.* Milton, Ont.

BARRON, Andy (speedskating); *b.* 2 May 1951, Penrith, Eng.; *given name:* Andrew James; Harry Ainley HS, U of Alberta, B.Ed.; began career as figure skater winning novice men's, pairs titles Alberta, juvenile Prairie titles 1960-64; mem. Jasper Place Swim Club 1968-69, competed Canadian championships Pointe Claire, Que., Canadian water polo championships, Quebec City; switched to speedskating, Canadian national team mem. 1971; represented Canada Sapporo Olympics 1972, Innsbruck Olympics 1976; won Canadian 1500m title 1973, men's division Canada-U S meet 1973; runner-up Canadian championships 1975-76; Canadian record holder 3000m, 5000m, 10 000m, also held 1500m mark 1973-74; winner six ISU medals in offical European competitions; Kinsman Salute to Youth Award 1971; *res.* Edmonton, Alta.

BARROW, John (football); *b.* 31 Oct 1935, Delray Beach, Fla.; *m.* Evangeline; *children:* Gregg, Elaine, Kyle; Georgia Military Academy, U of Florida; businessman; began football career as offensive end Georgia Military Academy; U of Florida offensive guard, middle guard, team captain final year; *Look* all-American, Atlanta TD Club Southeastern Conference lineman of year, first team Southeastern Conference AP, UPI, INS all-South first team recognition; third draft choice Detroit Lions (NFL) but chose CFL with Hamilton, in 14 years played in nine Grey Cup finals, four winners; EFC all-star 12 times, all-Canadian 11 times; nominated Schenley lineman of year eight times, won 1962, runner-up five times; lineman of century in CFL 1967; named to Hamilton all-star team of pro era 1950-67; general manager Toronto Argos 1971-75; mem. U of Florida, Canadian Football, Florida State Sports Halls of Fame; *res.* Burlington, Ont.

BARRY, Martin (hockey); *b.* 8 Dec 1904, St. Gabriel, Que., *d.* 20 Aug 1969, Halifax, N.S.; joined N Y Americans 1927, spent two seasons in minors rejoining NHL team 1929; five consecutive 20-goal seasons with Boston Bruins before trade to Detroit 1935; on Stanley Cup winners 1936-37 centring line of Larry Aurie, Herbie Lewis; Lady Byng Trophy 1937, all-star same season; final NHL season 1940 with Montreal Canadiens; NHL career total 195 goals in 12 seasons; became coach following retirement; *mem.* Canadian Hockey Hall of Fame.

BARWELL, Gord (football); *b.* 6 Sep 1944, Saskatoon, Sask.; *given name:* Gordon Keith; *m.* Nancy Phyliss; *children:* Jay, Jody; City Park HS; clothing salesman; national age-group honors HS T&F; one season Saskatoon Hilltops juniors then with Saskatchewan Roughriders in CFL 1964; defensive back, offensive flanker 10 years; in seven Western Conference playoffs, four Grey Cups; on receiving end of 102-yd TD pass from Ron Lancaster at Vancouver 1965; *mem.* Athletes in Action; *res.* Regina, Sask.

BATH, Doc (all-around); *b.* 9 Mar 1889, Bath, Eng.; *given name:* Leonard Harry; *m.* Helen; *children:* Gladys Helen, Valarie Doreen Jean; retired male nurse; participated in hockey, boxing, fastball, baseball, T&F; won Somerset Eng. 440, mile, six-mile, cross-country championships 1908; in British army 1910 claimed Aldershot command six-mile and 1911-13 six-mile North and South India champion, winner several 440, 220, 880 and mile races; emigrated to Canada 1925 where he turned to boxing, baseball, track; after retirement served as trainer Weyburn Beavers fastball team 13 years, also baseball, hockey trainer; coached oldtimers hockey three years; trainer Weyburn Red Wings hockey club 1961-75, Comets, Molson's Weyburn Canadians 1962-75 who won Canadian fastball title 1972; *mem.* Sask. Sports Hall of Fame; *res.* Weyburn, Sask.

BATHGATE, Andy (hockey); *b.* 28 Aug 1932, Winnipeg, Man.; *given name:* Andrew James; *m.* Merle Lewis; *children:* Sandra, Billy; captain junior hockey Guelph Memorial Cup winners 1951-52; turned pro NY Rangers organization 1952-53; minor league Vancouver (WHL), Cleveland (AHL); to Rangers in 1954-55 season, dealt to Toronto Maple Leafs during 1963-64 campaign; to Detroit Red Wings 1965-66, Pittsburgh Penguins 1967-68 for two seasons; played briefly in Switzerland, returned to coach and play briefly with Vancouver Blazers (WHA) 1974; early exponent of slapshot; among first to develop curved banana blade; captained Rangers; helped Leafs win 1964 Stanley Cup; won Hart Trophy 1959; twice first, second team all-star; NHL record 1,069 regular season games, 349 goals, 624 assists for 973 points plus 54 playoff games, 21 goals, 14 assists for 35 points; in eight all-star games scored three goals, three assists; West Side Trophy, Macbeth Trophy, Frank Boucher Trophy; prominent golfer; *res.* Bramalea, Ont.

BATSTONE, Harry (football); *b.* 5 Sep 1899, Hamilton, Ont., *d.* 11 Mar 1972, Kingston, Ont.; Central Tech, Queen's U, M.D.; physician; played football, baseball, hockey in various school, city leagues; age 20 invited to Argos tryout; in same backfield with Lionel Conacher led Argos to 1920 Interprovincial title, lost Grey Cup final to U of T; won Grey Cup 1921; with Pep Leadlay and Red McKelvey helped Queen's win three consecutive Intercollegiate titles, three Grey Cups; Queen's coach on three occasions; captain Argos 1921; *mem.* Canadian Football Hall of Fame.

BAUER, Bobby (hockey); *b.* 16 Feb 1915, Waterloo, Ont., *d.* 16 Sep 1964, Kitchener, Ont.; *given name:* Robert Theodore; *m.* Mar-

Bauer

guerite Bauer; *children:* Bobby, Bradley; St.Michael's College, U of Toronto; junior hockey Kitchener-Waterloo area where as right winger teamed with Woody Dumart, Milt Schmidt to form Sauerkraut line; trio joined Boston Bruins 1936-37 season, as Kraut Line helped Boston finish first four successive seasons, win Stanley Cup twice; coached K-W Dutchmen 1956 Olympics; made final Boston Gardens appearance 1951-52 season scoring goal, assist in special game as Kraut Line honored; among NHL leading scorers three times, four times NHL all-star, three times Lady Byng Trophy; nine-year NHL record 123 goals, 137 assists, 260 points; 11 playoff goals, 8 assists, 19 points.

BAUER, David (hockey); *b.* 2 Nov 1924, Waterloo, Ont.; *given name:* David William; St. Jerome's HS, St. Michael's College, U of Toronto, OCE, Notre Dame U; Basilian priest, teacher; brother Bobby mem. famed Kraut Line; played junior Toronto, Oshawa, Windsor; also played football, junior, senior baseball in K-W region; managed, coached St. Michael's Majors several years, won Memorial Cup; coached UBC hockey team and in 1964 conceived National Team plan which became basic concept for future Canadian international hockey participation evolving into Hockey Canada, of which he is a director; coached Austrian national team 1973 world tournament; since 1970 assisted with Japanese national team development; mem. Canadian Sports Hall of Fame; *res.* Vancouver, B.C.

BAUN, Bobby (hockey); *b.* 9 Sep 1936, Lanigan, Sask.; *m.* Sallie Krohn; *children:* Jeffrey, Gregory, Brian, Michele, Patricia; Scarborough HS; hockey coach; moved through Toronto Maple Leaf chain to Wes-

ton Dukes; played junior with Marlboros on two Memorial Cup winners; pro with Maple Leafs 1956; farmed to Rochester (AHL); returned to Leafs for 11 seasons on defence, on four Stanley Cup champions; picked by California in 1967 expansion draft, dealt to Detroit 1968-69; claimed on waivers by Buffalo 1970, traded to St. Louis then Toronto 1970; past pres. NHL Players' Association; coach Toronto Toros (WHA) 1975; played in 964 scheduled games scoring 37 goals, 187 assists for 224 points, 1,493 penalty minutes, 96 playoff games, three goals, 12 assists for 15 points, 171 penalty minutes; retired following 1972-73 season; *res.* Toronto, Ont.

BEACH, Ormand (football); *b.* 28 Oct 1910, Ponca City, Okla., *d.* 20 Sep 1938 Sarnia, Ont.; *m.* Marguerite Booth; Pawhuska HS, U of Kansas, McGill U; engineer; all-state fullback 1925-28; all-American at Kansas; as freshman described by Dr. James Naismith as 'an outstanding anatomical example of the perfect man'; helped Kansas tie Notre Dame 0-0 to give Jayhawkers first Big Six title, twice team captain; listed by Grantland Rice as one of all-time defensive greats in U S football; as flying wing and defensive linebacker helped Sarnia Imperials win four ORFU titles; three Grey Cup appearances, two winners; all-league, all-Canadian each year he played; Imperial Oil Trophy as ORFU MVP; died in refinery explosion at Sarnia; HS stadium named in his honor; mem. Canadian Football Hall of Fame.

BECK, Gary (autosport); *b.* 21 Jan 1941, Seattle, Wash.; *m.* Pennifer; pro drag racer; raced stock cars 12 years until he joined with Ray Peets of Edmonton and became drag racing success; in his eighth race in top fuel competition won National Hot Rod Association U S Nationals at Indianapolis 1972, 1973; 1974 won unprecedented three NHRA, two AHRA events (Winternationals, Pamona Calif., Springnationals Columbus Ohio, Grandnationals Montreal, Springnationals Spokane Wash., AHRA Nationals Boise Idaho); *Car Craft* top fuel driver of year, *Drag News* driver of year, NHRA world champion, all in 1974; won 1975 NHRA Winston Cup Series meet Cayuga Ont., WCS meet Minneapolis, Canadian Open, Winnipeg, runner-up NHRA Springnationals Englishtown N.J., Grandnationals Montreal; *res.* Edmonton, Alta.

BEDARD, Bob (tennis); *b.* 13 Sep 1931, St. Hyacinthe, Que.; *m.* Anne Stacey; *children:* Mark, Paul, Michael, Peter; Loyola U, B.A., U of Sherbrooke, B.E.; HS v.-principal, teacher; played semipro hockey earning MVP honors Quebec Senior League 1955-56; number one in Canadian tennis 1955-65; represented Canada Davis Cup 1953-61, 1967; Canadian Open champion 1955, 1956, 1958, sharing native record with Dr. Jack Wright; eight times Quebec Open titlist; scored at least one victory over every number one player from France, Sweden, Denmark, India, U S, Mexico, Cuba, Belgium, England, Brazil, Italy 1954-59; silver medal 1959 Pan-Am Games, gold medal 1969 Canada Games; with Don Fontana won Canadian men's doubles three times; with Mariette Laframboise won Canadian mixed title 1959; mem. Canada Fitness Council two years; pres. PQLTA three years, v.-pres. PQLTA three years; v.-pres. CLTA four years, honorary secretary CLTA two years; mem. AAU of C, Loyola College Halls of Fame; *res.* Aurora, Ont.

BEDECKI, Thomas (administrator); *b.* 4 May 1929, Glace Bay, N.S.; *m.* Ann McDonald; *children:* Ginni, Bruce, Dayna,

Clint; St. Ann's HS, St. Francis Xavier U, B.A., Springfield College, Ohio State U, Ph.D.; director National and International liaison Sport Canada; mem. McCurdy Cup rugby team, Allan Cup hockey team, Maritime baseball champions; coached hockey Colorado College (1957 NCAA champions), baseball Colorado, Ohio State; athletic director St. Ann's HS, U of Ottawa phys ed staff, phys ed instructor U of Florida, Ohio State; mem. American Coaches Association, American College of Sport Medicine, Federation of Provincial School Athletics, American and Canadian Association Health, Physical Education and Recreation; represented Sport Canada at numerous conferences and congresses and has attended major international sports events since 1965; played major role in development of Sport Canada policies, procedures, National Fitness Incentive Award program, Administrative Centre for Sport and Recreation, athletic grants-in-aid, Canadian athletes data bank, Canada Games sports exchange programs with USSR, China, Cuba, National Advisory Council; *res.* Kanata, Ont.

BEERS, John (track and field); *b.* 17 Aug 1952, Netherlands; *given name:* John Wiliam; *m.* Angela Elsaesser; U British Columbia, B.C. Institute of Technology; student; began high jumping career 1970 making Canadian national team same year; sixth 1972 Olympics and set Canadian record; bettered that record four times in 1973, best 7'4¼'' at time Canadian, Commonwealth record; fourth 1974 Commonwealth Games; silver medal 1975 Pan-Am Games; *res.* Merritt, B.C.

BEERS, William George (lacrosse); *b.* 5 May 1843, Montreal, *d.* 26 Dec 1900, Montreal, Que.; Phillips School, Lower Canada

College; dentist; prominent in outlining first laws of modern lacrosse and formation National Lacrosse Association 1867; toured British Isles with first Canadian lacrosse team to play in Britain 1876, played before Queen Victoria at Windsor; toured Britain again 1883; prominent in formation Montreal Amateur Athletic Association; wrote several books including *Lacrosse, the National Game of Canada* (1869); founder *Canada Journal of Dental Science* (1868), first dental journal in Canada; mem. Canadian Lacrosse Hall of Fame.

BEGIN, Terry (curling); *b.* 6 Mar 1938, Port Arthur, Ont.; Carleton U, B.Sc.; freelance broadcaster, writer, patent clerk; mem. executive Ottawa Granite, Navy Curling Clubs; winner many HS, university 'spiels; winner various major, minor bonspiels in Ontario, Quebec including Toronto 'spiel, Avonlea Beef-O-Rama, Toronto Royals; twice skipped City of Ottawa grand aggregate champions; three times represented Ottawa area in provincial Consols; mem. organizing committee 1974 Canadian Schoolboy, 1977 Montreal Brier; senior instructor rating, Curl Canada coaches development program instructing at clinics throughout Ontario, Quebec; handled broadcasts, radio and TV, written reports for *Ontario Curling Report* and *Canadian Curling News* since 1970; *res.* Ottawa, Ont.

BEILER, Egon (wrestling); *b.* 27 Mar 1953, Linz, Austria; *given name:* Egon Henry; U of Waterloo; U of Western Ontario, B.Sc., Lakehead U, B.P.H.E.; student; three times OFSAA wrestling champion; four times Canadian champion 136.5 lb division; gold medals Commonwealth Games 1974 New Zealand, Pan-Am Games Mexico 1975, World Cup Toledo 1976; silver 1975 world; bronze 1973 European championships; mem. 1972, 1976 Olympic teams; mem. St. Jerome's HS soccer title team, placed third in Ontario; chosen outstanding wrestler St. Jerome's HS Kitchener three times, U of Waterloo twice; athlete of year awards St. Jerome's 1971, City of Kitchener 1973, U of Waterloo 1974, Lakehead U 1976; *res.* Thunder Bay, Ont.

BELANGER, Frenchy (boxing); *b.* 17 May 1906, Toronto, Ont., *d.* 27 May 1969, Toronto, Ont.; *given name:* Albert; *m.* Ivy; *children:* Gerald, Leilani; pro fighter, waiter; began boxing career at 19 compiling impressive amateur and early pro record 1925-26; beat Newsboy Brown 10 rounds 1927 then Frankie Genaro in 10 to win vacant NBA world flyweight title 1927; defended successfully against Ernie Jarvis 1927, lost to Genaro 1928, lost rematch; two years as Canadian champion losing to Steve Rocco 1928; regained Canadian crown beating Rocco in rematch 1929; lost bid for U S flyweight title to Izzy Schwartz 1929; following 10-round loss to Genaro 1930 retired for one year; fought final pro bout 1932, seventh-round KO by Frankie Wolfram; pro record 62 bouts, winning 13 by KO, 24 by decision, seven draws, losing 15 decisions, one by foul and twice KO'd; nicknames, The Canadian Wolverine, The Canadian Tadpole; stroke 1964 left him paralyzed, speechless but with aid of friend Murphy Blandford spent final years involved with Belanger's Aces softball team; mem. Canadian Boxing, Sports Halls of Fame.

BELIVEAU, Jean (hockey); *b.* 31 Aug 1931, Trois-Rivières, Que.; *m.* Elise Couture; *children:* Hélène; graduating from Quebec Aces, Le Gros Bill joined the Montreal Canadiens 1953-54 until retirement 1971, team captain from 1961; scored 507 regular season goals (all-time record for centre) 79 more in playoffs; 712 regular season assists and record 97 in 162 playoff games; on 10 Stanley Cup winners; including playoffs, played in 1,287 NHL games; six times first team all-star, four times second team; scored 25 or more goals 13 seasons, had 80 game-winning goals, three four-goal games, 18 three-goal games; Art Ross trophy 1956 with career high 47 goals, 41 assists; twice Hart Trophy (MVP) 1956, 1964; Conn Smythe Trophy as playoff MVP 1965; record for consecutive years in playoffs, 16; French speaking athlete of year 1967; collected record 16 assists in 1970-71 playoffs; v.-pres. Canadiens; mem. Hockey Hall of Fame; *res.* Verdun, Que.

BELKIN, Mike (tennis); *b.* 29 Jun 1945, Montreal, Que.; U of Miami; teamed with Ron Seifert to win 1957 Canadian boys-13 doubles; won Canadian boys-15 singles 1959, U S national juniors 1960, U S boys-18 nationals (10th place in U S tennis), Canadian boys-18 singles 1962, U S Interscholastic singles 1963; played for Canada 1967-73 in Davis Cup; quarter-finalist 1968 Australian championships; three times won Canadian men's closed singles; top Canadian 1971 winning Virginia Slims Masters, semifinalist River Oaks Open, Tanglewood Classic; runner-up Florida championships 1972; *res.* Florida.

BELL, Marilyn (swimming); *b.* 19 Nov 1937, Toronto, Ont.; *m.* Joseph DiLascio; *children:* Lisa, Michael, Janet, Jodi; Loretto College School, McGill U, B.A., Rider College, M.A.; coached by Gus Ryder, at 15 was standout in 26-mile Atlantic City marathon swim; greatest achievement in 1954 when she became first person to conquer

Lake Ontario; swam 32 miles from Youngstown N.Y. to Toronto in 20:58; swam English Channel, other bodies of water before retirement; Lou Marsh Trophy 1953, Canadian female athlete of year (Velma Springstead Trophy) 1954, 1955; mem. Canadian Sports, U S Aquatic Halls of Fame; *res.* Willingsboro, N.J.

BELYEA, Arthur (rowing, skating); *b.* 31 Aug 1885, Saint John, N.B., *d.* 6 Jan 1968, Albany, N.Y.; *given name:* Hilton Arthur; provincial, Maritime, national, international awards in sculling and skating; starred as single sculler 1904-27 and as skater 1905-21; winner 35 silver cups and trophies, 33 medals; during 1924 Paris Olympics received special bronze medal from Olympic committee for good sportsmanship in single sculls; mem. N.B. Sports Hall of Fame.

BENEDICT, Clint (hockey); *b.* 1894, Ottawa Ont., *d.* 12 Nov 1976, Ottawa, Ont; *given name:* Clinton Stevenson; *children:* Graham; played with Ottawa Senators (NHA, NHL) 1913-24, Montreal Maroons 1924-30; habit of flopping on ice to block shot forced rule changes to make action legal; played 364 scheduled games, allowed 874 goals, 57 shutouts for 2.37 avg.; in playoffs 49 games, allowing 87 goals, 15 shutouts for 1.78 avg.; forced into retirement at 34 after stopping two bullet-like shots off stick of Howie Morenz, first shot shattered his nose, second injured his larynx; because of first shot, vision was impaired and he became one of first goalers to wear a face mask; mem. Greater Ottawa Sports, Hockey Halls of Fame.

BENNETT, Bruce (football); *b.* 13 Dec 1943, Valdosta, Ga.; *given name:* Lamar; *m.* Starling; *children:* Billy, Bobby, Bradley; U of Florida, B.S.; HS athletic director, football coach; all-American defensive safety U of Florida 1965; Saskatchewan Roughriders 1966-72; all-Canadian 1969, WFC all-star six seasons; recorded 35 interceptions during seven-year CFL career for 606 yds returned; longest single interception return 112yds vs Calgary at Regina 1972; played in four Grey Cup finals, one winner; *res.* Waycross, Ga.

BENSON, Lorne (football) *b.* 16 Sep 1930, Riverton, Man.; *m.* Betty Lane; *children:* Sherry, Bonnie, Lori, Robert, Linda; Daniel McIntyre HS; pipefitter B.C. railroad; nickname Boom Boom; Winnipeg minor football to Blue Bombers 1952 winning WFC Canadian rookie of year, Dr. Beattie Martin Trophy; CFL record six TDs single game 1953, later matched by clubmate Bob McNamara (since TDs were valued at five points, is one of four sharing second spot to McNamara for points in a game with 30), all six TDs were gained rushing, another CFL record; played hockey defence Winnipeg Maroons 1954-55, lacrosse 1947-48; Manitoba 100lb boxing title 1941; right-handed pitcher Calgary Purity 99ers, Grandview Maroons, two games Vancouver Mounties of PCL; with Winnipeg juniors pitched three successive no-hitters; played for Winnipeg Buffalos, Mandak League and Molson Canadians in winning 1967 Canadian title; as hockey coach guided Churchill Man. team to 28 straight victories, team won 35 of 38 games winning Northern Manitoba intermediate title; reached provincial playdowns in curling and was on rink which scored eight-ender in provincial Consols; *res.* Squamish, B.C.

BENTLEY, Doug (hockey); *b.* 3 Sep 1916, Delisle, Sask., *d.* 24 Nov 1972, Saskatoon, Sask.; *given name:* Douglas Wagner; *m.*

Betty Clark; *children:* Douglas Jr., Elaine, Patsy, Evelyn; Delisle HS; wheat farmer; one of four Bentley brothers dominating Prairie hockey 1938 at Drumheller, Alta., before Doug joined NHL 1939 with Chicago Black Hawks remaining there through 1953; retired after one season with NY Rangers; in 13 NHL campaigns played 566 games scoring 219 goals, 324 assists for 543 points and 217 penalty minutes; in 23 playoff games scored nine goals, eight assists for 17 points and eight penalty minutes; with Hawks played on Pony Line with brother Max and Bill Mosienko; NHL scoring title, Art Ross Trophy 1942-43; three times NHL all-star but never on Stanley Cup winner; played last minor pro hockey season 1961-62; *mem.* Hockey Hall of Fame.

BENTLEY, Max (hockey); *b.* 1 Mar 1920, Delisle, Sask.; *given name:* Maxwell Herbert Lloyd; *m.* Betty Miller; *children:* Lynn, Gary; Delisle HS; wheat farmer; began NHL career 1940 with Chicago Black Hawks; with brother Doug, Bill Mosienko formed Pony Line; nicknamed The Dipsy-Doodle Dandy for stickhandling ability; traded 1948 to Toronto Maple Leafs for five players; played on three Stanley Cup winners; concluded NHL career 1954 with NY Rangers; brief comeback with Saskatoon but finally retired 1956; in 12 NHL seasons appeared in 646 regular season games scoring 245 goals, 299 assists, 544 points, 179 penalty minutes; in 52 playoff games scored 18 goals, 27 assists for 45 points, 14 penalty minutes; twice won Art Ross Trophy (scoring) 1946, 1947; Hart Trophy (MVP) 1946, Lady Byng Trophy (most gentlemanly) 1943; tied Busher Jackson's 1934 record of four second-period goals 1943, later tied by Red Berenson 1968; *mem.* Hockey Hall of Fame; *res.* Delisle, Sask.

BERENSON, Red (hockey); *b.* 8 Dec 1939 Regina, Sask.; *given name:* Gordon Arthur; U of Michigan, B.A.; played junior Regina Pats then U of Michigan; earned all-American honors, scored 43 goals in one 28-game season, MVP Western Collegiate HA; at 20 joined Belleville McFarlands and led scorers world amateur tournament; turned pro Montreal 1961-62; with Hull-Ottawa (EPHL) 1962-63 before recalled by Canadiens; spent next two seasons with Quebec (AHL) and Montreal; traded to N Y Rangers for Ted Taylor, Garry Peters 1966; to St. Louis with Barclay Plager for Ron Stewart, Ron Attwell 1967; Detroit with Tim Ecclestone for Garry Unger, Wayne Connelly 1971; St. Louis for Phil Roberto, draft choice Blair Davidson 1974; leader in formation NHL Players' Association; nickname Red Baron; in NHL record book 1968 for scoring six goals in 8-0 St. Louis win over Philadelphia Flyers, tying record set 1944 by Detroit's Syd Howe vs Rangers; in same game tied record four goals in second period set 1934 by Busher Jackson, equalled 1943 by Max Bentley; NHL Western Division MVP; through 1976-77 seasons played 907 games, scored 248 goals, 372 assists for 620 points, 293 penalty minutes; in 81 playoff games scored 23 goals, 14 assists for 37 points, 45 penalty minutes; *res.* St. Louis, Mo.

BERGER, Sam (football); *b.* 1 Jan 1900, Ottawa, Ont.; *m.* Ilsa Marx; *children:* David, Robert, Julia; Lisgar CI, Osgoode Hall; lawyer; Eastern Football Conference legal advisor; p.-pres. Ottawa Football Club, Canadian Football League; purchased Montreal Alouettes football club 1970 building EFC champions three years, two Grey Cup champions; put CFL in big money market signing 'Ordinary Superstar' Johnny Rodgers for over $1 million; relinquished control of Alouettes to sons 1977; brought pro soccer to Montreal; *res.* Montreal, Que.

BERTIE, Gordon (wrestling); *b.* 20 Aug 1948, St. Gabriel de Brandon, Que.; *given name:* Gordon William; *m.* Joan Elizabeth Goldfinch; U of Alberta, B.Sc., B.Ed., Lakehead U; graduate student; at university won CIAU 118lb title 1971-73; won Canadian freestyle 105½ 1969, 114½ four times, 114½ Greco-Roman 1972; represented Canada 1971 Pan-Am Games placing seventh, 1975 Pan-Am Games; silver medal 1974 Commonwealth Games, sixth 1972 Munich Olympics, bronze medal 1974 Istanbul world finals, gold medal Toledo World Cup 1975, runner-up 1976, bronze 1974, silver 1975 Montreal pre-Olympics both freestyle, Greco-Roman; mem. 1976 Olympic team; *res.* Thunder Bay, Ont.

BERTOIA, Reno (baseball); *b.* 8 Jan 1935, St. Vito, Udina, Italy; *given name:* Reno Peter; *sep.; children:* Carl, Ruth, Gina; Assumption HS, U of Michigan, Assumption College, B.A.; HS history department head; played baseball Mic Mac League, Windsor, Class C Detroit Sandlot League; signed bonus contract Detroit Tigers, 1953; spring training 1956 earned him spot at third base but farmed to Charleston later in season; returned to Tigers 1957-58, dealt to Washington 1959 and moved with that club to Minnesota 1961; traded to Kansas City then Detroit 1961; started 1962 with Tigers then farmed to Denver, Syracuse; played 1963 season in Syracuse, spent two months of 1964 campaign in Japan before retiring; in 10 American League seasons .244 batting avg. playing 612 games, hitting 27 homeruns and driving in 171 runs; *res.* Windsor, Ont.

BEVAN, Eddie (football); *b.* 28 Sep 1924, Hamilton, Ont.; *given name:* Edward Charles; *m.* Ernestine Pallante; *children:* Marguerite; truck salesman; tried out with Hamilton juniors 1945, invited to join Hamilton Tigers in Big Four; in 1949 shifted to Wildcats; when Tigers and Wildcats amalgamated into Tiger-Cats 1950, played defensive guard with some offensive duties through 1959; captain 1953, 1955 teams; in four Grey Cup finals, won two; assistant coach 1960-61, another Grey Cup final; line coach McMaster U 1962-65; five times EFC all-star; in two East-West Shrine Games; *res.* Hamilton, Ont.

BEZIC, Sandra (figure skating); *b.* 6 Apr 1956, Toronto, Ont.; *given name:* Sandra Marie; student; (see brother Val for competitive record) torn ankle ligaments during 1975 training forced Sandra to forego 1976 Olympics and turn pro in 1975; with brother Val has performed almost in every major city of world, including London, Paris, Moscow, New York and Tokyo; coached by Ellen Burka, Ron Ludington, Bruce Hyland, Brian Foley; *res.* Willowdale, Ont.

BEZIC, Val (figure skating); *b.* 8 Dec 1952, Toronto, Ont.; *given name:* Val Nickolas; real estate agent; with sister Sandra one of Canada's and world's outstanding pairs skaters; Canadian novice title 1967; first year on international team, 1969, placed third Canadian senior pairs; won Canadian senior pairs 1970-74; ninth 1972 Olympics; injury to Sandra 1975 shattered dream of 1976 Olympic medal; represented Canada in world competition 1970-74, fifth 1974; won Zagreb Invitational 1973; turned pro 1975; *res.* Willowdale, Ont.

BISHOP, Jim (lacrosse, hockey); *b.* 14 May 1929, Toronto, Ont.; *given name:* James Gerrard; *div.* Lynn Boothby; *children:* Joe, Jim Jr., John, Anne, Gael; *m.* Vonnie Tennant; *children:* Lynn; Humberside CI, St. Michael's College; self employed; in lacrosse 1946 coached West Toronto peewee team to first of 19 Ontario championships; coached other title teams in Toronto, Oshawa, Huntsville and Windsor; coach, general manager Oshawa Green Gaels 1963-69, won seven Canadian junior A national titles and Minto Cup; coached both Green Gaels and Detroit Olympics 1968, guiding latter to Eastern division, National League finals; coach, general manager Toronto Tomahawks National Lacrosse League 1974, Montreal Québécois 1975; with Bruce Norris, Morley Kells helped found National Lacrosse League; v.-pres. in charge of internal administration Detroit Red Wings Hockey organization 1967-74; mem. executive Ontario, Canadian Lacrosse Associations; mem. Canadian Lacrosse Hall of Fame; *res.* St. Sauveur, Que.

BITTNER, Brigitte (track and field); *b.* 22 Sep 1955, West Germany; U of Ottawa; student; high jump specialist who won national junior title 1972-74, gold medal 1973 Canada Games 1.80m; bronze medal 1974 Commonwealth Games 1.80m; second national seniors 1973 1.75m; Canadian indoor record 1.87m 1976; bronze medal 1976 Olympic trials Montreal 1.80m; *res.* Ottawa, Ont, Elliott Lake, Ont.

BLACKMAN, Craig (track and field); *b.* 25 Mar 1951, Toronto, Ont.; *given name:* Craig Augustus; U of Oregon, B.Sc.; child care worker, psychiatric hospital; began track career under coach Lloyd Percival with Don Mills Track Club 1964; won at least one gold medal each year Canadian nationals 1964-72 (1971 excepted); personal bests: 22' 9" long jump age 18, 47' 9" triple jump age 17; 10.7 100m, 20.9 200m, 47.0 400m, 1:51.5 800m;

competed 1969 Pacific Conference Games placing fourth 440 at Silver Mile relays; two gold, one silver 400m in three meets involving Norway, Sweden, Canada 1970; gold medal 400m Canada vs Czechoslovakia; silver national finals 400m; fourth in mile relay 1971 Pan-Am Games running 44.9 split; ran 20.9 split 200m bronze NCAA mile relay; silver 1972 NCAA mile relay running 45.4 split; gold Canadian nationals 400m; competed 1972 Olympics running 45.5 split in mile relay in which Canada set record 3:04.2; *res.* Toronto, Ont.

BLACKWOOD, Marjorie (tennis); *b.* 1 May 1957, Ottawa, Ont.; Lisgar CI, Millfield School, Somerset Eng., U of Texas; student; Canadian junior singles title, doubles 1975; consolation winner 1975 Forest Hills Jr; Rothman's Pacific Coast Open senior title Vancouver 1975, Canadian under-21 title Winnipeg 1975; mem. Canadian under-21 team Soisbois Cup Italy 1975, 1976; Ottawa Associated Canadian Travellers tennis award 1973, 1975, Ontario Sports Achievement Award 1973-75, U of Texas tennis scholarship 1975; mem. Federation Cup team 1977; *res.* Ottawa, Ont.

BLAIR, Wren (hockey); *b.* 2 Oct 1925, Lindsay, Ont.; *given name:* Wren Alvin; hockey executive; nickname The Bird; won Ontario senior B title with Whitby Dunlops; refused senior A status by OHA clubs, Blair convinced B league to turn A and challenged for Allan Cup; won league title and beat Kitchener-Waterloo Dutchmen for Ontario title 1957; beat North Bay Trappers then Spokane for Allan Cup; Dunlops represented Canada 1958 world tournament beating USSR 4-2; repeated Allan Cup victory 1959; joined Boston Bruins organization, guided Kingston EPHL as general manager to 1963

league title; became Bruins' personnel director and signed Bobby Orr; played major role in revival Oshawa Generals OHA junior A team 1962 and with Orr as leader won 1965 Memorial Cup; simultaneously served as general manager Clinton Comets (EHL); coached, managed Minnesota North Stars (NHL) eight seasons; Saginaw Gears (IHL); since 1975 general manager Pittsburgh Penguins (NHL); three-year Minnesota coaching record 147 games, 48 wins, 65 losses, 34 ties for .442 percentage; reached playoffs once winning seven of 14 games played; *res.* Pittsburgh, Pa.

BLAKE, Toe (hockey); *b.* 21 Aug 1912, Victoria Mines, Ont.; *given name:* Hector; *children:* Mary Jane, Joan, Bruce; retired hockey executive; in youth played baseball Nickle Belt, Hamilton leagues, umpired in Quebec Provincial League; first organized hockey Sudbury Nickle Belt League 1929-30; started 1930-31 season in seniors but reverted to junior latter half 1931-32 helping team win Memorial Cup; played with Hamilton Tigers seniors until joining Montreal Maroons 1934; on bench as Maroons won 1935 Stanley Cup; joined Canadiens in trade from Maroons for Lorne Chabot 1936; nickname Old Lamplighter; for several years left winger Punch Line with Elmer Lach, Rocket Richard; scored 235 goals, 292 assists in 572 games; Hart Trophy 1939, Lady Byng Trophy 1946, Ross Trophy 1939; in 57 playoff games totalled 62 points; played on two Stanley Cup winners; three times first team, twice second team all-star; coached Houston to USHL title, Buffalo (AHL), Valleyfield (Provincial) to Alexander Trophy; rejoined Habs as coach 1955 and guided club to eight Stanley Cups before 1968 retirement; mem. Hockey Hall of Fame; *res.* Montreal, Que.

BOA, Gil (shooting); *b.* 8 Aug 1924, Montreal, Que., *d.* 7 Sep 1973 St. Catharines, Ont.; *m.* Kay Sillers; *children:* George, Anne, Victoria; Toronto Oakwood CI, U of Toronto, B.Sc.; civil engineer; mem. Canadian international smallbore rifle team age 16, remained 1946-51; mem. Canadian military rifle team 1949-52, Canadian international pistol team 1947; King's medal Connaught Ranges Ottawa 1949-51; King's Prize Bisley Eng. 1951; Governor-General's prize 1955 (matching father's 1948 performance), gold medal world championships Caracas Venezuela 1954; represented Canada five Olympics, won bronze medal 1956, fourth 1952, 1964; gold 1966 Commonwealth Games; two silver and bronze 1971 Pan-Am Games; Canadian smallbore rifle title 12 times; mem. Canadian Sports, Canadian Forces Sports Halls of Fame.

BOESE, Kurt (wrestling); *b.* 4 Nov 1929, Bremen, Germany; *m.* Wilhelmine Lange; *children:* Christa, Terry; plumber, steamfitter; began wrestling age 10 in Germany; North German junior champion 1944; competed 1952 German Olympic trials; emigrated to Canada 1952; won 11 Ontario titles in 154-171 lb range, Michigan Open three times, U of Guelph Open three times, three times third Eastern AAU championships; bronze medals 1962 Commonwealth, 1963 Pan-Am Games; mem. Canadian Toledo world team 1962, Commonwealth team 1958, Olympics 1960; volunteer coach Kitchener YMCA over 20 years guiding teams to six Ontario titles; five times convenor Ontario junior championships; coach Ontario team first Canada Winter Games Quebec City, 1972 Munich Olympics, Waterloo Lutheran U four years, U of Waterloo since 1966 winning OQAA title; national YMCA

leadership award 1967, FILA silver star for contribution to Canadian wrestling 1976; *res.* Kitchener, Ont.

BOLDT, Arnold (track and field); *b.* 16 Sep 1957, Osler, Sask.; *given name:* Arnold William; City Park HS; student; lost leg in grain auger at age three; through determined effort pursued athletic interests in swimming, skiing, volleyball, T&F; gold medal high jump, long jump at 1976 Olympiad for the Disabled Toronto; high jump of 6'1¼" set world record for one-legged jumper; surpassed that later same year with 6'4½" at Knights of Columbus indoor meet Saskatoon; mem. Canadian Sports Hall of Fame; *res.* Saskatoon, Sask.

BOLGER, Pat (wrestling, judo); *b.* 31 Jan 1948, Alexandria, Ont.; *given name:* Patrick John; U of Oklahoma, U of Waterloo; phys ed teacher; attended Oklahoma two years on wrestling scholarship; four times Canadian open wrestling champion; silver medal 1970 Commonwealth Games Edinburgh, bronze 1971 Pan-Am Games; fourth 1967 Pan-Am Games; eighth 1972 Munich Olympics; represented Canada 1968 Olympics, 1970-71 world championships; sixth University World Student Games Moscow; coached Canadian national wrestling team Tel Aviv international tournament commemorating 11 Munich massacre victims; twice Viscount Alexander award Canada's outstanding junior athlete; Canadian judo titlist four times; North American junior judo title Miami 1965; second North American HS championships San Jose, Calif.; third U S Open AAU 1969 championships; silver medal 1967 Pan-Am Games, bronze world finals 1967; won several European titles; quit judo team when refused permission to represent

Canada in both judo and wrestling Munich Olympics after having qualified for both teams; *res.* Toronto, Ont.

BONIFACE, George (baseball); *b.* 24 Nov 1926, Clifton, N.J.; *given name:* George Victor; *m.* Thelma Dwyar; *children:* Joanne; Clifton HS; service manager; pro baseball age 15 as shortstop, second baseman Jamestown (Pony) 1943 and over next two seasons played in Johnson City, Tenn., Rochester, Allentown; after WW2 service returned to baseball 1948 with Allentown and Pocatella, Idaho; played in Hamilton 1949 then Winston Salem where he was injured and retired; resumed baseball activity 1949 in Senior Intercounty ranks with Stratford, Kitchener-Waterloo until retirement 1964; led league in triples, runs scored once each, stolen bases twice; frequent all-star at second base, twice all-star second team manager while guiding Kitchener-Waterloo Dutchmen 1958-62; *res.* Kitchener, Ont.

BOON, Dickie (hockey); *b.* 14 Feb 1874, Belleville, Ont., *d.* 3 May 1961, Outremont, Que.; played junior hockey Young Crystals team Montreal; defenceman with Monarch HC 1897, Montreal AAA juniors 1898-1900, seniors 1901 helping win Stanley Cup against Winnipeg Victorias 1902; nickname Little Iron Man; manager Montreal Wanderers 1903, three Stanley Cups before retirement 1916; never played pro hockey; mem. Canadian Hockey Hall of Fame.

BOUCHER, Bill (hockey); *b.* 10 Nov 1899, Ottawa, Ont., *d.* 10 Nov 1958, Ottawa, Ont.; *m.* Theresa Payette; *children:* Bob, Bill, June; St. Joseph's SS; civil servant; turned pro Montreal Canadiens 1921 remaining through 1926; top scorer when Habs won 1924 Stanley Cup; with Boston 1926-27, NY Americans 1927-28; with Montreal played right wing on line with Howie Morenz, Aurel Joliat; career total 90 goals, 34 assists; mem. Ottawa, Hockey Halls of Fame.

BOUCHER, Bob (hockey); *b.* 23 Mar 1938, Ottawa, Ont.; *given name:* Robert Joseph; *m.* Anne Marie O'Niell; *children:* Trisha; U of Ottawa, Carleton U, St. Mary's U; following grounding in Ottawa minor hockey program joined Montreal Canadiens organization and led scorers on Ottawa-Hull junior Canadiens Memorial Cup team 1957-58; turned pro with Hull-Ottawa in Eastern Professional Hockey League; coach SMU 1969; guided team to seven consecutive conference championships; CIAU hockey coach of year 1976-77; *res.* Herring Cove, N.S.

BOUCHER, Frank (hockey); *b.* 7 Oct 1901, Ottawa, Ont.; *m.* Agnes Sylvester; *children:* Earl; hockey executive, farmer; early prominence in Ottawa's New Edinburgh area starring in hockey, baseball, football; began pro hockey career 1921 with Ottawa Senators; sold to Vancouver Maroons 1922, remained through 1926; joined NY Rangers, remained through 1938 before retiring to coach; coach NY Rovers (EAHL) 1938-39, Rangers 1939-43; during WW2 played 15 games with Rangers 1943-44; centred line of Bill and Bun Cook with Rangers; Lady Byng Trophy seven times in eight years, given permanent possession of original trophy; led U S division NHL scorers 1934 with 14 goals, 30 assists; pro career scoring record 219 goals, 298 assists; Western Canada Junior Hockey commissioner 10 years but was deposed 1968 over rules dispute; mem. Ottawa, Kingston, Madison Square Gardens, Hockey, Canadian Sports Halls of Fame; *res.* Kemptville, Ont.

BOUCHER, George (hockey); *b.* 12 Aug 1895, Ottawa, Ont., *d.* 17 Oct 1960, Ottawa, Ont.; *m.* Mabel Olsen; *children:* Earl (*d.*), Frank; hockey coach, farmer; eldest of famed Boucher brothers, nickname Buck; halfback at 15 with Ottawa Rough Riders; played three football seasons before hockey interests commanded all his time; played Ottawa City League; joined Senators 1915 and remained through four Stanley Cup victories between 1920-27; sold to Montreal Maroons 1928, Chicago 1930; retired 1934 with 122 career goals; coached Chicago, Ottawa, Boston, St. Louis, Springfield, Noranda, Quebec; coached Ottawa to 1949 Allan Cup; helped select, train 1948 Ottawa RCAF Olympic champions coached by son Frank; mem. Ottawa and Hockey Halls of Fame.

BOURASSA, Jocelyne (golf); *b.* 30 May 1947, Shawinigan, Que.; U of Montreal, B.A., U of Wisconsin, B.Sc.; nickname Frenchy; starred in basketball, volleyball, skiing, track at U of Montreal; began golf career as caddy for brother Gilles; Quebec junior champion 1963-65; Quebec ladies amateur champion 1963, 1969-71, runner-up 1964, 1968; Canadian ladies amateur champion 1965, 1971, runner-up 1968; Ontario ladies amateur champion 1971, runner-up 1967-68, 1970; mem. Canadian team winning World Cup in Spain 1970, runner-up 1971; won New Zealand amateur 1971; Canadian women's match champion 1965; turned pro 1972 winning LPGA rookie of the year; won La Canadienne LPGA tournament 1973 in playoff; mem. Canadian National Advisory Council 1971; Canadian female athlete of year and French Canadian athlete of year (first woman) 1972; elected LPGA treasurer 1975. *res.* Shawinigan, Que.

BOURNE, Munroe (swimming); *b.* 26 Jun 1910, Victoria, B.C.; *given name:* Frederick Munroe; *m.* Margaret Fairweather; *children:* Robert, Richard, Mary; McGill U, B.A., M.D., Oxford U, B.A., M.A.; physician; represented Canada 1928 Amsterdam, 1932 Los Angeles, 1936 Berlin Olympics; bronze medal 4x200m 1928, team captain 1936; gold 100yd, 4x200 relay 1930 British Empire Games Hamilton; winner 50m international student games 1933; winner 100m breast stroke, relay, Dublin 1928; winner several Canadian, Quebec intercollegiate championships; mem. McGill, Oxford swimming, water polo teams; pres. Oxford Swim Club 1934-35; mem. Montreal AAA; mem. London Otters Swim Club, twice won National team race title 1934-35; represented Oxford in Langlauf skiing 1934-35; coach McGill swim team 1938-40; Commander of Order of St. John 1975; *res.* Westmount, Que.

BOWDEN, Norris (figure skating); *b.* 13 Aug 1926, Toronto, Ont.; *given name:* Robert Norris; *m.* Joan; *children:* David, Kathy, Danny; U of Toronto, B.Sc., M.B.A.; chartered life underwriter; 1947 Canadian men's singles title, teamed with Frances Dafoe won both Canadian pairs and dance titles 1952; 1953 won Canadian, North American pairs titles; 1954 won Canadian, North American, world titles; repeated all three 1955; won North American pairs, silver medal 1956 Cortina Olympics; *res.* Toronto, Ont.

BOWER, Johnny (hockey); *b.* 8 Nov 1924, Prince Albert, Sask; *given name:* John William; *m.* Nancy Brain; *children:* John Jr, Cynthia; hockey executive; junior hockey in Prince Albert led to Providence and Cleveland Barons in AHL where, except for brief stints with NY Rangers in mid-50s, he remained until brought to Toronto Maple

Leafs 1958 at age 33; with Leafs through 1970 season appeared in 534 league games yielding 1,347 goals, posting 37 shutouts and 2.53 goals against avg.; in 72 playoff games allowed 184 goals, posted five shutouts and 2.58 avg.; once first team all-star; Vezina Trophy 1961, shared same with Terry Sawchuk 1965; three times Bickell Trophy as most valuable Leaf; with Cleveland 1945-56, five times AHL all-star; three times Hap Holmes Memorial Trophy as AHL MVP; three times Leslie Cunningham Trophy; with Vancouver (WHL) 1955 leading goaler award; following retirement became head scout for TML, later coaching assistant to Red Kelly; mem. Hockey Hall of Fame; *res.* Toronto, Ont.

BOWIE, Russell (hockey); *b.* 24 Aug 1880, Montreal, Que.; *d.* 8 Apr 1959, Montreal, Que.; weighed only 112 lbs when he joined Winnipeg Victorias 1898; remained amateur (CAHL, ECAHA) throughout career; scored 234 goals in 80 games over 10-year period; one of few ever to score 10 goals in single game; 38 goals in 10 games 1907, including eight in one game; led league scorers five times, perennial all-star; broken collarbone ended playing career, became referee; mem. Hockey Hall of Fame.

BOWMAN, Scotty (hockey); *b.* 18 Sep 1933, Montreal, Que.; *given name:* William Scott; *m.* Suella; *children:* Alicia, Stanley, Nancy, Bobby; hockey executive; playing career cut short by head injury during 1951-52 season while playing junior A, struck on head by J.G. Talbot's stick; turned to coaching with Canadiens' organization 1954-57 then became assistant to Sam Pollock as manager-coach Hull-Ottawa Canadiens; coached Peterborough Petes, Montreal Junior Canadiens in OHA junior A; eastern

Canadian scout for Habs three seasons before joining St. Louis Blues expansion team as coach-general manager 1965-66; remained with Blues four seasons, reached Stanley Cup finals first three years and second in Western Division 1970-71; rejoined Montreal organization 1971, coached club to three Stanley Cup victories; coached Canadian team in Canada Cup 1976 series; through 1976-77 NHL coaching record shows 418 wins, 166 losses, 128 ties for .782 percentage in regular season competition plus 72 wins, 47 losses for .605 avg. in playoffs; *res.* Montreal, Que.

BOX, Ab (football); *b.* 8 Mar 1909, Toronto, Ont.; *m.* Phyllis Malpass; *children:* Linda, Donald, Gary, Donald, Marilyn; retired; football with Malvern Grads 1928-29; protegé of Ted Reeve, played with Balmy Beach 1930-31 winning ORFU title, Eastern title, Grey Cup 1930; punter with Argos 1932-34 winning Grey Cup 1933; rejoined Balmy Beach 1935-38; frequent all-star; Jeff Russel Memorial Trophy as Eastern Big Four MVP 1934; baseball, softball player on several Canadian title teams; mem. Canadian Football, Canadian Sports Halls of Fame; *res.* Toronto, Ont.

BOYCE, Jim (tennis); *b.* 22 Jun 1951, Toronto, Ont.; *given name:* James Niell; Mississippi State U, B.Sc.; tennis pro; Ontario tennis recognition 1963 winning first of five provincial age-group titles at 12; five national titles including under-18 title three times; attended Mississippi State on tennis scholarship, all-South Eastern Conference team three years; in Ontario's top eight since junior days; 1974 Ontario men's title, 1975 Ontario closed; in Canada's top 15 since 1971; mem. Canadian Davis Cup team 1975, 1976; *res.* Ottawa, Ont.

BOYCE, Walter (autosport); *b.* 25 Oct 1946, Ottawa, Ont.; *m.* Leslie Bradbeer; *children:* Jennifer; Glebe CI, U of Ottawa; accountant; ninth and sixth respectively 1968-69 Canadian championships; with Doug Woods as navigator won Canadian title 1970-74, second 1975; only Canadian internationally rated, having won major events such as Press on Regardless rally for world title 1973, Rally of Rideau Lakes, Canadian Winter Rally; competed in Canada, U S, Africa; *res.* Ottawa, Ont.

BOYCHUK, Andy (track and field); *b.* 17 May 1941, Orono, Ont.; *given name:* Andrew Harry; *m.* Darlene Ann; U of Waterloo, B.Sc.; professional engineer; tenth Commonwealth Games marathon 1966; gold medal 1967 Pan-Am Games, Winnipeg; tenth 1968 Mexico Olympics, 1970 Commonwealth Games; four times Canadian marathon champion; best personal time for marathon 2:16.13 1975; outstanding harrier and track athlete of year 1967; Sarnia *Observer* citizen of year 1967; Sarnia area's outstanding man of year 1967; *res.* Sarnia, Ont.

BOYD, Barry (track and field); *b.* 12 Jan 1952, Calgary, Alta.; *given name:* Barry Allan; U of Alberta, B.Comm.; student; long jump specialist who won every indoor, outdoor Canadian age-group title since age 17; since 1969 has never finished out of medals in Canadian senior championship competition, indoor or outdoor; Canadian junior indoor long jump record 24′ 3¾″ and Canadian senior indoor record 25′ 3½″; ninth 1975 Pan-Am Games; best jump (wind assisted) 25′ 6″; *res.* Edmonton, Alta.

BOYLEN, Christilot (equestrian); *b.* 12 Apr 1947, Djakarta, Indonesia; *given name:* Christilot Hanson; *m.* James A. Boylen; *children:* Christa-Dora; Branksome Hall; language study in Europe, writer; nine times Canadian dressage champion; at 17 became youngest competitor to ride in Grand Prix dressage 1964 Tokyo Olympics; bronze medal 1967 Pan-Am Games; individual gold, team gold 1971 Pan-Am Games; individual gold, team silver 1975 Pan-Am Games; 1972 became first Canadian rider to win place among elite dozen riders in Olympic individual dressage, placing ninth; twice winner U S National championship; competed with distinction in Denmark, Netherlands, Tokyo, Munich, Canada, U S; three firsts Ohio Dressage Derby 1970; numerous Ontario, Quebec, Eastern U S dressage titles; twice honored as horsewoman of year by National Equestrian Federation of Canada; wrote book *Canadian Entry; res.* Cedar Valley, Ont.

BOYS, Bev (diving); *b.* 4 Jul 1951, Toronto, Ont.; U of Manitoba, U of Toronto; bank teller; various age-group titles from 11-16; Canadian senior titles 1966-75; silver, bronze medals 1966 Commonwealth Games Jamaica; silver 1967 Winnipeg Pan-Am Games; fourth 10m, seventh 3m 1968 Mexico Olympics; won U S 10m, Russian invitational 10m, East German international invitational 10m, British 3m and 10m 1969; second U S national 10m; gold medals 3m, 10m Commonwealth Games Edinburgh; won Bolanzo Italy international, Hungary international invitational 1970; silver, bronze medals Cali Colombia Pan-Am Games 1971; fifth Munich Olympics 1972; seventh Belgrade Yugoslavia world championships 1973; gold, silver 1974 Commonwealth Games Christchurch; competed in Cali world finals, second Ft. Lauderdale international 10m 1975; mem. Canadian 3m Olympic team 1976; *res.* Senneville, Que.

BRABENEC, Hana (tennis); *b.* 21 Jun 1928, Prague, Czechoslovakia; *given name:* Hana Veverka; *m.* Josef Brabenec; *children:* Josef; tennis coach; began playing age 12 and for 15 years among top 10 Czechoslovakian women tennis players; twice runner-up Czech national singles; four times winner national doubles; *res.* Vancouver, B.C.

BRABENEC, Josef (tennis); *b.* 29 Jan 1929, Prague, Czechoslovakia; *m.* Hana Veverka; *children:* Josef; Canadian national tennis coach; began playing tennis at 14, one of top juniors in Czechoslovakia; won Belgian junior international 1947, numerous European tournaments; with wife Hana, founded Prague tennis school for boys and girls 1963; since 1964 captained several Czechoslovakian national teams in Paris 1965, Wimbledon 1966, 1968, Rome 1967, Salisbury U S 1969; coached Czech national junior team at Florida Cup and Orange Bowl 1967; since 1970 head coach Jericho Tennis Club Vancouver; guided pupils to 15 junior titles, all age categories 1971-73; coach 1970 Canadian Federation Cup team; coached-managed B.C. team to two gold, two bronze Canada Summer Games 1973; head coach B.C. Tennis Association; third among Canadian veterans 1975; represented Canada several times in Jordan Cup action; wrote *Tennis for Children, Tennis—the Game for Everyone;* international secretary Czech LTA 1963-69; mem. committee of management ILTF 1969-71; Canadian national coach since 1975; *res.* Vancouver, B.C.

BRACK, Bill (autosport); *b.* 26 Dec 1935, Toronto, Ont.; *given name;* William Andrew; Parkdale CI; automotive dealer; sponsored by STP Corp. won Players' Challenge Series and Canadian championship 1973-75; competed in two Canadian Grand Prix Formula One events posting highest finish to that time by Canadian—eighth 1969 St. Jovite race; strong contender Formula 5000 series 1969-72; represented Canada in two Formula Atlantic races South Africa 1976, third in one and spun out in other; first Canadian title at 38; three times Formula Atlantic winner; operates Bill Brack Racing Enterprises and in 1976 sought to build racing stable; Wayne Kelly Trophy 1975 for driver best combining sportsmanship with ability; *res.* Toronto, Ont.

BRANCATO, George (football); *b.* 27 May 1931, Brooklyn, N.Y.; *m.* Barbara Thomson; *children:* Cindi, Wendy, George Jr., Alicia; Louisiana State, B.S., California State, M.A.; football coach; drafted 1953 by Chicago Cardinals (NFL) played two seasons; joined Montreal Alouettes for season then dealt to Ottawa Rough Riders 1956 where he played offensive and defensive halfback seven seasons; led EFC in pass interceptions 1957; EFC all-star 1961; retired and coached minor pro football until hired by Jack Gotta as defensive assistant 1970 with Riders; head coach 1974; CFL coach of year Annis Stukus Trophy 1975; International Italian of year in football 1976; coached Ottawa to Grey Cup 1976; *res.* Ottawa, Ont.

BRAUNSTEIN, Terry (curling); *b.* 18 Apr 1939, Winnipeg, Man.; *m.* Andrea Greenberg; *children:* Lisa, Danny; U of Manitoba, B. Comm.; clothing wholesaler; at 18 won Manitoba Consols and represented that province in Brier, youngest ever to do so; forced playoff before losing to Matt Baldwin 10-6; also forced revision of rules which prohibited schoolboys from competing for Canadian men's title; won provincial Consols 1965, Brier in Saskatoon; won Manitoba Bonspiel grand aggregate 1971; mem. Winnipeg Granite Club; *res.* Winnipeg, Man.

BRAZEAU, Howard (curling); *b.* 13 Mar 1938, Smith, Alta.; *given name:* Howard Charles; *m.* Catharine Mary Owens; *children:* Debbie, Kelly, Donna; Smith HS; Imperial Oil agent, assistant chief volunteer fire dept.; began curling 1955 Waterways (now McMurray) Alta.; moved to Fort Smith, N.W.T. where he became volunteer fireman; won Territorial men's title four times; skipped 1976 N.W.T. Brier entry posting 5-6 record; twice Territories mixed champion; three times N.W.T. firefighters champion; twice Canadian firefighters titlist; mem. several Territorial fastball championship teams as centrefielder; *res.* Fort Smith, N.W.T.

BREEN, Joe (football); *b.* 23 Apr 1897, Toronto, Ont.; *given name:* Joseph Melville; *m.* Winnifred Westman; *children:* Melwyn Joseph; U of Toronto, B.Sc.; civil engineer; captain U of T football team 1919-20 winning Grey Cup 1920; captain Toronto Argonauts, Parkdale Canoe Club 1921, 1924; coach UWO football 1929-34; mem. Canadian Football, Canadian Sports Halls of Fame; *res.* Montreal, Que.

BREWER, Carl (hockey); *b.* 21 Oct 1938, Toronto, Ont.; *given name:* Carl Thomas; *m.* Marilyn; Riverdale CI, McMaster U, U of Toronto, B.A.; Toronto minor hockey system to Weston junior B team to Marlboros junior A where he starred in 1956 Memorial Cup victory; MVP 1957-58; turned pro with Toronto Maple Leafs and played on three Stanley Cup winners in seven seasons; played with Leafs through 1964-65 season, twice lead NHL in penalty minutes; quit following disagreement with coach Punch Imlach; regained amateur status 1966 and played with Canadian National team 1966-67, outstanding defenceman 1967 world tournament;

player-coach Muskegon (IAHL) 1967-68, Finland 1968-69; Leafs sold his NHL rights to Detroit 1968 but he refused to play before 1969-70 season; played with St. Louis Blues 1970-72 then retired; named to NHL all-star first team once, second team twice; in 584 regular season NHL games scored 25 goals, 193 assists for 218 points, plus 72 playoff games scoring three goals, 17 assists for 20 points; in five all-star games; TV color commentator WHA hockey games; *res.* Toronto, Ont.

BRICKER, Cal (track and field); *b.* 1894, *d.* 1963, Grenfell, Sask.; *given name:* Calvin David; U of Toronto, D.D.S.; dentist; all-around champion U of T and individual Intercollegiate champion 1905-06; specialist in running broad jump (long jump) and hop, step and jump (triple jump); won both events 1908 Olympic trials setting record 24'1.5" in long jump which held 27 years; won long jump bronze with 23'3"; fourth triple jump London Olympics; qualified for 1912 Olympic team, won long jump silver medal with 23'7.75"; officer in charge of Canadian athletes in 1919 Paris Games for service personnel; mem. Canadian Sports Hall of Fame.

BRIGHT, Johnny (football); *b.* 11 Jun 1931, Fort Wayne, Ind.; *given name:* John Dee; *div.; children:* Darrell Michael, Deanie LaDette, Shaughna Darcine, Kandis Denita; Drake U, B.Sc., U of Alberta, B.Ed.; junior HS principal; all-state honors in football, track, basketball at HS in Fort Wayne; pitched Des Moines Iowa to state championships; at Drake established some 20 records in football, basketball, track; led all U S college ground-gainers, all-American honors; first draft choice 1951 Philadelphia Eagles; joined Calgary Stampeders 1952 playing two seasons before being dealt to Edmonton

Eskimos for Peter Lougheed; seven times WFC all-star, four times all-Canadian; Schenley Outstanding Player 1959; in 13 CFL seasons scored 71 TDs while carrying ball 1,969 times for 10,909 yds, 5.5 avg.; four times led CFL ground-gainers receiving Eddie James Memorial Trophy, and five times surpassed 1,000 yds one season; three times led CFL in total carries, five times surpassed 200-per-season; played on three Grey Cup winners in four finals; Drake U football player of century; Indiana silver anniversary basketball team; pro basketball Harlem Globetrotters; pitched perfect game Iowa State tournament; in U S East-West all-star game, Canadian all-star game; coached high school football, 74-27 record, basketball, 304-46; coach Edmonton Monarchs pro fastball team, 1972 coach of year; Edmonton athlete of year 1959; mem. Edmonton, Iowa, Canadian Football Halls of Fame; *res*. Edmonton, Alta.

BRILL, Debbie (track and field); *b*. 10 Mar 1953, Mission, B.C.; Garibaldi HS, U British Columbia; student; at 16 won high jump title Pacific Conference Games; originator of reverse jumping style known as Brill Bend; gold medal 1970 Commonwealth Games; represented Canada vs Norway, Sweden 1970 and won Canadian championship; gold medal 1971 Pan-Am Games; Canadian Open and native record 6'1¼'' 1971 becoming first Canadian, North American female to clear six-foot barrier; fourth 1975 Pan-Am Games with 1.81m (5'11¼'') jump; led 1976 Olympic qualifiers with Canadian record 1.89m (6'2½'') jump Quebec City; represented Canada 1972, 1976 Olympics; coached by Lionel Pugh; tied with Debbie Van Kiekebelt as 1971 Canadian female athlete of year in CP poll; *res*. Andergrove, B.C.

BROADBENT, Punch (hockey); *b*. 13 Jul 1893, Ottawa, Ont., *d*. 6 Mar 1971, Ottawa, Ont.; *given name:* Harold Lawton; *m*. Leda; *children:* Sally Ann; RCAF officer; played amateur hockey with New Edinburgh, Cliffsides; turned pro at 16; joined Senators 1912-13; after WWI rejoined Senators 1918, played five seasons before being sold to Montreal Maroons; returned to Senators 1927-28 then dealt to NY Americans following season; retired 1929; in 10 NHL campaigns scored 118 goals; played on three Stanley Cup winners with Ottawa, one with Maroons; led league scorers 1921-22 with 32 goals; scored one or more goals 16 consecutive games (record still stands); scored 25 goals and 32 assists in a 24-game schedule; mem. Ottawa, Canadian Forces, Hockey Halls of Fame.

BRODA, Turk (hockey); *b*. 15 May 1914, Brandon, Man., *d*. 17 Oct 1972, Toronto, Ont.; *given name:* Walter; *m*. Betty Williams; *children:* Barbara, Bonny, Betty; David Livingstone School; hockey player, coach; turned pro with Detroit serving first year as practice goaler after having starred with Brandon juveniles, juniors and Winnipeg Monarch juniors 1933-34; played with International League Detroit Olympics before being sold to Toronto Maple Leafs; played 16 seasons with Leafs winning Vezina Trophy twice and sharing another with Al Rollins; 13 shutouts in 101 playoff games (Stanley Cup record), 2.08 goals-against record; played on five Stanley Cup winners; retired 1952 and coached Toronto Marlboros to three league titles, two Memorial Cups in 11 seasons; coach London Nationals, Moncton N.B. juniors, Quebec Aces; mem. Hockey Hall of Fame.

BROOKS, Lela (speedskating); *b.* 7 Feb 1908, Toronto, Ont.; *given name:* Lela Alene; *m.* Russ Campbell *(d.); children:* Art, Carol, Donna, Dorothy; *m.* Clifford Bleich; Harbord CI, Kent Commercial; at 13 won Ontario under-18 440, mile titles; won under-16, under-18 senior mile titles 1924 Ontario indoor competition; won three Canadian titles, 220, 440 and under-18 880, then won 220, 440 and mile races in international competition Pittsburgh 1925; by end of 1925 had broken six world records; won three of four races and women's overall title 1926 world competition Saint John N.B.; continued to win Canadian, North American honors and set several world records including half-mile indoor, outdoor, three-quarter mile outdoor; broke mile record Detroit Mardi Gras Festival 1928; half-mile record set in Pittsburgh 1926 still stands; won 1935 North American indoor title Saint John; qualified for 1936 Olympics but chose retirement; coached by Harry Cody, Fred Robson; first woman admitted to Old Orchard Skating Club Toronto; from outset of career to retirement won all titles available to women speedskaters—Ontario indoor, outdoor, all-Canadian, international and world; mem. Canadian Speedskating, Sports Halls of Fame; *res.* Owen Sound, Ont.

BROSSEAU, Eugene (boxing); *b.* 1895, Montreal, Que., *d.* 1968, Montreal, Que.; post office employee; U S amateur middleweight title 1917; Canadian amateur welterweight title 1915, retained it and added U S amateur welterweight title 1916; fought series of San Francisco exhibitions on behalf of Red Cross 1917; turned pro following WW1; blow to back of neck in 1919 bout with George Chip caused left arm paralysis; returned to ring 1920 but never fully recovered; instructor to Canada's 1924 Olympic boxing team; in 27 pro bouts during two and one-half year span scored 17 KO's, won seven by decision, fought one no-contest, lost decision to Jack Bloomfield and was KO'd by Mike McTigue; only Canadian to win two U S amateur ring titles and be selected to halls of fame in both amateur, pro ranks; mem. Canadian Boxing, Sports Halls of Fame.

BROUILLARD, Lou (boxing); *b.* 23 May 1911, Eugene, Que.; dog breeder; began boxing Worcester Mass. at 16; following four successful years as amateur turned pro, won world welterweight title beating Jack Thompson in 15 rounds Boston 1931; lost crown to Jackie Fields Chicago 1932; won N Y Commission middleweight title KO'ing Ben Jeby in the seventh round 1933 at New York; lost title to Vince Dundee in 15 rounds Boston 1933; lost two more title bids to Marcel Thil in Paris, both on fouls, and barred from ring for year, manager received life suspension; won 60 of first 64 bouts — 44 by KO; in 140 pro bouts won 66 by KO, 43 on decision, one on foul and three draws; lost 24 decisions, two on fouls, once KO'd by Tiger Jack Fox; mem. Canadian Boxing, Sports Halls of Fame; *res.* South Hanson, Mass.

BROWN, Dick (football); *b.* 9 May 1925, Cleveland, Ohio.; *given name:* Richard Anthony; *m.* Anne Peetsalu; *children:* Mark Anthony, Melanie Louise; Cathedral Latin School, U of Toronto, B.A.; football coach, university facilities supervisor; all-city HS honors as end, punter; four years football U of T, Intercollegiate all-star tailback; turned pro Hamilton Tiger-Cats, remained five years before moving to Argos for two seasons, wound up career with Alouettes 1957; head coach Burlington Braves juniors two years; line coach, defensive coach Oakville Black Knights senior ORFU four years; head coach Hamilton Hurricanes juniors one year; offensive coordinator U of Guelph two years, head coach 1970; played 1953 Grey Cup champion Ticats; 15th CFL total career yardage on punt returns, Argo career punt return record 1,048yds, single season record 74 returns for 614yds 1955; 1953 CP Eastern all-star halfback, *New Liberty* all-pro safety, 1956 *Globe and Mail* Eastern all-star, Bulova Big Four player of week award 1955 Eastern playoff; cornerback Ticat Fabulous Fifties all-stars (players from 1950-60), also on Ticat 1950-70 dream team; punt returner on modern era (1945-73) all-Argos team; *res.* Guelph, Ont.

BROWN, George (rowing); *b.* 1839, Herring Cove, N.S., *d.* 8 Jul 1875, Halifax, N.S.; fisherman; began rowing as youngster under auspices of Halifax businessman James Pryor; lost to three-time winner George Lovett in Cogswell Belt race 1863; won that title 1864-68 and was awarded permanent possession of Cogswell Belt; 1871 competed on Pryor-assembled Halifax four and in single sculls vs Scottish, British, U S rowers; challenges issued world pro champion Joseph Sadler were avoided but Brown turned pro 1873; defeated Robert Fulton of Paris Crew fame 1873; same year defeated U S champion John Biglin; defeated U S singles champion Bill Scharff 1874 Boston; Brown bet all his life savings on himself and won race by six seconds; defeated Evan Morris of U S in Saint John N.B. 1874; while preparing for 1875 match with Sadler, suffered fatal stroke; mem. Canadian Sports Hall of Fame.

BROWN, Gord (curling); *b.* 27 Jul 1918, Manor, Sask.; *m.* Jean Busby; *children:* Michael, Denise, Frances; civil servant; Sas-

katchewan junior tennis title 1934; pres. Sask. Tennis Association 1961-62; after WW2 established reputation as curler winning three Sask. Legion titles, two Canadian Legion titles; twice won Regina grand aggregate, runner-up four times; Regina club pres. 1961-62; mem. Sask. Curling Association executive 1961-64; moved to Ottawa where he skipped rink to third place finish 1966 Ontario Consols; won 1966 televised Roarin' Game series Ottawa; Governor-General's (Canadian Branch Royal Caledonian Curling Club) double rink winner 1966, 1972; represented Ottawa Curling Club provincial Consols playdowns seven times in eight years, Ont. seniors; *res.* Ottawa, Ont.

BROWN, Louise (tennis); *b.* 19 Nov 1922, Dunnville, Ont.; *m.* Ross Brown; *children:* David, Chareen; Dunnville HS; insurance agent; won 1957 Canadian women's singles, teamed with Hilda Doleschell for doubles title; won 1962 national women's doubles with Ann Barclay; won Canadian women's senior singles (Ireland Cup) 1970-71; captain Canadian team's first Federation Cup appearance 1963, also played 1964, non-playing captain 1966-67, 1969; for 27 consecutive years among nation's top 10 players and dominated Ontario scene; women's representative on Players' Association; *res.* Mississauga, Ont.

BROWN, Ted (curling); *b.* 4 Oct 1937, Kingston, Ont.; *given name:* Edward James; *m.* Kathy; *children:* Jeff, Tim, Mike; Ottawa Technical HS; self employed furniture upholsterer; first major victory Ontario Governor-General's, Whitby Dunlop 'spiel 1969; won Royal Carspiel Toronto 1971—first carspiel in Ontario; three times in Ontario Consols, twice as skip; played third for Dr. Alex Scott, won Ontario title 1975, competed in Fredericton Brier; skipped Ontario entry Canadian mixed championships 1976; *res.* Kingston, Ont.

BRUCE, Ian (yachting); *b.* 7 Jun 1933, Jamaica, B.W.I.; *m.* Barbara Brittain; *children:* Tracy, Tobi; Trinity College School, McGill U, Syracuse U, B.I.D.; industrial designer, company pres.; captain TCS hockey team 1950-51; played McGill squash team 1951-53; mem. Canadian Olympic yachting team 1960 Finn Class, 1972 Star Class; team captain 1967 international 14 ft dinghy world team championships, won title, again 1968; Canadian International 14 ft dinghy title 1967, 1975, U S title 1958; major role in design and development of high performance lightweight sailing dinghy called Tasar; mem. Royal St. Lawrence Yacht Club; *res.* Dorval, Que.

BRUCE, Lou (football); *b.* 16 Jul 1933, Toronto, Ont.; *given name:* Lou Alexander; *m.* Janet Hanson; *children:* Heather, Wendy, Jennifer; Riverdale CI, Queen's U, B.A.; plastics manufacturer; Toronto all-star football and basketball 1950-52; mem. Frank Tindall's Queen's Golden Gaels, CIAU all-star 1954-55; turned pro Ottawa Rough Riders 1956, defensive end through 1961 season; three times all-star; *res.* Ottawa, Ont.

BRUNEAU, David (skiing); *b.* 17 Mar 1948, Montreal, Que.; U of Toronto, B.A., McGill U, B.Comm.; student; British junior ski titles 1962-63; won Taschereau 1966-67, Quebec championship 1966, Canadian junior slalom, Canadian Winter Games slalom 1967, Revelstoke slalom derby, Western Canadian championship, Lowell Thomas Classic Utah 1968; third Werner Classic, Steamboat Springs Colo.; won Vail Trophy

1968, Christmas Classic, Lake Louise slalom 1969; tenth Saalbaach Austria FIS B slalom 1969; represented Canada international team races France 1970; mem. Canadian national team 1967-70; *res.* Montreal, Que.

BRUNETEAU, Mud (hockey); *b.* 28 Nov 1914, St. Boniface, Man.; *given name:* Modère; graduated from junior ranks with Winnipeg K of C; turned pro 1934-35 with Detroit Olympics (IHL); to Red Wings late in 1935-36 season, scored only goal as Wings defeated Montreal Maroons 1-0 in longest game ever played in NHL (1936); except for brief stint with Pittsburgh (IAHL) 1937-38 remained with Detroit until 1945-46 scoring 139 goals, 138 assists in regular season play and 23 goals, 14 assists in playoffs; best season 1943-44, scored 35 goals in 39 games; after leaving NHL played in Indianapolis (AHL) Omaha (USHL).

BRUNO, Al (football); *b.* 28 Mar 1927, West Chester, Pa.; *given name:* Albert Paul; *m.* Marie Giosio; *children:* Mike, Maria, Lisa; West Chester HS, U of Kentucky, B.A.; football coach; played for Bear Bryant's Kentucky football team 1947-50; first college TD pass 1948 a 56yd toss from George Blanda; mem. Adolph Rupp's Kentucky NCAA basketball championship team 1948-49; participated 1950 Orange Bowl, 1951 Sugar Bowl; caught national record 10 TD passes, four in single game thrown by Babe Parilli 1950; mem. first Southeastern Conference title team for Kentucky 1950; all-conference, third-team all-American 1950; third round draft pick Philadelphia Eagles 1951; recruited by Frank Clair for Toronto Argos 1952, helped them win Grey Cup; top pass receiver, twice all-Canadian 1952-54; with Winnipeg Blue Bombers 1955-56; retired to coaching 1957; athletic director, football, basketball coach Toronto De La Salle CI, guided basketball team to provincial finals, football team to league title; player-coach London Lords (ORFU) 1958-60 reaching finals three years, winning title 1960; returned to Pennsylvania to teach, coach 1961-66; joined Ottawa Rough Riders as offensive coach under Frank Clair 1966-67, in one Grey Cup; joined Joe Restic on Hamilton Tiger-Cats coaching staff 1968-70 helping win 1970 Eastern Conference title, lost playoffs; since 1971 offensive coordinator for Restic at Harvard, helped team win Ivy League title 1974-75; *res.* Milford, Mass.

BRYDSON, Gordie   (golf); *b.* 3 Jan 1907, Toronto, Ont.; *m.* Dorothy Beamish; retired golf pro; flying wing, kicker Toronto Argonauts 1922-23; pro hockey right winger Toronto Maple Leafs, Chicago, Detroit 1924-38; golf pro from 1930; twice won Ontario Open, six times runner-up; twice Millar Trophy, once runner-up; won Quebec Open; twice Rivermead Cup, twice runner-up; twice CPGA titlist, three times runner-up; runner-up Canadian Open; twice CPGA seniors champion; four times Ontario PGA seniors title; club pro Mississauga Golf and Country Club 1931-72; CPGA life mem.; *res.* Mississauga, Ont.

BUCHAN, Ken   (curling); *b.* 9 Apr 1940, Harriston, Ont.; *given name:* Kenneth Donald; *m.* Deanne Catharine Girodat; *children:* Christine, Margaret; Waterloo Lutheran U, B.A., U of Waterloo, B.P.E.; teacher; played third for Bob Mann, Ontario Consols winner and Brier representative 1963-64, reached provincial finals again in 1965; became skip and guided own quartet to Ontario title 1969; Ontario Consols finals in 1970, 1973, 1975; Ontario Silver Tankard 1972, runner-up 1971; Ontario Seagram

mixed finals 1974; participant CBC Curling, Tournament of Champions; active in coaching Ontario Curl Canada program; *res.* London, Ont.

BUCYK, John   (hockey); *b.* 12 May 1935, Edmonton, Alta.; *given name:* John Paul; *m.* Ann Smith; *children:* three; hockey player; from Edmonton Oil Kings juniors turned pro with Edmonton (WHL), set rookie scoring record, league rookie of year; two seasons with Detroit Red Wings before being dealt to Boston for Terry Sawchuck 1957; with Vic Stasiuk, Bronco Horvath formed Uke Line; equalled Dit Clapper's Boston longevity record of 20 seasons with that club 1976-77 season; surpassed Milt Schmidt's Boston point record of 576 during 1968-69 season; first Bruins' 250-goal scorer; NHL's seventh 500-plus goal scorer 1975; second highest point scorer in NHL history; joined select circle of 50-goal scorers with 51 1970-71 season; in 22 NHL seasons played 1487 regular season games, scored 551 goals, 800 assists for 1351 points, 493 penalty minutes, plus 119 playoff games scored 41 goals, 61 assists for 102 points, 42 penalty minutes; first all-star team left wing once, second team once; twice winner Lady Byng Trophy, once Conacher Award; *res.* Boxford, Mass.

BUDGE, Susan   (orienteering); *b.* 2 Jun 1961, Montreal, Que.; *given name:* Susan Jane; Mount Royal HS, Laurentian Regional HS; student; Canadian under-14 championship 1972; Canadian junior title 1973-74; runner-up Canadian senior ladies' title 1975; winner Quebec senior, North American junior 1975; runner-up U S Open championship 1976, Denmark international 13-14-year-olds 1975; class A Laurentian Zone alpine ski racer; Mérite Sportif Québécois 1975; *res.* St. Sauveur des Monts, Que.

BURCH, Billy (hockey); *b*. 20 Nov 1900, Yonkers, N.Y., *d*. Dec 1950; turned pro Hamilton Tigers 1923, centred line of Green brothers, Redvers (Red), Wilfred (Shorty), and carried team to first place in NHL 1925; 1925 Hart Trophy; transferred with team to New York where he became captain; 1927 Lady Byng Trophy; remained with NY Americans until late in 1932 season when he was dealt to Boston then Chicago; broke leg in 1933 season and retired; team scoring leader five times; played 390 regular season games scoring 135 goals, 42 assists; mem. Hockey Hall of Fame.

BURKA, Petra (figure skating); *b*. 17 Nov 1946, Amsterdam, The Netherlands; won Central Ontario junior sectionals 1959; coached by mother Ellen, won Central Ontario senior sectionals 1960; 10th Canadian juniors; won Canadian juniors 1961, second seniors, fourth world 1962; won Canadian seniors, second North American 1963; won Canadian seniors, third world and Olympics 1964; won Canadian seniors, North American, world 1965; Canadian athlete of year (Lou Marsh Trophy) 1965; pro with Holiday on Ice 1966-69; sports consultant Sport Canada 1970-75; mem. Canadian Amateur Sports Hall of Fame; *res*. Toronto, Ont.

BURKA, Sylvia (speedskating); *b*. 4 May 1954, Winnipeg, Man.; Gordon Bell HS; student; 1967 Canadian juvenile title; 1969 Canadian junior champion; 1970 competed world, West Allis Wisc., won Canadian indoor, outdoor intermediate; 1971 competed ladies' world Helsinki, world sprints Germany, won Canadian indoor intermediate; 1972 won Canadian outdoor intermediate, competed Sapporo Japan Olympics (eighth of 33 in 100m), ladies' world Holland, world

sprints Sweden; world record 1973 175.050 points for 500m, 100m (twice) Davos Switzerland, junior world title Assen Holland, fourth of 29 world sprints Oslo, 12th of 26 world Sweden; sixth of 18 junior world Italy 1974, eighth of 26 world sprints Austria, 11th world Holland; won Canadian outdoor seniors 1975; fourth 1976 Olympics Innsbruck 500m; won worlds 1976, placed 15th 1977; won world sprints 1977; holds 35 Canadian, 23 Manitoba records; skater of year 1970, 1972-74; Manitoba junior athlete 1971; Manitoba sportswoman of year 1971, 1973; Order of Buffalo Hunt 1973, Government House honor 1973, City of Winnipeg honor 1973; began competitive cycling 1975 placing second Manitoba road championship, fifth Canadian road championship, second ladies' kilo, 300m pursuit, overall bronze medal; second 10-mile trail, fourth Criterium road race Western Canada Games; *res*. Winnipeg, Man.

BURKE, Desmond (shooting); *b*. 5 Dec 1904, Ottawa, Ont.; *d*. 11 Apr 1973, Oakville, Ont.; *given name:* Desmond Thomas; *m*. Marcella Frances Simpson; *children:* William Desmond; Lisgar CI, Queen's U, M.D.; radiologist; illness in youth prevented strenuous sports; aided by father and teacher, became proficient marksman and was placed in charge of cadet shooting training; youngest ever to win King's Prize Bisley 1924, lost 1929 shootoff for same award; accumulated more prizes and awards at Bisley than any other Canadian; qualified for 23 Bisley teams but was able to accept only 12 times; competed five Kalapore, three MacKinnon teams; mem. King's Hundred seven times; gold cross for grand aggregate twice, runner-up once; in total took 14 firsts, 11 seconds; many prizes in Canadian competitions; published *A Practical Rifleman's*

Guide (1932), *Canadian Bisley Shooting: An Art and Science* (1970); mem. Canadian Sports, Canadian Forces Sports Halls of Fame.

BURKHOLDER, Dave (football); *b.* 21 Oct 1936, Minneapolis, Minn.; *m.* Audrey; *children:* Heidi, David Matthew; U of Minnesota, B.B.A.; institutional sales representative; three football letters as tackle U of Minnesota, second Big 10 team, honorable mention all-American; in 1957 Blue-Grey and East-West games; joined Winnipeg Blue Bombers 1958, WIFU all-star 1958, 1960, 1961; Bombers' most valuable lineman (Dr. Bert Oja award) 1962; on four Grey Cup winners; retired following 1964 season; *res.* Hopkins, Minn.

BURNHAM, Faye (basketball); *b.* 2 Jun 1920, Vancouver, B.C.; *m.* James Eccleston; *children:* Glenn, Brian; U of British Columbia; retired phys ed teacher; mem. Canadian senior women's basketball championship teams — Westerns 1940, Hedlunds 1942-46; mem. Hedlunds B.C. women's softball champions during war, played third base; with Neons won 1944 World Series in Cleveland; rejected pro offers from Chicago Glamour League; centre forward on HS, B.C. women's field hockey teams, won Pacific Northwest titles; coached basketball, field hockey, T & F, softball, volleyball Magee HS Vancouver, Hudson Bay track team; former pres. B.C. branch Women's AAU of C, CAHPER; v.-pres. Canadian Camping Association; former director Vancouver YWCA; mem. National Advisory Council for Fitness and Amateur Sport; mem. B.C. Sports Hall of Fame; *res.* Vancouver, B.C.

BURNS, Tommy (boxing); *b.* 17 Jun 1881, Hanover, Ont.; *d.* 10 May 1955, Vancouver, B.C.; *given name:* Noah Brusso; *m.; children:* one; ordained minister; under Sam Biddle began ring career in Detroit at 19; scored seven straight KO's before adopting name Tommy Burns borrowed from jockey friend; KO's led to bout with Philadelphia Jack O'Brien and first loss; when Jim Jeffries retired Marvin Hart claimed vacant world heavyweight crown; Burns, O'Brien filed counter claims; first and only Canadian to hold world heavyweight boxing title, 1906; defended successfully 11 times including draw and win over O'Brien; lost title to Jack Johnson 1908; ended ring career 1920 with 36 KO's, nine wins on decisions, four losses on decisions, eight draws, one no-contest, once KO'd; two records: shortest heavyweight title bout, one minute, 28 second KO victory over Jem Roche 1908 in Dublin, and at 5'7" shortest ever heavyweight titlist; wrote *Scientific Boxing* 1908; mem. Canadian, U S Boxing, Canadian Sports Halls of Fame.

BUTT, Susan (tennis); *b.* 19 Mar 1938, Vancouver, B.C.; *given name:* Dorcas Susan; *m.* Dr. W.D. Liam Finn; *children:* Tara Susan, Donal Lee; U of British Columbia, B.A., M.A., U of Chicago, Ph.D.; psychologist, associate professor; for over 10 years one of Canada's leading tennis stars winning singles, doubles and mixed doubles in B.C., Ontario, Quebec, Canadian championships, Western Canadian, Pacific Northwest, U S intercollegiate, Holland Leider and Berlin titles; first in Canadian women's tennis 1960-61, 1967; gained third round at Wimbledon championships 1961 before losing to top-seeded Sandra Reynolds of South Africa; captain Canadian Federation Cup team 1970-72; v.-pres. Canadian Lawn Tennis Association 1971-72; wrote *A Psychology of Sport; res.* Vancouver, B.C.

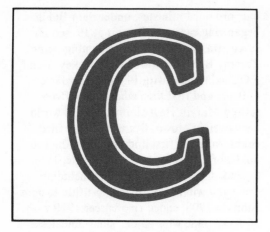

CAETANO, Errol (table tennis); *b*. 8 Aug 1953, Georgetown, Guyana; cable engineer; represented Canada world and Commonwealth Games 1971, 1973, 1975; mem. first team to visit China 1971; five times Canadian singles, men's doubles, six times mixed doubles titles; Caribbean singles, men's and mixed doubles titles 1972; Scandinavian open 1975; fifth ranked Commonwealth, 39th world; *res.* Toronto, Ont.

CAHILL, Leo (football); *b*. 30 Jul 1928, Utica, Ill.; *m*. Shirley; *children:* Steven, Christy Lee, Terry, Lisa Ann, Betty Lynn; U of Illinois, B.Sc., U of Toledo, M.A.; football coach; all-State centre in senior year HS; as Illinois freshman 1946 competed in Rose Bowl victory over UCLA; senior year all-Midwest guard, honorable mention all-American, Catholic all-American; played in Blue-Grey Game; coached football in Japan; freshman coach Illinois 1953; Lewis College line coach 1954-55; assistant coach Toledo 1956-57; U of South Carolina offensive coach 1958-59; joined Perry Moss as assistant Montreal Alouettes 1960-64; head coach Toronto Rifles, Continental League 1965, won division title, lost to Charleston in final;

tied for division title 1966 losing playoff to Philadelphia; coached Argos 1967-73 guiding them to playoffs first time since 1961; general manager Memphis Southmen (WFL) 1974; league official just before league folded 1975; returned to Argos as coach replacing Russ Jackson after 1976 season. *res.* Toronto. Ont.

CALLES, Ada (curling); *b*. 12 Oct 1920, Lancashire, Eng.; *given name:* Ada Davies; *m*. Samuel Calles; *children:* Dan, Sam; Trail HS, business college; began curling career 1951 Kimberley B.C.; with Ina Hansen 1956 won Primary Cup, Secondary Cup and grand aggregate 1957 and for nine consecutive years represented Kootenay District at B.C. championships; won B.C. and Canadian title 1962; runner-up to Ontario's Emily Wooley 1963; won Canadian title 1964 and defeated men's Canadian champion rink skipped by Lyall Dagg in special match; following seven-year break teamed again with Ina Hansen to take B.C. title and tie for first 1971 Canadian final, second in playoff; with Hansen at third, skipped winning B.C. entry in first Canadian ladies' seniors final Ottawa 1973; runner-up provincials 1974-75; mem. BCLCA executive 1960-67, from zone convenor to pres.; served as CLCA delegate; chairman 1976 B.C. girls' provincial championships; mem. Canadian Curling Hall of Fame; *res.* Kimberley, B.C.

CALLURA, Jackie (boxing); *b*. 24 Sep 1917, Hamilton, Ont.; Hamilton HS; Canadian amateur featherweight title 1931; represented Canada 1932 Olympics; turned pro 1936; won U S National Boxing Association featherweight, title beating Jackie Wilson in 15 at Providence 1943; defended twice before KO loss to Phil Terranova 1943 New Orleans; last pro bout Miami 1947; fought

100 pro bouts winning 13 by KO, 43 by decision, one on foul, 10 draws, 27 decisions lost, KO'd six times; mem. Canadian Boxing, Sports Halls of Fame; *res.* Hamilton, Ont.

CAMERON, Bev (rowing); *b.* 17 Jun 1953, Ottawa, Ont.; Laurentian HS, Nepean HS; student; third 1973 Canadian Henley single sculls; second 1974 Canadian Henley, Canadian championship single sculls; won 1975 Canadian national, Canadian Henley single sculls and, with sister Trice, Henley double sculls; second Canadian national, with Trice U S women's national double sculls; represented Canada 1976 Montreal Olympics; *res.* Ottawa, Ont.

CAMERON, Harry (hockey); *b.* 6 Feb 1890, Pembroke, Ont., *d.* 20 Oct 1953, Vancouver, B.C.; *given name:* Harold Hugh; one of first offensive defenceman, believed first player to curve a shot without aid of curved stick; scored 171 goals in 312 games over 14-year pro career; Toronto Blueshirts (NHA) 1913-17, Montreal Wanderers (NHA) 1917, Toronto Arenas 1918, 1920-24 (three Stanley Cups), Ottawa Senators 1919, Montreal Canadiens 1920; left NHL 1924, played in Vancouver, Saskatoon, Minneapolis, St. Louis; coach Saskatoon Sheiks in Prairie League 1932; mem. Canadian Hockey Hall of Fame.

CAMPBELL, Clarence (hockey); *b.* 7 Jul 1905, Fleming, Sask.; *given name:* Clarence Sutherland; *m.* Phyllis Loraine King; U of Alberta, B.A., LL.B., Oxford U, M.A.; hockey executive, lawyer; best known as administrator; played halfback Edmonton Eskimos in Provincial League, eventually owned club; at 17 organized Edmonton and district hockey association; catcher, outfielder in baseball; designed, built Renfrew Park, Edmon-

ton; at Oxford captain hockey team; in later years won several Canadian Branch of Royal Caledonian Curling Club competitions; refereed amateur hockey 1929-40, joined NHL 1936, officiated in 155 scheduled and 12 playoff games; NHL pres. 1946; prominent role in establishing NHL players pension plan, expansion program; Lester Patrick Trophy 1972; league created Clarence Campbell division in his honor; 1967 Centennial medal, MBE; mem. Canadian Sports, Canadian, U S Hockey Halls of Fame; *res.* Montreal, Que.

CAMPBELL, Colin (curling); *b.* 17 Jan 1901, Shedden, Ont.; *m.* Vera Smith; *children:* two sons, two daughters; Dutton HS, Queen's U; engineer, soldier, politician; mem. Ontario rink 1951 Macdonald Brier; captain Canadian Strathcona Cup team in Scotland 1960, 1970, Switzerland 1967; mem. Dominion (now Canadian) Curling Association since 1938, pres. 1947-48, chairman International Committee 1948-76; Macdonald Brier trustee since 1965; Canadian representative Scotch Cup Advisory Committee 1964-67; helped organize International Curling Federation 1966; Canadian representative to ICF since 1967, pres. since 1969; life mem. Hamilton Thistle Club, Manitoba CA, Quebec CA, Ontario CA, Canadian CA, Pacific Coast CA, Grand National CC of NA, German CA, Royal Caledonian CC; mem. Canadian Curling Hall of Fame; *res.* Keswick, Ont.

CAMPBELL, Garnet (curling); *b.* 11 Jan 1927, Avonlea, Sask; *given name:* William Garnet; *m.* DeVerne; *children:* Vern, Cassandra; farmer; represented Saskatchewan in unprecedented 10 Briers beginning 1947, skipped winner 1955; runner-up provincial playdowns three other times; skipped Saskatchewan in Canadian mixed finals 1976 tying for first and losing playoff to B.C. also 1977 Canadian mixed; winner six carspiels; grand aggregate champion Moose Jaw 'spiel seven times, Regina 'spiel five times, Weyburn, Ottawa, Vancouver Totem 'spiels once each; winner Quebec International, Windsor Invitational, Toronto Canada Life, Calgary Masters; twice won CBC keen-ice competition; mem. Canadian Curling Hall of Fame; *res.* Avonlea, Sask.

CAMPBELL, Hugh (football); *b.* 21 May 1941, Spokane, Wash.; *m.* Louise; *children:* Robin, Jill, Rick; Washington State U, B.S., M.Ed.; football coach; all-American end 1960-62 at WSU; drafted by San Francisco '49ers and joined Saskatchewan Roughriders from '49ers training camp 1963; with Saskatchewan in CFL through 1969 season, three times Western Conference all-star, twice all-Canadian flanker; CFL record 321 receptions for 5,425yds, 16.9yds per catch avg. and 60 TDs; shares CFL single season TD pass-catching record of 17 with Terry Evanshen; led WFC 1965 with 1,329yds on league-leading 73 receptions and 93.6 completion percentage; WFC scoring title 1966 with 109 points, Dave Dryburgh Trophy; coach several seasons Whitworth College; coach Edmonton Eskimos 1977; NAIA District One coach of year 1972, 1975; *res.* Edmonton, Alta.

CAMPBELL, Jerry (football); *b.* 14 Jul 1944, Binghampton, N.Y.; *m.* Betty; U of Idaho, B.Sc; football player, car salesman; nickname Soupy; Idaho lineman of year; all-Skyline team 1965; turned pro Calgary Stampeders 1966 as offensive guard, outside linebacker; traded to Ottawa Rough Riders 1968; all-Eastern six years, all-Canadian seven years; Washington pro athlete of year

1972-73, Idaho pro athlete of year 1972-74; traded to Calgary 1976, subsequently released; signed Hamilton 1977; assists Carleton U coaching staff; *res.* Ottawa, Ont.

CAMPBELL, R.D. (coaching); *b.* 12 Apr 1892, Ottawa, Ont., *d.* 4 Dec 1970, Ottawa, Ont.; *given name:* Robert Duncan; *m.* Annie Laurie McLaren (*d.*); *m.* Minnie Constance Currie (*d.*); *m.* Helen Mary Docksteader; *children:* Bruce; Woodstock HS; McMaster U, B.A., OCE; educator; set intercollegiate high jump record which stood many years; head phys ed Glebe CI until 1956; from 1930-53 won 16 senior, 11 junior city basketball titles, his teams won nearly 50 championships at all levels; coached Glebe Grads to 1938 Canadian senior title; won several juvenile, junior Canadian basketball titles; coached Glebe T & F athletes to Arthur Currie Trophy in national competition McGill eight times 1933-48; helped establish physical culture courses Hart House Toronto, Lake Couchiching for Dept. of Education; introduced team eligibility rules, forward pass, downfield blocking into Canadian game at HS level resulting in changes in Canadian football rules; sought by McMaster as athlete director in 1940s, by Ottawa Rough Riders as coach, but elected to stay with Ottawa HS sports; Ottawa sportsman of year; mem. selection committee Greater Ottawa Sports Hall of Fame; first HS stadium in Ottawa named in his honor; mem. Greater Ottawa Sports Hall of Fame.

CAMPBELL, Shirley (swimming); *b.* 21 Sep 1935, Fergus, Ont.; *given name:* Shirley Marguerite; *m.* William Richard Campbell; *children:* Gary, Sandra; Fergus HS; real estate agent; 5:13 record for Canadian 400 North Vancouver 1951; broke own record and qualified for 1952 Helsinki Olympics but illness forced her out; won Canadian mile at CNE 1952 then turned pro taking 1953, 1954 CNE three-mile pro swim titles, barely missing world record; at 19, coached by Max Hurley, attempted to beat Marilyn Bell's Lake Ontario swim record 1955 but was pulled from water one and one-half miles from goal after 21:27, 42 miles; second unsuccessful attempt under coach Bert Crockett 1956, after 18:44 pulled from lake 1,000yds from goal; gave up lake challenges and did some Sportman's Show swims; *res.* Caledon East, Ont.

CAMPBELL, Woody (basketball); *b.* 31 Jan 1925, Windsor, Ont.; *m.* Shirley; *children:* four daughters, two sons; U of Windsor, B.A.; sales executive; with Assumption College (U of Windsor) won Eastern Canadian Intercollegiate title 1946-47, 1948-49; with Tillsonburg Livingstons won 1952 Canadian senior men's title and represented Canada Helsinki Olympics; *res.* Tillsonburg, Ont.

CAPOZZI, Herb (football); *b.* 24 Apr 1925, Kelowna, B.C.; *given name:* Harold Peter; *m.* Dorothy Skelton; *children:* Paula, Greg, Sandra, Sheena; U of British Columbia, B.A., B. Comm., U of Italy, education degree; owns, operates men's athletic and recreation centre; played football UBC, received offers to play with N Y Giants (NFL) which he rejected to study in Italy; returned to Canada 1951, joined Calgary Stampeders, then three seasons with Montreal Alouettes; B.C. Lions' general manager 1957-66, won B.C's only Grey Cup 1964; chairman CFL, WFC general managers committees; briefly operated Vancouver Canucks NHL team; principal owner Vancouver Whitecaps in North American Soccer League; chairman Soccer Canada; with Bob Pickell 1973 Canadian Masters doubles racketball champion; *res.* Vancouver, B.C.

CARDINAL, Marc (weightlifting); *b.* 9 May 1956, Kingston, Ont.; *given name:* Donald Jean-Marc; Canterbury HS, U of Ottawa; medical student; 18 Canadian junior records and one Commonwealth junior record; only teenager to clean and jerk 400 lbs in Commonwealth competition; won class titles 1974 Ontario Winter Games, 1975 Canadian juniors, 1976 Canadian juniors, seniors, Ontario vs Eastern States; second 1975 Canada Winter Games, 1976 Ontario seniors; second 1977 Canadian championships with 340kg lift; *res.* Ottawa, Ont.

CARNWATH, Jim (badminton); *b.* 11 Feb 1935, Woodstock, Ont.; *given name:* James Dalziel; Woodstock CI, U of Toronto, B.A., LL.D.; lawyer; represented Canada Thomas Cup team 1958, 1961, 1964, 1967; Canadian mixed doubles champion 1963-64; Canadian Badminton Association pres. 1976-77; *res.* Woodstock, Ont.

CARPENTER, Keith (tennis); *b.* 3 Aug 1941, England; *given name:* Alan Keith; *m.* Judith Dianne; Sir George Williams U, B.Sc.; tennis court construction; won boys-18 doubles with Derek Penner 1958, Canadian Open doubles with Mike Carpenter 1966, Canadian Open mixed doubles with Eleanor Dodge 1962, with Vickie Berner 1963; Open singles runner-up 1963, Canadian Closed singles 1973, Closed doubles 1974; mem. Canadian Davis Cup team 1962-68, 1971; *res.* Toronto, Ont.

CARPENTER, Ken (football); *b.* 26 Feb 1926, Carlyle, Wash.; *given name:* Kenneth Leroy; *m.* Doris Jacobson; *children:* Kimberly, Kenneth Jr.; Oregon State U, B.A.; director of recreation; college football Oregon State 1946-49; pro Cleveland Browns, halfback 1950-53; Saskatchewan Roughriders 1954-59; versatile runner, passer, kicker and receiver; set Saskatchewan single-season, TD record with 18 in 1955, WFC MVP and leading scorer with 90 points; three times WFC all-star; six-year CFL career total 55 TDs; head coach Saskatchewan 1960; appeared in U S East-West Shrine Game, college all-star, NFL all-pro game and Canadian pro East-West Shrine Game; *res.* Indianapolis, Ind.

CARRUTHERS, Liz (diving); *b.* 14 Sep 1951, Edmonton, Alta.; *given name:* Elizabeth Ann; California State U; Canadian 11-12 100yd butterfly record 1963; third in Canada at 13 on balance beam, vaulting; held Alberta, Saskatchewan junior, novice, senior gymnastic titles; began diving age 11; national level 1967 with Alberta springboard titles, bronze in 3m at summer nationals and alternate's berth Pan-Am Games team; won Canadian junior 3m 1968, gold medal 3m Prague Czechoslovakia 1970; gold medals 1971 in 3m Cali Columbia Pan-Am Games, Canadian summer nationals, South African Cup, W. Germany/Canada dual meet, Russian International; competitive record includes 25 silver and 10 bronze in 1m, 3m springboard, Canadian, International 10m tower, including 1970 Commonwealth Games; represented Canada in U S, Czechoslovakia, E. and W. Germany, Mexico, Russia, Italy, Sweden, Finland, and South Africa; alternate 1968 Olympic team, competed in 1972 Munich Games; auto accident 1972 threatened athletic career but returned to competition late in 1975, fourth 1976 Olympic trials; *res.* Sherwood Park, Alta.

CARTER, Moe (autosport); *b.* 25 May 1924, Winnipeg, Man.; *given name:* Maurice Charles; *m.* Lois Tweed; *children:* Lesley, Susan, Kelly, Steven, Bradley; St. John's College; automobile dealer; began career in rallies, second 1964 Shell 4,000; moved into racing 1969 winning Canadian sedan title; only Canadian to win major U S races plus many on Canadian tracks; Canadian A Production title 1971-72; IMSA American Sedan & GT champion 1972-73; CRCA driver of year 1970; Canadian race driver of year 1971-72; *res.* Burlington, Ont.

CASEY, Tom (football); *b.* 1924, Ohio; Hampton Institute Virginia, U of Manitoba, M.D.; neurologist; played one year pro football N Y Yankees of all-American Conference; joined Hamilton Wildcats 1949, Winnipeg Blue Bombers 1950-55; nicknamed Citation while achieving all-star seven times; led 1950 WIFU rushers winning Eddie James Memorial Trophy; gained 100yds on single play 1952 vs Saskatchewan at Regina; same season gained 205yds in pass interception returns and set WIFU single season TD record of 16; Winnipeg citizen of year 1956; mem. Canadian Football Hall of Fame; *res.* New York, N.Y.

CASSAN, Gerry (speedskating); *b.* 5 Dec 1954; Ottawa, Ont.; *given name:* Gerard; Belcourt HS; civil servant; began speedskating career 1963 winning international competition Fort Henry N.Y.; through 1975 won eight Ontario indoor, 21 outdoor titles, four Canadian indoor, seven outdoor titles, two international indoor, 16 outdoor titles establishing many records; fastest 500m (40.19) by Canadian; represented Canada 1972 Olympics, 1973-74 world competitions; gold medal 500m junior world Cortina Italy 1974; played lacrosse Ontario champion Loisir St. Anne's 1964, Leduc Motors 1968; top scorer Overbrook Minto Colts minor football 1966; Ontario Junior Open cycling champion 1972; at eight youngest athlete honored by Ottawa

ACT; Ottawa Valley French Canadian athlete of year 1966, 1968; speedskater of year 1970-71; Ontario Sports Achievement Award 1969; honored by City of Ottawa three times; *res.* Ottawa, Ont.

CAVALLIN, Roy (lacrosse); *b.* 15 Sep 1919, Vancouver, B.C., *given name:* Roy Fred; *m.* Isabell; *children:* Timmie; played 16 years senior lacrosse; nicknames Fritzie, Rocky; with Vancouver Burrards Mann Cup winners 1949; during 30s played several seasons Coast League senior soccer with New Westminster Royals; senior A basketball with Lauries 1938; trainer for first Canadian soccer team to play in World Cup competition in Mexico; two years lacrosse referee; trainer B.C. Lions 1958-76; past pres. B.C. Athletic Trainers' Association; pres. B.C. Sports for the Retarded; mem. Canadian Lacrosse Hall of Fame; *res.* Vancouver, B.C.

CHABOT, Lorne (hockey); *b.* 5 Oct 1900, Montreal, Que. *d.* 10 Oct 1946, Montreal, Que.; in an era when diminutive goalers were the vogue, Chabot, at 6'1'', stood out; helped Port Arthur win Allan Cup then turned pro with N Y Rangers 1926; posted goals-against averages of 1.56 and 1.79 in two seasons with Rangers then moved to Toronto Maple Leafs 1928-33, Canadiens 1933-34, Chicago Black Hawks 1934-35, Montreal Maroons 1935-36, N Y Americans 1936-37; helped Rangers win 1928 Stanley Cup; 1935 Vezina Trophy, first team all-star.

CHAMBUL, Borys (track and field); *b.* 17 Feb 1953, Toronto, Ont.; *given name:* Borys Michael; U of Washington, B.A.; student; discus specialist; mem. Canadian junior team which toured Portugal 1973, Europe 1974; second in Canada 1975 with 58.98m; 1976

won Pacific Eight discus with 196'4'', NCAA title with 202'3'' (61.64m), Olympic trials Quebec City with 198'4'' (60.46m), Canadian, Commonwealth record of 214'7'' (65.40m) in Montreal (beat Pacific Eight record holder Jay Silvester of U S 65.40m-63.60m); holds NCAA record; represented Canada 1976 Olympics; most inspirational award U of Washington track team 1976; *res.* Scarborough, Ont.

CHAPMAN, Art (basketball); *b.* 28 Oct 1912, Victoria, B.C.; *given name:* Arthur St. Clair; *m.* Kathleen; *children:* Lyn Arthur, Jim; Victoria HS; salesman; HS aggregate T&F title 1931-32 in five events — high jump, long jump, hop, step and jump (triple jump), shot put and 120yd hurdles; mem. 1933 B.C. softball champions; at 16 batted .399 in senior A baseball league; with Victoria Blue Ribbons and Dominoes on five Canadian championship basketball teams; mem. 1936 Olympic silver medal team; mem. Dominoes 1946 team chosen B.C. team of century, won Canadian title without losing a game in league or playoffs; player-coach-manager Vancouver Hornets pro basketball 1947-48; in Canadian army 1945 helped unit win Canadian overseas titles basketball, volleyball, soccer; helped form juvenile football league; various executive positions in Little League, Connie Mack baseball; son Jim played three years Montreal Expos chain batting .311 in Triple A before being traded to Braves organization; with brother Chuck mem. B.C. Sports Hall of Fame; *res.* Qualicum Beach, B.C.

CHAPMAN, Chuck (basketball); *b.* 21 Apr 1911, Vancouver, B.C.; *given name:* Charles Winston; *m.* Emily Margaret; *children:* Clara Mary, Janet Kathleen, Fern Ruth; Victoria HS, Victoria College; retired; mem. B.C.

senior A softball, lacrosse, soccer championship teams; played for six B.C. championship basketball teams, captained five to Canadian titles; mem. Canadian silver medal team 1936 Olympics Berlin; captain Victoria Dominoes 1946 who won Canadian championship without losing league or playoff game; team chosen team of century for B.C.'s centennial year; mem. B.C. Sports Hall of Fame; *res.* Victoria, B.C.

CHAPMAN, John (harness racing); *b.* 25 Nov 1928, Toronto Ont.; *m.* Janice Feldman; *children:* Cynthia, Wendy, Cheryl, John Jr.; St. Michael's HS; harness driver, trainer; captain St. Michael's hockey team; won first harness race Dufferin Park 1947; through 1976 had over 3,300 wins with over $14 million in purses (sixth, all-time list), 25 sub-2:00 miles; winner Roosevelt International 1973-74; among better known horses Diller Hanover, Valiant Bret, Rising Wind, Skippers Dream, Delmonica Hanover, Meadow Flower; *res.* Westbury, N.Y.

CHEEVERS, Gerry (hockey); *b.* 7 Dec 1940, St. Catharines, Ont.; *given name:* Gerald Michael; *m.* Betty; *children:* Craig, Cheryl, Robby; St. Michael's College; St. Catharines minor hockey program to junior A with Toronto St. Michael's Majors to pro with Toronto Maple Leafs 1961-62; played minor pro Sault Ste. Marie (CPHL), Pittsburgh, Rochester (AHL), Sudbury (EPHL) Oklahoma (CPHL), then regular spot with Boston Bruins 1967-72; to WHA with Cleveland Crusaders for three and one-half seasons, then Boston 1975-77; mem. Team Canada 1974, 1976; set record of 32 unbeaten games with Bruins 1971-72; twice WHA all-star; Hap Holmes Trophy (AHL top goaler) 1965; CPHL top goaler 1967; WHA top goaler 1973; in 12 major league seasons played 458 games, 26,972 minutes allowed

1,333 goals, posted 31 shutouts for 2.96 avg., plus 65 games, 3,969 minutes, allowed 179 goals, posted six shutouts for 2.71 avg; owns string of thoroughbred racing horses including Royal Ski and has had some success at track; *res.* North Andover, Mass.

CHENARD, Line (swimming); *b.* 10 Apr 1957, Quebec City, Que.; student; 1975 Pan-Am Games gold medal 100m backstroke, silver medals 200m backstroke and 400m medley relay; toured Canada, Europe with national swim team 1974; *res.* Quebec City, Que.

CHENIER, Georges (snooker); *b.* 14 Nov 1907, Hull, Que., *d.* 16 Nov 1970, Toronto, Ont.; *m.* Bernadette Corrilla; North American snooker champion 1947, held title 22 years; twice failed to win world title placing second to England's Fred Davis 1950, 1958; world record match play break of 144 vs Walter Donaldson, England 1950; world record six century breaks vs Leo Levitt of Montreal during 1955 North American title matches Vancouver; world record run of 150 for pocket billiards against world champion Irving Crane 1963, NYC, later duplicated feat; stroke 1966 paralyzed left side restricting use of left arm; defended North American title 1968, 1970; mem. Canadian Sports Hall of Fame.

CHUVALO, George (boxing); 12 Sep 1937, Toronto, Ont.; *m.* Lynne; *children:* Mitchell, Steven, George Jr., Jesse, Vanessa; St. Michael's College; began boxing at 10 in St. Mary's Catholic Church hall; moved into amateur bouts at East York Arena, Palace Pier; Canadian amateur heavyweight title 1955; turned pro 1956; Canadian heavyweight title beating James J. Parker 1958; defended against Yvon Durelle then lost to Bob Cleroux 1960; regained title 1960 then lost it to Cleroux again 1961; regained it 1968 beating Jean Claude Roy, defended successfully through 1976; first U S bout lost to Pat McMurtry 1959; never tried for Commonwealth title but fought best in world including Muhammad Ali, Floyd Patterson, Ernie Terrell, Joe Frazier, George Foreman; career total 93 pro bouts, 65 won by KO, 9 by decision, one draw, lost 15 decisions, one on disqualification and TKO'd twice; never knocked off his feet; frequent TV boxing commentator; *res*. Weston, Ont.

CLAIR, Frank (football); *b*. 12 May 1917, Hamilton, Ohio; *m*. Pat Bausman; *children:* Robin, Holly (*d.*); Hamilton HS, Ohio State U, Miami of Ohio, B.Sc.; football executive; all-Big 10 end 1938 at Ohio State U; drafted by Washington Redskins, remained with club until war; assistant coach 71st Infantry Division in Europe; assistant coach Miami of Ohio 1946, Purdue 1947; U of Buffalo head coach 1948; coach Toronto Argos 1950-54, won two Grey Cups; assistant coach Cincinnati U 1955; head coach Ottawa Rough Riders 1956; guided Riders to four Grey Cup finals, won three; Riders general manager 1970; nickname The Professor; in 18 CFL seasons as coach compiled record of 172 wins, 125 losses, seven ties for .579 percentage; made playoffs 17 seasons, league final 12 times, six Grey Cups, winning five; CFL coach of year (Annis Stukus Trophy) 1966, 1969; *res*. Ottawa, Ont.

CLANCY, King (hockey); *b*. 25 Feb 1903, Ottawa, Ont.; *m*. Rae; *children:* Terry, Carol Ann, Judy, Tom; *given name:* Francis Michael; hockey executive; played amateur hockey St. Brigid's Ottawa; at 18 became pro Ottawa Senators, gained reputation as rushing defenceman; sold to Toronto Maple Leafs 1930 for unprecedented $35,000 and two players; led Leafs to first Stanley Cup

1931-32; twice named to each of first, second all-star teams; retired after 1936-37 season; coached Montreal Maroons first half 1937-38, switched to refereeing; 1950 joined Leafs as coach; following 1952-53 campaign became assistant manager, v.-pres.; nickname King inherited from athlete father Tom; mem. Hockey, Canadian Sports Halls of Fame; *res*. Toronto, Ont.

CLAPPER, Dit (hockey); *b*. 9 Feb 1907, Newmarket, Ont.; *given name:* Aubrey Victor; *m*. Lorraine Pratt; *children:* Donald, Marilyn; Aurora HS; office manager, accountant; played junior in Oshawa at 13; before joining Boston Bruin's at 19, played with Parkdale Canoe Club and Boston Tigers (CAHL); with Bruins became first NHL player to play 20 seasons with same club 1927-47; played nine years at right wing, 11 more on defence; scored 228 regular season goals, 246 assists plus 12 playoff goals and 23 assists; best season 1929-30, 41 goals in 44-game schedule; played on three Stanley Cup winners; three times first team, three times second team all-star; Bruins retired sweater No. 5 when he left club; played with Buffalo (AHL) after leaving NHL; came back to coach Bruins two seasons and Buffalo 1960 one season before retiring; mem. Hockey, Canadian Sports Halls of Fame; *res*. Peterborough, Ont.

CLARIDGE, Pat (football); *b*. 12 Jul 1938, Chilliwack, B.C.; U of Washington, stockbroker; twice appeared with Washington in Rosebowl game victories over Wisconsin 1960 and Minnesota 1961; all-Coast split end; pass receiver B.C. Lions 1961-66; with Calgary for 1968 Grey Cup; made 198 pass receptions for 2,497 yds; WFC all-star 1964, nominated top Canadian player; color commentary for CKNW broadcasts of Lions Games; *res*. Vancouver, B.C.

Clark

CLARK, Barbara (swimming); *b.* 24 Sep 1958, Coronation, Alta.; *given name:* Barbara Lynne; Stettler HS, U of Alberta; student; butterfly, freestyle specialist who trained under coach Larry Neilson with Cascade Swim Club; represented Canada 1975 world, sixth 100m butterfly; bronze medal 4x100m freestyle relay 1976 Montreal Olympics; retired from competition following 1976 Games; personal bests: 100m butterfly 1:03.88, 100m freestyle 58.37; Alberta outstanding swimmer award 1974, 1976, Governor-General's silver medal 1976; *res.* Stettler, Alta.

CLARKE, Bill (football); *b.* 25 Nov 1932, Regina, Sask.; *m.* Geraldine; *children:* Jim, Tara, Debbie, Peter, Robbie; Director Sport and Recreation, Dept. Culture and Youth, Saskatchewan; graduated from Regina Rams to pro with Saskatchewan Roughriders 1951, 14 years as centre, defensive tackle; all-star twice; prominent curler, won 1950 Canadian schoolboy title; *res.* Regina, Sask.

CLARKE, Bobby (hockey); *b.* 13 Aug 1949, Flin Flon, Man.; *given name:* Robert Earle; hockey player; through Flin Flon minor hockey to Junior Bombers; Philadelphia's second choice, 17th overall in 1969 amateur draft; led Flyers to two Stanley Cups; youngest NHL team captain; through 1976-77 NHL record 622 games played, 233 goals, 472 assists, 705 points, 758 penalty minutes plus 65 playoff games, 13 goals, 43 assists, 56 points, 94 penalty minutes; twice first team all-star centre, twice second team; mem. Team Canada 1972, 1976; Hart Trophy 1973, 1975, 1976; Bill Masterton Trophy 1972; Lester B. Pearson Award 1973; Canadian athlete of year 1975; Lou Marsh Trophy winner 1975. *res.* Philadelphia, Pa.

CLARKSON, Wendy (badminton); *b.* 11 Mar 1956, Glasgow, Scotland; *given name:* Wendy May; U of Calgary; student; won 1975 Canadian junior singles; with Tracey Vanwassenhove won Canadian junior girls' doubles; with Cam Dalgleish won mixed doubles; with Lorraine Thorne doubles runner-up; mem. Canadian Uber Cup team which defeated U S, Australia; won 1976 Canadian ladies' singles, Canadian Open; quarter-finalist 1977 all-England tournament; *res.* Edmonton, Alta.

CLAYTON, Harold (lawn bowling); *b.* 10 Jun 1916, Lang, Sask.; *given name:* Harold Wright; Lang, Regina HS; provincial civil servant; from 1945-60 among Saskatchewan's top curlers; Canadian singles lawn bowling title 1959, 1969, represented Canada 1970 British Commonwealth Games Edinburgh as singles competitor; mem. Saskatchewan Sports Hall of Fame; *res.* Regina Sask.

CLEGHORN, Odie (hockey); *b.* 1891, Montreal, Que., *d.* 13 Jul 1956, Montreal, Que.; *given name:* Ogilvie; unique distinction of playing major hockey as both forward and goaler, later referee; played for Canadiens 1918-25 then closed career with Pittsburgh Pirates for two seasons; nine-year NHL record 96 goals, 29 assists, 125 points; playoffs seven goals, two assists, nine points; as goaler one game, two goals, 2.00 avg.

CLEGHORN, Sprague (hockey); *b.* 1890, Montreal, Que., *d.* 11 Jul 1956, Montreal, Que.; played with N Y Crescents then moved to Renfrew (NHA) 1909-10; six years with Montreal Wanderers; began career as forward but with Renfrew shifted to defence with Cyclone Taylor; once scored five goals in single game; to Ottawa 1919-21, briefly to Toronto St. Pat's then back to Montreal to join Canadiens 1922-25; ended career with Boston Bruins 1926; in 17 seasons (missed 1918 with broken leg) scored 163 goals in 296 games; played on two Stanley Cup winners; mem. Hockey Hall of Fame.

CLIFF, Leslie (swimming); *b.* 11 Mar 1955, Vancouver, B.C.; U of British Columbia; student; won 15 Canadian titles, four British, one U S; three gold, two silver 1971 Pan-Am Games; two gold 1974 Commonwealth Games; silver 1972 Munich Olympics; specialist in 400m, 800m freestyle, 200m backstroke, 400m individual medley; Order of Canada award; B.C. swimmer of year 1971-73; *res.* Vancouver, B.C.

CLIFFORD, Betsy (skiing); *b.* 15 Oct 1953, Ottawa, Ont.; Philemon Wright HS, Algonquin College; began skiing at five, won consistently at eight in Gatineau area events; Canadian junior title age 12; Canadian women's title age 13; held Canadian slalom, giant slalom titles eight times through 1975; at 14 youngest Canadian skier ever in Olympics (1968 Grenoble); at 16 youngest person to win world ski title, with giant slalom gold medal Val Gardena Italy 1970; at 17 won women's special slalom title Val-d'Isère France; freak accident resulted in two broken heels in World Cup downhill 1972; returned to competition with Can-Am team 1973; 1974 silver medal world championship downhill St. Moritz Switzerland, third World Cup downhill Pfronten Germany, won Can-Am giant slalom, Thetford Mines Que., won Canadian slalom Owl's Head; won 1975 Canadian giant slalom; ACT (Ottawa) athlete of year twice; mem. Canadian Sports Hall of Fame; retired 1976; *res.* Old Chelsea, Que.

CLIFFORD, Harvey (skiing); *b.* 18 Sep 1926, Oak Point, N.B.; *m.* Ellen Vera; *children:* Christian, Heidi; Glebe CI, Queen's U; ski resort owner, operator; competed for Canada 1948 St. Moritz Olympics; coach, captain Canadian skiers 1950 world Aspen Colo; coach Canadian team 1952 Norway Olympics; ski school director Banff, Laurentians, New Zealand, Mt. Snow Vt.; chief examiner Canadian Ski Instructors Alliance; *res.* Waitsfield, Vt.

CLIFFORD, John (skiing); *b.* 13 Feb 1923, Ottawa, Ont.; *m.* Margaret Phillips; *children:* Betsy, Joanne, Stephen (*d.*), Susanne; Glebe CI, Ottawa Technical HS; ski area operator; despite schoolyard accident which left him almost blind in right eye, became skiing and water-skiing champion; won Chilean, Pan-Am titles 1946; three Canadian championships, two Quebec titles; Olympic alpine alternate 1948, 1952; competed world team Aspen Colo. 1950; Canadian water-ski title 1955; Quebec title four straight years; ninth world water-ski finals 1955; involved in development of ski areas Camp Fortune, Carlington, Mont Ste. Marie, Mt. Tremblant; *res.* Old Chelsea, Que.

COAFFEE, Cyril (track); *b.* 1897, Winnipeg, Man., *d.* 1945; won 100m final in 11.2 at 1920 Olympic trials but not named to team since funds available for only nine track representatives and he was 10th; Winnipeg supporters sent him to Antwerp Games and third place finish in qualifying heat; ran world record equalling 9.6 for 100yds 1922 which stood as Canadian standard more than 25 years; ran for Illinois Athletic Club Chicago, competed throughout U S, Europe 1923-24 then returned to Canada 1924 to qualify for Olympics; captain Olympic track team in Paris Games; equalled Olympic 10.8 mark for 100m in trials but failed to perform well in Paris; following Games faced many of world's top sprinters in series of British meets and had many victories at 100, 220yds; mem. Canadian Sports Hall of Fame.

COFFEY, Tommy-Joe (football); *b.* 1936, McAdoo, Tex.; West Texas State, B.S.; fine receiver, placement kicker; outstanding lineman 1959 Copper Bowl; eighth round draft choice of Baltimore Colts (NFL) 1959 but turned pro Edmonton Eskimos, quit after 1960 to enter business; returned to Eskimos 1962 and won Dave Dryburgh Trophy as WFC scoring champion; dealt to Hamilton Tiger-Cats 1967 and closed out 14-year CFL career 1973 with Toronto Argos; CFL career record 65 TDs, 204 converts, 108 field goals, 53 singles for 971 points, 650 pass receptions for 10,320yds, 15.9 avg., 63 TDs; CFL single season scoring record 148 points 1969 (since broken by Dave Cutler); three times WFC all-star, four times EFC all-star, eight times all-Canadian; WFC scoring champion once, EFC leader three times; WFC record 81 pass receptions 1964, 1965; three times runner-up Schenley outstanding player award; runner-up to Eagle Day 1962 Jeff Nicklin Award; played in 1960 Grey Cup with broken arm; in three Grey Cup finals, two winners; *res.* Hamilton, Ont.

COLE, Betty (golf); *b.* 21 Sep 1937, Calgary, Alta.; *given name:* Betty Stanhope; *m.* Gordon Cole; *children:* Jacqueline, Robert; won Alberta junior five times, Edmonton City Open 18 times, Alberta Open 12 times, Canadian Open 1957, Canadian Closed 1967, Canadian junior 1956, runner-up 1955, runner-up Canadian Closed three times; won Saskatchewan Open 1966; Eastern provinces championship 1964; mem. Alberta interprovincial team 18 times, Ontario and Saskatchewan teams twice, Canadian Commonwealth team 1963, 1971, Canadian world team 1964, 1974, 1976; number one

Canadian player 1974, 1976; Edmonton's outstanding athlete 1957; as curler skipped Alberta provincial champions 1970, 1973, runner-up 1972; Edmonton city title 1971, 1975; *res.* Edmonton, Alta.

COLEMAN, Lovell (football); *b.* 9 May 1938, Hamtramck, Mich.; Western Michigan U; lettered as college fullback 1957-59; honorable mention UPI all-American 1959; turned pro Saskatchewan Roughriders but never played there being traded to Calgary for Jack Gotta; played 11 CFL seasons with Calgary, Ottawa, B.C., three times rushing over 1,000yds-per-season and three times rushing ball more than 200 times in a season; scored 62 TDs, 42 rushing, while carrying ball 1,135 times for 6,566yds (5.8 avg.); best single season 1964 where he carried 260 times for 1,629yds, 10 TDs; same season recorded best single game with 238yds gained at Hamilton 1964; Calgary athlete of year 1964, Schenley Award as outstanding player.

COLLINS, Merv (football); *b.* 10 Aug 1933, Toronto, Ont.; *given name:* Mervyn Douglas; *m.* Christine Salvenmoser; *children:* David, Natalie, Steven; U of Alberta, B.Ed., U of Ottawa, M.Ed.; college teacher; played offensive guard, linebacker Balmy Beach in ORFU finals vs Sarnia Imperials 1952; only rookie to crack starting lineup with Grey Cup champion Argos 1953; traded to Hamilton Tiger-Cats 1955; moved to Ottawa 1956-65; played 1966 season with Edmonton Eskimos; retired 1967; played on 1960 Grey Cup champions; several times CFL all-star; founding mem. CFL Players Pension Fund; *res.* Ottawa, Ont.

COLMAN, Frank (baseball); *b.* 2 Mar 1918, London, Ont.; *m.* Anne; *children:* Frank, Jerry; H.B. Beal THS; maintenance;

played senior city baseball then joined London in Senior Intercounty League where he attracted pro offers; joined Toronto (IL) 1939 and moved through minor pro ranks to Wilmington Del. where he ran up a 7-0 record before contracting a sore arm; injury to Billy Southworth resulted in shift to right field; second to Elmer Valo in league batting .365-.363; rejoined Toronto two years then played with Pittsburgh (NL) 1942-46 before being traded to N Y Yankees who farmed him to Newark; played part of 1946-47 seasons with Yankees including a 19-game winning streak; sold to Seattle (PCL) 1948 but chose retirement; returned to action 1949-50 in Seattle hitting .319 with 18 home runs, 98 RBI 1949 and .310 in 1950; player coach Toronto Maple Leafs 1951-53 then retired and returned to London Majors (IC), bought franchise 1955-59; managed London to Intercounty title 1956, Great Lakes-Niagara championship 1958; IC batting title, MVP 1936; Major League record 271 games, 15 home runs, 106 runs batted in, .228 batting avg.; instrumental in formation Eager Beaver Baseball Association London, pres. several years; *res.* London, Ont.

COLVILLE, Neil (hockey); *b.* 4 Aug 1914, Edmonton, Alta.; *given name:* Neil MacNeil; played centre with younger brother Mac and Alex Shibicky on Bread Line with N Y Rangers 1936-42; served in Canadian Army, returned to Rangers 1946-47; switched to defence with Frankie Eddolls for 1948-49 campaign; coach Rangers 1950 but failed to make playoffs, retired; captain Rangers six years; played on one league championship, one Stanley Cup winner; three times all-star; while in service played with Ottawa's Allan Cup winner 1942; mem. Hockey Hall of Fame.

CONACHER, Charlie (hockey); *b.* 10 Dec 1909, Toronto, Ont., *d.* 30 Dec 1967, Toronto, Ont.; *given name:* Charles William; *m.* Sonny; *children:* Peter (Charles William Jr.), Brad, Scott; businessman; younger brother of Lionel Conacher; began as goaler but shifted to wing; captain 1926 Marlboros Memorial Cup winners; played with Toronto Maple Leafs 1929-38, Detroit 1938-39, N Y Americans 1939-41; coached Chicago 1948-50; Art Ross Trophy 1934, 1935; three times first team all-star, twice second team; played originally on line with Joe Primeau, Baldy Cotton; when Busher Jackson replaced Cotton, became known as the Kid Line, one of hockey's greatest combinations; NHL record 225 goals, 173 assists, 396 points, 17 playoff goals, 18 assists, 35 points; mem. Canadian Hockey Hall of Fame.

CONACHER, Lionel (all-around); *b.* 24 May 1902, Toronto, Ont., *d.* 26 May 1954, Ottawa, Ont.; *given name:* Lionel Pretoria; *m.* Dorothy Kennedy; *children:* three sons, two daughers; Duquesne U; pro athlete, politician; nickname Big Train; at 12 played in Toronto City Rugby League; at 18 was middle wing Toronto Central Y Ontario title team; at 16 won Ontario 125lb wrestling title; won Canadian light-heavyweight boxing title 1920 in first bout, later fought exhibition with Jack Dempsey; same year played senior city rugby, baseball, lacrosse; played with Toronto Maple Leafs 1926 when they won Triple A pro baseball title; played 1921 season with Toronto Argos, scored record 15 points in 23-0 Grey Cup vs Edmonton Eskimos; began skating at 16, joined NHL as defenceman 1925; played 11 seasons with Pittsburgh, Montreal Maroons, NY Americans, Chicago Black Hawks, scored 80 goals, 105 assists; on Stanley Cup winners Chicago 1934, Montreal 1935; retired from sport 1937; MLA (LIB); MPP (LIB); former Ontario Athletic Commissioner; Canada's athlete of half century 1950; mem. Canadian Sports, Football, Lacrosse Halls of Fame.

CONDON, Eddie (tennis); *b.* 18 Jul 1901, Ottawa, Ont., Lisgar CI, U of Ottawa; retired federal government auditor; in youth prominent cross-country skier, runner specializing in 1500m, mile; third both events 1920 Olympic trials; City of Ottawa, Eastern Ontario, Canadian Interscholastic titles both events; held Canadian, North American Intercollegiate, Eastern U S, Ottawa cross-country titles; officiated 1932 Olympics, 1950 world; chairman U S Olympic ski trials, North American championships; winner nine Ottawa tennis singles titles, N.B., P.E.I. provincial crowns; runner-up Ontario men's doubles with Maurice Margeson; semifinalist Quebec men's doubles with Harry Wright; organized first Canadian junior tennis championships 1949, served as chairman 25 years; v.-pres. Canadian Lawn Tennis Association; pres. OLTA; executive-director CLTA; mem. Greater Ottawa Sports Hall of Fame; *res.* Ottawa, Ont.

CONGALTON, Jim (curling); *b.* 26 Sep 1879, Guelph, Ont., *d.* 9 Oct 1947, Winnipeg, Man.; *m.* Blanche Hildegarde Dyson; *children:* Helen, Frances; salesman; at 12 youngest mem. in history of Guelph Curling Club, presented to Governor-General as youngest in Canada at time; skipped 1927 Winnipeg Granite rink which lost to Ossie Barkwell of Yellow Grass Sask. for right to represent West in 1927 inaugural Brier; won 1930 Brier as third then skipped 1932 Brier champions; *mem.* Canadian Curling Hall of Fame.

CONGALTON, William (baseball); *b.* 24 Jan 1875, Guelph, Ont., *d.* 19 Aug 1937, Cleveland, Ohio; *given name:* William Millar; *m.* Harriett; public utilities employee; outfielder with Chicago Cubs 1902, appeared in 47 games; following stint in minors played with Cleveland (AL) 1905-07 before being dealt to Boston 1907; returned to minors for a couple of seasons before retiring; major league record shows 309 games, six home runs, 95 runs batted in and career record .293 batting avg.

CONNELL, Alec (hockey); *b.* 8 Feb 1900, Ottawa, Ont., *d.* 10 May 1958, Ottawa, Ont.; *m.* Kay Muir; *children:* Bettianne; fireman; goaler, played early hockey for Ottawa area St. Brigid's, Gunners, Shamrocks and 1921 Allan Cup-winning Cliffsides; turned pro 1924 with Senators helping them win 1927 Stanley Cup; retired 1933 but made comeback 1934 with Montreal Maroons, won Stanley Cup; established NHL record six successive shutouts; retired again and coached St. Patrick's College, Senators (QHL) until illness forced him out 1949; noted for black cap he always wore while playing goal; baseball catcher with St. Brigid's city, interprovincial teams; played lacrosse 1920 with brother Charlie on Ottawa Senators who won eastern Canadian title; mem. Ottawa, Hockey Halls of Fame.

CONNELL, Charlie (lacrosse); 4 Dec 1897, Ottawa, Ont.; *m.* Ruth Edmonson; *children:* Frances, Elaine; St. Brigid's School; retired photoengraver; with Emmett Lacrosse Club won 1927-28 Mann Cup; captained Woodroffe team to 1922 Ottawa title; retired from field lacrosse at 35; won Val Cartier army camp middleweight boxing crown 1915 and Canadian Service Corps title at Thorncliffe Eng.; Canadian amateur middleweight title 1919-20; called up by Ottawa Rough Riders at 14 for 1912 playoffs and remained with club until age 34; played in government, city leagues; basketball with Ottawa Seniors, won district titles four times; refereed, coached football, lacrosse; mem. Ottawa, Canadian Lacrosse Halls of Fame; *res.* Ottawa, Ont.

CONNOLLY, Edward (boxing); *b.* 16 Nov 1876, Saint John, N.B., *d.* 1936, New York, N.Y.; British Empire lightweight champion 1896; world welterweight champion 1900; mem. N.B. Sports Hall of Fame.

CONYD, Magdy (fencing); *b.* 22 Jun 1939, Alexandria, Egypt; Aachen U, W. Germany; physical fitness consultant, director; began fencing competitively for Canada 1964; national foils titles 1964, 1971-72; holder highest foils rating in Canada 1968-70, 1972-73, 1975; Governor-General's international open foils titles 1965-70, 1972, runner-up 1974, third 1975; Ontario champion 1964-65; Quebec champion 1966; B.C. champion 1968-75; mem. Canadian world team four times, Olympic team twice, Commonwealth Games bronze medal team 1970; *res.* Vancouver, B.C.

COOK, Bill (hockey); *b.* 6 Oct 1896, Brantford, Ont.; *given name:* 'William Osser; played early hockey Kingston, Sault Ste. Marie; turned pro Saskatoon Sheiks 1922; won three WCL scoring titles in four years; in 1924-25 season scored 31 goals in 30 games; with demise of WCL, Bill and brother Bun were purchased by NY Rangers 1926 playing through 1937; played right wing on line with Bun and Frank Boucher; Art Ross scoring trophy twice; first team all-star three times, second team once; scored 228 regular season NHL goals, 140 assists and 16 goals,

10 assists Stanley Cup play; in WCL scored 87 goals, 58 assists; played on two Stanley Cup winners; mem. Hockey, Canadian Sports Halls of Fame.

COOK, Myrtle (all-around); *b.* 5 Jan 1902, Toronto, Ont.; *given name:* Myrtle Alice; *m.* Lloyd McGowan (*d.*); *children:* Donald; business college; retired sportswriter; excelled in T & F, paddling, softball, tennis, ice hockey, speedskating, cycling, basketball, lawn bowling; gold medal Amsterdam Olympics 1928 400m relay; world record 100m Halifax Olympic trials; gold medal 100m Paris, Philadelphia meets 1928; indoor 60yds winner New York, Chicago, Philadelphia, Montreal; won international mixed doubles tennis with Brendan Macken, Quebec mixed and ladies' doubles; Governor-General's medal Vancouver for track, 1967 Centennial medal; coached Hilda Strike, LA Olympics medal winner; mem. AAU of C, Canadian Sports Halls of Fame; *res.* Montreal, Que.

COOK, Wendy (swimming); *b.* 15 Sep 1956, Vancouver, B.C., *given name:* Wendy Elizabeth; *m.* Douglas Hogg; U of British Columbia; student; backstroke specialist, fifth Munich Olympics 100m 1:06.7; third 100m 1:06.2, sixth 200m 2:23 1973 world championships Belgrade Yugoslavia; two gold medals, 100m 1:06.2 and 200m 2:22; third gold in 400m medley relay world record 1:04.78; fifth 200 individual medley at 1974 Christchurch Commonwealth Games; same year won 200yd U S short course title 2:04.2, runner-up 100yd 0:59.7; won 200m U S long course nationals 2:18.8, runner-up 100m 1:04.9; fourth 100m, eighth 200m 1975 Cali Columbia world championships; bronze 4x100 medley 1976 Olympics; five firsts 1976 Canadian Nationals; Canadian records 1976 800m FS 8:26.00, 400m FS relay 3:52.98, 200m medley 1:59.16, 400m medley 4:18.80; B.C. junior athlete of year 1973; B.C. and Canadian female athlete of year 1974; Governor-General's silver medal 1976; *res.* Vancouver, B.C.

COOKE, Graham (golf); *b.* 11 Sep 1946, Belleville, Ont.; *given name:* Leonard Graham; Michigan State U; landscape architect, consultant Quebec Golf Association; began golfing at 14; won 1965 Ontario junior; medalist Canadian junior; NCAA all-American; three times runner-up Quebec amateur; won 1973 Duke of Kent; quarterfinalist Western Amateur bowing two and one to Ben Crenshaw; played frequently Canadian, U S amateurs; five times Quebec Willingdon Cup team; twice Quebec golfer of year; mem. Canadian Nation's Cup team, competed French Amateur 1977; *res.* Montreal, Que.

COOKE, Jack Kent (entrepreneur); *b.* 25 Oct 1912, Hamilton, Ont.; *m.* Barbara Jean Carnegie; *children:* Ralph, John; Malvern CI; publisher, promoter; began as football player on Ted Reeve's Malvern CI city champion team, Toronto and as hockey, baseball player; played clarinet, saxophone while leading own band Oley Kent and his Orchestra early 30s Toronto area; acquired substantial piece of Toronto Maple Leafs International League baseball franchise, won four pennants in seven years; Minor League executive of year 1952; unsuccessful in bids to purchase Toronto Argos, Detroit Tigers; quarter interest in Washington Redskins football franchise; with Branch Rickey, sought unsuccessfully to launch Continental Baseball League 1958; purchased Lakers NBA team 1965; when NHL expanded acquired LA franchise and formed Kings; constructed own arena, The Forum; acquired Springfield Indians (AHL) team from Eddie Shore; *res.* Los Angeles, Calif.

COOKSHAW, Brian (track); *b.* 12 Feb 1950, Swan River, Man.; *m.* Moira Watt; *children:* Denise Anne; Swan River HS, North Dakota U; sales supervisor; Manitoba 400m title 1969; silver medal Canadian senior 400m championships 1974, represented Canada vs France 1974; mem. gold medal 4x400m 1974 Prairies relay team; mem. gold medal 4x400m Prairie Golden Canadians 1975 relay team, set Canadian record indoor nationals; fourth 400m, silver medal 4x400 relay 1975 Canadian championships; switched to 800m, 1500m under new coach Gabor Simonyi 1976; *res.* Edmonton, Alta.

COOMBE, Eldon (curling); *b.* 8 May 1941, Kingston, Ont.; *given name:* Eldon James; *m.* Lynda Ann Jeffrey; *children:* Jeffrey James, Laurie Lynn; Glebe CI; survey technician; made first of seven Ontario Consols play-down appearances 1963 as lead for Bob Knippleburg; the Coombe quartet (Keith Forgues, Jim Patrick, Barry Provost) won Division One OCA title seven consecutive years; represented Ontario 1972 St. John's Nfld. Brier after winning Consols title in four-way playoff; three times winner Canadian Branch Royal Caledonian Curling Club Royal Victoria Jubilee; seven times Red Anderson Memorial Trophy winner; winner CBC curling classic 1972, runner-up 1973; winner Whitby Dunlop 'spiel 1972; top season in Branch competition 1966 when he skipped rink to Jubilee, Colts, Governor-General's titles; three times Ottawa ACT curler of year; *res.* Ottawa, Ont.

COPELAND, Royal (football); *b.* 12 Oct 1924, North Bay, Ont.; *given name:* Royal Hayward; *m.* Barbara Ann; *children:* Nola Jean, Cindy Ann; California State U, B.A., Azusa Pacific College, M.A.; teacher; ten years with Toronto Argonauts, combined with Joe Krol as the Gold Dust Twins; appeared in 111 regular season games, 14 playoff contests scoring 34 career TDs; led EFC scorers with 40 points 1945; tied Argos single-game TD record with four (all on passes from Krol) vs Montreal 1945, three interceptions vs Hamilton 1945; three times EFC all-star; Jeff Russel Memorial Trophy 1949; *res.* Oxnard, Calif.

COPP, Bobby (hockey); *b.* 15 Nov 1918, Port Elgin, N.B.; *given name:* Robert Alonzo; *m.* Mary MacMillan; *children:* Judith Ann, Bonnie Lynn; Mount Allison U, B.A., U of Toronto, D.D.S.; dentist; played rugby 1936-37, track 1938, hockey 1934-38 at Mount Allison winning 1938 Maritime Intercollegiate title; played with Amherst junior St. Pat's, won 1937 Maritime junior crown; with U of T 1938-40, won Intercollegiate 1940-41, senior Marlboros 1940-42, won Eastern Ontario 1941; turned pro Toronto Maple Leafs 1942-43; joined Canadian Army Dental Corps 1943 playing hockey with Maritime Champion RCAF Flyers Halifax, and Ottawa Commandos; played interservice hockey 1945; joined Ottawa Senators (QHL) 1946 as coach for two months until reinstated as amateur; reached Allan Cup finals 1948 bowing to Edmonton; won Allan Cup over Calgary 1949; from 1949-55 played for Senators except for two games with Toronto Maple Leafs 1950, three months with Smiths Falls Bears 1952; mem. N.B. Sports Hall of Fame; *res.* Ottawa, Ont.

CORSIGLIA, Robin (swimming); *b.* 12 Aug 1962, Kirkland, Ohio; *given name:* Robin Marie; Beaconsfield HS; student; breast stroke specialist; youngest mem. of Canadian Olympic swim team Montreal 1976, reached 100m semifinals, bronze medal 4x100 medley relay; won 200m breast stroke and broke own Canadian, Commonwealth record for 100m breast stroke 1976 Canadian nationals; Japan tour 1976; Canadian short course record 200m medley 2:05.20 1976. Canadian record 100m breast stroke 1:12.60 Paris meet 1977; Canadian record 200m breast stroke 2:33.27; Governor-General's silver medal 1976; *res.* Beaconsfield, Que.

COSENTINO, Frank (football); *b.* 22 May 1937, Hamilton, Ont.; *m.* Sheila; *children:* Tony, Mary, Teresa, Peter; U of Western Ontario, B.A., B.P.E., M.A., Ph.D.; director school of phys ed York U.; four years quarterback Western Ontario Mustangs; on two Intercollegiate championship teams; captain first Canadian championship team 1959; ten years in CFL—seven at Hamilton (five Grey Cup appearances, two winners), two years Edmonton, one Toronto; five years head football coach UWO, won two Canadian championships 1971, 1974; Intercounty senior baseball for Hamilton as pitcher; wrote, *Canadian Football: The Grey Cup Years,* with M.L. Howell *A History of Physical Education in Canada,* with Glynn Leyshon *Olympic Gold; res.* Toronto, Ont.

CÔTÉ, Gerard (track and field); *b.* 1913, St. Barnabe, Que.; first Boston Marathon bid 1936 but overtrained by running course two days before race; set record 2:28.28 1940 winning first of four Boston Marathons, won again 1942, 1943, 1948; three times U S AAU marathon champion; career record 264 races, won 112, second or third in 82 others;

leg cramps led to 17th finish in 1948 Olympics; set record 46 minutes snowshoeing eight-mile event St. Paul Minn. 1958; CP poll Canadian male athlete of year, Lou Marsh Trophy 1940; mem. Canadian Sports Hall of Fame. *res*. St. Hyacinthe, Que.

COTTON, Harry (football, boxing); *b*. 28 Jul 1909, Vancouver, B.C.; *given name:* Henry Ferguson; *m*. Olive Eve Wootton; *children:* Peter Ross, John Miles; Shawinigan Lake HS, Royal Military College; real estate agent, retired soldier; played football RMC 1928-29; mem. B.C. champions Vancouver AC 1930-31; Winnipeg Blue Bombers 1934-35; played English rugby Vancouver Rowing Club 1929-31; Garrison Football Club Winnipeg 1932-34; Manitoba all-stars 1933-34; runner-up British army middleweight boxing championship 1937; held Canadian army western division middleweight boxing title 1932-33; founded Little League baseball Rivers Man. 1950; district administrator Little League Eastern Ontario 1960-64; mem. winning rink Royal Victoria Jubilee 1963; *res*. Ottawa, Ont.

COUGHLAN, Angela (swimming); *b*. 4 Oct 1952, London, Eng.; *given name:* Angela Denise; *m*. Toomas Arusoo; assistant coach Oakville Aquatic Club; Canadian swim team mem. 1967-72; represented Canada 1967, 1971 Pan-Am Games; bronze 400m relay, sixth 400m freestyle (FS), seventh 800m FS 1968 Olympic Games; gold 100m FS, silver 200m FS 1970 Commonwealth Games; Velma Springstead Trophy (Canada's female athlete of year) 1970; Canadian female swimmer of 1970; *res*. Acton, Ont.

COULON, Johnny (boxing); *b*. 12 Feb 1889, Toronto, Ont., *d*. 1973 Chicago, Ill.; age 19 won vacant world bantam champion-ship, defended 12 times before losing to Kid Williams 1914, fought title matches twice within a three-week period, later three times in month; following loss to Williams retired, made comeback 1916-1918; nickname Chicago Spider; fought 96 pro bouts, won 24 by KO, 32 by decision, four draws, two decisions lost, twice KO'd, 32 no-decision bouts; boxing coach to age 73; mem. U S, Canadian Boxing, Canadian Sports Halls of Fame.

COULTER, Art (hockey); *b*. 31 May 1909, Winnipeg, Man.; *given name:* Arthur Edmund; began hockey career with Pilgrim AC 1924 and turned pro with Philadelphia 1929; entered NHL with Chicago Black Hawks 1931-32; defenceman, teamed with Taffy Abel to help Chicago win 1933-34 Stanley Cup; second team all-star 1935, dealt in mid-season 1935-36 to Rangers for Earl Seibert; succeeded Bill Cook as captain, three more times second team all-star; on 1940 Stanley Cup winner and ended career 1942 joining Canadian armed forces WW2; during 11 NHL seasons scored 30 goals, 82 assists; nicknamed Trapper because of penchant for talking fishing, hunting; mem. Hockey Hall of Fame; *res*. Winnipeg, Man.

COULTER, Bruce (football); *b*. 19 Nov 1927, Toronto, Ont.; *given name:* Bruce David; *m*. Joyce Brown; *children:* Susan, Bruce Jr., Douglas, John; Runnymede CI, U of Toronto; director of athletics, student affairs, Bishop's University; HS all-star in football, basketball, T & F; turned pro with Montreal Alouettes playing defensive half-back, quarterback 1948-57; nickname Bones; head coach McGill Redman 1958-61, Bishop's Gaiters 1962; past pres. Canadian Association of University Athletic Directors, Quebec University Athletic Association;

mem. board of directors Canadian Intercollegiate Athletic Union; *res.* Lennoxville, Que.

COULTER, Tex (football); *b.* 2 Oct 1924, Smith County, Texas; *given name:* Dewitt; *m.* Ruth; *children:* David, Ann, Jeff, Dena; West Point, Texas Christian U; artist, writer; all-Texas honors HS 1940-42; twice all-American while at West Point 1944-45; turned pro N Y Giants (NFL) 1946-52, all-pro three times; joined Montreal Alouettes 1953-56; three times all-Canadian; Schenley lineman of year 1955; appointed line coach to assist coach Peahead Walker 1955; mem. Texas Football Hall of Fame. *res.* Pierrefonds, Que.

COULTHARD, Bill (basketball); *b.* 29 Dec 1923, Buffalo, N.Y.; *m.* June Frances; *children:* Carol, Chris, Bruce, Betty, David; Assumption College, B.A.; personnel manager; all-city Windsor HS 1941; all-state Detroit Tech 1944; mem. Assumption College team 1947; Canadian champion Tillsonburg Livingston teams 1951-52; competed 1952 Helsinki Olympics; retired following 1952-53 season; *res.* Tillsonburg, Ont.

COURNOYER, Yvan (hockey); *b.* 22 Nov 1943, Drummondville, Que.; *given name:* Yvan Serge; *m.* Ginette; *children:* Marie-France, Yannik, Mélanie; hockey player, realty, oil business interests; early years played with Lachine, Montreal Junior Canadiens; joined Canadiens as right-winger for five-game trial 1963 scoring in first game; as NHL rookie 1964-65 scored seven goals; through 1976-77 NHL season played 885 games scoring 402 goals, 401 assists for 803 points, 241 penalty minutes and 132 playoff games scoring 57 goals, 59 assists for 116 points, 37 penalty minutes; scored 40 or more goals three successive seasons 1971-74; nine three-goal games; scored seven points (five goals, two assists) as Montreal beat Chicago 12-3 1975; four times second team all-star; Smythe Trophy 1973 playoffs; *res.* Montreal, Que.

COURTRIGHT, Jim (track and field); *b.* 16 Dec 1914, North Bay, Ont.; *given name:* James Milton; *m.* Marny Nora Roche; *children:* Joseph, James, Patricia, Stephen, John, Mary Ellen, Anthony, Frank; Glebe CI, U of Ottawa, B.A., Queen's U, B.Sc., Columbia U; v.-principal Queen's U; excelled in T & F (javelin), basketball, football; mem. Canadian Olympic team 1936 Berlin; gold medal 1937 Dallas Games, 1938 Commonwealth Games Sydney Australia; best individual performance British Empire vs U S relay and team match London Eng. 1936; played 12 years basketball Glebe CI, U of Ottawa, Montreal Oilers (1942 Canadian finalists); played five years football Glebe, U of Ottawa; Jenkins Trophy Queen's U 1941 as best combined athlete-student; Ames Trophy Glebe CI 1934 best athlete-student; Fink Trophy U of Ottawa 1937 best athlete-student; *res.* Kingston, Ont.

COUSINEAU, Alain (skiing); *b.* 28 Jul 1953, Montreal, Que.; *m.* Helene Ouellette; pro skier; mem. Laurentian Zone ski team 1969-70, Quebec team 1970-71, Canadian National team 1971-75; turned pro 1975-76 season; winner Quebec Kandahar 1971, 1974, Canadian Giant Slalom 1974; runner-up Can-Am giant slalom 1973, 1975, fourth 1972; third Canadian giant slalom 1973, 1975; competed in Bank of Montreal World Cup race 1972 (20th), 1974 (15th); 1974 world championships St. Moritz Switzerland; third 1975 dual slalom Waterville Valley; second Duvillard Masters pro slalom 1976; *res.* Brownsburg, Que.

COWAN, Gary (golf); *b.* 28 Oct 1938, Kitchener, Ont.; *m.* Elaine; *children:* three daughters, one son; insurance executive; won Ontario juvenile and junior, then national junior title; only Canadian to twice win U S amateur, 1966, 1971; won Canadian amateur 1961, runner-up five times; won Ontario amateur six times, runner-up five times; won Ontario Open 1968, second three times; won New Zealand Centennial Invitational, Porter Cup and U S North and South titles; individual low scorer in world amateur Japan 1962; low amateur U S Masters 1965; low amateur Canadian Open 1960; shared low medal with Jack Nicklaus 1962 America's Cup; sixteen times mem. Ontario Willingdon Cup team, five winners, four runners-up; six times on Canadian America's Cup team; seven times on Canadian world amateur team; four times Commonwealth team; mem. RCGA, Canadian Sports Halls of Fame; *res.* Kitchener, Ont.

COWAN, Jack (soccer); *b.* 6 Jun 1927, Vancouver, B.C.; *given name:* John Lawrence; *m.* Margaret; *children:* Gael Isobel, Lynn Jacqueline; Vancouver THS, U British Columbia, B.Sc., St. Andrews, Scotland; electrical engineer; won UBC Big Block 1945-49; played in Vancouver Coast League 1948-49, 1955-56; chosen to B.C. all-stars vs touring Newcastle United team; turned pro 1949 with Dundee in Scottish League first division, returned to Vancouver for 1955 season; Scottish League Cup medal 1951, runner-up 1952; won Canadian title with Vancouver Canadians 1955; toured Israel, Turkey, South Africa, East Africa as part of Scottish all-star team; mem. B.C. Sports Hall of Fame; *res.* Vancouver, B.C.

COWLEY, Bill (hockey); *b.* 12 Jun 1912, Bristol, Que.; *m.* Jessie; *children:* Jill, Jane, John, Dan; Glebe CI; hotel owner; played amateur hockey Primrose juniors, Shamrocks, toured Europe 1932 with Ottawa all-stars; joined Halifax Wolverines 1934; signed with St. Louis Eagles (NHL) as centre 1934; to Boston Bruins 1935-47; Art Ross Trophy (scoring) 1941; Hart Trophy (MVP) 1941, 1943; on three NHL title winners, won two Stanley Cups; lifetime record regular season 195 goals, 353 assists, playoffs 12 goals, 34 assists; four times first, once second team all-star; pres. Smiths Falls Rideaus three years; part-owner Ottawa 67's (OHA junior A) 1967-75; mem. Ottawa Sports, Hockey Halls of Fame; *res.* Ottawa, Ont.

COX, Ernie (football); *b.* 1894, Hamilton, Ont., *d.* 26 Feb 1962, Hamilton, Ont.; *m.* Cecilia Gibbs; *children:* Donald, Mrs. Ralph Hammel; retired firefighter; graduated from Hamilton sandlots to Hamilton Tigers; after WWI rejoined Tigers 1919, played 16 seasons; perennial league, all-Canadian all-star; first winner Jeff Russel Memorial Trophy 1928; played on Tiger Grey Cup champions 1928, 1929, 1932 and reached Eastern finals vs Balmy Beach twice; nickname the Iron Fireman; mem. Canadian Football Hall of Fame.

COY, Eric (track and field); *b.* 16 May 1914, Nottingham, Eng.; *m.* Margaret Helen Claudia Hindson; *children:* John, Rick, Judy; superintendent, technical service; during 30s held North American snowshoe sprint title 1933-41 (except 1938); won first Canadian title in javelin 1935 Winnipeg; Canadian javelin, discus, shot put titles 1938 for berth on British Empire Games team; gold medal discus, silver shot put in Australian Games; AAU of C athlete of year; selected 1940 Olympic team but games cancelled; following war again won Canadian discus, shot put titles; qualified for 1948 Olympic team; mem. Canadian Empire Games team 1950, 1954; football with Winnipeg Wanderers, Lew Hayman's RCAF Hurricanes Montreal; retired, coached T & F, wrestling and hockey; mem. Canadian Sports, AAU of C, Winnipeg Sports Halls of Fame; *res.* Winnipeg, Man.

CRAIG, Paul (track and field); *b.* 2 Sep 1953, Toronto, Ont.; *given name:* Paul Frederick; *m.* Judy Johnson; Don Mills CI, U of Texas; student; Canadian senior 1500m title 1973; won U S South-West Conference mile 1973-74; represented Canada 1974 European track tour, best time 3:39.9 in 1500m; qualified for Canadian track team 1976 Montreal Olympics; *res.* Don Mills, Ont.

CRANHAM, Scott (diving); *b.* 8 Sep 1954, Toronto, Ont.; Indiana U; student; athletic scholarship to Indiana, competed for university diving team and Pointe Claire Diving Club; represented Canada 1972 Munich Olympics finishing 14th; eighth in both 3m, 10m at 1973 world Belgrade Yugoslavia; Canadian national 1m, 3m, 10m titles 1973; runner-up 10m platform 1974 Finnish Cup Helsinki; silver medal 3m springboard, bronze 10m platform 1974 Christchurch Commonwealth Games; third U S 1974 Nationals establishing Canadian record 520 points on 10m platform; 1m, 3m, 10m titles 1974 Canadian championships; fractured ankle in 1974 skydiving accident; won 1975 Canadian Pan-Am trials but weak ankle kept him from springboard events; fifth 10m 1975 Mexico Pan-Am Games; qualified for 1976 Olympics in 3m, 10m; *res.* Bloomington, Ind.

CRANSTON, Toller (figure skating); *b.* 20 Apr 1949, Hamilton, Ont.; Ecole des Beaux Arts, Montreal; skater, artist; began skating at eight; launched national competitive career 1964 winning Canadian junior; 1967 won Quebec Winter Games; 1968-69 third Canadian seniors; 1969 third Grand Prix International St. Gervais France, sixth North American; 1970 second Canadian seniors, 13th world; 1971 won Canadian seniors, second North American, 11th world; 1972 won Canadian seniors, ninth Olympics, fifth world (won freestyle portion of singles); 1973 won Canadian seniors, fifth world, won Skate Canada; 1974 won Canadian seniors; third world (won freestyle singles); 1975 won Canadian seniors, fourth world (won freestyle); mem. ISU winter and summer tour 1971-74; coaches: Eva Vasak (1960-67), Ellen Burka; choreographer: Brian Foley; launched own pro ice show 1976; mem. Canadian Sports Hall of Fame; *res.* Toronto, Ont.

CRAWFORD, Judy (skiing); *b.* 22 Dec 1951, Toronto, Ont.; *given name:* Judith MacPherson; U of Toronto; student; mem. Canadian National ski team 1968-75; won Canadian championships 1971, 1973, U S title 1971, European Cup race France 1973; third World Cup slalom Grindelwald Switzerland 1973; fourth Sapporo Japan winter Olympics slalom 1972; fourth world downhill Val Gardena Italy 1970; fourth world combined St. Moritz Switzerland 1974; John Semmelink Trophy for achievement in skiing, sportsmanship; *res.* Toronto, Ont.

CRAWFORD, Rusty (hockey); *b.* 7 Nov 1884, Cardinal, Ont., *d.* 19 Dec 1971; *given name:* Samuel Russell; as amateur played with Verdun Que. three seasons before shifting to Prince Albert Sask. two seasons and Saskatoon one season; joined Quebec Bulldogs 1912-13 helping them win Stanley Cup; remained with Quebec 1917-18, joined Ottawa for four games, shifted to Toronto Arenas and another Stanley Cup victory; with Saskatoon 1920, Calgary to 1925, moved to Vancouver 1926; ended career at 45 with Minneapolis 1929; mem. Hockey, Sask. Halls of Fame.

CREBER, Bill (curling); *b.* 30 Nov 1935, Toronto, Ont.; *m.* Carol Anne Ward; *children:* Brad, Jill; sales representative; best known for marathon loss to London's Ken Buchan 1969 Ontario Consols at London Ivanhoe; lead winning Ontario Silver Tankard rink 1964-65; skipped Tankard winner 1974, runner-up 1967; skipped three Toronto Curling Association championships, three southern Ontario all-star titles, skipped rinks to variety of major bonspiel victories in Ontario such as Whitby, Peterborough, St. Catharines, Orillia, Royals Classic, Avonlea Beef O'Rama, Parkway Open; *res.* Agincourt, Ont.

CREIGHTON, Dale (baseball, football, basketball); *b.* 12 Jun 1934, London, Ont.; *m.* Marion Thompson; *children:* Matthew, Paul, Lyndsey; U of Western Ontario, B.A.; v.-pres., executive-director marketing London Life; first baseman, catcher, outfielder; mem. six Ontario baseball title teams City of London 1948-58; captained three title teams; senior baseball Great Lakes-Niagara, Intercounty League London Majors; second team all-star 1958; mem. Alexandra PS city basketball title team 1948; Central CI junior, senior basketball teams, captained one, won three city titles, led city league scorers twice; twice city all-star; mem. one junior, three senior London District HS Conference football title teams; twice WOSSA champions; 1952 Red Feather tournament titlists; twice captained HS football teams, three times all-conference scoring leader, all-star; standout fullback UWO Mustangs 1954-57; twice Intercollegiate all-star; mem. London Lords ORFU 1956 earning all-star while leading league rushers, third in scoring; mem. Kitchener-Waterloo Dutchmen 1958; team MVP, ORFU all-star inside linebacker; retired from sports 1959; *res.* London, Ont.

CRONIN, Carl (football); *b.* 18 Oct 1908, Chicago, Ill.; *given name:* Carl Michael; *m.* Ruth Harmon; *children:* Michael, Pat (*d.*), Dennis (*d.*), Thomas (*d.*); Notre Dame U; retired, electrical business; exhibited early athletic skills in HS football and in pole vault, javelin; at Notre Dame 1929-31 played halfback, quarterback; first U S import with Winnipeg 1932 as player-coach guided Winnipeg to Western title 1933, losing 13-0 to Toronto Argos; became Calgary Broncos' coach 1935; in five seasons made Calgary contender; returned to Chicago 1942 and retired from business 1973; mem. Canadian Football Hall of Fame; *res.* Vancouver, B.C.

CROOKALL, John (lacrosse); *b.* 6 Feb 1889, Toronto, Ont.; *d.* 31 May 1965, Snug Cove, Bowen Island, B.C.; outstanding field lacrosse star with Vancouver teams 1911-1925; mem. five Minto Cup champions, including five in succession 1911-15; turned pro 1919; several years baseball umpire; mem. Lacrosse, B.C. Sports Halls of Fame.

CROTHERS, Bill (track); *b.* 24 Dec 1940, Markham, Ont.; *m.* Morven; *children:* Margaret Grace; Agincourt HS, U of Toronto; pharmacist; OFSSA senior 440yd and Canadian junior 440 titles 1959; from 1961-68 competed regularly in both indoor and outdoor meets in Canada, U S, Europe, leading field in 440 and 880yd; at one time held all Canadian records from 440 to 1500m; in 75 indoor meets won 65 times; represented Canada 1964 Tokyo, 1968 Mexico Olympics, silver medal 800m Tokyo; gold medal 800m 1965 World Student Games Budapest; first in world at distance by *Track and Field News;* U S 880yd title in record 1:46.8 1963; same year posted world's two fastest 880s; represented Canada in Commonwealth Games Australia, Jamaica and Pan-Am Games Winnipeg; 1961-65 held Canadian senior titles in 440 and 880; last international race 1968; mem. National Sports Advisory Council; *res.* Markham, Ont.

CROWLEY, Maureen (track); *b.* 26 May 1953, Brampton, Ont.; *given name:* Maureen Adele; Simon Fraser U; student; mem. Canada vs Italy team 1971; represented Canada on junior team vs Portugal, Spain 1973; junior, senior 800m Canadian titles 1973; in 1974 New Zealand Commonwealth Games placed sixth 800m, bronze medal team mem. 4x400m relay; Canadian 400m title 1974; second 1500m, 800m in New Zealand Games; mem. European tour 1975; injuries 1976 removed her from Olympic team contention; *res.* Burnaby, B.C.

CRUTCHFIELD, Linda (skiing, water-skiing, luge); *b.* 3 Apr 1942, Shawinigan, Que.; *div.* Robert Bocock; Sir George Williams U, Burke Mountain Academy; student, teacher; at 17 competed in first major ski race, Taschereau on Mt. Tremblant, won by 11 seconds; invited by Vic Emery 1967 to test run a luge (one-man toboggan), made four runs, won Canadian title; 10th 1968 Olympics; qualified for national teams in skiing,

water-skiing, luge; mem. national alpine ski team 1960-65 including 1964 Olympics; 14 water-ski titles, established several jump records; first Canadian woman to clear 100ft in water-ski jump; represented Canada four world water-ski championships; ski school director ten years, water-ski school director three years; John Semmelink Trophy 1964; Canadian alpine champion 1962, 1964; Canadian luge champion 1967-68; North American luge champion 1968; Velma Springstead Trophy (Canadian female athlete of year) 1969, 1973; *res.* East Burke, Vt.

CULVER, Diane (skiing); *b.* 14 Sep 1952, Montreal, Que.; *given name:* Diane Mary; McGill U; ski coach; won Pontiac Cup 1969; competed for national Alpine ski team 1970 world championships, 11th in downhill; mem. Canadian World Cup ski team 1970-72; eighth giant slalom World Cup final 1970 Voss Norway; coached women's Can-Am ski team 1975-76; *res.* Montreal, Que.

CURRIE, Andy (football); *b.* 5 Jun 1911, Brandon, Man.; *m.* Thelma Wright; *children:* David, Roger; St. John's College School, U of Manitoba, B.A.; retired deputy minister; coached HS, U of Manitoba, Regina Pats; refereed 15 years in Winnipeg area; with Saskatchewan Roughriders in 1928 Grey Cup at 17; week later helped Pats win Canadian junior title; played with U of Manitoba 1929, 1931, Roughriders 1928, 1930, St. John's seniors 1932, Winnipeg football club 1933; director of phys ed for Winnipeg schools 1951; Province of Manitoba director of PE & R 1957; Director Parks and Recreation Greater Winnipeg 1961; WIFU official 20 years, supervisor of officials 14 years; mem. Canadian Football Hall of Fame; *res.* Winnipeg, Man.

Curtis

CURTIS, Ulysses (football); *b.* 10 May 1926, Albion, Mich.; *m.* Catherine; *children:* Carol, Sylvia, Warren; Florida A & M, B.A., B.P.H.E., McMaster U; HS teacher; Negro all-American 1948-49; turned pro Toronto Argos 1950-54, appeared in 57 league, nine playoff games; three times led Argos in scoring, set single season TD record of 16 in 12 games 1952; scored total 235 points in five-year CFL career, 47 TDs (27 rushing, 20 on pass receptions); played on two Grey Cup winners; twice EFC all-star; coached Toronto junior football league 12 years, won three Eastern Canadian titles; coached backfield York U three years; five years teacher-counsellor, program coordinator Ontario Athletic Leadership Camp; *res.* Willowdale, Ont.

CUSTIS, Bernie (football); *b.* 23 Sep 1929, Philadelphia, Pa.; *given name:* Bernard Eugene; *m.* Lorraine DeFoe; John Bartram HS, Syracuse U; PS principal; played football, baseball on scholarship at Syracuse; drafted as quarterback by Cleveland Browns but joined Hamilton Tiger-Cats where he played quarterback and halfback five seasons; Ottawa Rough Riders one season; coached in Toronto then with Oakville Black Knights (ORFU) six years; coached Burlington Braves juniors eight years, three national finals; coached Sheridan Community College football since 1971, three national finals; *res.* Burlington, Ont.

CUTLER, Dave (football); *b.* 17 Oct 1945, Biggar, Sask.; *given name:* David Robert Stuart; *m.* Barbara; *children:* Rob, John; Mountain View HS, Simon Fraser U; teacher, pro footballer; in college NAIA District One all-star, receiving honorable mention Little All-American as linebacker; twice team inspiration award; number one draft by

Edmonton 1969 but elected to sign with Green Bay Packers (NFL); cut by Packers, joined Eskimos; CFL record for longest field goal (59yds) 1970; CFL scoring record 1975 with 169 points on 40 field goals, 36 of 36 converts and 13 singles; Dave Dryburgh Memorial Trophy as WFC scoring champion 1973-75; Beattie Martin Trophy as WFC top Canadian 1973; runner-up Canadian Schenley Award 1973; CFL record through 1976, 228 converts, 214 field goals, 96 singles, 966 points; *res.* Victoria, B.C.

CYR, Louis (weightlifting); *b.* 1863, Montreal, Que., *d.* 1912, Montreal, Que.; *m.* Melina; legend that at 17 he pulled loaded wagon from mud by lifting it on his back and decided to become a travelling strongman; challenged David Michaud, Canada's strongest of period, to rock lifting contest, Cyr won lifting 480lb boulder; at 22 joined Montreal police force but resigned when attacked on beat with an axe; signed by promoter Richard Fox and billed as world's strongest man; took on all challengers and never lost; toured Europe 23 months becoming household name in Western world; tour highlight came 1889 at London's Royal Aquarium Theatre when he lifted a 551lb weight with one finger, lifted 4,100lbs on platform stretched across his back, lifted 273¼lbs with one hand to shoulder level then above head and with one hand lifted 314lb barrel of cement to shoulder; Marquis of Queensbury (father of modern boxing rules) offered him horse if he could hold a pair of horses tied to his arms to a standstill, Cyr won the horse; most astounding feat Boston 1895 when he lifted 18 fat men on a plank on his back in what is claimed to be the greatest lift ever made by a man—4,337lbs; died at 49 of Bright's disease; *mem.* Canadian Sports Hall of Fame.

CZAJA, Mitch (basketball, curling); *b.* 4 Aug 1935, Winnipeg, Man.; *given name;* Mitchell Peter; *m.* Mary Gail Langdon; *children:* Clinton, Aaron, Ainsley; Gordon Bell HS, U of Manitoba; mechanical engineer; began curling at Strathcona Club 1951; provincial schoolboy title; lost 1954 Canadian championship to Bayne Secord on last rock; curled with Norm Houck, Bruce Hudson, reached provincial Consols, lost in 1956 finals; 1959 joined London Curling Club; with Ken Buchan played second, won 1969 Ontario consols, represented province Oshawa Brier; once won Ontario Tankard, frequent provincial Consols contender; played HS basketball 1951-52, reached Canadian junior finals with Winnipeg Light Infantry team 1953; played senior with Winnipeg Kodiaks, lost to Montreal in Canadian finals 1957; played with Tillsonburg Livingstons 1960, represented Canada Chicago Pan-Am Games; *res.* London, Ont.

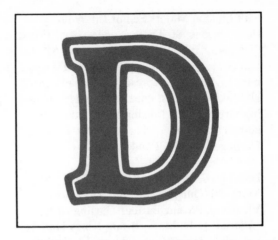

DAIGNEAULT, Doug (football); *b.* 4 Aug 1936, Montreal, Que.; *given name:* Douglas John; *m.* Jane DeCoste; *children:* Betsy, Debbie, Lois, Vickie, Julie; Franklin Academy, Clemson U, B.Sc.; football, basketball coach, assistant athletic director; at Franklin won all-State, honorable mention all-American football, basketball senior year; played league champion baseball, basketball, football; at Clemson leading scorer freshman basketball; participated Orange, Sugar, Bluebonnet Bowls; coached basketball South Carolina Textile League; mem. Ottawa Rough Riders 1960-64, 1960 Grey Cup champions; Montreal Alouettes 1964-66; coached Concordia U basketball teams, won 271 games, including 66 consecutive league games, lost 99 while winning seven league titles, participated five national championships; coach Concordia U football 1971-75, 20-15-2 record, 1972 league title, participated in Western Bowl; *res.* Pierrefonds, Que.

DALTON, Chuck (basketball); *b.* 1 Sep 1927, Windsor, Ont.; *given name:* Charles Harwood; *m.* Marcia Lawton; *children:* Karen Ann, Charles Scott; South CI, U Western Ontario; sales manager, real estate; baseball with London Majors Senior Intercounty three seasons, St. Thomas one season, Frood, Ont. (N.O.); basketball with Johnny Metras' UWO Mustangs; two seasons with Tillsonburg Livingstons; represented Canada 1952 Helsinki Olympics; knee injury ended playing career; coach London intermediate basketball team one season; past pres. London Curling Club; *res.* London, Ont.

DARLING, Dora (golf); *b.* 11 Aug 1904, Montreal, Que.; *given name:* Dora Jean Virtue; *m.* Arthur Balfour Darling (*d.*); *children:* Judy, Mary, Brian; Kings Hall School; began golfing at 14 at Whitlock CC; won women's Canadian Open, runner-up Canadian women's Closed 1936; three times Quebec women's title, three times runner-up; three times won Canadian senior women's, twice runner-up; *res.* Montreal, Que., Florida.

DARLING, Judy (golf); *b.* 6 Oct 1937, Montreal, Que.; *given name:* Judith Kathleen; *m.* John Douglas Evans; *children:* Kathy, Cindy, Tracey, Daphne; The Study, McGill U, B.Sc.; Quebec ladies' title 1957-61, 1972, runner-up once; Canadian junior women's titlist 1957 beating Mary Ellen Driscoll on second extra hole after having been runner-up 1956; runner-up Canadian women's Closed beating Janet MacWha in playoff on third extra hole 1960; Canadian women's Open championship 1960-61; *res.* Montreal, Que.

DARRAGH, Jack (hockey); *b.* 4 Dec 1890, Ottawa, Ont., *d.* 28 Jun 1924, Ottawa, Ont.; *given name:* John Proctor; *m.* Elizabeth; *children:* Aileen, Frances, Marion; accountant, poultry breeder; as amateur played Ottawa church league, Fort Coulonge Pontiac League and Cliffsides; turned pro Otta-

wa 1911 Stanley Cup champions, mem. Super Six, captain several Ottawa teams playing on three Stanley Cup winners-1920, 1921, 1923; on line with Frank Nighbor, Cy Denneny, when Punch Broadbent joined line shifted to left wing; scored 24 goals one 22-game season, 195 pro total; mem. Ottawa, Hockey Halls of Fame.

DARWIN, Howard (entrepreneur); *b.* 10 Sep 1931, Ottawa, Ont.; *given name:* Howard Joseph; *m.* Constance Goudie; *children:* Kim, Nancy, Jack, Jeff; St. Joseph's HS; jewellery business owner; after 30-35 amateur boxing bouts with Beaver Boxing Club, switched to refereeing, promoting fights; promotions included wrestling, closed circuit boxing matches; invested in OHA junior A hockey with formation of Ottawa 67's becoming part-owner, operator of Ottawa franchise; 1968 bought London Gardens and London OHA junior A hockey franchise; *res.* Ottawa, Ont.

DAVIDSON, Scotty (hockey); *b.* 1892, Kingston, Ont., *d.* 6 Jun 1915, France; *given name:* Allan; learned hockey under game's originator James T. Sutherland in Kingston; led Kingston Frontenacs to OHA title honors 1910-1911; turned pro Toronto Blueshirts (NHA) 1912-14; scored 19 goals in 20 games 1912-13, 24 goals in 1913-14 leading Toronto to Stanley Cup; killed in action WW1; mem. Hockey Hall of Fame.

DAVIES, Jack (administrator); *b.* Paris, France; *m.* Winnifred Hurdman; *children:* John Bruce; retired businessman, soldier; competed from childhood until 1963 in T & F, swimming, waterpolo, badminton, tennis, table tennis, boxing, sailing, equestrian winning approx. 300 trophies, medals and prizes; mem. Canadian T & F committee nearly 20 years, officiated 1934 British Empire Games; co-founder, councillor Western Hemisphere Athletic Commission; many times mem., director, manager Commonwealth, Pan-Am, Olympic Games teams from 1934-76; official Canadian delegate International Amateur Athletic Federation 14 times; official delegate British Empire and Commonwealth Games Federation 11 times; v.-pres. Quebec Branch AAU of C 17 years; co-founder Quebec Amateur T&F Assoc.; pres., life mem. AAU of C; six four-year terms and only Canadian ever elected to IAAF; first Canadian v.-pres. Commonwealth Games Federation 1970-76; pres. Commonwealth Games Assoc. of Canada since 1953; mem. advisory board, life mem. Canadian Olympic Assoc.; Chairman Commonwealth records committee since 1952; first Canadian, charter mem. world T&F Statisticians Assoc. since 1950; life mem.: Canadian Olympic Assoc., Canadian T&F Assoc., Quebec Amateur T&F Assoc., International Lawn Tennis Club (Canada), Quebec Lawn Tennis Federation, British Olympic Assoc., Amateur Athletic Union of U S, Canadian Bobsled and Luge Assoc., Sports Federation of Canada, Canadian Amateur Wrestling Assoc.; Chairman AAU of C Hall of Fame; some awards: Commonwealth Games Federation Shield, News of World plaque, AAU of C plaque, LA Rose Bowl, Helms Hall of Fame plaque, Expo '67 sports medal, COA Centennial medal, Baron de Coubertin Centennial medal, Order of Canada, special awards from Supreme Sports Council of Africa, Nigeria, U S, Australia, France; co-founder MAAA mixed badminton club; co-founder K of C badminton club; owner, coach Notre Dame de Grace badminton club; mem. AAU of C, Canadian Aquatic, Helms Halls of Fame; *res.* Montreal, Que.

DAVIES, Jim (cycling); *b.* 8 Jan 1906, London, Eng.; *given name:* James Arthur; *m.* Vera Beatrice Newport; *children:* Shirley Edith, Diane Estelle; Vancouver HS; retired sales representative; B.C. bicycle champion 1925-28, Canadian champion 1927-28; represented Canada 1928 Amsterdam Olympics equalling world record; *Vancouver Province* Cup, *Victoria Colonist* Cup; competed in numerous six-day races Vancouver, Portland Ore., Montreal; administrative positions B.C. Track Cycle Association; mem. B.C. Sports Hall of Fame; *res.* Burnaby, B.C.

DAVIES, Mike (football); *b.* 28 Feb 1937, Toronto, Ont.; Royal York HS; manager, broadcast sales company; quarterbacked Toronto Parkdale Lions to 1957 Canadian junior football title; with B.C. Lions 1958-59, Winnipeg Blue Bombers 1960; held Ontario HS hurdles record; *res.* Vancouver, B.C.

DAVIS, Pat (coaching); *b.* 15 Jan 1936, Windsor, Ont.; *given name:* Patricia Ann; U of Toronto, B.P.E., U of North Carolina, M.Ed., OCE; phys ed teacher; played varsity basketball at U of T, softball, basketball in Windsor, during HS days was competitive badminton player; since 1967 assistant director women's athletics U of Waterloo, coach Athena volleyball team; coached Waterloo AA senior women's team to provincial title 1975, Waterloo junior women's team to provincial runner-up 1976; at W.F. Herman CI 1958-66 coached volleyball, basketball, track, gymnastics teams; coaching committee chairman, level IV certificate holder, Canadian Volleyball Association; first regional director region three South-west Ontario; past coaching chairman Ontario Volleyball Association; held numerous committee chairmanships in Ontario Women's Intercollegiate Athletic Association and chaired committee which formulated amalgamation of OQWCIA and WIAU to form OWIAA; *res.* Waterloo, Ont.

DAWSON, Bob (football); *b.* 4 Feb 1932, Windsor, Ont.; *m.* Louise Bennett; *children:* Debbie, Lori; Walkerville HS; operates TV advertising sales company; leading scorer Windsor AKO three consecutive seasons including Canadian junior title 1952; Hamilton Tiger-Cats rookie of year 1953; remained active through 1959 season then turned to coaching; guided Burlington Braves to junior league title 1960; coached McMaster to four league titles 1961-65; *res.* Ancaster, Ont.

DAY, Eagle (football); *b.* 2 Oct 1932, Columbia, Miss.; *given name:* Herman Sidney; U of Mississippi, B.Sc.; quarterback at Mississippi, MVP 1955 Cotton Bowl; turned pro Winnipeg 1956 but kidney ailment sidelined him 1957, lost 1958 comeback bid to Jim Van Pelt; dealt to Calgary 1959 for Jimmy Morse but joined Washington Redskins (NFL) 1959-61, Calgary fall of 1961; dealt to Toronto Argos 1966; seven season CFL totals: 1,753 passes thrown, 1,015 completions, 14,405yds gained, 71 interceptions for .579 percentage (second only to Peter Liske), 74 TDs; WFC, all-Canadian all-star 1962; Jeff Nicklin Memorial Trophy as WFC MVP 1962.

DAY, Hap (hockey); *b.* 14 Jun 1901, Owen Sound, Ont.; *given name:* Clarence; U of Toronto; pharmacist; played junior hockey Midland, Ont. then moved to Hamilton senior Tigers for two years; turned pro Toronto St. Pat's 1924 and spent the next 33 years involved with hockey as player, coach,

referee, general manager; with Leafs teamed with King Clancy on defence; record four goals one game by defenceman 1929, broken 1977 by Leafs' Ian Turnbull; captained first Toronto Maple Leafs team to Stanley Cup 1931-32, scored three goals in semifinals; career NHL mark 86 goals, 116 assists; coached West Toronto Nationals to 1936 Memorial Cup then closed competitive career 1937-38 with N Y Americans; refereed two seasons then rejoined Leafs as coach guiding them to five Stanley Cups, three in succession; Leafs' manager 1950-57; mem. Hockey Hall of Fame; *res.* St. Thomas, Ont.

DAY, James (equestrian); *b.* 7 Jul 1946, Thornhill, Ont.; *sep.* Dinny; *children:* Catherine, Richard; car salesman, farm manager; first international competition 1964 Pennsylvania National; mem. gold medal team 1968 Olympics, fourth individual jumping; team sixth Prix des Nations 1972 Munich Olympics; competed 1976 Montreal Olympics in jumping, three-day events; individual gold medal 1967 Pan-Am Games; team bronze Prix des Nations; team silver 1975 Mexico Pan-Am Games; tied world puissance record 7'3" New York, Toronto 1966, 1968; mem. winning Prix des Nations team 1970 world; North American three-day champion 1973; through 1976 winner 11 Rothmans Grand Prix events; Canadian Equestrian Team challenge trophy as leading rider 1974; five times open jumping champion, four times intermediate, twice preliminary jumping; horseman of year 1966-68; competitive mounts Steelmaster, Out of Sight, Southern Cat, Easy Doc, Deep South, Viceroy, Mr. Super Plus, Sympatico; *res.* Hornby, Ont.

DAY, Mike (orienteering); *b.* 27 Oct 1934, London, Eng.; *m.* Mary Nolan; *children:* Erin, Kevin, Mike, Christina; Quintin

School; flight operations officer; placed 83rd with 2:40.18 1970 Boston Marathon; Canadian, Ontario Veteran Class Orienteering champion 1975; pres. Canadian Orienteering Federation; manager Canadian Orienteering team 1974 Denmark world championships; mem. Canadian team 1972 Czechoslovakian championships; *res.* Ottawa, Ont.

DEAN, Bob (football); *b.* 17 Dec 1929, Pittsburgh, Pa.; *given name:* Robert Wadsworth; *m.* Shirley Anne Donaldson; *children:* Geoffrey, Matthew, Clayton; U of Maryland, B.Sc., U of Alberta, B.Ed., M.Ed.; school administrator; played with Washington Redskins then joined Edmonton Eskimos 1954; contributed field goal and game winning convert in Edmonton's 26-25 1954 Grey Cup win over Montreal; Ted Reeve's all-Canadian rating 1955; mem. Alberta's national volleyball team five years; *res.* Edmonton, Alta.

DEKDEBRUN, Al (football); *b.* 11 May 1921, Buffalo, N.Y.; *given name:* Allen Edward; *m.* Corinne Scoones; *children:* Gregory, Rick; Cornell U, B.Sc.; sporting goods proprietor; all-American quarterback at Cornell 1945; MVP East-West Shrine Game 1946; mem. college all-star team 1946; played three years all-American conference in U S; six seasons in Canada with Toronto, Hamilton, Ottawa; mem. 1950 Argos Grey Cup champions; coached at Canisius College, U of Buffalo; *res.* Williamsville, N.Y.

DELAHEY, Wally (football); *b.* 23 Sep 1932, Toronto, Ont.; *given name:* Wallace Allan; *m.* Patricia Ann; *children:* Karen, Diane, Jill, Brian; U of Western Ontario, B.P.H.E., OCE; assistant professor; played entire Humberside CI football career on team which never lost game; also excelled at

basketball, T&F, gymnastics, swimming; four years college football, one year swimming; coach West Hill CI two years, Kitchener CI four years, U of Waterloo 13 years, nine as head coach; pres. K-W branch CAHPER 1963-64; pres. Canadian Football Coaches Association 1969; mem. all-Canadian football selection committee 1972-76; chairman Canadian Red Cross Society water safety services Kitchener branch 1964-69; secretary-treasurer Twin City HS Athletic Association 1962-66; waterfront director Camp Tawingo Huntsville 1969-76; mem. rules committee Canadian Amateur Football Association 1977; *res.* Kitchener, Ont.

DELAMARRE, Victor (weightlifting); *b.* 1888, Lac St. Jean, Que., *d.* 1955, Montreal, Que.; *m.; children:* four sons, six daughters; pro strongman, wrestler, policeman; following footsteps of idol Louis Cyr, joined Montreal police force despite size—5'6, 145lbs; began giving exhibitions of strength; lifted world record 309½lbs one hand 1914; with one finger lifted 201lbs; lifted platforms with 60 people weighing 7,000lbs; October 1928 lifted 30 Quebec City policeman, each weighting at least 200lbs; turned to pro wrestling 1931, reported to have had 1,500 bouts; mem. Canadian Sports Hall of Fame.

DELANEY, Jack (boxing); *b.* 18 Mar 1900, St. Francis, Que., *d.* 27 Nov 1948, Katanah, N.Y.; *given name:* Ovila Chapdelaine; turned pro at 19 taking name when ring announcer, having trouble with Chapdelaine, called him Jack Delaney; first fight, second round KO of Tom Nelson; lost to Paul Berlenbach 1925 for world light heavyweight title at Madison Square Garden; beat Berlenbach in 15 1926 to take title but never defended; fought last bout as heavyweight Hartford Conn. 1948, KO'd Leo Williams in first; pro record 86 bouts, winning 42 on KO's, 27 on decision, one by foul, three draws, seven decisions lost, three times KO'd, two no-decisions, one no-contest; beat many top names including Tommy Loughran, Tiger Flowers; mem. Canadian Boxing, Sports Halls of fame.

DELVECCHIO, Alex (hockey); *b.* 4 Dec 1931, Fort William, Ont.; *given name:* Alexander Peter; *m.* Teresa De Guiseppe; *children:* Kenneth, Janice, Corrine; hockey executive; played for Ft. William Junior Hurricanes then moved to OHA junior A Oshawa Generals where he scored 51 goals, 69 assists for 120 points 1950-51 season; turned pro with Detroit, after six games at Indianapolis (AHL) moved to centre with Red Wings; second player in NHL history to play over 20 seasons with same club; played left wing with Gordie Howe, Norm Ullman; in 1,549 league games scored 456 goals, 825 assists for 1,281 points, 383 penalty minutes; in 121 playoff games scored 35 goals, 69 assists for 104 points, 29 penalty minutes; Detroit captain 1961 until retirement as player 1973; coached Wings 1973, general manager 1974-77; twice second team all-star; Lady Byng Trophy three times; Lester Patrick Award once; three year coaching record 200 games, 69 wins, 104 losses, 27 ties for .413 percentage, no playoffs; mem. Michigan Hall of Fame; *res.* Detroit, Mich.

DENNENY, Cy (hockey); *b.* 23 Dec 1891, Farran's Point, Ont., *d.* 10 Sep 1970, Ottawa, Ont.; *given name:* Cyril Joseph; *m.* Malvina K. Eastman (*d.*); *m.* Isobel Clark; *children:* Kathlyn, Janet, Alma (*d.*); Cornwall HS; civil servant; early hockey Cornwall County League; joined Russell Ont. team Lower Ottawa Valley League 1912; following year with O'Brien Mine team in Cobalt Mining League turned pro 1914 Toronto Shamrocks; joined Ottawa Senators 1916-28; on five Stanley Cup winners, scored 246 goals; player, coach, assistant manager one year with Boston Bruins, refereed one year in NHL; coach junior, senior amateur teams Ottawa 1931-32; coach 1932-33 Ottawa Senators; on line with Frank Nighbor, Punch Broadbent; scored seven goals single game 1921-22 season; exponent of curved stick; mem. Ottawa, Hockey Halls of Fame.

de ST. CROIX, Ted (orienteering); *b.* 30 Aug 1957, St. Catharines, Ont.; Beamsville DHS; student; boys under-14 Ontario title; second North American championships for boys 15-16 1971; Ontario boys 15-16 title 1972; North American junior men's, placed 11th Sweden boys 15-16 finals 1973; men's 17-18 Göteborg Sweden; 17th Swedish five-day, third Canadian elite 1974; North American elite title, second Canadian, third Ontario, fourth Quebec (top Canadian), fourth Swedish 19km open class, first Swedish men's 17-18, men's Ontario overall elite 1975; U S elite title, second Canadian national team trials 1976; *res.* Vineland, Ont.

DESCHAMPS, Claude (softball); *b.* 7 Aug 1934, Ottawa, Ont.; *m.* Dolorese Seguin; *children:* Marc, Lucie, Louise; Guiges School, LaSalle Academy; played 1964 season as second baseman Hull Que.; helped organize Hull Volant team 1971, Atlantic Seaboard Major Fastball League, 1973 Canadian men's senior softball championships Hull; played major role senior fastball in Ottawa area with organization of Metropolitan Major Fastball League; six years secretary-general of Hull International Softball tournament; appointed CASA executive-director 1975; *res.* Ottawa, Ont.

DESJARDINS, Paul (football); *b.* 12 Sep 1943, Ottawa, Ont.; *given name:* Paul Robert; *m.* Vona Elizabeth Freeman; *children:* Michelle, Steven, Jason; U of Ottawa, B.Sc., U of Manitoba, M.Sc., Ph.D.; clinical chemist; played football U of Ottawa Gee-Gees 1960-65; turned pro Winnipeg Blue Bombers 1965-70, Toronto Argos 1971-73; CFL all-star centre (East) 1971-73, all-Canadian 1973; 1968 Winnipeg MVP; best all-around athlete U of Ottawa 1963-64; top volleyball player U of O 1964-65; Gil O. Julien trophy French Canadian athlete of year 1965; *res.* Winnipeg, Man.

DESMARTEAU, Etienne (track and field); *b.* 1877, Montreal, Que., *d.* 1905, Montreal, Que.; policeman, smallest of five brothers at 6'1", 225lbs; with brother Zacharie competed in police games held annually in Toronto, New York, Montreal and Boston; specialized in 56lb weight toss, similar to today's hammer throw; competed 1904 St. Louis Olympics sponsored by MAAA and became first Canadian Olympic gold medalist winning weight toss, event discontinued following 1920 games; world record with 15'9" height and 36'6.5" distance; 1976 Olympic facilities named in his honor; mem. Canadian Sports Hall of Fame.

DEVAL, Gordon (fly, bait casting); *b.* 18 Jan 1930, Winnipeg, Man.; *m.* Britta; *children:* Ronald, Randall, Connie, Wendy; Meisterschaft College, U of Toronto, Shaw Business School; insurance agent; all-Canadian distance casting records since 1955; all-around champion since 1955; runner-up to world champion Steve Rajeff San Francisco 1975; represented Canada world tournament South Africa 1975 finishing in top 10; holder world record one ounce spin distance and ⅝ ounce unrestricted bait distance 531 and 384ft respectively; *res* Scarborough, Ont.

DEWAR, Phyllis (swimming); *b.* 1916, *d.* 1961; *m.* Murray Lowery; *children:* four; four gold medals — 100yd, 400yd freestyle, 300yd medley, 400yd relay, 1934 British Empire Games London Eng.; qualified for 1936 Olympics swim team but contracted flu and performed poorly; gold medal 400yd freestyle 1938 British Empire Games Australia; Velma Springstead Trophy (Canadian female athlete of year) 1934; mem. Canadian Sports Hall of Fame.

DEWITTE, Marcel (curling); *b.* 27 Nov 1927, Belgium; *given name:* Marcel George Maurice; *m.* Joan Ann Newell; *children:* John Charles, Jacqueline Alice; arena and parks manager, refrigeration engineer; began as curling ice maker Simcoe Curling Club 1958; moved to Sarnia Golf and Curling Club 1961; ice superintendent 16-sheet Ivanhoe Curling Club London Ont. 1963-76; Ontario Legion playdowns Zone A representative at North Bay 1968; one of Canada's most competent curling ice makers, conducted clinics under OCA auspices; served on 1974 London Brier, London Silver Broom steering committees; chief ice maker 1974 London Brier, 1978 Sault St. Marie Canadian Lassie; *res.* Burgessville, Ont.

DIACHUN, Jennifer (gymnastics); *b.* 14 Aug 1953, Toronto, Ont.; *given name:* Jennifer Marie; U of Toronto, U of British Columbia; student; senior Canadian title 1969-72 and 1974; Canadian Intercollegiate title 1973, 1976; represented Canada 1968, 1972 Olympics, 1970, 1974 world tournament; two bronze 1971 Pan-Am Games; fourth on bars 1973 World Student Games Moscow; competed as Canadian team member in China, Russia, Canadian tours; mem. 1973 Moscow News Invitational, sixth in vault; Ontario Gymnastics Federation outstanding person in gymnastics 1975; *res.* East Delta, B.C.

DIONNE, Marcel (hockey); *b.* 3 Aug 1951, Drummondville, Que.; *given name:* Marcel Elphege; hockey player; junior career with St. Catharines Black Hawks, twice lead junior OHA in scoring; Detroit's first draft choice, second overall in 1971 amateur draft; NHL rookie record with 28 goals, 49 assists for 77 points 1971-72 season; as free agent acquired by Los Angeles Kings with Bart Crashley for Terry Harper, Dan Maloney and LA's second choice in 1976 amateur draft; Lady Byng Trophy 1975 even though playing out option; through 1976-77 NHL record: 469 games, 232 goals, 350 assists for 582 points 109 penalty minutes plus 18 playoff games, 11 goals, 10 assists, 21 points; played for Team Canada 1976, won Canada Cup; ranked as one of NHL's top scoring centres; *res.* Los Angeles, Calif.

DIXON, George (boxing); *b.* 29 Jul 1870, Halifax, N.S., *d.* 6 Jan 1909, New York, N.Y.; at 16 KO'd Young Johnson 1886 at Halifax; nickname Little Chocolate; in 1888 claimed vacant world bantam title which he defended twice; recognized 1891 as featherweight champion after beating Cal McCarthy in 22 rounds Troy N.Y.; defended three times before losing to Solly Smith in 20 rounds 1897 San Francisco; regained title beating Dave Sullivan in 10 at NYC 1898; lost to Terry McGovern 1900 then, when McGovern couldn't make weight, fought Abe Attel for vacated crown losing in 15 1901 at St. Louis; last bout 1906, 15-round loss to Monk Newsboy; pro career totalled 158 bouts (estimated he fought some 800 times including barnstorming), won 30 by KO, 55 by decision, one on foul, 38 draws, 21 decisions lost, four times KO'd and nine no decisions; longest fight 70 round draw with McCarthy; mem. U S, Canadian Boxing, Canadian Sports Halls of Fame.

DIXON, George (football); *b.* 19 Oct 1933, New Haven, Conn.; *m.* Carol Grant; *children:* Kirk, Eric; U of Bridgeport; promotions; drafted by Green Bay Packers (NFL)· joined Montreal Alouettes 1959 and through seven CFL seasons scored 59 career TDs, including 18 in 1960 season; 896 carries for 5,615yds, 6.3 avg.; best single season 1962 with 216 carries for 1,520yds, 7.0 avg., 11 TDs; twice rushed for over 1,000yds one season; shares CFL record with Willie Fleming longest single play gain 109yds 2 Sep 1963 vs Ottawa; 1962 Schenley outstanding player award, Jeff Russel Memorial trophy; Lord Calvert trophy; frequent EFC, all-Canadian all-star halfback; mem. Canadian Football Hall of Fame; *res.* Montreal, Que.

DOCKERILL, Sylvia (swimming); *b.* 17 Sep 1951, Vancouver B.C.; *given name:* Sylvia Elizabeth; West Vancouver HS, U of British Columbia, B.H.E., teaching certificate; home economics teacher; mem. Canadian national team 1969-72; competed U.K., N.Z. tours 1968-69, German, Russian national tours 1972, China tour 1974, 1972 Munich Olympics, 1971 Pan-Am Games, 1970 Commonwealth Games; gold medal 100m breast stroke 1971 Pan-Am Games; seventh medley relay 1972 Olympics; *res.* Victoria, B.C.

DOJACK, Paul (football); *b.* 24 Apr 1917, Winnipeg, Man.; *given name:* Paul Stanley; *m.* Ellen Annie Dawson; director Saskatchewan Boys' School; one of founders Dales Athletic Club, starred as softball pitcher, quarterback city champion juvenile football team and Dales team in Saskatchewan junior league; past manager, secretary-treasurer, coach, pres. of Dales; as coach directed Dales to four consecutive Western Canadian titles, 1938 Canadian junior championship;

coached basketball, softball, officiated football with Regina Rifles; recruited by WIFU as official 1947; retired from football officiating as WFC supervisor of officials 1973; officiated in close to 600 games, including 15 Grey Cups, nine as head referee; wrote syndicated sports column on football rules; chairman 1967 Canadian junior championships, Regina Centennial Bantam Football tournament; mem. Sask. Sports Hall of Fame; *res.* Regina, Sask.

DOMIK, Bob (softball); *b.* 8 Jun 1942, Duparquet, Que.; *m.* Ann Purdy; *children:* Dawn Darlene, Sunday Rozalee, Davita Dorothy; King CI; partner in cartage business; mem. 1972 Canadian world championship team Manila Philippines, pitched no-hitter and voted world's best pitcher with 0.00 earned run avg.; pitched in six Canadian championships since 1958, twice won titles; established in one seven-inning game a record 14 consecutive strike outs, 18 of 21 outs in game 1975; now wears uniform No. 14; played softball in every Canadian province, most U S states, Philippines, Japan, New Zealand, Nassau; designed pitching program available through Canadian Amateur Softball Association Ottawa; *res.* Scarborough, Ont.

DOMONKOS, Mariann (table tennis); *b.* 12 Feb 1958, Budapest, Hungary; CEGEP student; four times Canadian junior girls champion; won 1973 Canadian Open women's singles; North American junior girls title; North American women's doubles champion 1972; Scandinavian Open mixed doubles finalist 1975; eighth in Commonwealth 1975; won Canadian women's singles 1977, Canadian women's doubles 1976-77; *res.* Chateauguay, Que.

DONOHUE, Jack (basketball); *b.* 4 Jun 1931, New York, N.Y.; *m.* Mary Jane Choffin; *children:* Carol, John Joe, Kathy, Mary Beth, Bryan, Maura; Fordham U, B.A., New York U, M.A.; employed Sport O'Keefe, commissioner, head coach Canadian Amateur Basketball Association; began coaching career St. Nicholas of Tolentine NYC 1954, shifted to Power Memorial NYC; HS coaching record 250-46 including string of 71 consecutive victories due largely to efforts of Lew Alcindor (Kareem Abdul Jabbar); head coach Holy Cross College 1965-71 compiling 108-65 record; Eastern region coach of year 1970; accepted CABA post 1972; coached Canadian women's national team briefly; guided Canadian men's team to fourth place 1976 Olympics; noted raconteur; *res.* Kanata, Ont.

DORSCH, Henry (football); *b.* 11 Nov 1940, Weyburn, Sask.; *m.* Helen Patricia; *children:* Douglas, Natalie, Debra; U of Tulsa, B.Sc.; hospital administrator; played two years Regina Rams then U of Tulsa, starred as fullback; joined Saskatchewan Roughriders 1964 as backup fullback, played nine years as defensive back with occasional action on offence; *mem.* Saskatchewan Roughrider management committee 1975; played in four Grey Cup finals, one winner; *res.* Regina, Sask.

DOTY, Frederick (football); *b.* 25 Oct 1924, Toronto, Ont.; *m.* Beverly Brown; *children:* Cole, Tobin; U of Toronto, B.Sc.; v.-pres. Canadian Johns-Mansville; played junior football Calgary 1944 and basketball with RCAF Calgary 1943-44; turned pro Toronto Argos 1945-49; played for both Argos and Toronto Varsity 1946; in three Grey Cups; *res.* Mississauga, Ont.

DOUCETTE, Gerry (football); *b.* 18 Sep 1933, Toronto, Ont.; *given name:* Gerald David; *m.* Mildred Ruth Grosse; *children:* Mike, Steve, Jill, Sue; Etobicoke HS; salesman; led Etobicoke Rams to TDIAA title then spent season with Balmy Beach ORFU 1953; moved up to Argos 1954-59 as backup quarterback, punter, placement specialist; appeared in 75 regular season, two playoff games; threw 366 passes, completing 180 for 2,558yds, 14 TDs, 30 interceptions; totalled 158 kickoffs, including 62 in 1956 season, for 8,458yds; punted 180 times for 6,691yds; *res.* Oakville, Ont.

DOUTHWRIGHT, Joyce (basketball); *b.* 25 Apr 1950, Moncton, N.B.; *given name:* Joyce Ann; U of New Brunswick, B.P.E., B.A.; technical director N.B. Amateur Basketball Association; mem. national women's basketball team since 1969, N.B. Canada Games basketball team 1971, 1975, N.B. field hockey team 1969-74; MVP UNB field hockey team 1970-71; represented Canada women's basketball Montreal Olympics 1976; UNB athlete of year 1973-74; *res.* Riverview N.B.

DOWDS, Maureen (track and field); *b.* 3 Jul 1948, Whitehorse, Yukon; *given name:* Maureen Joan; St. James CI, U of Manitoba, U of Western Ontario; HS phys ed teacher; top female athlete in HS, U of Manitoba twice; Red River shot put title 39'3'' 1964; Canadian junior shot put title 1967; placed second Canadian seniors, bronze Pan-Am Games with Canadian junior record 47'1'' 1967; Canadian shot put title, first vs Sweden, Norway on Canadian team tour 1968; semi-retired 1969 but returned to competition winning Ontario College title 1972; second Canadian championships 1974-75, fourth Pan-Am Games 1975

with personal best 16.46m to tie Canadian record; injury forced her out of 1976 Olympics; *res.* Winnipeg, Man.

DRAYTON, Jerome (track); *b.* 10 Jan 1945, W. Germany; *given name:* Jerome Peter Buniak; McMaster U, B.A.; Ontario civil servant; first of five Canadian 10 000m titles 1968, set Canadian record for distance 28:25.8 June 1970; Canadian 5000m title 1970; Canadian marathon champion 1972; won Fukuoka Japan marathon 1969, 1975, 1976; Boston marathon 1977; world record indoor three-mile 13:06.0 1975, 10-mile track record 46:37.6 1973; represented Canada in Commonwealth Games, six Boston marathons; *res.* Toronto, Ont.

DRILLON, Gord (hockey); *b.* 23 Oct 1913, Moncton, N.B.; *given name:* Gordon Arthur; *m.* Barbara Alice Lee; N.B. government consultant; played junior hockey with Moncton Athletics, Moncton Wheelers, Toronto Young Rangers, Toronto Lions, senior hockey with Pittsburgh Yellow Jackets 1935; turned pro Toronto Maple Leafs chain playing with Syracuse Stars for short time before joining Leafs 1936-42; with Montreal Canadiens 1942-43; seven NHL season record 155 regular season goals, 139 assists for 294 points, 62 penalty minutes, plus 26 playoff goals, 15 assists for 41 points, 10 penalty minutes; twice first, second team all-star; Art Ross Trophy as NHL's leading scorer 1937-38 with 26 goals, 26 assists for 52 points; Lady Byng Trophy 1937-38; hockey fan trophy as most popular NHL player 1939; mem. 1941-42 Stanley Cup champions; with Leafs teamed with Syl Apps, Bob Davidson to form DAD line, alternately known as Leaf Dynamite; with Canadiens played left side on line with Buddy O'Connor, Ray Getliffe; pitched southpaw softball for Toronto Danforth Aces in Davisville senior softball league, Maritime CNR softball league; competed in Eastern Canadian tennis championships; honored by city of Saint John; mem. N.B. Sports, Hockey Halls of Fame; *res.* Saint John, N.B.

DRINKWATER, Graham (hockey); *b.* 22 Feb 1875, Montreal, Que., *d.* 26 Sep 1946, Montreal, Que.; *given name:* Charles Graham; McGill U; played junior hockey (MAAA) taking 1892-93 title; following year played with McGill junior football champions, McGill intermediate hockey titlists; joined Montreal Victorias 1895, winning Stanley Cup that year, lost 1896, then three more winners in succession; captained 1898-99 Stanley Cup champions; although he played on four Stanley Cup winners, never turned pro; mem. Hockey Hall of Fame.

DRYDEN, Ken (hockey); *b.* 8 Aug 1947, Hamilton, Ont.; *given name:* Kenneth Wayne; *m.* Lynda; *children:* Sarah; Etobicoke CI, Cornell U, U of Manitoba, McGill U, LL.B.; hockey player, lawyer; played junior B Etobicoke; third choice of Boston Bruins, 14th overall in 1964 amateur draft; chose Cornell, three times all-American goaler while posting record of 71 wins, four losses, one tie and 1.65 goals-against avg.; Eastern Collegiate Athletic Association tournament MVP; Boston U outstanding opponent award 1969; played with Canadian national team as amateur then turned pro with Montreal Voyageurs (AHL) 1970-71; called up by Canadiens late in season, starred in Stanley Cup playdowns, won Conn Smythe Trophy, scored assist in playoffs; 1971-72 Calder Memorial Trophy as league's top rookie; 1973 Vezina Trophy; sat out 1973-74 season completing law studies,

playing defence in Toronto Industrial League, doing TV commentary for Toronto Toros of WHA; returned to NHL play with Canadiens 1974-75; Vezina Trophy 1976, 1977; twice first team, once second team all-star goaler; played for Team Canada 1972 vs USSR; through 1976-77 NHL record 298 games played, 17,467 minutes, 657 goals allowed, 36 shutouts, 2.26 avg. plus 81 playoff games for 4,937 minutes, 204 goals allowed, eight shutouts, 2.48 avg.; *res.* Montreal, Que.

DUBOIS, Theo (rowing); *b.* 19 May 1911, Brussels, Belgium; *given name:* Theo Alfred; Provencher CI, U of Manitoba, B.Arch.; architect; won Canadian junior singles St. Catharines 1938, CAAO singles and senior doubles 1939; qualified for cancelled 1940 Olympics; same year won NAAO senior doubles with Albert Riley; won U S singles 1940 and both U S, Canadian singles 1941; retained Canadian singles and won Eastern Rowing Association singles 1942; won 1947 U S singles, Canadian doubles with Derry Riley; competed 1948 London Olympic trials St. Catharines but did not qualify although his trial time was faster than winning Olympic time; retired from competitive rowing 1948; twice defeated Eastern U S champion cyclist Adolph Velthuysen Detroit Velodrome 1934 after beating him in 10-mile road race the previous day; representing Ottawa YMCA won Eastern Ontario light heavyweight boxing title 1943; Lou Marsh Trophy, Canadian athlete of year, 1941; *res.* Winnipeg, Man.

DUFF, Dick (hockey); *b.* 18 Feb 1936, Kirkland Lake, Ont.; *given name:* Terrance Richard; St. Michael's College, Assumption College, B.A.; played two seasons St. Michael's College junior B, two junior A scoring 99 goals; turned pro with Toronto Maple Leafs 1954-63, played left wing on line with Tod Sloan, George Armstrong; traded to N Y Rangers 1964 with Bob Nevin, Bill Collins, Arnie Brown, Rod Seiling for Andy Bathgate, Don McKenney; dealt to Montreal Canadiens 1964 for Bill Hicke; played with Los Angeles, Buffalo Sabres before retiring; in 18 NHL campaigns played 1,030 games scoring 283 goals, 289 assists for 572 points and 743 penalty minutes; in 114 playoff games scored 30 goals, 49 assists for 79 points, 78 penalty minutes; best season with Leafs 1958-59, scored 29 goals; five times scored 20 or more goals in a season; *res.* Montreal, Que.

DUFRESNE, Coleen (basketball); *b.* 15 Feb 1953, Halifax, N.S.; Vaudreuil Catholic HS, U of Ottawa, B.P.E.; teacher; Nova Scotia, Quebec records in shot put, javelin, triple jump; four years with U of O women's basketball team, lead OUAA scorers four years; Canadian women's national team 1974; competed in 1975 world Columbia, 1975 Pan-Am Games Mexico, 1976 Olympics Montreal; mem. Quebec team 1971, 1975 Canada winter games; all-Canadian 1975; Ottawa region basketball athlete of year 1974-75; *res.* Montreal, Que.

DUGGAN, Herrick (yachting); *b.* 1862, Toronto, Ont., *d.* 1946; *given name:* George Herrick; Upper Canada College, U of Toronto; construction engineer; assisted in formation of Toronto Yacht Club 1880, Lake Yacht Racing Association; as mem. Royal St. Lawrence Yacht Club Montreal 1896 challenged for Seawanhaka Cup; designed five of 18 challengers and skippered his Glencairn I to cup victory; defended successfully against U S, English challengers; designed unusual yacht Dominion-claimed as

single-hulled with two waterlines although opponents said it was double-hulled catamaran; in his time considered best designer of small boats in world; designed, built total of 142 boats; mem. Canadian Sports Hall of Fame.

DUGRE, Lou (curling); *b.* 9 Apr 1945, Moncton, N.B.; *given name:* Louis Joseph Marcel; *m.* Elizabeth; *children:* Jean Paul; marketing, supply procedures Canadian Forces; represented N.B. 1971 Legion championships, won Canadian title at Charlottetown; followed with Canadian Forces Atlantic Zone title Cornwallis N.S. 1972; runner-up Canadian Legion final Winnipeg 1972, third Toronto 1973; N.B. men's provincial title, tied for third 1973 Edmonton Brier; third 1974 Canadian Legion finals, fourth provincial title; skipped Ottawa rink to 1975 Ontario Legion and Canadian Legion championships; won fifth event 1975 Whitby Sun Life 'spiel; runner-up Division One OCA Consols 1976; qualified for Ontario Consols by winning Ontario Challenge Round at Orillia; in third place tie with 5-4 record Peterborough 1976 Consols; *res.* Ottawa, Ont.

DUGUID, Don (curling); *b.* 21 Oct 1935, Winnipeg, Man.; *m.* Georgina Tucker; *children:* Terry, Dale, Dean, Randy, Kevin; Daniel McIntyre HS; auto dealership manager; played six years with Terry Braunstein rink; played second for Howie Wood Jr., won 1957 Manitoba Consols, third place tie in Brier; with Braunstein played third claiming 1965 Manitoba Consols and Brier title; teamed with Rod Hunter, Jim Pettapiece and Bryan Wood to win back-to-back Manitoba, Canadian, world championships 1970-71; several years color commentator with CBC on major curling event coverage;

three times Manitoba bonspiel grand aggregate champion; mem. Canadian Curling Hall of Fame; *res.* Winnipeg, Man.

DUKOWSKI, Albin (track); *b.* 4 Jun 1954, Vancouver, B.C.; U of Oregon, B.Sc.; student; Western Canadian 100, 200m titles 1975; junior, juvenile Canadian records in 200m (21.1); mem. Canadian 4x100m relay team 1975 World Student Games Rome which won silver medal in 39.8; mem. 1975 Pan-Am Games team Mexico, bronze in 4x100m relay, established Canadian record 38.86; mem. Canadian Olympic team 1976; *res.* Vancouver, B.C.

DUMELIE, Larry (football); *b.* 7 Dec 1936, Lafleche, Sask.; *given name:* Lawrence; *m.* Karen Marie; *children:* Michele, Bobby, Sherrie, Doug, James; U of Arizona, B.A., B.Sc.; product promotion manager; defensive back with Saskatchewan Roughriders 1960-68 competing in two Grey Cup finals; second in WFC 1964 with six interceptions; also led Riders in interceptions 1965-66; Saskatoon Hilltop football coach 1969; pres. Saskatoon Handball Association 1969, doubles champion that year; coached minor hockey London Ont. 1973-74; *res.* Markham, Ont.

DUNDERDALE, Tommy (hockey); *b.* 6 May 1887, Benella, Australia, *d.* 1960 Winnipeg, Man.; learned hockey fundamentals in Ottawa, joined Shamrocks (NHA) 1910 then moved to Quebec Bulldogs 1911; joined Victoria 1912 and remained in PCHA through 1923 concluding career with Saskatoon, Edmonton in WCHL 1924; while in PCHA played four years at Victoria, three at Portland then five more with Victoria; twice led league scorers; during 12 PCHA

seasons scored more goals than any other player in league; scored in each of Victoria's 15 league games 1914, league all-star centre; career total 225 goals in 290 games plus six goals in 12 playoff games; following retirement coached, managed teams in Los Angeles, Edmonton, Winnipeg; mem. Hockey Hall of Fame.

DUNLAP, Frank (football, hockey); *b.* 10 Aug 1924, Ottawa, Ont.; *given name:* Frank Egan; *m.* Mary Kathryn Heney; *children:* David, Michael, Patrick, Daniel; St. Patrick's College, B. Comm., Osgoode Hall, LL.B.; county court judge; hockey with St. Michael's College Majors 1942-44, brief stint 1943 with Toronto Maple Leafs; Ottawa Commandos (QSHL) 1944, Hull Volants (QSHL) 1945, Ottawa Senators (QSHL) 1946, Pembroke Lumber Kings 1947; football Ottawa Trojans 1942, Ottawa Combines 1943, pro with Ottawa Rough Riders 1944-47, 1950-51, Toronto Argos 1948-49; all-Canadian quarterback 1946; with 1951 Ottawa Grey Cup champions; mem. Canada Fitness Council 1967-69; *res.* Ottawa, Ont.

DUNLAP, Moffat (equestrian); *b.* 31 Mar 1941, Toronto, Ont.; *m.* Margaret Humphrey; *children:* Louise, John; Upper Canada College, U of Western Ontario, B.A.; real estate broker; mem. Canadian Equestrian team since 1958; on bronze medal Nations' Cup team 1967 Pan-Am Games; gold medal team world championships France 1970; mem. several Nations' Cup winning teams International Fall Circuit; leading rider Pennsylvania National Horse Show three times and holds Puissance record 7'½'' that show; board mem. Canadian Horse Council, Canadian Horse Shows Association, administrative committee Royal Horse Show; frequent Grand Prix winner, Cleveland,

Hornby, Memphis, Atlanta; competitive horses include Scotch Valley, Mexteco, Stoic, Cousin Albert; *res.* Newmarket, Ont.

DURELLE, Yvon (boxing); *b.* 14 Oct 1929, Baie Ste. Anne, N.B.; first recorded bout Chatham N.B. 1948, KO'd Sonny Ramsay in second; Canadian light heavyweight title 1953 with 12 round decision over Gordon Wallace Sydney N.S.; lost title in 12 to Doug Harper Calgary 1953; regained title from Harper 1954 Newcastle N.B.; defended twice; fought some top names: Floyd Patterson, Jimmy Slade, Yolande Pompey, KO'd by each; won British Empire light heavyweight title 1957, KO'd Wallace in second, Moncton N.B.; defended once; challenged Archie Moore for world light heavyweight title 1958 at Montreal but Moore won on KO in 11th; rematch 1959 in Montreal, Moore scored third round KO; met George Chuvalo Toronto 1959 for Canadian heavyweight title but was KO'd in 12th; retired to try hand at wrestling 1951; brief boxing comeback 1963 scoring two KOs; last bout 1963, KO'd Phonse La Saga at Trois-Rivières; pro record 105 bouts, 44 won by KO, 38 by decision, 10 lost on decision, three on fouls, nine by KO and one no contest; mem. Canadian Boxing, Sports Halls of Fame; *res.* Baie Ste. Anne, N.B.

DURNAN, Bill (hockey); *b.* 22 Jan 1915, Toronto, Ont.; *d.* 31 Oct 1972, Toronto, Ont.; *m.* Amanda; *children:* Deanna, Brenda; gained early reputation as goaler with Sudbury juniors 1933-34 OHA finals; played three seasons with NOHA contenders before joining Allan Cup-winning Kirkland Lake Blue Devils 1940; ambidextrous brilliance caught eye of Montreal scouts who convinced him to join Royals; moved to Canadiens winning Vezina Trophy in rookie pro season 1943-44; played seven seasons with Habs winning Vezina six times; first team all-star six times; played on four league champions, two Stanley Cup winners; 1948-49 established modern NHL record for consecutive shutouts, four, playing 309 minutes, 21 seconds of shutout hockey; played 383 scheduled games allowing 901 goals for 2.36 goals against avg., 34 shutouts; also softball pitcher with at least 14 no-hitters to his record; once fanned 24 in nine-inning game; pitched Montreal to four successive provincial titles; mem. Hockey Hall of Fame.

DYE, Babe (hockey); *b.* 13 May 1898, Hamilton, Ont., *d.* 3 Jan 1962, Chicago, Ill.; *given name:* Cecil Henry; foreman, contract paving firm; played halfback Toronto Argos, baseball with Toronto; played junior hockey Aura Lee Ontario champions 1917; joined Toronto St. Pat's 1919 scoring 11 goals in 21 games; remained seven seasons then joined Chicago Black Hawks 1926; broken leg sidelined him 1927, retired after 1928 with N Y Americans; four times Art Ross Trophy winner as NHL leading scorer; twice scored five goals in single game, twice had 11-game scoring streaks; played on one Stanley Cup winner; scored nine goals in five playoff games; had highest goals-per-game record in NHL history — 200 in 255 games; on retirement coached Chicago Shamrocks in American Association, refereed five years in NHL in late 30s; mem. Hockey Hall of Fame.

EAGLESON, Alan (hockey); *b.* 24 Apr 1933, St. Catharines, Ont.; *given name:* Robert Alan; *m.* Nancy Elizabeth Fisk; *children:* Trevor Allen, Jill Anne; Mimico HS; U of Toronto, B.A. LL.B.; lawyer; agent for several pro athletes including Bobby Orr; director of Hockey Canada; active role in Team Canada 1972 series, organized Canada Cup 1976 tournament; executive-director NHL Players' Association; director-secretary Bobby Orr Enterprises Ltd.; Etobicoke outstanding young man award twice; Vanier award as one of Canada's five outstanding young men 1968; University College bronze award and Arts Trophy for athletics 1957; *res.* Mississauga, Ont.

EBBELS, Bill (tennis); *b.* 20 Jul 1922, Saskatoon, Sask.; *given name:* William Dennis; *m.* Ruth Hutchison; *children:* Harold, John, James, William, Virginia, Andrea; U of Saskatchewan, B. Comm.; investment dealer; initial recognition on tennis courts with Sask. under-13 title 1935; runner-up 1940, winner 1941 U of Sask. singles; played junior A hockey with Saskatoon Chiefs, basketball with U of Sask. Huskies; Halifax Naval College net honors 1942; U of Sask.

hockey 1946-47, mem. five man team runner-up to McGill U in only national university tennis championships 1946; eight times Sask. men's singles champion (record), runner-up seven times; winner Sask. men's doubles seven times, runner-up four times; Regina city men's singles four times, doubles four times; Regina Civil Service Tennis Club champion once, runner-up twice; seven times Sask. men's veterans singles champion, six times doubles winner; only player to claim provincial men's and veteran's singles same year 1967; represented province in Canada Summer Games 1971 winning seven, losing five matches in men's singles although at 49 was oldest competitor; Regina Squash racquets champion 1967-68; variety of administrative roles from 1947 including two terms pres. Sask. LTA; Regina B'nai B'rith Sportsman's Award 1972; mem. Sask. Sports Hall of Fame; *res.* Regina, Sask.

ECKEL, Shirley (track and field); *b.* 3 Feb 1932, Toronto, Ont.; *given name:* Shirley Gretchen; *m.* Dr. William H. Kerr (*d.*); *children:* Gretchen, Christopher, Elizabeth, Thomas; U of Toronto, B.A.; at 12 fourth internationally in 50m hurdles; gold medal 1945-46 junior Olympics; at 20 held Canadian 80m hurdles title and record, eighth in world and mem. Canadian Olympic team; 1953 Canadian 80m title; mem. Canadian team 1954 British Empire Games, placed fifth, set new Canadian record; Canadian 80m title 1955; throughout career was North American champion; *res.* Islington, Ont.

ECUYER, Al (football); *b.* 1938, New Orleans, La.; Notre Dame U; insurance executive; captain Notre Dame; twice all-American guard; drafted by N Y Giants (NFL); joined Edmonton Eskimos 1959, was cut then recalled, became all-star; with

Eskimos 1959-65, co-captain 1964; to Toronto Argos 1966, Montreal Alouettes 1967-68; twice nominated by Eskimos as outstanding player, outstanding lineman; twice named to coaches all-Canadian (second team); Vancouver *Sun* all-stars as interior linebacker; twice named to Blue Bombers' all-opponents team; wrestled professionally.

EDGE, Ken (bowling); *b.* 16 Jun 1927, Hamilton, Ont.; *given name:* Kenneth Mills; *m.* Phyllis Veronica; *children:* Patricia, Linda; Central HS; electrical contractor, politician; one of founders Hamilton Bowlers' Association 1963; helped establish O'Keefe Bowler of Month tourney; pres. Ontario Bowlers Congress; founded Crippled Children's Bowling tourney Hamilton; Builders of Bowling Industry award; *res.* Hamilton, Ont.

EDWARDS, Jake (curling); *b.* 7 May 1921, Kingston, Ont.; *given name:* Jack Leisk; *m.* Lois Smith; *children:* Sandra, Tracy; *m.* Joan Whalen; Kingston H.S.; auto dealer; knuckleball pitcher with variety Kingston area baseball teams; rejected pro contract with Jersey City Giants; while serving four years with Ordnance Corps WW2 helped team win Canadian Army overseas baseball title; retired from game at 28; proficient golfer twice winning Amherstview Club title, twice seniors champion; Alcan Seniors titlist 1976; won Ontario Governor-General's, Silver Tankard titles once each, runner-up once each; twice won Burden, *Globe and Mail* trophies in provincial curling play; six times competitor Ontario Consols winning 1960 title and was only rink to defeat Ernie Richardson 1960 Brier; competed in Ontario Intermediate championships; twice won Ontario Seniors title; won 10 straight games two consecutive years City of Ottawa championships claiming grand aggregate once, runner-up twice; mem. National Fitness Council 1964-67; *res.* Kingston, Ont.

EDWARDS, Phil (track); *b.* 13 Sep 1907, Georgetown, British Guiana, *d.* 6 Sep 1971 Montreal, Que.; New York U, McGill U, M.D.; physician; captain track teams at NYU, McGill; national middle-distance titles in Canada, U S, Ireland, Poland, Latvia; represented Canada 1928 Amsterdam Olympics, fourth 800m; at Los Angeles 1932 Olympics won bronze 800, 1500m; represented British Guiana in 1934 British Empire Games, won 880 yd gold; captain Canadian track team 1936 Berlin Olympics, won 800m bronze, beat world record but finished fifth 1500m in eight Olympic finals in total; part-time coach McGill track team; first winner Lou Marsh Trophy 1936 as Canada's top athlete; same year Canada's top male athlete in CP poll, top athlete Canadian Amateur Athletic Union; mem. AAU of C Hall of Fame.

EKDAHL, Trevor (football); *b.* 3 Apr 1942, Weyburn, Sask.; *given name:* Trevor Harold; *m.* Moira Christine; *children:* Trevor Kenneth; Mount Royal College, Utah State U; heavy equipment sales; turned pro B. C. Lions 1967, played offensive guard through eight seasons, retired after 1974 campaign; all-star 1973; Canadian Football League Players' Association player representative for Lions; *res.* Williams Lake, B.C.

ELDER, Jim (equestrian); *b.* 27 Jul 1934, Toronto, Ont.; *m.* Marianne; *children:* Michael, Mark, Elizabeth, Erin; Upper Canada College, U of Toronto, B.A.; owner commercial refrigeration distributors; 1956 Olympic bronze medal, 1968 gold medal; gold Pan-Am Games 1959, 1971, bronze team

1967; gold 1970 world; captain Canadian team several years; individual international champion Royal Winter Fair three times; high score award for Canada 1965-67; four times Eastern Canadian champion; team development series champion 1965-66; represented Canada 1976 Montreal Olympics; *res.* Elderberry Hill Farm, Aurora, Ont.

ELFORD, Gear (football); *b.* 4 Apr 1902, Hamilton, Ont.; *given name:* Harold Norman; *m.* Alice; *children:* Estelle; retired; played with Canadian Rugby Union intermediate champion Hamilton Tigers 1921; outstanding lineman seven years 1922-30 with Tigers in ORFU, Interprovincial Rugby Union; with Hamilton Rowing Club for 1923 ORFU title, with Tigers for five IPRU titles, two Grey Cups; played basketball Hamilton City, church leagues; recorded Hamilton's first perfect five-pin bowling 450 in 1937; mem. best-of-century Tiger team as lineman 1967; *res.* Hamilton, Ont.

ELIOWITZ, Abe (football); *b.* 15 Nov 1910, New York, N.Y.; *m.* Ida Lachman; *children:* Susan, Linda; Michigan State U, retired teacher; as southpaw passer and punter played for Ottawa Rough Riders 1933-35 before joining Montreal 1936-37; also played baseball with Ottawa Crains in St. Lawrence League; in football played fullback, halfback, flying wing; led Big Four scorers 1935 with 62 points; four times all-star; Jeff Russel Memorial Trophy (MVP) 1935; retiring to Detroit coached HS football, baseball, cross-country running, won two city football, three city baseball titles; mem. Canadian Football Hall of Fame; *res.* Detroit, Mich.

ELLIOTT, Bob (all-around); *b.* 29 Mar 1910, Kingston, Ont.; *d.* 21 May 1970, Kingston, Ont.; *given name:* Robert Fawcette; *m.* Sarah Delia 'Deed' Whitney; *children:* Robert Whitney, Elizabeth Mae; Queen's U, B.A.; purchaser aluminum co.; son of hockey Hall of Famer Chaucer Elliott; standout halfback, offensive end, corner linebacker Queen's, on two Intercollegiate title teams; five Q's for Queen's athletic efforts; lost eye 1934 playing football; senior ORFU football Balmy Beach 1935; coached RMC, Garrison, Queen's football teams during WW2, guided Garrison to Ontario Intermediate title 1940, intercollegiate football official five years; helped Queen's win 1929 Intercollegiate basketball title; helped Kingston YMCA take two Ontario Intermediate basketball titles; semi-pro baseball Brockville, Smiths Falls, Delora Seniors, Creighton Mines, Kingston Ponies 1924-38 winning numerous batting titles; coached Kingston juniors, juveniles to three city titles, Kingston Centennials to 1967 Ontario Baseball Association title; played on three Ontario Curling Association Governor-General's Trophy winners, two Ontario Silver Tankard rinks; mem. Jake Edwards' 1960 Ontario Brier rink; life mem. Kingston CC from 1968; honored by peers with Bob Elliott appreciation day 1968; Kingston sportsman of year (Wally Elmer Memorial Trophy); Kingston distinguished achievement award; Ontario Achievement award.

ELLIOTT, Chaucer (hockey, football); *b.* 1879, Kingston, Ont., *d.* 13 Mar 1913 Kingston, Ont.; *given name:* Edwin Smith; *m.* Elizabeth Montague; *children:* Robert Fawcette; played point, captain Queen's U; captain Granites football team, Canadian title 1899; joined Toronto baseball team 1903; coach Toronto Argos football team; guided 1906 Hamilton Tigers to Canadian title; joined Montreal AAA; organized semipro baseball league which included Kingston team; owned, organized, managed St. Thomas in Canadian Baseball League; hockey referee 1903, for 10 years considered one of finest officials in OHA; mem. Hockey Hall of Fame.

ELLIS, Ron (hockey); *b.* 8 Jan 1945, Lindsay, Ont.; *given name:* Ronald John Edward; York U; operates automotive agency, Sand Lake resort; influenced by father Randy, mem. 1948 RCAF Flyers Olympic champions, played peewee with Ferris Flyers in North Bay and through Ottawa Cradle League where he was scouted by Bryan Lynch and sent to Weston Dukes junior B team at 15; switched from centre to right wing when he joined junior A Marlboros; starred for Marlies in 1964 Memorial Cup victory and with Pete Stemkowski shared OHA MVP; TML regular 1964-65 and was runner-up to Roger Crozier in Calder Memorial Trophy voting; on suggestion of Ace Bailey, whose sweater No. 6 had been retired with him in 1934, Ellis reactivated No. 6 although he'd worn No. 8 at outset of NHL career; mem. Team Canada 1972, 1976; in 12 NHL seasons appeared in 805 games scoring 276 goals, 258 assists for 534 points, 172 penalty minutes plus 48 playoff games scoring 14 goals, five assists for 19 points, 18 penalty minutes; *res.* Toronto, Ont.

ELSBY, Ted (football); *b.* 3 Jan 1932, Galt, Ont.; *given name:* Edward Ernest; *m.* Pauline Patricia Pepper; *children:* Elaine, Paul, Steven, Gary; Galt HS; business forms salesman; played HS and Brantford Indians junior football; turned pro Montreal Alouettes 1954-65 as defensive tackle; competed 1956-57 East-West Shrine Game; EFC all-star 1964; first-ballot nominee 1964 for three Schenley Awards—best Canadian, best lineman, best player; following retirement coached football U of Montreal four years, Sir George Williams U one year, Beaconsfield HS two years; *res.* Beaconsfield, Que.

EMERSON, Eddie (football); *b.* 11 Mar 1892, Cordeil, Ga., *d.* 27 Jan 1970, Ottawa, Ont.; *m.* Heasley Parker; *children:* Marilyn; automobile salesman; played first game with Ottawa Rough Riders 1909, flying wing on offence, inside wing on defence; played 26 years unpaid, retired 1937; twice Ottawa club pres., as player 1930, again 1947-50; Big Four pres. 1948-49; also noted auto racer; Ottawa area pool champion; played city league hockey; mem. Ottawa Sports, Canadian Football Halls of Fame.

EMERY, John (bobsledding); *b.* 4 Jan 1932, Montreal, Que.; *m.* Phyllis; *children:* Allison, John David; Trinity College School, Queen's U, M.D.; plastic surgeon; competed in track, football, received Stubb's Trophy from Duke of Edinburgh as best all-around athlete in RCN(R); with brother Victor formed Laurentian Bobsledding Association 1957; 13th in field of 16 in world championships St. Moritz 1959; Emery brothers, Doug Anakin and Peter Kirby teamed to win gold medal 1964 Olympics at Innsbruck; 1970 won over-190lb 13-mile California mountain race (Double Dipsea); ran sub-four hour marathon Burlingame 1974; ninth Squaw Valley Triathlon (five-mile cross-country skiing, cycling, kayak); second over-40 Great Race, competed in six-mile kayak leg of three-man event; swam across Golden Gate Bridge entrance 1975; mem. Canadian Sports Hall of Fame; *res.* San Francisco, Calif.

EMERY, Victor (bobsledding); *b.* 28 Jun 1933, Montreal, Que.; *m.* Jenifer Wontner; *children:* Vanessa, Samantha, Alistair; Trinity College School, U Western Ontario, B.A., L'Alliance Française, Harvard U, M.B.A.; businessman; interests: skiing, skating, car driving, aerobatic flying, diving, wrestling, running, tennis, squash; involved internationally in sailing (Olympic Finn class), skiing (class A four-way in 50s and 60s), bobsledding (pilot Canadian gold medal team 1964 Olympics, 1965 world championships); mem. Canadian Olympic Association, Chef de Mission-Adjoint, Canadian Winter Olympic team 1968; since 1970 TV commentator on bobsleigh, luge, cross-country skiing during world, Olympic competitions; mem. Canadian Sports Hall of Fame; *res.* Montreal, Que.

EON, Suzanne (synchronized swimming); *b.* 19 Feb 1924, Montreal, Que.; St. Mary's Academy, Bart's Business College; director synchronized swimming Quebec YWCA; coached synchronized swimming since 1950 guiding competitors to 104 national titles in open and closed competition; coached entries in Pan-Am Games 1955, 1959, 1963, 1971, international invitationals 1957, 1970, 1974 in New York, Denmark, Ottawa, Japan, world championships Belgrade Yugoslavia 1973, Pan-Pacific Games Hawaii 1974, Canada Games 1967, 1971, 1975; international coaching record since 1955: seven gold, 13 silver, six bronze medals; produced top Canadian team, Dick Ellis trophy, 1975; Quebec City press coach of year 1963; Canadian Confederation medal 1967; CASSA distinguished service award, Canadian Council for cooperation in aquatics award, Quebec coach of year, Sport and Fitness coach of month 1974; Standard Brands award 1975, runner-up Air Canada amateur coach of year 1973; *res.* Lac St. Charles, Que.

ERVASTI, Ed (golf); *b.* 13 Jan 1914, Minneapolis, Minn.; *given name:* Edward Walker; *m.* Jane Bradshaw; *children:* Thomas, John, David; Royal Oak HS, Wayne State U; general manager; reached finals Salt Lake City and Utah amateurs 1943; won 1947 Michigan State amateur; St. Louis District title; lost 1953 Michigan State final but qualified for U S Open, only Michigan amateur to do so; twice low amateur Erie Pa. Open; London District title 1966; three times Sunningdale champion, once London Hunt Club champion; winner several London Hunt Invitation tournaments; twice Canadian seniors champion, twice runner-up; runner-up seniors championship of Canada for Rankin Memorial Trophy 1973; twice Ontario seniors champion, three times runner-up; 1975 U S seniors title; fifth 1974 international seniors; *res.* London, Ont.

ESPOSITO, Phil (hockey); *b.* 20 Feb 1942, Sault Ste. Marie, Ont.; *given name:* Philip Anthony; *div.* Linda; hockey player; played through Sault Ste. Marie minor hockey chain to Sarnia Ont. junior B club, St. Catharines Teepees junior A team; pro Chicago organization 1961 playing with Sault Ste. Marie, St. Louis (EPHL, CPHL) before graduating to Hawks as winger in 1963; traded with Ken Hodge, Fred Stanfield to Boston for Gilles Marotte, Pit Martin, Jack Norris 1967; became first player in NHL history to score 100 points in single season 1968-69, 49 goals, 77 assists for 126 points; surpassed that mark 1970-71 with record 76 goals and 76 assists for 152 points; five consecutive 100-plus point seasons, six in seven years, missed 1969-70 by one point; tied Frank Mahovlich for most Stanley Cup playoff points with 27 1969-70 season; scored 50 or more goals five successive seasons; twice Hart Trophy, five times Ross

Trophy; Lester B. Pearson Award 1972; with Carol Vadnais traded to NY Rangers for Brad Park, Jean Ratelle, Joe Zanussi 1975; through 1976-77 NHL campaign appeared in 1002 league games scoring 596 goals, 737 assists for 1,333 points, 727 penalty minutes, plus 100 playoff games, 50 goals, 60 assists for 110 points, 105 penalty minutes; six times first team, twice second team all-star centre; standout role in Team Canada 1972 series vs USSR also in Team Canada 1976 Canada Cup victory; mem. Team Canada 1977; brother Tony goaltender with Chicago Black Hawks; Canadian male athlete of year in CP poll 1972-73; Lou Marsh Trophy 1972; played on two Stanley Cup winners; *res.* New York, N.Y.

ETCHEVERRY, Sam (football); *b.* 20 May 1930, Carlsbad, N.M., *m.* Juanita Louise Mulcahy; *children:* Steve, Mike, Jim, Nancy, Jennifer; St. Edwards HS, U of Denver, B.A.; stockbroker; appeared in 1950 Pineapple Bowl; turned pro Montreal Alouettes 1952; nickname The Rifle; CFL record begun in 1954 shows 1,630 completions on 2,829 passes for 25,582yds for .576 avg., 163 interceptions, 174 TDs; holds CFL single season passing mark 4,723yds 1956, completion total of 276 in 446 attempts for .619 avg.; shares CFL record for longest completed pass 109yds to Hal Patterson against Hamilton at Montreal 1956; played in three Grey Cup finals; traded to Hamilton 1960 with Patterson for Bernie Faloney and Don Paquette but joined NFL St. Louis Cardinals for two seasons; coached Quebec Rifles (UFL) 1964, Alouettes to 1970 Grey Cup victory; six times EFC all-star; Canadian Schenley player of the year 1954; Jeff Russel Memorial Trophy (EFC MVP) 1954, 1958; mem. Canadian Football Hall of Fame; *res.* Montreal, Que.

EVANS, Art (football); *b.* 29 Jul 1915, Toronto, Ont.; *m.* Dorothy Rule; *children:* Sandra Louise; Runnymede CI; packing plant manager; played lacrosse in HS, junior ranks in early 30s; football with Toronto Argos 1935-39 as tackle, end, middle linebacker; mem. 1937-38 Grey Cup champions; captain Argos 1938; mem. RCAF 1942 Hurricanes Grey Cup winners; v.-pres. Calgary Stampeders 1975-76, pres. 1977-78; *res.* Calgary, Alta.

EVANS, Clay (swimming); *b.* 28 Oct 1953, El Bagre, Colombia; *given name:* Thomas Clayton; Huntingdon Beach HS, UCLA; student; represented Canada 1972, 1976 Olympics, silver medal 4 x 100 medley, sixth 100m butterfly, personal best 55.65; two firsts Canadian Nationals 1976; Canadian record 2:13.29 in 200m IM; mem. Japanese tour team 1976; 13th ranked 100m butterfly world 1976, played water polo with UCLA until third shoulder separation; Governor-General's silver medal 1976; *res.* Huntingdon Beach, Calif.

EVANSHEN, Terry (football); *b.* 13 Jun 1944, Montreal, Que.; *given name:* Terrence Anthony; *m.* Lorraine Galarneau; *children:* Tracy Lee, Tara; D'Arcy McGee HS, Utah State U; football player, restaurateur, furniture manufacturer; failed to make Alouette lineup 1964, joined Portland Seahawks (Atlantic Coast Conference); with Alouettes 1965 as halfback, EFC rookie of year; traded to Calgary 1966; traded back to Alouettes 1970; won Grey Cup; traded to Hamilton Tiger-Cats 1975; twice Schenley top Canadian, once runner-up; twice EFC all-star, four times WFC all-star, once all-Canadian; set CFL record for receptions single season with 96 and tied Hugh Campbell for CFL TD passes in single season with 17 1967; tied record for longest pass reception combining with Jerry Keeling for 109yd scoring play Calgary vs Winnipeg 1966; in 11 CFL seasons amassed 76 TDs (CFL record for receivers), caught 550 passes for 9,009yds; caught four TD passes vs Ottawa 1975; played three Grey Cups, two winners; *res.* Montreal, Que.

EVON, Russ (baseball); *b.* 15 Aug 1917, Windsor, Ont; *given name:* Russell Phillip; *m.* Hellen; W.D. Lowe VCI; owner laundry, dry cleaning business; in teens among top five fastballers in Canada; played in Border Cities Softball Federation 1938, fanned record 25 consecutive batters and posted many no-hitters; twice competed in world tournaments, winning one and batting over .400 in both; joined Senior Intercounty Baseball League with London Majors 1943; through 18 seasons with London, St. Thomas, amassed .345 lifetime avg., lead circuit in hitting 1946 (.383), 1952 (.361), in runs batted in five times, home runs twice, hits three times, triples five times, total bases three times; mem. three provincial basketball championship teams; competed city, industrial, OHA intermediate, International Hockey League, outstanding player in latter 1940-41; refereed hockey London area 30 years; strong swimmer credited with saving nine lives, seven in one boating accident Port Stanley Lake Erie 1946; as bowler competed in numerous local, provincial, national, international tournaments; *res.* London, Ont.

EXELBY, Clare (football); *b.* 5 Nov 1937, Toronto, Ont.; *given name:* Clare Douglas; *m.* Maureen Girvin; *children:* Julie Lynn, Randy Allan; Bloor CI, U of Toronto, B.A.; teacher; played with Dominion finalist Parkdale Junior Lions 1956 and Canadian champions 1957; joined Toronto Argos 1958;

traded to Calgary Stampeders 1960; Western Conference all-star defensive back, lead league in interceptions; traded to Argos 1961-63; dealt to Montreal Alouettes, all-Canadian defensive back 1964; *res.* Weston, Ont.

EYNON, Bob (swimming); *b.* 16 Aug 1935, North Bay, Ont.; *given name:* Robert Barrie; *m.* Mary Ellen Thompson; *children:* Susan, Robert, Patrick; U Western Ontario, B.A.; U of Illinois, M.Sc.; associate professor, head swimming coach; coach Canadian women's swim team 1967 Winnipeg Pan-Am Games, Canadian team Crystal Palace Coca-Cola meet England 1973, 1974; twice Canadian College swim coach of year 1966, 1975; treasurer Canadian Amateur Swimming Association 1960-73; chairman Ontario Swimming Coaches Association 1966-73; chairman Canadian College Swimming Coaches Assoc. since 1973; Ont. merit award 1970, Canadian Red Cross Society merit award 1971; *res.* London, Ont.

FABRE, Edouard (track and field); *b.* 1885, Montreal, Que., *d.* 1939 Montreal, Que.; construction worker; in 30 years of competition ran 315 major races, won hundreds of trophies and medals; in one 24-hour event was matched against a horse to see who could run furthest, Fabre won; competed in 1906 Athens marathon; after 1908 competed throughout North America; represented Canada 1912 Stockholm Olympics; entered his first Boston Marathon 1911, won on fifth attempt 1915 in 2:31.41; in 1930, age 45, won 200-mile, six-day snowshoe marathon Quebec to Montreal, in 34:46.24 averaging just under six miles per hour; mem. Canadian Sports Hall of Fame.

FABRIS, Lucio (badminton); *b.* 7 Nov 1957, Sudbury, Ont.; *given name:* Lucio Mario; St. Charles College; U of Toronto student; won Canadian junior mixed doubles, Ontario junior men's doubles 1973; won men's mixed doubles 1974 Toronto Granite junior tournament; won 1974 singles, mixed doubles Oakville junior invitational; won 1974 singles, men's doubles Ontario junior; won 1974 singles Kitchener senior invitational; won 1974 men's doubles, singles finalist

Canadian junior; won 1974 singles all-Ontario HS; men's doubles semifinalist Mexican Open and was mem. St. Charles Canadian junior title team 1974; singles finalist Niagara Falls seniors; junior men's doubles champion Toronto Granite; singles finalist, mixed doubles winner Kitchener seniors; singles, men's, mixed doubles champion Ontario juniors; singles finalist Ontario seniors; triple Canadian junior champion; Canadian senior men's doubles semifinalist 1975; Canadian mixed doubles 1976 with Lillian Cozzarine; represented Canada internationally vs England, Indonesia, China, Mexico, Jamaica; honored by Ontario, municipal governments for outstanding achievement in sport; *res.* Creighton Mines, Toronto, Ont.

FAIRHOLM, Larry (football); *b.* 15 Dec 1941, Montreal, Que.; *m.* Joyce Street; *children:* Jeff, Randy, Joy; U of Arizona, B.Sc.; businessman; led Rosemount Bombers to 1960 Canadian junior title; played four years on athletic scholarship Arizona, 1963 South-West all-American; captain University team 1964; turned pro Montreal Alouettes 1965 and developed into one of CFL's most respected defensive backs; Eastern all-star 1968; all-Canadian 1969; Jeff Russel Award 1968; mem. 1970 Grey Cup champions; *res.* Montreal, Que.

FALONEY, Bernie (football); *b.* 15 Jun 1932, Carnegie, Pa.; *m.* Janet Wallace; *children:* Bernie Jr., Wally; U of Maryland, B.Sc.; businessman; all-American football player of year Atlantic Coast Conference; played in 1952 Sugar Bowl, 1953 Orange Bowl; quarterbacked, co-captained Maryland to undefeated season, national championship, first choice San Francisco '49ers 1953; Dapper Dan award 1953; Washington D.C. Touchdown Club award 1953; turned pro with Edmonton Eskimos guiding them to 1954 Grey Cup victory over Montreal; quarterbacked Bolling AFB Generals to two service titles 1955-56; played for Hamilton 1957-65 then dealt to Montreal Alouettes for Hal Patterson and Sam Etcheverry; passed and punted Hamilton to eight Grey Cup finals, won three; closed 12-year pro career with B.C. Lions 1967; CFL record: 1,493 completions in 2,876 attempts for 24,264yds and 151 TDs, 201 interceptions for a .519 completion percentage; CBC football color commentator 1968 season; Canadian Schenley Award outstanding player 1961, runner-up 1959; Jeff Russel Award 1965; quarterback Hamilton all-pro team 1950-67; U of Maryland man of year 1971; competed in Canadian Shrine all-star game; twice chosen to Ted Reeve all-Canada team and Hamilton Quarterback Club most popular player several times; coached CFL all-stars vs Grey Cup champions in winning effort 1973; mem. Canadian Football Hall of Fame; *res.* Dundas, Ont.

FARLEY, Phil   (golf); *b.* 27 Mar 1912, Toronto, Ont., *d.* 10 Apr 1974, Toronto, Ont.; *m.* Ruth; *children:* Maureen, Michael, Diane, Philip Edward; Toronto Commerce HS; stockbroker; won Ontario junior 1930, first of six Ontario amateurs 1931, runner-up three times; won Ontario Open twice, Quebec amateur twice, runner-up once; runner-up Canadian amateur three times; won 1961 Ontario best ball (Phil Brownlee); won Ontario seniors three times, runner-up once; won RCGA seniors twice; won Canadian Seniors Golf Association three times, runner-up once.

FARMER, Jim   (football); *b.* 28 Nov 1916, Glasgow, Scotland; *given name:* James Gordon; *m.* Joan; *children:* Brian, Peter, Sarah; Patterson CI, Assumption College, U of Western Ontario, OCE; salesman; undefeated four years at one-quarter, one-half, one, two, eight miles, Windsor, Detroit swim meets; all-star HS football, basketball; senior individual T & F honors 1934; twice HS junior, senior swim champion; Patterson CI all-time all-round athlete; mem. junior A baseball champions 1935 and pitched junior, senior A softball; at Assumption competed in both football, basketball reaching Canadian finals in latter before losing to Fords, Canadian 1936 Olympic representatives; captain 1937-38 CIAU basketball champions; OQAA all-star fullback 1938; pro football Toronto Argos 1939; basketball Broadview YMCA; director Windsor Rockets (ORFU) 1947; mem. Intercollegiate football rules committee 1959-75; seven years referee-in-chief OQAA; ten years editor, rules interpreter OQAA, OUAA, CIAU; *res.* London, Ont.

FARMER, Ken   (hockey); *b.* 26 Jul 1912, Westmount, Que.; *m.* Lorayne Strachan; *children:* Howard, Ian, Cynthia, Pamela; McGill U, B.Comm.; chartered accountant; played hockey with McGill 1931-34; mem. Canadian Olympic hockey team 1936; Canadian Intercollegiate tennis doubles champion; pres. Canadian Olympic Association 1953-61; Chairman National Advisory Council on Fitness and Amateur Sport 1962-65; v.-pres. Commonwealth Games Association of Canada since 1974; director Montreal Organizing Committee for XXI Olympiad; *res.* Montreal, Que.

FAUL, Adam   (boxing); *b.* 18 Apr 1929, Regina, Sask.; *m.* Marjorie Evelyn Shaw; *children:* Kevin Darrell, Cheryl Lynn, Mark Perry, Gregory Shaw; Moose Jaw HS, business school; municipal secretary-treasurer;

won 1945 Sask. light heavyweight title, retained 1946-47; Canadian light heavyweight title 1947; won Western Diamond Belt heavyweight title, Canadian heavyweight title, Olympic trials 1948; represented Canada 1948 London Olympics; played football for Saskatchewan Roughriders 1944, junior football with Regina Eastend Bombers; mem. Sask. Sports Hall of Fame; *res.* Spy Hill, Sask.

FAUQUIER, Harry (tennis); *b.* 28 Aug 1942, Toronto, Ont.; *given name:* Henry Edmund; *m.* Lindsay; *children:* Sarah; Oakwood CI, U of Michigan, B.A.; tennis entrepreneur; Canadian junior title 1959-60; Big 10 title 1961-62; captain Michigan team 1963-64; represented Canada 1963 Pan-Am Games; seven times mem. Canadian Davis Cup team, twice captain; with John Sharpe won Canadian men's doubles 1968; among Canada's top five 10 years; five years number one Ontario seed; competed in all major world tournaments, Forest Hills, Wimbledon, France, Italy; won international tournaments in US, South America, Europe, Canada; *res.* Toronto, Ont.

FEAGAN, Ron (harness racing); *b.* 10 Mar 1942, Goderich, Ont.; entire life centred around harness racing with grandfather George, father Keith and brother Gary forming Feagan racing stable; considerable talent in sulky; Canadian co-horseman of year 1965; first Canadian driver to win 200 races one season; Canada's leading race winner 1966, 1969, 1970; top Canadian money winner 1968, 1970; Golden Horseshoe Circuit dash and money winner 1972, 1973; since 1964 has amassed more than 2,000 wins, $3 million in purses; *res.* Goderich, Ont.

FEAR, Cap (football); *b.* 11 Jun 1901, Old Sailbury, Eng.; *given name:* Alfred Henry John; *m.* Gertrude Lilian Farr; Central Technical HS; retired construction superintendent; joined Toronto Argos 1920 as outside wing, remained for three league titles, one Grey Cup; mem. of team which lost only one game in 1921-22 seasons; Hamilton Tigers 1928-32, two league titles, two Grey Cups; played hockey with Aura Lee senior OHA and Ontario Hydro Toronto Mercantile League; runner-up North American welterweight boxing title; with Argonaut Rowing Club stroked lightweight eights, fours to Canadian Henley victories same day; also won at Lachine, Detroit, Dominion Day regattas; named to Hamilton best-of-century (1867-1949) amateur era all-star football team; mem. Canadian Football Hall of Fame; *res.* St. Catharines, Ont.

FEDORUK, Sylvia (curling, track, softball); *b.* 5 May 1927, Canora, Sask.; Walkerville CI, U of Saskatchewan, B.A., M.A., Ph.D.; physicist, professor; two gold, one silver, one bronze and T. Eaton Trophy as top individual performer 1947 Dominion T & F championships; mem. Saskatoon Ramblers 1948 provincial women's softball champions, Regina Gorins 1954, Saskatoon Ramblers 1955 Western Canadian softball champions; mem. 12 Intervarsity championship teams (5 basketball, 2 track, 3 volleyball, 2 golf) 1946-51; 1951 Intervarsity golf title; Governor-General's gold medal U of Sask. 1949; coached university volleyball, curling teams two years; played third Joyce McKee rink winning 1960-61 Canadian titles, runner-up 1962; three times provincial titlists, Western Canadian champions 1960; six times Saskatoon & District titlists; pres. Canadian Ladies Curling Association

1971-72, Sask. LCA 1959, women's athletic board U of Sask. 1949; mem. Curling Hall of Fame; *res.* Saskatoon, Sask.

FERGUSON, John (hockey); *b.* 5 Sep 1938, Vancouver, B.C.; *given name:* John Bowie; *m.* Joan; *children:* Christina, Catherine, John Jr.; hockey executive; able lacrosse player; stick boy Vancouver Canucks (WHL); played junior hockey Melville Sask. at 18 under coach Bill 'Legs' Fraser; played hockey Ft. Wayne Komets seniors, then signed by Jackie Gordon for Cleveland Barons pro team; Montreal Canadiens' policeman 1963-64, left winger eight seasons; NHL playoff record for penalties in season with 80 minutes 1969; eight year NHL record 500 games played, scored 145 goals, 158 assists for 303 points, 1,214 penalty minutes, plus 85 playoff games, 20 goals, 18 assists, 38 points and 260 penalty minutes; assistant coach Team Canada 1972; coach, general manager NY Rangers 1976; played on five Stanley Cup winners; operated Montreal Québécois in pro lacrosse league; keen interest in horse racing; *res.* New York.

FERGUSON, Merv (lacrosse); *b.* 1 Jul 1909, London, Ont.; *m.* May; King Edward HS; all-around HS athlete; sprinting, middle distance running, soccer, softball, marksmanship; stricken by polio he entered sports administration; secretary B.C. Lacrosse Association; eight years mem., chairman Vancouver Athletic Commission; governor Pacific National Exhibition Sports Committee; mem. B.C. Branch AAU of C 1948; mem. ten years B.C. amateur boxing commission; nine years treasurer B.C. amateur sports council; chairman B.C. Sports Hall of Fame; pres. AAU of C 1963-65; secretary-treasurer AAU of C national boxing committee; ten years executive mem. Pan-Am Games Association; mem.-at-large British Commonwealth Games Association; three years pres. Canadian Amateur Sports Federation; assistant manager Canadian Pan-Am team 1967, manager 1971; mem. Canada Games Council; chairman technical advisory board Canada Summer Games 1973; mem. COA; pres. B.C. Lacrosse Association 1943-58, Canadian Lacrosse Association 1962-63; Canadian Lacrosse Association liaison officer to International Amateur Lacrosse Federation 1967-72; B.C. Sportsman award 1967-68, Air Canada amateur sports executive of year; mem. B.C. Sports, Canadian Lacrosse Halls of Fame; *res.* Vancouver, B.C.

FERGUSON, Reid (curling); *b.* 16 May 1953, Toronto, Ont.; *given name:* William Reid; Wilfrid Laurier U, B.A.; student; Toronto HS hockey all-star; university golf team; East York Ontario junior baseball champions; lead with Paul Savage rink winning Ontario Consols, competing in Brier 1977; won Thunder Bay cash 'spiel 1976; *res.* Agincourt, Ont.

FERGUSON, Rich (track); *b.* 3 Aug 1931, Calgary, Alta.; *div.* Kathleen Mavis McNamee; *children:* David, Jeanne, John; Leaside HS, U of Iowa, B.S., B. Comm., U of Western Ontario, M.B.A.; businessman; finished third to Roger Bannister and John Landy in 1954 Vancouver Miracle Mile with 4:04.6; equalled that time in 1955 NCAA championships in California; Canadian male athlete of year 1954 CP poll; *res.* Phoenix, Ariz.

FERRANGE, Claude (track and field); *b.* 14 Oct 1952, Montreal, Que.; U of Laval, student; high jump specialist under coach

Michel Portmann; Quebec indoor titles 1973-74; won Canadian indoor titles 1973-75; third Canadian outdoor 1973-74; gold medals Canada vs Russia indoor meet 1973, Canada vs France 1974, Canada vs W. Germany, Canada vs Great Britain 1976; bronze 1974 Commonwealth Games; mem. Canadian 1975 Pan-Am Games, 1976 Olympic teams; set Canadian indoor record 2.23m 26 Feb 1977 in Montreal, record subsequently surpassed by Robert Forget week later; *res.* Montreal, Que.

FERRARO, John (football); *b.* 18 Dec 1910, Buffalo, N.Y.; *given name:* John James; *m.* Edna Winifred Letts; *children:* John Jr., Robert Letts, Linda Joan; Cook Academy, Cornell U, B.Sc.; retired oil company sales supervisor; at Cornell captain 1933 football team, all-American 1931-33; captain Cornell basketball 1933-34, Ivy League scoring title, Eastern Intercollegiate all-star; joined Hamilton Tigers as coach-player 1934; on 1935 Grey Cup team losing to Winnipeg; Orm Beach Trophy 1934; to Montreal 1936, played five years with Nationals, Alouettes; seven times all-Canadian; quarterback Hamilton best-of-century (1867-1949) amateur era team; Lew Hayman's best-of-30s dream team; Dave Walsh (Cornell) 30-year (1912-42) all-Intercollegiate team; Eastern Intercollegiate League 50-year (1901-51) all-star team; manager-player, scoring leader Dominion Douglas basketball team, Eastern Canadian title 1936-37; coach Queen's basketball team 1937-38; player, leading scorer McGill Grads in Montreal League 1939-40, team won Canadian title; manager-player-coach Oilers basketball team, won Canadian title 1941-42; mem. Canadian Football Hall of Fame; *res.* Westfield, N.J.

FIELDGATE, Norm (football); *b.* 12 Jan 1932, Regina, Sask.; *given name:* William Norman; *m.* Doreen Caughlin; *children:* Carey, Lesley, Janine; automotive parts distributor; from Sask. junior ranks, joined original B.C. Lions team 1953; played 14 seasons with club and was last of originals; one of two B.C. Lions players honored with 'day' 1962 (also By Bailey); co-captained Lions several seasons, played offensive, defensive end, corner linebacker, made 37 career interceptions; three-time WCF all-star, once all-Canadian; Lions' MVP three times; most popular Lion 1965; director B.C. Lions football club; mem. B.C. Sports Hall of Fame; *res.* North Vancouver, B.C.

FILCHOCK, Frank (football); *b.* 1916, Crucible, Pa.; Grindstone HS, U of Indiana; all-around HS athlete capable of sprinting 100 yds in 10 seconds flat; turned pro with Steelers, played with Washington Redskins, N Y Giants; suspended over gambling charge, cleared by NFL officials but moved to Canadian football with Hamilton, Montreal; coached, quarterbacked Hamilton Tigers to 1948 final vs Ottawa but lost when he broke wrist early in game; joined Alouettes 1949, won Grey Cup, outstanding player of year; ORFU Imperial Oil Trophy as MVP; head coach Edmonton Eskimos 1952 guiding them to WIFU title and losing Grey Cup; coach Sask. Roughriders 1953-57, in playoffs four consecutive years; mem. Canadian Football Hall of Fame.

FILION, Herve (harness racing); *b.* 1 Feb 1940, Angers, Que.; *m.* Barbara Ann; *children:* four; harness race driver; drove 407 winners 1968 eclipsing world standard 386 set by W. Germany's Eddie Freundt; drove 605 winners 1972 then posted 634 wins with purses totalling $3.5 million 1974; known to drive as many as 20 races per day; drove seven winners Windsor Raceway 1972; five winners clocked at 1:59.4 or less for mile 1970 Brandywine; owns, operates 46 acre Capital Hill Farms Lachute Que.; through 1976 had 5,845 recorded lifetime victories with winnings totalling over $20 million; frequently named Canada's outstanding French-speaking athlete; Lou Marsh trophy 1971; Order of Canada; Hickok pro athlete of month Nov 1971; Harness Tracks of America driver of year since 1969; world harness racing champion 1970; international drivers' stakes winner Sydney Australia 1971; twice winner Realization Pace; won Little Brown Jug, Dexter Cup, Sheppard Pace, American National Pace; mem. Canadian Sports, Canadian Horseracing, Living Horsemen's Halls of Fame; *res.* Lachute, Que.

FINDLEY, John (harness racing); *b.* 2 Sep 1924, Braeside, Ont.; *m.* Mary Jane Chateauvert; Ontario Veterinary College; veterinarian, horse breeder, driver, trainer; won eight driver titles in eight years on Ontario's Golden Horseshoe Circuit (Greenwood, Mohawk, Garden City tracks); led North American drivers 1969 with .441 UDRS avg., runner-up 1970; career record over 900 wins, over $1.5 million in purses; among horses he has bred, trained or raced are Dalyce Blue (first Canadian-bred two-year-old trotter to better 2:10 mile), Peaches Atom (first Canadian-bred three-year-old trotter to better 2:05 mile), Autumn Frost, Crimson Duchess (two-year-old Canadian trotter of year), The Black Douglas, Canny Choice and Moon Magic (whose 1:59.1 mile fastest by Findley-bred pacer); *res.* Arnprior, Ont.

FINNAMORE, Arthur (baseball); *b.* 13 Dec 1882, Fredericton, N.B.; *m.* Aletha Sallaws MacLean; U New Brunswick; re-tired, Dept. of Agriculture; nickname Flying Frederictonian for performances in 100, 220 yd track events; at 14 received $5.00 per game to play baseball for Doaktown, Boisetown teams thereby becoming pro; officially joined pro ranks at 23 catching for Glace Bay in Cape Breton League, later played in Western Canada; with Fredericton Tartars senior team at 16, Caribous, Houlton, St. Stephen; captained, coached Glace Bay to Cape Breton League title 1913; later became highly respected baseball umpire; university rugby star; as mountain climber scaled Bald Mountain, Mount Carleton; mem. N.B. Sports Hall of Fame; *res.* Saint John, N.B.

FIRTH, Sharon (skiing); *b.* 31 Dec 1953, Aklavik, N.W.T.; *given name:* Sharon Anne; with twin sister Shirley has become one of Canada's finest cross-country skiers; 1969 Canadian championships placed third in junior 5km, mem. of winning 3x5 relay team; won 1970 10km, 3x5 relay, second senior and junior 5km; 1971 won senior 10km, 3x5 relay and was second 5km; duplicated feat 1973-74 then in 1975 won 5km and relay and finished second 10km; won 1976 20km and relay and finished third 10km; represented Canada 1970 world championships Czechoslovakia, 1972, 1976 Olympics, 1974 world Sweden; won 1974 North American 10km, 5km, 3x5 relay; several U S titles; *res.* Banff, Alta.

FIRTH, Shirley (skiing); *b.* 31 Dec 1953, Aklavik, N.W.T.; *given name:* Shirley Anne; twin Firth sisters, Shirley and Sharon, among the finest cross-country skiers in Canada; won 1969 junior 5km; since 1969 has won Canadian senior 5km five times, 10km twice, runner-up four times; won U S junior 5km three times, runner-up once, U S senior 10km once, runner-up once, runner-up

5km twice; won North American 5km three times, runner-up three times, 10km four times, runner-up twice, 20km once; represented Canada 1970, 1974 world, 1972, 1976 Olympics; won several races senior and junior classes on European tours since 1969; *res.* Banff, Alta.

FISHER, Joan (track); *b.* 26 Sep 1949, Ottawa, Ont.; *given name:* Barbara Joan; *div.;* Carleton U, U of Ottawa, B.Sc.; personnel administrator; set 1965 Canadian midget records for 60yds (7.0), 100yds (10.9), 220yds (25.0); retained Canadian midget women's 60, 220 records 1966; set 1967 Canadian juvenile record in 100yds (10.8), 220yds (24.6); represented Canada 4x100 relay team 1967 Pan-Am Games; set Canadian junior 220yd record (23.9) 1968; in 1968 Olympic trials won Canadian 200m, 400m titles; semifinalist 400m 1968 Mexico Olympics; *res.* Ottawa, Ont.

FITZGERALD, Billy (lacrosse); *b.* 1888, St. Catharines, Ont., *d.* 1926; at 19 joined Senior Athletic Lacrosse Club St. Catharines, team won Globe Shield 1905-12, played 1907-08 campaigns undefeated; played for Conn Jones in Vancouver, led team to Minto Cup; following year joined Toronto Lacrosse Club; after war returned briefly to play in Vancouver, helped organize St. Catharines team in Ontario semipro league; coached at Hobart College, Geneva N.Y., Swathmore College, West Point; coached St. Catharines youngsters and refereed in OALA senior division; *mem.* Canadian Sports, Lacrosse Halls of Fame.

FLEMING, Dave (football); *b.* 9 Mar 1945, Pittsburgh, Pa.; *given name:* Joseph David; *m.* Susan Jane Dickson; *children:* Jill Suzanne, Joseph David Jr.; coach; moved from HS and sandlot football to 1965 Pittsburgh Steelers training camp; joined Hamilton Tiger-Cats 1965 for three games as receiver; played defence first time 1966 and intercepted three passes; used both ways 1967 then strictly on offence 1968, leading team in total yardage; rushed for 641yds 1969, 614 1970 and caught 56 passes for 692yds; caught 108yd TD pass from Joe Zuger vs Toronto 1971; captain Tiger-Cats two years; Hamilton MVP three years; 10 seasons with Hamilton reaching playoffs each year, played on three Grey Cup champions; EFC, all-Canadian all-star 1970; Tiger-Cats player representative CFL Players' Association; *res.* West Homestead, Pa.

FLEMING, Willie (football); *b.* 2 Feb 1939, Detroit, Mich.; Iowa U; all-city halfback in HS 1956, AP all-Big 10 at Iowa 1957 where he tied single season TD record with 11; starred in Iowa's 1959 Rose Bowl victory over California; signed with B.C. Lions 1959; nickname Will-of-the-Wisp; twice surpassed 1,000yd rushing mark single season; twice teamed with Joe Kapp for 106yd TD pass; set 1963 CFL rushing record averaging 9.7yds-per-carry, gained 2,027 total yds, 1,234 rushing, 639 on passes, returned kickoffs for 154; eight-year CFL record: 86 TDs, 1 convert for 517 points, 868 carries for 6,125yds, 7.1 avg. and 37 TDs, 231 receptions for 4,480yds, 19.4yds avg.; scored decisive TD in B.C. Grey Cup victory over Hamilton 1964; sought by Minnesota Vikings in exchange for Jim Young but elected to retire; three times chosen most popular Lion by B.C. fans; three times WFC all-star, once all-Canadian.

FLETCHER, Douglas (lacrosse); *b.* 18 Nov 1892, Leicester, Eng.; *m.* Ethel Maud; *children:* Dorothy, Joan; hotel and meat market proprietor; played nine years Albion Cricket

Club scoring numerous centuries, and represented B.C. vs Australian team which defeated England in 1912 test matches; played for Five C's, Victoria teams until retiring at 50; pres. Greater Victoria League 1942-68; organized minor lacrosse 1944, coached and/or managed 35 provincial champions; pres. BCLA 1948; v.-pres. CLA 1957; refereed both junior A, senior B games several years; with late Ivan Temple organized Victoria Minor Hockey Association 1943; pres. Vancouver Island Senior Hockey League several years; played soccer Empress Hotel team, retired from game at 40; won 12 consecutive games as pitcher Sons of England 1934 softball league champions; scored two holes-in-one during golf career which began 1929; five years pres. Uplands GC; life mem. since 1942; holds record most holes played one day-72; fewest putts 18 hole round-24; BCAHA Diamond Hockey Stick Award 1964; numerous honors including Sid Thomas Memorial Trophy 1952; Memorial Arena Plaque 1960; Centennial medal 1967; Victoria sportsman of year 1968; *Sport Magazine* plaque 1968; life mem. Greater Victoria Lacrosse Association 1968; mem. Canadian Lacrosse, B.C. Sports Halls of Fame; *res.* Victoria, B.C.

FLETCHER, Pat (golf); *b.* 18 Jun 1916, Clacton-on-Sea, Eng.; *m.* Dorothy; *children:* two sons, one daughter; retired golf pro; runner-up Alberta Open 1944, 1946-47; won first of three Sask. Opens 1947, CPGA title 1952; low Canadian 1953 Canadian Open, in 1954 first Canadian to win Canadian Open since 1914; former golf pro Saskatoon Golf and Country Club and Royal Montreal; won Quebec Spring Open 1956-57; represented Canada four Hopkins Trophy matches; CPGA pres. 1962-65; mem. RCGA, Canadian Sports Halls of Fame; *res.* Pointe Claire, Que.

FOLEY, Jim (football); *b.* 27 Oct 1947, Ottawa, Ont.; *m.* Lesley Cheryl Scharf; *children:* Rodney James; U of P.E.I., B.A.; program director, athletic club; turned pro with Montreal Alouettes 1971 as running back and wide receiver; Gruen Trophy as EFC rookie of year; traded to Ottawa Rough Riders 1973; Hiram Walker award 1974 as players' player; Schenley award as CFL's top Canadian 1975, Lew Hayman Trophy 1975; mem. Ottawa Grey Cup champions 1973, 1976; *res.* Ottawa, Ont.

FONTANA, Don (tennis); *b.* 18 Jun 1931, Toronto, Ont.; *given name:* Donald Anthony; Northern VCI, UCLA; tennis consultant; reached semifinals in his first tournament, Ontario 15-and-under finals; twice won Ontario Open singles, with Bob Bedard Quebec Open doubles; with Bedard won Canadian men's doubles three times; reached finals 1956 Canadian men's singles; mem. Canadian Davis Cup team 1955-60, 1962, captain 1962, 1974-76; played twice at Wimbledon, 11 times at Forest Hills, once in French Open; organized Canadian championships for CLTA; chief consultant for Rothmans Canadian Grand Prix tennis tournaments; TV color commentator CBC Canadian championship; *res.* Toronto, Ont.

FOOT, Fred (track and field); *b.* 28 Oct 1916, Folkestone, Kent, Eng.; *given name:* Frederick Albert; *m.* Mary Betty Reid; *children:* Angela, Deborah; East York CI; Metro Toronto Police; since late 40s has been one of Canada's top track coaches; coached East York Track Club, University of Toronto, 1956 Canadian Olympic team, 1962 Commonwealth Games team; prominent athletes he has coached are Bill Crothers, Dave Bailey, Tiny O'Halloran, Joe Foreman, George Shepherd, Jackie McDonald, Bruce Kidd and Sue Bradley; *res.* Toronto, Ont.

Ford

FORD, Alan (football); *b.* 2 Jul 1943, Regina, Sask.; *given name:* Robert Alan; *m.* Sally Ann; *children:* Tracy, Robby, Jill; U of Pacific, B.A.; football player, teacher; accepted basketball scholarship U of Pacific but turned to football; pro with Sask. Roughriders 1965; played split end, halfback, flanker, cornerback, defensive back and tight end; through 11 seasons (1975) handled majority Sask. punting, kicking ball 1,041 times for 41,880yds, 40.23yd avg. and 23 single points; fourth in career punting in CFL records; played in every league, playoff game 1966-75; twice Sask. nominee for Canadian Schenley award; holds record for longest punt and kickoff return in Grey Cup history; appeared in four Grey Cup finals, one winner 1966; *res.* Regina, Sask.

FORGET, Robert (track and field); *b.* 15 Jan 1955, Montreal, Que.; second place finishes 1975 Canadian junior, senior championships and in 1976 Canada vs Great Britain meet; personal best 2.20m jump in Quebec City Olympic trials led to participation 1976 Montreal Olympics; set Canadian indoor record 2.26m 3 Mar 1977 in Toronto surpassing Claude Ferrange mark of 2.23 set week earlier; *res.* Montreal, Que.

FORGO, Christine (table tennis); *b.* 19 Oct 1959, Montreal, Que.; *given name:* Christine Mary; student; U S Open, North American junior 13 title 1972; won Canadian Closed junior 15 1974; won Quebec Closed junior 17, Canadian Open junior 17 1975; Quebec Closed mixed doubles 1976; third among Canada's top 12 women's A category 1976; won Canadian women's doubles with Mariann Domonkas 1976-77; *res.* St. Laurent, Que.

FORGUES, Keith (curling); *b.* 17 Sep 1942, Vulcan, Alta.; *m.* Carole Pender; *children:* Lisa, Michael; U of Alberta, B.Sc.; chemist; 1963 City of Edmonton Consols zone title, played third; Ottawa District Consols title seven consecutive years 1968-74, 1971 as skip; with Eldon Coombe rink won Ontario Consols 1972, runners-up 1968; four-time winner Canadian Branch Royal Victoria Jubilee, once as skip; twice won Branch Governor-General's Trophy, once as skip; played second for Terry Begin winning City of Ottawa bonspiel 1973; won CBC cross-country curling series 1972, runner-up 1973; won Whitby Invitational 1972; won Northern Ontario Curling Association bonspiel 1975; won Branch Colts 1966; seven time winner Red Anderson Memorial Trophy; *res.* Ottawa, Ont.

FORHAN, Bob (hockey); *b.* 27 Mar 1936; Newmarket, Ont.; *m.* Sandra O'Rourke; *children:* Bobby, Michael, Scott, Joe; Newmarket HS, U of British Columbia, B.P.E.; teacher, politician; with OHA junior B champion Weston Dukes 1952-53; leading scorer OHA junior A Guelph Biltmores 1953-56; OHA senior A Sudbury Wolves, Kitchener-Waterloo Dutchmen who won Olympic silver medal Squaw Valley 1960; with Trail Smoke Eaters in world tournament Sweden, Canada's national team 1964 Innsbruck Olympics, 1965 world tournament Finland; *res.* Newmarket, Ont.

FOWLIE, Jim (swimming); *b.* 26 Jul 1956, Prince George, B.C.; *given name:* James Kenneth; *m.* Lynn Bengtson; Sentinel HS; student; butterfly, freestyle (FS), individual medley (IM) specialist, competed in 1973 Canadian championships; Canadian 800 FS relay record 7:56.94 1974 Canadian championships; Canadian, Commonwealth 400

IM record 4:35.70, 800 FS relay 7:55.20, 1975 Canadian championships; Canadian short course record 400 IM 4:26.25 1976; represented B.C. 1973 Canada Games, silver 400 IM, bronze 200m butterfly; 1974 Commonwealth Games; 1975 world championships; *res.* Prince George, B.C.

FOXCROFT, Bob (fencing); *b.* 17 Aug 1934, London, Ont.; *given name:* Robert Samuel; Sir Adam Beck CI; salesman; Ontario foil, épée, sabre champion 12 times; Canadian sabre champion five times; represented Canada in 1959, 1967, 1971 Pan-Am Games; bronze team foil 1959, fourth individual épée, bronze team sabre 1967; represented Canada in 1962, 1966, 1970, 1974 Commonwealth Games; bronze team sabre 1966; sixth individual sabre 1970; silver team sabre 1974; represented Canada 1964, 1972 Olympic Games, 1958, 1967 world championships; holds international B card in all three weapons; coach Seneca College, London Sword Club, U of Western Ontario; first v.-pres. AAU of C at its dissolution; pres. Ontario Fencing Association; Ontario Achievement Award 1965; *res.* Toronto, Ont.

FOYSTON, Frank (hockey); *b.* 2 Feb 1891, Minesing, Ont., *d.* 24 Jan 1966 Seattle, Wash.; entered organized hockey with Barrie Dyment Colts at 17; at 20 with Eatons of Toronto won 1911-12 OHA senior crown; turned pro 1912 with Toronto (NHA); played centre on 1913-14 Stanley Cup winners; moved to Seattle 1915-16 for nine seasons, guided first U S Stanley Cup champions 1916-17; two seasons in Victoria, on 1924-25 Stanley Cup winner; retired after two seasons in Detroit 1928; in six Stanley Cup finals, winning three; mem. Hockey Hall of Fame.

FRACAS, Gino (football); *b.* 28 Apr 1930, Windsor, Ont.; *given name:* Gino Mark; *m.* Leona Deck; *children:* Mark, Michael, Gina, Paul, Donna; U of Western Ontario, B.A., U of Alberta, B.Ed., U of Michigan, M.A.; professor, head football coach; played four seasons Western Mustangs as fullback, linebacker 1951-55; all-star three times, OQAA scoring champion twice, MVP 1955; pro Edmonton Eskimos (1955-62) as fullback, linebacker; co-captain, defensive signal caller 1961-62, played in three Grey Cup finals, two winners; head coach U of Alberta 1963-66, won three league titles, defeated Queen's in Golden Bowl 1963, start of East-West College Bowl games; met U of Toronto in first official College Bowl 1965; since 1967 head coach U of Windsor Lancers, 1969 Western Division CCIFC titlists, 1975 OQIFC West Division champions; v.-pres. Canadian Football Coaches Association 1969-70; life mem. Alberta Football Coaches Association; *res.* Windsor, Ont.

FRANK, Bill (football); *b.* 13 Apr 1938, Denver, Colo.; *m.* Barbara; *children:* Jeffrey, Kari-Lynn; San Diego Jr. College, U of Colorado; retired football player; award-winning college wrestler; West Coast and junior college all-American; named to Colorado all-time all-star team; turned pro B.C. Lions 1963-64; joined Toronto Argos 1965-68; following tryout with Denver (NFL) joined Winnipeg Blue Bombers midway through 1969 season, retired 1976; all-Canadian offensive tackle seven times; Blue Bombers lineman of year 1970-75; Dr. Bert Oja Award 1970; six times Schenley Award nominee; named to Argos quarter-century team 1974, Winnipeg all-time dream team; mem. Athletes In Action; player representative Canadian Football Players' Association; *res.* Winnipeg, Man.

Fraser

FRASER, Alexa Stirling (golf); *b.* 5 Sep 1897, Atlanta, Ga., *d.* 15 Apr 1977, Ottawa, Ont.; *m.* Dr. Wilbert A. Fraser; *children:* Sandra, Alin Robert, Richard Douglas; won women's southern championships 1915, 1916, 1919; won US women's amateur 1914, 1919, 1920, runner-up 1921, 1923, 1925, semifinalist 1915, 1927; Canadian women's amateur champion 1920, 1934, runner-up 1922, 1925; teamed with Bobby Jones on 1918 Red Cross fund-raising tour; mem. Ottawa, RCGA Halls of Fame.

FRASER, Bud (basketball, track); *b.* 16 Oct 1923, Bridgewater, N.S.; *given name:* Arthur; *m.* Ella Thomson; *children:* Geoffrey, Robin, Judy, Terry, Jill, Scott; McGill U, B.Sc., U of Minnesota, M.A.; director of athletics U of T; Nova Scotia HS high jump title 1940; armed forces high jump title 1942-43; Southeast Asia armed forces champion in six events 1945; CIAU basketball all-star 1948-50; Montreal city basketball all-star 1948-50; captain McGill U basketball team, won four letters 1948-50; silver award McGill athletic council, three track letters; coached Maritime intermediate hockey champion Brookfield Elks 1950-51, Western Canadian Intercollegiate basketball champions U of Manitoba 1954-57, U of Minnesota freshman basketball team; Winnipeg basketball coach of year 1953-54; former senior consultant Sport Canada; *res.* Mississauga, Ont.

FRASER, Cam (football); *b.* 16 Feb 1932, Hamilton, Ont.; *given name:* Cameron Donald; *m.* Betty Robertson; *children:* Donna Sandra; Westdale CI; steel company employee, businessman; 12-year CFL career 1952-62, 1969; kicked lifetime total 101 singles; during 10 recorded seasons from 1954, punted 987 times for 44,287yds, 44.9 avg.; holds CFL record most punting yds single season with 7,222 on 157 punts 1957; runner-up with 7,108yds on 156 punts 1958; retired following 1962 season, at age 37 was back as interim punter when Joe Zuger broke wrist 1969; since 1973 coached champion girls' softball team, Ancaster; named punter Tiger-Cats pro era (1950-67) team; *res.* Ancaster, Ont.

FRASER, Frank (football); *b.* 26 Dec 1935, Montreal, Que.; *m.* Janet Beers; *children:* Gregory, Natalie; Ohio State U, Tennessee A & I; mechanical engineer; played junior A hockey Quebec Frontenacs, Jonquière; junior baseball Laval U in Montreal League; Montreal HS and U S college football; eight years 1956-63 as halfback with Montreal, Ottawa, Regina, Edmonton, Winnipeg in CFL; led Canadian pass receivers 1959, 1960; *res.* Kanata, Ont.

FRASER, Hugh (track); *b.* 10 Jul 1952, Kingston, Jamaica; *given name:* Hugh Lloyd; *m.* Ann Kennedy; Queen's U, B.A., U of Ottawa, LL.B., gold medal 100m Canada vs Italy meet 1971, repeat vs Great Britain 1974; Canadian national 100m title in 10.1 1974, 100m and 200m titles 1975; Canadian indoor 300yd record 31.0; Canadian automatic timing record 200m 20.86 1975 Pan-Am Games beating Harry Jerome's 1968 Olympic 21.22; 15th in world 1975; mem. 4x100 bronze medal relay team 1975 Pan-Am Games setting Canadian record 38.86; mem. 1976 Olympic team; football U of O 1976, drafted by Toronto Argos 1976; *res.* Ottawa, Ont.

FREDRICKSON, Frank (hockey); *b.* 11 Jun 1895, Winnipeg, Man.; *m.;* Kelvin HS, U of Manitoba; retired insurance agent; captain U of Manitoba team; after war service joined Winnipeg Falcons, won Allan Cup and 1920 Antwerp Olympics gold medal on 2-0 final game win over U S, Fredrickson scored both goals; joined Lester Patrick with Victoria Aristocrats, later Cougars, scored upset Stanley Cup victory over Montreal Canadiens 1925; lost to Montreal Maroons in 1926 final; sold to Boston but signed with Detroit, played half season before shifting to Boston where he sparked Bruins to Stanley Cup final vs Ottawa; finished third in NHL scoring; led PCL, WCL scorers twice; sold to Pittsburgh Pirates 1930 becoming first NHL player-coach-manager; led NHL scorers through first seven games before check from Rangers' Bill Cook damaged his knee, ended playing career; coached Winnipeg 1931-32, Princeton 1933-35, seven years UBC; first player to write instructional articles on hockey for newspaper *(Toronto Star)* 1932: mem. Canadian Hockey Hall of Fame; *res.* Vancouver, B.C.

FRIESEN, Ron (diving); *b.* 13 Feb 1949, Saskatoon, Sask.; *given name:* Ronald George; U of Saskatchewan, B.P.H.E.; recreation director; Canadian Intercollegiate 3m title 1969, 1m and 3m titles 1970, 1971; bronze medal 3m Edinburgh Commonwealth Games 1970; Canadian 1m, 3m, 10m tower titles 1971, repeat latter two 1972; mem. World Student Games team Turin Italy 1969, Pan-Am Games team, Cali Colombia 1971, Munich Olympic team 1972; named most distinguished graduate U of Sask. school of phys ed 1971; *res.* Victoria, B.C.

FRITZ, Bill (track); *b.* 14 Aug 1914, Ferry Bank, Alta.; *given name:* William Duncan; *m.* Kathleen Nickell; *children:* David, Jim, Barbara; Walkerville CI, Queen's U, B.Sc.; engineer; began career as HS quarter-miler, broad jumper; intermediate titles both events in Windsor regional meets; WOSSA intermediate quarter-mile, broad jump, mile relay champion; senior 220, quarter-mile setting Windsor, WOSSA records; failed in bid for 1932 Olympic team; won Intercollegiate quarter-mile, 220, placed in 100m and competed on relay team Queen's U; fourth 1934 British Empire Games quarter-mile; ran for Toronto Beaches Olympic Team, West End Y; represented Canada 1936 Olympics placing fourth in relay, fifth 400m; mem. 1936 British Empire Games 1600m relay team which beat U S in London meet; Scandinavian tour won 500m, 400m; silver medal 1938 British Empire Games quarter-mile, gold relay; set Victoria State record 47.4 winning Melbourne Australia quarter-mile handicap race 1938; third, U S championships 1938; won Melrose, Boston indoor 600m 1938; *res.* London, Ont.

FRITZ, Bob (football); *b.* 29 Jul 1909, International Falls, Minn.; *given name:* Robert Francis; *m.* Phyllis Marcille; Concordia College, B.A., U of Minnesota; retired, sporting goods business; all-conference fullback 1931-34; UPI all-American 1934; joined Winnipeg Rugby Club as head coach-quarterback-fullback guiding them to West's first Grey Cup 1935, named all-Canadian quarterback; coached and played for Bomber team which lost Grey Cup 4-3 to Toronto Argos 1937; head coach-quarterback-fullback Edmonton Eskimos 1938-40; coached, played for Western Canada Air Force team which lost 1942 Grey Cup to Argos (East Air Force); backfield coach Concordia College 1948-54; life mem. Blue Bomber Alumni Association; Blue Bombers certificate of merit 1970; *res.* Fargo, N.D.

FROST, Barclay (track and field); *b.* 6 Jun 1941, Pembroke, Ont.; *given name:* Barclay William; *m.* Janet Small; *children:* Kendra, Kevin, Kirk; Carleton U, B.A.; teacher; mem. 1960 HS football champions; set HS high jump, long jump records; Ottawa HS boys' singles badminton title 1961; outstanding HS athlete 1961; mem. intermediate, senior city basketball league, West Carleton senior men's fastball league; goaler Carleton teachers hockey league; coached pole vaulters Ottawa Harriers; in two Canadian national T & F championships, placed third in 1962 long jump; triple jump measuring duties 1976 Montreal Olympics; coached championship teams in every sport as phys ed teacher; coached Greenbank Senior PS to eight consecutive cross-country T & F titles; *res.* Ottawa, Ont.

FROST, Stanley (shooting); *b.* 2 Sep 1939, Montreal, Que.; *m.* Anne; Queen's U, B.Sc.; health physicist; mem. Canadian team for Pershing matches Camp Perry Ohio 1965; gold master's badge 1970 world English match rifle championships; bronze medal 1973 Benito Juarez Games 300m free rifle team; three-position Ontario indoor champion; prone champion 1974 Ontario indoor; silver master badge English match at world; shooting Federation of Canada executive committee member 1968-69, v.-chairman SFC match rifle section 1970-75; *res.* Port Hope, Ont.

FULTON, Jack (lacrosse); *b.* 30 Jul 1926, New Westminster, B.C.; *m.* Jean Kemp; *children:* Craig, Jackie; Marine College; fire captain; manager New Westminster Salmonbellies 1956-66; executive mem. Canadian Lacrosse Association 1967-74, pres. 1971-72; governor Canadian Lacrosse Hall of Fame 1967-73; Lacrosse Hall of Fame chairman 1974-77; treasurer junior Salmonbellies 1975-77; *res.* New Westminster, B.C.

FURLONG, Jim (football); *b.* 13 Apr 1940, Lethbridge, Alta.; Lethbridge CI, Tulsa U; played with Calgary junior Bronks earning Tulsa U scholarship; offensive end, punter, Missouri Valley Conference all-star 1962; joined Calgary Stampeders 1962 as linebacker, punter 12 seasons; punted 707 times for 28,898yds, 40.9 avg.; 1964 game avg. 59yds per punt vs Edmonton, second best ever in CFL; WFC all-star 1965. *res.* Calgary, Alta.

GABLER, Wally (football); *b.* 9 Jun 1944, Royal Oak, Mich.; *given name:* Wallace Gabler III; *m.* Jacqueline Bescoby; *children;* Wallace IV, Tamara, Melissa; New Mexico Military Institute, U of Michigan, B.A.; investment dealer; HS all-State defensive back; junior college all-American at New Mexico Military Institute; at Michigan played quarterback, won Rose Bowl 1965; turned pro Toronto Argos 1966; Winnipeg Blue Bombers 1969; Hamilton Tiger-Cats 1971 and back to Argos to close out 1972 season before retiring; best single season 1968, passed for 3,242yds; seven-year CFL career record shows 1,690 passes thrown with 854 completed for 13,080yds and 61 TDs; *res.* Burlington, Ont.

GABRIEL, Tony (football); *b.* 11 Dec 1948, Hamilton, Ont.; *given name:* Tony Peter; *m.* Diane Ellen Gaudaur; *children:* Benjamin Daniel, Laura Daniele; Burlington Central HS, Syracuse U, B.Sc.; football player, chemical company representative; split end with Syracuse, broke nearly all major pass receiving records for school; four TDs one game vs Miami; NCAA record scoring two TDs in just over two minutes; joined Hamil-ton Tiger-Cats 1971, 1972 season led Hamilton receivers as tight end with 49 receptions for 733yds and three TDs; three last-minute catches set up Hamilton 13-10 Grey Cup victory over Sask.; CFL playoff record with 15 receptions vs Ottawa in semifinals 1974; led EFC receivers with 61 receptions; traded to Ottawa Rough Riders 1975, led EFC receivers with 65 catches; four times Schen-ley Canadian player award, winner 1974, 1976; all-East tight end five times, all-Canadian four times; caught winning TD pass from Tom Clements, Canadian player of game 1976 Grey Cup; Shopsy award 1976; won Canadian Superstars TV series 1976; *res.* Burlington, Ont.

GADSBY, Bill (hockey); *b.* 8 Aug 1927, Calgary, Alta.; *given name:* William Alex-ander; as 12-year-old was aboard torpedoed Athenia 1939 and spent five hours in Atlant-ic before rescue; played Edmonton junior hockey; turned pro as defenceman Chicago Black Hawks 1946-54, N Y Rangers 1954-61, Detroit Red Wings 1961-66; coach Detroit 1968-69; three times NHL first team all-star, four times second team; collected close to 600 stitches during his 20 year NHL career, never played on Stanley Cup winner; while captain 1952 Black Hawks was strick-en by polio but returned to become third man in NHL history to play 20 years; at one stage shared NHL record with Pierre Pilote for most assists by defenceman single season and led NHL defencemen lifetime assists with 437, since topped by Bobby Orr; played 1,248 regular season games scoring 130 goals, 437 assists for 567 points, 1,539 penalty minutes; 67 playoff games, four goals, 23 assists, 27 points, 92 penalty mi-nutes; coach Edmonton Oil Kings two sea-sons, league title 1966-67; mem. Hockey Hall of Fame; *res.* Florida.

GAGNIER, Ed (gymnastics); *b.* 1 Feb 1936, Windsor, Ont.; *m.* Carolyn; *children:* Bonnie, Becky; U of Michigan. B.S., M.A.; gymnastics coach; Canadian junior athlete of year 1954; represented Canada 1956 Olympics; Big 10 all-around champion 1957; U of M Yost honor award 1957-58; Iowa State coach 1961 and three times NCAA coach of year; coach U S World Student Games team Italy 1970; coach 10 Big Eight conference winners, three NCAA national championship teams; *res.* Ames, Iowa.

GAINES, Gene (football); *b.* 26 Jun 1938, Los Angeles, Calif.; *given name:* Eugene Carver; *m.* Marion Backstrom; *children:* Ellen Courtney, Eugene Jr., Elaine Carla; UCLA; football coach; pro Montreal Alouettes 1961; traded to Ottawa Rough Riders 1962; back to Montreal as player-assistant coach 1970-76; outstanding defensive back with 41 career interceptions, 655yds returned; returned kickoff 128yds in playoff vs Hamilton 1966; Jeff Russel Memorial Trophy 1966; mem. six Grey Cup finalists, four winners; *res.* Montreal, Que.

GAIRDNER, Bill (track and field); *b.* 19 Oct 1940, Oakville, Ont.; *given name:* William Douglas; *m.* Michele Lesavre; *children:* Christine, Emilie; U of Colorado, B.A., Stanford U, M.A., Ph.D.; pres. Fitness Institute; silver medal decathlon 1963 Sao Paulo Pan-Am Games; 11th same event 1964 Tokyo Olympics; sixth 400m hurdles 1966 Commonwealth Games Kingston Jamaica, 1970 Commonwealth Games Edinburgh Scotland; gold medal 400 hurdles Italy vs Canada 1971; numerous national, provincial, Eastern Canadian championships, record holder in variety of events; personal bests: 7,147 points decathlon Tokyo 1964, 14.2 in 110 hurdles, 51.3 in 400 hurdles, 10.9 in 100m, 22' long jump, 49'2'' shot put, 5'10'' high jump, 48.8 400m, 156' discus, 12'6'' pole vault, 196'8'' javelin, 4:24.5 1500m; ran personal best 400 hurdles in Winnipeg at age 32; only Canadian to compete in national T&F championships Sudbury 1975 and national cross-country 15km ski championships Sudbury same season; TV commentator 1976 Olympics; first degree black belt in judo, Japan 1965; *res.* Unionville, Ont.

GARAPICK, Nancy (swimming); *b.* 24 Sep 1961, Halifax, N.S.; *given name:* Nancy Ellen; Cornwallis Jr. HS; student; in 1974 placed third 100, 200m backstroke finals at Canadian championships; world record 2:16.33 for 200m backstroke 1975 and Canadian standard for 100m backstroke in 1:04.30; Olympic record 1:03.28 for 100m backstroke in heats; eight firsts 1976 Ontario short course championships; four firsts, two seconds Pointe Claire Canada Cup meet 1977; three firsts Netherlands Speedo meet 1977; three firsts, two seconds Paris meet 1977, set three Canadian records 100m FS (56.93), 100m butterfly (1:02.63), 200m IM (2:17.5); two bronze medals 1976 Montreal Olympics; Canadian female athlete of year 1975; Governor-General's silver medal 1976; US short course 400yd IM record 4:19.05 1977; *res.* Halifax, N.S.

GARDINER, Chuck (hockey); *b.* 31 Dec 1904, Edinburgh, Scotland, *d.* 13 Jun 1934, Winnipeg, Man.; *given name:* Charles Robert; goaler intermediate hockey at 14, joined Selkirk seniors 1925 and turned pro Winnipeg Maroons 1926; Chicago Black Hawks 1927-34; during seven season NHL career played in 315 games allowing 673 goals for 2.13 avg., 42 shutouts; played in 21 Stanley Cup contests recording five shutouts and allowing 35 goals for 1.66 avg.; twice won

Vezina Trophy; three times first team all-star, once second team; two months after helping Chicago win Stanley Cup, allowing just 12 goals in eight games for 1.50 avg., died of brain tumor at 30; mem. Hockey Hall of Fame.

GARDINER, Herb (hockey); *b.* 8 May 1891, Winnipeg, Man., *d.* 11 Jan 1972; *given name:* Herbert Martin; began hockey career 1908 with Winnipeg Victorias then played with Northern Crown Bank in Bankers' League two seasons; out of hockey next eight seasons, returned to Calgary Rotarians 1919; Calgary Tigers (WCL) 1920-25; after team met Canadiens for Stanley Cup challenge, Montreal signed him at age 35; played with Montreal 1926-29 then loaned to Chicago as manager; recalled by Habs for playoffs 1929 then sold to Boston; manager-coach Philadelphia Arrows of Canadian-American League; 1949 coached Ramblers, Falcons; with Arrows won 1933 title on 29-12-7 record; NHL MVP, Hart Trophy 1927; mem. Hockey Hall of Fame.

GARDNER, Jimmy (hockey); *b.* 21 May 1881, Montreal, Que., *d.* 7 Nov 1940, Montreal, Que.; *given name:* James Henry; played left wing on Montreal hockey club's Little Men of Iron for 1901-02 Stanley Cup victory; with Montreal Wanderers won 1910 Stanley Cup; to Calumet Michigan two seasons, Pittsburgh, back to Montreal with Shamrocks and Wanderers, New Westminster (PCL) for two seasons, Montreal for two seasons with Canadiens; retired as player and coached Canadiens two years; officiated in minors 1917-18, WCL 1923-24; coach Hamilton Tiger-Cats 1924-25; mem. Hockey Hall of Fame.

GARROW, Alex (basketball); *b.* 3 Jan 1937, St. Regis, Que.; *m.* Carol Harris; *children:* Terry, Kathy, Patrick; Bishop Fallon HS, U of Alabama, Algonquin College; student; nickname Chief; all-Catholic City of Buffalo all-star basketball in HS; scored over 1,000 points in HS career; attended Alabama on basketball scholarship 1957-58; joined Tillsonburg Livingstons 1960-61 winning Canadian title and representing Canada 1960 Olympics; planned to turn pro with Elmer Ripley's Washington D.C. ABA team but home injury sidelined him 1962 season; joined Vince Drake's 1963 Yvon Coutu Institute team Montreal, senior league MVP 1963-64; captain first Quebec team 1967 Canada Winter Games; plays Ottawa city league basketball and coaches Nepean bantam basketball; *res.* Ottawa, Ont.

GARVIE, Gord (wrestling); *b.* 25 Oct 1944, Saskatoon, Sask.; *given name:* Gordon Taylor; *m.* Joan Katherine Willness; *children:* Trona Lee, Lana Katherine, Carla Vi, Barton Minor; U of Saskatchewan, B.A., B.Ed., M.Sc.; technical director Canadian Wrestling Assoc.; played football Nutona Blues 1959-61, Saskatoon Hilltops 1962-65, Saskatchewan Huskies 1966-69, all-star seven years, MVP with Blues, Hilltops; played hockey to junior A level before moving to wrestling at university; Canadian university title 1967-69, Canadian title 1969, U of Sask. athlete of year 1966-69; represented Canada 1968 Olympics, 1969 world championships; player-coach Thunder Bay Mustangs football team 1970-71; wrestling coach Lakehead U 1970, produced nine CIAU champions, 17 runners-up, five Canadian open medalists, one Canadian open titlist in five year span; manager World Student Games team Moscow 1973; assistant coach World Cup team 1973; Commonwealth

Games team coach 1974, five gold medalists; World Cup team coach 1974-76, two gold, silver, bronze medalists; coach 1976 Olympics; *res.* Ottawa, Ont.

GAUDAUR, Jake Jr. (football); *b.* 5 Oct 1920, Orillia, Ont.; *given name:* Jacob Gill Jr.; *m.* Isobel Grace Scott; *children:* Jacqueline Gaye, Diane Ellen, Janice Arlene; football executive; son of former world pro rowing champion, won 1938 North American Schoolboys rowing singles at Princeton, Canadian junior singles; played for 1939 Canadian junior lacrosse champions Orillia Terriers; at 19 played first pro football season with Hamilton Tiger-Cats; joined Toronto Argos 1941; same year won Canadian senior mile rowing title; played with 1942 Grey Cup champion RCAF Hurricanes; one of eight players who purchased, operated Toronto Indians in Ontario Rugby Football Union 1945-46; simultaneously played pro lacrosse with Hamilton Tigers; co-captain 1947 Montreal Alouettes and played lacrosse with Quebec Montagnards; captain 1948-49 ORFU champion Hamilton Tigers; captain 1950-51 Hamilton Tiger-Cats; retired to become Hamilton club director; reactivated 1953 to centre Hamilton to Grey Cup victory; retired to club pres. 1954, pres.-general manager 1956-58; Eastern Football Conference pres. 1959; CFL pres. 1962; chairman Canadian Football Hall of Fame 1963; CFL commissioner 1968; chairman CFL Players Pension advisory board, CFL rules committee; *res.* Burlington, Ont.

GAUDAUR, Jake Sr. (rowing); *b.* 3 Apr 1858, Orillia, Ont.; *d.* 11 Oct 1937, Orillia, Ont.; *given name:* Jacob Gill; *m.* Cora Coons (*d.*); Ida Harris (*d.*); Alice Grace Hemming (*d.*); *children:* six sons, six daughters; pro oarsman, boat livery, fishing guide business; rowed first pro race at 17; finished third to world titlist Ned Hanlan, James Riley in first significant race in shell 1879 Barrie regatta; challenged Hanlan's conqueror, William Beach, losing by length; at 30 won North American title vs Hanlan; 1887-97 set new records nearly every time he rowed; from 1892 was world's best oarsman; three-mile record 19:6 Austin Tex. 1893; lowered mark 1894 to 19:1.5 (still stands); beat Jim Stanbury for world's pro title 1896 London Eng.; defended 1898 vs R.N. Johnson Vancouver; retired after loss to Australia's George Towns 1901; mem. Canadian Sports Hall of Fame.

GAY, Mary (golf); *b.* 16 Sep 1931, Toronto, Ont.; supervisor payroll and records; won Ontario Open 1952, runner-up three times; five times runner-up Canadian Open, three times runner-up Canadian Closed; Alberta Open runner-up twice; mem. Canadian ladies' team to Britain twice; mem. Ontario ladies' team interprovincial matches three times, Alberta team twice; skip 1962-63 Ontario Business Girls curling champions; last competitive play 1965 Canadian ladies; *res.* Waterloo, Ont.

GAYFORD, Tom (equestrian); *b.* 21 Nov 1928, Toronto, Ont.; *m.* Martha West; *children:* Margaret, Mary, Janet, Virginia, Elizabeth; U of Toronto; stockbroker; began riding at two, competing at seven; with father, Major Gordon Gayford, became first father-son combination to compete internationally; represented Canada 1959, 1967, 1971 Pan-Am Games, 1970 world, 1952, 1960, 1968 Olympics; coached Canadian Equestrian team 1972 Olympics; gold medals 1959 Pan-Am Games three-day team; 1968 Prix des Nations Mexico Olympics; 1971 captain Pan-Am Games Prix des Nations team; 1970 captain Prix des Nations world team; won Rothmans modified Grand Prix, National Horse Show jumping title 1972; won U S Horse Show N.Y. puissance three successive years; competitive horses Dreamy Joe, Snow Witch, Big Dee, Regardez, Moonstep, Red Admiral; mem. Canadian Sports Hall of Fame; *res.* Gormley, Ont.

GENEREUX, George (trapshooting); *b.* 1 Mar 1935, Saskatoon, Sask.; *given name:* George Patrick; *m.* Lee; *children:* Andrea, George; U of Saskatchewan, B.A., McGill U, M.D.; diagnostic radiologist; at 13 won first major competition — Midwestern International Handicap; followed with three successive Manitoba-Saskatchewan junior titles; won North American junior championship at Vandalia Ohio and Sask. title; tied for second place world finals at Oslo; gold medal 1952 Helsinki Olympics; 1952 Canadian athlete of year, Viscount Alexander Trophy (junior athlete of year), Saskatoon citizen of year; mem. AAU of C, Canadian Sports, Sask. Sports Halls of Fame; *res.* Saskatoon, Sask.

GENOIS, Rejean (tennis); *b.* 30 Dec 1952, Quebec City, Que.; *given name:* Joseph George Rejean; *m.* Marie Falardeau; Arthur Gagnon HS, Florida State U; tennis pro, accountant; 1971 junior Davis Cup title; joined pro tour 1975 after using successful junior career to win tennis scholarship at Florida State; leading player on 1976 Rothman's Grand Prix tour; four times Davis Cup team mem.; Quebec City athlete of year 1973; *res.* Loretteville, Que.

GEOFFRION, Bernie (hockey); *b.* 14 Feb 1931, Montreal, Que.; *m.* Marlene Morenz; *children:* Linda, Robert, Danny; broadcaster, hockey executive; nickname Boom Boom; started as defenceman in church league; turned pro Montreal Canadiens playing 18 games in 1950-51 season; Calder Trophy rookie of year 1951-52 as right winger; career almost ended 1958 when he ruptured bowel in collision with Andre Pronovost; second player to score 50 goals in single season 1960-61; retired following 1963-64 campaign, spent two seasons coaching Quebec City to consecutive pennants; drafted by N Y Rangers, made comeback 1966-68 before ulcers stopped him; Ranger coach briefly; coach with expansion Atlanta Flames 1972 for two and one-half years; resigned, rejoined Flames 1976 as TV color commentator, publicity director; NHL career record 882 league games, 393 goals, 429 assists for 822 points, 689 penalty minutes, in 131 playoff games, 58 goals, 59 assists, 117 points, 88 penalty minutes; Ross Trophy twice, Hart Trophy once; played on seven Prince of Wales Trophy winners, six Stanley Cup winners; mem. Hockey Hall of Fame; *res.* Montreal, Que., Atlanta, Ga.

GERARD, Eddie (hockey); *b.* 22 Feb 1890, Ottawa, Ont., *d.* 7 Aug 1937, Ottawa, Ont.; *given name:* Edward George; *m.* Lillian Mackenzie; *children:* Ailsa, Margaret; printer; as youth with Ottawa New Edinburgh league hockey team, Ottawa New Edinburgh Canoe Club, Printing Bureau team in mercantile baseball league, Ottawa cricket team; with Don Mackenzie won Dominion canoe tandem title at 15; backfield for Ottawa Rough Riders 1909-13; turned pro Ottawa Senators hockey club 1913, 11 seasons on defence; captain Senators 1920-21; played on four Stanley Cup winners, one on loan to Toronto St. Pat's; coached Montreal Maroons to 1926 Stanley Cup; managed N Y Americans 1930; returned to Maroons 1933;

joined St. Louis Eagles 1934 but illness forced him out mid-season; mem. Ottawa, Hockey Halls of Fame.

GERELA, Ted (football); *b.* 12 Mar 1944, Powell River, B.C.; Spokane HS, Washington State U.; played soccer as youth but was conventional style placement kicker with Washington State; discovered Gogolak brothers NFL success with soccer-style placement kicking, changed own style; turned pro B.C. Lions 1967 as running back, placement kicker; Dr. Beattie Martin Trophy (WFC rookie of year); CFL record 30 field goals single season 1968; twice kicked five field goals in single game; seven-year CFL record 132 converts, 123 field goals, 67 singles for 569 points; *res.* Powell River, B.C.

GERIS, Harry (wrestling); *b.* 22 Nov 1947, Netherlands; *given name:* Harry Ted; *m.* Jo-Anne Kathleen Knight; *children:* Jason Scott, Shawn Joseph; H.B. Beal Technical HS, Joliet Junior College, Oklahoma State U, B.Sc.; insurance salesman; Ontario HS title 1966, 1967; five times Canadian Open freestyle champion; three times Canadian Open Greco-Roman champion in unlimited class; U S national junior college heavyweight title 1968, runner-up 1969; silver medals 1972 AAU heavyweight Cleveland, USWF heavyweight Stillwater Okla.; bronze medals 1975 Pan-Am Games Mexico; AAU heavyweight Cleveland 1976; fourth 1966 Commonwealth Games, 1973 World Student Games Moscow, 1972 NCAA championships; ninth 1972 Munich Olympics; mem. 1976 Olympic team; *res.* London, Ont.

GERVAIS, Hec (curling); *b.* 4 Nov 1933, St. Albert, Alta.; *given name:* Hector Joseph; *m.* Helen Bowman; *children:* Janet, Sandy, Hector Jr, Stanley, Kim; St. Albert HS;

retired farmer; played football Edmonton Wildcats, tryout with Eskimos 1953; also played juvenile hockey; nine times represented Northern Alberta in provincial curling playdowns, won title four times; Brier titles 1961, 1974, once world champion; won several Carspiels, Calgary Masters twice, Toronto Tournament of Champions, many regional competitions; known for push shot; mem. Canadian Curling Hall of Fame; *res.* St. Albert, Alta.

GETLIFFE, Ray (hockey, golf); *b.* 3 Apr 1914, Galt, Ont.; *m.* Lorna; *children:* John, Lorna; textiles company executive; played junior hockey Western Ontario area; Boston Bruins 1936-39; Montreal Canadiens 1939-45; on two Stanley Cup winners; scored five goals for Canadiens 1943 game vs Bruins; mem. Ontario Willingdon Cup champions 1938; pres. Quebec Golf Association 1960, Royal Canadian Golf Association 1969; Governor RCGA 1961-75; mem. Canadian Seniors Golf Association, American Seniors Golf Association, U S Eastern Seniors Golf Association; *res.* Montreal, Que.

GETTY, Don (football); *b.* 30 Aug 1933, Westmount, Que.; *given name:* Donald Ross; *m.* Margaret Inez Mitchell; *children:* Dale, David, Darin, Derek; Sir Adam Beck CI, U of Western Ontario, B.A.; politician, investment counsellor, oil consultant; joined Edmonton Eskimos 1954 in backfield with Jackie Parker, Johnny Bright and Normie Kwong; quarterbacked 1956 Eskimos to Grey Cup victory over Montreal; topped WIFU in yds-per-completed pass 1959, runner-up to Ottawa's Russ Jackson for Canadian player of the year; topped WIFU with completion percentage 54.7 1961; second to Parker as Eskimos MVP; present director

Eskimos football club; since 1967 MLA, Minister Energy and Natural Resources since 1975; *res.* Edmonton, Alta.

GIARDINO, Wayne (football); *b.* 7 Nov 1943, Peterborough, Ont.; *given name:* Wayne Maurice; *m.* Nancy Von Fielitzsch; *children:* Nicole, David; Florida State U, B.A.; salesman; captain Florida State, all-State running back; rejected Dodgers invitation for football scholarship; played baseball college world series Omaha 1965; turned pro with Ottawa Rough Riders 1967, linebacker, occasional fullback until 1976 retirement; EFC rookie of year (Gruen Trophy) 1967; Hiram Walker Trophy, nominee for outstanding Canadian (Schenley award) 1971; frequent all-star; *res.* Almonte, Ont.

GIBSON, Cheryl (swimming); *b.* 28 Jul 1959, Edmonton, Alta.; *given name:* Cheryl Ann; Strathern Junior HS, McNally HS; student; since 1974 mem. Canadian national swim team; mem. Canadian Dolphins Swim Club under coach Deryk Snelling; silver medals 200m butterfly, 400m individual medley (IM), bronze 200m backstroke, 200m IM and fourth 100m backstroke 1975 Pan-Am Games; seventh 400 IM 1975 world; silver 400m IM with personal best, Canadian record 4:48.10 1976 Montreal Olympics, fifth 100m backstroke, sixth 200m butterfly; four firsts Canadian nationals, record 3:52.98 for 400m FS relay, 8:26.00 800m FS relay; four firsts, one second Pointe Claire Canada Cup meet 1977; two firsts Netherlands Speedo meet 1977; three firsts, Canadian record 2:15.30 for 200m backstroke, 1977 Paris meet; Governor-General's silver medal 1976; *res.* Edmonton, Alta.

GIBSON, George (baseball); *b.* 22 Jul 1880, London, Ont.; *d.* 25 Jan 1967, London, Ont.; *m.* Margaret McMurphy; *children:* Marguerite, George Jr.; William; pro baseball player, bricklayer; nickname Mooney because of round face; began career London industrial league, joined Pittsburgh Pirates (NL) 1905; played over 1,000 games before being traded to NY Giants 1917; in 1,203 major league games had .236 lifetime batting avg., 15 home runs, 331 runs batted in; best season with Pirates 1914, batted .285 in 102 games; managed Pirates 1920-22 and 1932-34, Chicago Cubs 1925; coached Toronto (IL); Canada's baseball player of half century 1950 CP poll; all-time all-star catcher with Pirates; mem. Canadian Sports Hall of Fame.

GILBERT, Bob (curling); *b.* 29 Jan 1915 Rosetown, Sask.; *given name:* Robert Lorne; *m.* Jean Irene Groves; *children:* Diane, Bob Jr.; Royal Oak HS; retired gasoline co. executive; began curling 1937, earned reputation as one of Western Ontario's best shotmakers; won Ontario Tankard, City of London, Sarnia Imperial, Highland Tartan, Highland Mixed, St. Thomas Early Bird, Chatham City, Toronto City, Hamilton Centennial 'spiel; played second for father winning Ontario Consols, represented province in 1953 Brier; *res.* London, Ont., Florida.

GILBERT, Don (curling); *b.* 28 Jun 1930, St. Thomas, Ont.; *given name:* Donald Alexander. *m.* Patricia Marie Anderson; *children:* Michael, David, Stephen, Jeffrey; U of Toronto, D.D.S.; dentist; played second on Ontario Colts title rink, Harvey J. Sims Trophy, 1959; skipped Albert E. Dunker Trophy winner 1963 OCA Colts competition; played third 1961 OCA Governor-General's trophy winner; twice winner OCA Silver Tankard, three times runner-up; winner Burden trophy OCA Tankard competition, also runner-up; skipped 1968 Ontario

Consols champion posting 6-4 record Kelowna Brier; through 1977 appeared in Ontario Consols playdowns six times, winning once, runner-up once; semifinalist OCA Rose Bowl competition 1965; winner numerous major bonspiels including City of London, Sarnia Imperial, St. Thomas Early Bird, Welland Banana Belt, Lambton Masters. *res.* St. Thomas, Ont.

GILBERT, Don (football); *b.* 6 Oct 1943, Buffalo, N. Y.; *given name:* Don Alan; *m.* Patricia Gale Tananbaum; *children:* Eric Jonathon, Kara Ann; Bennett HS, State University of NY at Buffalo, B.Ed., M.Ed.; public relations, coach; as school athlete played football, basketball, baseball, won 12 major athletic letters, various community awards; six major letters in college — three football, one basketball, two baseball; Dom Grossi Award (outstanding athlete Buffalo U) 1965, Penn State Award (outstanding student-athlete) 1965; joined Ottawa Rough Riders as defensive halfback, reserve quarterback 1966; traded to Winnipeg Blue Bombers 1968; head football coach U of Ottawa 1971-75, won conference titles five consecutive years, Canadian College Bowl championship 1975; Canadian college football coach of year 1975; coach Ottawa Rough Riders 1974 CFL all-star game victory; past coaching assistant Edmonton Eskimos training camp; *res.* Buffalo, N.Y.

GILBERT, Gord (curling); *b.* 25 Apr 1918, Rosetown, Sask.; *given name:* Gordon Luton; *m.* Alma Jeffery; *children:* Peter; Royal Oak HS; retired gasoline co. executive; played third for father Peter 1949 provincial Consols title, represented province in Hamilton Brier; repeated Consols victory 1953 with father as skip and brother Bob at second; *res.* Chatham, Ont., Florida.

GILBERT, Peter (curling); *b.* 13 Jan 1880, Orwell, Ont., *d.* 31 Jul 1961, Chatham, Ont.; *given name:* Peter Lorne; *m.* Grace Ingram; *children:* Bob, Gord; businessman; twice won Ontario championship 1949, 1953; represented Ontario in Brier; former owner Chatham Curling Club.

GILBERT, Rod (hockey); *b.* 1 Jul 1941, Montreal, Que.; *given name:* Rodrigue Gabriel; *m.* Arunee Leeaphorn; minor hockey Montreal to junior OHA as NY Rangers prospect with Guelph Junior Royals; led OHA scorers, won Red Tilson Memorial Trophy as most gentlemanly player in OHA; turned pro with Trois-Rivières (EPHL), Kingston-Waterloo (EPHL) then to NY Rangers as regular 1962-63, first and second team all-star once each; West Side Association Trophy as Rangers' MVP; through 1976-77 appeared in 1046 NHL games scoring 404 goals, 608 assists for 1012 points, 502 penalty minutes plus 79 playoff games, 34 goals, 33 assists, 67 points and 43 penalty minutes; Bill Masterton Memorial Trophy 1976; *res.* New York, N.Y.

GILMOUR, Billy (hockey); *b.* 21 Mar 1885, Ottawa, Ont., *d.* 13 Mar 1959, Montreal, Que.; *given name:* Hamilton Livingstone; *m.* Merle Woods; *children:* Germaine; McGill U; engineer; joined Ottawa Silver Seven 1902-03 season, right wing three consecutive Stanley Cup winners; 10 goals in seven games plus five in four playoff contests in rookie season; retired for year following 1905-06 campaign; joined Montreal Victorias of Eastern Canada Amateur HA 1907-08; rejoined Ottawa (renamed Senators) 1908-09, won Stanley Cup, scored 11 goals in 11 games; retired six more seasons; tried 1915-16 two-game comeback with Senators, scored in game against Georges Vezina, then retired; mem. Ottawa, Hockey Halls of Fame.

GILMOUR, Buddy (harness racing); *b.* 23 Jul 1932, Lucan, Ont.; *given name:* William; *m.* Gwen Harner; *children:* four; Ridgeway HS; harness race driver; drove first race 1952 Toronto's Dufferin Park; posted first win with Money Maker same year; Batavia Downs fire 1961 destroyed almost his entire stable but rebuilt to one of North America's finest; Roosevelt Raceway dash winning record 1:56 set in 1973; through 1976 has won more than 3,500 races with purses totalling more than $12 million; has driven over 30 sub-two-minute miles; twice won Al B. White Trophy as Roosevelt dash winner; won Roosevelt Futurity with Strike Out 1971; as trainer had greatest success with George Campos-owned pacer Myakka Prince 1973 tying Roosevelt track record for aged geldings with 1:59 mile, $166,980 in winnings; became second driver in history to top $1.8 million in single season winnings 1973 (other was Herve Filion); *res.* Westbury, N.Y.

GLASSER, Sully (football); *b.* 25 Oct 1922, Regina, Sask.; *given name:* Sullivan John; *m.* Terry; *children:* Donna, Brenda, Sullivan, Jill, Marsha, Grant; chartered life underwriter; backfielder with Saskatchewan Roughriders mid-40s to mid-50s; WFC all-star 1946; scored TD against Ottawa 1951 Grey Cup; played six years senior baseball, junior hockey; *res.* Regina, Sask.

GLOAG, Norman (basketball); *b.* 9 Jul 1919, Vancouver, B.C. *given name:* Norman Grainger; *m.* Elizabeth Jones; *children:* John, Mary; air line executive; played senior men's basketball Vancouver 1938-48 excluding 1942-45; played for Vancouver Cloverleafs senior A men on Philippines tour, won Canadian senior men's championship 1948; manager Canadian basketball team 1956 Melbourne Olympics; Canadian representative world basketball tournament 1959 Santiago Chili; Canadian representative 1960 Rome Olympics; manager Canadian basketball team Manila world championships 1962; Canadian basketball representative Olympics Tokyo 1964, Mexico 1968, Munich 1972; since 1951 chairman Vancouver Amateur Basketball Association; two terms pres. CABA 1970-74; mem. Pan-Am Games committee; director COA, director Vancouver/Garibaldi Olympic Committee; mem. women's commission FIBA; mem. B.C. Sports Hall of Fame; *res.* Vancouver, B.C.

GMOSER, Hans (skiing, mountaineering); *b.* 7 Jul 1932, Austria; *m.* Margaret Grace MacGougan; *children;* Conrad, Robson; Harvard Business School; mountain guide, businessman; first ascents in Canadian Rockies; first ascent of 16,525ft Mt. Blackburn Alaska; first ascent Wickersham on Mt. McKinley; second ascent East Ridge Mt. Logan (at 19,850ft highest in Canada); developed alpine ski touring in Western Canadian mountains, helicopter skiing in the Bugaboos, Cariboos and Monasuees; *res.* Banff, Alta.

GOLAB, Tony (football); *b.* 17 Jan 1919, Windsor, Ont.; *given name:* Anthony Charles; *wid.; children:* son and daughter; Kennedy CI, U of Puget Sound; retired air force officer, Sport Canada official; played basketball for Dominion champion Windsor Alumni; with Sarnia Imperials for 1938 Ontario Rugby Football Union title; halfback with Ottawa Rough Riders 1939-41, 1945-50; Jeff Russell Memorial Trophy 1941 as Big Four MVP; played on 1940 Grey Cup champions and in 1939, 1941, 1948 finals; coached Hamilton ORFU Panthers 1952-53, RMC football teams to three successive conference titles 1954-57; Atlantic Conference v.-pres. 1959; general manager Montreal Alouettes 1968; consultant Sport Canada 1972; Canadian Football, Canadian Sports Halls of Fame; *res.* Ottawa, Ont.

GOODFELLOW, Ebbie (hockey); *b.* 9 Apr 1907, Ottawa, Ont.; *given name:* Ebenezer Ralston; all-star centre with Ottawa Montagnards as amateur before being picked up by Detroit; all-star with Olympics of International League 1928-29; with Red Wings 1929-43; played centre then defence; coach Wings during 1942 Stanley Cup finals with Toronto; coach Chicago Black Hawks 1950-52 before retiring; Hart Trophy (MVP) 1940; twice first team all-star, once second team; mem. three Stanley Cup winners; in 575 NHL games scored 134 goals, 190 assists for 324 points; mem. Hockey Hall of Fame selection committee; mem. Ottawa, Hockey Halls of Fame; *res.* Florida.

GOODMAN, Russell (skiing); *b.* 5 May 1953, Montreal, Que.; McGill U; student; through age-group ranks as alpine skier, international status 1973, best international slalom rating among Canadians Feb 1973 to May 1975; 10th 1974 slalom world championships St. Moritz for best finish by Canadian male skier in Olympic, World Cup or world championship competition; runner-up 1972 Canadian slalom final, 1974, 1975 giant slalom; won 1975 Can-Am giant slalom, Canadian spring slalom Rossland B.C. 1975, Hunter Mountain Can-Am giant slalom 1975, Waterville Valley Can-Am dual slalom 1975; runner-up Killington Can-Am giant slalom 1975; third 1975 Can-Am overall title; competed in European Cup 1973-74, fourth Andora slalom 1973, seventh Cas-

poggio, Sella Nevea, Czechoslovakia slaloms 1973, sixth Sella Nevea giant slalom, ninth slalom 1974; *res.* Montreal, Que.

GORDON, Jack (hockey); *b.* 3 Mar 1928, Winnipeg, Man.; hockey executive; 17 years as player, coach, manager Cleveland minor league; played New Haven (AHL) 1947-50, Cincinnati (AHL) 1950-51 and at times NY Rangers 1948-51; with Cleveland won four Calder Cups; four years assistant general manager NY Rangers; coached Minnesota North Stars three seasons, part of two others, did some scouting and since 1974 general manager; in two NHL seasons as player appeared in 36 games, scored three goals, 10 assists for 13 points plus nine playoff games, one goal, one assist, two points; in five years as NHL coach guided team through 290 regular season games, 116 wins, 124 losses, 50 ties for .486 percentage, plus 25 playoff games, 11 wins, 14 losses for .440 percentage; *res.* Edina, Minn.

GORMAN, Charles (speedskating); *b.* 6 Jul 1897, Saint John, N.B.; *d.* 12 Feb 1940, Saint John, N.B.; won U S national amateur outdoor and international three-mile Lake Placid NY 1924; lost both titles 1925, came back 1926 to beat 1924 Olympic champion Clas Thunberg of Finland for world title; won mid-Atlantic title, tied for first U S outdoor, won Canadian indoor, retained world title breaking record for one-sixth mile and shaving second from own 440yd standard 1927; seventh in 500m 1928 Winter Olympics when another skater fell in his path; denied another heat, left games in protest; record 200yd indoor, 400yd indoor, outdoor and one-sixth mile times still stand; once won 16 events in 11-day period; mem. N. B., Canadian Speedskating, Canadian Sports Halls of Fame.

GORMAN, T. P. Tommy (entrepreneur); *b.* 9 Jun 1886, Ottawa, Ont.; *d.* 15 May 1961, Ottawa, Ont.; *given name:* Thomas Patrick; *m.* Mary Elizabeth Westwick; *children:* Betty, Frank, Joe; sportswriter, coach; at 22 youngest mem. 1908 Olympic lacrosse gold medal team; one of five men involved in 1917 birth of National Hockey League; introduced hockey to NYC with old Americans; as coach-owner Ottawa Senators won titles 1920-21, 1923, with Chicago Black Hawks 1934, Montreal Maroons 1935, Canadiens 1944, 1946; coached and/or managed seven Stanley Cup winners; left NHL 1946 to take over Ottawa Auditorium; Ottawa Senators pres. in Quebec Senior Hockey League, won 1949 Allan Cup; assistant general manager Aqua Caliente race track Mexico 1929-32, and in 40s acquired Connaught Park Ottawa, introduced harness racing; involved with Ottawa entry International Baseball League; mem. Ottawa, Hockey Halls of Fame.

GOSSELIN, Gus (softball); *b.* 24 Feb 1919, Ottawa, Ont.; *given name:* Hubert; *m.* Ida Thibeault; *children:* Pierre, Claire, Louise, Monique, Denise, Paul; Notre Dame College; civil servant; as pitcher played with various title-winning service and Ottawa area teams 1937-74; MVP 1940, 1941, 1973-74; top pitcher awards 1941 (16-1), 1951 (14-2) two no-hitters 1951; led Ottawa Valley league hitters 1948 with .497 avg.; *res.* Luskville, Que.

GOTTA, Jack (football); *b.* 1932, Ironwood, Mich.; *m.* Joan Patterson; *children:* Jeff, Tony, Jake, Gia; Oregon State U; football coach; pass receiver, Oregon State; service football with Hamilton AFB; captain 1955 USAF team, all-service all-star, league MVP, caught 44 passes for eight TDs; last cut by Cleveland Browns 1956, joined Calgary Stampeders for final seven games; played in 1957 Shrine Game; Saskatchewan Roughriders 1960, led receivers 1961-63 until he broke arm; Montreal Alouettes 1964; retired, became assistant to Eagle Keys at Sask. 1965-66; joined Ottawa as assistant to Frank Clair 1967, head coach 1970; guided Ottawa to Grey Cup victory 1973; twice Annis Stukus Trophy CFL coach of year; joined World Football League as Birmingham coach 1974; coach Calgary Stampeders 1977; nine year CFL playing record 253 receptions for 4,317yds, 17.1 avg., 20 TDs; twice WFC all-star; *res.* Calgary, Alta.

GOULDING, George (track and field); *b.* 1885, England, *d.* 1966, Toronto, Ont.; *given name:* George Henry; on 1908 Olympic team as marathon runner, mile walker, 19th in marathon, fourth in walking; won 300 race victories at distances from 1-40 miles; won 1912 Stockholm Olympics 10 000m race in record 46:28.4; twice set world mile records including 6:25.8 at Eaton Games Hanlan's Point Toronto 1911; in many stunt races; won over 10 miles at Guelph Ont. against man driving horse and buggy; defeated four-man U S relay team in four mile N.Y. walk; covered eight and one-quarter miles in hour walk around Toronto Varsity oval; 1916 set record for seven miles, 50:40 at Rutgers U; mem. Canadian Sports Hall of Fame.

GRAHAM, Charles (boxing); *b.* 13 Mar 1896, Carlisle, Eng.; *m.* Ivy; *children:* two daughters; boxed and coached in England as amateur and pro; coached in Edmonton from 1954-73; guided champions in every division from flyweight to heavyweight except light middleweight; coached Marv Arneson in 1968 Olympics and to five Canadian titles, and Billie McGrandle, Edinburgh Empire Games titlist; mem. Alberta Amateur Sports Hall of Fame; *res.* Edmonton, Alta.

GRANT, Bud (football); *b.* 20 May 1927, Superior, Wisc.; *given name:* Harry Peter; *m.* Pat; *children:* five; U of Minnesota; football coach; two seasons pro basketball with Minneapolis Lakers; turned football pro with Philadelphia Eagles; joined Winnipeg Blue Bombers as offensive end 1953, topped WFC pass receivers three of four years played; three times WFC all-star; for a time held WFC record for receptions single season with 68; turned to coaching 1957 and remained with Blue Bombers 10 years posting 122 wins, 66 losses, three ties for .647 percentage; made playoffs eight seasons, league final eight times, Grey Cup final six times, won four; nickname The Iceman; coach Minnesota Vikings (NFL) guiding them to four Super Bowl appearances; U of Minnesota athlete of half century 1951; *res.* Minneapolis, Minn.

GRANT, Mike (hockey); *b.* 1870s, Montreal, Que., *d.* 1961 Montreal, Que.; captain Montreal Victorias, Stanley Cup 1894, 1896-98; played with Victorias in CAHL 1899-1900, 1902; Shamrocks 1901; retired to refereeing following 1902 season; mem. Hockey Hall of Fame.

GRANT, Tommy (football); *b.* 9 Jan 1935, Windsor, Ont.; *m.* Ida Gagnon; *children:* Colette, Lisa, Tommy Jr., Michelle; Patterson CI; car salesman; outstanding HS, junior (AKO) football career led to pro ranks Hamilton Tiger-Cats 1956 where he won EFC rookie of year, Gruen Trophy; played 14 seasons in CFL with Hamilton, Winnipeg as halfback; caught 329 passes for 6,542yds, 19.9 avg., 51 TDs; most productive season 1964 when he caught 44 passes for 1,029yds, 23.4 avg.; returned kickoff vs Montreal 105yds 1962; frequent all-star; one year pro baseball as outfielder in Detroit Tigers chain with Jamestown, Idaho Falls; *res.* Burlington, Ont.

GRAY, George (track and field); *b.* 1865, Coldwater, Ont.; *d.* 1933, Sault Ste. Marie, Ont.; Coldwater HS; At 1885 Canadian Amateur Athletic Association meet Toronto he put shot 41'5.5'' with first toss in first competition and won title, held it 17 years; acclaimed world champion; eldest brother John twice won two-oared rowing title of America; two cousins were rower Jake Gaudaur Sr., all-around athlete and track coach Harry Gill; world shot put record with 43'11'' 1887, held it through 1902, broke record several times himself; at retirement had won 188 medals, trophies for shot put; mem. Canadian Sports Hall of Fame.

GRAY, Herb (football); *b.* 12 Jun 1934, Baytown, Tex.; *given name:* Herbert William; *m.* Joy; *children:* James Kevin, Stephen Craig, Bryan David; Robert E. Lee HS, U of Texas, B.S.; sales executive; as HS athlete won all-district title three years, all-Southern, all-American in senior year; at U of Texas won all-Southwest Conference four years, lineman of year, all-American senior year; turned pro with Winnipeg Blue Bombers, all-star guard and end seven times, all-Canadian several times; defensive captain Blue Bombers nine years; played in Senior Bowl, Canadian and U S Shrine Games; in six Grey Cup finals, four winners; 1960 Schenley Award outstanding lineman in CFL; 1965 Dr. Bert Oja most valuable Bomber lineman award; *res.* San Antonio, Tex.

GRAVES, Richard (ski jumping); *b*. 22 Apr 1955, Montreal, Que.; *given name:* Richard MacFarlane; Gloucester HS, U of Guelph; student; at 14 junior B alpine racer, mem. Ottawa junior cross-country team; switched to jumping 1970; mem. Canadian national jumping team 1972, won junior championship 1972-73; runner-up U S juniors, third seniors 1973; 37th in world ski flying championships with 410ft Oberstdorf Germany 1973; 20th world junior Leningrad same year; flew 136m Ironwood 1973 tournament; 1974 finished 13th Grand Prix des Nations Cortina Italy, seventh Garmisch International, 13th Swiss Le Brassus; 1975 second North American plastic jumping championships, Canadian 70m, third Canadian 90m, 26th world ski flying, 22nd LeBrassus; 1976 won Canadian 70m, third 90m but overlooked in Canadian Olympic team selections; won O'Keefe international 1976; *res*. Ottawa, Ont.

GREEN, Art (football); *b*. 18 Sep 1949, Atlanta, Ga.; *m*. Adrine; Albany State College; pro football player, recreational director; in senior HS gained 1,400yds rushing and 26 TDs; MVP in college junior year; turned pro New Orleans Saints in NFL then to New York Jets; joined CFL with Ottawa Rough Riders 1973 as running back, led EFC rushers with 1,188yds 1975, Rider's MVP 1975; mem. 1973, 1976 Grey Cup winners; led EFC rushers 1976 with 1,257yds on 234 carries, 13 TDs while playing out option; signed with Philadelphia NFL 1977; *res*. Decatur, Ga.

GREEN, Ron (curling); *b*. 11 Apr 1947, Toronto, Ont.; *given name:* Ronald Lawrence; *m*. Lynda; *children:* Leslie; advertising sales representative; with Paul Savage won Ontario junior title 1966; with Bill Creber runner-up to London's Ken Buchan in 1969 Consols; with Savage won Ontario Consols, 1970, 1973, 1974, 1977, competed in Brier each time, runner-up 1970; won 1973, 1974 Royal Canadian carspiel; competed CBC Curling Classic 1973-74, 1975 Century Curling Classic Calgary; skipped own rink to 1976 Canada Life 'spiel title Toronto; all-star lead 1973-74 Briers; *res*. Agincourt, Ont.

GREEN, Shorty (hockey); *b*. 17 Jul 1896, Sudbury, Ont.; *d*. 19 Apr 1960; *given name:* Wilfred Thomas; began with Sudbury Intermediates in NOHA 1914-15; after WW1 joined Hamilton Tigers, won 1919 Allan Cup; returned to Sudbury until 1923; turned pro Hamilton Tigers 1923, won league title 1925 and, as captain, spokesman for players who refused to participate in playoffs unless club paid $200 per player; club owners refused and Toronto and Montreal were forced to meet for title; Hamilton franchise was shifted to N Y and Green scored first goal in Madison Square Garden Dec 1925; coached through 1933 before retiring; mem. Hockey Hall of Fame.

GREENE, Nancy (skiing); *b*. 11 May 1943, Ottawa, Ont.; *m*. Al Raine; *children:* twin sons Charles, William; began skiing at three; 22nd 1960 Squaw Valley downhill; seventh downhill, 15th slalom 1964 Innsbruck Olympics; 1967 World Cup, retained title 1968 adding Olympic giant slalom gold at Grenoble France; retired after Olympics; mem. Task Force on Canadian Sport for Federal government; prominent as sports ambassador; with husband (Canadian National Ski Team coach 1969-73) active in development of Brandywyne ski area near

B.C.'s Whistler Mountain; Canada's female athlete of year 1967, 1968; Lou Marsh Trophy Canada's top athlete 1968; mem. Canadian Sports Hall of Fame. *res.* Rossland, B.C.

GREENSHIELDS, Henry (canoeing); *b.* 25 Aug 1898, Montreal, Que.; *given name:* Henry Clifton; *m.* Edith Florence Aslin; *children:* Ian; retired, Eaton's Ltd; winner Dominion senior singles, senior tandem titles 1923; represented Canada 1924 Paris Olympics; life mem. Montreal Amateur Athletic Association, Longueuil Boating Club; *res.* Piedmont, Que.

GREGOIRE, Hélène (water-skiing); *b.* 10 Mar 1953, Hull, Que.; *given name:* Hélène Madeleine; U of Montreal; dental student; dominated girls' division Canadian championships 1969-70, gold medal slalom, jumping, tricks; joined national team 1970, represented Canada in Group One Pan-Am Games Mexico; 1972 Canadian title, bronze Group One jumping; fourth jumping 1973 world Bogota Colombia, three gold Can-Am competition, Canadian championship; gold 1974 Canadian jumping championships, silver slalom, tricks, combined; fourth slalom, jumping, seventh tricks 1974 California World Cup; repeated 1975 Canadian championships; overall champion Canadian finals with gold jumping, tricks, combined, silver slalom; fifth jumping, sixth combined world championships; gold 1976 Canadian finals jumping, silver slalom, tricks, combined; gold jumping, slalom, combined, silver tricks 1976 Can-Am; Gilles O. Julien French Canadian amateur athlete of year 1970; water-skiing sports merit award 1974 from Quebec Sports Federation; as alpine skier won gold 1969 Canadian junior championships giant slalom; *res.* Hull, Que.

GRIFFIN, Audrey (swimming); *b.* 16 Jun 1902, Burgess Hill, Sussex, Eng.; *given name:* Audrey Mildred; *m.* John Russell Kieran; St. Anne's Academy; from 1915-30 held Canadian, Pacific Northwest titles and never lost a B.C. women's championship entered; won Victoria mixed three mile swims nine times in 12 attempts; mem. B.C. Sports Hall of Fame; *res.* Victoria, B.C.

GRIFFING, Dean (football); *b.* 1910, Council Grove, Ka.; *m.* Bea Metcalfe: *children:* three; Kansas State U; played centre Chicago Cardinals 1935; to Regina 1936, won title but CRU eligibility rules were allegedly broken so forfeited Grey Cup challenge; nickname Bad Man; three times all-Canadian centre; Saskatchewan team player-coach through 1943 before joining Toronto Balmy Beach as player-line coach 1944; coach Calgary 1945-47; manager Riders 1954-56; briefly manager Denver Broncos (AFL); mem. Canadian Football Hall of Fame; *res.* Plano, Ill.

GRIFFIS, Si (hockey); *b.* 1883, Onaga, Kansas, *d.* Jul 1950, Kenora, Ont.; *given name:* Silas Seth; rover, defence for Rat Portage (Kenora) Thistles 1903-07; retired following 1907 season, returned 1912-18 with Vancouver Millionaires (PCHA); helped Kenora claim league titles 1900-04, Stanley Cup 1906; captained Millionaires to Stanley Cup final 1915; nickname Sox; as oarsman, stroked junior fours to Canadian Henley title 1905; mem. Hockey Hall of Fame.

GRIFFITH, Harry (coaching); *b.* 19 Sep 1878, Hamilton, Ont.; *d.* 9 Dec 1960, Toronto, Ont.; *given name:* Henry Crawford; *m.* Ethel Clare Wright; *children:* son and daughter; Ridley College, Trinity College,

B.A., M.A.; educator; quarterback varsity football team; coached Trinity College 1907-10 to two consecutive Grey Cup victories; returned to Ridley 1911, coached rugby, cricket until retirement 1949; mem. Canadian Football Hall of Fame.

GRINNELL, Rae (skiing); *b.* 24 Apr 1921, Toronto, Ont.; *m.* Betty Heron; *children:* Eric, Jane, Douglas, Sheila; Riverdale CI, U of New Brunswick, B.Sc.F.; forest economist; won zone, provincial, CIAU titles; developed ski clubs in several areas of Canada; Ontario Zone, Division pres. CASA 12 years, national pres. 1961-64; first Canadian, second North American on FIS Council 1963-71; involved with National Ski Museum; executive mem., v.-pres. Canadian Amateur Sports Federation eight years; *res.* Manotick, Ont.

GROARKE, Louis (track); *b.* 18 Jul 1953, London, Eng.; Colorado State U, B.A., U of British Columbia; student; Canadian junior 3000m title, Canadian record 8:27 in 1970; second Canadian 5000m championships 1973, 1975, both Canadian Olympic trials 1976; B.C., Alberta cross-country titles 1976; fifth Canadian cross-country 1976; won Western Canada games 10 000m 1975, eight mile Chandler Road Race 1976; outstanding cross-country runner Colorado State 1971-74; Alberta T & F athlete of year 1975; *res.* Calgary, Alta.

GROUT, Cameron (swimming); *b.* 23 Oct 1939, Montreal, Que.; *m.* Marsha Leigh Beaton; *children:* Christi, Robin; McGill U, B.Sc., investment dealer; holder of 21 national swim titles in various categories; medalist British Empire Games, Cardiff Wales 1958, Chicago Pan-Am Games 1959; finalist Rome Olympics 1960; coach Montreal Amateur Athletic Association 1963-64; Quebec all-star team 1964; director Quebec section Canadian Amateur Swimming Association 1964-65, Nova Scotia section 1973-75; pres. Nova Scotia section CASA 1970-72; national director CASA 1973-75; first pres. Sport Nova Scotia 1970-73; director Olympic Club of Canada 1973-75, pres. 1973-74; director Canadian Olympic Association 1974; director Sport Federation of Canada 1972-73; chairman Nova Scotia Kinsmen Special Olympics 1973; Province of Nova Scotia award of recognition for sport and recreation administration 1975; honorary life mem. Sport Nova Scotia; Canadian swimmer of year 1958-59; Montreal athlete of year 1958-59; outstanding athlete McGill U 1958; mem. Montreal AAA Hall of Fame; *res.* Oakville, Ont.

GROUT, Glen (diving); *b.* 31 May 1952, N. Vancouver; Simon Fraser U; student; junior Canadian 1m, 3m springboard titles 1969; gold 3m 1972 winter nationals; bronze 2m, silver 10m 1973 summer nationals; silver 10m 1973 winter nationals; gold 10m 1975 winter nationals; represented Canada 1973, 1975 world, 1974 Commonwealth, 1976 Olympics; competed in Canada Cup, GDR, Mexican meets; *res.* Vancouver, B.C.

GUEST, Jack (rowing); *b.* 28 Mar 1906, Montreal, Que., d. 12 Jun, 1972, Toronto, Ont.; *given name:* John Schofield; *m.* Mary Macdonald; *children:* John Jr., Donald; Central HS of Commerce; business executive; won junior and association singles St. Catharines 1927; joined Argonaut junior eights under coach Joe Wright Sr., twice lost to Joe Wright Jr. in diamond sculls competition 1928-29; with Joe Jr. won 1928 Olympics silver in double sculls; won Canadian single sculls 1929; defeated Boetzeler, German champion, by nearly 200yds to win 1930 diamond sculls; retired from competition 1930; Don Rowing Club pres. 1938-52; pres. Dominion Day Regatta Association 1946-56; pres. Canadian Association of Amateur Oarsmen 1955-56; director Canadian Olympic Association 1960-68; manager Canadian rowing team 1956 Melbourne Olympics; assistant manager Canadian rowing teams British Empire Games 1962, 1966; first Canadian elected to governing body of world rowing (FISA) 1969; mem. Canadian Sports Hall of Fame.

GURNEY, Jack   (football); *b.* 9 Apr 1923, Brantford, Ont.; *given name:* John Thomas; *m.* Doreen Melba Shaw; *children:* Diane Charlene, Elizabeth Ann; Brantford CI, McMaster U, B.A.; Bell Canada management; refereed all levels of basketball to college level since 1942; officiated minor league football 1944-52, all leagues through college level 1952-73, since 1973 OUAA referee-in-chief; *res.* Ottawa, Ont.

GUROWKA, Joe   (curling); *b.* 28 Apr 1933, The Pas, Man.; *m.* Shirley Young; *children:* Jim, Kim; U of Manitoba, B.Sc., U of Western Ontario, M.B.A.; civil engineer, general manager; represented Dixie Curling Club in provincial playdown competition 18 years; nine times finalist Ontario Consols, won provincial title twice, runner-up 1966 Brier; Canada Life bonspiel champion 1969, won various competitions throughout Southern Ontario; *res.* Mississauga, Ont.

GURR, Donna-Marie   (swimming); *b.* 18 Feb 1955, Vancouver, B.C.; student; five gold 1969 British national; four gold, one silver Canadian nationals and five gold, one silver Canada Summer Games Halifax; silver, two bronze in backstroke 1970 Edinburgh Commonwealth Games; three gold 100m, 200m backstroke, 400m medley relay, silver 4x100m freestyle 1971 Pan-Am Games Cali Colombia; bronze 200m backstroke 1972 Munich Olympics; silver 100m backstroke, bronze 200m backstroke 1974 Commonwealth Games Christchurch N.Z.; 1969-72 Barber Trophy for Canadian 100m backstroke championship; *res.* Vancouver, B.C.

GWYNNE, Lefty   (boxing); *b.* 5 Oct 1912, Toronto, Ont.; *given name:* Horace; *m.* Henrietta; *children:* John, Gordon, Larry; retired, recreation centre employee; gold medal 118lb bantamweight Los Angeles Olympics 1932; pro bantamweight competitor 1935-39; pro Canadian bantamweight title 1938, retired undefeated 1939; 26 years jockey, trainer, jockey's agent; mem. Canadian Boxing, Sports Hall of Fame; *res:* Waubaushene, Ont.

HAHN, Robin (equestrian); *b.* 19 Jun 1933, Regina, Sask.; *m.* Maureen; *children:* Apryl, Amber, Jaysen; U of British Columbia; farmer; has shown horses in Western Canada since age 17; represented Canada three-day event 1967, 1971 Pan-Am Games, 1968, 1972, 1976 Olympics; fifth 1967 Pan-Am Games three-day aboard Warden; ninth 1968 Olympics aboard Taffy; won 1969 Canadian three-day event trials, 1970, 1972 Canadian three-day title; *res.* Belle Plaine, Sask.

HAINSWORTH, George (hockey); *b.* 26 Jun 1895, Toronto, Ont.; *d.* 9 Oct 1950; played goal Kitchener juniors, Allan Cup 1918; turned pro with Saskatoon 1923-24; joined Montreal Canadiens 1926-27, remained in NHL 11 seasons; Vezina trophy first three seasons with Canadiens; during 1928-29 campaign allowed just 43 goals in 44-game schedule, posted 22 shutouts as team won 22 games; traded to Toronto Maple Leafs for Lorne Chabot in early 30s, retired midway through 1936-37 season; mem. Hockey Hall of Fame.

HAIST, Jane (track and field); *b.* 1 Mar 1949, Thornhill, Ont.; Pelham HS, York U; student; represented Canada 1974 Commonwealth games, won gold medals, established Canadian, Commonwealth records shot put and discus; bronze medal discus 1975 Pan-Am Games; 1975 Canadian record 60.70m for discus vs Sweden; 11th with 59.78m 1976 Montreal Olympics; best shot performance 16.15m 1974 Cardiff Wales; Rowell Trophy as outstanding Canadian amateur athlete in jumping, weight events 1974; *res.* St. Laurent, Que.

HALDER, Wally (hockey, tennis); *b.* 15 Sep 1925, Toronto, Ont.; *given name:* Wallace Edwin; *m.* Joyce; *children:* Gregory, Christina, Matthew; U of Toronto, B.A., O.C.E.; pres. Olympic Trust; captain U of T hockey team; mem. 1948 Olympic gold medal hockey team; swimming, diving instructor Ontario Athletic Commission; coach U of T, Trinity College hockey teams; Canadian senior doubles tennis champion; represented Canada on Gordon Trophy tennis teams; Biggs Trophy U of T; *res.* Toronto, Ont.

HALL, Glenn (hockey); *b.* 3 Oct 1931, Humboldt, Sask.; *given name:* Glenn Henry; *m.* Pauline Patrick; *children:* Patrick, Leslie, Tammy, Lindsay; Humboldt HS; farmer; centred, captained PS team then shifted to goal age 10; two years juvenile, one year Humboldt junior Indians before attending Detroit Red Wings camp at 15 and being assigned to Windsor Spitfires juniors, MVP; turned pro Indianapolis AHL 1952; Edmonton 1953-55 with brief stints Detroit until becoming regular 1956; led league with 12 shutouts 1956-57; helped Wings win 1957 Prince of Wales Trophy; dealt with Ted Lindsay to Chicago Black Hawks for John Wilson, Forbes Kennedy, Bill Preston, Hank

Bassen 1957; helped Hawks win 1961 Stanley Cup; drafted by St. Louis Blues 1967; retired following 1970-71 season; five times led NHL in shutouts; three times Vezina Trophy winner; Calder rookie of year; Conn Smythe Trophy; seven times first team, four times second team all-star; in 18 NHL seasons appeared in 891 games, including 552 in succession, allowing 2,239 goals for 2.51 avg., 84 shutouts; 113 playoff games, 321 goals, 2.79 avg., six shutouts; 13 all-star games, 27 periods, 22 goals for .81 avg.; mem. Hockey Hall of Fame; *res.* Stony Plain, Alta.

HALL, Joe (hockey); *b.* 3 May 1882, Staffordshire, Eng., *d.* 5 Apr 1919, Seattle, Wash.; *given name:* Joseph Henry; hockey player; played with Winnipeg Rowing Club and Rat Portage until turning pro 1905-06 with Kenora; with Quebec Bulldogs 1910-16 won Stanley Cup twice; finished career with Montreal Canadiens winning NHA title 1918-19, to Seattle for Stanley Cup; influenza epidemic ended series and took Hall's life; mem. Hockey Hall of Fame.

HALL-HOLLAND, Kelly (equestrian); *b.* 10 Jan 1951, London, Ont.; *m.* Richard K. Hodge; Neuchâtel, U Western Ontario; chartered accountant; 1974 won 16 ribbons including the only first for Canada against international teams from Germany, U.K., US and Mexico; three firsts on Regardez, two on R.S.V.P. in Royal Winter Fair open jumper; international junior honors 1968; won CNE jumper sweepstakes, CNE and Sutton open jumper, Rothmans, Quebec, Hamilton, Aurora Grand Prix; twice leading rider at Hornby; other horses: Paynester, Raffles IV, Reserve, Raffles, Dutch Harlem; TV commentator 1976 Olympics; *res.* London, Ont.

HALTER, G. Sydney (football); *b.* 18 Apr 1905, Winnipeg, Man.; U of Manitoba, B.A., LL.B.; lawyer; with Frank Hannibal, Joe Ryan helped reorganize Winnipeg football club; pres. Amateur Athletic Union of Canada 1938-46; deputy commissioner WIFU 1952, commissioner 1953; key role in amalgamation of WIFU and Eastern Big Four Leagues; registrar Canadian Football Council 1956; Canada's first national football commissioner 1958, retired 1966; chairman Manitoba Horse Racing Commission 1965-75; mem. AAU of C, Canadian Football Halls of Fame; *res.* Winnipeg, Man.

HAMILTON, Jack (administration); *b.* 11 Jun 1886, Caledonia, Ont.; *d.* 5 Aug 1976, Regina, Sask.; *given name:* John Welch; *m.* Elsie White Greason; *children:* Donald, Hugh; general-manager lumber company; organized construction of 3,500 seat hockey rink Saskatoon 1918; coached Regina Vics hockey club 20s, later club pres.; Sask. Amateur Hockey Association pres. 1925-27; CAHA pres. 1930; involved in football administration as secretary Regina Roughriders 1923-27, pres. WIFU 1928; pres. Sask. branch CAAU several years, national pres. 1937; headed Queen City Gardens Co. which raised funds to install artificial ice in Regina hockey rink, operated rink 11 years; headed operation to construct 3,500-seat rink in Moose Jaw 1957; numerous honors from world of sport, business community, nation; King George VI coronation medal for work on behalf of athletics; Jack Hamilton rink in Regina; Regina Optimist sportsman of year; CAHA medal of merit; honorary life mem. SAHA; mem. Sask., AAU of C, Canadian Sports Halls of Fame.

HAMMOND, Alvin (hockey, track); *b.* 1892, North Dakota; *given name:* Richard Alvin; *m.* Grace Wood; *children:* Richard

Alvin Jr., Margery; retired salesman; all-around track athlete, won Saskatchewan titles in 100, 220, 440yds sprints, running broad jump, hop, step and jump; titles in these events three times in Saskatoon, Regina, Moose Jaw, once Swift Current; represented Sask. three times in Olympic trials; played hockey with Victoria club, 1914 world amateur title Regina; mem. Sask. Sports Hall of Fame; *res.* Regina, Sask.

HAMMOND, Gord (lacrosse); *b.* 5 Mar 1926, Toronto, Ont.; *m.* Yvonne Burnie; *children:* Bob, Joanne, Abbie, Nola, Steve, Ken; Parkdale CI, Ryerson Polytechnical Inst.; buildings manager; played minor lacrosse age 10 with St. Vincents through 1942 with St. John's Toronto, Mimico Ontario CYO, OLA midget champions; senior A lacrosse with Mimico Brampton 1943, Mimico 1944, Orillia 1946, 1952-53; won Ontario title 1943, Eastern Canadian 1952; intermediate lacrosse Orillia 1947, 1949, Midland 1948, Alliston 1950-55; switched to refereeing 1956-64; secretary, treasurer, referee-in-chief OLA 1964-67; with CLA since 1967 as secretary-treasurer, v.-pres., pres.; governor Lacrosse Hall of Fame; helped reactivate international competition dormant since 1928 with 1967 world tournament Toronto, 1974 Australian tour; hockey with Toronto Navy juniors 1943-44, Orillia Terriers senior B 1947-49; refereed in OHA 1950-60; Alliston MVP 1950; OLA Mr. Lacrosse award 1967; CLA Lester B. Pearson Award 1976; *res.* London, Ont.

HANLAN, Ned (rowing); *b.* 12 Jul 1855, Toronto, Ont.; *d.* 4 Jan 1908, Toronto, Ont.; *m.* Margaret Gordon Sutherland; *children:* two sons, six daughters; pro oarsman, politician; first major win U S centennial singles Philadelphia 1876; beat Wallace Ross Saint John N.B. 1877 for Canadian title; beat Eph Morris 1878 for U S title; by 1879, Boy in Blue, nickname referred to rowing outfit, was North American rowing king; first oarsman to master sliding seat; world rowing title six years before losing to Australian William Beach 1884; retired from racing 1901; one end of Toronto Island re-christened Hanlan's Point; town in Australia named in his honor; 20ft statue erected in his memory 1926 at CNE; in over 350 races lost only six; Toronto alderman; mem. Canadian Sports Hall of Fame.

HANSEN, Ina (curling); *b.* 7 Nov 1920, Boissevaine, Man.; *given name:* Georgina Rutherford; *m.* Alvin Hansen; *children:* Lynn Vernon, Joanne Candace; U of Saskatchewan; city clerk; first major victory 1950 playing third on Rossland Nelson Cup winner, grand aggregate in East-West Kootenay competition; represented Kootenays in B.C. provincial play 12 consecutive years, 18 in total; seven times provincial champion, three times Canadian titlist, runner-up twice; once beat men's world champion Lyall Dagg rink; represented East Kootenay as zone convenor; B.C. Ladies' Curling Association executive officer 1955-57, pres. 1957; junior delegate to Western Ladies' Curling Association 1958, senior delegate 1959; B.C. delegate in establishment of Canadian championships; director WCLCA; B.C. title 1971, second to Sask. in Canadian final playoff; playing third for Ada Calles won Canadian senior ladies 1973, runner-up 1974, 1975, third 1976; among first women named to Canadian Curling Hall of Fame 1975; *res.* Kimberley, B.C.

HANSEN, Warren (curling); *b.* 15 Feb 1943, Edmonton, Alta.; *given name:* Warren Richard; Northern Alberta Institute of

Technology; telecommunications technician, sports promotions; offensive guard with Edmonton Huskies 1962-64 Canadian junior football champions; briefly with Edmonton Eskimos 1965; coached junior football seven years; began curling at 14 reaching provincial finals 1961; joined Hec Gervais' rink 1972 as second, won Brier 1974 London Ont.; with Jim Pettapiece formed Silver Broom Curling School 1972 now nationwide; 1974 director Canadian Curling Association instructor training program; *res* Edmonton, Alta.

HANSON, Fritzie (football); *b.* 1912, Perhan, Minn.; *given name:* Melvin; Perhan HS, Dakota State U; joined Winnipeg Blue Bombers 1935; in Grey Cup game vs Hamilton ran back punts for over 300yds on seven returns, including spectacular 78yd TD run through entire Hamilton team; Hanson's achievements over next decade established East-West rivalry which has made the annual Grey Cup clash a focal point of Canadian unity; mem. Canadian Football Hall of Fame; *res.* Calgary, Alta.

HARE, William (shooting); *b.* 14 May 1935, Ottawa, Ont.; *given name:* William Edward; *m.* Frances; Lisgar CI, Carleton U, B.A., Queen's U, B.D.; United Church minister; pistol specialist, competed world shooting championships 1962, 1970, 1974, Pan-Am Games 1963, 1967, 1971, 1975, team silver 1963, 1971; fourth overall 1967 Canada Winter Games; Ontario handgun title 1970; competed national handgun finals 1965-71, Olympics 1964, 1968, 1972; gold medal team standard pistol, silver team air pistol 1973 Confederation of Americas shoot; gold medal rapid fire 1974 Commonwealth Games; chairman handgun section SFC 1969-72, SFC director 1973-76; *res.* Renfrew, Ont.

HARRINGTON, Ed (football); *b.* 8 Feb 1941, Speer, Okla.; *given name:* Edison Dean; *m.* Alda Yvonne Moore; *children:* Wendy, Dusti Lia; Langston U, B.Sc.; investigator for ombudsman; Oklahoma state weightlifting titles 1960-62; turned pro Houston Oilers 1962, joined Toronto Argos as offensive guard 1963; EFC all-star 1964; joined Toronto Rifles of Continental League 1965, returned to Argos 1967-71; three times all-Eastern, all-Canadian; *res.* West Hill, Ont.

HARRIS, Lesley (badminton); *b.* 18 Oct 1954, Kuala Lumpur, Malaya; *given name:* Lesley Elizabeth; Trafalgar School, McGill U; student; Canadian junior singles, doubles badminton titles 1973-74; Canadian ladies' singles finalist 1975; mem. Uber Cup team 1975 semifinalist Indonesia; bronze medal ladies' singles 1971 Canada Winter Games; as tennis player teamed with Mila Zaruba to win 1971 girls-18 Canadian doubles; *res.* Montreal, Que.

HARRIS, Wayne (football); *b.* 4 May 1938, Hampton, Ark.; *given name:* Carrol Wayne; *m.* Anne Dearth; *children:* Wayne Jr., Heather Wynelle, Andrew Cooper; U of Arkansas; manager sales and contracts drilling and exploration co.; began football career as linebacker, guard Eldorado junior HS, all-State 1952-53; HS all-State 1955-56, all-Southern, all-American 1956; Arkansas HS all-star game outstanding lineman 1956; attended U of Arkansas on scholarship 1957-60; all-Southwest Conference 1959-60; all-American 1960; Houston *Post* award outstanding Southwest Conference player; Arkansas, Louisiana, Texas athlete of year 1960; played in 1960 all-American Bowl, Cotton Bowl, 1959 Gator Bowl; Arkansas Association Neil Gibson Martin Victory

Trophy 1960; drafted by Boston Patriots; turned pro Calgary Stampeders 1961; played 12 seasons CFL with Calgary; all-Western Conference 11 times, all-Canadian nine times; four times Schenley outstanding lineman, once runner-up; played in three Grey Cups, one winner; outstanding player 1971 Grey Cup; Demarco-Becket trophy winner; Calgary athlete of year 1967; twice most popular player award; twice Calgary Stampeder president's award; sweater No. 55 retired by club on Wayne Harris Day 1973; roasted by CFL Player's Association 1976; coached junior football 1973; HS football 1975-76; mem. Canadian Football Hall of Fame; *res.* Calgary, Alta.

HARTLEY, Errol (field hockey); *b.* 16 Mar 1940, Allahabad, India; *given name:* Errol Patrick; *m.* Patricia Ann; *children:* Adrian Christopher; London U, P.Eng., M.I.E.E., B.Sc.; engineer; represented B.C. four consecutive interprovincial title-winning teams 1968-71; coached B.C. to 1972 interprovincial title; coached Canada to bronze medal 1971 Pan-Am Games, silver 1975 Pan-Am Games; coach Canadian national team on all tours since 1970; coached 1976 Olympic team to 10th place; *res.* West Vancouver, B.C.

HARTMAN, Barney (shooting); *b.* 2 Nov 1916, Swan River, Man.; *m.* Joahanna; *children:* Shelley Jo-Anne; sales promotion; considered world's greatest skeet shooter; from 1957 10 times captain of NSSA all-American skeet team; four times scored perfect 100x100 with 410 gauge; won nearly 30 world titles in 12 gauge, 20 gauge, 28 gauge, 410 gauge and all-around categories; 1966 missed only five of 400 setting world record .9875 avg. with 410; 1968 established world record .9991 avg., 1,049 of 1,050 targets in 12 gauge (mark broken 1971 by U S marksman with perfect 1.000); 1969 shot record .9980, 499 of 500, with 28 gauge; 1971 broke 599 of 600 for .9983 20 gauge avg. breaking own 1958 record of .9950; 1966-73 avg. .99038 in all-around category; once broke string of 2,002 clay targets without a miss; wrote 1967 instruction book *Hartman on Skeet; res.* Brownsburg, Que.

HARTZELL, Irene (swimming); *b.* 19 Oct 1922, Winnipeg, Man.; *m.* Dr. George D. Athans; *children:* George Jr., Greg, Gary; during 40's won Manitoba breast stroke title, established Canadian record; Manitoba synchronized swimming title four consecutive years; competed nationally both sports; *res.* Kelowna, B.C.

HARVEY, Doug (hockey); *b.* 19 Dec 1924, Montreal, Que.; *given name:* Douglas Norman; *m.* Ursula; *children:* five; Gilson HS; two seasons Border Baseball League with Ottawa, led league hitters with .351 one season; rejected offers from Boston Braves, entered pro hockey with Canadiens 1947-61; seven times Norris Trophy winner, 10 times first, once second team all-star defenceman; NY Rangers 1961-64, Detroit 1966-67, St. Louis Blues 1968-69, frequent minor league stints; coach Rangers 1961-62; played on six Stanley Cup winners with Habs; mem. Montreal Royals Allan Cup winner; mem. Hockey Hall of Fame; *res.* Montreal, Que.

HAUCH, Paul (swimming); *b.* 27 Dec 1903, Tokyo, Japan; *m.* Marion Louise Bole; *children:* Jon, Bill; Kitchener HS, U of Western Ontario, M.D., Royal College of Physicians and Surgeons, D.M.R.(D.); radiologist; captain UWO football team 1931; first recipient G. Howard Ferguson award as UWO outstanding athlete, scholar; captain

UWO basketball team 1929, swim team 1932; runner-up freshman tennis champion Northwestern U 1925; swim coach London YMCA 1946-73; pres. Ontario section CASA 1945-59, secretary 1959-68; v.-pres. ASUA 1959; director-v.-pres. COA, chairman medical advisory committee 1960-69; mem. COA 1969-76; mem. technical swim committee FINA 1956-68, mem. FINA bureau 1968-72, honorary secretary FINA 1972-76; Air Canada amateur sports executive of year 1967; Ontario Athletic Commission award 1968; mem. National Fitness Advisory Council 1965-66; manager, physician three Canadian Olympic teams; Centennial medal 1967; *res.* London, Ont.

HAWKINS, John   (track and field); *b.* 8 Jun 1949, Kelowna, B.C.; *given name:* Francis John Alexander; Courtney HS, U of British Columbia, B.P.E.; student; high jump specialist; B.C. midget title 1964 with 5'6''; juvenile title 1965 with 6'1''; won B.C. junior 1967 with 6'1'' 1967; switched from scissor jump to Fosbury Flop, first Canadian to clear 7' Seattle 1971; Commonwealth Games silver 1970 with 6'11½'' scissors style; fourth 1971 Pan-Am Games, same year second Italy, Germany establishing Canadian records; 1972 Canadian indoor title, second in Olympic trials, ninth Olympics with 2.15m; 1973 WCIAU, Pan-Pacific Games titles tying Canadian record 2.18m, bronze World University Games Moscow, silver Canadian championships; fifth 1974 Commonwealth Games; injury in 1975 curtailed activity with best showing 2.14m; mem. 1970 CIAU basketball champions World Student Games Italy 1970; B.C. athlete of year 1971; *res.* Courtenay, B.C.

HAWLEY, Sandy   (horse racing); *b.* 16 Apr 1949, Oshawa, Ont.; *given name:* Sanford Desmond; *m.* Sherrie; jockey; in HS runner-up Ont. 96lb wrestling title; began pro riding career 1968 with four wins; Canada's leading jockey 1969 with 230 victories, retained Canadian riding honors each year since; North American riding title 1970 with 452 wins, repeat 1972-73; surpassed Bill Shoemaker's 1953 record of 485 winners with 515 victory total 1973 (Chris McCarran ahead 1974 with 547); four times Queen's Plate winner, five times Canadian Oaks; at 27 youngest jockey to ride 3,000 winners 1976; fourth North American riding title in six years with 413 winners 1976; lifetime winning percentage 25.6 best in the sport; mem. Order of Canada; Lou Marsh Trophy twice, U S racing's Eclipse Award; mem. Canadian Sports Hall of Fame; *res.* Mississauga, Ont.

HAY, George   (hockey); *b.* 10 Jan 1898, Listowel, Ont., *d.* 13 Jul 1975, Stratford, Ont.; *given name:* George William; began hockey in Winnipeg with Junior Monarchs 1915-16, joined Regina Vics 1920-21; turned pro with Regina Caps, scored 87 goals, 57 assists in four years; moved to Portland Rosebuds, scored 18 goals before being sold to Chicago; Detroit for 1927-28 season; with Cougars led with 22 goals, 13 assists, named to coaches' dream team as left winger on line with Howie Morenz and Bill Cook, King Clancy and Eddie Shore on defence, Roy Worters in goal; retired following 1933 season having scored 73 goals, 54 assists in NHL play; mem. Hockey Hall of Fame.

HAYES, Cheryl   (swimming); *b.* 18 Dec 1958, Saskatoon, Sask.; *given name:* Cheryl Lynn; Saskatoon HS; deaf since birth, won swimming honors since 14; began competitive swimming 1969 as mem. Saskatoon Kinsmen Goldfins Swim Club; represented Canada 12th Games for Deaf Malmo Sweden 1973, silver in butterfly, bronze 400 individual medley; represented Canada first Pan-Am Games for Deaf Maracaibo Venezuela 1975, won four gold, 100m backstroke, 100m butterfly, 100m breast stroke, 100m freestyle, silver 200m backstroke; world records for 50m pool 100m butterfly (1:15.89), 100m backstroke (1:19.11), 200m individual medley (2:47.3); coached by Harry Bailey; Saskatoon Goldfin Swim Club most valuable swimmer 1976; *res:* Saskatoon, Sask.

HAYES, George (hockey); *b.* 7 Sep 1920, Montreal, Que.; *given name:* George William; *m.* Judy; *children:* Bill, George Jr., Susan; H.B. Beal THS; retired hockey official, freelance writer; junior hockey Ingersoll, Woodstock Ont., in baseball played outfield, first base with Stratford, Ingersoll, Woodstock, Tillsonburg teams; played football Woodstock Ontario junior champions 1936; began refereeing rural, minor hockey 1940; NHL debut as linesman 1946; remained 19 seasons as referee, linesman officiating in 1,549 league and 149 playoff games; *res.* Ingersoll, Ont.

HAYES, John (soccer); *b.* 25 Mar 1913, Belfast, Northern Ireland, *d.* 3 Sep 1974, Saskatoon, Sask.; *given name:* John Fielding; *m.* Doris Roegele; *children:* Faye, Brian, Cheryl; railway carman; played with Sons of England to 1932, Saskatoon Thistles 1933-35, Legion Sons 1937-47, Saskatoon Ahepa 1948-49; won Sask. Shield 1949; with Saskatoon Legionnaires 1950-51, won Sask. Shield each year; with Saskatoon Thistles 1952-53, Sask. Shield 1952, runner-up 1953; with Saskatoon United 1954-60, Sask. Shield 1955, 1959, runner-up 1956-58; played goal against touring Charlton Athletic 1937, Corinthians 1940, Tottenham Hotspur 1952; coached Mayfair Rangers to three provincial junior titles and became permanent possessor

of *Star-Phoenix* Trophy, later returned it to league for annual competition; coached Westmount United to provincial midget honors 1962 and Westmount PS to Saskatoon city title 1962-63; coached Mount Royal CI to 11-0-1 record and city, provincial title 1965, repeat 1966 with 12-0; repeated city, provincial title wins MRCI 1971; played with Shamrock Rovers 1966-67, Saskatoon United (indoors) 1972; played goal for Saskatoon United broomball team 1954-73, city title seven successive years; medal, trophy Saskatoon Soccer Association for 25 years of playing, coaching 1955; trophy in his honor awarded by Saskatoon United to city HS champions since 1975; mem. Sask. Sports Hall of Fame.

HAYMAN, Lew (football); *b.* 30 Sep 1908, Paterson, N.J.; *given name:* Lewis Edward; *m.* Joan; New York Military Academy, Syracuse U; football executive; came to Canada 1932 to join Warren Stevens as U of T coach; coach Toronto Argos 1933 guiding them to Grey Cup victory, repeat 1937, 1938; coached RCAF Hurricanes to 1942 national title; after war became part owner, chief executive Montreal Alouettes 1946, Grey Cup champions 1949, general manager through 1954; moved to Toronto Argos 1957; coached five Grey Cup winners, first at age 25; CFL pres. 1949-50; responsible for several CFL firsts, televised games, night games, Sunday games, break in color bar; mem. Canadian Football Hall of Fame; *res.* Toronto, Ont.

HAYWARD, Bob (speedboat racing); *b.* 27 Oct 1928, Embro, Ont., *d.* 10 Sep 1961, Detroit River, Mich.; joined Jim Thompson's Miss Supertest hydroplane crew as mechanic 1957, as driver 1959 won St. Clair international trophy; upset Maverick 1959 in record

104.098 mph to break 30-year US hold on Harmsworth Trophy; successfully defended title 1960, 1961 establishing 116.464 mph record 1960; killed driving Miss Supertest 11 in Detroit River Silver Cup race; Thompson retired from racing and Miss Supertest 111 was enshrined in Canadian Sports Hall of Fame at CNE grounds; Hayward awarded 1960 Sport Medal of Honor by Union of International Motor Boating of Ghent Belgium; mem. Canadian Sports Hall of Fame.

HEANEY, Brian (basketball); *b.* 9 Mar 1946, Brooklyn, N.Y.; *m.* Liana Hynes; *children:* Pamela Jane, Jennifer Christine, Brian Niles; Acadia U, B.Sc.; head coach Canadian women's national basketball team; at Acadia 1965-69 established eight all-time scoring records including 74 points single game, 52 in one-half, single season scoring avg. 34.5; turned pro Baltimore Bullets (NBA) 1969-70; combined NY HS teaching career with pro play Sunbury Mercs (EPBL) 1970; as starting guard avg. 19.5 points-per-game, 26 in playoffs; head coach St. Mary's U 1971; only person to win CIAU championship as player (1965) and coach (1973); coached team to title 1973, national finals 1974-75; Canadian college coach of year 1973; coached women's national team 1976 Olympics; *res.* Halifax, N.S.

HEAP, Alan (table tennis); *b.* 10 Mar 1947, Bolton, Lancashire, Eng.; Hull U, Eng., B.A., McMaster U, M.A.; teacher; British Universities champion 1966, 1968, 1969; Lancashire Closed champion 1972; mem. Ontario provincial team 1974-76; semifinalist Canadian Closed championships 1975; National Capital Open champion 1973, 1976; semifinalist, finalist numerous Ontario and Quebec Open tournaments 1972-76; *res.* Toronto, Ont.

HEBENTON, Andy (hockey); *b.* 3 Oct 1929, Winnipeg, Man.; *given name:* Andrew Alex; *m.* Gael; *children:* Clayton, Theresa; five years with Victoria Cougars in Western League before Muzz Patrick acquired him for NY Rangers, missed only three games in 280 team played; joined Rangers 1955, established NHL record playing in 630 consecutive league games scoring 189 goals, 202 assists for 391 points, plus 22 playoff games, six goals, five assists, 11 points; played with Rangers 1955-63, Boston 1963-64, then to minors with Portland Buckaroos, frequent all-star, twice Fred J. Hume Trophy as WHL most gentlemanly player; runner-up NHL rookie of year 1956; Lady Byng Trophy 1957; Rangers Players' Prize.

HEES, George (football); *b.* 17 Jun 1910, Toronto, Ont.; *m.* Mabel Dunlop; *children:* Catherine, Martha, Roslyn; Royal Military College, U of Toronto, Cambridge U; politician; played with Toronto Argos 1934 and again with Grey Cup championship team 1938; Progressive Conservative MP since 1950; Minister of Transport 1957-60, Minister Trade and Commerce 1960-63; *res.* Cobourg, Rockcliffe, Ont.

HEGGTVEIT, Anne (skiing); *b.* 11 Jan 1939, Ottawa, Ont.; *m.* Ross Hamilton; *children:* Timothy, Christianne; Lisgar HS; v.-pres. sporting goods company; father Halvor former Canadian cross-country champion, uncles Bud Clark, Bruce Heggtveit former Olympic skiers; at age seven won Gatineau Zone senior women's slalom, combined; by 1954 had won every Ottawa area competition; first international success 1954 Holmenkollen giant slalom Norway, at 15 youngest in event's 50-year history; competed 1956 Cortina Olympics; won 1959 two-stage combined St. Moritz, Arlberg-Kandahar at Garmisch-Partenkirchen; gold 1960 Squaw Valley Olympic slalom; Canadian female athlete of year 1959-60 CP poll; Lou Marsh Trophy top Canadian athlete 1960; mem. US Skiing, Ottawa, Canadian Sports Halls of Fame; *res.* Montreal, Que.

HEIKKILA, Bill (track and field); *b.* 17 Aug 1944, Toronto, Ont.; *m.* Pat; *children:* Kirsti, Kaarina; U of Oregon, B.A., M.P.E.; sports consultant; five times Canadian senior javelin champion; gold medal Canada Games 1969; Canadian juvenile, senior record holder; represented Canada 1967 Winnipeg Pan-Am Games, 1968 Mexico Olympics, 1970 Edinburgh Commonwealth Games; Oregon all-American 1967; *res.* Ottawa, Ont.

HEIMRATH, Ludwig (autosport); *b.* 11 Aug 1934, Munich, Germany; *m.* Brigitte Wlochowitz; *children:* Ludwig Jr., Karin; auto dealer; Canadian driving champion three times, runner-up three times; Ontario driving champion seven times; began racing career on motorcycles in native Germany 1952; competed in first Players' 200 race 1961 at Mosport and since then has won more than 200 Mosport races; represented Canada in USAC, USRRC and Can-Am events; runner-up to Trans-Am champion Peter Gregg 1974; *res.* Scarborough, Ont.

HENDERSON, Gil (shooting); *b.* 5 Sep 1926, Toronto, Ont.; *given name:* Gilbert James; *m.* Molly; mechanical contractor; trapshooting specialist, has held Canadian singles, doubles, handicap titles several times, also several US honors; represented Canada 1960 Olympics, 1966, 1974 world championships, 1971 world moving target championships, 1975 championship of Americas; past pres. Canadian Trapshooting

Association, v.-pres. Shooting Federation of Canada; coach-manager shotgun team 1972 Olympics, Christchurch N.Z. Commonwealth Games shooting team 1974; manager shotgun events 1976 Olympics; *res.* Rexdale, Ont.

HENDERSON, Paul (yachting); *b.* 17 Nov 1934, Toronto, Ont.; *given name:* Paul Franklin; *m.* Mary Katherine Lynn McLeod; *children:* John, Martha; Lawrence Park CI, U of Toronto, B.Sc.; engineer; first of four Aphrodite Cup Canadian junior team race titles 1945; since 1945 mem. Royal Canadian Yacht Club; junior club champion, fleet captain 1950; twice Canadian Intercollegiate titlist; English, US, Bermuda, world, Alexander of Tunis International 14 ft dinghy titles; Dutch, US, twice Canadian Flying Dutchman Olympic Class centreboarder titles; twice Canadian Finn Olympic Class single-handed centreboarder title; US Midwest Tempest Olympic Class keel boat title; US Atlantic Coast Soling Olympic Class keel yacht title; North American Fireball title; represented Canada 1964, 1968 Olympics; coach 1972 Olympic yachting team; founding director Water Rat Sailing Club; third in world 1974 in Flying Dutchman, top in Canada 1975 Soling Class; director Canadian National Sailing team 1970-71; Ontario squash open doubles semifinals 1973; Ontario yachtsman of year 1974; mem. National Fitness Advisory Council 1974-76; director CYA, International Yacht Racing Union, Ontario Sailing Assoc., Canadian Squash Racquets Assoc.; *res.* Toronto, Ont.

HENDERSON, Scott (skiing); *b.* 4 Apr 1943, Calgary, Alta.; *given name:* George Scott Robert; *m.* Patricia; alpine ski coach; mem. Canadian alpine ski team 1962-69 until injuries retired him; three times Canadian, three times US alpine champion; won 1967 international races Australia, top 10 Europe several times 1968-69; turned pro, became Lange racing director 1970-72; coach Canadian men's alpine team since 1972, produced World Cup winners 1975-76; *res.* Nederland, Colo.

HENDRICKSON, Lefty (football); *b.* 27 Apr 1943, Squamish, B.C.; *given name:* Lynn Alfred; *m.* Carol Anne; *children:* Craig Stephen, Scott Patrick; U of Oregon, B.Sc.; auto dealer; basketball all-star Howe Sound District 1959-62; played all-star junior football North Shore Cougars 1960-63; Pacific Eight honorable mention as Oregon tight end 1967-68; turned pro B.C. Lions 1968 as outside linebacker but switched to receiver second season; caught 123 passes for 1,669yds, 13.5 avg. and seven TDs during six-year CFL career; WFC all-star 1973; all-star softball first baseman Brandon 1976; v.-pres. for sports 1979 Canada Winter Games Brandon Man.; *res.* Alexander, Man.

HENDRY, Joan (track); *b.* 14 May 1945, Glasgow, Scotland; *given name:* Joan Lynn; U of Ottawa, B.A.; teacher; launched international competitive career with 20'3/4'' long jump 1967 Winnipeg Pan-Am Games; competed in long jump, relay 1968 Mexico Olympics; relay silver medal 1969 Tokyo Pan-Pacific Games; two bronze Edinburgh Commonwealth Games 1970 with 20'7¼'' Canadian record long jump and Canadian record 44.6 relay; Canada's top sprinter over 100m 1972 with 11.4; named to Munich Olympic team but injury forced withdrawal; began running again 1975; Ontario record 100m 11.4; co-holder Canadian indoor 50m 6.2; 1967-71 held Canadian women's long jump mark; *res.* Ottawa, Ont.

HENLEY, Garney (football); *b.* 21 Dec 1935, Elgin, N.D.; *m.* Phyllis Diekmann; *children:* Pamela, Lori, Jody, Garney Kyle; Huron College, B.A.; University athletic director; many awards in HS and college basketball, T & F, baseball and football; most prolific scorer in history of American college football with 394 points in 31-game, four-year career; drafted by Green Bay Packers (NFL), New York (AFL) 1960; played part of 1960 season with Packers before joining Hamilton Tiger-Cats; through 16 seasons as player holds all-time CFL interception record with 59 for record 916yds; shares CFL record for catching TD passes single game with four; career total 364 punts returned for 2,844yds including 83 in 1966 season; ten times EFC all-star, all-Canadian; six times Schenley nominee, winner 1972; Jeff Russel Memorial Trophy twice; named to Ticats best-of-century team 1967; played in seven Grey Cup finals, four winners; Ticats assistant coach 1976; athletic director Mount Allison U 1977; mem. US College Football S.D. Sports Halls of Fame; coach basketball 10 years Guelph U, won 1974 CIAU title; *res.* Sackville, N.B.

HENNYEY, Donna (fencing); *b.* 10 Apr 1942, New York, N.Y.; *given name:* Donna Jean Atkinson; *m.* Alex Richard Hennyey; *children:* Mark Alexander, Allison Marijke; U of Toronto, B.A., M.A.; food sciences lecturer; mem. Canadian fencing team since 1967, represented Canada at world three times, Pan-Am Games three times, team silver Mexico 1975, Martini Rossi Torino Italy five times, German international once, De Beaumont Cup London Eng. once, Austrian international once, 1972, 1976 Olympics, Martini Rossi NY three times; twice Ontario women's champion, six times runner-up; twice Eastern Canadian titlist, once runner-up; three times Canadian champion; five times Heroes International winner, once runner-up; three times Governor-General's title, once runner-up; four times Harmonie International champion; winner Golden Foil, Dell Open events; mem. three Ontario title teams, five national team champions, three times runner-up; Norman Craig award Ontario female athlete of year 1968; *res*. Toronto, Ont.

HENNYEY, Imre (fencing); *b*. 14 Jul 1913, Cattaro, Yugoslavia; *m*. Ilona; *children:* Alex, Sheilah; Ludovika Academy, U of Toronto, B.Sc.; teacher; world university épée title 1939 Vienna; Hungarian épée title 1941, 1943, 1947; represented Hungary 1948, 1952 Olympics; coached 1953-54 Hungarian modern pentathlon fencing team; coached U of Manitoba fencing team three years, U of Toronto fencing team since 1961, 1968 Canadian Olympic fencing team, 1970 Commonwealth Games team; *res*. Toronto, Ont.

HENRY, Camille (hockey); *b*. 31 Jan 1933, Quebec City, Que.; *given name:* Camille Wilfrid; *m*. Aimée Sylvestre (Dominique Michel); rejected baseball in favor of hockey; stickboy with father's Sherbrooke Saints team in Quebec senior provincial league; began play at 11 in Quebec bantam league, after three years with Quebec Citadel juniors invited to Rangers' training camp; scored four against Terry Sawchuk in single game, Calder Memorial Trophy as NHL's leading rookie 1954; to Quebec, Providence next two seasons, rejoined Rangers 1956-57; nickname The Eel; from Rangers to Chicago 1964-65; refused to go to minors, sat out 1966-67 season, rejoined Rangers 1967-68, closed out career with St. Louis Blues 1968-70; coached NY Raiders-Golden

Blades- Jersey Knights in WHA 1972-74; Lady Byng Trophy 1958; second team all-star left winger 1958; in 14 NHL seasons appeared in 817 league games scoring 279 goals, 249 assists for 528 points, plus 48 playoff games scoring six goals 12 assists for 18 points; appeared in three all-star games; *res*. Quebec City, Que.

HEPBURN, Doug (weightlifting); *b*. 16 Sep 1926, Vancouver, B.C.; Vancouver HS; health food distributor; born with clubbed foot, went on body building program, put 300lbs on 5'10'' frame, earned title of world's strongest man; turned competitive 1948 pressing Canadian record 300lb in Vancouver; US national title Los Angeles 1949; world heavyweight title Stockholm 1953 with lift of 1,030lbs; 1954 British Empire Games gold; Lou Marsh Trophy winner; B.C. man of year 1954; mem. B.C., Canadian Sports Halls of Fame; *res*. Vancouver, B.C.

HERLEN, Ossie (boxing); *b*. 26 Nov 1918, Star City, Sask., *d*. 9 June 1944; *given name:* Ernst Osborne; Saskatoon THS; played football with Saskatoon Tech winning 1937 title; started boxing at 15; began ring career scoring fourth round TKO over Babe Brown of Regina 1935; former ring name Biff Bapp; fought for Saskatchewan amateur title vs Lawrence Anderson losing decision Regina 1936; stopped Sask. lightweight titlist Billy Moore in second round Regina 1937; won Sask. welterweight title vs Bob Hughes Regina 1938; outpointed by Howard Bulmer in Canadian welterweight title bout 1938 but Bulmer later disqualified; boxed in service winning Toronto Garrison welterweight title; ring record 33 fights, 12 won by KO, 12 by decision, three TKO, one draw, lost five by decision; never KO'd in nine years of boxing;

in 30s frequently sparred with sister; v.-pres. Saskatoon Golden Gloves Boxing Club at formation 1938; mem. Sask. Sports Hall of Fame.

HERN, Riley (hockey); *b.* 5 Dec, 1880, St. Mary's, Ont., *d.* 24 Jun 1929, Montreal, Que.; *given name:* William Milton; business executive; started as goaler with hometown OHA junior team and moved through intermediate and senior ranks with London Ont. as forward; in first nine years of hockey played on seven championship teams; pro with Portage Lake team Houghton Mich., 1904 as goaler then joined Montreal Wanderers 1906 helping them win 1906, 1908, 1910 Stanley Cups; retired as player 1911; referee, goal judge several years; twice won Rosemere golf club title; pres. St. Rose Boating Club; mem. Hockey Hall of Fame.

HEVENOR, George (golf); *b.* 4 Aug 1904, Saint John, N.B.; *m.* Martha; *children:* George Jr.; Toronto Central THS; stockbroker; mem. Balmy Beach (ORFU) football team 1925-26; canoe racer Island Aquatic Paddling Association; mem. Toronto Central Y basketball champions five years; three times Ontario seniors golf champion, four times runner-up; three times RCGA seniors, once CSGA champion; five times Ontario Parent-Child titlist; *res.* Toronto, Ont.

HEXTALL, Bryan Sr. (hockey); *b.* 31 Jul 1913, Grenfell, Sask.; *given name:* Bryan Aldwyn; *m.* Gertrude Lyon; *children:* Bryan Jr., Dennis, Richard, Heather, Randy; Poplar Point HS; lumber, hardware business; played minor hockey at Poplar Point Man. winning 1930 juvenile title; played junior with Winnipeg Monarchs, Portage La Prairie before turning pro with Vancouver Lions in Western Hockey League 1934; on WHL

champions 1936 then joined Philadelphia Ramblers briefly before being called up to NY Rangers during 1936-37 campaign; remained in NHL through 1947-48 season; in 449 league games scored 187 goals, 175 assists; Art Ross Trophy 1942 with 56 points; scored 20 or more goals in seven of 12 NHL seasons; scored winning overtime goal in 1940 Stanley Cup final vs Toronto; three times first team, twice second team all-star; mem. Hockey Hall of Fame; *res.* Poplar Point, Man.

HEYDENFELDT, Bob (football); *b.* 17 Sep 1933, Santa Monica, Calif.; *given name:* Robert Marshall; *m.* JoAnn Good; *children:* Linda Jo, Robert Tad, Richard Daniel, Dina Marie; Canoga Park HS, UCLA, B.Sc.; furniture wholesaler and jobber; top college punter in US 1954; played in Rose Bowl, North-South Shrine games as UCLA junior 1954; passed up by NFL when refused to play football on Sundays, joined Edmonton Eskimos winning WFC punting title and helping them win 1955 Grey Cup; played in first Canadian East-West all-star game Toronto 1955, kicked single which gave West 6-6 tie with East; *res.* Lafayette, Calif.

HIBBERD, Ted (hockey); *b.* 22 Apr 1926, Ottawa, Ont.; *given name:* Thomas Edward; *m.* Anna Smith; *children:* Lesley, Wendy, Nancye, Jeffrey, Laurie; HS of Commerce; underwriting supervisor; played junior hockey New Edinburgh, Ottawa Montagnards, Hull and Intermediate Senators; played with 1948 RCAF Flyers winning world, Olympic hockey title; *res.* Ottawa, Ont.

HILDEBRAND, Ike (lacrosse, hockey); *b.* 27 May 1927, Winnipeg, Man.; *given name:* Isaac; *m.* Helen Alpin; *children:* Isaac Jay, Jody Ann, Daniel, Heidi, Melanie; Oshawa

HS; sporting goods manufacturer's rep.; began playing lacrosse at 14; youngest mem. at 15 of 1943 New Westminster Salmonbellies winning Mann Cup; in 16 seasons senior lacrosse with New Westminster, Mimico, Peterborough scored over 900 goals, 700 assists while playing on seven successive Mann Cup finalists, five winners with Peterborough; at 17 youngest player ever to win Mike Kelly Mann Cup MVP award; MVP, twice scoring champion both East, West leagues; senior hockey at 17 Seattle Ironmen; OHA junior A Oshawa Generals 1945-47; senior Toronto Marlboros; nine years pro, parts of three seasons NY Rangers, Chicago Black Hawks; US League scoring champion Kansas City 1951, AHL top scorer Cleveland 1953; mem. Cleveland AHL Calder Cup champions 1952-53; first team all-star right wing US League 1951, AHL 1953; leading scorer Belleville McFarlands Allan Cup, world champions 1959-60; pro career 185 goals, 209 assists, 394 points; coach Peterborough Mann Cup winner 1954; Belleville McFarlands 1959 Allan Cup, 1960 world championship; twice Green MVP Trophy; junior A hockey coach six years Peterborough, London, Oshawa; senior hockey six years Pembroke, Belleville, Orillia; Allan Cup Orillia 1969; active Toronto NHL Oldtimers; mem. Canadian Lacrosse Hall of Fame; *res.* Thornhill, Ont.

HILL, Craig (autosport); *b.* 9 Jan 1934, Hamilton, Ont.; *given name:* Richard Craig; *m.* Jean McCallum; *children:* Michael, Mark; F.R. Close THS, Delta CI; sales marketing coordinator; progressed through stock cars, super modifieds, sprint cars; won Canada's first pro road race, CRDA 500, in D-type Jaguar Harewood Ont. 1959; several times Canadian sports car, open wheel champion; CTV color commentary Players' Challenge Series; *res.* Mississauga, Ont.

HILL, Harvey (weightlifting); *b.* 16 Dec 1897, Shaw's Lane, Eng.; *m.* Elsie; retired; active as competitor 1925-27 then switched to coaching, officiating and administrating weightlifting; coach Verdun Weightlifting Club 1928-42, South-Western YMCA Verdun 1942-53; manager-coach first Canadian team to world championships Philadelphia 1947; manager-coach first Canadian team to Olympics London Eng. 1948; manager-coach first Canadian team to British Empire Games Auckland N.Z. 1950; refereed North American championships 1936-58, Federation Halterophile Canadien 1927-54, variety of regional, provincial, national and international meets 1927-58; founded Quebec Weightlifters Association 1936, secretary 1936-58; introduced weightlifting to AAU of C 1936; organized secretary weightlifting contests 1936-58; founded Canadian Weightlifters Association, secretary 1948-58; national weightlifting chairman AAU of C 1950-52; chairman at founding of British Empire Weightlifting Federation, v.-pres. 1948; *res.* Fulford, Que.

HILLER, John (baseball); *b.* 8 Apr 1943, Scarborough, Ont.; *given name:* John Fredrick; *m.* Janis Patricia Baldwin; *children:* Wendy Louise, Joseph Scott, Danielle Patricia; Scarborough HS; baseball player; southpaw pitcher who moved through Toronto minor baseball ranks to pro ranks signing with Detroit Tigers organization 1962; played minor baseball in Detroit chain with Jamestown, Duluth, Knoxville, Montgomery, Syracuse and Toledo before joining Tigers to stay 1968; relief pitching specialist; heart attack 1971, missed entire season and part of 1972; amazing comeback 1973 earning Hutch Award, American League comeback player of year, Major League fireman of year, Tiger of year, King Tiger award and placed fourth in Cy Young, MVP voting; set AL record for victories by relief pitcher with 17 in 1974, major league record of 31 decisions for fireman 1974 with 17-14 record; arm injury caused him to miss much of 1975 season; 12-8 won-lost record, 2.38 ERA 1976; through 1976 season led all Tigers with 94 career saves; 30th on all-time major league list; holds major league record 38 saves one season; Tiger club record finishing 60 games one season; following 215 consecutive relief appearances made first start, hurling four-hit shutout over Milwaukee; *res.* Duluth, Minn.

HILLMAN, Larry   (hockey); *b.* 5 Feb 1937, Kirkland Lake, Ont.; *given name:* Larry Morley; *m.* Marjorie; *children:* Laurie, Valerie, Darryn, Peter; hockey player; defenceman, junior hockey in Windsor, Hamilton before turning pro with Detroit Red Wings 1955; played Buffalo (AHL), Edmonton (WHL) before rejoining Detroit 1956; drafted from Detroit by Chicago then claimed on waivers by Boston 1957; farmed to Providence (AHL), Eddie Shore award as league's top defenceman 1959-60; drafted by Toronto from Boston 1960 and spent time between Leafs, Rochester, Springfield until put on NY Rangers' reserve list 1968; drafted by Minnesota, claimed on waivers by Pittsburgh, traded to Montreal for Jean Guy Legrace, all in 1968; drafted from Montreal by Philadelphia 1969 and traded to Los Angeles, then Buffalo 1971; WHA Cleveland Crusaders 1973-75, Winnipeg Jets 1975-76; NHL record 790 games, 36 goals, 196 assists for 232 points, 579 penalty minutes, plus 74 playoff games, two goals, nine assists, 11 points, 30 penalty minutes; in WHA has played 192 games, scoring six goals, 49 assists, 55 points, 182 penalty minutes; played on six Stanley Cups, one Calder Cup; former AHL all-star; *res.* Beamsville, Ont.

HINDMARCH, Robert   (hockey); *b.* 27 May 1930, Nanaimo, B.C.; *given name:* Robert George; *m.* Jean; *children:* Robert Bruce, David Stephen; U of British Columbia, B.P.E., Oregon U, M.S., D.Ed.; university professor; played football, hockey while attending college, later turned to coaching and administration; Dr. Gordon Burke award for football UBC 1952; Bobby Gaul Trophy as UBC outstanding athlete 1953; assistant coach UBC football 1955-62; UBC hockey coach since 1965; manager Canadian Olympic hockey team 1964; chairman Hockey Development Council since 1974; director Canadian Amateur Hockey Association since 1975; *res.* Vancouver, B.C.

HINTON, Tom   (football); *b.* 19 Mar 1936, Ruston, La.; *given name:* William Thomas; *m.* Patsy Nelson; *children:* Steve, Janet, Terry; Louisiana Tech, B.A.; general manager; all-State T&F (shot put, discus), football; all-American HS football; all-Conference guard three successive years in college; as senior voted Gulf State Conference athlete of year; first from conference to play North-South game, all-American; drafted by NFL Chicago Cardinals; pro B.C. Lions 1958-1966; WFC all-star guard five times, all-Canadian twice; several times Lions' fans most popular player; several times Lions' Schenley nominee; on retirement served six years Lions' director; *res.* North Vancouver, B.C.

HOBKIRK, Alan   (field hockey); *b.* 7 Nov 1952, Vancouver, B.C.; *given name:* Alan Arthur; University Hill HS, U of British Columbia, B.A., Oxford U, M.A.; Rhodes scholar, student; mem. B.C. junior team 1966-70, captain two years, v.-captain one; B.C. seniors 1970-73; won Canadian championship three times; captain Oxford team 1975-76; captain British Universities all-star team 1975-76; captain Folkestone International Festival winners 1976; mem. Canadian national team since 1971 winning 55 caps; bronze 1971 Pan-Am Games Cali Colombia; silver 1975 Pan-Am Games Mexico; competed in Bavaria, England, Wales, New Zealand, Malaysia, Japan, Argentina, Australia, Colombia, Mexico, W. Germany, Holland and Canada; *res.* Oxford, Eng., Vancouver, B.C.

HODGINS, Clint (harness racing); *b.* 18 Jun 1907, Clandeboye, Ont.; driver, trainer, breeder; drove more than 2,000 winning races in U S and Canada; led U S dash winners 1949 with 128, money winners with $184, 108; drove 42 sub two-minute miles; won Little Brown Jug, Messenger Pace, Kentucky Futurity, Cane Pace (twice); drove Adios Butler to 1:59.2 mile, first sub two-minute clocking in Little Brown Jug history 1959; among best he's bred, trained, driven are Bye Bye Byrd (1959 horse of year), Elaine Rodney, Skipper Thorpe, Sing Away Herbert, Pat's Bye Bye, Terry Parker, Acrasia and Proximity; mem. Horseman's Living Hall of Fame; *res.* Orlando, Fla.

HODGSON, George (swimming); *b.* 12 Oct 1893, Montreal, Que.; *m.* Adythe Harrower (*d.*); *children:* George Jr., Thomas; McGill U; retired stockbroker; at 18 represented Canada in Festival of Empire Games London 1911, defeated world mile record holder Sid Battersky of Britain; became first Canadian swimming gold medalist 1912 Stockholm Olympics taking 400, 1500m freestyle

events in record times; represented Canada 1920 Olympics; mem. Canadian Sports Hall of Fame; *res.* Montreal, Que.

HOFFMAN, Abby (track); *b.* 11 Feb 1947, Toronto, Ont.; *given name:* Abigail; U of Toronto, B.A., M.A.; university professor; stirred sports controversy at 11 playing goal for Toronto boys' team in peewee hockey tournament; represented Canada internationally since 1962 competing in four Olympics, four Pan-Am Games, two Commonwealth Games, three World Student Games and one Maccabiah Games; eight times Canadian 800m title, runner-up 1500m 1975; Canadian record holder 800m 1962-75 cutting time from 2:10.8 to 2:00.2, 440yd 1963-76 with 54.4, Canadian indoor 1500m 4:13.3; gold medal 1966 Jamaica Commonwealth 880yd, 1963 Brazil, 1971 Colombia Pan-Am Games 800m, 1969 Tel Aviv Maccabiah 400m, 800m; silver medal 1975 Mexico Pan-Am Games 800m, 1967 Tokyo Student Games 800m, bronze medal 1967 Winnipeg Pan-Am Games 800m, 1975 Mexico Pan-Am Games 1500m, 1965 Budapest Student Games 800m; finalist 800m 1968 Mexico, 1972 Munich Olympics, set Commonwealth record 2:00.2 in latter; City of Toronto Civic Award of Merit 1976, Ontario Award of Merit 1975; *res.* Toronto, Ont.

HOHL, Elmer (horseshoes); *b.* 16 Jan 1919, Wellesley, Ont.; *m.* Hilda; *children:* Sandra, Susan, Richard, Karen, Steve; farmer, carpenter; since 1956 held Canadian championship 15 times, Ontario title 19 times and world championship four times; one of two in World Horseshoe Pitching Association history (formed 1903) to pitch perfect game of 30 consecutive ringers in competition; pitched 69 consecutive ringers, three short of world mark held by Ted Allen, Boulder

Colo., with whom he shares perfect game record; best performance 1968 world tournament scoring 572 of maximum 600 to break world record 571 set by Harold Reno, Sabrina Ohio; ringer percentage of 88.5 broke 1969 standard 87.5 set by Casey Jones, Waukesha Wisc.; son Steve won 1973 Canadian junior title; five-pin bowler with 260 avg.; Ontario four-game men's record 1,376 posted 1971; frequent Canadian five-pin championship competitor; *res.* Wellesley, Ont.

HOLLOWAY, Sue (canoeing, skiing); *b.* 19 May 1955, Halifax, N.S.; Brookfield HS; student; Canadian junior cross-country ski title 1972 and qualified for both skiing, canoeing Canadian national teams 1973; 29th junior European ski championships 1973; won Canadian senior, 21st junior European, 28th world 1974; won Canadian junior, senior K1, (kayak singles), senior K2, K4, ninth world K2, third junior world K1, fifth K2, third North American K1, second K2, K4 1973; won Canadian senior K1, K2, K4, North American K1, K2, sixth world K4, seventh K1, K2 1974; won Canadian K1, K2, K4, seventh world K2, bronze medal Pan-Am Games K1 500m 1975; represented Canada in Innsbruck winter Olympics cross-country and Montreal summer Olympics K1, K2 1976; twice Ottawa ACT amateur athlete of year; Velma Springstead, Elaine Tanner trophies; *res.* Ottawa, Ont.

HOLMES, Derek (hockey); *b.* 15 Aug 1939, Ottawa, Ont.; *m.* Louise Cornu; *children:* Sean, Katherine; St. Michael's College, Carleton U, B.A.; executive-director, treasurer Hockey Canada; played all level of minor hockey Kemptville Ont., junior hockey St. Mike's, Ottawa Montagnards, college hockey Carleton; player, captain Canadian

Eastern National Team 1967-70; player, coach with teams in Austria, Switzerland; national coach Finland 1961-62; Olympic, national coach Switzerland 1972-74; general manager Team Canada 1977 Vienna world championships; *res.* Ottawa, Ont.

HOLMES, Hap (hockey); *b.* 1889, Aurora, Ont., *d.* 1940, Florida; *given name:* Harry; starred in all five leagues he played goal-National Hockey Association, Pacific Coast Hockey Association, Western Canadian Hockey League, Western Hockey League, National Hockey League; turned pro 1912-13 with Toronto and played 15 seasons with Toronto, Seattle, Victoria, Detroit during which he posted a 2.90 goals-against avg. in 409 games; played on seven league championship teams, four Stanley Cup winners-twice Toronto, once each Seattle, Victoria; Holmes Memorial Trophy presented annually to best goaltender in American Hockey League; mem. Hockey Hall of Fame.

HOLZSCHEITER, Herb (golf); *b.* 8 Jan 1946, West Hill, Ont.; West Hill CI, CPGA business school; tournament director CPGA; mem. HS golf team, won TDIAA title 1964, runner-up 1963; Scarborough GC caddy champion 1963; worked part-time for Bob Gray at Scarborough GC 1963-65, assistant pro 1965-67; playing pro Thunderbird GC 1968-76; conducted April golf school for GM employees 1973-76; won BIC Open 1970; runner-up Newfoundland Open 1972; third Alberta Open 1969, Ontario Open 1973-74; won Molson-Spec Invitational 1973-74; Ontario PGA; Hunt Trophy for OPGA scoring avg. 67.3 1975; course record 66 Spruce Needles Timmins 1969, 66 Brockville 1974, 64 Thunderbird (old) 1972, (new) 1974, 63 Board of Trade CC 1976; tournament player's rep. on Peter Jackson golf tour, mem. CPGA board of directors 1975-76; *res*. West Hill, Ont.

HOMENUIK, Wilf (golf); *b*. 30 Dec 1937, Kamsack, Sask.; *m*. Jean Young; *children:* Gwen, Scott, Jason; golf pro, teacher; three times runner-up then won Sask. junior 1954; won Sask. amateur 1953; won 1956-57 Manitoba amateurs; represented Manitoba in Willingdon Cup play; turned pro 1958 joining US tour 1966; won Manitoba Open 1961, 1972, Alberta Open 1961, 1965, CPGA 1965, 1971, Peru Open 1965, Panama Open 1966, Millar Trophy 1967, 1968, East Ridge 1971, Labatt Invitational 1973, Lake Michigan Classic 1973; Dauphin pro-am 1975; mem. Canada's World Cup team 1971, 1974; head pro London Highlands 1976; *res*. London, Ont., West Palm Beach, Fla.

HOMER-DIXON, Marjorie (canoeing); *b*. 10 Aug 1945, Indochina; Port Credit HS; McMaster U, B.P.E.; supervisor women's fitness centre, kayak coach; won Canadian K2 (kayak doubles), bronze medal Pan-Am Games Winnipeg 1967; Canadian record in Canadian K1 singles, retained K2 title, third K4 in 1968; represented Canada 1968, 1972 Olympics; silver 1968 North American championships K2; mem. of first Canadian K4 girls' team to win North American gold 1969, also took silver in Canadian K1; semifinalist 1971 world Yugoslavia; competed in Munich international regatta; turned to coaching after 1972; TV color commentator 1976 Olympics; *res*. Mississauga, Ont.

HOOPER, Tom (hockey); *b*. 24 Nov 1883, Rat Portage (now Kenora), Ont. *d*. 23 Mar 1960; *given name:* Charles Thomas; with Tommy Phillips helped Kenora Thistles win

1901 Manitoba, Northwestern League titles; Thistles challenged for Stanley Cup 1903, 1905, 1907 achieving success latter year but two months later lost Cup to Montreal Wanderers; played final season with Wanderers 1907-08 again winning Stanley Cup; mem. Hockey Hall of Fame.

HORNER, Red (hockey); *b*. 28 May 1909, Lynden, Ont.; *given name:* George Reginald; played defence with Toronto Marlboros, Brokers' League before joining Toronto Maple Leafs 1928; 12 years with Leafs; led NHL in penalty minutes eight successive seasons; record 167 penalty minutes in 43 games 1935-36 season which stood 20 years; career total 1,254 penalty minutes; captain Leafs 1937-38; scored 42 goals, 110 assists during career; mem. Hockey Hall of Fame; *res*. Toronto, Ont.

HORTON, Tim (hockey); *b*. 12 Jan 1930, Cochrane, Ont., *d*. 21 Feb 1974, Toronto, Ont.; *given name:* Myles Gilbert; *m*. Dolores Michalek; *children:* Jeri-Lyn, Kim, Kelly, Tracy; Cochrane, Sudbury HS, St. Michael's College; hockey player, franchise donut chain owner; played midget hockey in Sudbury, with Copper Cliff Redmen 1946-47, then St. Mike's Majors where he led OHA junior badmen first year; signed by Toronto Maple Leafs 1949 and spent much of next three years with Pittsburgh Hornets in AHL, won Calder Cup, all-star defensive berth; Toronto Maple Leaf regular 1952-70; dealt to NY Rangers 1970-71, Pittsburgh Penguins 1971-72, Buffalo Sabres 1972; twice first team, three times second team all-star; played on five Stanley Cup winners; in 22 NHL seasons played in 1,446 regular season games scoring 115 goals, 403 assists for 518 points, 1,611 penalty minutes, plus 126 playoff games, 11 goals, 39 assists, 50 points, 183 penalty minutes; killed in single car accident; sweater No. 2 retired by Sabres in his memory; J.P. Bickell trophy as Toronto Maple Leaf MVP 1969.

HOWARD, Tom (track); *b.* 20 Sep 1948, Vancouver, B.C.; *given name:* Thomas George; *m.* Cheryl Lynne Spowage; U of British Columbia; transit operator; third 1973 Canadian marathon championships, represented Canada World Student Games Moscow finishing 11th 5000m, 13th 10 000m; competed in both events 1974 European tour, won Canadian marathon in 2:17.57, second Canadian outdoor 10 000m; fourth 1975 Boston Marathon; bronze 1975 Pan-Am Games Mexico marathon; 30th 1976 Montreal Olympics marathon; *res.* Surrey, B.C.

HOWE, Gordie (hockey); *b.* 31 Mar 1928, Floral, Sask.; *given name:* Gordon; *m.* Colleen Joffa; *children:* Marty, Mark, Murray, Cathleen; hockey player, executive; at 15 attended NY Rangers camp Winnipeg; first pro contract 1945 with Omaha Knights (USHL) then joined Detroit Red Wings 1946; first NHL goal 1946; wore sweater No. 9 1951-71 which retired with him; right wing with Red Wings in 25 NHL seasons scoring in 1,687 regular season games 786 goals, 1,023 assists for 1,809 points, 1,643 penalty minutes; in 154 playoff games totalled 67 goals, 91 assists for 158 points, 218 penalty minutes; six times Hart Trophy (MVP); six times Art Ross Trophy (scoring); Lester Patrick Trophy 1967; 12 times first team, nine times second team all-star, all-star selectee 15 consecutive years; played in 22 all-star games scoring 10 goals, eight assists for 18 points, 25 penalty minutes; co-holder all-star points in single-game mark of four 1965; following retirement served two

years as Red Wings v.-pres. before joining sons Marty, Mark with Houston Aeros (WHA) 1973-74; despite age, 45, chosen WHA MVP 1974; helped Aeros win two Avco Cups, all-star each season; major hockey's first playing club pres. 1975-76; in four WHA campaigns (through 1976-77) played 313 games scoring 132 goals, 274 assists for 406 points, 315 penalty minutes; with sons joined WHA New England Whalers 1977; Canadian male athlete of year 1963 CP poll; *Sport Magazine* hockey player of quarter century 1971; mem. Hockey, Canadian Sports Halls of Fame; *res.* Detroit, Mich.

HOWE, Syd (hockey); *b.* 28 Sep 1911, Ottawa, Ont., *d.* 20 May 1976, Ottawa, Ont.; *given name:* Stanley Harris; *m.* Frances; *children:* Shirley; Glebe CI; civil servant; mem. first Ottawa team to play in Memorial Cup final losing 1928 to Regina; played senior 1929; turned pro Ottawa Senators (NHL) 1930, then played with Philadelphia Quakers, Toronto Maple Leafs before returning to Ottawa 1932; went with franchise to St. Louis 1935; purchased by Detroit Red Wings that season and remained until 1946 retirement; NHL lifetime record 237 goals, 291 assists over 16 seasons; set modern record 1944 scoring six goals in game vs Rangers at Detroit, mark since equalled by Red Berenson, Darryl Sittler; on ice when Mud Bruneteau scored goal that ended Stanley Cup's longest game; played on three league champions, three Stanley Cup winners; mem. Ottawa, Hockey Halls of Fame.

HOWELL, Harry (hockey); *b.* 28 Dec 1932, Hamilton, Ont.; *given name:* Henry Vernon; *m.* Marilyn Gorrie; *children:* Danny (*d.*), Cheryl; Westdale CI, Guelph CI; hockey executive; junior hockey with Guelph Biltmores; turned pro with Rangers playing single game with Cincinnati (AHL) 1951-52 then joined Rangers as defenceman 1952-69; established Rangers record by playing over 1,000 games with that team; sold to Oakland 1969, Los Angeles 1971 where he remained through 1972-73 season before moving to WHA with NY Raiders (then Golden Blades), Jersey Knights and San Diego Mariners; player-coach Mariners 1974-75, released summer of 1975; assistant general manager Cleveland Barons (NHL) 1976, general manager 1976-77; in 21 NHL seasons played 1,411 regular season games, scored 94 goals, 324 assists for 418 points and 1,298 penalty minutes, plus 38 playoff games scored three goals, three assists for six points, 32 penalty minutes; James Norris Memorial Trophy 1966-67 as best NHL defenceman; first team all-star once; *res.* Carlyle, Ont.

HOWELL, Ron (football, hockey); *b.* 4 Dec 1935, Hamilton, Ont.; *given name:* Ronald John; *m.* Ruth Jean Moore; *children:* Robin, Lisa, Cathy, Tracey; Westdale CI; furrier; played with Guelph Biltmores OHA junior A, Tilson Award 1955-56 season; played senior hockey Kitchener-Waterloo then turned pro Rochester AHL; played in minors with Vancouver (WHL), Long Island (EHL) until retirement 1964; pro football Hamilton Tiger-Cats 1954-62 before trade to B.C. Lions 1962; sat out 1963 season then moved to Toronto 1964-65 and completed 13 years in CFL with Montreal 1966; in 13 CFL seasons returned 458 punts for 2,742yds, 6.0 avg., five TDs; played in four Grey Cup finals, one winner; Gruen EFC rookie of year award 1954; Schenley outstanding Canadian player award 1958; *res.* Burlington, Ont.

HOWSON, Barry (basketball); *b.* 17 Jun 1939, London, Ont.; *given name:* Barry Franklin; *m.* Janet; *children:* Micheline, David, Bryan; Sir Adam Beck CI, U Western Ontario, B.A., Wayne State U, M.Ed.; HS phys ed teacher, department head; mem. all-Ontario HS champions 1957-58, OQAA champions Western 1960; with 1961 Tillsonburg Livingstons-London Fredericks who won Eastern Canadian senior A title but lost to Lethbridge in Canadian final; with Montreal Yvan Coutu Huskies Eastern Canadian titlists 1962; London 5B Sports 1963; mem. 1964 Tokyo Olympic team, Toronto Dow Kings senior A champions; Sarnia Drawbridge Knights 1966-68 winning Ontario senior latter year; gold medal 1966 Canada Winter Games; mem. 1967 Pan-Am Games team; London Host-Rent-A-Car team 1969-70; Canadian national team world championships Yugoslavia 1971; Ontario senior A champion London Celtics 1972-73; Sarnia Trader Bryan intermediate A Bullets 1975; Sarnia Northgate Bowl intermediates 1976; coach St. Patricks's HS basketball, football, track, tennis, Lambton College basketball; *res.* Sarnia, Ont.

HSU, Gloria (table tennis); *b.* 7 Oct 1956, South Africa; student; Canadian women's Closed doubles champion 1974; mem. Ontario team Canadian Closed championships 1974; Canadian national team world championships 1975; *res.* Don Mills, Ont.

HUDSON, Bruce (curling); *b.* 13 Nov 1928, Winnipeg, Man.; *m.* Verla Scott; *children:* Diane, Gordon, Elaine, Scott; Gordon Bell HS, U of Manitoba; civil servant; competed in 11 provincial championships reaching finals four years in succession 1964-67 matching record of Ken Watson 1941-44; represented Manitoba in Brier 1964, 1967; winner Manitoba bonspiel 1961; honorary life mem. Manitoba Curling Association; *res.* Winnipeg, Man.

HUDSON, Gordon (curling); *b.* 5 Jan 1894, Kenora, Ont., *d.* 10 Jul 1959, Winnipeg, Man.; *m.* Flora MacLean; *children:* Bruce, Margaret; Kenora HS; manufacturers agent; early recognition as catcher in senior baseball Kenora area; at 20 won first of five Manitoba Bonspiel titles; skipped Brier winners 1928, 1929 winning 18 of 20 games played; past pres., honorary life mem. Manitoba, Dominion Curling Associations; mem. Canadian Curling Hall of Fame.

HULL, Bobby (hockey); *b.* 3 Jan 1939, Pointe Anne, Ont.; *given name:* Robert Marvin; *div.* Judy Learie; *children:* Terry; *m.* Joanne McKay; *children:* Bobby Jr., Blake, Brett, Bart, Michelle; hockey player, cattle farmer; played junior B Hespeler, Woodstock and Galt, junior A St. Catharines Black Hawks 1955-57; turned pro with Chicago Black Hawks 1957-58 season playing left wing in NHL through 1971-72 campaign before shifting to Winnipeg Jets of WHA; briefly player-coach before returning to playing only; second to Gordie Howe in goals, points scored; in 15 NHL seasons played in 1,036 regular schedule games scoring 604 goals, 549 assists for 1,153 points, 640 penalty minutes; in 116 playoff games scored 62 goals, 67 assists for 129 points and 102 penalty minutes; in four WHA seasons played in 330 games, scored 255 goals, 261 assists, 516 points, 160 penalty minutes; five 50-plus goal seasons with Chicago; first team all-star NHL 10 times, WHA four times; second team NHL twice; Art Ross Trophy (scoring) three times; Hart Trophy (NHL MVP) twice; Lady Byng Trophy (most gentlemanly NHL) once; Lester Patrick Award (service to hockey in US) once; Gary Davidson Trophy (WHA MVP) twice; nickname Golden Jet; fastest left-handed slap shot 118.3 mph, fastest skater 29.7 mph; Cana-da's male athlete of year 1965, 1966; *res.* Winnipeg, Man.

HUMBER, Bruce (track); *b.* 11 Oct 1913, Victoria, B.C.; *m.* Anne; *children:* Richard, Leslie Anne; U of Washington, B.A.; sales manager; all-time Seattle prep school records of 9.9, 21.8 in 100, 220yds; at University ran 9.6 and 20.8; mem. fourth place Canadian Olympic relay team 1936 Berlin Olympics; coach 1950 Canadian British Empire Games track team, 1952 Olympic team; mem. U of Washington, B.C. Sports Hall of Fame; *res.* Victoria, B.C.

HUME, Fred (lacrosse, hockey, soccer); *b.* 2 May 1892, Sapperton, B.C., *d.* 17 Feb 1967, Vancouver, B.C.; *given name:* Frederick; player, later pres. New Westminster Salmonbellies; pres. New Westminster Royals soccer team which won three Canadian championships; helped form Western Hockey League; owned, operated New Westminster Royals, later Vancouver Canucks in WHL; dominant role in bringing British Empire Games to Vancouver 1954; mem. B.C. Sports, Hockey, Lacrosse Halls of Fame.

HUNGERFORD, George (rowing); *b.* 2 Jan 1944, Vancouver, B.C.; *given name:* George William; *m.* Jane; *children:* Geordie, Michael, Andrew; U of British Columbia, B.A., LL.B.; lawyer; teamed with Roger Jackson to win pairs without cox gold medal 1964 Tokyo Olympics; Lou Marsh Trophy winner with Jackson 1964; trustee, secretary B.C. Sports Hall of Fame; director, v.-pres. Olympic Club Canada; mem. 1975 Pan-Am Games committee; mem. B.C., Canadian Sports Halls of Fame; *res.* Vancouver, B.C.

HUNT, Claudia (canoeing); *b.* 12 Mar 1950, Montreal, Que.; *m.* Sebastien Cardarelli; U of Ottawa, B.Sc.; student; at 16 competed internationally 1966 North American placing fifth K1 (single kayak); fifth K1 1967 Winnipeg Pan-Am Games, 1968 Mexico Olympics; campaigned in Canada 1969 winning K1, K2, K4 titles, North American K4 and placing second K1, third K2; Canadian K4 title 1970-74; competed 1970-71 Copenhagen, Belgrade world; represented Canada 1972 Munich Olympics, 1973 Finland world, 1974 Mexico world; *res.* Ottawa, Ont.

HUNT, Helen (volleyball, swimming); *b.* 28 Dec 1938, Vancouver, B.C.; *given name:* Helen Stewart; *m.* Ted Hunt; *children:* Shelley; U of British Columbia, B.E.; teacher; silver medal 1954 Commonwealth Games in 4x100 medley relay; gold medal 100m freestyle 1955 Pan-Am Games; represented Canada 1956 Melbourne Olympics; silver 1959 Pan-Am Games 4x100 freestyle relay; Canada's outstanding female swimmer 1955-56; B.C. athlete of year 1955; turned to volleyball and competed as mem. Canadian national women's team, Canadian women's championship B.C. team 1964-74; represented Canada 1967, 1971 Pan-Am Games volleyball competition; mem. B.C. Sports Hall of Fame; *res.* Vancouver, B.C.

HUNT, Ted (all-around); *b.* 15 Mar 1933, Vancouver, B.C.; *given name:* Edmund Arthur; *m.* Helen Stewart; *children:* Shelley; Lord Byng HS, U of British Columbia, B.P.E., M.P.E., Ed. D., U of Washington, M.A.; school administrator; captain B.C. in rugby victories over Australia 1958, Japan 1961; mem. McKechnie Trophy winning team; mem. Burrards Mann Cup Canadian champion lacrosse team 1961, 1964; B.C. Lions' halfback 1957-58; Lions' rookie of year 1957, candidate for CFL top Canadian 1958; mem. 1952 Canadian Olympic ski jumping team, 1954 FIS team, eighth 1954

Swedish national championships; while at UBC held light heavyweight boxing title four years; B.C. athlete of year 1957; Bob Gaul Memorial Award 1958; Howie McPhee Memorial Award 1961; mem. B.C. Sports Hall of Fame; *res.* Vancouver, B.C.

HUNTER, Gord (orienteering); *b.* 20 Jan 1946, Montreal, Que.; *sep.* Anne; *children:* Philip; Ridgemont HS, Dalhousie U, B.A.; phys ed teacher; played junior football 1970 Ottawa Sooners, rugby with Ottawa Indians 1969-73; involved in orienteering as novice 1970, B class 1971, elite class since 1973; second Ontario championships 1973-74, North American finals 1973, 1975; Canadian title 1972-74; 59th 1972 world Czechoslovakia, 48th 1974 world Denmark; *res.* Ottawa, Ont.

HUNTER, Jim (skiing); *b.* 30 May 1953, Shaunavon, Sask.; *given name:* James Mack; *m.* Gail Jespersen; farmer; began skiing at 12 winning first race he entered - Happy Valley Alta.; mem. Canadian World Cup team since 1970; bronze medal combined 1972 Sapporo Olympics; four times winner giant slalom Canadian championships, once combined winner, twice slalom; won US Snowmass giant slalom; twice winner Pontiac Cup giant slalom, once slalom; third World Cup downhill Wengen 1975; 10th downhill Innsbruck 1976 Olympics; Alberta athlete of year; nickname Jungle Jim; mem. Canadian World Cup team 1970-77; turned pro 1977; *res.* Calgary, Alta.

HUNTER, Malcolm (cross-country skiing); *b.* 23 May 1950, London, Eng., *given name:* Malcolm Wes; Carleton U, B.A.; ski coach; Canadian junior title 1968; Canadian senior 15km title 1969-70, 30km title 1971; represented Canada 1970 world Nordic ski championships, 1972 Olympics; *res.* Ottawa, Ont.

HUNTER, Rod (curling); *b.* 24 Aug 1943, Norwich, N.Y.; *given name:* Roderick George McLean; *m.* Patricia Gail Karman; *children:* Onalee, Charlene; Kelvin HS, U of Winnipeg, B.Sc.; transportation and purchasing manager; began curling 1957 as junior; under skip Don Duguid won Manitoba Consols, Brier and world Silver Broom championships 1970-71; skipped 1973 Manitoba Brier entry; won CBC televised curling series 1971-72, runner-up 1976; won 1970 Heather carspiel, International Crystal Trophy Zurich Switzerland; won Manitoba bonspiel grand aggregate 1970, 1975, Birks Trophy same 'spiel four times; *res.* Winnipeg, Man.

HURDIS, John (speedskating); *b.* 27 Apr 1927, Birmingham, Eng.; *m.* Mary Kathleen; *children:* Lynda, Janette, John; manager, professional development service; club skater in England beginning 1943; secretary National Ice Racing League of National Skating Association of Great Britain and GBNSA skating judge; v.-pres. Canadian Amateur Speedskating Association 1962-64, pres. 1967-70, 1972-76; coordinator several Canadian indoor, outdoor championship meets and Barrie Winter Carnival 1960-65; editor *The Racer,* Canada's official speedskating newspaper; governor National Centre for Sports and Recreation Ottawa; mem. COA Organizing Committee for 1976 Innsbruck Olympics; Centennial medal 1967; life mem. Birmingham Mohawks, US Amateur Skating Assoc., Polish Skating Assoc.; played major role in club development Toronto, K-W; *res.* Toronto, Ont.

HUTTON, Bouse (hockey, football, lacrosse); *b.* 24 Oct 1877, Ottawa, Ont., *d.* 27 Oct 1962, Ottawa, Ont.; *given name:* John Bower; goaler hockey, lacrosse, fullback football; mem. three Canadian championship teams 1907 (Minto Cup, Grey Cup, Stanley Cup); lacrosse Ottawa Capitals, won Minto Cup, toured England; fullback Ottawa Rough Riders, goaler Silver Seven; Ottawa intermediate hockey champions 1898-99, Silver Seven two games that season; with Silver Seven six seasons posting 2.90 goals-against avg. in 36 games; scored league's only two regular season shutouts 1901-02 season; allowed 28 goals in 12 playoff games; helped Silver Seven win two Stanley Cups; coach junior, senior hockey Ottawa several years; mem. Hockey Hall of Fame.

HUTTON, Ralph (swimming); *b.* 6 Mar 1948, Ocean Falls, B.C.; Colorado State U; nickname Iron Man; began swimming Ocean Falls 1960 under coach George Gate; freestyle, backstroke specialist; one-time holder of 11 Canadian records, one world mark 4:06.5 for 700m freestyle; represented Canada 1964, 1968, 1972 Olympics, 1963, 1967, 1971 Pan-Am Games, 1966, 1970 Commonwealth Games, won medals in all but Olympics; best showing 1967 Pan-Am Games with one gold, five silvers, three bronze; mem. 1972 Olympic 800m relay team which placed sixth and set Canadian record; mem. B.C., Canadian Sports Halls of Fame; *res.* Vancouver, B.C.

HYLAND, Harry (hockey); *b.* 2 Jan 1889, Montreal, Que., *d.* 8 Aug 1969, Montreal, Que.; early hockey Montreal Galics, St. Ann's, Shamrocks; pro with latter 1908-09 although still of junior age; scored twice in first pro game; joined Wanderers in time to play right wing on Stanley Cup winner; PCHL 1911-12 with New Westminster scoring 16 goals in 12 games as team won league title; rejoined Wanderers 1913 scoring eight goals in game vs Quebec, 28 for season; joined Ottawa 1918; mem. Hockey Hall of Fame.

IMLACH, Punch (hockey); *b.* 15 Mar 1918, Toronto, Ont.; *given name:* George; *m.* Dorothy; *children:* Brent, Marlene; hockey executive; played as teenager with Young Rangers Juniors, Toronto Marlboros, Toronto Goodyears Seniors; earned nickname Punch with Goodyears when he was knocked out in a game and swung punches at his team trainer; led army team in scoring one season as centre; brief trial with Detroit Red Wings following WW2; 11 years as player, coach, manager and eventually part-owner Anglo-Canadian Pulp and Paper Mills Quebec City; joined Bruins organization one year as manager-coach Springfield Indians then accepted manager-coach position with Toronto Maple Leafs 1958-69; coached Leafs to four Stanley Cups; sports columnist *Toronto Telegram* 1969-70 season then returned to hockey as general manager-coach Buffalo Sabres 1970, retired as coach 1971; *res.* Toronto, Ont.

ION, Mickey (hockey, lacrosse); *b.* 25 Feb 1886, Paris, Ont., *d.* 26 Oct 1964, Seattle, Wash., *given name:* Frederick; prominent lacrosse, baseball player in youth; pro lacrosse Toronto Tecumsehs, Vancouver, New

Westminster; refereed amateur hockey and attracted attention of Frank Patrick who moved him into pro ranks 1913; became top official in Pacific Coast League then NHL; refereed Howie Morenz Memorial game Montreal Forum 1937; retired 1941; mem. Hockey Hall of Fame.

IRVIN, Dick Sr. (hockey); *b.* 19 Jul 1892, Limestone Ridge, Ont., *d.* 16 May 1957, Montreal, Que.; *given name:* James Dickenson; *m.* Bertha Helen Bain; *children:* Dick Jr, Fay; hockey executive; played with Winnipeg Strathcona juniors, intermediate Monarchs; turned pro Portland Rosebuds (PCHL) 1915-16; reinstated amateur Regina Vics after WWI then turned pro again Regina Caps (WCHL), four seasons later moved to Portland; when club became Chicago Black Hawks 1926 Irvin went with them at age 34; in initial NHL season finished point behind Rangers' Bill Cook in scoring race; retired as player after skull fracture 1927 season; began coaching 1929 and put Hawks into playoffs first two years; joined Toronto and coached Maple Leafs to Stanley Cup; remained nine seasons with Leafs before joining Montreal Canadiens; coaching innovator, first to rotate three intact lines, employ goalie shuttle system; coach four Stanley Cup winners; mem. Hockey Hall of Fame.

IRVING, Wendy (equestrian); *b.* 11 Nov 1951, Ottawa, Ont.; *m.* George Dell; Champlain HS; riding instructor; three-day team event specialist; 1970 won Lou-Don Va., Delaware Valley Pa., Blue Ridge Va., Dalmohoy Montreal, fifth Eastern Canadian, second Ontario; 1971 won Joker's Hill, team gold Pan-Am Games, third Canadian championships, ninth Delaware Valley, seventh individual Pan-Am Games; 1972 sixth Canadian championships, 44th of 75 competitors Munich Olympics; *res.* King, Ont.

IRWIN, Cathy Lee (figure skating); *b.* 4 Sep 1952, Vancouver, B.C.; Havergal, Seneca College; figure skating teacher; seventh Canadian junior singles at 11; won Canadian junior singles 1966; gold medal 1967 Quebec Winter Games; won ladies' singles St. Gervais France Grand Prix 1970; second 1971 Richmond Trophy England; third Canadian women's 1972; represented Canada 1972 Olympics, world; won 1972 Moscow Skate; second Canadian women's, competed in 1973 world; turned pro with Holiday on Ice; second world pro championships Japan; winner several B.C., Ontario regional honors during amateur career; Centennial medal 1967; *res.* Whitby, Ont.

IRWIN, Dave (skiing); *b.* 12 Jul 1954, Thunder Bay, Ont.; Thunder Bay HS, Simon Fraser U; student; mem. national team since 1971, competed two years in Can-Am series, three in World Cup; one of two Canadian men to score World Cup downhill victory December 1975 winning Schladming Austria race; eighth downhill 1976 Innsbruck Olympics; Thunder Bay athlete of year 1973, 1975; Ontario athlete of year 1975; runner-up Canadian athlete of year 1975; *res.* Thunder Bay, Ont.

IVAN, Tommy (hockey); *b.* 31 Jan 1911, Toronto, Ont.; began pro career as scout for Detroit Red Wings organization; coach Omaha Knights (USHL) 1945-46, Indianapolis (AHL) 1946-47, Detroit Red Wings 1947-48; guided Wings to six consecutive NHL titles (Prince of Wales Trophy) and three Stanley Cups in seven seasons; joined Chicago Black Hawks as general manager 1954-55, coach following death of Dick Irvin, credited with building Hawks into a strong club through farm system; under his management Hawks have won one Stanley Cup, six division titles; responsible for many NHL rule changes; pioneered in tapping college ranks for talent; co-manager Team USA in Canada Cup 1976 series; nine-year coaching record shows 610 scheduled games, 302 wins, 196 losses, 112 ties for .587 percentage; in seven playoffs coached 67 games, won 36, lost 31 for .537 percentage; Lester Patrick Award 1975; mem. Hockey Hall of Fame; *res.* Lake Forest, Ill.

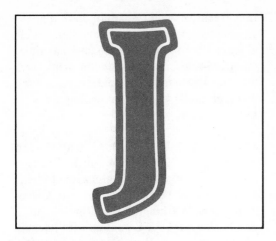

JACKSON, Busher (hockey); *b.* 19 Jan 1911, Toronto, Ont., *d.* 25 Jun 1966, Toronto, Ont.; *given name:* Harvey; product of Toronto junior Marlboros, turned pro Toronto Maple Leafs 1930; with Charlie Conacher, Joe Primeau formed Kid Line; played on three league champions, one Stanley Cup winner; five times NHL all-star, four times first team; Art Ross Trophy as NHL scoring leader 1932-33 with 28 goals, 25 assists; traded to NY Rangers 1939, Boston 1942 where he closed career 1943-44 season; played 633 regular season NHL games scoring 241 goals, 234 assists for 475 points and 72 playoff games with 18 goals, 12 assists for 30 points; mem. Hockey Hall of Fame.

JACKSON, Don (archery); *b.* 25 Oct 1932, Lindsay, Ont.; *given name:* Donald Arthur; operates archery business; self-taught archer who began shooting 1965, won Canadian Field Archery title 1966; runner-up field, target grand aggregate 1967; won both Canadian, Ontario indoor same year and placed ninth world target in Holland; won Ontario indoor, Canadian target, field, aggregate 1968, 1969, placed sixth world field,

ninth target; won Canadian target, runner-up field 1970; won Ontario indoor 1970-71, 10th world target in England; won Canadian Olympic trials 1972, sixth Munich Games; holds numerous Canadian records; *res.* Lindsay, Ont.

JACKSON, Donald (figure skating); *b.* 2 Apr 1940, Oshawa, Ont.; *m.* Joanne Diercks; *children:* one son; skating pro; winner Canadian junior 1955; seventh world 1957, fourth 1958, second 1959; won 1959 North American, Canadian seniors; bronze medal 1960 Olympics, won Canadian, second world; won 1961 Canadian, North American, 1962 world, Canadian senior championships; first of three skaters ever to perform triple lutz in competition Prague 1962; skated pro Ice Follies 1962-68; world pro champion 1970; Lou Marsh Trophy 1962; mem. AAU of C, Canadian Sports Halls of Fame; *res.* Agincourt, Ont.

JACKSON, Robbie (golf); *b.* 25 Mar 1955, Montreal, Que.; *given name:* Robert Donald; Lower Canada College, Indiana U; won 1970 Canadian juvenile, 1971-73 Quebec junior, 1972-73 Canadian junior, 1973-76 Alexander of Tunis, 1974-76 Quebec amateur, 1974 Kentucky Invitational, 1974-75 mem. Big 10 conference golf champions; tied for first 1976 Southern Intercollegiate but lost playoff; Les Bolstead Award for Big 10 conference low avg. 1975; four times Quebec Willingdon Cup team; mem. Canadian World Cup team 1976; twice Quebec golfer of year; *res.* Town of Mount Royal, Que.

JACKSON, Roger (rowing); *b.* 14 Jan 1942, Toronto, Ont.; *given name:* Roger Charles; *m.* Linda; *children:* Christopher; U of Western Ontario, B.A., U of British Columbia, M.P.E., U Wisconsin, Ph.D.; director Sport Canada; mem. 1960-63 university national rowing eights champions; teamed with George Hungerford to win gold medal coxless pairs 1964 Tokyo Olympics; second cox-fours 1965 Lucerne International regatta; with R. Fieldwalter won 1965 Scandinavian coxless pairs; competed 1966 coxless fours in Yugoslavia world; finalist single sculls 1968 Mexico Olympics; competed in 1970 St. Catharines world; competed cox-fours 1972 Munich Olympics; with Hungerford won Lou Marsh Trophy as Canada's outstanding athletes 1964; coordinated Sport Canada's Game Plan 1976; mem. Canadian Sports Hall of Fame; *res.* Lucerne, Que.

JACKSON, Russ (football); *b.* 28 Jun 1936, Hamilton, Ont.; *given name:* Russell Stanley; *m.* Lois Hendershot; *children:* Kevin, Suzanne, Nancy; McMaster U, B.A., M.A.; HS principal; played Senior Intercounty baseball with Hamilton; joined Ottawa Rough Riders 1959, starting quarterback 1963; retired 1969; in 12 pro playing seasons attempted 2,511 passes completing 1,341 for 23,341yds, .533 percentage, 125 intercepted and 184 caught for TDs; led CFL Eastern Conference passers six times; as runner carried 738 times for 5,045yds, 6.6 avg., scored 55 TDs for 330 points; guided Ottawa to Grey Cup finals four times, winning three; Schenley Award as outstanding player three times; top Canadian four times, runner-up twice; Jeff Russel Memorial Trophy twice; CP Poll Canadian male athlete of year twice; Lou Marsh Trophy 1969; coach Toronto Argonauts 1975-76; mem. Canadian Football Hall of Fame; *res.* Toronto, Ont.

JACOBS, Dave (skiing); *b.* 1 Oct 1933, Montreal, Que.; *given name:* David Lloyd; *m.* Helen Faye; *children:* Bernard, William Kelly, Tracy; St. Lawrence U, B.Sc.; corporate executive; won Canadian downhill championship 1957; mem. Canadian national team 1957-61; head coach national alpine team 1964-66; since 1961 senior mem. Canadian Ski Instructors Association; since 1964 mem. National Coaches Association; *res.* Boulder, Colo.

JACOBS, Jack (football); *b.* 1920, Holdenville, Okla., *d.* 12 Jan 1974 North Greensboro, N.C.; Oklahoma U; nickname Indian Jack; National Football League with Cleveland Rams, Washington Redskins, Green Bay Packers; led NFL punters with Packers 1947; quarterback Winnipeg Blue Bombers 1950-54; completed 709 of 1,330 passes for 11,094yds, 104 TDs, punted 518 times for 21,248yds, 41.0 avg., 57 singles; prolific passer, completed 31 of 48 vs Hamilton 1953, six TD passes vs Calgary 1952; scouted for Bombers 1955; coached London Lords (ORFU) two seasons; assistant coach Hamilton, Montreal, Edmonton; Jeff Nicklin Memorial Trophy (MVP) 1952; twice guided Bombers to Grey Cup final but lost both; twice all-star; mem. Canadian Football Hall of Fame.

JAMES, Eddie (football); *b.* 30 Sep 1907, Winnipeg, Man., *d.* 26 Dec 1958, Winnipeg, Man.; *given name:* Edwin; *m.* Moira Kathleen FitzGerald; *children:* Don, Gerry; Charleswood HS; nickname Dynamite; offensive, defensive halfback with Winnipeg, Regina Pats, Winnipeg St. John's and Regina Roughriders through 20s and early 30s; trophy in his honor awarded annually to WFC leading rusher; charter mem. Canadian Football Hall of Fame.

JAMES, Gerry (football, hockey); *b.* 22 Oct 1934, Regina, Sask.; *given name:* Gerald Edwin; *m.* Margaret Petrie; *children:* Debra,

Tracy, Tara, Kelly, Brady; Kelvin HS; store proprietor; son of Dynamite James; HS football to CFL at 17; played 11 seasons with Winnipeg, Sask. 1952-64, scored 63 TDs, 143 converts, 40 field goals, 21 singles for 645 points; carried 995 times for 5,554yds (5.6yd avg.), 57 TDs; twice rushed for 1,000-plus yds in one season; CFL season record for TDs scored rushing with 18 1957; scored one other on pass reception same season to tie Pat Abbruzzi with 19; twice Dave Dryburgh Trophy as WFC scoring leader, once runner-up; twice WFC all-star; twice Canadian Schenley Award; played junior hockey with Toronto Marlboros and turned pro as right wing with Toronto Maple Leafs 1954-55 season; played five NHL seasons appearing in 149 regular season games, scoring 14 goals, 26 assists for 40 points and 257 penalty minutes; in 15 playoff games scored one goal; coach Melville Millionaires junior A team; *res.* Yorkton, Sask.

JANZEN, Henry (football); *b.* 7 Jun 1940, Winnipeg, Man.; *m.* Judy Munro; *children:* Dean, Joanne; U of North Dakota, B.Sc., U of Northern Colorado, M.A., Ph.D.; university athletic director; joined Winnipeg Blue Bombers 1959, Dr. Beattie Martin Trophy as WFC rookie of year; outstanding Canadian on Blue Bombers 1962, 1965; all-Canadian 1965; led WFC in punt return yardage 394, and best avg. runback 7.3yds; retired 1966; coached U of Manitoba Bisons to Canadian College Bowl championship 1969-70; Canadian college coach of year 1969; *res.* Winnipeg, Man.

JARDIN, Anne (swimming); *b.* 26 Jul 1959, Montreal, Que.; *given name:* Anne Elizabeth; Pointe Claire HS, U of Houston; student; freestyle (FS), butterfly specialist who worked way through age-group ranks to national team 1974; competed in 1974 Canadian championships, fourth 100m FS 1974 Commonwealth Games; silver medal 400m FS relay, bronze 200m FS, fourth 100m FS 1975 Pan-Am Games; seventh 1975 world 100m FS; competed with national team in Holland 1975-76; bronze 4x100 FS relay, 4x100 medley relay 1976 Montreal Olympics; personal bests: 100m FS 57.48 (Canadian, Commonwealth record), 200m FS 1:49.11 (Canadian record), 400m FS 4:28.08; mem. Houston U swim team; Governor-General's silver medal 1976; *res.* Pointe Claire, Que.

JAUCH, Ray (football); *b.* 11 Feb 1938, Mendota, Ill.; *m.* Sarah; *children:* four sons; Iowa U, B.Sc.; football executive; mem. 1959 Iowa Rose Bowl team; turned pro Winnipeg Blue Bombers 1960; turned to coaching after leg injury 1961; coach Winnipeg junior Rods 1962, Iowa U 1964; joined Edmonton Eskimos 1966 as assistant to Neill Armstrong, head coach 1970-76; Annis Stukus Trophy as CFL coach of year in rookie season; guided Eskimos to WFC title 1973-75 winning Grey Cup 1975; *res.* Edmonton, Alta.

JELINEK, Maria (figure skating); *b.* 16 Nov 1942, Prague, Czechoslovakia; *m.* Paul Harrington; *children:* one son; U of Michigan; teamed with brother Otto in pairs competition, (see Otto Jelinek for record); pro skater 1963-69 Ice Capades; mem. Canadian Sports Hall of Fame; *res.* Toronto, Ont.

JELINEK, Otto (figure skating); *b.* 20 May 1940, Prague, Czechoslovakia; *m.* Leata; Appleby College, Swiss Alpine Business College; politician, real estate broker, sporting goods manufacturer; with sister Maria won

1955 Canadian junior pairs; third 1957-58 world, fourth 1959, second 1960; fourth for Canada 1960 Olympics; won 1961 North American, Canadian senior pairs, 1962 Canadian senior, world; pro skater Ice Capades 1963-69; Lake Placid pro pairs title 1964; MP(PC) for Hyde Park since 1972; mem. Canadian Sports Hall of Fame; *res.* Carp, Ont.

JENKINS, Ferguson (baseball); 13 Feb 1943, Chatham, Ont.; *m.* Cathy Henson; *children:* two daughters; Chatham CVI; baseball player; at 16 played Western Counties senior baseball Chatham; signed with Philadelphia Phillies organization 1962; four seasons in minors, 43-26 won-lost record mostly in relief roles; traded to Chicago Cubs 1966 where Leo Durocher installed him as starter; Cub record six 20-victory campaigns, National League Cy Young award 1971 for 24-13 record; dealt to American League Texas Rangers 1974, 25-12 record, Cy Young award runner-up to Catfish Hunter, AL comeback player of year, fifth in AL MVP voting; traded to Boston Red Sox 1976 where Achilles tendon injury cut short pitching season; through 12 Major League seasons (1976) recorded 203 victories, 150 losses; four times CP poll Canadian male athlete of year; Lou Marsh Trophy 1974; gaining reputation as hunting dog breader; *res.* Blenheim, Ont.

JENSEN, Al (golf); *b.* 24 Jan 1938, Montreal, Que.; *given name:* Allan Howard; *m.* Mary Ellen Clark; *children:* Allan Jr., Jimmy; Rosemount HS; golf pro; runner-up Canadian Assistants championships 1975; won four pro tournaments 1976 and Earl Stimpson Shield for best overall tournament performance among Ottawa Valley pros;

three competitive course records: 59 Poplar Grove, 70 Petawawa, 66 Hylands South course; *res.* Ottawa, Ont.

JEROME, Harry (track); *b.* 30 Sep 1940, Prince Albert, Sask.; *given name:* Henry Winston; *div.* Wendy; U of Oregon, B.Sc., M.A.; teacher; in 1960 ran 100m in 10.00 to share world record with Germany's Armin Hary; tied world 100yd sprint with 9.3 Corvallis Ore. 1961; twice in Canada ran 9.2, tied Bob Hayes' world record 9.1 in Edmonton 1966; won 1962 NCAA 220yd in 20.8; anchored Oregon team that equalled world 440yd relay record of 40.00 on course with two turns; represented Canada 1960, 1964, 1968 Olympics; bronze medal 100m in 10.1 1964, fourth 200m; ran 100m in 10.1 1968 but finished seventh; gold 100m 1967 Winnipeg Pan-Am Games in 10.2; at one time held six world sprint records; for several years Sport Canada consultant; mem. Order of Canada; mem. B.C., AAU of C, Canadian Sports Halls of Fame; *res.* Vancouver, B.C.

JOHNSON, Ching (hockey); *b.* 7 Dec 1897, Winnipeg, Man.; *given name:* Ivan Wilfrid; defenceman Winnipeg Monarchs 1919 then moved to Eveleth Minn. Miners for three seasons followed by three more campaigns with Minneapolis Millers; purchased by N Y Rangers 1926, won two Stanley Cups during 11-year tenure; played final two NHL seasons with N Y Americans, retired at 41; continued to play hockey until 46 with Minneapolis Minn., Marquette Mich., Washington D.C. and Hollywood Wolves; as player-coach with Wolves won Helms Award; during 1926-38 NHL career appeared in 463 scheduled games scoring 38 goals, 48 assists for 86 points and 969 penalty minutes; represented Rangers in first NHL all-star game 1934; three times first team all-star, twice second team; mem. Hockey Hall of Fame; *res.* Takoma Park, Md.

JOHNSON, Moose (hockey); *b.* 1886, Montreal, Que., *d.* 25 Mar 1963, White Rock, B.C.; *given name:* Ernest; began playing junior hockey around 1900, by 1903-04 was playing left wing, defence for Montreal MAAA; turned pro Montreal Wanderers and played on four Stanley Cup winners; moved to New Westminster Royals 1912; played 11 years in PCL with Portland, Victoria Maroons, Los Angeles scoring 123 goals in 270 games and earning all-star 10 consecutive years; PCL staged special Moose Johnson night in his honor; mem. Hockey Hall of Fame.

JOHNSON, Tom (hockey); *b.* 18 Feb 1928, Baldur, Man.; *given name:* Thomas Christian; began with Winnipeg junior Monarchs 1945, went to Montreal senior Royals, then spent 1948-50 seasons with Buffalo (AHL); joined Canadiens' defensive corps 1949-50 for playoffs and remained with Habs until 1963 when he went to Boston Bruins until retirement 1965; in 15 NHL seasons played 978 games, scored 51 goals, 213 assists; played on six Stanley Cup winners; first team all-star 1959, second team 1956; Norris Trophy (top NHL defenceman) 1959; coached Boston to first Prince of Wales Trophy in 30 years 1970-71, repeated 1971-72 winning Stanley Cup also; assistant to general manager 1973; mem. Hockey Hall of Fame; *res.* Boston, Mass.

JOHNSTON, John (golf); *b.* 19 May 1925, Vancouver, B.C.; *m.* Elizabeth; *children:* Gregory, John, David; Lord Byng HS; real estate salesman; won 1953 New Westminster, 1959 Canadian amateur beating Gary

Cowan one up; won Mexican amateur, Penticton Open, B.C. Open 1967; same year named to Canadian Commonwealth team; six times B.C. Willingdon Cup team mem., four times America's Cup team; mem. B.C. Sports Hall of Fame; *res.* Vancouver, B.C.

JOLIAT, Aurel (hockey); *b.* 29 Aug 1901, Ottawa, Ont.; *given name:* Aurel Emile; *m.* Berthe *(d.)*, *m.* Yvette; retired railway employee; kicking fullback with New Edinburgh (Ottawa), Ottawa Rough Riders and Regina Wascana Boat Club before turning to hockey; early experience New Edinburgh, Iroquois Falls, Saskatoon Shieks; Canadiens traded Newsy Lalonde for Joliat 1922-23 season; played left wing for Canadiens until retirement 1938; nicknames Mighty Atom, Little Giant; scored 270 goals over 16 NHL seasons; played on three Stanley Cup winners; Hart Trophy 1934; first all-star team once, second team three times; mem. Ottawa, Canadian Sports, Hockey Halls of Fame; *res.* Ottawa, Ont.

JONAS, Don (football); *b.* 3 Dec 1938, Scranton, Pa.; *given name:* Donald Walter; *m.* Rosemary Eisman; *children:* Jaudon, Jennifer; West Scranton HS, Penn State U, B.S.; public relations; all-American in college; turned pro as running back with Philadelphia Eagles 1962; cut after first league game, joined Atlantic Coast League earning MVP; played with Newark Bears, Orlando Panthers Continental League, MVP three consecutive seasons; led Panthers to four pennants, two league titles; set Continental single-game record 63 pass attempts, 25 completions; single-season record 41 TD passes, kicked 56 consecutive converts 1968-69; joined CFL with Toronto Argos, Winnipeg Blue Bombers, Hamilton Tiger-Cats 1970-74; CFL record 1,930 passes, 997 completions, 15,064yds, .516 percentage, 130 interceptions, 98 TDs; Jeff Nicklin (WFC MVP), Dave Dryburgh (WFC scoring), Schenley (CFL outstanding player) awards 1971; twice WFC all star, once all-Canadian; mem. Scranton Sports Hall of Fame; *res.* Casselberry, Fla.

JONES, Diane (track and field); *b.* 7 Mar 1951, Vancouver, B.C.; *given name:* Diane Helen; U of Saskatchewan, B.E.; student; Canadian pentathlon champion 1969, 1972, 1976, junior titlist 1970; fourth world with electronic timing; Canadian senior indoor long jump champion 1974; pentathlon gold 1975 Pan-Am Games Mexico, silver 1974 Commonwealth Games New Zealand, bronze 1973 World Student Games; represented Canada 1972 Munich Olympics (10th pentathlon), 1976 Montreal Olympics (fourth pentathlon), also competed in long jump; since 1968 has represented Canada in all major Games excluding 1968 Olympics, 1971 Pan-Am Games; Polish, Czechoslovakian pentathlon titles 1974 European tour; broke world indoor pentathlon record Edmonton national championships 1975 with 4,540; personal best (outdoors) 4,673 winning 1975 Pan-Am Games; Canadian indoor 50m hurdle record 7.1m, Canadian long jump 6.37m, shot put 16.23m; nickname Saskatoon Sunflower; *res.* Saskatoon, Sask.

JOY, Greg (track and field); *b.* 23 Apr 1956, Portland, Ore.; *given name:* Gregory Andrew; Laura Secord HS, Vancouver THS, U of Texas; student; Canadian Interscholastic record 2.12m; competed in 1973 Canada Games scoring personal best jump; in Sweden scored another personal best vs Dwight Stones; fourth Canadian championships 1973 with 6'9¾", second 1974 Canadian

championships with 6'10¾"; toured Europe with Canadian track team 1974; in Athens improved personal best with 7'2" jump; silver 1976 Olympics with 7'3¾"; personal best indoors 1.914m, outdoors 7'5", 7'6" in practice; mem. Optimist Striders Track Club coached by Steve Spencer; Governor-General's silver medal 1976; Norton Crowe Trophy as Canadian amateur male athlete of year 1976; *res.* Vancouver, B.C.

JUCKES, Gordon (hockey); *b.* 20 Jun 1914, Watrous, Sask.; *given name:* Gordon Wainwright; *m.* Clara Thompson; *children:* two daughters, two sons; Melville HS; mem. Saskatchewan AHA 1948-60; pres. CAHA 1959-60; executive director CAHA 1960-77; *res.* Ottawa, Ont.

KAILL, Bob (orienteering); *b.* 12 Dec 1942, Liverpool, N.S.; *given name:* Robert Douglas; *m.* Kristina Eriksson; *children:* Erik; U of Waterloo, B.A., U of Gothenburg, Sweden; teacher, writer; top Canadian at Canadian championships 1971; never beaten by a North American in major European competition; top Canadian world championships Czechoslovakia 1972, Denmark 1974; only Canadian competitor E. Germany world 1970; editor *National Orienteering; res.* Guelph, Ont.

KARCZ, Zeno (football); *b.* 16 Mar 1935, Toronto, Ont.; *given name:* Zenon Peter; *m.* Ethel Cullen; Windsor Patterson CI, U of Michigan, B.A.; sales manager; played baseball Detroit Federation League; after two seasons with Windsor AKO received football scholarship to Michigan; turned pro Hamilton Tiger-Cats 1956, no regular action until 1958; equally adept as halfback, end, corner linebacker; EFC all-star three times; *Globe and Mail* all-Canadian defensive team linebacker 1964; Schenley Canadian Award 1965; played in eight Grey Cup games, three winners; coach Windsor minor hockey, AKO football, Hamilton minor hockey, football; *res.* Burlington, Ont.

KARRYS, Steve (football); *b.* 20 Jun 1924, Montreal, Que.; *m.* Helen Bazos; *children:* Anita Elaine, Steven James; Northern HS, U of Toronto; wholesale distributor; Toronto Argos 1945-46, 1951-52, U of T 1947, Ottawa Rough Riders 1948-50; in four Grey Cup finals, three winners; defensive back Argos modern era all-stars (1945-73); *res.* Willowdale, Ont.

KASTING, Robert (swimming); *b.* 28 Aug 1950, Ottawa, Ont.; Yale U, B.A., Stockholm, Dip. Social Science, McGill U; law student; all-Ivy honors with Yale swim team 1970-72, all-American 1970, 1972; captain Yale swim team 1972; silver 400m freestyle (FS), 800m FS relays, fourth 100m FS 1967 Pan-Am Games; captain Canadian 1972 Olympic swim team winning bronze 400m medley relay, 10th 100m FS, butterfly; silver 400m FS, 800m FS relays 1966, 1970 Commonwealth Games; gold 400m medley relay 1970 Commonwealth Games; bronze 100m FS, silver 400m FS, 800m FS, 400m medley relays 1971 Pan Am Games; fourth 400m medley relay, eighth 100m FS 1975 world championships; *res.* Montreal, Que.

KAUFMANIS, Eric (golf); *b.* 29 Sep 1960, Toronto, Ont.; Wake Forest U, student; outstanding T & F, basketball star Philemon Wright HS Hull Que.; all-Ottawa Valley honors; won Quebec golf association boys-10-12, 12-14 titles; Glenlea GC men's title 1974; quarterfinalist East Aurora N.Y. junior invitational 1975, winner 1976; won Quebec juvenile 1975-76; runner-up Canadian juvenile 1975-76; won Ottawa District junior 1975-76; Ottawa District men's 1976; competed Miami Junior Orange Bowl invitational 1976; mem. Royal Ottawa, Rideau View GC; *res.* Aylmer East, Que.

KEATING, Murray (track and field); *b.* 28 May 1952, Manning, Alta.; *given name:* Kenneth Murray; *m.* Sheila Punshon; Simon Fraser U, B.A.; assistant manager contracting co.; hammer throw specialist; B.C. HS, Canadian juvenile titles 1970; second Canadian junior 1971; Canadian junior title with record 59.22m (194'3"), second NAIA nationals 1972; Canadian senior record 64.30m vs Japan, US, Australia, N.Z., competed in World Student Games Moscow; won NAIA title 1973; Canadian title 1975 with 67.46m record, fourth Pan-Am Games with 64.06; Canadian record 68.30 and represented Canada 1976 Montreal Olympics placing 19th with 65.68m; *res.* Victoria, B.C.

KEATS, Duke (hockey); *b.* 1 Mar 1895, Montreal, Que., *d.* 16 Jan 1972; *given name:* Gordon Blanchard; at 17 turned pro with Toronto (NHA); returned to amateur briefly with Peterborough then rejoined Toronto; played amateur hockey with Edmonton, pro 1919-20 with Patricks, led WCL in scoring 1922-23; sold to Boston (NHL), transferred to Detroit midway through season, joined Chicago 1927; to Tulsa American Association, won scoring title; remained in hockey several more seasons with various Western Canada League teams; scored 119 goals in 128 games prior to playing in NHL where he added 30 goals in two seasons; mem. Hockey Hall of Fame.

KELLOND, Lyn (track); *b.* 18 Nov 1953, Hamilton, Ont.; Sheridan CI; secretary; Canadian junior title 100m 1971-73; third 100m Canadian senior championships 1972-74; represented Canada vs Portugal 1973, Commonwealth Games 1974, vs Romania, Poland, Greece, France, England, Wales, Germany 1975, Pan-Am Games 1975; personal bests: 11.4 for 100m, 24.1 for 200m; Olympics 1976; *res.* Toronto, Ont.

KELLS, Morley (lacrosse); *b.* 26 Jan 1936, Midland, Ont.; *given name:* Morley Cecil; *m.* Gloria Pellegrin; *children:* Christine, Bradley, Terrence, Louise; Mimico HS; pres. sports services co.; began playing lacrosse at 16, turned to coaching, administration at 24; helped lead Long Branch Monarchs to 1955 Minto Cup as player; coached Brantford Warriors to 1971 Mann Cup; coach, general manager Rochester Griffins winning 1974 Nations Cup; with Jim Bishop, Bruce Norris, helped create National Lacrosse League 1973; first recipient CLA Lester B. Pearson Award for contribution to game 1973; *res.* Etobicoke, Ont.

KELLY, Con (football, speedskating); *b.* 15 Jan 1934, Edmonton, Alta.; *m.* Marlene McDermott; *children:* Con Jr., Vincent, Nancy Lee; plumber; nickname Shipwreck Kelly; all-star HS basketball 1951; Saskatchewan, Alberta junior speedskating titles 1946-47; played junior football with Edmonton Wildcats, appeared in 1952 Little Grey Cup final Windsor Ont.; three years with Edmonton Eskimos as fullback, played in 1955-56 Grey Cup finals; *res.* Edmonton, Alta.

KELLY, Red (hockey); *b.* 19 Jul 1927, Simcoe, Ont.; *given name:* Leonard Patrick; *m.* Andra McLaughlin; *children:* four; Norfolk DHS, St. Michael's College; hockey coach; began career with St. Michael's junior B club which won three successive titles; joined Detroit Red Wings 1947 and played 12½ seasons before trade to Toronto Maple Leafs 1959-67; retired to coach Los Angeles Kings; coach Pittsburgh Penguins 1970-73, Leafs since 1973; during 20 NHL seasons played 1,316 regular season games scoring 281 goals, 542 assists for 823 points and only 327 penalty minutes; four-time Lady Byng

Trophy winner; in 164 playoff games scored 33 goals, 59 assists for 92 points, 47 penalty minutes; played on nine Prince of Wales Trophy winners, eight with Wings; played on eight Stanley Cup winners, four with Wings, four with Leafs; first winner Norris Trophy as NHL's best defenceman; six times first team all-star, twice second team; *Hockey News* NHL coach of year 1970; MP(Lib) York-West 1962-65; mem. Canadian Sports, Hockey Halls of Fame; *res.* Toronto, Ont.

KEMP, Sally (coaching); *b.* 15 Sep 1939, Montreal, Que.; *given name:* Sally Elizabeth; MacDonald College, Sir George Williams U, B.A., SUNY Cortland, M.Sc.; phys ed teacher; outstanding athlete in senior HS year; at MacDonald played basketball two years, MVP soccer and hockey; played basketball with YWCA Blues 1964-68, Harmony, Jackson Five teams Kitchener winning frequent city titles; coach women's basketball, volleyball, badminton at Sir George Williams 1965-68, basketball, field hockey Waterloo since 1968, basketball, volleyball at YM-YWCA Leadership camps, Camp Cuyaga; pres. Montreal Women's Basketball League 1966-68, East-West Conference Intercollegiate athletics 1967-68; past pres. Ontario Women's Intercollegiate Athletic Association; mem. executive committee OLBA 1972-74, pres. 1974-75; v.-pres. Waterloo regional sports council since 1974; *res.* Waterloo, Ont.

KENNEDY, Bill (swimming); *b.* 26 Oct 1952, London, Ont.; *given name:* William Ray; *m.* Deborah Stock; U of Michigan, U of Western Ontario, B.A., U of Ottawa; student; held Canadian records 10 through 14 age groups; at 14 youngest mem. 1967 Pan-Am Games team placing seventh 100m backstroke; three gold Halifax Canada Games 1969; two gold 1970 Edinburgh Commonwealth Games; bronze 100m backstroke 1971 Cali Colombia Pan-Am Games; mem. 1972 Olympic team placing 15th 200m backstroke; three times Canadian Intercollegiate titlist; *res.* Ottawa, Ont.

KENNEDY, Louise (swimming); *b.* 16 Aug 1949, London, Ont.; *given name:* Helen Louise; *m.* James Glen Cross; *children:* Cameron James; U of Western Ontario, B.A., represented Canada 1964 Tokyo Olympics; toured W. Germany, Holland, France and England with Canadian swim team 1965; mem. Canadian world record 440yd freestyle relay team Commonwealth Games Jamaica 1966; toured South Africa with national team 1967; *res.* Oakville, Ont.

KENNEDY, Ted (hockey); *b.* 12 Dec 1925, Humberstone, Ont.; *given name:* Theodore; nickname Teeder; played juvenile, senior hockey Port Colborne Ont.; joined Toronto Maple Leafs at 16, captain at 22 and led Leafs to five Stanley Cup victories; Hart Trophy (MVP) 1954-55 season; led Leaf scorers 1946-47 with 28 goals, 32 assists for 60 points in 60 games; following season had eight goals, six assists in nine playoff games; in 696 league games scored 231 goals, 329 assists for 560 points; in 74 playoff games scored 28 goals, 28 assists for 56 points; centred Leafs' second Kid Line of Vic Lynn, Howie Meeker; retired following 1955 season but returned briefly 1957 to help injury-riddled Leafs; coached briefly at Upper Canada College and Peterborough Petes in OHA junior; twice J.P. Bickell Memorial Trophy as Leaf's MVP; mem. Hockey, Canadian Sports Halls of Fame; *res.* Toronto, St. Mary's, Ont.

KEON, Dave (hockey); *b.* 22 Mar 1940, Noranda, Que.; *given name:* David Michael; *m.* Lola; *children:* David, Anne, Marie, Kathleen, Tim; hockey player, business executive; played with Noranda Mines juveniles; tryout at 15 Red Wings' camp Burlington Ont.; played three years with Toronto St. Mike's; four-game stint with Sudbury (EPHL) before joining Toronto Maple Leafs as centre, right wing 1960-61; Calder Memorial Trophy as NHL's top rookie; twice Lady Byng Trophy; Conn Smythe Trophy in 1967 playoffs; twice second team all-star centre; captain Leafs; in 15 NHL seasons appeared in 1,062 games scoring 365 goals, 493 assists for 858 points, 75 penalty minutes, plus 89 playoff games, 32 goals, 35 assists, 67 points and six penalty minutes; with Billy Harris operates successful summer hockey school; WHA with Minnesota, New England 1975-77; WHA record: 145 games, 56 goals, 108 assists, 164 points and 16 penalty minutes; mem. Team Canada 1977; *res.* Toronto, Ont.

KER, Michael (swimming); *b.* 21 Jul 1957, Vancouver, B.C.; *given name:* Michael Gordon; student; four gold, one silver 1973 Canada Games; holds Canadian senior records in 400m, 800m, 1500m, 500yd, 1,000yd, 1,650yd FS events; winner Canadian national championship 1500m 1973, 1975; represented Canada 1973, 1975 world championships, 1976 Olympics; four gold, one bronze 1975 Western Canada Games; *res.* Vancouver, B.C.

KERN, Ben (golf); *b.* 11 Aug 1946, Rolandia, Brazil; *m.* Janet; New Mexico College; runner-up 1965 Ontario amateur, 1967 Ontario Open; won 1968-69 New Mexico intercollegiate, 1969 New Mexico college invitational, 1968 New Mexico Open; turned pro 1969; in 1974 won New Mexico PGA and was low Canadian in Canadian Open; twice mem. Canadian World Cup team; best finish 10th 1973 Sahara Open; tied second Sun City Open, sixth Sea Pines Open on satellite tour; *res.* Clarkson, Ont.

KERN, Laurie (track and field); *b.* 6 Feb 1957, Vancouver, B.C.; U of British Columbia; student; javelin specialist; B.C. bantam title 1971 with record 136' 8½'' toss; Canadian record 152'2'' 1972 Western Canada midget title; record 161'4'' Canada Games 1973; won Canadian senior, WAAA championship England same year; mem. Canadian national team on 1974 European tour; Canadian record 164'2'' 1975 Canadian junior title; topped previous standard 1976 with 174'9¾''; *res.* Richmond, B.C.

KERNS, John (football); *b.* 17 Jun 1923, Ashtabula, Ohio; *m.* Faye Radman; *children:* Lynne, Deborah, John; Ohio U; life insurance salesman; turned pro with Toronto Argos 1950 helping club win Grey Cup that season; player, line coach 1951, line coach 1952-53; *res.* Toronto, Ont.

KERR, Bobby (track); *b.* 1882, Ireland, *d.* 1963, Hamilton, Ont.; won 100yd, 440yd, 880yd races Hamilton Coronation Games 1902; 1903-04 won 100yd, 220yd events in Canadian championships; competed in 1904 St. Louis Olympics, won 100yd heat before being eliminated; 100yd, 220yd Canadian titles 1907 and 41 firsts in other races; Canadian record 9.4 for 100yd; in 1908 set Canadian 50yd record, won London Olympics gold 200m, bronze 100m; prior to Olympics competed in British Stamford Bridge meet winning 100yd, 220yd events and Harvey Gold Cup as meet's outstanding athlete; defended both titles 1909 Dublin, became

Irish champion; selected for Stockholm Olympics but chose retirement; during competitive career won nearly 400 awards, trophies, set six Canadian records; mem. Canadian Sports, AAU of C. Halls of Fame.

KERR, Dave (track); *b.* 1 Jun 1946, Toronto, Ont.; *m.* Anne Sauasvous; Ball State U, Miami of Ohio, B.Sc.; teacher; middle distance specialist; all-American cross-country college champion 1967; mem. all-American track team 1968, all-American indoor track team 1969; runner-up 1500m Olympic trials 1968; won NCAA 1500m, record holder 1968; represented Canada 1974 European tour; *res.* Scarborough, Ont.

KERWIN, Gale (boxing); *b.* 9 Jan 1935, Ottawa, Ont.; *given name:* Gale Allen; *m.* Joyce Payne; *children:* Allen, Kathleen, Shawn, Christine; politician, real estate broker; competed as amateur 1947-53 attaining finals twice in Olympic trials; turned pro 1954 KO'ing Vic Compos of Brooklyn in first round; Canadian welterweight title 1958 KO'ing Bobo Fiddler in the 12th; lost bid for world lightweight title to Joe Brown on fourth round TKO 1959; challenged 1960 for world middleweight title, lost to Ralph Dupas on seventh round TKO; lost bid for world junior welterweight title 1961 to Julio Loi in Milano Italy on sixth round TKO; never KO'd in pro career but in all three title bouts was stopped on TKO, the result of cuts; won British Empire welterweight division, 10th world welterweight division; retired from ring following first round KO of Frank Marvin 1962; pro record: 47 bouts, won 12 by KO, 21 by decision, three draws, lost three on TKOs, eight on decision; *res.* Ottawa, Ont.

KEYS, Eagle (football); *b.* 4 Dec 1923, Tompkinsville, Ky.; *m.* Joyce White; *children:* Betty, Buddy, Dale, Janice, Karen; Western Kentucky State College, B.S., U of Kentucky, M.A.; football coach; turned pro in CFL as centre with Montreal Alouettes 1949; moved to Edmonton Eskimos 1952, all-Western 1952-54; following 1954 Eskimos Grey Cup win retired to coach; head coach Eskimos 1959 guiding them to Grey Cup final 1960; joined Sask. Roughriders as assistant 1964, head coach 1965-70, guided club to Grey Cup victory 1966, finals 1967, 1969; head coach B.C. Lions 1971-75; Annis Stukus Trophy as CFL coach of year 1968; *res.* Burnaby, B.C.

KIDD, Bruce (track); *b.* 26 Aug 1943, Ottawa, Ont.; *div.;* U of Toronto, B.A., U of Chicago, M.A.; assistant professor; Commonwealth six-mile championship 1962; Canadian one-mile title 1961, 1963, three-mile title 1961, 1962, 1964, six-mile 1962, 1964, cross-country 1960, 1961, 1963; won US three-mile indoor 1961-62, six-mile 1962, cross-country 1961, 1963; won British two-mile indoor 1964; Lou Marsh Trophy 1962; CP poll Canadian male athlete of year 1961-62; mem. Canadian Sports Hall of Fame; *res.* Toronto, Ont.

KIEFER, Eniko (diving); *b.* 12 Aug 1960, Montreal, Que.; student; gold medal 3m 1974 junior national; silver 1m 1974 summer national; gold 1971 Belgium world 12-and-under 3m, bronze 1m, 10m; gold 1969 10-and-under; 1972 11-12; 1973 13-14 US 1m international; gold 1971 Bolzano Italy 14-and-under 1m; gold 1970 U S 10-and-under 3m, 1972 11-12, 1973 13-14 3m; gold 1971 15-16 Bolzano 10m; represented Canada in Canada Cup since 1974 and various international meets DDR,

USSR, Mexico, Finland, Cuba, Italy and 1976 Montreal Olympics; *res.* Dollard des Ormeaux, Que.

KIHN, Richard (gymnastics); *b.* 15 Aug 1935, Alzenau, Bavaria; *m.* Tina; *children:* Marcus, Britta; accountant, hospital comptroller; won Canadian men's title four years; won world trials 1962 but unable to compete as he was not Canadian citizen; represented Canada 1964 Tokyo Olympics, highest score ever by Canadian gymnast in international competition (107.95); treasurer Ontario, Canadian gymnastic associations; meet director annual Ontario Milk Meet; *res.* Toronto, Ont.

KILREA, Brian (hockey); *b.* 21 Oct 1934, Ottawa, Ont.; *given name:* Brian Blair; *m.* Judy Ringer; *children:* William, Dianne, Linda; Lisgar HS; hockey coach, manager; through Ottawa minor hockey ranks to Troy Senior Bruins; pro Edmonton (WHL) 1957-58; centre Vancouver (WHL), Rochester, Springfield (AHL), Tulsa (CHL) through 1968-69 season; in brief NHL appearances with Detroit (1957), Los Angeles (1967) scored three goals, five assists; in nine seasons Springfield (AHL) with Eddie Shore won three Calder Cups; coach, manager Ottawa 67's Ontario Major junior A League since 1973, OHA title 1977; *res.* Ottawa, Ont.

KING, Mike (football); *b.* 13 May 1925, Toronto, Ont.; *m.* Allisen Allan; *children:* Glen, Gary; Central Tech; company manager; began football career with Toronto Indians Beaches 1944-49 then joined Edmonton Eskimos 1950 as fullback; carried 201 times for 910yds 1951, WFC all-star fullback 1950-51; closed career 1957 playing defensive guard final two seasons; played East-West Shrine all-star game 1955; on three Grey Cup winners; *res.* Edmonton, Alta.

KIRBY, Bruce (yachting); *b.* 2 Jan 1929, Ottawa, Ont.; *m.* Margo Dancey; *children:* Janice, Kelly; Lisgar CI; yacht designer; competed for Canada 1956, 1964 Finn Class, 1968 Star Class Olympics sailing; International 14 championship 1963-64; mem. three-boat team winning world team title International 14 Class 1958, 1961; designed Laser 1969, world's most popular sailboat; *res.* Rowayton, Conn.

KIRBY, Peter (bobsledding, skiing); *b.* 17 Dec 1931, Montreal, Que.; *given name:* Peter Murray; *m.* Lynnette Castonguay; *children:* Gillian, Martha; Dartmouth College, B.A.; McGill U; geologist, importer ski equipment; Canadian junior alpine ski title 1953; mem. Canadian FIS team 1954; captain Dartmouth College ski team 1956; involved in bobsledding 1961-66, Olympic gold on 1964 four-man team, fourth two-man team; mem. 1965 world title four-man team; *res.* Beaconsfield, Que.

KIRKCONNELL, Herb (badminton); *b.* 6 Sep 1925, Toronto, Ont.; *m.* Lois; U of Toronto; student affairs director; seven times winner Canadian men's senior doubles; three times Ontario men's doubles champion; eight times Ontario senior men's doubles title; mem. Canadian Thomas Cup team 1961; past pres. Ontario Badminton Association; past director Canadian Badminton Association; *res.* Oshawa, Ont.

KNIGHT, Pete (rodeo); *b.* 1904 Philadelphia, Pa., *d.* 1937, Hayward, Calif.; rode in first Calgary Stampede 1924, shared championship honors; rode six bucking horses in one day at Winnipeg 1926 to win world championship; 1930 reserve championship American Rodeo Association and after 1934 world tour won world title again 1935, 1936; defending title 1937 at Hayward was thrown and killed.

KNOX, Walter (track and field); *b.* 1878, Listowel, Ont., *d.* 3 Mar 1951, St. Petersburg, Fla.; Beloit College, U of Illinois; pro athlete, coach; from 1896-1933 competed in many races winning 359 firsts, 90 seconds, 52 thirds in formal competition; in single afternoon 1907 won five Canadian championships (100yd dash, broad jump, pole vault, shot put, hammer throw); in single meet beat Canadian world class athletes Ed Archibald (pole vault), Dr. Cal Bricker (broad jump), Bobby Kerr (1908 Olympic sprint champion) in their own specialties while each was at peak of his career; held Canadian titles at 9.6 for 100yd dash (tieing world record), 22.8 for 220yd, 46'5" for shot put, 12'6" for pole vault, 24'2" for running broad jump, 10'7.5" for standing broad jump, 128' for discus; in British tour 1911 won 57 firsts, 23 seconds, 31 thirds; coach Canadian Olympic track team Stockholm Games; competed in England and Scotland taking 40 firsts, 15 seconds, 15 thirds; American all-pro 1913 defeating US champion John A. MacDonald in match contest Hanlan's Point Toronto; competed vs British Empire champion F.R. Cramb for world all-around title 1914 at Manchester winning six of eight events; coach 1916 British Olympic team but war cancelled games; Canadian Olympic coach 1920 Antwerp Games; chief coach Ontario Athletic Commission several years; mem. Canadian Sports Hall of Fame.

KNUDSON, George (golf); *b.* 28 Jun 1937, Winnipeg, Man.; *m.* Shirley; *children:* three; golf pro; won Manitoba junior 1954, Manitoba and Canadian junior 1955; mem. Manitoba Willingdon Cup team 1956-57; won Manitoba Open 1958-60, Ontario Open 1960-61, 1976, Atlantic Open 1976, CPGA five times; PGA tour victories include 1961 Coral Gables, 1962 Maracaibo, Puerto Rico, 1963 Portland, Panama, 1964 Fresno, Caracas, 1967 Greater New Orleans, 1968 Phoenix, Tucson (back-to-back), 1970 Robinson Open, 1972 Kaiser Open; individual low and International Trophy 1966 World Cup Japan; with Al Balding won 1968 World Cup; tied second U S Masters 1969, won Australian Wills Masters 1969, runner-up 1970; winner in playoff with Stan Leonard Shell Wonderful World of Golf 1963-64, in playoff with Balding 1964-65, runner-up to Gene Littler 1965-66, Al Geiberger 1967-68, winner over Lee Edler, George Archer 1969-70 then lost to Roberto de Vincenzo in semifinal; Peter Jackson Cup 1976; *res.* Willowdale, Ont.

KOLAR, Stanley (golf); *b.* 1 Nov 1922, Czechoslovakia; *m.* Ethel Marie Barlow; *children:* Terence, Lynn, Tracey; golf pro; runner-up Manitoba junior 1939; won Thunder Bay amateur 1941; won Lachute Open twice, Rawdon Open, Quebec Open (1964); ninth two CPGA championships; runner-up CPGA seniors twice; Canada's third master pro 1977; *res.* Lucerne, Que.

KOSMOS, Mark (football); *b.* 28 Oct 1945, Baltimore, Md.; *given name:* Markus Michael; *m.* Nikki Marie Zaharis; *children:* Markus Michael Jr.; U of Oklahoma, B.A.; sales rep.; HS all-league in football, wrestling, lacrosse; all-league football Eastern Oklahoma Junior College; Oklahoma U two seasons, Pottstown Firebirds (ACFL) two seasons earning all-league and 1969 championship; turned pro Montreal Alouettes 1970, Hamilton Tiger-Cats 1972, Ottawa Rough Riders 1973; all-Canadian, Eastern Schenley lineman of year nomination 1971; all-Eastern 1975, 1976; played on four Grey Cup champions, three different teams; *res.* Ottawa, Ont.

KOVITS, Herman (rowing); *b.* 20 Jan 1933, Lashburn, Sask.; *given name:* Joseph Herman; *m.* Brenda; *children:* Carolyn Andrea, Eric; U of British Columbia, B.A., McGill U, D.D.S.; dentist; UBC Big Blocks award for rowing; mem. 1954 British Empire Games gold medal eight-oared crew; mem. class B B.C. fastball champions 1956; mem. B.C. Sports Hall of Fame; *res.* Vancouver, B.C.

KRAEMER, Bob (football); *b.* 31 May 1950, Winnipeg, Man.; *m.* Beverly; U of Manitoba, B.P.E.; athletic association director; conference all-star quarterback, team MVP, twice conference MVP; guided U of Manitoba Bisons to Canadian College Bowl title 1969-70; outstanding player 1969 College Bowl; first round draft pick Winnipeg Blue Bombers, WFC rookie of year 1971 as wide receiver; caught 47 passes 1973 setting single game Bombers record with 11 receptions; retired 1975 to devote full time to Athletes in Action; *res.* Abbotsford, B.C.

KREINER, Kathy (skiing); *b.* 4 May 1957, Timmins, Ont.; student; at 12 youngest ever to win Taschereau downhill Mt. Tremblant; at 14 joined older sister Laurie on Canadian World Cup team and competed in 1972 Sapporo Japan Olympics; gold medal World Cup giant slalom Pfronten W. Germany 1974; Canadian giant slalom title 1974, 1976; won Canadian downhill, slalom, FIS giant slalom Invermere 1975; gold medal

giant slalom Innsbruck Olympics 1976; mem. Canadian Sports Hall of Fame; *res.* Timmins, Ont.

KREINER, Laurie (skiing); *b.* 30 Jun 1954, Timmins, Ont.; *given name:* Lauren Margaret; *m.* Ron Vaillancourt; student; Canadian downhill title Whistler Mt. 1969; won giant slalom US national Aspen Colo 1971; fourth giant slalom 1972 Sapporo Japan Olympics; fourth downhill World Cup Pfronten W. Germany 1973; fifth World Cup giant slalom St. Gervais France; 10th World Cup slalom Badgastein Germany; second Europa Cup downhill La Plague France 1974; 1975 Roch Cup Aspen, overall downhill title 1975 Can-Am series; ninth slalom 1975 world series Jackson Hole Wyo.; second overall Canadian championships Jasper Alta.; represented Canada 1976 Innsbruck Olympics; Ontario Achievement Award, Timmins sportswoman of year 1972; *res.* Timmins, Ont.

KROL, Joe (football); *b.* 20 Feb 1919, Hamilton, Ont.; *m.* Pat; *children:* Richard, Peter; Windsor Kennedy CI, U of Western Ontario, B.A.; government consultant; nickname King; runner, passer, kicker, helped UWO win 1939 Intercollegiate title, Hamilton Wildcats to Canadian final 1943; with Argos 1945-52 played on five Grey Cup champion teams; with Royal Copeland formed Gold Dust Twins; Jeff Russel Trophy 1946; CP poll Canadian male athlete of year 1946-47; Lou Marsh Trophy 1946; Grey Cup record 30 points; mem. Canadian Football, Sports Halls of Fame; *res.* Toronto, Ont.

KROLL, Horst (autosport); *b.* 16 May 1936, Germany; *m.* Hildegard Schmelzle; *children:* Birgit; operator auto service business; began racing as amateur in Germany; won under two-litre title 1967, placed third

Canadian championship; retained under two-litre and won Canadian championship 1968; Germany's Algemeiner Deutscher Automobil Club gold medal with diamonds for distinguished service to international autosport 1968; since 1969 raced in Formula 5000 series in Canada, U S; twice runner-up to Eppie Wietzes in Canadian championships; 14th tie with Al Unser in 1974 championship series; three times Canadian Formula Vee champion; *res.* Scarborough, Ont.

KROUSE, Bob (football); *b.* 21 Feb 1943, Hamilton, Ont.; *given name:* Frank Robert; *m.* Marjorie Hughes; *children:* Robert Joseph, Paul Edgar; Hamilton Central HS, McMaster U, B.A., B.P.E., U of Buffalo, M.A.; HS phys ed teacher; twice all-city fullback, defensive back in HS; mem. first Canadian HS mile relay team to post sub-3:30 indoor mile (3:27.9); pro with Hamilton Tiger-Cats 1963 playing backup defensive back, fullback; starting corner linebacker 1967-75; called defensive signals 1971-75; captained Ticats 1973, player-coach 1975; EFC all-star 1967; *res.* Grimsby, Ont.

KULAI, Dan (soccer); *b.* 10 Nov 1907, Ladysmith, B.C.; *m.* Margaret; *children:* one son, one daughter; Vancouver HS: retired fire chief; mem. New Westminster Royals Canadian soccer championship teams 1927-28; forward, later goaler with B.C. Select soccer teams several seasons; retired as player and switched to refereeing for 25 years, officiated in World Cup, Pan-Am Games and most of world's top soccer matches; several years held Vancouver city handball championships in singles and doubles; mem. B.C. Sports Hall of Fame; *res.* Vancouver, B.C.

KWONG, Normie (football); *b.* 24 Oct 1929, Calgary, Alta.; *given name:* Lim Kwong Yew; *m.* Mary; *children:* Gregory, Bradley, Martin, Randy; Mount Royal Junior College; real estate broker; nickname The China Clipper; played 14 years with Calgary, Edmonton; in 11 years of recorded CFL statistics (from 1950) scored 74 TDs, gained 9,022 yds averaging 5.2 yds per carry (third highest in league history); Eddie James Memorial Trophy as WFC leading rusher three times; on three successive Grey Cup winners 1954-56; five times all-star; twice Schenley award as outstanding Canadian 1955-56; CP poll Canadian male athlete of year 1955; mem. Canadian Football, Sports Halls of Fame; *res.* Calgary, Alta.

KYLE, Doug (track); *b.* 22 Jul 1932, Toronto, Ont.; *given name:* Douglas Haig; *m.* Carol Hemmings; *children:* Suzanne, Bobby; U of British Columbia, B.A., U of Michigan, M.S.; economist; four times Canadian three-mile, six times six-mile champion; once 10-mile, marathon and three times Canadian cross-country title; 10 Canadian records in two, three, five, six, 10, 15 miles and 3000, 5000, 10 000 and 25 000m; nine Alberta records from one-10 miles and US six-mile record; represented Canada 1954 British Empire Games, 1956, 1960 Olympics, 1959, 1963 Pan-Am Games; silver 10 000m, bronze 5000m 1959 Pan-Am Games; silver 7000m Sao Paulo Brazil 1959; Fred Tees award outstanding college athlete 1954; Jack Davies award outstanding Canadian track athlete 1956, 1959; Norton Crowe award outstanding AAU of C athlete 1956; national track team coach 1967 Pan-Am Games, 1968 Olympics; Calgary athlete of year 1959; Calgary sportsman of year 1968; mem. AAU of C Hall of Fame; *res.* Calgary, Alta.

LABLANCHE, George (boxing); *b.* 17 Dec 1856, Point Levi, Que., *d.* 10 May 1918, Lawrence, Mass.; fought Jack (Nonpareil) Dempsey for middleweight title 1886, was KO'd in 13; met Dempsey again 1889 and although Dempsey scored 32nd round KO he was disqualified for an illegal punch; Lablanche claimed title but claim was not allowed; KO'd in four by Bert Woods, Toledo O. in last bout 1898; record: 69 bouts, won 17 by KO, 18 by decision, six draws, 10 decisions lost, 14 times KO'd, two lost on foul, one no decision, one no-contest.

LACH, Elmer (hockey); *b.* 22 Jan 1918, Nokomis, Sask.; *given name:* Elmer James; public relations director; played junior hockey with Regina Abbotts, senior with Weyburn Beavers, Moose Jaw Millers; turned pro 1940-41 with Montreal Canadiens; missed the next season when broken arm, first of a series of major injuries which were to earn him the nickname Elmer the Unlucky, sidelined him; returned to first line; teamed with Rocket Richard, Toe Blake on wings to form Punch Line; played 14 seasons with Habs

appearing in 646 games scoring 215 goals, 408 assists for 623 points, plus 76 playoff games scoring 19 goals, 45 assists for 64 points; in three all-star games; three times first team, twice second team all-star; on three Stanley Cup winners, four league champions; led league scorers 1944-45, won Art Ross Trophy with 80 points, repeat 1947-48; Hart Trophy 1944-45; coach Loyola College, Junior Canadiens, Montreal Royals (QHL); mem. Sask. Sports, Hockey Halls of Fame; *res.* Montreal, Que.

LAFLEUR, Guy (hockey); *b.* 20 Sep 1951, Thurso, Que.; *given name:* Guy Damien; *m.* Lise; *children:* Martin; hockey player; spotted by scouts while leading Thurso team to class C title in 1962 Quebec international peewee tournament; at 14 joined Quebec City junior B team; following year played eight junior A games scoring first of 315 junior A goals with Quebec Ramparts; in first full junior campaign scored 30 goals, added 50 next year, 103 third season; scored 130 goals, 79 assists for 209 points in final junior season; Montreal's first choice and first overall in 1971 amateur draft; scored 29 goals as rookie and in six years three times has cleared 50 goals; through 1976-77 in 445 games scoring 243 goals, 312 assists for 555 points, 221 penalty minutes, plus 67 playoff games scoring 32 goals, 44 assists for 76 points, 38 penalty minutes; three times first team all-star right winger; Art Ross Trophy 1976, 1977; Lester B. Pearson Trophy 1976, 1977; mem. Team Canada 1976; Conn Smythe Trophy 1977; *Sport Magazine* playoff MVP award 1977; *res.* Montreal, Que.

LALLY, Joe (lacrosse); *b.* 1868, Cornwall, Ont., *d.* 1956, Cornwall, Ont.; *given name:* Patrick Joseph; manufacturer; player, referee, equipment manufacturer, instrumental in establishing Canadian Lacrosse Association 1925; donated Lally Perpetual Trophy 1930 to be awarded annually to teams representing Canada and the US; mem. Canadian Sports, Lacrosse Halls of Fame.

LALONDE, Newsy (hockey, lacrosse); *b.* 1888, Cornwall, Ont., *d.* 21 Nov 1971; *given name:* Edouard; reporter, printer; began lacrosse career in Cornwall at 16 travelling country with various teams through 1912 season; pro hockey at 18 with Sault Ste. Marie of International League; with Renfrew Millionaires 1910-11 scored 38 goals in 11 games; played for Montreal Canadiens 1913-1922; four times led league in scoring; led 1916 team to Stanley Cup win over Portland; player-manager 1919, won Stanley Cup over Seattle; traded to Saskatoon Shieks of WHL 1922 where he served four years as player-manager; concluded career 1926 in Vancouver with 441 career goals in 365 games; coached NY Americans, Montreal Canadiens, Ottawa Senators; mem. Canadian Hockey, Lacrosse Halls of Fame.

LAMB, Joe (hockey); *b.* 18 Jun 1906, Sussex, N.B.; *m.* Marguerite Gillis (*d.*); *children:* Joann Isobel, Margot Elizabeth; retired soldier; played hockey Sussex Dairy Kings seniors 1922-25 winning N.B., P.E.I. championships, Maritime championship 1924; played for Royal Bank Montreal Bankers League 1925-27; turned pro 1928 Montreal Maroons playing 11 years NHL with various clubs, scored 101 goals; only player to appear in two longest NHL games (1932-33 Boston Bruins vs Toronto Maple Leafs, 1935-36 Montreal Maroons vs Detroit Red Wings); with Montreal in 1928 Stanley Cup loss to NY Rangers; Ottawa District class A golf champion 1949; secretary-manager Ottawa Valley Curling Assoc.

1968-76, Ottawa District Golf Assoc. 1965-76; mem. Governor General's Curling Club; mem. N.B. Sports Hall of Fame; *res.* Ottawa, Ont.

LAMB, Willie (golf); *b.* 15 Dec 1902, Montrose Angus, Scotland, *d.* 28 Jan 1969, St. Petersburg, Fla.; head pro Toronto Uplands 1929-33, Lambton Golf Club 1934-64; five times CPGA champion, runner-up once; winner Ontario Open 1932, three times runner-up; winner Quebec Open 1931-33; CPGA Millar Trophy 1930, runner-up 1953; pres. CPGA 1929, Ontario PGA 1948-50; on 1964 retirement made CPGA life mem., mem. Canadian Golf Hall of Fame.

LANCASTER, Ron (football); *b.* 14 Oct 1938, Fairchance, Pa.; *m.* Beverly Vaughan; *children:* Lana, Ronald David, Robert Lee; Wittenberg (Ohio) College, B.Ed.; teacher, coach; turned pro with Ottawa Rough Riders 1960; competed with Russ Jackson as quarterback until traded to Sask. Roughriders 1963; through 1976 totalled 2,924 completions on 5,394 passing attempts for 44,786yds and 54.2 percentage; has had 349 interceptions and completed 304 for TDs; Sask. record for passing yds and completions in a single season (3,869 on 297 completions 1976), and TDs single season (28 1966); quarterbacked Sask. to playoffs in each of 13 seasons totalling 146 wins, five Grey Cup finals, 1966 winner; best single game against Calgary 1963 when he passed for 492yds; six times WFC all-star, four times all-Canadian; four times Jeff Nicklin Memorial Trophy as WFC MVP; winner Schenley outstanding player award 1970, runner-up 1966; *res.* Regina, Sask.

LANGFORD, Sam (boxing); *b.* 12 Feb 1880, Weymouth, N.S., *d.* 12 Jan 1956, Cambridge, Mass.; nickname Boston Tar

Baby; fought almost 300 bouts, many not recorded; among opponents were Jack McVey, Jack Johnson, Stanley Ketchel, Joe Jennette, Young Peter Jackson, Joe (the original) Walcott, Jack Blackburn; held Negro heavyweight title losing it 1919 to Harry Wills in 15; no records, but believed to have had 22 bouts with Wills, 16 of which Langford won by KO; ranked by *Ring Magazine* as one of top 10 all-time heavyweights; stood 5'5'' with 84'' reach; partial record: 252 bouts, 99 won by KO, 37 by decision, one on foul, 31 draws, 19 lost on decision, four by KO, 59 no decisions, two no-contests; mem. Canadian Boxing, U S Boxing, Canadian Sports Halls of Fame.

LANGLOIS, Al (curling); *b.* 4 Aug 1915, Winnipeg, Man.; *given name:* Allan David; Kelvin HS; retired; skipped inter-HS curling champions 1934 and guided rink to variety of junior honors in Manitoba; winner variety of events Manitoba Bonspiel; played third for Billy Walsh winning Manitoba Consols, Brier 1952, 1956; mem. Canadian Curling Hall of Fame; *res.* Winnipeg, Man.

LAPTHORNE, Whitey (baseball); *b.* 1 Apr 1942, London, Ont.; *given name:* David James; *m.* Mary Jane McDonald; *children:* Andrea, Heather, Joseph; Sir Adam Beck CI, U of Western Ontario, B.A., M.A., OCE; PS v.-principal; through Eager Beaver Baseball Association minor ranks to London juniors and then London Majors (Senior Intercounty) where he has excelled at every infield position since 1960; in 17 senior seasons has .275 lifetime avg.; best season 1963 with .346; twice first team all-star third baseman; once first, once second team all-star first baseman; mem. Ontario team Canadian baseball championship, Pan-Am Games playdowns Brandon Man. 1970; *res.* London, Ont.

LARGE, Bert (lacrosse); *b.* 12 May 1907, Brampton, Ont.; *m.* Alice Gibson; *children:* Alberta, Margi-Fay; plumber; played for Brampton Ontario Amateur Lacrosse Association senior champions 1926; mem. Mann Cup-winning Brampton team 1930; turned pro Toronto Maple Leafs 1931 and joined Toronto Tecumseh pro team 1932; mem. Mimico-Brampton Combines Mann Cup winner 1942, Mike Kelly Memorial Medal as MVP in Mann Cup playoffs; mem. Ontario champion Mimico-Brampton Combines 1943; mem. Canadian Lacrosse Hall of Fame; *res.* Brampton, Ont.

LASHUK, Mike (football); *b.* 9 Dec 1938, Edmonton, Alta.; U of Alberta, B.P.E., Southern Illinois U, M.Sc.; associate professor; won Edmonton City junior golf title, provincial HS shot put; played junior A hockey with Edmonton Oil Kings; turned pro Edmonton Eskimos 1957-63, Dr. Beattie Martin Trophy as WFC rookie of year 1957; corner linebacker, twice selected by teammates as top Canadian player; coached HS football five years; head coach U of Calgary Dinosaurs seven years leading team to National College Bowl final 1975, losing to U of Ottawa; *res.* Calgary, Alta.

LAVIOLETTE, Jack (hockey, lacrosse); *b.* 27 Aug 1879, Belleville, Ont., *d.* 10 Jan 1960, Montreal, Que.; played amateur hockey 1899 in Montreal with Overland juniors; with CP Telegraphs 1900 then Nationals of Federal League in both hockey, lacrosse; with formation of first pro league International 1904 played four seasons U S Sault Ste. Marie team, captain 1906; when league disbanded 1907 played with Montreal Shamrocks, lacrosse with Nationals; with Newsy Lalonde mem. 1910 team which lost Minto Cup to New Westminster; with formation

1909 of NHA involved in recruiting, managing oldest pro hockey team still in existence in Canada, Montreal Canadiens; played forward for Canadiens' first Stanley Cup 1916; became referee after injury 1917; mem. Canadian Sports, Hockey, Lacrosse Halls of Fame.

LAVOIE, Marc (fencing); *b.* 29 Apr 1954, Hull, Que.; Carleton U, U of Paris; student; won French handball, baseball championships, class B golf title while attending HS in Paris; won Ontario, Canadian junior sabre titles 1973-74, Canadian Universities title 1974-75; at 21 youngest ever Canadian senior sabre champion 1975, also won 1976, 1977; represented Canada world championships 1973-75, Pan-Am Games 1975, Olympics 1976; bronze medal team sabre 1974 Commonwealth championships, fourth individual; Carleton U athlete of year 1974-75; Ottawa ACT fencer of year 1974; *res.* Hull, Que.

LAY, Marion (swimming); *b.* 26 Nov 1948, Vancouver, B.C.; *given name:* Marion Beverly; California State Polytechnic College, B.A., California State U, M.A.; acting manager technical programs Sport Canada; Canadian 100m freestyle (FS) title 1964-68, competed nationally and internationally; fifth 100m FS 1964 Tokyo Olympics; toured Europe with 1965 Canadian swim team setting British Open 100m FS record Blackpool Eng.; captain Canadian swim team, won two gold, set world record 4x110yd FS relay Kingston Jamaica Commonwealth Games 1966; captain Canadian team Winnipeg Pan-Am Games winning four silver 1967; bronze medal 100m FS US Long Course Nationals 1967; toured South Africa with Canadian team 1968 setting South African Open 100m FS record Capetown; captain

Canadian Olympic swim team Mexico 1968 placing fourth 100m FS, bronze 4x100m FS relay; coached UWO 1971-72 swim team to fourth place 1972 CWIAU championships; color commentary for CBC amateur swimming coverage; since 1972 assistant coach with Ottawa Kingfish Swim Club; director Institute for Study of Sport in Society 1971-75; involved in sport research; *res.* Ottawa, Ont.

LEACH, Al (all-around); *b.* 12 Jul 1917, Richmond, Ont.; *given name:* Alvin Douglas; *m.* Valerie Evelyn Bennett; *children:* Douglas John, Patricia Gail; Oakwood CI; chief mechanical inspector, plan examiner; HS swimming champion 1935-37; Kiwanis juniors Big Four football champions 1937; Oakwood Indians ORFU intermediate titlists 1938-39; Toronto Commercial Hockey League seniors 1938-40; Ottawa football clubs (Combines, Trojans, Rough Riders) 1941-47; Ottawa District Football (soccer) Association 1943-48, ODFA title 1948; Ottawa Mercantile Softball League 1943-46, Eastern Ontario title 1945; Ottawa Valley Curling Association director, past pres.; mem. Governor-General's Curling Club; *res.* Ottawa, Ont.

LEADLAY, Pep (football); *b.* 7 Mar 1898, Hamilton, Ont.; *given name:* Frank Robert; *m.* Vera Esther Rymal; Queen's U, B.Sc.; retired civil engineer; Hamilton Tigers intermediate Canadian champions 1915; with Hamilton Tigers Interprovincial Union 1919-20, Queen's 1921-25 winning Canadian college title, Grey Cup 1922-24, OQAA title 1922-25; Hamilton Tigers 1926-30, league title 1927; ORFU, Canadian title 1928-29, Interprovincial Union title 1930; captain Queen's, Hamilton teams; on Golden Gaels team which won 26 consecutive victories; mem. Canadian Football, Canadian Sports Halls of Fame; *res.* Hamilton, Ont.

LEAR, Les (football); *b.* 22 Aug 1918, Grafton, N.D.; *m.* Betty Louise Neill; Pinkham, Daniel McIntyre HS; played football Deer Lodge juniors; with Winnipeg Blue Bombers 1937-42, all-star lineman three times; helped Bombers win WIFU titles 1937-39 and Grey Cup 1939; US pro football tryout with Cleveland Rams summer 1942, played with that club through 1947, moved with franchise to Los Angeles 1946; second team US pro all-star 1945; traded to Detroit Lions 1947 but retired to coach Calgary Stampeders in CFL; guided Stampeders to Grey Cup 1948; following season won West but lost Grey Cup final to Montreal; mem. Canadian Football Hall of Fame; *res.* Hollywood, Fla.

LEARN, Ed (football); *b.* 30 Sep 1935, Welland, Ont.; *m.* Marilyn; *children:* Billy, Paul, Janice; Welland HS; automobile dealer; K-W Dutchmen 1956-57; twelve-year defensive halfback with Montreal, Toronto; punt return specialist with 506 for 3,091yds, 6.1 avg., 578yds returning 51 pass interceptions; all-Eastern three times, all-Canadian once; Montreal nominee for Canadian player of year 1961; led EFC in interceptions 1968 with seven; defensive back modern era Argo all-star team (1945-73); *res.* Ridgeville, Ont.

LEDDY, Jack (golf); *b.* 27 Oct 1912, Saskatoon, Sask.; *given name:* John Edward; *m.* Rita Wilkinson; *children:* three; Saskatoon HS, U of Saskatchewan, McGill U; surgeon; runner-up 1930 Sask. junior boys championship; runner-up 1968 Sask. seniors title; pres. Royal Canadian Golf Association 1962; non-playing captain Canadian team

which finished second world amateur tournament Japan 1962; mem. Sask. Sports Hall of Fame; *res.* Saskatoon, Sask.

LEE, Peter (hockey); *b.* 2 Jan 1956, Chester, Eng.; *given name:* Peter John; Carleton U; student; scored most OHA junior A career goals (215), most career points (451), and in 1975-76 most goals single season (81) with Ottawa 67's; OHA MVP, Tilson Trophy, and highest scoring right winger, Mahon Trophy 1976; honored by Peter Lee Day Ottawa Civic Centre 1976; Ottawa ACT amateur hockey player of year 1975, 1976; pro Nova Scotia Voyageurs 1976-77; *res.* Ottawa, Ont.

LEFAIVE, Lou (administration); *b.* 13 Feb 1928, Windsor, Ont. *m.* Winnifred; *children:* Louise, Michelle, Marie, Jacqueline; St. Peter's Seminary, U of Ottawa, St. Patrick's College; pres. National Sports and Recreation Centre; college football, basketball, semipro softball Windsor; coached basketball U of Ottawa, St. Patrick's College; director Sport Canada 1968-1975; founding mem. Hockey Canada, Coaching Association of Canada, Canada Games Council; *res.* Ottawa, Ont.

LEHMAN, Hughie (hockey); *b.* 27 Oct 1885, Pembroke, Ont., *d.* 8 Apr 1961, Toronto, Ont.; *given name:* Frederick Hugh; nickname Old Eagle Eyes; goaler; Pembroke 1905, Sault Ste. Marie in international pro league 1906, Pembroke semipro 1907, Berlin (Kitchener) in Ontario Pro Hockey League 1908-10, New Westminster Royals 1911-13, Vancouver Millionaires (PCL) 1914-25, Chicago (NHL) 1926-27; played on eight Stanley Cup challengers, won with Vancouver 1914-15; shares record with Percy LeSueur of having played on two different

Stanley Cup challengers within two months (Galt vs Ottawa and Berlin vs Wanderers 1909-10); mem. Hockey Hall of Fame.

LEHMANN, Ken (football); *b*. 13 Jan 1942, Louisville, Ky.; *m*. Bonnie Ross; *children:* Eric, Heidi, Bridget; Xavier U, B.S.; radio advertising salesman; captain, most valuable lineman two years in college; Xavier legion of honor award; turned pro Ottawa Rough Riders 1964-72; Schenley lineman of year 1968, runner-up 1966; six times EFC all-star, five times all-Canadian; played on three Grey Cups, two winners; assistant football coach U of Ottawa one season; *res.* Ottawa, Ont.

LEINWEBER, Judi (skiing); *b*. 13 Jun 1950, Kimberley, B.C.; *given name:* Judi Lea; *m*. Currie Chapman; Notre Dame U; HS phys ed teacher; Canadian junior championship at 12 and 15; Canadian senior title Whistler Mt. 1969; second U S championships 1968; fifth World Cup slalom 1968 Oslo; mem. Olympic team; *res.* Nelson, B.C.

LEMHENYI, Dezso (water polo); *b*. 9 Dec 1917, Budapest, Hungary; *m*. Olga Tass; *children:* Cjilla; coach; competed internationally for Hungarian water polo team 1940-52; international referee 1940-64; coach Hungarian national team 1952-60 winning two Olympic gold, one bronze and numerous European championships; national coach France 1961-68; director Centre Institute of Sports Budapest 1969-72; coach Quebec Elite, 1973 Canadian champions; Canadian national team coach 1974, 1976 Montreal Olympics; wrote *Training Techniques of Water Polo; res.* Budapest, Hungary.

LENARD, Al (football); *b*. 6 Jan 1921, Windsor, Ont.; *given name:* Aldon Lewis; *m*. Jean Louise Bidwell; *children:* James Aldon; Queen's U, B.A., B.P.H.E., U of Michigan, M.A., U of Illinois, Ph.D.; professor, director of athletics; Silverwood Trophy, WOSSA T & F MVP in hs 1938; played ORFU football Hamilton Wildcats 1940-42, 1945, Imperial Oil Trophy as MVP 1941; Eastern Canada scoring leader 1941, 1942; quarterback Queen's football team 1946-49; first captain chosen twice at Queen's 1947-48; assistant coach 1954-70; pres. Canadian Athletic Directors Association 1972; v.-pres. CIAU 1973; chairman CIAU administrative committee 1973-74; chairman OUAA administrative council 1974-76; coached intercollegiate champions in curling, golf; 1957 Kingston golf champion; *res.* Kingston, Ont.

LEONARD, Stan (golf); *b*. 2 Feb 1915, Vancouver, B.C.; *m*. Chris; *children:* Linda; retired golf pro; won first tournament he entered, 1932 B.C. Amateur, repeat 1935; semifinals Canadian Amateur 1936-37; six times B.C. Willingdon Cup Team mem.; touring pro 1955-63; won 1957 Greater Greenboro Open, 1958 Tournament of Champions, 1960 Western Open; teamed with Jules Huot as runner-up 1953 World Cup; low individual 1953, 1959 World Cup; eight CPGA titles, five times runner-up; Rivermead Cup as low Canadian in Canadian Open nine times; won B.C. Open five times, Alberta Open nine times, Sask. Open twice, Millar Trophy once; nine times Canada Cup team mem., six times on Canadian Hopkins Trophy team; third 1958 US Masters; mem. Royal Canadian Golf, Canadian Sports Halls of Fame; *res.* Calif.

LESSARD, Lucille (archery); *b*. 26 May 1957, Quebec City, Que.; CEGEP de Limoilou; student; Canadian women's champion,

1974, 1975; world field champion 1974; Champion of the Americas 1975; seventh in target world championship 1975; Elaine Tanner Trophy, Quebec athlete of year 1974; mem. Canadian Sports Hall of Fame; *res.* Loretteville, Que.

LESUEUR, Percy (hockey); *b.* 18 Nov 1881, Quebec City, Que., *d.* 27 Jan 1962, Hamilton, Ont.; *m.* Georgia Steele; *children:* Steve Douglas; Quebec City HS; hockey executive; nickname Peerless Percy; played junior with Quebec Victorias, senior with Quebec; originally right winger but shifted to goal 1904; Ottawa Silver Seven 1906-13, won Stanley Cup twice; captain team three seasons, managed, coached club part of 1913-14; Toronto Arenas 1914; career spanned 50 years as player, coach, manager, referee, equipment designer, arena manager, broadcaster, columnist; designed gauntlet-type goaler's gloves and net used by NHA, NHL 1912-25; original mem. radio's Hot Stove League; retired 1946; mem. Hockey Hall of Fame.

LEVANTIS, Steve (football); *b.* 28 Jul 1916, Montreal, Que.; *m.* Lillian; Jarvis, Northern HS, Assumption College; sales and marketing; played with three TDIAA champions while attending HS; played baseball with Mahars winning Ontario senior title; Toronto Argos 1936-41, 1945-49; in 76 league, 23 playoff games; mem. five Grey Cup champions-four with Argos, one with St. Hyacinthe Donnacona Navy 1944; EFC all-star 1945; all-Argo team as tackle 1921-41; *res.* Ancaster, Ont.

LEWINGTON, Nancy (track); *b.* 10 Apr 1941, Hamilton, Ont.; *given name:* Nancy Helen; McMaster U, B.A.; HS teacher; Canadian 100m record 11.8 1960; represented Canada 1960 Rome Olympics; *res.* Hamilton, Ont.

LEWIS, Bill (curling); *b.* 8 Feb 1921, Angusville, Man.; *given name:* William Morris; *m.* Avis Skitch; *children:* Patricia, Dale, Guy; *m.* Carol Devereaux; real estate salesman; twice won Ontario Silver Tankard, runner-up once; twice won Burden trophy; twice competed in Ontario Consols, runner-up once; Ontario mixed finalist; won Ontario Legion title; City of Ottawa grand aggregate champion, runner-up once; third stone for Jake Edwards (delivering final rocks each end) two Ontario seniors championship rinks; *res.* Kingston, Ont.

LEWIS, Elinor (curling); *b.* 16 Nov 1918, Thurso, Que.; *m.* Ray Lewis; *children:* Terry, Shirley; won Hope, Crystal Pebble Molson, Woods Dubuc, Tweedsmuir trophies also Rideau mixed, numerous regional events; pres. Ottawa Hunt curling section 1968-69, v.-pres. District Two LCA 1969-70; charter mem. Ottawa Crystal Pebble committee; publicity director CLCA senior championships 1973; past pres. EOLCA, OLCA; Ontario delegate to CLCA meetings Moncton, Winnipeg, Halifax; executive CLCA; charter mem. Ontario Curling Development Council; first woman director National Capital Region Amateur Sports Council; *res.* Ottawa, Ont.

LEWIS, Leo (football); *b.* 4 Feb 1933, Des Moines, Iowa; *given name:* Leo Everett Jr.; *m.* Doris Marie; *children:* Leo III, Marc, Barry; Lincoln U, B.Sc., U of Missouri, M.Ed.; instructor, coach Lincoln U; all-city in football, basketball John Marshall HS; all-Midwest Athletic Association first team all-star as running back 1951-54; *Pittsburgh Courier* all-American three times; AP Little all-American twice; Philip Morris all-American 1953; 4,457yds rushing in four-year college career, including 245yds single game,

1,239yds single season, carried ball 623 times for 7.15yd avg.; record longest kickoff return (100yds); had 95yd TD run from scrimmage; 64 career TDs, 22 single season, four times scored four one game, 132 scoring points one season, all Lincoln U records; pro Winnipeg Blue Bombers 1955-66; CFL career record 8,856yds rushing on 1,351 carries for 6.57 avg., 48 TDs; twice rushed over 1,000yds single season; 234 passes caught for 4,251yds, 18.2 avg., 26 TDs; CFL leader career kickoff returns with 187 for 5,444yds, 29.1 avg., one TD; 75 career TDs, five converts, one single for 450 CFL points; six times CFL all-star; mem. all-decade Blue Bomber team of 60s; six Grey Cup finals, four winners: head football coach Lincoln U 1973-75; director intramural sports, golf coach Lincoln U; mem. Canadian Football Hall of Fame; *res.* Columbia, Mo.

LEWIS, Ray (track); *b.* 8 Oct 1910, Hamilton, Ont.; *given name:* Raymond Gray; *m.* Vivienne; *children:* Larry; government chauffeur; won HS 100yd, 220yd, 440yd, mile relay in single day 1929; twice Canadian 440yd title; bronze 1600m relay 1932 Olympics; silver 1934 British Empire Games mile relay; 600yd indoor title five years; several firsts Penn Relays, Marquette Relays; *res.* Hamilton, Ont.

LEYSHON, Glynn (wrestling); *b.* 2 Aug 1929, Hamilton, Ont.; *given name:* Glynn Arthur; *m.* Judith; *children:* Sian, Gar, Rhysa, Tal; U of Western Ontario, Ph.D.; university phys ed assistant dean; twice Canadian Intercollegiate wrestling champion; referee 1967 Pan-Am Games; wrestling coach UWO since 1964, produced five league championships; coach Canadian team world championships Toledo Ohio 1966, Tehran Iran 1973, World Student Games Moscow 1973, World Cup of wrestling Toledo 1973, 1975; CIAU wrestling coach of year 1975; wrote (with Frank Cosentino) *Olympic Gold; res.* London, Ont.

L'HEUREUX, Bill (hockey, football); *b.* 28 Feb 1918, Port Arthur, Ont.; *given name:* Willard Joseph; *m.* Viola M. Suitor; *children:* Susan, Mary, Bill Jr.; Assumption College, B.A., U of Michigan, M.A., U of New Brunswick, LL.D.; university professor; played hockey Assumption College 1934-36, Windsor Seniors 1937, Chatham Maroons 1938, U of T Blues 1939, Maxville Millionaires ODHA intermediate 1940, Cornwall Flyers Quebec senior 1941-43, Arnprior, Hull, Renfrew, Cornwall, Alexandria ODHA 1945-49; coach Maxville HS 1939, Cornwall CIVS 1940-43, Ottawa Tech 1945-48, Ottawa St. Patrick's 1949-50, UWO Mustangs 1950-55, 1963-65; since 1975 coach UWO women's intercollegiate hockey squad; played football Assumption 1934-37; coached Cornwall 1940-43, Galt CIVS 1943-45, Ottawa Tech 1945-50, assistant UWO 1950-56; chairman National Advisory Council on Fitness and Amateur Sport 1966-69; CAHPER Tait Mckenzie honor award 1967; Hockey Canada development committee 1972-75; OHA coaching consultant 1975-76; wrote several books on hockey; *res.* London, Ont.

LIDSTONE, Dorothy (archery); *b.* 2 Nov 1938, Wetaskiwin, Alta.; *given name:* Dorothy Carole Wagar; *div.;* Dunstable HS; archery equipment manufacturer; competed in first Canadian championship 1963; three provincial, four Pacific Northwest titles; Canadian title, world championship 1969; mem. Canadian Sports Hall of Fame; *res.* Vancouver, B.C.

LINDLEY, Earl (football); *b.* 13 Mar 1933, Wellsville, Utah; *given name:* Earl Leishman; *m.* Marilyn Jensen; *children:* Greg, Teresa, Lance, Corey, Wade; Utah State U, B.S., M.S.; teacher, football coach; 11 HS letters in football, basketball, T & F and baseball; all-State two years in HS football; led US scorers senior year; linebacker, drafted by Chicago Bears NFL, but played for Edmonton Eskimos 1954-57; all-star 1956; played on three Grey Cup winners; head coach Idaho Falls HS three years; assistant coach Brigham Young U seven years; since 1968 head coach Sky View HS, Logan Utah; *res.* Smithfield, Utah.

LINDSAY, Ted (hockey); *b.* 29 Jul 1925, Renfrew, Ont.; *given name:* Robert Blake Theodore; *sep.; children:* three; plastics manufacturer, hockey coach; played early hockey in Kirkland Lake Holy Name League, season with St. Mike's Majors; picked up by Oshawa to help win 1944 Memorial Cup; at 19 to NHL with Detroit Red Wings, played left wing on line with Sid Abel, Gordie Howe; led by this Production Line combination the Wings won seven straight NHL league titles and four Stanley Cups; led league in penalties; nickname Tempestuous Ted, Terrible Ted or Forever Furious; with Wings 13 seasons, traded to Chicago Black Hawks 1957-58; retired following 1959-60 campaign but made comeback 1964-65 with Wings winning Prince of Wales Trophy; eight times first, once second team all-star; in 17 NHL seasons appeared in 1,068 games scoring 379 goals, 472 assists for 851 points, 1,808 penalty minutes, plus 133 playoff games, 47 goals, 49 assists for 96 points; in 11 all-star games scored five goals, five assists for 10 points; past pres. NHL Players' Association; coach Detroit Red Wings 1977; mem. Hockey Hall of Fame; *res.* Detroit, Mich.

LISKE, Peter (football); *b.* 24 May 1941, Plainfield, N.J.; Penn State U; drafted by Philadelphia Eagles but chose to play with NY Jets as quarterback, defensive back; late cut 1965, joined Argos; to Calgary 1966 for Pete Manning, Bobby Taylor and remained with Stampeders through 1968; two seasons with Denver Broncos then traded to Philadelphia Eagles for two seasons; rejoined Stampeders 1973 and was dealt to B.C. Lions; set CFL record 508 pass attempts, 303 completions and 40 TD passes 1967; seven-year CFL record 2,571 passes thrown, 1,449 completed for 21,266yds and .564 percentage, 133 interceptions, 130 TDs; Schenley outstanding player award 1967, Jeff Nicklin WFC MVP award 1967; *res.* New Jersey.

LOARING, John (track, swimming); *b.* 3 Aug 1915, Winnipeg, Man., *d.* 20 Nov 1969, Windsor, Ont.; *given name:* John Wilfrid; *m.* Ellen Selina Ruston; *children:* Mary Ellen, David John (*d.*), George Robert John, David Charles, Esther Ann; Kennedy CI, Huron College; pres. construction co.; won 440yd dash, 120yd high hurdles 1934, Ontario interscholastic championships 1935; won high hurdles, anchored mile relay winner 1934 Inter-Empire schoolboy games Melbourne Australia; silver low hurdles 1936 Berlin Olympics; gold medal 440yd hurdles, 440yd relay, mile relay 1938 British Empire Games; won 1935 senior intercollegiate 100yd, 220yd low hurdles, 440yd, third high hurdles; won Ontario 440yd hurdles 1936; fourth 1937 Pan-Am Games 400m; Canadian senior intercollegiate track champion, intermediate intercollegiate swim champion four times; mem. 1939 intermediate intercollegiate harrier title team; held Canadian native, open 400m hurdles records; won numerous service competitions during WW2 stint in navy; equalled British 440yd hurdles record 1942 Portsmouth; helped form Windsor Swim Club, pres. 1947-52; officiated many Windsor track meets, Jamaica Commonwealth Games 1966; executive mem. Commonwealth Games Association, AAU of C, COA, Windsor recreation commission; coach Windsor Swim Club water polo team several years; athletic coordinator Windsor-Detroit Freedom Festival 1963; J.W. Davies track trophy 1938; Windsor Scout executive award 1958; Windsor Swim Club award 1969; U of Windsor annually presents awards in his honor to HS swim champions, Kennedy relays 400m dash winners; numerous swimming pool design awards; mem. AAU of C Hall of Fame.

LOCKHART, Gene (swimming, football); *b.* 18 Jul 1891, London, Ont., *d.* 31 Mar 1957, Santa Monica, Calif.; *m.* Kathleen Arthur; *children:* June; St. Michael's College, De LaSalle Institute, Brompton Oratory School London Eng.; actor; captain St. Mike's hockey team; played football for Toronto Argos and in 1909 held Canadian mile swimming title; appeared in about 300 motion pictures, numerous stage plays.

LOGAN, Tip (football); *b.* 30 Nov 1927, St. Thomas, Ont.; *given name:* John Robert; *m.* Helen Marie Batt; *children:* Timothy John, Claudia Marie; Fort Erie HS, Queen's U; securities salesman; played amateur football St. Catharines Rams juniors, Queen's U, pro Hamilton Tiger-Cats 1950-55; twice CIAU all-star; led Big Four scorers one year; placement specialist, held Canadian record for 85 consecutive conversions; Big Four all-star one year; played on 1953 Grey Cup champions; since 1957 intercollegiate football official, in six College Bowls; played minor, intermediate baseball Fort Erie, pro

in Brooklyn Dodger chain in class D Florida State, Pony Leagues; mem. Welland senior OBA champions 1949, mem. COSSA basketball champions 1948; officiated HS basketball games 10 years; in curling runner-up 1973 Ontario Colts championships; skipped Hamilton City championship rink 1975-76; founder, pres. Hamilton Minor Football Association; pres. Lakeshore Football Officials Association; pres. Ontario Minor Football Association; *res.* Hamilton, Ont.

LOMBARDO, Guy (speedboat racing); *b.* 19 Jun 1902, London, Ont.; *m.* Lilliebelle Glenn; St Peter's School; band leader, Guy Lombardo and his Royal Canadians; won 1946 International Gold Cup and National Sweepstakes for unlimited hydroplanes with his Tempo boats; US national champion 1946-49; past secretary American Power Boating Association; began racing 1938 winning every major trophy in Gold Cup unlimited class for 20-40 ft propellor driven boats; set then speed record 119.7mph 1948; retired 1952, returned 1955-56 winning national titles; mem. US Speedboat Hall of Fame; *res.* Freeport, N.Y.

LONEY, Don (football); *b.* 16 Nov 1923, Ottawa, Ont.; *given name:* Donald John; West Hill HS, North Carolina State U; real estate salesman; service football Montreal and Halifax 1943-44, nine years pro football Montreal, Toronto, Ottawa, Calgary, playing in three Grey Cup finals, two winners; retired 1955; Jeff Russel Memorial Trophy 1950; frequent Eastern all-star, once all-Canadian; coached three years Ottawa HS, three years Navy, 17 years college football winning three service league titles, 10 college conference titles, 1966 national college title; coached football St. Francis Xavier U 1957-74, record of 133 wins, 31 losses, two ties; CAFA-CFL plaque 1973; Confederation Medal 1967; CIAU trophy presented annually in his honor to Atlantic Bowl MVP; *res.* Jasper, Alta.

LONG, Bill (hockey); *b.* 2 Jan 1918, Barrie, Ont.; *given name:* William Edwin; *m.* Dorothy Catharine Wiles; *children:* Terry; Barrie CI; hockey executive; began playing career in Barrie Church League then played three years junior B in Barrie, one year senior with Port Colborne; turned pro with Pittsburgh organization remaining three months before shifting to Kansas City; joined Hap Emms as junior B coach 1950-51 season; worked with junior A team as 'Sunday coach' before moving with Emms to Niagara Falls 1960; coach Ottawa 67's 1967-71; coach, general manager London Knights 1972; coach junior B champions 1951, juvenile champions 1954, Memorial Cup finalists 1963, Memorial Cup junior A champions 1965; *res.* London, Ont.

LONGBOAT, Tom (track); *b.* 4 Jun 1887, Brantford, Ont., *d.* 9 Jan 1949, Brantford, Ont.; *given name:* Thomas Charles; *m.* Lauretta Maracle; outran horse over 12-mile course 1906; won 15-mile Toronto marathon three consecutive years; Boston Marathon 1907, setting record; as marathon pro beat Italian champion Dorando Pietri, Britain's Alf Shrubb several times; competed 1908 Olympics; last major race 1912; victim of exploitation by promoters; mem. Canadian Sports Hall of Fame.

LOOMER, Lorne (rowing); *b.* 1937, Penticton, B.C.; *given name:* Lorne Kenneth; *m.* Elisabeth Baess; *children:* Lise-Lotte, Anne-Lise; Nelson HS, U of British Columbia, B.A., B.Sc., Ph.C.; pharmacist; gold 1956 Melbourne Olympics coxless four; gold eights 1958 British Empire Games Cardiff

Wales; represented Canada 1960 Rome Olympics; mem. B.C., Canadian Sports Halls of Fame; *res.* Vancouver, B.C.

LOUGHEED, Peter (football); *b.* 26 Jul 1928, Calgary, Alta.; *given name:* Edgar Peter; *m.* Jeanne Estelle Rogers; *children:* Stephen, Andrea, Pamela, Joseph; U of Alberta, B.A., LL.B., Harvard U, M.B.A.; Premier of Alberta; played end for Edmonton Eskimos; traded to Calgary for Johnny Bright; *res.* Calgary, Alta.

LOVELL, Jocelyn (cycling); *b.* 19 Jul 1950, England; *given name:* Jocelyn Bjorn; won 22 Canadian titles; represented Canada 1967, 1971, 1975 Pan-Am Games, 1968, 1972, 1976 Olympics, 1969-71, 1974-75 world, 1970 Commonwealth Games; gold, silver, bronze medals Commonwealth Games Edinburgh 1970; gold Pan-Am Games 1971, 1975; fifth 1975 world Belgium; Canadian male amateur athlete of year 1975; 15th Canadian speedskating championships Saskatoon 1975; *res.* Toronto, Ont.

LOVEROCK, Patty (track); *b.* 21 Feb 1953, Vancouver, B.C.; *given name:* Patricia Elaine; U of British Columbia, B.R.E.; recreologist; Canadian record holder 100m (11.1), 200m (22.6), 4x100 (43.63); bronze 4x100 Commonwealth Games 1970; silver 100m, bronze 4x100 1975 Pan-Am Games; represented Canada 1976 Montreal Olympics; *res.* Vancouver, B.C.

LOWRY, Ron (orienteering); *b.* 29 Nov 1955, Halifax, N.S.; *given name:* Ronald William; Clarke HS, McMaster U; student; 1968 Ontario, Quebec junior titles; four Canadian titles, 1971 North American title; mem. European tour 1971; competed world student championships 1974, world orienteering championships Denmark 1974; runner-up Canadian men's championships 1974; Canadian men's title 1975; competed 1976 world championships Scotland; Ontario Athletic Achievement Award; *res.* Newcastle, Ont.

LUFTSPRING, Sammy (boxing); *b.* 14 Mar 1916, Toronto, Ont.; *given name:* Yisrael; *m.* Elsie Goodman; *children:* Brian, Orian; Central Tech; restaurant, night club manager; began boxing Toronto club matches 1932; lost just two of 24 amateur bantamweight bouts 1933; protesting Germany's treatment of Jews, rejected 1936 Olympic team trials; under guidance Harry Sniderman began Spanish tour but stopped by civil war; launched pro career 1936 stopping Mannie Hill in three; after seven pro bouts met Gordon Wallace for Canadian welterweight title 1937 losing split decision; under manager Al Weill won Canadian welterweight title with 13th round TKO over Frank Genovese 1938 Toronto; world ranking 1938 beating third-ranked Salvy Saban; prepping to fight Henry Armstrong for world title, met Steve Belloise in warm-up bout 1940 Bronx Coliseum; accidental thumb in eye ended ring career and cost him left eye; turned to refereeing; over 1,000 bouts to his credit including several world class matches; wrote *Call Me Sammy;* mem. Canadian Boxing Hall of Fame; *res.* Toronto, Ont.

LUMLEY, Harry (hockey); *b.* 11 Nov 1926, Owen Sound, Ont.; *m.* Frances Buckley; *children:* Kerri Ann, James, Frank, Harry Jr.; livestock auction manager; started career as defenceman in Owen Sound minor leagues, shifted to goal and remained there until NHL retirement 1964; played intermediate in Owen Sound, junior in Barrie; pro with Indianapolis (AHL) 1943-44, Detroit Red Wings 1945-50, Chicago Black Hawks 1951, Toronto Maple Leafs 1952-56; Vezina Trophy with 1.85 avg.; J.P. Bickell Memorial Gold Cup as Leafs' MVP and first team all-star 1954-55; Boston Bruins 1957-61; final years with Kingston (EPHL), Winnipeg (WHL), and local league Collingwood Senior Shipbuilders; in 16 NHL seasons appeared in 803 regular season games, allowed 2,210 goals, posted 71 shutouts, 2.75 avg.; in 76 playoff games allowed 199 goals, seven shutouts, 2.62 avg.; played on one Stanley Cup winner; *res.* Owen Sound, Ont.

LUMSDEN, Neil (football); *b.* 19 Dec 1952, London, Ont.; *given name:* Neil James; Trinity College, Northern CI, U of Ottawa; athlete of year at every school he attended; at U of Ottawa set CIAU record 410 points scored, OUAA records 148 single season points, 36 lifetime field goals, 103 lifetime converts, 41 single season converts, 15 single season TDs, 31 lifetime TDs (equalled record of Eric Walter of McGill, Toronto); league all-star four times, all-Canadian three times; three times Omega Trophy (OUAA MVP); Ted Morris Trophy (MVP) in Canadian College Bowl 1975 in which U of Ottawa won Vanier Cup; team also won Yates Cup that year; holder of school records in all departments of offence including lifetime yds rushing 3,111; U of Ottawa outstanding running back four times, MVP three times; athlete of year 1975; ACT (Ottawa) athlete of year 1975; joined Toronto Argonauts 1976; runner-up 1976 CFL rookie of year; EFC rookie of year 1976; *res.* Toronto, Ont.

LUMSDON, Cliff (swimming); *b.* 13 Apr 1931, Toronto, Ont.; *div.; children:* Kim; Humber College; parks and recreation supervisor; at 18 claimed first of five world marathon swim championships by beating field of 70 in CNE 32-mile swim; won

Atlantic City 26-mile marathon 1956; became first to conquer Straits of Juan de Fuca 1956; regarded as king of pro swimmers; coached by Gus Ryder; coaches daughter Kim and has assisted Cindy Nicholas, Diane Nyad; manages Lakeshore Swim Club, works with crippled children; Lou Marsh Trophy Canada's athlete of year 1949; mem. Canadian Sports Hall of Fame; *res.* Etobicoke, Ont.

LUMSDON, Kim (swimming); *b.* 3 Feb 1957, Toronto, Ont.; Branksome Hall; swimming teacher, coach; began swimming at two; under coaching of father Cliff entered first competition at nine; sixth AAU long distance (three miles) nationals 1973; first woman, fifth overall Rio de la Plate Argentina five-mile swim 1974; second woman, fifth overall Lac St. Jean five-mile swim 1975; cold water, exhaustion ended 1975 Lake Ontario bid; third woman, 10th overall Lac St. Jean 25-mile swim 1976; conquered 32-mile Lake Ontario despite 4-6 ft waves 1976 in 21:27; fourth best women's marathon swimmer in world 1976; won Gus Ryder, Borough of Etobicoke awards for Lake Ontario swim; *res.* Etobicoke, Ont.

LUNSFORD, Earl (football); *b.* 19 Oct 1933, Stillwater, Okla.; *m.* Margot; *children:* Brenda, Lamar; Oklahoma A&M, B.A., M.A.; football executive; all-American 1955; drafted by Philadelphia Eagles but turned pro with Calgary Stampeders 1956 leading club in scoring first season; carried 183 times for 1,034yds and 10 TDs 1959 season; single-game WFC rushing record 211yds 1960; first player to gain more than a mile rushing single season 1961 with 296 carries for 1,796yds; twice won Eddie James Trophy as WFC leading rusher; six-year CFL record 1,199 carries for 6,994yds, 56 TDs; five TDs vs Edmonton Sep 1962; five times 1,000-plus

yds in season, three times 200-plus carries in season; general manager Winnipeg Blue Bombers 1967; *res.* Winnipeg, Man.

LYLE, Dulcie (golf); *b.* 25 Mar 1918, Allan's Corners, Que.; *given name:* Dulcie Isabella Jessie Logan; *m.* Robert Lyle; Notre Dame Ladies College; Canadian javelin record in HS; equalled Canadian 100yd breast stroke mark during British Empire Games trials; with Marian Macdonald won MAAA, Montreal & District badminton doubles title three times; MAAA squash titlist, played frequent international matches; began golfing age 31, reduced handicap to four in two years; won Kaniwaki club title 14 times, six times Montreal & District, four times Montreal & District seniors, once Quebec Open, five times Quebec seniors, twice Quebec mixed, six times Quebec two-ball and best ball; won 1960 Canadian Closed, 1971 Canadian seniors, 1973 US seniors; mem. Quebec interprovincial team 14 times, interprovincial seniors five times; non-playing captain Canadian World Cup team Australia 1968; semifinalist Doherty 1962; third US North-South Pinehurst 1972; *res.* Montreal, Que., Florida.

LYON, George S. (golf); *b.* 27 Jul 1858, Richmond, Ont., *d.* 11 May 1938, Toronto, Ont.; *given name:* George Seymour; *m.* Annette M. Martin; *children:* George S. Jr., Fred M; at 18 held Canadian pole vault record; in cricket for Toronto Rosedale vs combined Peterborough-Toronto team carried bat for 238, Canadian record; began golf age 38, in 16-year span won eight Canadian amateurs, runner-up twice; at 46 only person in history to win Olympic gold medal in golf beating US champion Chandler Egan three and two St. Louis 1904; mem. RCGA, Canadian Sports Halls of Fame.

MABEY, Hap (curling); *b.* 25 Oct 1939, Saint John, N.B.; *given name:* Harold Arthur; *m.* Lina Petrea Andersen; *children:* Joy, Kim, Nathalie, Tanya, Adonica, David, Peter; sporting goods agent; early recognition baseball 1953 Maritime midget title team; 1955 N.B. juvenile baseball honors; runner-up N.B. Schoolboy curling finals 1956, title 1957; mem. Maritime junior baseball champions 1959, Maritime senior A baseball, fastball champions 1960; five times winner N.B. men's curling title and Brier representative, five times runner-up for provincial title; winner various regional competitions in curling, baseball, fastball, golf; plays with Oldtimers hockey team; mem. N.B. Sports Hall of Fame; *res.* Riverview, N.B.

MACDONALD, Gary (swimming); *b.* 15 Dec 1953, Mission, B.C.; *given name:* Gary Wayne; Mission HS, Simon Fraser U; student; began competitive swimming 1972 under coach Deryk Snelling with Canadian Dolphins Swim Club; represented Canada World Student Games Moscow 1973, Commonwealth Games 1974 figuring in gold, two bronze medal performances; 1975 Pan-Am Games won silver 400m freestyle (FS) relay,

fourth 200m individual medley, fifth 100m FS; silver 4x100m medley relay; 13th 100m FS semifinals 1976 Olympics; four gold 1976 Canadian Nationals; personal bests: 100m FS 53.31; 200m FS 1:38.51; Canadian records 400m FS relay 3:33.42, 400m medley relay 3:55.69; Governor-General's silver medal 1976; *res.* Mission, B.C.

MACDONALD, Irene (diving); *b.* 22 Nov 1933, Hamilton, Ont.; *given name:* Irene Margaret; provincial diving development coordinator; 15 Canadian national titles 1951-61, six US national 1957-60 and two Mexican 1958-59; bronze 3m springboard 1954, silver 1958 Commonwealth Games; fourth 1955, 1959 Pan-Am Games; bronze 1956, sixth 1960 Olympics; Ontario 3m title 1951-55, B.C. 1961, Quebec 1956; Velma Springstead Trophy (Canadian female athlete of year) 1957; past director B.C. Sports Federation; chairman Diving for Canada 1962-66; diving coach Canadian Commonwealth team 1966, European tour team 1971, world championship team 1973-75; trustee B.C. Sports Hall of Fame; CADA technical director 1967-69; mem. B.C. Sports, National Aquatic Halls of Fame; *res.* Vancouver, B.C.

MACDONALD, Jackie (track and field); *b.* 12 Oct 1932, Toronto, Ont.; *m.* Bill Gelling; *children:* Andrew, Steven; Carleton U, B.A.; teacher; Ontario junior diving title 1945; played with junior basketball champion Toronto Globetrotters 1949-50; Canadian shot put title 1953; Canadian shot put record, silver medal Vancouver British Empire Games 1954; fifth discus Mexico Pan-Am Games 1955; beat own Canadian record placing 10th shot put 1956 Melbourne Olympics; only Canadian representative

Macdonald

Moscow World Youth Games 1957; bronze medal 1958 Commonwealth Games; *res.* Ottawa, Ont.

MACDONALD, Kilby (hockey); *b.* 6 Sep 1913, Ottawa, Ont.; *m.* Mary Hayes; *children:* Kilby Jr., Ann, Terry, Allan; University of Ottawa HS; regional sales manager; mem. U of O HS Canadian title football team; hockey Lasalle juniors 1926, Montagnard juniors 1928-32, Kirkland Lake seniors 1933-36, Noranda Copper Kings 1937; pro NY Ranger chain, season with Rovers, two with Philadelphia Ramblers; won Calder Memorial Trophy as top NHL rookie with Rangers 1940; except for 1942-44 WW2 army service remained with Rangers through 1945; Eastern Ontario scout for Rangers five years; coach at West Point, Arvida, Baltimore, Quebec; Memorial Cup finalists vs Barrie 1951; helped with Ottawa Cradle League; coach St. Anthony seniors; manager-coach Babe Ruth baseball teams winning Ontario, Canadian titles, competing in Washington D.C. world championships; *res.* Windsor, Ont.

MACDONALD, Noel (basketball); *b.* 1915, Mortlach, Sask.; *m.* Harry Robertson; joined Edmonton Grads 1933 playing until 1939 retirement; in 135 games scored 1,874 points for 13.8 points-per-game avg., best in club's history; CP poll Canadian female athlete of year 1938; mem. Canadian Sports Hall of Fame.

MACDONNELL, Wayne (badminton); *b.* 28 Jun 1940, Vancouver, B.C.; *given name:* Wayne Barry; personnel manager; record six times Canadian men's singles champion 1962-67; Canadian doubles champion 1963; eight times B.C. singles, five times B.C. doubles, seven times Vancouver singles champion; three times Oregon State, 11 times Washington State singles champion; won 1966 US mixed doubles, 1971 Irish Open singles; record six times mem. Canadian Thomas Cup team; *res.* Burnaby B.C.

MACFARLANE, Angus (basketball); *b.* 19 Feb 1925, Montreal, Que.; McGill U, B.A., B.Ed.; teacher, politician; general manager Canadian national basketball team 1969-70; coached at Verdun, Mount Allison; National Association of Basketball Coaches of Canada merit award; resource officer National Sports and Recreation Centre; MP (LIB) Hamilton Mountain; *res.* Ottawa, Ont.

MACKAY, Craig (speedskating); *b.* 1 Apr 1927, Banff, Alta.; *given name:* Craig Innis; *m.* Gwen Bibbey; *children:* Kim, Heather, Terri, Craig Jr., Cam, Tom; Westmount, Bedford Rd HS; road building contractor; joined Saskatoon Lions Speedskating Club at 16 and became city, provincial champion following year setting provincial mile record, repeat 1945; 1947 Alberta senior men's 220yd record, gold medal Canadian senior men's three-mile same year; *Star-Phoenix* Road Race three-mile mark 1948; Alberta champion 1951; runner-up numerous Canadian events through 25-year competitive career; represented Saskatoon 1967 Canada Winter Games Quebec City; represented Canada 1948 St. Moritz; 11th in 5000m, 13th 10 000m 1952 Oslo Olympics, marks unequalled by Canadian men to date; was alternate 1956, 1960 Olympic Games; represented Canada 1950 world placing seventh 500m, ninth 1500m; helped institute Olympic trials for skaters; key role in North American outdoor speedskating championships Saskatoon 1957; mem. International Speedskating Association; two years pres. Saskatchewan branch Canadian Amateur

Speedskating Association; two years v.-pres. CASA; chairman 1968 Canadian outdoor championships Saskatoon; chairman Canada Winter Games Speedskating committee 1970-71; chairman CASA Hall of Fame committee since 1968; chairman 1973 Canadian indoor championships Saskatoon; Saskatoon sportsman of year 1973; mem. Saskatchewan Sports, Canadian Speedskating Halls of Fame; *res.* Saskatoon, Sask.

MACKAY, Mickey (hockey); *b.* 21 May 1894, Chesley, Ont., *d.* 21 May 1940, Nelson, B.C.; *given name:* Duncan McMillan; as junior, played senior hockey in Edmonton, Grand Forks B.C.; nickname The Wee Scot; Vancouver Millionaires (PCL) 1915, missed scoring title by single point in rookie season with 33 goals; remained with Vancouver through 1925-26 season, three scoring titles, 202 goals in 242 games, on one Stanley Cup winner; Chicago team's leading scorer 1927-28; played half of 1928-29 season in Pittsburgh then joined Boston Bruins, won Stanley Cup; retired 1930 to Boston business manager; mem. Hockey Hall of Fame.

MACKEN, Brendan (tennis); *b.* 21 Jan 1923, Montreal, Que.; *given name:* Brendan Hubert; *m.* Elizabeth Gillam; *children:* Nancy, Ginny, Peggy, Helen, Bren Jr.; College of William and Mary, B.Sc.; owner chemical co.; competed for Canada 1946-52 on Davis Cup team, captain 1954; only Canadian to beat an Australian in Davis Cup play (Billy Sidwell 1949); one of two Canadians to beat a US player in Davis Cup action (Bob Perry 1952); Canadian men's singles title 1950; with brother Jim won Canadian men's doubles 1947, repeat 1951 with Lorne Main; Quebec, Ontario singles, doubles, mixed doubles titles 1952; retired 1954; first chairman Canadian Lawn Tennis Association junior

development; 1967 chairman Davis Cup selection committee; two years pres. QLTA; Canadian veteran squash doubles title with late Paul Ouimet 1968-69 and was US runner-up each year; currently A ranked in squash singles representing Canada in matches against US, Australia; past pres. MAAA; *res.* Thornhill, Ont.

MACKEN, Jim (tennis); *b.* 29 Jul 1925, Montreal, Que.; *m.* Audrey Maureen; *children:* Gerald, Kathy, Chris, Patrick, Tony; College of William and Mary, B.A., McGill U; distributor; captained William and Mary to NCAA title 1949; playing mem. Canadian Davis Cup team 1948, non-playing captain 1963, 1965; with brother Bren won Canadian doubles title 1946; nationally ranked in top 10 1946-58; Nova Scotia, Quebec, Ontario, B.C. provincial titles; Vancouver, B.C., Pacific Northwest, Pacific Coast squash titles; mem. 1943-44 McGill Redmen hockey team; pres. Canadian Lawn Tennis Association 1964-66; Centennial medal 1967; *res.* Vancouver, B.C.

MACKEN, Patricia (tennis); *b.* 5 Jul 1928, Montreal, Que.; *div.* Eldon Smart; *children:* Jennifer, Sheila; St. Paul's Academy, College of William and Mary; junior provincial titles Quebec, Ontario 1943-45; Vermont State ladies' singles, doubles, mixed doubles (with Clark Taylor) titles 1948; Quebec senior ladies' singles champion three times; Ontario ladies' singles, doubles five times; Montreal City & District ladies' singles, doubles seven times; Canadian ladies' Open singles, doubles, mixed doubles (with brother Brendan) 1947; mem. Canadian Wightman Cup team vs Britain 1948; Alberta, Manitoba ladies' doubles, mixed titles; 1950 CP poll Canadian female tennis player of half century; *res.* Vancouver, B.C.

MACKENZIE, Ada (golf); *b.* 30 Oct 1891, Toronto, Ont.; *d.* 25 Jan 1973, Richmond Hill, Ont.; Havergal College; first of five Canadian ladies' Open titles 1919; won three successive Havergal Cups; instrumental in formation Toronto Ladies' Golf Club 1924; five Canadian ladies' Closed titles, eight Canadian ladies' seniors, nine Ontario ladies, two Ontario seniors, 10 Toronto and district titles; twice reached semifinals US women's amateur; won Bermuda twice; competed internationally for Scotland and Canada; last seniors title 1969 at age 78; since 1971 Canadian seniors have competed for Ada MacKenzie Trophy; Canadian female athlete of year 1933; mem. RCGA, Canadian Sports Hall of Fame.

MACKENZIE, Shanty (football); *b.* 27 Aug 1920, Scotland; *given name:* Donald; *m.* Audrey Lock; *children:* Mary Louise, Catherine, Marion, William Hugh; Toronto Western Tech; building superintendent; Toronto Argos 1940-41; with Canadian army team vs US Army in two games London Eng. 1944; Toronto Balmy Beach (ORFU) 1946-49, player-coach 1949; rejoined Argos 1950-53, captain 1950 Grey Cup champions; played on two Grey Cup champions; line coach Parkdale Junior Lions (1957 champions), North York Knights, Scarboro Rams 1955-63; Jimmy Keith Memorial Trophy; *res.* Agincourt, Ont.

MACKINNON, Dan (harness racing); *b.* 12 Nov 1876 Highfield, P.E.I., *d.* 24 Dec 1964, Charlottetown, P.E.I.; *m.; children:* Morris; pharmacist, fox farmer, publisher; won Maritime mile run 1896-98; Governor-General's medal for shooting 1920; during 12-day period 1915 won 15 of 16 starts with pacer Helen R.; his horse Volo Rico upset previously unbeaten US-owned Eula H. 1931 Charlottetown; world ice racing record Mt.

Clemens Mich. 1923 with The Yank; Eastern harness racing promotor 1930; USTA director, promoter 1930-61; mem. Canadian Sports Hall of Fame.

MACLEOD, Tammy (diving); *b.* 3 Aug 1956, Vancouver, B.C.; U of British Columbia; student; gold medal 1m 1971 nationals 13-14 age-group; bronze 3m 1972 winter nationals; bronze 10m 1974 summer nationals; silver 10m 1971 world age-group finals Italy; silver 3m, 10m 1971 Bolzano competition; gold 1m, 3m 1973 Australian junior nationals, silver 10m; bronze 1m 1973 Australian senior nationals; bronze 3m 1974 USSR; bronze 10m 1975 New Zealand Games; represented Canada 1976 Montreal Olympics; *res.* Vancouver, B.C.

MACPHERSON, Kitch (basketball); *b.* 11 Jun 1916, Hamilton Ont.; *given name:* Herbert Horatio Kitchener; *m.* Jessie Park; *children:* Catharine, Edward; Westdale HS; stereotyper; officiated 27 years, first Canadian to hold international referee card; officiated Chicago Pan-Am Games 1959, Russian national team tour of US 1960, 1962, Manila world games 1962, Pan-Am Games 1967, Philadelphia World Cup 1968; current supervisor Western Division OUAA referees; Canadian Universities Coaches award, CYO special award, IAABO award, Ontario service to basketball award; *res.* Hamilton, Ont.

MAGNUSSEN, Karen (figure skating); *b.* 4 Apr 1952, North Vancouver, B.C.; Simon Fraser U; pro skater; won Canadian junior singles 1965; fourth Canadian seniors 1966; second Canadian seniors, fourth North Americans, 12th world 1967; won Canadian seniors, seventh world, Olympics 1968; second Canadian seniors, North American 1969; won Canadian seniors, fourth world 1970; won Canadian seniors, North American, third world 1971; won Canadian, second world, Olympics 1972; won Canadian, world 1973 then turned pro with Ice Capades to 1977 retirement; B.C. junior athlete of year 1967; B.C. sports merit award 1970; Sports Federation of Canada female athlete of year 1971-72; B.C. athlete of year 1972; CP poll Canadian female athlete of year 1973; Order of Canada; mem. B.C., Canadian Sports Halls of Fame; *res.* Vancouver, B.C.

MAHONY, Bill (swimming); *b.* 16 Sep 1949, New Westminster, B.C.; *given name:* William Victor; U of British Columbia, B.Sc.; sports physiologist; bronze medal 200m breast stroke 1966 Commonwealth Games; silver 4x100 medley relay 1967 Pan-Am Games; semifinalist 100m breast stroke 1968 Olympics; three gold in 100m, 200m breast stroke, 4x100 medley 1970 Commonwealth Games; silver 4x100 medley 1971 Pan-Am Games; bronze 4x100 medley, semifinalist 100m breast stroke 1972 Olympics; gold 4x100 medley 1974 Commonwealth Games; first Canadian to break 2:40 and 2:30 breast stroke barriers; *res.* Coquitlam, B.C.

MAHOVLICH, Frank (hockey); *b.* 10 Jan 1938, Timmins, Ont.; *given name:* Francis William; *m.* Marie; *children:* Michael, Nancy, Teddy; St. Michael's College, Assumption College; hockey player, travel agent; moved through minor hockey ranks at Schumacher Ont. to St. Michael's College junior B and A teams; OHA junior all-star, Red Tilson Memorial Trophy winner as MVP 1956-57; scouted by pros at 13; baseball talents attracted pro offer from Boston Red Sox; also strong competitive swimmer; three-game stint with Toronto Maple Leafs 1956-57 season then turned pro that club 1957-58 winning Calder Memorial Trophy

as NHL rookie of year; with Leafs until 1968 when traded with Garry Unger, Pete Stemkowski to Detroit for Paul Henderson, Norm Ullman, Floyd Smith; dealt to Montreal for Mickey Redmond, Guy Charron, Bill Collins 1971; three times NHL first team, six times second team all-star left winger; tied Phil Esposito for Stanley Cup playoff points one year with 27, including record 14 goals; through 1973-74 NHL record 1,181 games played scoring 533 goals, 570 assists for 1,103 points, 1,056 penalty minutes, plus 137 playoff games 51 goals, 67 assists, 118 points, 163 penalty minutes; best single season 1968-69 with Detroit scoring 49 goals; played with brother Pete while with Montreal; mem. Team Canada 1972; joined WHA with Toronto (later Birmingham) 1974-75; through 1976-77 played in 165 games scoring 75 goals, 119 assists, 194 points, 53 penalty minutes; *res.* Toronto, Ont.

MAHOVLICH, Pete (hockey); *b.* 10 Oct 1946, Timmins, Ont.; *given name:* Peter Joseph; *m.* Candy; *children:* Peter Jr., Jeffrey, Margaret-Ann; graduated from OHA junior A ranks with Hamilton Red Wings to pro Detroit Red Wings 1965 after being chosen first by Wings, second overall 1963 amateur draft; with brief stints at Pittsburgh (AHL), Fort Worth (CPHL) remained with Detroit until 1969 when traded to Montreal with Bart Crashley for Garry Monahan and Doug Piper; played briefly with Montreal Voyageurs (AHL) and since 1969-70 starred at centre for Canadiens; through 1976-77 appeared in 646 NHL games scoring 229 goals, 341 assists for 580 points, 741 penalty minutes, plus 73 playoff games, 26 goals, 36 assists for 62 points, 115 penalty minutes; mem. Team Canada 1972, 1976; four Stanley Cups; *res.* Montreal, Que.

MAIN, Lorne (tennis); *b.* 9 Jul 1930, Vancouver, B.C.; *given name:* Lorne Garnet; *m.* Ivy Malloy (*d.*); *children:* Kelly, Kevin, Kristine, Kasey; McGee HS, U of California (Berkeley); tennis pro; first title B.C. under-15; won Canadian junior singles 1946, 1947, 1948; with Jim McGregor won 1946 junior doubles; with Brendan Macken won 1951 Canadian men's doubles and with Luis Ayala again 1954; with Barbara Knapp won 1950 Canadian mixed doubles; playing mem. Canadian Davis Cup team 1949-55, non-playing captain five times; won Monte Carlo International, Belgium Open and (with Gil Shea of US) Irish Doubles 1954; with Bob Bedard defeated Chile, Australia and US team of Vic Seixas, Hugh Stewart to win 1976 Stevens Cup; mem. Canadian Gordon Cup title team 1976; *res.* Halifax, N.S.

MAKOLOSKY, Randy (track); *b.* 26 Jul 1953, Calgary, Alta.; *given name:* Randall Samuel; *div.;* U of Calgary; supervisor, distribution centre; held Canadian junior 800m mark of 1:48.9 (1970); with Bill Crothers Canadian senior 800m indoor mark of 1:49.5 (1974); three times Canadian senior indoor 800m champion; represented Canada indoor international dual meets 1973 vs Russia, France 1974, W. Germany 1975; mem. Canadian team which toured Europe, South Africa 1974; *res.* Calgary, Alta.

MALCOLM, Andrew (all-around); *b.* 15 Sep 1901, Saint John, N.B.; *m.* Jean Harding; *children:* Jean, Bruce; Saint John HS; retired; basketball, T&F, baseball and rugby main sports; captain Saint John HS rugby, basketball team and co-captained T&F team; intermediate basketball through 1921 then played for Trojan senior teams until retirement 1932; captain 11 years during which they won nine N.B., eight Maritime, one Eastern title; beat Windsor Ont. for 1932 Eastern Canadian title but lost national title to Winnipeg Toilers; led scorers in each series they played; coached Saint John HS basketball team 1928-33; refereed basketball several years including Canadian Inter-scholastic championships 1933, Canadian senior championships 1930; Maritime shot put record 1924, Canadian title same year in Montreal, repeat 1927 Toronto; six medals 1925 Canadian championships Halifax scoring three firsts, one second, two thirds, high individual winner; led city league baseball batters 1922; nominated 1950 CP poll athletes of half century; Andrew Malcolm Trophy awarded annually by YMCA to Saint John male athlete of year; mem. N.B. Sports Hall of Fame; *res.* Saint John, N.B.

MALONE, Joe (hockey); *b.* 28 Feb 1890, Quebec City, Que.; *d.* 15 May 1969, Montreal, Que.; tool maker; began playing organized hockey 1907 with Crescent juniors, pro with Waterloo 1909, Quebec 1910-17, Montreal Canadiens 1917-19, back to Quebec 1919-20, Hamilton 1920-22 and back to Canadiens 1922-24; NHL scoring record seven goals in single game with Quebec Bulldogs vs Toronto St. Pats 1920; 1917-18 counted 44 goals in 22-game schedule; 1919-20 scored 39 goals, six assists in 24-game schedule; pro career record 379 goals; captained Quebec to Stanley Cup 1912, 1913; coached Quebec 1912-13; nickname Phantom Joe; nine goals vs Sydney Millionaires 1913 Stanley Cup playoff game, eight goals one game vs Wanderers 1917; mem. Hockey Hall of Fame.

MANAHAN, Cliff (curling); *b.* 11 Oct 1888, Fort William, Ont., *d.* 20 Mar 1970, Edmonton, Alta.; *given name:* Clifford Ross; *m.* Elizabeth Ann Jones, (*d.*), *m.* Mary Watson McAndrew Eckert; *children:* Ross (*d.*), Robert, Donald, Doris, Kathleen, June,

Marjorie, Dawn; civil servant; competed in first Edmonton 'spiel 1927; won Alberta championship eight times, Northern Alberta title nine times and represented province in five Briers scoring victories 1933, 1937, second twice, third once; seven times winner Alberta CA and grand aggregate, eight times Edmonton grand challenge title; winner of numerous other events in annual provincial play; in total claimed 65 major championships; winner of numerous Manitoba bonspiel honors; life mem. Alberta Curling Association, Royal Glenora CC, Granite CC of Edmonton; mem. Edmonton Sports, Alberta Amateur Sports, Canadian Curling Halls of Fame.

MANN, Avard (curling); *b.* 18 Sep 1894, Elgin, N.B.; *m.* Mable; *children:* Lloyd (*d.*), Bob, Phyllis; retired; class AA Maritime skeet title 1938; three times Nova Scotia junior curling champion; represented N.S. three times in Brier; N.S. seniors title 1965, competed in finals five times, twice runner-up; Maritime Johnson senior championship; *res.* Truro, N.S.

MANN, Bob (curling); *b.* 5 Jan 1922, Truro, N.S.; *m.* Lena; *children:* Bob, Susan, Patricia, Sandy; regional sales manager; N.S. junior hockey champions 1939-40; six years senior hockey with Truro Bearcats; refereed Big Six League 1950-51; N.S. class A skeet title 1948; three times N.S. Consols finalist, five times Ontario finalist; represented N.S. 1960 Brier, Ontario 1963-64; Ontario Silver Tankard 1968, Ontario intermediate 1972, finalist Ontario seniors 1975-76; third Tournament of Champions Maple Leaf Gardens 1964; *res.* Mississauga, Ont.

MANN, Dave (football); *b.* 6 Feb 1932, Berkeley, Calif.; *given name:* David Carl; *m.* Gail; *children:* Angela, Melissa; Oregon

State U; salesman, actor; Chicago Cardinals three years; Argos 1958 as offensive back, carried ball 107 times for 556yds, caught 33 passes for 319yds; appeared in 155 league, 13 playoff games; second in Argos all-time scoring records with 435 points (33 TDs, 73 converts, 22 field goals, 98 singles); punter 1960-70 with 1,261 punts for 55,745yds including one for 102yds; twice scored TDs on punt returns; handled 139 kickoffs for 7,862yds and as returner carried 36 for 755yds; EFC all-star 1960-61; punter on Argos modern era all-star team 1945-73; *res.* Mississauga, Ont.

MANNING, Peter (track and field); *b.* 6 Apr 1931, Romford, Essex, Eng.; *given name:* Peter George; *m.* Myra Laycock; *children:* Helen Jane, Gillian Claire, Sarah Louise; U of London, U of Manitoba; director, product management; director Manitoba CTFA 1967-70, CTFA coach of year 1974, runner-up Air Canada award 1974; coached 1600m relays 1976 Olympics; *res.* Guelph, Ont.

MANTHA, Sylvio (hockey); *b.* 14 Apr 1903, Montreal, Que., *d.* 1974, Montreal, Que.; played with Notre Dame de Grace juniors 1918-19 then moved through intermediate, senior ranks to Nationals in Quebec Senior League before turning pro; played forward as amateur then shifted to defence as pro with Montreal Canadiens 1923-24; played on nine Prince of Wales Trophy winners, three Stanley Cup champions; player-coach with Habs 1935-36 then moved to Boston until retirement 1936-37; two seasons as NHL linesman, AHL referee; coach junior, senior teams for several years; twice named to second team all-stars; during NHL career scored 63 goals, 72 assists; mem. Hockey Hall of Fame.

MARCHILDON, Phil (baseball); *b.* 25 Oct 1913, Penetanguishene, Ont.; *given name:* Philip Joseph; *m.* Irene Patience; *children:* Dawna, Carol; Penetanguishene HS, St. Michael's College; hospital furnishing co. employee; pitched Penetang intermediates to Ontario finals in 30s and Creighton Mines to Nickle Belt title and provincial finals 1938; two seasons with Toronto Maple Leafs (IL), part of one with Cornwall (Can-Am) before joining Connie Mack's Philadelphia Athletics 1940; posted 17-14 record with A's 1942; honored by fans with Marchildon Night Philadelphia 1945; 19-9 record 1947 with one-hitter and two two-hitters; wound up career with Boston Red Sox 1950; played in Senior Intercounty with Guelph, Waterloo; in 185 major league games posted 68-75 won-lost record, four shutouts; mem. Canadian Sports Hall of Fame; *res.* Toronto, Ont.

MARCOTTE, Bill (track); *b.* 22 Jan 1954, Toronto, Ont.; *given name:* William Dale; Parkdale CI, Ryerson Polytechnical Inst.; student; Canadian junior 5000m title 1974; mem. Canadian European touring team 1975; *res.* Toronto, Ont.

MARION, Alain (shooting); *b.* 23 Dec 1946, Pointe Gatineau, Que.; *m.* Mireille; Hull CGEP; police officer; won Quebec match rifle prone title four times, match rifle three position twice; mem. national smallbore prone team title twice, Bisley team nine times; competed in Australia, New Zealand 1968 championships, Canadian championships four times; represented Canada 1974 Commonwealth Games; Queen's silver medal 1972, Bisley grand aggregate silver cross 1973; *res.* Gatineau, Que.

MARSHALL, Jack (hockey); *b.* 14 Mar 1877, St. Vallier, Que.; *d.* 7 Aug 1965, Montreal, Que.; Caledonia Cup (soccer) three times 1890s; played rugby for championship Britannia club 1897; hockey forward, defenceman in 17-year career with seven different teams, five Stanley Cup winners; Winnipeg Victorias 1901, Montreal Victorias 1902-03, Montreal Wanderers 1904-05, 1907, 1910-12, 1916-17, Montagnards 1907, Shamrocks 1908-09, Toronto Arenas 1913-15; twice led league scorers; player-manager Arenas 1913-14, guided club to 1914 Stanley Cup; scored 99 career goals in 132 league games, 13 in 18 playoff games; scored six goals in one game, five goals in two others; mem. Hockey Hall of Fame.

MARTEL, Marty (bowling); *b.* 1887, Cape Breton, *d.* 1958, Halifax, N.S.; *given name:* Wilbert; world candlepin record for single string 213, total 496 for three strings; helped form Nova Scotia Wolverines, Allan Cup winners; mem. Canadian Sports Hall of Fame.

MARTIN, Carol (track and field); *b.* 19 Apr 1948, Toronto, Ont.; *given name:* Carol Lynne; Simon Fraser U, York U, B.A.; bronze medal discus 1966 Commonwealth Games 159'3''; silver 1967 Pan-Am Games 156'3''; mem. Canadian team 1968 Scandinavian tour; silver 1969 Pan-Pacific Games; bronze 1970 Commonwealth Games 158'10''; won 1972 Olympic trials setting Canadian record 55.45m; competed Munich Olympics; gold medal 1973 Pan-Pacific Games; bronze 1974 Commonwealth Games, personal best 56.60m; toured Europe with Canadian team 1975; *res.* Toronto, Ont.

MARTIN, Flora Greenwood (curling, softball); *b.* 21 Jun 1916, Treherne, Man.; *given name:* Flora Mae Greenwood; *m.* Geoff Martin; *children:* Bill; mem. Treherne softball team which won eight of nine Manitoba tournaments 1938-39; won Vancouver Island ladies' curling playdowns nine times, Victoria Club ladies' championship eight times; skipped B.C. ladies' playdowns 1974, 1975 in both Macdonald Lassies and ladies' seniors; runner-up B.C. ladies' seniors 1973; represented B.C. winning Canadian ladies' seniors 1974-75; mem. Vancouver Island O'Keefe mixed championship rink 1964; in lawn bowling won Vancouver Island novice title 1969, Vancouver Open singles 1974, runner-up 1975; runner-up provincial pairs championships 1974-75; master athlete of year finalist B.C. Sports Federation 1974-75; mem. Canadian Curling Hall of Fame; *res.* Victoria, B.C.

MARTIN, John (bowling); *b.* 30 Nov 1919, Toronto, Ont.; *given name:* John Martyn; *sep.* Winnifred Vale; *children:* Patricia, Wayne (*d.*), Calvin, Michael, Ronald, Randall, John Jr., Kevin; Central Tech; bowling proprietor; five-pin bowler, entered business with opening of O'Connor Bowl Toronto 1951; major role in elimination of counter pin and adoption of new scoring system; through his efforts bowling became regular CBC-TV feature for nine years; annual O'Connor Open among country's top competitions since 1957; staged attractions such as Canadian Invitational Singles, Rotary '50' Marathon; founding mem. Bowling Proprietors Associations of Ontario, Canada, past pres. of each; Builders of Bowling Industry Award 1974; *res.* Toronto, Ont.

MARTIN, Peter (football); *b.* 20 Oct 1940, Toronto, Ont.; *given name:* Peter Thomas Ross; *m.* Wendy Warwick; *children:* Cindy, Kristi, Peter James, Jennifer; Winston Churchill HS, U Western Ontario, B.P.H.E.; phys ed teacher; co-captain UWO Mustangs 1963, MVP same season; first college draft choice Ottawa Rough Riders 1964; picked

up by Argos, played with East York Argos Canadian senior champions 1964; CFL Argos linebacker 1965-72; played in 103 league, 10 playoff games: *res.* Mississauga, Ont.

MARTIN, Pit (hockey); *b.* 9 Dec 1943, Noranda, Que.; *given name:* Hubert Jacques; *m.* Pat Gurniss; hockey player; 1958 NOHA title team then joined Hamilton junior Red Wings in OHA; single-game trial with Detroit Red Wings 1961; two seasons with Pittsburgh (AHL) before becoming Detroit regular 1963-64; except for 16-game stint with Pittsburgh remained with Wings until traded to Boston for Parker MacDonald 1965; traded to Chicago with Gilles Marotte, Jack Norris for Phil Esposito, Ken Hodge, Fred Stanfield 1967; most productive season 1972-73, scored 29 goals, 61 assists for 90 points; 32 goals 1975-76 campaign; 14 NHL seasons (through 1976-77) has played in 963 games scoring 296 goals, 439 assists for 735 points, 549 penalty minutes, plus 97 playoff games, 27 goals, 30 assists for 57 points, 54 penalty minutes; Bill Masterton Memorial Trophy 1970; *res.* Chicago, Ill.

MASTERS, Wally (football, baseball); *b.* 28 Mar 1907, Pen Argyl, Pa.; *given name:* Walter Thomas; *m.* Ruth Anna Newman; *children:* Walter Thomas Jr.; U of Pennsylvania; public relations; all-American college baseball righthander 1931 winning 15 in row, 28-3 record; same year chosen to Knute Rockne football all-American team; played pro baseball one year each Washington, Philadelphia Athletics American League, Philadelphia Phillies National League; pitched for Ottawa Nationals Border League 1947; pro football as quarterback with Philadelphia Eagles, Chicago Cardinals-Pittsburgh Steelers combined teams; 1932 season with Ottawa Rough Riders, all-Canadian; coached Ottawa Rough Riders 1933-34 (simultaneously managed Ottawa Crains Can-Am baseball league), St. Patrick's College 1935, Ottawa Trojans ORFU 1947, Rough Riders 1948-50; coached Wilmington Delaware Clippers in American Association 1937-39; overall football coaching record 88 wins, 22 losses, two ties; ORFU title 1947 with Trojans, guided Riders to 1948 Grey Cup bowing to Calgary 12-7; *res.* Ottawa, Ont.

MAXWELL, Steamer (hockey); *b.* 19 May 1890, Winnipeg, Man., *d.* 11 Sep 1975, Winnipeg, Man.; *given name:* Fred; skating prowess earned him nickname Steamer; rover Winnipeg Monarchs Allan Cup champions 1914-15; retired as player 1917, coach Monarchs two seasons; coached Winnipeg Falcons to 1919 Allan Cup, 1920 Olympics, world championships, Winnipeg Rangers to Manitoba title 1925-26, Winnipeg Maroons (APHL) 1926-28 then returned to amateur with junior, senior teams; guided Elmwood Millionaires to junior, senior Manitoba titles 1929-30; Monarchs to world title 1935; officiated many games, amateur and pro 1910-40; mem. Hockey Hall of Fame.

MAYER, Alfons (shooting); *b.* 1 Feb 1938, Weiler, Germany; *div.* Mary; *children:* Anita, Linda; *m.* Irngard; mechanical foreman; several Canadian, Ontario rifle championships; gold medal English Match 1967 Pan-Am Games tieing world record; fourth world English Match competition; 1968 N.Y. State title; bronze 1971 Pan-Am Games English Match; represented Canada 1968, 1972 Olympics, 1966, 1974 world; *res.* Kitchener, Ont.

MCBLAIN, Liz (track and field); *b.* 30 Jan 1948, Bandung, Indonesia; *given name:* Elizabeth Vanderstam; *m.* William McBlain; U of Lethbridge, U of Alberta, B.P.E.; teacher; represented Canada in pentathlon vs USSR, US, Austria; best performance 3,951 points through 1976; personal best 400m hurdles 61.2, 400m 54.9, 53.88 in relay leg; outstanding Calgary athlete 1967, outstanding U of Lethbridge athlete 1971; *res.* Edmonton, Alta.

MCCAFFREY, Jimmy (football); *b.* 1895, Alexandria, Ont., *d.* 29 Oct 1966, Alexandria, Ont.; *m.* Ella Krock (*d.*); *children:* Patricia; government registrar of trademarks; managed St. Brigid's hockey club; past pres. Ottawa Senators in Quebec Senior League; manager Ottawa Rough Riders 1923, amalgamated with St. Brigid's Club of Ottawa City League; managed Riders 1925-1959 (except war years); saw Riders win four Grey Cup titles while losing in finals three times; Big Four pres. 1940, 1956; helped form Eastern Football Conference; Schenley award trustee 1955; mem. Ottawa, Canadian Football Hall of Fame.

MCCANCE, Ches (football); *b.* 19 Feb 1915, Winnipeg, Man., *d.* 8 May 1956, Winnipeg, Man.; *given name:* Chester William; *m.* Frances Elizabeth Carson *children:* William Robert, Margaret Elizabeth; Daniel McIntyre HS; wine salesman; in CFL with Winnipeg Blue Bombers, Montreal Alouettes, played in eight Grey Cup finals, winning three; kicked two field goals, two singles as Bombers edged Ottawa 18-16 1941 final; field goal, three converts, one single as Als beat Calgary in 1949 final; played third Ken Weldon's Quebec entry 1952, 1953 Briers; lost title playoff 1953; coached Isaac Newton Junior HS to Manitoba football title 1940; assistant coach Blue Bombers 1943.

MCCONACHIE, John (football, hockey); *b.* 18 Jul 1941, Montreal, Que.; *given name:* John Alexander; *m.* Diane Gregory; *children:* Sean, Ryan; Sir George Williams U, B.A.; assistant executive-director Canadian Intercollegiate Athletic Union; male athlete of year 1958-60 Royal George HS Greenfield Park; junior football Rosemount Bombers winning 1960 national title, 1961 national finalists; mem. 1963-64 SGW national finalist hockey team; three years head coach South Shore Colts juvenile football team; competed interscholastic gymnastics, badminton (singles, mixed doubles titles), soccer (team captain two seasons), volleyball (team captain); pres. South Shore Colts football club two years; outstanding defenceman award South Shore intermediate hockey league 1966-67; *res.* Stittsville, Ont.

MCCREADY, Earl (wrestling); *b.* 1908, Lansdowne, Ont.; Oklahoma A & M, B.P.E.; masseur; Canadian heavyweight title 1926; U S national intercollegiate title 1928-30, U S national amateur title 1930; represented Canada 1930 British Empire Games Hamilton, Canadian wrestlers took all seven gold medals; by 1930 won every amateur wrestling title available in Canada, U S, British Commonwealth; lost bid for world pro championship 1932 to Jim Londos; mem. U S, Canadian Wrestling, Sports Halls of Fame; *res.* Seattle, Wash.

MCCUBBINS, Chris (track); *b.* 22 Nov 1945, Enid, Okla.; *given name:* Raymond Chris; Enid HS, Oklahoma State U, B.S., U of Manitoba; teacher; third Oklahoma State AA mile 1963; second outdoor Big Eight mile, third indoor Big Eight two-mile, fifth Big Eight cross-country 1964-65; won Big Eight outdoor three-mile, second Big Eight indoor two-mile 1965-66; won 1966-67 Big Eight cross-country, indoor two-mile, outdoor three-mile, NCAA steeplechase, U S Pan-Am Games steeplechase trials; gold medal 1967 Winnipeg Pan-Am Games steeplechase (record 8:38.2); won Canadian Steeplechase 1971-72, Canadian cross-country 1976; best times 1000m 28:16.6, 5000m 14:08.8; won Canadian Olympic 10 000m trials in 29:29.0, third 5000m in 14:27.2; represented Canada 1976 Montreal Olympics; *res.* Winnipeg, Man.

MCCULLOCH, Jack (speedskating); *b.* 1872, Winnipeg, Man., *d.* 1918, Winnipeg, Man.; skate manufacturer; hockey with Winnipeg Victorias who won nine of 11 games on Eastern tour and outscored rivals 76-36 1890; first Canadian speedskating title 1893; won U S nationals St. Paul 1896; world title Montreal 1897; turned pro 1898 and barnstormed for several years; mem. Canadian Sports Hall of Fame.

MCDONALD, Joan (archery); *b.* 23 Feb 1943, Toronto, Ont.; *given name:* Joan Gallie; *div.* Alan McDonald; *children:* David, Christopher; winner Canadian freestyle target 1962, 1964-67, freestyle field 1964-66, grand champion 1964-66; mem. Canadian world team 1965, 1967, 1975; figure skating judge; *res.* Toronto, Ont.

MCDONALD, Vern (basketball); *b.* 5 Jul 1910, Winnipeg, Man.; *given name:* Vern Henry; *m.* Ethel Fines; retired; coached basketball teams to five city, three Ontario, one Canadian championship; also coaches lacrosse; honored by Ontario Government for contribution to sport, by Canadian Coaches Association for contribution to basketball, by International Association of Approved Basketball Officials for work on behalf of basketball in Canada; *res.* Hamilton, Ont.

MCFARLANE, Bob (track, football); *b.* 28 May 1927, London, Ont.; *given name:* Robert Malcolm; *m.* Patricia Jean Henderson; *children:* Janie, Wendy, Laurie; Ridley College, U of Western Ontario, M.D.; plastic surgeon, professor of surgery; backfielder UWO team which won CIAU titles 1945-47, 1949-50; mem. intercollegiate, Eastern Canadian all-star teams; ran 880yd relay 1:27.1, 440yd 47.5, mile relay 3:17.1 1947; ran 400m 47.3 1948; ran 500yd 58.00, 1,000yd 2:18.1, mile relay 3:32.4, 300yd 30.00, 880yd 1:53.2 1950; represented Canada 1948 London Olympics, mem. 4x100m relay team which placed fifth; Lou Marsh Trophy (Canadian athlete of year) 1950; John W. Davies trophy (AAU of C) 1947, 1950; *res.* London, Ont.

MCFARLANE, Don (football, track); *b.* 18 May 1926, London, Ont.; *given name:* Donald Cecil; *m.* Frances Smith; *children:* David, Donald, Karen, Joanne; Ridley College, U of Western Ontario, M.D.; ocular surgeon; with brother Bob mem. UWO Mustangs powerhouse backfield 1944-50 winning Canadian title 1945-47, 1949-50; intercollegiate, Eastern Canadian all-star; George McCullough MVP Trophy; mem. UWO track team 1946-49 specializing 200m, 400m, 800m events; competed Eastern Canada vs Eastern US track meets 1946-47; mem. 4x100m fifth place Canadian relay team 1948 Olympics; mem. British Empire vs US track team London Eng. 1948; qualified 1950 British Empire Games team but did not compete due to medical residency training; *res.* London, Ont.

MCGEE, Frank (hockey); *b.* 1882, Ottawa, Ont., *d.* 16 Sep 1916, Courcelette, France; *given name:* Francis; played centre, rover with Ottawa Silver Seven 1903-06 winning three consecutive Stanley Cups; scored 71 goals in 23 regular season games; in 22 Stanley Cup playoff games scored 63 goals including 14 in a single game against Dawson City 1905 as Ottawa won 23-2, eight consecutive goals in span of eight minutes, 20 seconds; seven times scored five goals in a game; mem. Hockey Hall of Fame.

MCGILL, Frank (all-around); *b.* 20 Jun 1894, Montreal, Que.; *given name:* Frank Scholes; *m.* Margaret Williamson; *children:* Isabel, Nancy, John; McGill U; retired Air Vice Marshall; participated in hockey, football, swimming, water polo, sailing, squash, racquets, golf, tennis, baseball; quarterbacked Montreal Big Four 1919 title team calling signals in French; broke Canadian 100yd outdoor record 1912; captained MAAA water polo team to three Canadian titles; mem. George Hamilton crew which represented Canada in international sailing races vs U S at St. Paul Minn.; past pres. Interprovincial Football Union, MAAA Football Club; Sir Vincent Meredith Trophy as best all-around MAAA athlete; CFL Schenley awards trustee; CB (companion of Bath), Haakon VII Cross of Liberation, Order of Lafayette; mem. Canadian Football, Canadian Sports Halls of Fame; *res.* Montreal, Que.

MCGIMSIE, Billy (hockey); *b.* 7 Jun 1880, Woodsville, Ont.; *d.* 28 Oct 1968, Calgary, Alta.; *given name:* William George; played through Kenora minor, church league, mercantile ranks before joining Thistles where he starred at centre 10 years; entire major league career with one club; four times competed for Stanley Cup, won once; dislocated shoulder in Ottawa exhibition contest ended career; mem. Hockey Hall of Fame.

MCINTOSH, Pam (orienteering); *b.* 23 Mar 1949, Beaverlodge, Alta.; *given name:* Pamela Jean; U of Guelph B.Sc., U of Toronto, B.Ed.; phys ed teacher; Ontario elite ladies' title 1972, second in Canadian finals; 1973 Ontario, Ohio titles, third Canadian; 1974 Ontario title; mem. national team, placed 35th (top Canadian) world championship Denmark; Canadian elite title 1975, second New England championships; Ontario Athletic Commission Award; *res.* Ridgeway, Ont.

MCKAY, Roy (baseball); *b.* 1 Aug 1933, London, Ont.; *given name:* Roy Alexander; *m.* Ruth McPherson; *children:* Alex, Rosemary (*d.*), Jim (*d.*); Central CI; specifications writer; pitching talents attracted pro baseball scouts, signed with Detroit Tigers organization following 1952 trials with Dodgers at Vero Beach; played in Douglas Ga., Idaho Falls part of 1953, 1955 seasons; Senior Intercounty baseball with London Majors 1952, pitched 13 seasons that league; one season with London, Great Lakes-Niagara League, most valuable pitcher 1957; best season 1958 with 10-6 record, 2.79 ERA; in 13 senior seasons posted 20 wins, 32 losses with 4.02 ERA; led in complete games with 13 in 1958; topped circuit in hit batsmen with 16 in 1958; manager London club 1969 guiding them to first place 1969, 1970; excluding 1973 campaign has managed London since 1969; twice chosen Intercounty all-star manager; *res.* London, Ont.

MCKAY, Willie (track and field, football); *b.* 30 Mar 1930, Toronto, Ont.; *given name:* William Earl; *m.* Barbara Ethel Askew; *children:* Robin, Paul; Western Tech, U of Ottawa, OCE; HS art teacher; played football up to semipro 15 years, coached HS nine, officiated seven; pres. Oakville Black Knights 1958-60; ran 100yds 10.2, 220yds 22.4 in junior Olympics; twice won Canadian Forces grand aggregate; coached Oakville track team 1962-67; javelin referee Montreal Olympics; Ontario Fitness & Amateur Sport achievement award 1964; Oakville award of merit 1968; Alan Klarer Trophy for leadership in sports (Oakville Recreation Dept.); *res.* Ottawa, Ont.

MCKEE, Joyce (curling); *b.* 29 Oct 1933, Asquith, Sask.; *given name:* Helen Joyce; stock control operator; mem. several Saskatchewan, Western Canadian championship softball teams early 50s; eight Sask. ladies' curling titles, five as skip, three as second; six times Canadian champion, three times as skip, three as second; runner-up 1962 Canadian finals; winner numerous regional competitions; participated 1954 British Empire Games Vancouver; Saskatoon sportswoman of year 1969; mem. Sask. Sports, Canadian Curling Halls of Fame; *res.* Saskatoon, Sask.

MCKENNA, Ann (field hockey); *b.* 27 Oct 1943, Christchurch, N.Z.; *m.* William McKenna; *children:* Kerry, Derek; U of Canterbury, N.Z., B.Sc.; coach national women's field hockey team; competed internationally for New Zealand in field hockey 1967-71, cricket 1969; *res.* Belcarra Park, B.C.

MCKENNY, Jim (hockey); *b.* 1 Dec 1946, Ottawa, Ont.; *given name:* James Claude; *m.* Christine; *children:* Mia, Jason; hockey player; at 15 played junior A hockey regularly with Toronto Marlboros, helped win 1964 Memorial Cup; in four seasons twice OHA all-star; third Toronto Maple Leaf choice and 17th overall in 1963 amateur draft; made four attempts as defenceman with Leafs but spent more time in minor pro ranks with Tulsa, Rochester, Vancouver until full-time with Toronto Maple Leafs 1969-70 season; played three weeks on loan from Vancouver with Canadian National team 1969, MVP in game vs Finland; Leafs' player representative to NHL Players' Association; seven-season NHL record 503 regular season games, 65 goals, 213 assists, 278 points and 248 penalty minutes, plus 28 playoff games, seven goals, seven assists for 14 points and eight penalty minutes; *res.* Toronto, Ont.

MCKENZIE, Tait (physical educator); *b.* 26 May 1867, Almonte, Ont., *d.* 28 Apr 1938, Philadelphia, Pa.; *given name:* Robert Tait; *m.* Ethel O'Neil; McGill U, B.A., M.D., Springfield College, M.P.E.; developed own frail frame through exercise establishing foundation upon which he developed programs leading to recognition as the father of phys ed programs in North America; held college title in high jump; among forerunners in orthopedic surgery 1892; British army medical corps WWI; contributions to sport art through sculpting without peer; among best known works which exemplified perfection in physical development are The Onslaught, Brothers of the Wind; many of his works used in design of Olympic medals; also noted for war memorials; wrote books on physical education, sports medicine; twice pres. American Physical Education Association; mem. American Academy of Physical Education, Philadelphia St. Andrews Society; instrumental in development Philadelphia playground system, Boy Scout movement.

MCKENZIE, Tom (baseball); *b.* 11 Apr 1942, London, Ont; *m.* Cheryl MacDonald; *children:* Kerry-Sue, Tommy-Jay; Sir Adam Beck CI, U of Western Ontario, B.A., U of Oregon, M.A.; teacher; all-Ontario HS honors as hockey goaler, in track, football; minor baseball London; London Majors Senior Intercounty (IC) team 1960-65; Kitchener from 1966; Senior IC 17-year batting avg. .301; twice led league hitters, .446 in 1970, .434 in 1971; managed Kitchener 1966-67 compiling 41-15 record; IC MVP 1970; led IC in hits, triples once, runs scored, stolen bases twice; three times first team all-star shortstop, six times second team, once each first, second team manager; mem. Ontario team 1970 Canadian championships Brandon Man.; 1967, 1971 Canadian Pan-Am Games team; 1970, 1971 Canadian world amateur team; *res.* Kitchener, Ont.

MCKEOWN, Bob (football); *b.* 10 Oct 1950, Ottawa, Ont.; *given name:* Robert Duff; *m.* Alice Ramo; *children:* Robert III; Brookfield HS, Yale U; CBC-Radio commentator; winner Canadian discus age-group title 1965; played varsity football at Yale; turned pro as centre with Ottawa Rough Riders 1971-75; Eastern Conference all-star 1974; mem. Grey Cup champions 1973; *res.* Ottawa, Ont.

MCKIBBON, John (basketball); *b.* 14 Sep 1940, Sudbury, Ont.; *m.* Patricia; *children:* Jeffrey, Tommy; Sheridan Tech, Laurentian U, B.A., U of Toronto, M. Div.; United Church minister; mem. Canadian national team 1959 Pan-Am Games Chicago, 1960 Rome Olympics, 1964 Tokyo Olympics, 1972 People's Republic of China tour; head basketball coach Laurentian U 1967-69; Laurentian U athlete of year 1970, 1972; *res.* Alma, Ont.

MCKILLOP, Bob (baseball, hockey); *b.* 1 Jun 1942, Toronto, Ont.; *given name:* Robert Cummings; *m.* Margaret; *children:* Robert,

Barbara; U of Waterloo, B.A., B.P.E.; phys ed teacher; catcher, pitcher Toronto People's Jewellers junior team 1959; pro Chicago White Sox organization 1960-64; Kitchener Senior Intercounty (IC) 1966 as catcher-pitcher; through 11 Senior IC seasons .342 lifetime batting avg., 34-11 won-lost record, 2.37 ERA; managed Kitchener 1968-69, 1971, posting 56-24 record and winning 1971 pennant; three times IC home run, five times RBI, twice total bases leader; led IC hitters 1969 with .381, pitchers 1966 with 0.93 ERA; seven times first team all-star catcher, first team right-handed pitcher, manager once each, four times MVP; mem. Ontario gold medal team 1969 Canada Games Halifax; Canadian team 1967 Pan-Am Games Winnipeg; Since 1968 head hockey coach, assistant football coach U of Waterloo; *res.* Kitchener, Ont.

MCKINNON, Archie (all-around); *b.* 19 Aug 1896, Glasgow, Scotland; *m.* Dorothy Bell; *children:* Dorothy Joan, Isabel Ann, Heather Anne; U of Washington; YMCA phys ed director; competed or coached Commonwealth teams 1928-61; Olympic competitor 1928, diving coach 1932, T&F coach 1936, swimming, diving coach 1948, swimming coach 1952; various awards including naming of Victoria YM-YWCA pool, U of Victoria athletic complex in his honor; mem. B.C. Sports Hall of Fame; *res.* Victoria, B.C.

MCLAREN, Grant (track); *b.* 19 Aug 1948, Paris, Ont.; *m.* Janet Manley; Paris DHS, U of Guelph, B.Sc., U of Western Ontario, Ph.D.; teacher; won CWOSSA two-mile 1965, Canadian junior cross-country 1967, OQAA three-mile 1968, Canada Games steeplechase, 5000m 1969, OQAA 1500m, 5000m, steeplechase 1970, Philadelphia two-mile, Drake Relays three-mile

1972, Pan-Pacific Games 5000m 1973, Montreal France-Canada dual meet 3000m 1974; mem. Toronto Olympic Club; U of Guelph athlete of year 1968-69; outstanding Canadian university track athlete 1970; UWO athlete of year 1972-73; held Canadian records for indoor two-mile, outdoor three-mile, 3000m, 5000m, steeplechase, 2000m; 3:59 mile clocking 1972; mem. Canadian teams 1971, 1975 Pan-Am Games, 1970, 1974 Commonwealth Games, 1972, 1976 Olympics; *res.* London, Ont.

MCLARNIN, Jimmy (boxing); *b.* 19 Dec 1907, Belfast, Ireland; *m.* Lilliam Cupitt; *children:* four; retired, chromium plating business; began boxing age 12, turned pro at 16; won initial fight in four rounds 1923 vs George Ainsworth; unbeaten 19 bouts through 1924; lost first pro bout to Bud Taylor in 10, won rematch on foul in second; protegee of Pop Foster who guided him through success and left him a fortune; lost world lightweight title bid in 15 to Sammy Mandell 1928 NYC; KO'd Young Corbett III in first to win world welterweight title 1933 LA; lost title in 15 to Barney Ross 1934 NYC; regained title beating Ross in 15 1934; again lost crown to Ross in 15 1935 NYC and retired from ring 1936; pro record 77 fights winning 20 by KO, 42 on decision, one on foul, three draws, losing 10 on decision, KO'd once; Canada's boxer of half century 1950 CP poll; mem. US, Canadian Boxing, Canadian Sports Halls of Fame; *res.* Glendale, Calif.

MCLAUGHLIN, Sam (horse racing); *b.* 8 Sep 1871, Enniskillen, Ont., d. 6 Jan 1972, Oshawa, Ont.; *given name:* Robert Samuel; *m.* Adelaide Louise Mowbray (*d.*); *children:* five daughters; automobile executive, manufacturer, philanthropist; won many cycling awards as youth; 1925 as yachtsman won Richardson Cup and championship of Great Lakes; entered first horse show 1926 with jumpers; won 1,500 ribbons, 400 trophies on Canada, US circuit; switched to horse racing; produced King's Plate winners Horometer 1934, Kingarvie 1946, Moldy 1947; mem. Canadian Sports Hall of Fame.

MCMAHON, Gary (shooting); *b.* 25 Feb 1932, Roland, Man.; *given name:* Garfield Walter; *m.* Ruby Bertha Fulton; Brandon U, B.Sc., U of British Columbia, M.Sc.; research scientist; won first of three Canadian open handgun titles 1958; Nova Scotia handgun title 1959-66; represented Canada 1960 Rome, 1964 Tokyo Olympics, 1962 Cairo (fifth free pistol), 1966 Weisbaden world, 1959, 1963, 1967, 1971 Pan-Am Games, 1966 Commonwealth Games; bronze individual centrefire, team free pistol 1959 Pan-Am Games; three silver, one bronze individual centrefire 1963 Pan-Am Games; bronze free pistol 1966 Commonwealth Games; silver centrefire team 1972 Pan-Am Games; best international performer 1962 world; *res.* Dartmouth, N.S.

MCMILLAN, Leigh (football); *b.* 8 Nov 1935, Edmonton Alta.; *given name:* Herbert Leigh; *m.* Aline Baril; *children:* Linda, Karen, John; U of Denver, B.Sc., U of Alberta, B.Ed.; teacher; fullback, safety Edmonton Eskimos 1956-58, avg. 5.4yds per carry on 66 punt returns while playing for 1956 Grey Cup champions; mem. Lacombe intermediate A Rockets hockey team 1961-63, U of Alberta Golden Bears hockey team 1963-64; coaches minor league football, hockey, soccer; *res.* Edmonton, Alta.

MCMILLAN, Roy (curling); *b.* 1 Apr 1893, Stratford, Ont.; *m.* Helen Belyea; *children:* Jean, Dorothy, Catherine, Donald;

Stratford CI, U of Toronto; chemical engineer, retired teacher; won Royal Victoria Jubilee, Royal Caledonia; won Branch Governor-General's three times, runner-up four times, seniors twice; twice reached Ontario seniors playdowns; mem. Governor-General's CC; life mem. Canadian Branch, OCA, Rideau CC; *res.* Ottawa, Ont.

MCMURRAY, Mary (curling); *b.* 6 Mar 1896, Newcastle, N.B.; *m.* Andrew M. McMurray (*d.*); *children:* Betty; curled 41 consecutive years; mem. Canadian Curling Hall of Fame; *res.* Bathurst, N.B.

MCNAMARA, Bob (football); *b.* 12 Aug 1931, Hastings, Minn.; *m.* Annette; *children:* Anne, Suzy, Bobby; U of Minnesota B.S.; all-American halfback Minnesota 1954; Winnipeg Blue Bombers 1955-58; Denver Broncos 1960-61; all-Canadian 1956 with 1,101yds rushing on 178 carries for 13 TDs; CFL record 36 points single game at Vancouver 1956 tieing Lorne Benson for most TDs single game (six); US paddleball doubles title 1958, singles 1970; *res.* Minneapolis, Minn.

MCNAMARA, George (hockey); *b.* 26 Aug 1886, Penetang, Ont.; *d.* 10 Mar 1952, Sault Ste. Marie, Ont.; initial appearance major organized hockey with Michigan Soo team; Montreal Shamrocks (ECL) 1908-09, Halifax Crescents (MPL) three seasons; Toronto Tecumsehs 1912-13 and following one game with Ottawa moved to Toronto Ontarios for balance 1913-14 campaign; Canadian Army 228th Sportsman's Battalion team in NHA; coached Soo Greyhounds to 1924 Allan Cup; mem. Hockey Hall of Fame.

MCNAUGHTON, Duncan (track and field); *b.* 7 Dec 1910, Cornwall, Ont.; *given name:* Duncan Anderson; *m.* Eileen Frances

Garrioch; *children:* Diane, Sheila, Ellen; King Edward HS, U of Southern California, B.A., Ph.D., Cal Tech, M.Sc.; consulting geologist; captain, coach 1929 provincial basketball champions; same year won individual titles Vancouver HS track meet, B.C. HS Olympiad; mem. USC track team; disqualified for illegal jumping techniques 1930 British Empire Games; style change to conventional Western roll resulted in California State title, setting new State record with winning high jump; won US national intercollegiate high jump title 1933; gold medal 1932 Los Angeles Olympics clearing 6'6", mem. Canadian Sports Hall of Fame; *res.* Dallas, Tex.

MCPHERSON, Donald (figure skating); *b.* 20 Feb 1945, Windsor, Ont.; *given name:* John Donald; Stratford HS; figure skating teacher; entered first competition at eight; won Western Ontario novice 1957, senior 1958-59, Canadian junior 1959; first Canadian to win Canadian, North American, world amateur titles in single year (1963); world pro title 1965; 10th 1960 Olympics; 11 years with Holiday on Ice show; since 1974 has taught skating in English, French, German, Italian; mem. Canadian Sports Hall of Fame; *res.* Lugano, Switzerland.

MCQUARTERS, Ed (football); *b.* 16 Apr 1943, Tulsa, Okla.; *given name:* Eddie Lee; *m.* PaulElla; *children:* Ed Jr., Mike; U of Oklahoma; advertising supervisor; set HS discus, shot put records; won State wrestling title; second Big Eight wrestling tournament 1962; played in Gator Bowl 1963; St. Louis Cardinals 1964-65; Saskatchewan Roughriders 1966-74; Schenley award as lineman of year 1967; all-Canadian three years; WFC outstanding lineman twice; *res.* Regina, Sask.

MCRAE, Ed (cycling); *b.* 13 Apr 1953, Kamloops, B.C.; *given name:* Edward Renner; Simon Fraser U, B.A.; industrial sales rep.; won North American junior 1970; five times B.C. road racing champion; mem. Canadian team 1971 Pan-Am Games, 1972 Olympics, 1973 world; only Canadian to win gold medal in international Grand Prix (US1973); *res.* Vancouver, B.C.

MCTAVISH, Boyd (curling); *b.* 13 Jul 1917, Winnipeg, Man.; *given name:* William Boyd; *m.* Ann; *children:* Jamie, John, Gordon, Billy; U of Manitoba, B.Sc., M.D.; general practitioner; in Winnipeg Bonspiel 1950 had 22 consecutive victories winning Birks, Eatons, grand aggregate and British Consols trophies; represented Manitoba 1950 Brier, placing second; Manitoba seniors winner 1973-74, Canadian seniors 1973; *res.* Winnipeg, Man.

MCWHIRTER, Cliff (boxing); *b.* 19 Apr 1913, London, Ont.; *given name:* Clifford Gilbert; *m.* Mary Warback; *children:* Lloyd Gary, David Clifford; H.B. Beal Technical HS, Wells Business Academy; retired insurance co. supervisor; appeared in first amateur bout at 14 winning Western Ontario featherweight title; later claimed several Golden Gloves titles while boxing as amateur until he turned pro 1932; fought throughout Canada, US, Cuba, South America under ring name of Babe La Varre; fought on first boxing card ever staged at Toronto's Maple Leaf Gardens; career total 157 bouts, won 136, lost 17, four draws; never KO'd; after war became trainer, manager, promoter; among fighters he handled were Jackie 'Spider' Armstrong, Teddy Swain, Gil Geekie, all of Toronto; mem. Canadian Boxing Hall of Fame; *res.* London, Ont.

MEAGHER, Aileen (track); *b.* 26 Nov 1910, Edmonton, Alta.; *given name:* Aileen Alethea; Sacred Heart Convent, Dalhousie U, B.A.; retired teacher; qualified 1932 Olympics as sprinter but severe charley horse prevented participation; gold medal 660yd relay, silver 440yd relay, 220yd 1934 London British Empire Games; bronze 400m relay, fourth 100m semifinal 1936 Berlin Olympics; silver 440yd, bronze 660yd relay, fourth 220yd finals Sydney Australia British Empire Games 1938; Norton Crowe Trophy, Velma Springstead Trophy 1935; mem. AAU of C Hall of Fame; *res.* Halifax, N.S.

MEDLAND, Pam (track); *b.* 13 Mar 1958, Vancouver, B.C.; *given name:* Pamela Rita Aline; Simon Fraser U, Capilano College; student; Canadian midget 800m record 2:06.9; won Canadian junior indoor 400m, third Canadian junior outdoor 400m 1975; fifth Canadian senior 800m, seventh 400m 1975; bronze 1976 Olympic trials 400m; fifth 1976 Canadian senior indoor 400m; mem. Canada vs Britain vs Poland 4x400m relay team 1976; *res.* West Vancouver, B.C.

MEEKER, Howie (hockey); *b.* 4 Nov 1924, New Hamburg, Ont.; *given name:* Howard William; TV commentator; joined Toronto Maple Leafs 1946, formed part of second generation Kid Line with Vic Lynn, Teeder Kennedy; NHL rookie of year, Calder Trophy 1946-47; played on four Stanley Cup winners; coached Stratford 1952, Pittsburgh (AHL) 1953-54 to Calder Cup victory; youngest coach in Toronto Maple Leaf history at 32 1956-57; five months Toronto Maple Leaf general manager before being fired by Stafford Smythe; operates boys' hockey schools St. John's Nfld, Parksville B.C., Calgary Alta., Stanstead Que., Port Hope and London, Ont.; wrote several hock-

ey instruction books; MP (Lib) Waterloo South 1951-53; *res.* St. John's, Nfld.

MEISSNER, Ernie (diving); *b.* 29 May 1937, Belgrade, Yugoslavia; U of Michigan; pres. travel bureau chain; Ontario, Canadian titles 1m, 3m, 10m 1958-62; 1m Ontario, Canadian titles 1964, 1968; bronze 3m 1962 Commonwealth Games; fifth 3m 1960 Rome Olympics; *res.* Kitchener, Ont.

MELESCHUK, Orest (curling); *b.* 11 Apr 1940, St. Boniface, Man.; *m.* Patricia Frances McSherry; *children:* Sean, Karin; Nelson McIntyre HS, United College; engineering technician; nickname Big O; won Manitoba university championship, Charleswood carspiel, CBC televised series once, runner-up once; won most major Manitoba 'spiels at least once; won 1974 Grey Cup 'spiel Toronto; competed in eight provincial championships winning Manitoba Consols, Brier, Silver Broom 1972; won Sudbury Superspiel 1976; *res.* St. Boniface, Man.

MESSNER, Joe (water-skiing); *b.* 1 Mar 1924, Solbad Hall, Tirol, Austria; *m.* Linda Ohm-Meier; *children:* Peter, Bill, Patricia; Ferdinand Franzens U Innsbruck, Handelsakademie Austria; executive director Children's Aid Society; competitive record includes 77 firsts, 20 seconds, nine thirds and 11 special awards including five Ontario Sports Awards, five Ontario Achievement Awards, one Command Sports Award; *res.* Ottawa, Ont.

MESSNER, Pat (water-skiing); *b.* 17 Mar 1954, Hamilton, Ont.; *given name:* Patricia Marilynn; Gloucester HS, McGill U, Carleton U; musician; 1967-1975 won 99 firsts, 24 seconds, five thirds; 14 Canadian, 18 Ontario records; Canadian girls' title 1968, Ontario

Open five times, Ontario Closed six times, Canadian National twice, Upper Canada Open twice, Eastern Canada Open, National Capital Open, Rob Principe Memorial, Carl Fischer International Cup, Can-Am women's twice, Ontario-Quebec Open; competed in Canada Summer Games 1969, California International Cup 1972; first Canadian woman to win medal (bronze, 1975 slalom) in world water-ski tournament; bronze women's slalom 1972 Olympics; top Canadian 1972 championship of the Americas; Canadian women's slalom record 1972; Ontario Sports Achievement Award six times, Summer Games certificate of merit, Ottawa ACT Sports Achievement Award three times; total of 26 special awards; *res.* Ottawa, Ont.

METRAS, John (football, basketball); *b.* 8 Apr 1909, Dowagiac, Mich.; *given name:* John Pius; *m.* Shirley Goodheart; *children:* three; U of Detroit; liaison officer UWO; all-State HS halfback; all-American mention as centre U of D; with St. Michael's College starred in ORFU 1933-34; joined Bill Stern as assistant coach UWO 1935, head coach 1939-69; 30-year football coaching record 106 wins, 76 losses, 11 ties, nine league titles; teams once had undefeated run of 29 games; basketball teams won or shared 14 titles, once 24 league-game winning streak; UWO athletic director 1945-72; nickname The Bull; various official capacities in football, basketball rules-making bodies Canada and US; hon.-pres. Association of Canadian Intercollegiate Football Coaches; trophy in his honor awarded to Canadian college football lineman of year; *res.* London, Ont.

MICHIENZI, Peter (wrestling); *b.* 22 Feb 1934, Curinga, Italy; *m.* Margaret; *children:* Peter (Piero), Marina; H.B. Beal Technical HS (night school); printer; won 10 Canadian freestyle titles, five Greco-Roman titles (15 titles a Canadian record); won Jewish Invitational Buffalo, Michigan State title; silver medal 1962 British Empire Games Australia; bronze 1966 Jamaica Commonwealth Games; Canadian team 1962 Toledo world, 1963, 1967 Pan-Am Games, 1968 Olympics; captain Canadian national team 1966-68; outstanding wrestler 1966 Canadian championships Edmonton; Ontario Fitness and Sport Award 1966, 1969; Ontario medallion of excellence in sport 1967; Italo-Canadian sports award 1973; London Jaycees young man of year 1967; volunteer coach since 1957 guiding London Y to three provincial titles, UWO to Canada Games gold medal as Ontario representatives 1971; coach London Amateur Wrestling and Athletic Club; A1 status as international amateur wrestling referee; director Olympic Club of Canada; mem. Canadian Amateur Wrestling Hall of Fame; *res.* London, Ont.

MIKITA, Stan (hockey); *b.* 20 May 1940, Sokolce, Czechoslovakia; *given name:* Stanislas Gvoth; *m.* Jill; *children:* Scott, Meg, Jane Elizabeth; Central HS, hon. doctorate Brock U; hockey player, restaurateur; nickname Stash; learned to skate in Czechoslovakia on blades which curled above toes and were screwed to bottom of boot; played school hockey, scored 16 goals in one neighborhood game scouted by Rudy Pilous; won 1954 scoring title with Legion team; played junior with St. Catharines Teepees; three times OHA all-star, MVP once, 1958-59, scoring title; three games with Chicago Black Hawks 1958-59, stayed 1959-60; NHL's first triple crown winner, (Ross, Hart and Lady Byng trophies) in single season 1966-67, repeat 1967-68; won Ross (scoring) four times, Hart (MVP) and Lady Byng (most gentlemanly) twice each: six times first team all-star centre, twice second team; 19 NHL season record (through 1976-77) 1,236 games, 502 goals, 843 assists, 1,345 points, 1,189 penalty minutes, plus 149 playoff games, 56 goals, 90 assists, 146 points, 169 penalty minutes; inventive player, developed suspension helmet, curved stick; with Ab McDonald, Ken Wharram formed Scooter Line; scored record 21 playoff points in 12 games, record 15 assists; *res.* Elmhurst, Ill.

MILES, Johnny (track); *b.* 30 Oct 1905, Halifax, Eng.; *m.* Elizabeth Connon; manager of manufacturing, fibre and twine; won Canadian five-mile, Halifax *Herald* 10-mile 1925, Boston Marathon 1926; repeat 1929 in record 2:33.8; won Canadian 10 000m Toronto 1928; bronze 1930 British Empire Games Hamilton; represented Canada 1928 Amsterdam, 1932 Los Angeles Olympics; in 1926 competed in 20 races winning 15, second four times, fourth once; mem. Canadian Sports Hall of Fame; *res.* Hamilton, Ont.

MILES, Rollie (football); *b.* 16 Feb 1928, Washington, D.C.; *m.* Marianne; *children:* Rolanda, Tony, Monica, Mario, Michelle, Rollie Jr., Brett; North Carolina State U, St. Augustine College, B.A., U of Arizona, M.Ed.; phys ed supervisor; all-American NC State 1950; 10 athletic letters baseball and track; to Regina 1951 for class A baseball with Boston Braves farm team; joined Edmonton Eskimos same year, remained 12 seasons through 1962; CFL career record: 278 punts returned for 2,085yds and 7.5 avg., 88 kickoff returns for 2,131yds, 24.2 avg. including 100yds for TD, 38 interceptions returned for 547yds; eight times WFC all-star, four times all-Canadian; three times club MVP; held variety of club records: most

TDs one season, most yds gained single game, most interceptions one season; mem. Edmonton Hall of Fame; *res.* Edmonton, Alta.

MILLAR, Ian (equestrian); *b.* 6 Jan 1947, Halifax, N.S.; *m.* Lynn Doran; *children:* Johnathan Livingstone, Amie Lynn; businessman; won 1970 Sutton, London Grand Prix, 1971 Open jumper Royal Horse Show, 1972 reserve jumper Edmonton, jumper Calgary, 1973 reserve jumper CNE, Open jumper Ottawa horse show winning five classes; 1974 two Grand Prix titles Rothman's tour, CNE jumper; 1975 Jacksonville Fla., Hamilton, Ottawa, Sundance Farms grand prix winner, Bolton jumper classic, jumper titles Syracuse, Buffalo, Sutton, CNE, Sundance Farms horse shows; mem. Canadian equestrian team 1972, 1976 Olympics, 1975 Pan-Am Games; Ottawa (ACT) equestrian of year 1975; leading Grand Prix rider in Canada 1975; won International jumper stakes Jacksonville 1977; competitive horses include Country Club, Bandit, Count Down, Julio, Brother Sam, 21; *res.* Perth, Ont.

MILLER, Dave (yachting); *b.* 18 Sep 1943, Vancouver, B.C.; *given name:* David Sidney; *m.* Susan Jean; U of British Columbia, B.Comm.; sailmaker; with crew Colin Park, Kenneth Baxter, won 1960 North American junior sailing title and Sears Cup; skippered 1964 Star Class entry for Canada in Tokyo Olympics age 19; crew mem., tactician fourth place Dragon Class entry 1968 Mexico Olympics; skippered bronze medal Soling Class entry 1972 Munich Olympics; *res.* Mississauga, Ont.

MILLER, Doug Jr. (bowling); *b.* 25 Nov 1927, Peterborough, Ont.; *given name:* James Douglas; *m.* Colleen Smith; *children:*

Doug Jr., Carol, Dan, Dave, Anne Marie; Peterborough CIVS; tool designer, product manager; played minor lacrosse, junior, intermediate, senior football, hockey, boxing; played pro lacrosse two seasons with Toledo 1948-49; coached Peterborough juvenile team to Ontario lacrosse title 1952; built Allencourt Lanes Richmond Hill and remained as manager 1960-62, launched World Bantam Bowling tournament; played key role in eliminating counter pin, establishing new scoring system as executive director BPAO 1962-69; in *Ripley's Sports Oddities* for snapping football which didn't touch ground but resulted in TD for opposition when it hit goal post and bounced into arms of opposing team mem.; played series of pool matches 1963 in New Orleans vs world champion Willie Mosconi, won three or four games of the 50-60 played; Ontario Sports Achievement Award, Builders of Bowling Industry Award; *res.* Scarborough, Ont.

MILLER, Doug Sr. (lacrosse); *b.* 1904, Peterborough, Ont.; *given name:* Thomas Douglas; *m.* Alice Mary Ebbs; *children:* Douglas, Adele, Marilyn; retired contractor; played two seasons with Wallaceburg then returned to Peterborough, played 27 years; final game of senior play marked beginning of senior play for son Doug as both appeared on the field the same day; constructed first outdoor lacrosse stadium, Miller Bowl; mem. Lacrosse Hall of Fame; *res.* Largo, Fla.

MILLER, Russ (curling, darts); *b.* 13 Sep 1918, London, Ont.; *given name:* Russell Edward; *m.* Frances Elizabeth Blakey; *children:* Bonnie Jean; H.B. Beal Technical HS; sheet metal worker; won London Curling Club championship 26 times, Ontario Tankard 1948, 1954, numerous City of London bonspiel titles; with wife Fran, won Auld London mixed, Tillsonburg Tobacco Belt; scored three eight-enders; Ontario Points championship 1958-59; six times in Ontario Consols; won first Masters Curling Classic London Ivanhoe 1969-70; Royal Canadian Legion zone title 12 times, provincial 1959, fourth in nationals; *London Free Press* sportsman of year 1959; mem. Ontario champion dart teams 1955, 1974 and winner many city titles; numerous perfect 180 scores with either hand; flag-bearer 1974 London Brier; life mem. LCC; ranked in London's top 10 five-pin bowlers 1962; *res.* London, Ont.

MILNE, Howie (hockey, football, baseball); *b.* 1903, Park River, N.D.; *given name:* Howard; *m.* Violet Benallick Bartlett; Central CI; retired; began playing hockey at 16 with Regina junior Vic's two seasons, Pat's two seasons, on four provincial junior champions; mem. losing Pat's in 1922 Memorial Cup series with Ft. William; played centre, defence senior Vic's 1923-24; replaced Al Ritchie as coach Monarchs 1927 winning Memorial Cup; reorganized senior Vic's and coached one season; officiated 1933 Western Canada junior final series; football with YMCA Regina Winners in junior 1918-20, twice won provincial title; at 22 player-coach Roughriders three seasons, fourth as coach; first Western official to work Grey Cup final 1931; Canadian football all-stars 1923; shortstop, third base with Y Winners in North Side Baseball League intermediate, later senior divisions; mem. Champ's Hotel team 1919-27; best season 1923 leading Southern Baseball League batters with .423, pro offers from Minneapolis Millers of American Association; also played with Probus club and Regina Balmorals, a semipro outfit with whom he played only on the road and under name of Phillips to protect amateur status; some basketball with Moose Jaw, Saskatoon and with Regina winning two provincial titles but losing Canadian finals to Winnipeg Toilers 1925; one of few to play, coach in Memorial Cup final, play, officiate in Grey Cup final; pres. Regina Juvenile Baseball League 1926; Regina outstanding athlete 1923, 1924; mem. Sask. Sports Hall of Fame; *res.* Weyburn, Sask.

MITCHELL, Ray (bowling); *b.* 22 Mar 1931, Peace River, Alta.; *given name:* Raymond Harold; *m.* Mari Dillon; *children:* Adrienne, Jocelyn; systems operations manager; played variety of sports in England winning several regional boxing, swimming titles; 1951 began bowling in Toronto Bell men's five-pin league; started 10-pin bowling in early 60s; won various Toronto area tournaments; 1967-68 Southern Ontario singles, third Canadian singles; mem. Scarborough league champions who established Canadian three-game, five-man record score of 3,385; 1972 Southwestern Ontario, Canadian singles titles, world 10-pin title Hamburg Germany; mem. world team medal champions in England; technical coordinator Canadian 10-pin Federation, national coach; coached in Japan, Philippines, South America and Canada; bowling column in *Globe and Mail;* mem. Canadian Sports Hall of Fame; *res.* Scarborough, Ont.

MITRUK, Steve (gymnastics); *b.* 17 Jan 1947, Hamilton, Ont.; *given name:* Stephen Frederick; *m.* Brigitte; *children:* Terry, Christopher; McMaster U, B.A., U of Toronto, B.Ed; HS teacher; while in HS competed 1967 Canada Winter Games, 1968 Mexico Olympics; won Werry Cup, Ontario Intercollegiate gymnast of year award record five consecutive years 1969-73; represented Canada 1969 Cup of Americas Mexico,

1970 world Yugoslavia, world invitational Winnipeg, World Student Games Italy, 1971 Colombia Pan-Ams Games, 1972 Munich Olympics, 1973 pre-World Games Bulgaria, World Student Games Russia, 1974 world Bulgaria, China tour; McMaster athlete of year 1972; *res.* Burlington, Ont.

MONNOT, Ray (basketball); *b.* 24 May 1932, Pittsburgh, Pa.; *div.; children:* Christopher, Sandra, Susan; Etobicoke HS, U Western Ontario, B.A.; management consultant; mem. Toronto Nortown Tri-Bells, Canadian senior champions 1953-54; UWO intercollegiate titlists 1954-55, captain UWO 1955-57; UWO record 44 points one game 1956-57; UWO career high scoring record; competed in Olympic trials Vancouver; with Tillsonburg Livingstons Canadian champions 1958-59, Pan-Am Games Chicago; with Livingstons 1960 Canadian champions, represented Canada Rome Olympics; UWO outstanding athlete 1957; *res.* Ottawa, Ont.

MONTMINY, Claude (track); *b.* 23 Sep 1953, Drummondville, Que.; University of Quebec, B.A.P.E.; student; shares Canadian 50yd record 5.2 with Harry Jerome; mem. Canadian junior team Portugal tour 1973; mem. 4x100m Canadian senior men's relay team 1974-75; second 50yd Canada vs USSR 1973, Canada vs France 1974, winner Canada vs Great Britain 1976; Quebec record holder 100m 10.2, 50m 5.7; *res.* Cap de la Madeleine, Que.

MOORE, Bob (track); *b.* 11 Nov 1940, Doveridge, Eng.; *given name:* Robert William; *m.* Barbara Jane McVicar; *children:* Fiona; U of Leeds, B.Sc., Ph.D., U of Toronto, Dip. Clinical Chemistry; clinical biochemist; Canadian 10-mile title 1969-73;

competed four Boston Marathons placing fifth once, seventh three times; competed international road races in San Juan Puerto Rico, Sao Paulo Brazil, San Blas Puerto Rico, cross-country races Vichy world championships, Pan-Am Games 1971; international marathons in Antwerp, Toronto, Japan, 1970 Commonwealth Games; fourth in marathon 1976 Olympic trials; best personal times: 3km 8:09, 5km 14:22, 10km 29:49, 10 miles 48:49, 1 mile 4:19, 3 miles 13:40, marathon 2:16.45; *res.* Toronto, Ont.

MOORE, Dickie (hockey); *b.* 6 Jan 1931, Montreal, Que.; *given name:* Richard Winston; led Montreal Royals, then junior Canadiens to Memorial Cup victories; Royals of Quebec senior league 1951-52; pro Canadiens midway through season and remained with them until retirement after 1962-63; out of retirement, Toronto Maple Leafs 1964-65, St. Louis Blues 1967-68; Art Ross Trophy (NHL scoring leader) 1958, 1959; following season broke by one point record 95 points held by Gordie Howe; twice first team all-star left winger, once second team; in 719 league games scored 261 goals, 347 assists for 608 points; in 135 playoff games scored 46 goals, 64 assists; in 12 seasons with Canadiens played on six Stanley Cup winners; mem. Hockey Hall of Fame; *res.* Montreal, Que.

MOORE, Gail Harvey (golf); *b.* 13 Jun 1943, Toronto, Ont.; *given name:* Gail Harvey; *m.* Dr. James B. Moore; *children:* Dana, Julie; U of Toronto, B.P.H.E.; won Canadian junior 1958-60, Canadian Closed 1964-65, runner-up 1963 Canadian Open, Closed; won Canadian Open, B.C. titles 1970; represented Canada women's world team four times, Commonwealth team twice; mem. Ontario

interprovincial team 1958-66, B.C. interprovincial team 1968-72, 1974-75; *res.* Coquitlam, B.C.

MOORE, George (football, hockey); *b.* 4 Apr 1933, Saskatoon, Sask.; *given name:* George Alan; *m.* Patricia Prenty; *children:* Chris, Keith, Colleen; U of North Dakota, B.A., M.S., Cornell U, Ed.D.; university professor; Winnipeg HS 100yd dash in record 10.1 1952; college football U of N. Dakota 1952-55; pro Winnipeg Blue Bombers 1955-56; college hockey and pro Grand Forks Redwings 1955; coached St. James CI to Manitoba HS basketball championship 1959; *res.* Kanata, Ont.

MORAN, Paddy (hockey); *b.* 11 Mar 1877, Quebec City, Que., *d.* 14 Jan 1966, Quebec City, Que.; *given name:* Patrick Joseph; began organized hockey at 15 with city league Sarsfield juvenile team; two years Quebec Dominion juniors then Crescent intermediates 1895-1901, winning Canadian intermediate title; one of hockey's great standup goalers; Quebec Bulldogs 1901-02 and, except for 1909-10 season when he played in Haileybury, remained with Bulldogs 16 seasons posting 5.4 avg. for 201 games; helped Bulldogs win successive Stanley Cups 1912-13; mem. Hockey Hall of Fame.

MORENZ, Howie (hockey); *b.* 21 Sep 1902, Mitchell, Ont., *d.* 8 Mar 1937, Montreal, Que.; *given name:* Howarth; *m.* Mary McKay; *children:* two sons, one daughter; Stratford HS; nickname Stratford Streak or Mitchell Meteor; Stratford OHA juniors at 18 and 19; Montreal Canadiens 1923-1934; briefly with Chicago and NY, then returned to Canadiens 1936; died of hockey injury; in 14 seasons scored 270 goals, 197 assists for

Morris

467 points; Art Ross Trophy (NHL scoring leader) 1927-28, 1930-31; Hart Trophy (MVP) three times; played on five league championship teams, three Stanley Cup winners; Canada's hockey player of half century in 1950 CP poll; mem. Hockey Hall of Fame.

MORRIS, Jim (all-around); *b.* 15 Dec 1911, Tacoma, Wash.; *given name:* James Henry; *m.* Mary Isabel; *children:* Gary Wayne, James Thomas; personnel officer; T&F, baseball, lacrosse, hockey, basketball, swimming, fastball, soccer, rugby, curling; mem. eight B.C. hockey title teams including 1938 Trail Allan Cup winners, 1939 world champion Trail Smoke Eaters; mem. three Blaylock Bowl soccer title winners; pitched no-hitter, batted .400 one year; played with variety lacrosse, baseball, fastball, basketball championship teams; Jim Morris Award presented annually to Trail sportsman of year; mem. B.C. Sports Hall of Fame; *res.* Trail, B.C.

MORRIS, Price (weightlifting); *b.* 22 Oct 1941, Frankford, Ont.; *given name:* Ernest Price; *m.* Louise Mills; *children:* Jacqueline, Price Jr; U of Guelph; farmer; began lifting at 14, competed 17 years; won Canadian teenage contest 1958; won Canadian titles 1965, 1967, 1968, 1971, 1972; fourth 1967 Pan-Am Games breaking own Canadian clean and jerk (C & J) mark of 386lbs with 392lbs; top points Tri-Country meet with France, Britain; first Canadian to lift 400lbs and set 406½lb C & J record; second to Russ Prior 242lb class, qualified for Commonwealth Games 1970, won bronze and set Games record 402lbs C & J; 22nd in world; 363lb Canadian press record 242lb class 1971; qualified for 1971 Pan-Am Games, set 410lb C & J mark, four bronze medals;

qualified for 1972 Olympics two classes; broke four Canadian records, 382½lb press (set by Doug Hepburn), 308lb snatch (John Lewis), C & J 413lb (own record), 1,058 total lbs; first Canadian to unofficially total 1,102lbs and to that time had lifted 400lbs more times than any other Canadian in history; *res.* Frankford, Ont.

MORRIS, Teddy (football); *b.* 1910, Toronto, Ont., *d.* 5 Sep 1965, Toronto, Ont.; career spanned three decades as football player, coach; at 16 played softball Toronto Industrial League and halfback with brother Gord's junior team; moved to Winnipeg at 18 and joined Winnipeg Native Sons; captained team to Western junior title but lost Canadian title to junior Argos; returning to Toronto made junior Argos as reserve halfback; earned berth as regular in brilliant performance vs Hamilton; with Argos 1931-41; backfield coach last two years; coach HMCS York team WW2 winning 1944 service title; rejoined Argos as coach 1945-49; helped Argos win three Grey Cups as player, three more as coach; Jeff Russel Memorial Trophy 1937; mem. Canadian Football Hall of Fame.

MORRISON, Lee (softball, curling); *b.* 14 Oct 1938, Regina, Sask.; *given name:* Lenore; *m.* Larry Morrison; *children:* Lance, Layne; U of Toronto, B.P.H.E., U of Saskatchewan, B.Ed., U of Oregon, M.Sc.; professor; softball with 1958, 1960 Regina Lexiers, 1964 Saskatoon Imperials winning Saskatchewan provincial title; mem. U of T women's ice hockey team 1960, U of Sask. volleyball team 1961-62; mem. winning rinks Saskatoon ladies' bonspiel 1965-69; with club, city, Northern, provincial and Canadian championship rinks 1969, 1971-73; mem. city reps Northern provincial playdowns

1970; competed in CBC-TV match against Brier champions, won 1972; participated in 1973 CBC championship curling series; coach U of Sask. women's curling team 1962-73 winning six conference titles, three times runner-up; coach 1972-73 National Girls' champions; coach U of Sask. women's field hockey team 1967-70 winning one conference title, once runner-up, senior T award U of T; mem. Saskatchewan Sports, Canadian Curling Halls of Fame; *res.* Saskatoon, Sask.

MORROW, Suzanne (figure skating); *b.* 14 Dec 1930, Toronto, Ont.; *div.; children:* Kristen Lyn Francis; Ontario Veterinary College; veterinarian; only woman in Canadian figure skating history to hold senior national titles in singles (1949-51), pairs (1947-48) and dance (1948); North American pairs champion with Wally Diestelmeyer 1947; bronze Olympic pairs, world championships 1948, 1950-52; fifth ladies' singles 1952 Olympics; judge 1964, 1976 Innsbruck Olympics, 1966 Davos world, 1971 pre-Olympics Sapporo, 1972 Calgary world, South African championships; director CFSA; Doberman Pinscher breeder; *res.* Bolton, Ont.

MOSIENKO, Bill (hockey); *b.* 2 Nov 1921, Winnipeg, Man.; amateur with Torbans, Sherburns, Winnipeg Monarchs juniors; pro at 18 Chicago organization; minor pro Providence, Kansas City; Chicago Black Hawks 1941-55; right winger on Pony Line with Max, Doug Bentley; Lady Byng Trophy 1945; twice second team all-star; set record 21 seconds for fastest three goals one game vs NY Rangers Mar 1952; in 14 NHL seasons played 711 games scoring 258 goals, 282 assists for 540 points; in 1,030 pro games over 20-year span accumulated only

129 penalty minutes; with Alf Pike launched pro hockey in Winnipeg; their Warriors won Edinburgh Trophy in inaugural season 1956; played with Warriors through 1959, coach 1960; mem. Hockey Hall of Fame; *res.* Winnipeg, Man.

MULLINS, Peter (basketball); *b.* 9 Jul 1926, Sydney, Australia; Washington State U, Ed. D.; university associate professor; sixth 1948 London Olympics decathlon; mem. Canadian national basketball team 1959 world tournament Chile; coached Canadian national basketball team 1969-71; coach UBC basketball, T&F since 1955; *res.* Vancouver, B.C.

MUNRO, Johnny (football); *b.* 27 Sep 1913, Toronto, Ont.; *given name:* John McCulloch; *m.* Bette Gilmour; *children:* Michael John, Elizabeth Anne, Brian Gilmour; Queen's U, B.A., U of Toronto, Cambridge U; senior v.-pres. life assurance co.; mem. numerous local Toronto baseball teams; three years HS all-star, one year all-Canadian with Queen's; with 1933-1938 Argo Grey Cup champions; played hockey Marlboro juniors, four years Queen's, leading college scorer; CFL referee 14 years in Eastern Conference; *res.* Toronto, Ont.

MURPHY, Mike (football); *b.* 6 Jul 1955, Moncton, N.B.; *given name:* Michael Paul; St. Pat's HS, Hillcrest HS, U of Ottawa; student; mem. two Ottawa HS football championship teams; mem. U of Ottawa 1975 College Bowl champions, scored winning TD in championship game; mem. 1976 Conference champions losing 18-16 to Acadia in Atlantic Bowl; MVP Ottawa HS championship 1973, Hillcrest Hawks MVP 1973; Canadian Intercollegiate rushing record of 1,060yds with U of O 1976; Ontario-

Murphy

Quebec Intercollegiate Football Conference scoring title with 144 points; tied ex-teammate Neil Lumsden's single season TD standard with 15; Omega Award (conference MVP), Atlantic Bowl MVP (Don Loney Trophy) with 239yds rushing, OQIFC all-star, all-Canadian 1976; on Rough Rider protected list 1977; *res.* Ottawa, Ont.

MURPHY, Pat (cycling); *b.* 7 Nov 1933, South Norwich Twp, Ont.; *given name:* James Patrick; *m.* Marlene; Delhi HS; sales executive; winner Canadian amateur track 1952, pursuit 1953; represented Canada 1954, 1958 British Empire Games, 1956 Melbourne Olympics; winner, record holder 1956 Quebec-Montreal road race; *res.* Schaumburg, Ill.

MURPHY, Ron (football); *b.* 13 Jun 1932, Hamilton, Ont.; *m.* Betty; *children:* Paula Jane, Douglas Paul, Gregory Ronald; Cathedral HS, McGill U, B.Sc., M.Ed.; educator, football coach; outstanding HS football career 1946-52 playing two years junior and three seasons senior, captain two years; MVP, most sportsmanlike player; twice in Red Feather HS tournament winning championship, MVP 1951; twice league all-star; with junior Tiger-Cats 1952, Grey Cup champion Ticats 1953; McGill Redmen 1954-58, MV lineman 1954; three seasons senior Redmen, all-star; joined McGill athletic staff 1958-64; played pro ball Alouettes; retired following 1961 campaign; assistant coach McGill 1962, OUAA title; U of Toronto phys ed staff, assistant coach Blues 1964; head football coach Toronto Varsity 1966; Old Crow Society CIAU coach of year 1974; *res.* Toronto, Ont.

MURRAY, Ben (football); *b.* 22 Jul 1916, St. Thomas, Ont., *d.* 1976, St. Thomas, Ont.; *given name:* Benjamin; *m.* Helen Foley; *children:* William, James, Margaret; railroad police sergeant; played junior, senior HS football, four years St. Thomas ORFU juniors; intermediate basketball St. Thomas Y, Orioles; pitched softball intermediate, senior OASA clubs; for several years intercollegiate football official.

MURRAY, Dave (skiing); *b.* 5 Sep 1953, Montreal, Que.; *given name:* William David; ski instructor, coach; Canadian World Cup team 1973-74, top 10 in two World Cup events, eighth St. Moritz downhill, ninth Aspen slalom, won Edelweiss FIS slalom; second in Canadian downhill 1974-75; three times in top 10 World Cup downhill events Europe 1976; silver giant slalom, bronze slalom 1976 Canadian championships; represented Canada Innsbruck Olympics 1976, 18th in downhill; *res.* Abbotsford, B.C.

NAIRN, Bill (football); *b.* 16 Nov 1912, Winnipeg, Man.; *m.* Stella Patricia King; *children:* Herbert Gordon; regional manager; Deer Lodge juniors 1931-33; Winnipeg Blue Bombers as guard, placement specialist 1934; Winnipeg Victorias 1935; returned to Blue Bombers 1936-40, officiated 1941-70 including 20 Western finals, 18 Grey Cups; mem. Howie Wood curling rink 20 years; *res.* Winnipeg, Man.

NAISMITH, James (basketball); *b.* 6 Nov 1861, Almonte, Ont., *d.* 28 Nov 1939, Lawrence, Kan.; *m.* Maude Sherman; *children:* two sons; McGill U, B.A., D.D., Presbyterian Theological College, Springfield College, Gross Medical School, M.D., U of Kansas; played football under Amos Alonzo Stagg at Springfield; top McGill athlete for gymnastics; briefly McGill phys ed director; inventor of basketball 1891 using soccer ball and pair of peach baskets; Naismith Memorial Basketball Hall of Fame, Springfield Mass., completed 1968; mem. Basketball, Canadian Sports Halls of Fame.

NAKAMURA, Hiroshi (judo); *b.* 22 Jun 1942, Tokyo; *m.* Keiko Maruyama; *children:* Emi, Yumi; Chuo U, B.Ec., Kodokan Judo Institute (sixth dan); judo coach; mem. Japanese national team 1962-67; Japanese Cambo middleweight champion 1966; among top 10 Japanese open championships 1964, 1966; head coach Quebec Judo Association 1968-70; coached Canadian team 1975 Pan-Am Games, 1976 Olympics; *res.* Pierrefonds, Que.

NANSEN, Elizabeth (dogsledding); *b.* 4 Dec, Providence, R.I.; *given name:* Elizabeth Miller; *div.* Edward Ricker; *children:* Edward, Susan Elizabeth; *m.* Kaare Nansen; *children:* Peter; Dana Hall, Wellesley; prominent socialite who emerged as one of few women sled dog racers during 20s, 30s; *res.* Ottawa, Ont.

NASH, Jack (golf); *b.* 18 Dec 1911, London, Ont; *m.* Kelly; *children:* Becky, John, Rob, David; London Central CI, U of Toronto, U of Western Ontario; jeweller; runner-up Ontario junior 1929-30; won first of three Ontario amateurs 1930, runner-up twice; with father John A. won Ontario father-son title 1935; claimed same title five more times, twice each with sons Rob, David, once with son John C; mem. 12 Ontario Willingdon Cup teams; won London Hunt and Country Club championship 13 times; three times Ontario seniors champion, twice runner-up; once Canadian seniors titlist, twice runner-up, member London Hunt George S. Lyon Trophy team 1960; with Colin Brown won two Ontario badminton doubles titles; finalists Canadian championships; began curling 1938 winning two Ontario Silver Tankards with London Curling Club, competed four Ontario Consols playdowns; *res.* London, Ont.

NATTRASS, Sue (trapshooting); *b.* 5 Nov 1950, Medicine Hat, Alta.; *given name:* Susan Marie; Ross Shepperd HS, U of Alberta, B.A., M.A., Waterloo U; student; consecutive fourth place finishes in women's world championships 1969-70, silver medal 1971, world title 1974-75 establishing world records 143 of 150 targets Bern Switzerland 1974, 188 of 200 targets Munich 1975; gold medals 1973 Championship of the Americas, 1975 Benito Juarez international championships Mexico; four times captain women's all-American team in American style competition; second woman to shoot perfect 200 twice; first woman to win both high overall, all-around honors from 27yds; Canadian women's championship winner since 1968; three times women's all-around North American avg. champion; first woman trapshooter to compete in Olympic Games 1976 Montreal; mem. Canadian international trapshooting team since 1969; coached volleyball Waterloo, skiing Cornell, McMaster, Blue Mountain; Order of Delta Gamma Rose Award 1976, City of Edmonton award since 1968, Province of Alberta award annually since 1970, Province of Ontario award of merit twice; mem. AAU of C, Canadian Sports Halls of Fame; *res.* Waterloo, Ont.

NEILSON, Scott (track and field); *b.* 31 Jan 1957, New Westminster, B.C.; *given name:* Robert Scott; New Westminster HS, U of Washington; student; Canadian juvenile record with 12lb hammer throw 72.34m, Canadian junior 16lb hammer 67.06; North American HS 12lb record with 70.30m; bronze medal 1975 Pan-Am Games; NCAA hammer title 1976; *res.* New Westminster, B.C.

NESBITT, Keith (skiing); *b.* 14 Jan 1930, Montreal, Que.; *div.; children:* Keran, Brian, Christopher; Sir George Williams U; execu-tive-director Canadian Ski Association; introduced to skiing at 15 and became active in competitive skiing through 1952; became involved in officiating 1948; Laurentian ski zone official 1953, pres. 1956; pres. Quebec Division two terms; National Alpine chairman 1963-65; became first full-time manager Canadian Ski Association 1967 evolving into executive-director; helped create permanent national ski team 1958; instrumental in bringing international ski racing to Canada through 1966 Du Maurier series; created coaching certification program, official suppliers program for national ski team, athletic grading or classification system, first officials courses; active in Sports Federation of Canada, Canadian Olympic Association; *res.* Ottawa, Ont.

NESUKAITIS, Violetta (table tennis); *b.* 28 Mar 1951, Toronto, Ont.; bank teller; among 28 junior titles won Ontario midget girls, Ontario Open, Closed, girls under-15; won over 100 Canadian, US titles in singles, women's and mixed doubles including 10 Canadian singles titles; finalist Commonwealth mixed doubles 1975; has trained in Europe, Japan; made promotional instruction film for Prudential; top ranked in Canada, sixth in Commonwealth; *res.* Toronto, Ont.

NETTLES, Ray (football); *b.* 1 Aug 1949, Jacksonville, Fla.; *given name:* Ernest Ray; *m.* Ewin; U of Tennessee; college all-star; B.C. Lions 1972-76; traded to Toronto Argos 1977; 1973 WFC, CFL Schenley Award as outstanding lineman; WFC all-star four times; *res.* Jacksonville, Fla.

NEVILLE, Bill (volleyball); *b.* 28 Apr 1945, Seattle, Wash.; *given name:* William James; *m.* Suzette; *children:* Cory Jo, Russell Shane; George Williams College, Whitworth College, B.S.; coach Canadian men's volleyball team; twice Midwest college volleyball all-star; 1967 player of year; assistant coach US Olympic team 1968, US men's team 1970-73; as player three years Pacific Northeast all-star; coached Canada 1975 Pan-Am Games, 1976 Montreal Olympics; *res.* Winnipeg, Man.

NEWMAN, Bernard (gymnastics); *b.* 4 Aug 1914, Windsor, Ont.; *m.* Lee Werbowecki; *children:* Bernard Jr, Leeann, Jane, Gary, Patricia; Assumption College; teacher, politician; while teaching school in Windsor 1934-58 gained reputation as fine gymnastics coach; among protegees were Canadian champions Ernestine Russell, Ed Gagnier; national chairman of gymnastics AAU 1955-56; coach Canadian gymnastics team 1956 Olympics, 1958 world games, 1959 Pan-Am Games; MLA (Lib) Windsor since 1958; *res.* Windsor, Ont.

NEWTON, Jack (football); *b.* 2 Jun 1887, Sarnia, Ont., *d.* 23 Dec 1967, Sarnia, Ont.; *m.* Eleanor Watson; *children:* John, Fred; Sarnia CI, U of Toronto; educator; led U of T to Grey Cup 1909, all-star; turned to coaching and guided varsity to two interprovincial titles, 1914 Grey Cup; head coach Sarnia CI, directed teams to several Ontario championships; coached Sarnia intermediates eight years winning numerous Ontario, Canadian championships; head coach Sarnia Imperials; mem. Canadian Football Hall of Fame.

NEZAN, Andy (golf); *b.* 10 Nov 1926, Ottawa, Ont.; *m.* Rose Sydor; *children:* Diane, Greg; LaSalle Academy, Ottawa Technical HS; engraver; twice Quebec amateur champion; four times won ODGA match, twice ODGA medal; twice (with Glen Seely) ODGA best ball; twice winner Collie Cup; eight times Rivermead Club, once Chaudière champion; mem. 1969 Quebec Willingdon Cup team; won O'Keefe Open Chaudière, Renfrew, Buckingham Invitationals twice each, invitation tournaments at Rideau Glen, Smiths Falls, Deep River, Cornwall, Thurso, Outaouais, Pembroke, Petawawa, Maniwaki, Hawkesbury; twice Ottawa ACT golf award; ACT amateur athlete of year 1964; Charles Daoust French speaking amateur athlete of year 1965; *res.* Ottawa, Ont.

NICHOLAS, Cindy (swimming); *b.* 20 Aug 1957, Toronto, Ont.; *given name:* Cynthia Maria; U of Toronto; student; best remembered for 15:10 record conquest of Lake Ontario 16 Aug 1974; amateur recognition with provincial, national age-group records in freestyle, backstroke, butterfly; record 9:46 swim of English Channel from France to England 1975; October 1975 swam 25km race in first international Syrian swim from Jablak to Lattakia, set record; won women's division 1976 Chibougama single-day three-swim competition (10 miles, five miles, one and one-half miles); won women's division 25-mile Lake St. John swim; swam English Channel from England to France in 10:20 1976; English Channel England to France in 10:24 becoming first Canadian to swim it three times; best world avg. times for Channel swim; World Federation of Swimming title of world's women's international swimming champion 1976; Scarborough, Toronto, Ontario, Canadian government awards; *res.* Scarborough, Ont.

NIELSEN, Ken (football); *b.* 10 May 1942, Hanna, Alta., *m.* Marsha Murray; *children:* Alana, Jennifer, Grant, Keith; U of Alberta,

D.D.S.; dentist; Winnipeg Blue Bombers 1965-70 as halfback, end; Western Conference all-star three times; 1968 Schenley Award as outstanding Canadian; caught CFL record-tieing 109yd TD pass from Kenny Ploen at Calgary 1965; career total 280 passes for 4,340yds (15.5 avg.) and 31 TDs; Manitoba male athlete of year 1967; *res.* Winnipeg, Man.

NIGHBOR, Frank (hockey); *b.* 26 Jan 1893, Pembroke, Ont., *d.* 13 Apr 1966, Pembroke, Ont.; *m.* Dorothy Slattery (*d.*); *children:* Frank Jr.; *m.* Ann Heney (*d.*); *children:* Patrick, Pauline, Catharine; insurance executive; Port Arthur for 1910-11 season, turned pro Toronto 1913; with Vancouver Millionaires Stanley Cup winners 1914-15, Ottawa Senators 1915-29, Toronto 1929; with Senators on four Stanley Cup winners; nickname Flying Dutchman, Pembroke Peach; tied for 1917 scoring lead 41 goals in 20 games; scored 233 goals in 281 regular season games, 16 in 33 playoffs; first recipient Lady Byng Trophy 1925, repeat 1926; first recipient Hart Trophy 1924; mem. Hockey Hall of Fame.

NIGHTINGALE, Lynn (figure skating); *b.* 5 Aug 1956, Edmonton, Alta.; Immaculata HS; third Eastern Ontario sectionals 1968, second 1969; won EO senior 1970-72, Canadian junior 1972, Skate Canada, Prague Skate 1973; 10th world 1973; won Canadian senior, Skate Canada, Moscow Skate, sixth world 1974; won Canadian senior, seventh world 1975; won Canadian senior, ninth Olympics, seventh world 1976; won Ont.-Que. divisionals, Canadian senior, eighth world 1977; rejected 1976 pro offer from Toller Cranston show; turned pro Ice Capades 1977; coached by Marilyn Thompson, Ellen Burka, Don Jackson, Carlo Fassi; honored by City of Ottawa 1972-74; Ottawa ACT athlete of year 1974; *res.* Ottawa, Ont.

NOBLE, Reg (hockey); *b.* 23 Jun 1895, Collingwood, Ont., *d.* 19 Jan 1962, Alliston, Ont.; *given name:* Edward Reginald; mem. Collingwood juniors 1915 OHA group titlists, provincial semifinalists; helped Toronto Riversides take OHA senior title 1916; pro Toronto 1916-17 but when team disbanded went to Montreal Canadiens; Toronto Arenas at inception of NHL 1917-18, scored 28 goals in 22 games, helped team win Stanley Cup; team became St. Pat's and Noble helped them win 1921-22 Stanley Cup; traded to Montreal Maroons 1924, on Stanley Cup winner 1925-26; traded to Detroit Cougars and played five years on defence before returning to Maroons 1933; scored 170 NHL goals; played one season Cleveland (IHL) then refereed two seasons NHL; mem. Hockey Hall of Fame.

NOONEY, John (gymnastics); *b.* 21 Jun 1921, Bendon, Ireland; *m.* Patricia; Christian Brothers College, Ireland; senior civil servant Ontario; involved gymnastics from age eight; 14 years as PTI (all sports) RAF; emigrated to Canada 1950 becoming early pioneer Ontario Gymnastics Association; wrote first gymnastics handbook for YMCA; coach Etobicoke; international judge at Pan-Am Games; technical director Ontario men's gymnastics; Ontario judging chairman; executive mem. Ontario Gymnastics Federation; historian OGF, CGF; Canadian reporter *Modern Gymnast* magazine; mem. British Olympic Committee; considered father of gymnastics in Ontario; *res.* Mississauga, Ont.

NORMAN, Moe (golf); *b.* 10 Jul 1930, Kitchener, Ont.; *given name:* Murray; pro golfer; began career as caddy Kitchener Rockway; became student of Lloyd Tucker; outstanding amateur in Western Ontario region; won Canadian amateur 1955-56; turned pro 1956; tied Stan Leonard as low Canadian pro 1957 Canadian Open; twice won Ontario Open, Saskatchewan Open, Manitoba Open, three times Alberta Open, twice CPGA, once Quebec Open, once Millar Trophy; set competitive record nine-hole 29 on back nine CPGA final Old Ashburn Halifax; mem. Ontario Willingdon Cup teams, Canadian America's Cup teams, Rockway's George S. Lyon team matches; considered by peers most proficient shotmaker despite impatient behavior; popular with fans due to running repartee throughout round; *res.* Gilford, Ont.

NORTHCOTT, Ron (curling); *b.* 31 Dec 1935, Innisfail, Alta.; *given name:* Ronald Charles; *m.* Gerry McKay; *children:* Karen, Greg; Vulcan HS; assistant manager steel company; launched curling career at Vulcan junior HS; played in 1963-64, 1966-69 Briers, won last three; three times world champion; nickname The Owl; mem. Canadian Sports, Curling Halls of Fame; *res.* Calgary, Alta.

NUNNS, Brenda (tennis); *b.* 13 Sep 1945, Toronto, Ont.; *m.* John Michael Shoemaker; *children:* Adam, Alexandra, John, David, Victoria; Bishop Strachan School, Trinity College; father Gilbert eight times Canadian Davis Cup team mem., mother Beatrice Eastern Canadian champion; with Faye Urban won Canadian girls-15 doubles 1960, girls-18 doubles 1961-62, Canadian women's doubles 1965; won Canadian Intercollegiate women's singles 1963-66, Ontario under-18 singles 1962; with Cynthia Nowlan won National Capital women's doubles 1975; mem. Canadian Federation Cup team 1966; member Rockcliffe Lawn Tennis Club; *res.* Ottawa, Ont.

NUNNS, Gilbert (tennis); *b.* 30 Jun 1907, Leeds, Eng.; *m.* Beatrice Symons; *children:* Mary, Margot, Ruth, Brenda; Lower Canada College, U of Toronto, B.A.; retired advertising agency v.-pres.; at 15 won Quebec boys' championship; won both Ontario, Quebec junior titles; eight times Canadian Davis Cup team mem., captain 1934; *res.* Toronto, Ont.

NUTTER, Janet (diving); *b.* 2 Apr 1953, Winnipeg, Man.; U of Manitoba; student; bronze 1m, gold 3m 1973 Canada Games; gold 3m CIAWU 1973 championships; bronze 3m 1973 summer nationals; silver 10m 1975 USSR, Mexico; represented Canada vs DDR, USSR, CSSR, Australia, Mexico, New Zealand Games, World Student Games Moscow 1973 and Canada Cup; *res.* Winnipeg, Man.

OAKLEY, Alex (track); *b.* 26 Apr 1926, St. John's, Nfld.; *given name:* Alexander Harold; G.M. of Canada; competed 1960, 1964, 1972, 1976 Olympics, sixth 1960; gold 20km walk 1963 Pan-Am Games Brazil; competed in two Commonwealth Games; Ontario athlete of year 1960; *res.* Oshawa, Ont.

OBECK, Vic (football); *b.* 28 Mar 1921, Philadelphia, Pa.; Springfield College, B.Sc., Columbia U, M.A., New York U, Ph.D.; owner public relations firm; college letters in football, track, wrestling, swimming, lacrosse, boxing; pro football three years with Chicago Cardinals, Brooklyn Dodgers; coach, athletic director McGill 1947-55; general manager Montreal Alouettes two years; athletic director NYU 12 years; public relations officer 1976 Olympics; *res.* Montreal, Que.

O'BILLOVICH, Bob (football, basketball); *b.* 30 Jun 1940, Butte, Montana; *m.* Judy Ristow; *children:* Tracy, Jodi, Coy, Robert Jr.; U of Montana, B.A.; football coach; lettered in football, basketball, baseball Montana, all-Skyline Conference in each; twice won Grizzly award for combining academic-athletic excellence; Dragstedt award, basketball MVP, 1960-61; all-American football honorable mention; led US colleges pass interceptions 1960; Earhart award best defensive basketballer Montana 1961-62; Montana athlete of decade 1960-70; St. Louis Cardinals draftee; late cut AFL Denver Broncos; all-star defensive back United League Indianapolis, led league in interceptions 1962; Ottawa Rough Riders as defensive back, backup quarterback 1963-67; twice EFC, once all-Canadian; twice led EFC interceptions, CFL once; basketball coach Eastern Ontario Institute of Technology (later Algonquin) 1965-69; football coach U of Ottawa 1970 guiding team to College Bowl; basketball coach, sports information officer Carleton U 1971-73; basketball coach, coordinator intercollegiate athletics U of O 1973-77; coach Ottawa Rough Riders since 1976; mem. Montana Grizzlies Basketball Hall of Fame; *res.* Ottawa, Ont.

O'BRIEN, J. Ambrose (hockey); *b.* 27 May 1885, Renfrew, Ont., *d.* 25 Apr 1968, Ottawa, Ont.; *m.* Mary Adele Gorman (*d.*); *children:* Lawrence (*d.*), Brian, Barry, Justin, Gerald; U of Toronto; retired businessman; junior, intermediate, senior hockey Renfrew and U of T; organized National Hockey Association; with father, Sen. M.J. O'Brien, financed four clubs including Renfrew Millionaires, Montreal Canadiens; mem. Ottawa, Hockey Halls of Fame.

O'BRIEN, John (baseball); *b.* 15 Jul 1866, West Saint John, N.B., *d.* 13 May 1913, Lewiston, Me.; nickname Chewing Gum; National Baseball League 1891-99 hitting .256 lifetime avg. in 492 games; played with Brooklyn, Chicago, Louisville, Washington, Baltimore, Pittsburgh.

O'CONNOR, Larry (track); *b.* 22 Sep 1916, Toronto, Ont.; *given name:* Lawrence Gerard; *m.* Helen Elizabeth Conway; *children:* Lawrence Jr., Thomas, Jane; Cobourg HS, U of Toronto, Osgoode Hall, LL.B.; lawyer; won Canadian Intercollegiate 120yd high hurdles 1935-37; mem. Canadian team 1936 Berlin Olympics, fifth 110m hurdles; mem. Canadian team 1938 British Empire Games Sydney, silver 120yd high hurdles, gold 440yd relay; world record 60yd indoor hurdles 1937; Norton Crowe Memorial Trophy 1939; member AAU of C Sports Hall of Fame; *res.* Chatham, Ont.

O'CONNOR, Zeke (football); *b.* 5 Feb 1926, New York; *given name:* William; *m.* Nancy Jean Seffing; *children:* Cathie, Karen, Christopher; Notre Dame U, B.Sc., Columbia U, M.A.; business executive; all-American 1944; captain Great Lakes Naval football team under Paul Brown, mem. Great Lakes basketball team under Weeb Ewbank 1945; turned pro Buffalo Bills 1948, Cleveland Browns 1949, NY Yankees 1950-51, Toronto Argos 1952-53, with 1952 Grey Cup champions; head coach Balmy Beach ORFU 1954-56; radio football commentator since 1958; *res.* Streetsville, Ont.

O'HARA, Jane (tennis); *b.* 24 Jul 1951, Toronto, Ont.; *given name:* Jane Ellen; U of Toronto, B.A.; newspaper writer; won girls-12 Closed singles 1963; through 1969 won girls-14, 16, 18 (twice) Closed singles, Canadian Open girls-18 singles and 18 doubles (with Karen Will); four times Wimbledon competitor reaching quarterfinals mixed doubles 1970; six times mem. Canadian Federation Cup team; number one Canadian woman tennis player 1975; *res.* Toronto, Ont.

OLIVER, Harry (hockey); *b.* 26 Oct 1898, Selkirk, Man.; helped Selkirk seniors win Western Canadian championship 1917-18; turned pro with Calgary in WHL 1920-26; sold to Boston Bruins, on 1929 Stanley Cup winner; traded to NY Americans 1934-37; with Calgary scored 91 goals, 49 assists, in 11 NHL seasons recorded 127 goals, 95 assists; mem. Hockey Hall of Fame; *res.* Winnipeg, Man.

O'MALLEY, Terry (hockey); *b.* 21 Oct 1940, Toronto, Ont.; *m.* Deborah Suzanne Hindle; *children:* Kathleen, Frank, Bridget; U of British Columbia, U of Manitoba; St. Michael's College 1961 Memorial Cup team; Canadian national team Olympic program 1963-70; since 1971 player-coach in Japan; *res.* Tokyo, Japan.

O'NEILL, John (rowing); *b.* 1877, Ketch Harbor, N.S., *d.* 1967, Halifax, N.S.; 1904 Halifax harbor sculling title; Middle States regatta singles title 1905, 1907; US Association singles 1908; US single sculls 1909; mem. Canadian Sports Hall of Fame.

O'NEILL, Tip (baseball); *b.* 25 May 1858, Woodstock, Ont., *d.* 31 Dec 1915, Montreal, Que.; *given name:* James Edward; early baseball in Ontario leagues then semi-pro Detroit; major leagues with NY, St. Louis, Chicago, Cincinnati as pitcher-outfielder; 11-year big league record of 16-16 as pitcher and .340 avg. through 1,038 games; played in 38 World Series games; in 1887 compiled all-time record .492 single season avg.

ONESCHUK, Steve (football); *b.* 22 Nov 1930, St. Catharines, Ont.; *m.* Marilyn McIntosh; *children:* Douglas, James; U of Toronto, B.P.H.E.; HS principal; mem. St. Catharines junior Athletics (1948 Minto

Cup finalists), senior Athletics 1949, 1950; U of T football all-star four years; Johnny Copp Memorial Trophy 1954; George M. Biggs Trophy 1953-54; Hamilton Tiger-Cats 1955-60, co-captain three years; twice in East-West Shrine game; EFC, *Globe and Mail* Canadian all-star three times; led Ticat scorers 1957 as halfback, placement kicker; in three Grey Cup finals, one winner; assistant coach Ticats 1961; *res.* Hamilton, Ont.

O'QUINN, Red (football); *b.* 7 Sep 1925, Bluett Falls, N.C.; *given name:* John William; *m.* Dorothy Brown; *children:* Kathy, John III; Wake Forest U, B.S., M.A.; marketing manager; moving from HS to service ball earned Wake Forest scholarship; pass-catching talents earned him all-Southern; pro Chicago Bears two seasons; Montreal Alouettes as tight end 1952-59, combined with Sam Etcheverry for 377 receptions for 5,679yds, 24 TDs (figures cover from 1954 when EFC records were kept); frequent all-East, all-Canadian; honored by Montreal fans with 'day' 1959; in three Grey Cup finals; best season 1955 with 78 receptions; general manager Ottawa Rough Riders 1962-69, Montreal Alouettes 1970-71; with Etcheverry Montreal sportsman of year for 1970 Grey Cup victory; *res.* Montreal, Que.

ORGAN, Gerry (football); *b.* 4 Dec 1944, Cheltenham, Eng.; *m.* Lore; *children:* Jamey, Leah; U of Guelph, B.Sc.; pres. athletic club; all-Canadian with U of Guelph Gryphons; place kicker Ottawa Rough Riders from 1971 winning EFC scoring title four times in five years; led CFL scorers 1972 with 131 points; shares CFL record six field goals single game 1973 with Edmonton's Dave Cutler; also kicked five against Toronto 1974; CFL single-season record 36 field goals 1974; Schenley Award outstanding Canadian 1973, runner-up 1972; CFL record through 1976: 2TDs, 186 converts, 159 field goals, 42 singles for 717 points; mem. Athletes in Action; *res.* Ottawa, Ont.

ORR, Bobby (hockey); *b.* 20 Mar 1948, Parry Sound, Ont.; *given name:* Robert Gordon; *m.* Peggy; *children:* Darren; hockey player, business executive; shortstop MacTier Ont. provincial champion junior baseball team 1963; from hometown minor hockey ranks to Oshawa Generals OHA junior A club at 14; led team to OHA title 1966; with help of Alan Eagleson signed reported $70,000 pro contract Boston Bruins Sep 1966; deal considered cornerstone for NHL Players' Association; Calder Memorial Trophy as NHL rookie of year 1967; twice Art Ross scoring title; three times Hart MVP Trophy; twice Conn Smythe Trophy; eight times James Norris Memorial Trophy; eight times first team, once second team all-star defenceman; NHL regular season assist record of 102 in 1970-71; record point total for defenceman of 139 same season; playoff assist record with 19 1971-72; playoff point record for defenceman same season with 24; regular season goals record for defenceman with 46 1974-75; helped Bruins win two Stanley Cups; played out option, signed by Chicago Black Hawks 1976; six knee operations make future play questionable; assistant coach Chicago 1976-77; MVP Canada Cup 1976; through 1976-77 played 651 regular season games scoring 268 goals, 643 assists for 911 points, 949 penalty minutes, plus 74 playoff games, 26 goals, 66 assists for 92 points, 107 penalty minutes; with Mike Walton operates hockey camp; Lou Marsh Trophy 1970; Canadian CP poll male athlete of year 1970; *Sport Magazine, Sports Illustrated* athlete of year awards; *res.* Boston, Mass.

OSBORNE, Bob (administrator); *b.* 10 Apr 1913, Victoria, B.C.; *given name:* Robert Freer; *m.* Dorothy Beatrice McRae; *children:* Wayne McRae, Robert David; U of British Columbia, B.A., B.Ed., U of Washington, university professor; mem. 1936 Canadian Olympic basketball team; phys ed director for men UBC 1945; director school of phys ed and recreation UBC 1952; pres. AAU of C 1950-51; manager Olympic track team 1956, Commonwealth Games team 1958, Pan-Am Games team 1959, 1963; chairman B.C. Sports Council 1967-70; coach 1968 Olympic basketball team; v.-pres. COA, chairman Pan-Am Games Committee; mem. AAU of C, B.C. Sports Halls of Fame; *res.* Vancouver, B.C.

OUELLETTE, Gerry (shooting); *b.* 14 Aug 1934, Windsor, Ont., *d.* 25 Jun 1975, Windsor, Ont.; *m.* Judith, *children:* Mark; W.D. Lowe Vocational HS; teacher; Canadian junior and cadet service rifle titles 1951; Lieutenant-Governor's medal 1952; gold 1956 Olympics Melbourne Australia; Canadian service pistol title 1957; gold, two silver 1959 Pan-Am Games, silver 1967 Pan-Am Games; sixth 1968 Olympics; mem. Canadian Bisley team 15 times; Queen's final eight times, finished in top 25 12 times; Canadian high-powered titlist three times, grand aggregate winner four times; seventh world masters 1958; mem. Canadian Sports Hall of Fame.

PAGE, Percy (basketball); *b.* 14 May 1887, Rochester, N.Y., *d.* 2 Mar 1973, Edmonton, Alta.; *m.* Maude Roche; *children:* daughter; Queen's U; teacher, politician; coached Edmonton Grads 1915-40, team played 522 games, won 502 for 96.2 percentage; attended Olympics Paris 1924, Amsterdam 1928, Los Angeles 1932, Berlin 1936, won 27 consecutive games; during team's 25-year existence recorded victory streaks of 147 and 78 games; MLA (PC) 1952-59; Lt. Gov. Alta. 1959-66; mem. Canadian Sports, Alberta Amateur, Dr. Naismith Memorial Basketball Halls of Fame.

PALMER, Lillian (track and field); *b.* 23 Jun 1913, Vancouver, B.C.; *given name:* Lillian Emily; *m.* Charles Collingwood Alderson; *children:* Donald, Blake; set records in PS, HS 50, 100yd dash, high and broad jump; as ineligible 15-year-old beat 1928 Olympics seniors, set world record 50yd 5.4; competed in 1932 Olympics on silver medal relay team; with Hilda Strike and two British runners beat US gold medal team in post-Olympic match San Francisco; 1932 B.C. women's 200m title, repeat 1934 in 26.4 to equal British Empire Games trials standard; mem. gold medal relay team British Empire Games, set record; captain Canadian team, fourth 200m, carried flag 1934 Women's World Games; hole-in-one Point Grey Club 1972; mem. B.C. Sports Hall of Fame; *res.* Vancouver, B.C.

PALMER, Marilyn (golf); *b.* 17 Dec 1946, Vancouver, B.C.; U of British Columbia, B.Ed.; teacher; won B.C. junior 1963-65, B.C. ladies' seven times, Canadian ladies' Closed 1966, Canadian Open runner-up twice, third once; Canadian Open medalist 1969; Pacific Northwest Golf Association title 1973, medal 1966, 1972; with Jocelyne Bourassa won New Zealand Foursomes title 1971; with Dale Shaw won Canadian Foursomes 1975, International Fourball 1972; low amateur women's titleholder tournament 1972; mem. Canadian ladies' Commonwealth team three times, World Cup team three times, B.C. interprovincial team 1964-75; *res.* Vancouver, B.C.

PANASIUK, Bob (golf); *b.* 20 Oct 1941, Windsor, Ont.; *m.* Dolores; *children:* Melissa; pro golfer; began career as caddy; won Ontario junior, best ball, Canadian junior 1958, Ontario amateur 1959, Ontario junior 1960; turned pro 1960; twice won Brooks Bursary; won Quebec Open 1974, Alberta Open 1974-75, Saskatchewan Open 1974, Newfoundland Open 1973, Atlantic Open 1975, Northern Ontario PGA 1966, Canadian PGA 1972-73, Canadian Tar Sands tournament of champions 1976, Peter Jackson Cup order of merit 1975; limited success on US pro tour; mem. Canadian World Cup team 1972, 1973, 1974; Canadian golfer of year 1974; *res.* Windsor, Ont.

PAPROSKI, Steve (football); *b.* 23 Sep 1928, Lwow, Poland; *given name:* Steven Eugene; *m.* Mary Elizabeth Coburn; *chil-*

dren: Patrick, Peter, Annamarie, Alexandra, Elizabeth; U of North Dakota, U of Arizona, Banff School of Advanced Management; chief opposition whip House of Commons; college football N. Dakota, Arizona; turned pro Edmonton Eskimos 1949-54; Alberta HS heavyweight wrestling champion 1943, runner-up Canadian heavyweight championship 1943-44; MP (PC) from 1968; *res.* Edmonton, Alta., Ottawa, Ont.

PARK, Brad (hockey); *b.* 6 Jul 1948, Toronto, Ont.; *given name:* Douglas Bradford; *m.* Gerri; *children:* two sons; hockey player; played Scarborough Lions, spotted by pro scouts at 17, first choice of NY Rangers in former juvenile draft 1965; played junior with Toronto Marlboros then turned pro with Rangers organization; played 17 games with Buffalo (AHL) 1968-69 before being called up to NHL team where he starred on defence until dealt to Boston Bruins with Jean Ratelle, Joe Zanussi for Phil Esposito, Carol Vadnais 1975; mem. Team Canada 1972; four times first team all-star, twice second team; eight season NHL record, 508 regular season games, 111 goals, 320 assists, 431 points, 833 penalty minutes, plus 75 playoff games, 15 goals, 40 assists, 55 points, 143 penalty minutes; *res.* Lynnfield, Mass.

PARKER, Jackie (football); *b.* 1 Jan 1932, Knoxville, Tenn.; *given name:* John Dickerson; *m.* Peggy; *children:* Jere Jo, Peggy Mae, Jack Jr.; Mississippi State U; all-American, 1952-53 Southeastern Conference MVP, scoring record 120 points 1952; halfback, quarterback, wide receiver, placement kicker and punter Edmonton Eskimos 1954-62 leading club to three Grey Cup wins vs Montreal Alouettes; Toronto Argos 1963-65; coach Toronto Rifles Continental League 1966; B.C. Lions' assistant coach 1968, head coach 1969, general manager 1970-75; seven times winner Jeff Nicklin Memorial Trophy (WFC MVP), three times Schenley outstanding player; eight times WFC, CFL all-star; CFL 13-year record 88 TDs, 103 converts, 40 field goals, 19 singles for 750 points, 5,210yds rushing, 135 receptions for 2,308yds, threw 2,061 passes completing 1,089 for 16,476yds and 88 TDs; mem. Canadian Sports, Football, Edmonton, Mississippi Halls of Fame; *res*. Vancouver, B.C.

PARKER, Valerie (track and field); *b*. 28 Apr 1944, St. Boniface, Man.; *given name:* Valerie Jerome; *m*. Ronald Parker; *children:* Stuart; U of British Columbia; teacher; Canadian senior 60m, 100m, long jump titles, on B.C. champion 4x100 relay team, placed third in high jump 1959; same summer represented Canada Chicago Pan-Am Games, placed fourth 100m, seventh 60m, won relay bronze, all at age 15; competed 1960 Rome Olympics; competed 100m, 200m sprints with Canadian track team in variety of European dual meets 1968; chief judge 1976 Montreal Olympics; personal bests: 100m 11.6 1968, 200m 24.2 1968, high jump 1.55m 1971, long jump 5.64m 1967, 100m hurdles 15.3 1973; *res*. Vancouver, B.C.

PARKIN, Lorne (football); *b*. 3 Oct 1919, Toronto, Ont.; *m*. Ella Grace; *children:* John, Robert; retired policeman; Toronto Indians 1947, Toronto Indians Beaches in ORFU 1948; turned pro Argos 1949-55 appearing in 58 league, 10 playoff games including Grey Cup victories 1950, 1952; coached Toronto Police tug-of-war team to North American championship 1960 until 1973 retirement; *res*. Toronto, Ont.

PARKS, Arnold (shooting); *b*. 14 Jun 1930, Saint John, N.B.; *given name:* Alfred Arnold; *m*. Zola Sypher; *children:* Victoria, Sonya Jane; certified general accountant; Canadian cadet smallbore outdoor title 1948; numerous N.B. shooting honors including Prince of Wales Cup, Governor's Cup four times; winner N.B., Atlantic Rifle championships; mem. Canadian Bisley team 10 times, adjutant 1968 team; mem. Canadian Palma team several times but accepted only three times; mem. N.B. Inter-Maritime team 19 times, coach three times, titles twice; mem. N.B. team shooting in Ottawa 22 times; won Governor-General's match twice; at Bisley won Century match 1967, Clock Tower match 1969, St. George's Silver Cross 1973; Queen's prize 1968, fifth same event 1970; in Queen's Hundred five times; mem. several Kolapore, MacKinnon match teams, several winners; N.B. indoor smallbore champion several times; Canadian (DCRA) smallbore title 1970; life mem. DCRA, N.B. Rifle Associations; pres. NBRA, Saint John Garrison Military Rifle Association; held various executive roles with DCRA, NBRA; coached juniors, cadets; mem. N.B. Sports Hall of Fame; *res*. Saint John, N.B.

PARNELL, William (track and field); *b*. 14 Feb 1928, Vancouver, B.C.; *given name:* Comer William; *m*. Joan Mary; *children:* John, Leslie, Keith, Jacqueline; N. Vancouver HS, Washington State U, B.Sc., U of British Columbia, teacher's certificate; educator; all-American as WSU miler; third US nationals in 4:09.6; represented Canada 1948, 1952 Olympics, 1950, 1954 Commonwealth Games; gold medal for 4:11 mile 1950 Games at Auckland N.Z.; NCAA three-mile title, several national titles and records; captain Canadian T&F team 1954 British Empire Games Vancouver; Norton

H. Crowe Memorial Award, Canadian male athlete of year 1949; mem. B.C. Sports Hall of Fame; *res.* Vancouver, B.C.

PARRY, Jack (football, track, baseball); *b.* 18 Jun 1922, Windsor, Ont.; *given name:* John Clayton; *m.* Anne Huffman; *children:* Jann, Jay, Jill, Jon; U of Western Ontario, M.D.; physician; Windsor, WOSSA, Ontario records in sprints several years; two years Windsor all-city football; 1942 Grey Cup with Toronto Hurricanes; UWO Mustangs 1947-49; mem. Canadian Olympic relay team 1948 London Games; Canadian 100m, 200m records 1948 as mem. UWO track team; outfield for London Majors in Senior Intercounty baseball league; *res.* Chatham, Ont.

PATAKY, Bill (basketball); *b.* 12 May 1930, Windsor, Ont.; *given name:* William Andrew; *m.* Joan T. Monaghan; *children:* Maureen, Joanne, Monica, Margaret, Jane; U of Windsor, U of Western Ontario, OCE; HS v.-principal; Windsor all-city football backfielder, basketball forward 1948-49; shortstop Windsor junior Ontario finalists 1948-49; halfback Assumption College (U of Windsor) junior ORFU all-Ontario finalists; varsity basketball Assumption College 1949-50; shortstop Frood Mine baseball team Sudbury 1951; UWO Mustangs all-star 1951-52; mem. Tillsonburg Livingstons basketball team representing Canada in Helsinki Olympics; football with Sarnia Imperials ORFU 1953; senior basketball 1953-65 in Sarnia-Port Huron area; *res.* Sarnia, Ont.

PATRICK, Frank (hockey); *b.* 23 Dec 1885, Ottawa, Ont., *d.* 29 Jun 1960; *m.* Catherine Porter; *children:* Joseph, Gloria, Frances; McGill U; hockey executive; defenceman with Montreal Victorias (CAHL) 1904, Westmount (CAHL) 1905, Montreal Victorias (ECAHA) 1908, Renfrew Millionaires (NHA) 1910, Vancouver Millionaires (PCHA) 1912-18, Vancouver Millionaires (WCHL) 1925; coach Boston Bruins 1934-36; created Vancouver Millionaires, manager-captain when they won 1915 Stanley Cup; coach Boston three seasons then managed Canadiens; mem. B.C. Sports, Hockey Halls of Fame.

PATRICK, Lester (hockey); *b.* 31 Dec 1883, Drummondville, Que., *d.* 1 Jun 1960, Victoria, B.C.; *m.* Grace Victoria Linn; *children:* Lynn, Murray; McGill U; hockey executive; defenceman Brandon Man. 1903, Westmount (CAHL) 1905, Montreal Wanderers (ECAHA) 1906-07, captain for two Stanley Cup wins; captain Nelson B.C. team through 1909; joined Renfrew Millionaires 1910; formed Victoria Aristocrats, helped establish Pacific Coast League, organized clubs and built artificial ice arenas in all league centres; played with Victoria 1912-16, 1919-26, Spokane 1917, Seattle 1918; NY Rangers manager-coach and sometime player 1926-39, general manager through 1946; seven times in eight seasons NHL all-star coach; with Aristocrats defeated Quebec for 1913 world title although Stanley Cup not at stake; won Stanley Cup 1924 with Victoria Cougars vs Canadiens; with Rangers won three Stanley Cups; trophy in his memory for service to US hockey since 1966; division of NHL given his name 1974; nickname Silver Fox; mem. B.C., Hockey Halls of Fame.

PATRICK, Lynn (hockey); *b.* 3 Feb 1912, Victoria, B.C.; *given name:* Joseph Lynn; *div.* Dorothy Davis, *m.* Bernice Pachal (*d.*); *children:* Lester Lee, Craig, Karen, Glenn, Dean; hockey executive; mem. Canadian champion Blue Ribbons basketball team, B.C. Reps rugby team, Winnipeg Blue Bombers; NY Rangers 1935-46 except war services 1943-45; first team all-star 1942, helped Rangers win 1940 Stanley Cup; coached Rangers to 1950 Stanley Cup finals, lost to Detroit in second sudden-death overtime in seventh game; Boston Bruins 1950-53, coach-general manager to 1965; St. Louis Blues 1966 as coach-general manager, executive v.-pres. 1967-77; *res.* St. Louis, Mo.

PATRICK, Muzz (hockey); *b.* 28 Jun 1915, Victoria, B.C.; *given name:* Frederick Murray; *m.* Jessie Farr; *children:* Lynda, Richard, Paul, Lori; defenceman NY Rangers 1937-41, 1945-46; coach Rangers 1954-55, general manager 1955-64, later v.-pres.; mem. Victoria Dominoes basketball champions; Canadian amateur heavyweight boxing title 1936; with Art Coulter became one of Rangers' toughest defensive units; following war coached, managed in minors; competing for Victoria Y under coach Archie MacKinnon won city interscholastic mile, half-mile same day; mem. B.C. Sports Hall of Fame; *res.* Riverside, Conn.

PATTERSON, Hal (football); *b.* 1933, Rozel, Kansas; *given name:* Harold; Kansas U; nickname Prince Hal; Kansas U all-star baseball, basketball, football player; Montreal Alouettes 1954-60, Hamilton Ticats 1961-67; began pro career as defensive back, switched to receiver; in 14 CFL seasons caught 460 passes for 9,473yds, 20.6 avg., 64 TDs, also returned 105 kickoffs for 2,871yds, 27.3 avg., three majors, scored total 75 TDs for 432 points; best single season 1956 with 88 passes for CFL record 1,914yds; best game 29 Sep 1956 with CFL record 338yds in receptions; longest single gain on reception

109yds; longest kickoff return 105yds; Lord Calvert Trophy (Montreal MVP) three times; Jeff Russel Memorial Trophy 1956; Schenley outstanding player award 1956, runner-up 1957; eight times EFC all-star, twice all-Canadian; competed nine Grey Cup finals, won three; mem. Canadian Football Hall of Fame; *res.* Larned, Kansas.

PAUL, Robert (figure skating); *b.* 2 Jun 1937, Toronto, Ont.; *m.* Sally Ann Welsh; skating choreographer, coach; five Canadian, two North American, four world titles, 1960 Olympic gold medal; Ice Capades 1961-64; since 1965 coached US world and Olympic competitors; choreographer for 1968 Olympic gold medalist Peggy Fleming; with Barbara Wagner shared 1959 Lou Marsh Trophy as Canada's outstanding athletes; mem. Canadian Sports Hall of Fame; *res.* Beverly Hills, Calif.

PAULSON, Jamie (badminton); *b.* 26 Apr 1948, Calgary, Alta.; U of Calgary, B.Comm., U of Western Ontario, M.B.A.; real estate executive; won Canadian junior singles four times, national singles four times; with Yves Pare took national men's doubles five times; twice singles, doubles champion Jamaican, Mexican Opens; led Canada to first North American title over US 1969; bronze medal Singapore world championships; gold singles, bronze doubles 1970 Commonwealth Games Edinburgh; silver 1974 Commonwealth Games Christchurch N.Z.; twice Thomas Cup team mem.; flag-bearer 1974 Commonwealth Games; among top five singles players in world five consecutive years; *res.* Toronto, Ont.

PEARCE, Bobby (rowing); *b.* 30 Sep 1905, Sydney, Australia, *d.* 20 May 1976, Toronto, Ont.; *m.* Velma Hilda; *children:* Jon Robert,

Jill Elizabeth, Robert Ernest; salesman; Australian army heavyweight boxing champion 1926; world amateur sculling champion with gold medal 7:01 record 1928 Amsterdam Olympics, repeat 1932; British Empire Games amateur sculling title 1930 Hamilton, Ont.; won 1931 diamond sculls at Henley Eng. representing Canada; competed for Australia 1932 Olympics although Canadian resident; pro world title at CNE 1933; lost only two races in pro career; Lou Marsh Trophy as Canada's outstanding athlete 1938; Australia's athlete of past 200 years 1970; second only to Joe Wright Sr. as Canada's outstanding oarsman of half century 1950 CP poll; mem. Canadian Sports Hall of Fame.

PEARSON, Mike (football, hockey, baseball); *b.* 23 Apr 1897, Toronto, Ont. *d.* 27 Dec 1972, Ottawa, Ont.; *given name:* Lester Bowles; *m.* Maryon Moody; *children:* son, daughter; Victoria College, B.A., St. John's College Oxford, B.A.; former Prime Minister of Canada; intercounty baseball with Guelph; interfaculty rugby, basketball, football, hockey, lacrosse at Oxford; coach senior hockey 1926-27, senior football, lacrosse 1926-27, senior ORFU football 1927-28; Nobel Peace Prize 1957; trophy in his name presented annually by CIAU.

PEDEN, Doug (all-around); *b.* 18 Apr 1916, Victoria, B.C.; *given name:* James Douglas; *m.* Trudy; sports editor; competed professionally in bike racing, basketball, baseball; in cycling rode 37 six-day races, won seven, second nine times; Canadian pro sprint title 1939 Montreal; toured with House of David baseball team; joined Pittsburgh organization playing and managing several minor league teams; led class B Interstate league hitters with .357 avg. York

Pa. 1946; guard with Victoria, three Canadian basketball titles; top scorer Windsor Fords, 1936 Olympic silver medal; pro basketball with Buffalo Bisons, Vancouver Hornets; numerous B.C. junior tennis titles; B.C. rugger fullback, punter, place kicker; 120yd high hurdler; several regional swimming titles; mem. B.C. Sports Hall of Fame; *res.* Victoria, B.C.

PEDEN, Torchy (cycling); *b.* 16 Apr 1906, Victoria, B.C.; *given name:* William John; *m.* Annamae; *children:* four; retail sporting goods; competed 1928 Amsterdam Olympics after winning Canadian titles at one, five miles and tieing for all-around Canadian amateur title; one-third, one-half, one, two, five mile Canadian amateur indoor titles setting records in four 1929; English 103-mile record of 1:39.39; competed in Warsaw, London, Paris, Glasgow; pro 1929-48 with 38 wins in 148 six-day races; US record for mile with 73½ mph Minneapolis 1931; mem. Canadian, B.C. Sports Halls of Fame; *res.* Northbrook, Ill.

PELKEY, Arthur (boxing); *b.* 27 Oct 1884, Chatham, Ont., *d.* 18 Feb 1921, Ford City, Ont.; *given name:* Andrew Arthur Peletier; fought Tommy Burns, Jess Willard, Jim Coffey to no decisions; KO victory 1913 resulted in death of opponent Luther McCarty, Pelkey never again won a bout; only title challenge 1914 Daly City Calif., KO'd by Gunboat Smith; in 50-bout career won 12 by KO, nine by decision, four draws, lost one decision, KO'd 13 times, 11 no decisions.

PERCIVAL, Lloyd (all-around); *b.* 3 Jun 1913, Toronto, Ont.; *d.* 23 Jul 1974, Montreal, Que.; *m.* Dorothy Macdonell; *children:* Janet; North Toronto HS; physical educator;

nickname Ace; cricket, boxing, lacrosse, tennis, hockey, T&F, football; Canadian junior tennis finals at 16; Canadian bantam Golden Gloves boxing title, qualified for Olympics but too young to participate; high scorer 1936 Canadian cricket team touring England; coached 1932 National Sea Flea midgets to undefeated hockey season; launched Sports College 1941, at peak of program 800,000 students were registered; began Canadian Amateur Sports and Physical Fitness Development Service 1956; founder Fitness Institute; T & F coach; formed Don Mills TC; Coronation medal from Queen Elizabeth.

PERRY, Gordon (football, curling); *b.* 18 Mar 1907, Moncton, N.B.; *m.* Jessie Keith; *children:* Gordon Jr., Marilyn, Patricia; retired bank employee; Quebec city league baseball, hockey, Montreal Westward football intermediates; Montreal Winged Wheelers 1928-34, captained 1931 unbeaten, untied team to Grey Cup 22-0 vs Regina; Jeff Russel Memorial Trophy same year; Royal Victoria Jubilee curling title in both irons, granites 1953, 1956, Branch Governor-General's 1961; mem. Ottawa District, New Brunswick, Quebec, Canadian Football, Canadian Sports Halls of Fame; *res.* Ottawa, Ont.

PERRY, Norm (football); *b.* 1 Jun 1904, Sarnia, Ont., *d.* 17 Nov 1957, Sarnia, Ont.; *m.* Marie McPhail; *children:* Don, Dick; safety supervisor; running halfback in eight seasons junior, intermediate football; eight seasons with senior ORFU Sarnia Imperials winning seven titles, one Grey Cup; captain 1934 Grey Cup champions, MVP that season; perennial all-star; ORFU executive officer several years, CRU pres. 1953; term as mayor of Sarnia; mem. Canadian Football Hall of Fame.

PETTAPIECE, Jim (curling); *b.* 7 May 1943, Saskatoon, Sask.; *given name:* James Kenneth; U of Nevada; owner International Curling Promotions; Saskatchewan junior, senior championship baseball teams, baseball scholarship at Nevada; mem. Don Duguid Manitoba Consols, Brier, Silver Broom championship rinks 1970-71, 1973; with Dan Fink on 1973 Manitoba Consols winner, Brier entry; all-star Brier second 1970-71; instructor with Silver Broom Curling Schools, Curl Canada Clinics 1971-75; mem. Curling Hall of Fame; *res.* Winnipeg, Man.

PETTIGREW, Vern (wrestling); *b.* 30 Mar 1908, Durham, Ont.; *given name:* John Vernon; *m.* Jean Saunderson; *children:* Robert, Donald, Heather, Ronald; stonecutter, firefighter; 1933-40 won six Canadian titles; fourth featherweight class (134lbs) 1936 Berlin Olympics; wrestling instructor Regina City Police 1935-37; referee-in-chief Canadian wrestling championships 1955; mem. AAU of C, Sask. Sports, Canadian Wrestling Halls of Fame; *res.* Regina, Sask.

PETTINGER, Glen (basketball); *b.* 27 Sep 1928, Toronto, Ont.; *given name:* Glen Murray; *m.* Nancy Louise Hayman; *children:* Wendy, Kim, Jill, Christopher; U of Western Ontario, B.A.; HS principal; mem. East York Collegiate Ontario Golden Ball champions 1946, York Belting Canadian junior titlists 1947; CIAU all-star U of T 1949; UWO Mustangs Canadian Intercollegiate winners 1952 earning all-Canadian; mem. Tillsonburg Livingstons 1952 Olympics Helsinki; captain Nortown Tri-Bells Canadian senior basketball titlists 1953; Canadian Pan-Am Games team Chicago; mem. Ottawa Fellers 1959 Canadian finalists; *res.* Ottawa, Ont.

PEZER, Vera (curling); *b.* 13 Jan 1939, Melfort, Sask.; *given name:* Vera Lois; U of Saskatchewan, M.A., Ph.D.; assistant professor; won intercollegiate titles; with Joyce McKee rink won 1969 Canadian ladies' title; skipped Canadian champion rinks 1971-73; coach Canadian junior champions 1975; Western intercollegiate champions three years; mem. Saskatoon Imperials 1963-69 provincial women's softball champions; won 1969 Canadian title; mem. Saskatchewan interprovincial golf team 1970-77; Saskatoon sportswoman of year 1968; mem. Sask. Sports, Curling Halls of Fame; *res.* Saskatoon, Sask.

PHIBBS, Bob (basketball); *b.* 26 May 1927, Windsor, Ont.; *given name:* Robert James; *m.* Mary; *children:* Lizabeth Jean, Christine Louise, Richard James; U of Western Ontario, B.A.; company v.-pres.; Ontario discus, javelin titles 1946; three UWO intercollegiate football title teams, four basketball championship teams; captain 1952 Canadian senior men's basketball champions, Canadian Olympic team; Claude Brown Memorial Trophy 1949 as UWO outstanding athlete; *res.* Calgary, Alta.

PHILLIPS, Alf Jr. (curling); *b.* 10 Sep 1938, Toronto, Ont.; *given name:* Alfred John; *m.* June Doreen Carnell; *children:* Cliff, Steve, Wayne; Ryerson business school; v.-pres. Canadian Cocklin Shows; Ontario under-17 100yd freestyle swimming title; won Ontario junior tankard 1958; three times Ontario Silver Tankard winner; skipped Canadian Brier winners Ottawa 1967; City of Ottawa champion 1975; publisher *Ontario Curling Report* since 1974; mem. Canadian Curling Hall of Fame; *res.* Toronto, Ont.

PHILLIPS, Alf Sr. (diving, curling); *b.* 27 Jul 1908, Durham, Ont.; *m.* Margaret Dobson; *children:* Alf Jr., Dave; company pres.; Ontario springboard, platform fancy diving champion 1926-34, Canadian champion 1926-34 retiring undefeated; represented Canada 1928 Olympics Amsterdam (seventh platform), 1932 Olympics Los Angeles (fourth springboard); first double winner 1930 British Empire Games Hamilton; four times Ontario Silver Tankard winner; twice Canada Life title, five times Canada Life seniors; won Toronto International, Canadian seniors; skip 1956 Ontario champions, lost Moncton Brier extra-end playoff; mem. Canadian Curling, AAU of C Halls of Fame; *res.* Toronto, Ont.

PHILLIPS, Dave (curling); *b.* 29 Feb 1944, Toronto, Ont.; *given name:* David Edmund; *m.* Earline Kathryn Laroche; Forest Hill CI; curling club manager; 1970 Ontario Consols championship; second for Tom Cushing 1972 Canadian mixed finals; *res.* Agincourt, Ont.

PHILLIPS, Peter (curling); *b.* 9 May 1943, Toronto, Ont.; *given name:* Peter Edward; *m.* Beverley Johnstone; *children:* Monica, Ryan; U of Waterloo, Ryerson Polytechnical Inst.; v.-pres. information services; Ontario men's champion runner-up 1972; twice winner Ontario Tankard; five times provincial championship competitor; *res.* Agincourt, Ont.

PHILLIPS, Tommy (hockey); *b.* 22 May 1880, Kenora, Ont., *d.* 5 Dec 1923, Toronto, Ont.; *given name:* Thomas Neil; McGill U, U of Toronto; Toronto Marlboros 1904, OHA senior title; captained Kenora Thistles to two Stanley Cup challenges losing to Ottawa 2-1 1906; scored 13 goals in six playoff games as Kenora won Stanley Cup 1907; Ottawa Senators 1907, scored 26 goals in 10 games; on six Stanley Cup challengers, won once; closed career with Vancouver Millionaires 1912; *mem.* Hockey Hall of Fame.

PHILP, Jerry (football); *b.* 6 Jun 1932, Windsor, Ont.; *m.* Joanne Lawrence; *children:* John, Mark, Ann; Florida State U; HS teacher; all-city basketball Detroit 1950; Toronto Argos 1958-63, Montreal Alouettes 1964; coach Toronto De LaSalle, Windsor Assumption, 15-year record of 108 wins, 17 losses, two ties; *res.* Harrow, Ont.

PHOENIX, Skip (diving); *b.* 9 Apr 1948, Addis Ababa, Ethiopia; phys ed instructor; bronze medal 3m springboard 1973 winter, 1974 summer nationals; silver 1974 summer nationals, bronze 1975 winter nationals 1m; represented Canada twice in Canada Cup, twice vs USSR, DDR, Mexico, and 1976 Montreal Olympics; *res.* Toronto, Ont.

PIASKOSKI, Jim (football); *b.* 10 Oct 1948, Levack, Ont.; *given name:* James Peter; *m.* Nancy Ross; Eastern Michigan College; Sudbury Spartans juniors to offensive, defensive tackle Ottawa Rough Riders 1972; *mem.* 1973, 1976 Grey Cup champions; *mem.* 1976 City of Ottawa grand aggregate curling champions; *res.* Ottawa, Ont.

PICKELL, Bob (basketball); *b.* 2 Jul 1927, Kovna, Lithuania; *given name:* Bernard; *m.* Wendy; *children:* Al, Stephen; U of Portland; salesman; HS all-star; U of Portland four years, in three NIT tournaments; *mem.* five Canadian championship teams; five times team MVP; *mem.* Canadian Pan-Am Games team 1959, Canadian Olympic teams 1952, 1956; Edmonton Eskimos 1951-52, B.C. Lions 1954; AAU basketball 1951-52 Hawaii; toured Far East with Universal

Motors team 1952-53; won Vancouver City handball singles, doubles twice; with Herb Capozzi won Canadian Masters doubles in racketball 1973; drove in Shell 4,000 rally four times; *res.* Vancouver, B.C., Toronto, Ont.

PICKELL, Stephen (swimming); *b.* 11 Aug 1957, Vancouver, B.C.; *given name:* Stephen John; Capilano College; student; 28 national championships 1973-76; *mem.* Canadian world competition team since 1973; gold, silver medals 1974 Commonwealth Games; silver 4 x 100m medley relay 1976 Olympics; nine firsts 1976 Canadian nationals; seventh in world 100m backstroke, 13th in 200m backstroke, 15th 100m FS; Canadian records 100m, 200m backstroke, 200m freestyle, 200m individual medley; world record 100m butterfly short course 54.25 1977; *res.* Vancouver, B.C.

PICKERING, Bob (curling); *b.* 19 Sep 1932, Regina, Sask.; *given name:* Robert Hugh; *m.* Dorothy Somerville; *children:* Laurie, Pattie, Sheri; farmer; nickname Peewee; six times provincial champion and Brier representative finishing second several times; 1964 Massey-Ferguson Canadian Farmers' title, Canadian Elks 1975; twice winner Canadian Open Carspiel Edmonton; twice Calgary Masters champion; *mem.* Canadian Curling Hall of Fame; *res.* Milestone, Sask.

PILON, Claude (wrestling); *b.* 13 Jun 1950, Ottawa, Ont.; *m.* Rosalie; *children:* Jean-Marc; U of Ottawa; program operations officer Sport Canada; Canadian junior discus, hammer titles 1969-70; defensive end for Ottawa Sooners Canadian junior, senior ORFU finalists 1970-71; Canadian junior heavyweight wrestling title 1969, light heavyweight 1970, heavyweight 1972-75; mem. Pan-Am Games team 1971, 1975; bronze medal 1970 Commonwealth Games; silver World Cup 1975; Canadian Intercollegiate champion 1971-74; gold 1974 Commonwealth Games; represented Canada 1973 World Student Games Moscow; alternate Canadian Greco-Roman team 1976 Olympics; pro football Ottawa Rough Riders 1977; *res.* Ottawa, Ont.

PIOTROWSKI, Irene (track); *b.* 9 Jul 1941, Skaudvile, Lithuania; *given name:* Irena Macijauskas; *div.* Heinz Piotrowski; U of British Columbia; teacher; won B.C. cross-country and set Canadian 100yd record 1963; won indoor 880yd 1964 finishing second to Abby Hoffman in 2:15.9; same year set Canadian, world record 11.4 for 100m and competed Tokyo Olympics; also set world indoor 300yd, 300m records; silver 100yd, bronze 220yd 1966 Commonwealth Games; five firsts, set Canadian 220yd 23.5 mark B.C. vs Oregon meet; silver, bronze 1967 Winnipeg Pan-Am Games; Canadian record 11.3 100m 1968 Mexico Olympics; Yukon Flour Packing title 1974 backpacking 500lbs 100ft, 600lbs 50ft; carried 342lbs 50ft 1975 Powell River Sea Festival; women's 1974 European tour manager; best times record 100yd 10.4, 100m 11.3; *res.* Vancouver, B.C.

PIRNIE, Bruce (track and field); *b.* 20 Sep 1942, Boston, Mass.; *m.* Karen Hayton; *children:* Elizabeth, Catherine; Yankton College, B.A., South Dakota State U; track coach; college all-conference track, football; all-league defensive end St. Vital Bulldogs, Canadian senior champions 1968; in shot put represented Canada vs Norway 1970, Italy 1971; co-captained 1972 Olympic team placing 17th overall; silver medal Pan-Pacific

Games 1973; bronze Commonwealth Games 1974; gold Pan-Am Games 1975; five times Canadian indoor, outdoor shot put champion; mem. 1976 Montreal Games team; *res.* Winnipeg, Man.

PITRE, Didier (hockey, lacrosse); *b.* 1884, Sault Ste. Marie, Ont.; *d.* 29 Jul 1934, Sault Ste. Marie, Mich.; pro defenceman with Nationals of Federal Amateur Hockey League; played with Jack Laviolette in international pro league, pair teamed on defence with Shamrocks 1908; with Lester Patrick's Edmonton team 1909; first player signed when Laviolette formed Montreal Canadiens 1909-10 and remained with that club until 1923 retirement except for 1913-14 season when he played with Vancouver; moved to right wing 1911, teamed with Laviolette, Newsy Lalonde to form a top line which led Canadiens to 1915-16 Stanley Cup, team became known as Flying Frenchmen; most productive season 1915 when he scored 30 goals; in 19 seasons played in 282 games scoring 240 goals, plus 14 goals in 27 playoff games; lacrosse player with variety of teams; nickname Cannonball; mem. Canadian Lacrosse, Hockey Halls of Fame.

PLANTE, Jacques (hockey); *b.* 17 Jan 1929, Mt. Carmel, Que.; *m.* Jacqueline; *children:* Michel (*d.*), Richard; minor hockey Shawinigan Falls Que., junior Quebec City; minor pro Montreal Royals (QHL), Buffalo (AHL); he starred in goal Montreal Canadiens 1952-63; with NY Rangers 1963-65, St. Louis Blues 1968-70, Toronto Maple Leafs 1970-73, Boston Bruins 1973, Edmonton (WHA) 1974-75; coach Quebec Nordiques (WHA) 1973-74; Hart Trophy (MVP) 1962, seven times Vezina Trophy, including five in succession 1956-60; three times first team, four times second team NHL all-star;

revolutionized netminding methods; pioneered modern-day goaler's masks; Montreal junior league commissioner; assistant coach California Seals 1967-68; led Quebec minor pro baseball league hitters several seasons; *res.* Switzerland.

PLOEN, Ken (football); *b.* 3 Jun 1935, Lost Nation, Iowa; *m.* Janet Newcomer; *children:* Kendra, Douglas, Carol; U of Iowa, B.S.; radio retail marketing manager; all-American at Iowa, in 1957 Rose Bowl game; Winnipeg Blue Bombers 1957-67; as defensive back 1959 established club interception record with 10; as quarterback completed 1,084 of 1,916 passes for 16,470yds 119 TDs and 56.6 completion avg; 1962 completion avg. 65.8 with 137 of 208 passes; 106 intercepted passes during 11-year career; shares CFL record for longest completed pass-109yds to Ken Nielsen 1965; three times WFC all-star; appeared in six Grey Cup finals, four winners; quarterbacked West to 9-3 all-star victory over East 1958; mem. Canadian Football Hall of Fame; *res.* Winnipeg, Man.

PLUMMER, Reg (field hockey); *b.* 6 Aug 1953, Sudbury, Ont.; *given name:* Reginald Frederick; Nepean HS, Carleton U, U of British Columbia, B.Sc.; student; three seasons with Ottawa; 1973 toured England, Wales with Canadian national team; toured N.Z., Argentina, Chile with 1974 Canadian team; silver medal 1975 Pan-Am Games team; toured England, Germany, Holland and represented Canada in 1976 Montreal Olympics; MVP Lahr Germany international tournament 1976; *res.* Vancouver, B.C.

POCE, Paul (track); *b.* 19 Sep 1929, Toronto, Ont.; *given name:* Paul Francis; *m.* Ethel McKnight; Central Tech, U of Toronto; as distance runner competed three, six miles, cross-country throughout Ontario, Buffalo, Detroit, won several provincial honors in early 60s; coach Canadian team 1966, 1970 Commonwealth Games, 1967, 1975 Pan-Am Games, 1972, 1976 Olympic Games; coach Canadian teams 1968 Scandinavia, 1971 Italy, 1974 European tour; *res.* Toronto, Ont.

POLLOCK, Sam (hockey); *b.* 15 Dec 1925, Montreal, Que.; *m.* Mimi; *children:* Rachel, Sammy Jr., Mary; coached junior Canadiens 1947-53; general manager Hull-Ottawa Canadiens (EPHL) 1959-62; general manager Montreal Canadiens since 1965; won eight Stanley Cups; general manager Team Canada 1976; Montreal sportsman of year 1976; *res.* Montreal, Que.

PORTER, Lewis (football); *b.* 3 Jul 1947, Clarksdale, Miss.; *m.* Christine Hendrix; *children:* Patricia; Connie; Southern U, B.A.; real estate agent; 29th among running backs in US HS; MVP Mississippi 1965; all-conference three years, all-American twice; Denver Broncos 1969, Kansas City Chiefs 1970-71; joined Hamilton Tiger-Cats during 1971 season; as cornerback was all-Canadian 1973, all-Eastern 1975; returned kick-off 98yds for TD 1972; *res.* Hamilton, Ont.

PORTER, Muriel (curling); *b.* 1903, Toronto, Ont.; *given name:* Muriel Kathleen Steen; *m.* Dr. Alvin B. Porter *(d.);* *children:* Robert Thomas, Charles Beverly; Dauphin CI, U of British Columbia; teacher; organized Vancouver Ladies Curling Club 1948, pres. two years; helped organize B.C. Ladies Curling Association 1950; gold medal best HS female athlete; mem. Canadian Curling Hall of Fame; *res.* Vancouver, B.C.

POST, Sandra (golf); *b.* 4 Jun 1943, Oakville, Ont.; *div.* John Elliott; pro golfer; inspired by LPGA tournaments in Florida began playing golf at five, coached by father Cliff and Elmer Prieskorn; won Canadian junior 1964-66, Ontario junior three times, Ontario Open, South Atlantic once each; turned pro 1968; 1968 LPGA championship Sutton Mass., beat Kathy Whitworth in playoff; LPGA rookie of year 1968; won Colgate Far East tournament 1974, 10th LPGA ranking; hole-in-one 1968 at Cypress Creek Club Boynton Fla.; nickname Post-O; *res.* Boynton, Fla.

POTVIN, Denis (hockey); *b.* 29 Oct 1953, Hull, Que.; *given name:* Denis Charles; *m.* Debbie Taylor; Rideau HS; junior hockey with Ottawa 67's at 14; from Overbrook Minor Hockey Association to six years in junior, twice OHA junior A Max Kaminsky Trophy as top defenceman; first choice NY Islanders and first pick overall 1973 amateur draft; Calder Memorial Trophy NHL rookie of year 1974; James Norris Memorial Trophy as top NHL defenceman 1976; twice first team all-star; through 1976-77 NHL record shows 314 regular season games, 94 goals, 214 assists, 308 points, 483 penalty minutes, plus 42 playoff games, 16 goals, 27 assists for 43 points, 82 penalty minutes; in Team Canada's Canada Cup 1976 victory; with brother Jean stages annual golf tournament at Outaouais Golf Club to raise funds for student athletes; *res.* Vanier, Ont.

POTVIN, Jean (hockey); *b.* 25 Mar 1949, Hull, Que.; *given name:* Jean Rene; *m.* Lorraine Paluck; La Salle Academy, Rideau HS, U of Ottawa; midget A in Overbrook organization at 14; two seasons with Hull Hawks in Central Junior A league, two months with Canadian national team, joined Ottawa 67's for two seasons; turned pro Springfield (AHL) 1969-70; four games with Los Angeles Kings then spent balance of season 1970-71 with Springfield; started 1971-72 season with LA then was traded with Bill Flett, Ed Joyal, Ross Lonsberry to Philadelphia for Bill Lesuk, Jim Johnson, Serge Bernier 1972; traded to NY Islanders 1973 with Glen Irwin for Terry Crisp to link forces on blueline with brother Denis; through 1976-77 NHL record shows 425 regular season games with 50 goals, 169 assists for 219 points, 324 penalty minutes, plus 39 playoff games, two goals, nine assists for 11 points, 17 penalty minutes; with brother Denis stages annual Outaouais Golf Club tournament to help raise funds for student athletes; *res.* Vanier, Ont.

POUND, Richard (swimming); *b.* 22 Mar 1942, St. Catharines, Ont.; *given name:* Richard William Duncan; *m.* Mary Sherrill Owen; *children:* William Trevor Whitley, Duncan Robert Fraser, Megan Christy; McGill U, B.Comm., B.C.L., Sir George Williams U, B.A.; lawyer; four times Canadian freestyle (FS), once Canadian butterfly, three times Canadian relay champion; Canadian records in 40, 50, 100, 110, 200yd, 100m FS; six times provincial FS champion holding records in 40, 50, 100, 200, 220yd, 100, 200m; intercollegiate FS champion five years holding records in 50, 100, 200, 220yds; represented Canada 1959 Chicago Pan-Am Games; sixth 100m FS 1960 Rome Olympics, fourth 400m medley relay; gold 110yd FS in record 55.8 1962 Commonwealth Games, silver medals 880yd FS relay, 440yd FS relay, bronze 440yd medley relay; pres. Canadian Olympic Association 1977; mem. Canadian Swimming, Sports Federation of Canada Halls of Fame; *res.* Montreal, Que.

POWER, Dale (tennis); *b.* 2 Oct 1949, Toronto, Ont.; *given name:* Dale Thomas; *m.* Joan Kathryn Westman; Oklahoma City U; tennis pro; Canadian boys-18 Closed title 1967; same year signed first Ontario Hockey Association junior A contract with St. Catharines; traded for Dick Redmond to Peterborough Petes 1968; fifth in first universal draft by Montreal Canadiens 1969; OCU tennis scholarship 1970; played for Canada in 1972 Davis Cup tie vs Mexico; returned to hockey as pro with Fort Wayne Komets (IHL); retired following one season to concentrate on tennis 1974; in Canada's top 10 singles players since 1968; Canadian men's doubles champion 1973; top men's singles player on 1975 Rothman's Summer Grand Prix tour; represented Canada 1976 Davis Cup play; *res.* Toronto, Ont.

PRATT, Babe (hockey); *b.* 7 Jan 1916, Stoney Mountain, Man.; *given name:* Walter; public relations assistant Vancouver Canucks; during 26 years of hockey from juvenile to Stanley Cup was mem. of 15 championship teams; with Elmwood Maple Leafs won Manitoba midget, juvenile titles; with Kenora juniors won Manitoba title; turned pro with Philadelphia in Rangers' farm system then moved to Rangers as defenceman 1935-36 until traded to Toronto Maple Leafs 1942-43; with Leafs through 1945-46 then closed NHL career with Boston 1946-47; in 12 NHL seasons appeared in 517 games scoring 83 goals, 209 assists, 292 points, plus 64 playoff games, 12 goals, 17 assists, 29 points; on leaving NHL played with Hershey, New Westminster, Tacoma; Hart Trophy as NHL MVP 1944, mem. first, second all-star teams once each; with 1940 NY Stanley Cup champions, 1942 Prince of Wales Trophy winners; mem. Hockey Hall of Fame; *res.* Vancouver, B.C.

PRESTON, Ken (football); *b.* 29 Oct 1917, Portland, Ont.; *m.* Dorothy Barber; *children:* William, Douglas, Richard, Donna; Queen's U, B.Comm.; general manager Saskatchewan Roughriders; football Queen's 1936-39; turned pro Sask. 1940; Winnipeg Blue Bombers 1941 playing in Grey Cup victory; Ottawa Rough Riders 1945 then back to Sask. 1946-48; Roughrider general manager 1958; *res.* Regina, Sask.

PRIESTLEY, Gladys (swimming); *b.* 17 Jun 1938, Montreal, Que.; *given name:* Gladys Jean; *m.* Ross Watson; *children:* Ray Allan, Lori Anne; Canadian freestyle (FS), relay titles in record times 1950-58; represented Canada 1952 (silver medal FS, medley relay), 1956 Olympics; silver 400m FS 1954, silver relay 1958 British Empire Games; FS finalist 1955 Pan-Am Games; *res.* Arundel, Que.

PRIESTNER, Cathy (speedskating); *b.* 27 May 1956, Windsor, Ont.; *given name:* Catherine Ann; student; six times Canadian national champion; gold medal 400m, silver 500m 1971 Canada Games; silver 500m 1973 world sprints; bronze 500m 1974 world sprints; silver 500m, 1000m 1975 junior world; fifth overall world championships Assen Holland 1975 with silver 500m, bronze 1000m, 14th 1500m, 3000m; third overall 1975 world sprint championships Göteborg Sweden with gold 500m, fourth 1000m, sixth 500m, 1000m; silver 500m, sixth 1000m 1976 Innsbruck Olympics; Canadian open records 500m, 1000m; fastest 500m award three times; 1975 skater of year; 1975 Calgary athlete of year; Governor-General's silver medal 1976; *res.* Calgary, Alta.

PRIMEAU, Joe (hockey); *b.* 29 Jan 1906, Lindsay, Ont.; *m.* Helen Marie Meagher; *children:* Joe Jr., Bill, Bob, Anne, Richard;

St. Michael's College; hockey coach, businessman; centre with St. Michael's College juniors; Toronto Ravinas 1927 winning Canadian pro league scoring title; Maple Leafs 1928-1936; centred Kid Line with Charlie Conacher, Busher Jackson; twice runner-up NHL scoring race; Lady Byng Trophy 1932; second team all-star 1934; coach for 23 years, won Memorial, Allan and Stanley Cups; played on 1932 Stanley Cup champions; coached 1951 titlists; mem. Hockey, Canadian Sports Halls of Fame; *res.* Toronto, Ont.

PRIMROSE, John (trapshooting); *b.* 28 May 1942, Ottawa, Ont.; U of Alberta, B.P.E., Ph.D.; eight times mem. Canadian team world championships, title 1975; represented Canada 1968, 1972, 1976 Olympics; gold medal 1974 Commonwealth Games; Canadian doubles champion 1969 Pan-Am Games; mem. 1975 Pan-Am Games team, Benito Juarez Mexico championships; six times Canadian international style trap title; Canadian record 386x400 1968, 296x300 1970; mem. Edmonton Gun Club, director 1964-70; pres. Alberta International Style Trap Association 1972-74; director Shooting Federation of Canada 1973-75; chairman shooting technical committee 1978 Commonwealth Games Edmonton; founding committee mem. Alberta Federation of Shooting Sports; mem. Canadian Sports Hall of Fame; *res.* Edmonton, Alta.

PRIOR, Russ (weightlifting); *b.* 11 Jul 1949, Hamilton, Ont.; McMaster U, Carleton U; student; 16 Commonwealth, 56 Canadian records; holds all Canadian, Commonwealth standards in heavyweight, super heavyweight classes; gold medal 1970 Commonwealth Games heavyweight; ninth 1973 world championships; North American

champion 1974; gold Commonwealth heavyweight class with 352.5kg lift 1974; gold Pan-Am Games heavyweight with 365kg lift 1975; mem. Canadian 1976 Olympic team; set Canadian, Commonwealth record snatch 170kg 1977; *res.* Ottawa, Ont.

PRONOVOST, Marcel (hockey); *b.* 15 Jun 1930, St. Theophile du Lac, Que; *given name:* Joseph Rene Marcel; *m.* Cindy Lapierre; *children:* Michel, Brigitte, Leo; hockey coach; Windsor Spitfire juniors to pro Omaha (USHL) 1949-50; Detroit Red Wings in playoffs helping them win Stanley Cup same season; Indianapolis (AHL) 1950-51 remaining part of season before being recalled to Red Wings where he became defensive star for 14 seasons; dealt to Toronto Maple Leafs with Autry Erickson, Larry Jeffrey, Ed Joyal, Lowell MacDonald for Andy Bathgate, Billy Harris, Garry Jarrett May 1965; with Leafs through 1969-70 season then two more years Tulsa (CHL); coach Hull Que. juniors from 1975-76; in 19 NHL seasons played 1,206 regular season games, scoring 88 goals, 257 assists for 345 points and 851 penalty minutes, plus 134 playoff games, eight goals, 23 assists, 31 points and 104 penalty minutes; mem. eight Prince of Wales Trophy (league title) winners, five Stanley Cup winners; twice first, second team all-star; *res.* Ottawa, Ont.

PROULX, Rita (curling); *b.* 16 Jun 1919, Quebec City, Que.; *given name:* Rita Couture; *m.* Jean Noel Proulx; organized Province of Quebec Ladies Curling Association 1956; six-time provincial champion, twice runner-up; twice Quebec senior ladies title, once runner-up; second v.-pres. Canadian Ladies Curling Association 1976; mem. Canadian Curling Hall of Fame; *res.* Quebec City, Que.

PROVOST, Barry (curling); *b.* 15 Mar 1944, Ottawa, Ont.; *given name:* Barry Michael; *m.* Nancy Carol Jeffrey; *children:* James Warren; Beaver River HS, Gould Business College; marketing rep. insurance group; won North Eastern Alta. Schoolboy title 1963; joined Eldon Coombe rink Ottawa as lead winning seven consecutive Division One Ontario Curling Association titles; Ontario Consols title and Brier berth 1972; three Canadian Branch Royal Caledonian Curling Club Royal Victoria Jubilee titles; seven Red Anderson Memorial championships; won CBC Curling Classic 1972; won Whitby Dunlop 'spiel 1972; three times Ottawa Associated Canadian Travellers curler of year; rated one of Canada's outstanding leads and sweepers; *res.* Ottawa, Ont.

PUGH, Bob (football, hockey); *b.* 29 Oct 1928, Montreal, Que.; *given name:* Robert Wesley; *m.* Thora Doreen Sheppard; *children:* Paige, Stacey, Wesley, Corrie; Springfield College, B.Sc.; executive-director Canadian Intercollegiate Athletic Union; quarterbacked Verdun Bulldogs, Westmount Warriors, 1948 Dominion Intermediate champion HMCS Donnacona; senior fastball Verdun Crawford Park; junior B hockey Verdun Maple Leafs; director of athletics 14 years Macdonald College, head football coach 14 years, hockey coach 10 years; pres. Ottawa St. Lawrence Athletic Association six years; pres. CIAU two years; director Hockey Canada, Sports Federation of Canada; director school of sports administration Laurentian U; Chef de Mission 1973 World Student Games; with John McConachie played major role in elevating several intercollegiate sports to national championship status; *res.* Pakenham, Ont.

PUGH, Lionel (track and field); *b.* 1 Apr 1922, Wales; *given name:* David Lionel; *m.* Irene Samuel; *children:* Jane; U of Wales, B.A., U of Leeds, P.E.; associate professor, T&F coach UBC; represented Wales in javelin setting school records; colors in rugby, soccer, squash, boxing; captain boxing team; played first class rugby for Headingley and Swansea; national T&F coach Great Britain 1952-62; coach Oxford U T&F 1962-64; national T&F head coach Canada 1969-73; coach Nigerian Commonwealth Games team 1958, Canadian Commonwealth Games team 1970, Pan-Am Games team 1971, Olympic team 1972; wrote three T&F books; coach of 45 top international athletes in Britain, Canada; Air Canada Canadian coach of year 1973; *res.* Vancouver, B.C.

PUGLIESE, Dan (administrator); *b.* 7 May 1931, St. Catharines, Ont.; *given name:* Daniel Joseph; *sep.; children:* four; Linwell HS, McMaster U, B.A., B.P.H.E., Buffalo U, M.E.; pres. Sport Devco; college letters in football, basketball; several years executive administrator National Sports and Recreation Centre Ottawa; coached basketball, football, baseball, T&F at community, HS, university levels; designed numerous sports, recreation programs and facilities in Kitchener-Waterloo region and Ottawa; with Jim Rose wrote *Basketball for the New Coach; res.* Ottawa, Ont.

PULFORD, Bob (hockey); *b.* 31 Mar 1936, Newton Robinson, Ont.; *given name:* Robert Jesse; *m.* Roslyn McIlroy; McMaster U, B.A.; hockey coach; played Toronto Marlboros winning two successive Memorial Cups; pro with Toronto Maple Leafs 1956-70, Los Angeles Kings 1970-72; in 16 seasons as player appeared in 1,079 games scoring 281 goals, 362 assists for 643 points, 792 penalty minutes, plus 89 playoff games, 25 goals, 26 assists for 51 points, 126 penalty minutes; as coach Los Angeles Kings 1972-77 won 178, lost 150, tied 68 for .542 percentage, plus 11 playoff wins, 15 losses for .423 percentage; mem. four Stanley Cup winners; NHL coach of year 1974-75; coach Team USA 1976; mem. Brampton Canadian junior lacrosse champions, Weston CI football all-stars; *res.* Los Angeles, Calif.

PULFORD, Harvey (all-around); *b.* 22 Apr 1875, Toronto, Ont., *d.* 31 Oct 1940, Ottawa, Ont.; *given name:* Ernest Harvey; *m.* Jean Davison; *children:* Harvey P., Lawrence Moore; insurance salesman; HS championship hockey, football, paddling, lacrosse teams; prizes boxing, rowing, squash; mem. Ottawa Silver Seven 1893-1908 playing on three Stanley Cup winners; Ottawa Rough Riders backfielder 1893-1909 playing on four Canadian title teams; lacrosse with Capitals 1896-1900 winning Canadian titles 1897-1900; Eastern Canadian light heavyweight, heavyweight boxing titles 1896-98; Eastern Canadian double, single blade paddling champion 1898; mem. 1900 war canoe title crew; Canadian title St. Catharines, US title at National regatta; mem. team winning Hanlan Memorial, Canadian Henley, US International 1910; stroked Ottawa eight to 1911 English Henley semifinals; Ottawa squash title 1922-24; mem. Ottawa, Hockey Halls of Fame.

PULLEN, Tom (football); *b.* 3 Jan 1945, Ottawa, Ont.; *given name:* Thomas Robert; *m.* Judith Lynn O'Neil; *children:* Tracey-Lynn, Kevin Thomas; Glebe CI, U of Michigan, B.Sc., U of Ottawa; regional sales manager; junior hockey Ottawa Montagnards; provincial, city track meets in high jump, hurdles; Golden Ball basketball tournament with Glebe; *Journal* Trophy 1961 as Ottawa HS lineman of year; turned pro as tight end with Ottawa Rough Riders 1968; traded to Montreal 1970 and back to Ottawa 1972; closed eight-year CFL career with Toronto Argos 1975; coach Carleton U 1976; in seven-year span played on four Grey Cup winners; *res.* Ottawa, Ont.

PULLEN, Wayne (archery); *b.* 27 Feb 1945, St. Thomas, Ont.; *m.* Anne-Marie; *children:* Jason, Shannon; St. Thomas Tech.; machinist; Canadian men's title 1970, 1971, 1973; 41st for Canada 1972 Munich Olympics, 28th 1973 Grenoble world, 28th 1975 Switzerland world; mem. Ambassador Cup-winning team 1970; two gold in field events Orlando Fla. Championship of Americas 1973; Canadian record 1,200, field 1972, broke both 1974; FITA record Joliette 1973; only competitor to win Indian John trophy five times (shooting double field course of 60 targets); fifth 1975 pre-Olympics Montreal; *res.* Dorchester, Ont.

PURCELL, Jack (badminton); *b.* 24 Dec 1903, Guelph, Ont.; *m.* Helen Colson (*d.*); *children:* William, Nancy, Peter, Philip; Guelph CI; stockbroker; five consecutive Ontario singles titles, numerous men's, mixed doubles titles 1927-31; Canadian singles champion 1929, 1930; turned pro 1932, unbeaten world pro champion until 1945 retirement; runner-up to Bud Thomas for Canadian junior tennis title 1922; Canadian badminton player of half century 1950 CP poll; mem. Canadian Sports Hall of Fame; *res.* Toronto, Ont.

PYZER, Doug (football); *b.* 8 Oct 1923, Toronto, Ont.; *m.* Noreen; *children:* Jeannie, Douglas, Ruth Linda; U of Toronto; manager; Toronto Indians 1942, RCAF Hurricanes 1943-44, Toronto Indians 1945-46, Toronto Argos 1947, Toronto Beaches Indians 1948, Argos 1949, Edmonton Eskimos 1950, Argos 1951-53; played on two Grey Cup champions; player-coach Toronto Beaches senior A fastball 1949-55 winning championships twice; with Columbus Boys' Club Ontario bantam baseball champions 1938, Webber Machinery Ontario junior titlists 1940; firsts in 100yd, 220yd dashes Ontario RCAF track championships 1940-41, repeat RCAF Eastern Canadian championships 1943; mem. Toronto, Ontario midget hockey champions 1939; mem. Toronto, provincial intermediate A basketball champions 1950; *res.* Toronto, Ont.

QUILTY, Silver (football); *b.* 8 Feb 1891, Renfrew, Ont., *d.* 2 Dec 1976, Toronto, Ont.; *m.* Irene Boyle; *children:* John (*d.*), Helen (*d.*), Bernadine, Ken, Bob, Renfrew HS, U of Ottawa, B.A., McGill U; retired insurance executive, civil servant; HS rugby-football player; outside wing on U of O Senior Intercollegiate champions 1907; Ottawa Rough Riders 1913; college football McGill 1914; refereed intercollegiate, interprovincial football five years; coached Ottawa Rough Riders; pres. Canadian Amateur Hockey Association 1924-26; mem. Canadian Football, Ottawa, Canadian Sports Halls of Fame.

QUIRK, Wendy (swimming); *b.* 29 May 1959, Montreal, Que.; John Abbott CEGEP; student; eighth 400m freestyle (FS) national championships 1972; three seconds, two thirds 1973 championships; represented Canada 1974 Commonwealth Games, silver 400m FS; same year mem. Canadian champion 400m, 800m FS relay teams setting records in each; records 100m butterfy (1:04.69), 400m medley relay; toured New Zealand 1975 winning two gold; mem. 400m

record-setting FS medley relay team 1975
Canadian spring championships, Commonwealth mark of 4:24.42 in medley; five gold,
record 200m, 400m FS relays 1975 Canadian championships; silver 400m medley,
bronze 100m butterfly 1975 Pan-Am Games;
personal bests 1976 in 100m butterfly
1:01.54, 200m butterfly 2:13.68, 400m FS
4:19.81, 800m FS 8:57.07; represented Canada 1976 Montreal Olympics placing fifth
200m butterfly, sixth 100m butterfly, ninth
400m, 800m FS; Canadian records 100m,
200m butterfly, 200m FS relay 1:49.11,
200m medley relay 2:05.20; world ranking
1976, fifth 200m, sixth 100m butterfly, 16th
800m FS, 21st 400m FS; *res.* Pointe Claire,
Que.

RACINE, Moe (football); *b.* 14 Oct 1937,
Cornwall, Ont.; *given name:* Maurice Joseph;
m. Donna Donihee; *children:* Tom, Scott,
Lee Ann, Bruce; St. Lawrence HS; insurance
executive; tackle Ottawa Rough Riders 17
seasons; as placement kicker recorded 176
converts, 62 field goals; played in five Grey
Cup finals, four winners; four times EFC
all-star, once all-Canadian; Gil O. Julien
trophy 1962 as outstanding French Canadian
athlete, Cornwall outstanding athlete award;
honored by 'day' Oct 1974 when his jersey
No. 62 was retired; mem. Cornwall Hall of
Fame; *res.* Ottawa, Ont.

RAE, Al (basketball); *b.* 26 Dec 1932,
Weyburn, Sask.; *given name:* Allen Gordon;
m. Edna Beryl Bright; *children:* Allan Gordon William; Carleton U, B.A.; sport consultant; officiated 1964 Tokyo Olympics,
1965 Canadian women's championships Edmonton, 1966 Canadian men's Winnipeg,
CIAU finals Calgary, Indian Nationals
Bombay, Asian Games Bangkok Thailand,
1967 Pan-Am Games Winnipeg, World Student Games Tokyo, Asian men's finals Seoul
Korea, 1968 Japanese nationals Tokyo, Mexico Olympics, 1969 Asian men's Bangkok,

1970 Asian Youth Seoul, 1971 Pan-Am Games Cali Colombia, Canadian men's, women's nationals Vancouver, 1972 Munich Olympics, 1973 Asian men's Manila, CIAU Waterloo, 1974 Asian Games Teheran, Asian women's, CIAU Waterloo, 1975 European men's Belgrade, Pan-Am Games Mexico, CIAU Waterloo, 1976 Montreal Olympics; *res.* Ottawa, Ont.

RAINE, Al (skiing); *b.* 22 Oct 1941, Dauphin, Man.; *m.* Nancy Greene; *children:* Charles, William; Burnaby HS; ski development coordinator; coach national alpine ski team 1968-70; Canadian Ski Association program director 1970-73; *res.* Burnaby, B.C.

RANKIN, Frank (hockey); *b.* 1 Apr 1889, Stratford, Ont, *d.* 23 Jul, 1932, Toronto, Ont.; rover in seven-man hockey era; led Stratford juniors to three consecutive OHA titles; captained Eaton Athletic Association to Ontario titles 1910-11, 1911-12, lost Allan Cup to Winnipeg Victorias each time; with Toronto St. Mike's in OHA finals 1912-13, 1913-14, lost to Toronto R&AA each time; coached Toronto Granites to 1924 Olympic title Chamonix France; mem. Hockey Hall of Fame.

RANKINE, Scotty (track); *b.* 6 Jan 1909, Hamilton, Scotland; *given name:* Robert Scade; *m.* Edna May Hodgkiss; *children:* Ian, Lynne, Craig; Shakespeare Supplementary HS Scotland; retired deputy sheriff; twice won Canadian marathon titles; three times competed in Boston Marathon placing fourth, fifth, seventh; twice won US 15km title, once 20km; Canadian 5000m title to qualify for 1932 Olympics, reached 5000m finals; represented Canada 1936 Olympics but leg cramps at 7500m mark of 10 000m

race forced him out, silver six-mile, fourth three-mile 1934 British Empire Games London Eng.; silver six-mile, bronze three-mile 1938 British Empire Games Sydney Australia; CP poll Canadian male athlete of year 1935; Norton Crowe Memorial Trophy as Canada's outstanding amateur athlete 1937; *res.* Wasaga Beach, Ont.

RATELLE, Jean (hockey); *b.* 3 Oct 1940, Lac St. Jean, Que.; *given name:* Joseph Gilbert Yvon Jean; *m.* Nancy; *children:* three daughters; hockey player; left Guelph Junior Royals with teammate Rod Gilbert 1959-60 season; five seasons with Trois-Rivières, Kitchener-Waterloo (EPHL), Baltimore (AHL), then NY Rangers 1964-65; as baseball player in Senior Intercounty league attracted offers from Milwaukee Braves, Los Angeles Dodgers organizations; star centre with Rangers until dealt with Brad Park, Joe Zanussi to Boston for Phil Esposito, Carol Vadnais 1975; second team all-star centre once; Bill Masterton Memorial Trophy; Lester B. Pearson Trophy; WBZ radio's No. 1 star award; twice Lady Byng Trophy; through 1976-77 NHL seasons appeared in 1007 games scoring 400 goals, 601 assists, 1001 points, 230 penalty minutes, plus 91 playoff games, 22 goals, 53 assists, 72 points, 22 penalty minutes; *res.* Boston, Mass.

RATHGEB, Chuck (all-around); *b.* 2 Dec 1921, Trois-Rivières, Que.; *m.* Rosemary; Upper Canada College, U of Toronto; board chairman; toured England 1935 with Canadian Commonwealth cricket team; mem. 1950-51 team which climbed Mount Edith Cavell, Mount Robson; founding mem. Canadian Bobsled, Luge Association; competed 1959-61 world bobsled championships; organized, coached Canadian Olympic gold medal team Innsbruck Austria 1964; manager-driver Comstock auto racing team; with late Peter Ryan driving won first Canadian Grand Prix; twice won Shell Trans-Canada rally, three times Canadian Winter rally; first Canadian to campaign cars at Daytona, Sebring, LeMans in world class races, at 52 finished 10th 1973 Targa Florio road race Sicily; drove 1975 Trans-Sahara World Cup rally; founding mem., first pres. Balloon Club of Canada; entry Trans-Canada balloon race Calgary to Winnipeg; flew over Alps by balloon from Zurich to Milan 1967; entry London to Monte Carlo powerboat race 1972; won Canadian Handicap Gulfstream Park Fla. on Canada Day 1972; one of three Canadians to have taken the Big Six animals, lion, leopard, elephant, buffalo, rhino, tiger, in big game hunting; Canadian entry International Tuna championships; *res.* Toronto, Ont.

READ, Ken (skiing); *b.* 6 Nov 1955, Ann Arbor, Mich., *given name:* Kenneth John; U of Calgary; student; competed in Pontiac Cup 1970-72; won Swiss Romande region championship and competed in Europa Cup events 1972-73; eighth World Cup downhill Megève France 1975; Canadian downhill title, second Argentinian downhill championships 1975; won downhill Val-d'Isère 1975, Canadian downhill 1976, dual slalom titles, second combined Canadian championships; fifth downhill Innsbruck Olympics; *res.* Calgary, Alta.

REARDON, Ken (hockey); *b.* 1 Apr 1921, Winnipeg, Man.; *given name:* Kenneth Joseph; hockey executive; with Winnipeg under-12 champions, junior in Edmonton; signed by Montreal Canadiens prior to WW2; with Ottawa Commandos won Allan Cup 1943; played in Britain, Belgium; returned to Canadiens 1945-46, all-star defenceman; on one Stanley Cup winner; seven-year NHL record 341 league games, 26 goals, 96 assists, 122 points; in three all-star games; following retirement 1950 became executive Montreal Canadiens' organization; mem. Hockey Hall of Fame; *res.* Montreal, Que.

REAY, Billy (hockey); *b.* 21 Aug 1918, Winnipeg, Man.; *m.* Clare; *children:* Adele, Billy Jr.; hockey executive; unique among NHL coaches because he coached before he played; player-coach Quebec Aces 1943-44, guided Quebec senior hockey league team to Allan Cup winning every playoff series entered; four games with Detroit over two seasons then joined Montreal Canadiens, centre eight years; in 479 scheduled games scored 105 goals, 162 assists for 267 points, 202 penalty minutes; in 63 playoff games scored 13 goals, 16 assists for 29 points, 43 penalty minutes; retired following 1952-53 season, coached Victoria Cougars (WHL) two seasons, Seattle (WHL) one, Rochester (AHL) one before becoming Toronto Maple Leaf coach 1957-58; replaced by Punch Imlach early following season, joined Chicago organization and coached Sault Ste. Marie entry in EPHL one season, Buffalo (AHL) two seasons; 1963-77 guided Black Hawks leading team to 1967 Prince of Wales Trophy, Clarence Campbell Bowl 1971-73; in 15 NHL coaching campaigns had 532 wins, 366 losses, 170 ties for .578 percentage in regular season play, plus 57 wins, 60 losses for .487 in playoffs; *res.* Chicago, Ill.

REBHOLZ, Russ (football); *b.* 9 Nov 1908, Portage, Wisc.; *m.* June; *children:* Ted, Tom, Tim, Bonnie; U of Wisconsin, B.S., M.S.; retired teacher, coach; nickname Doss; three letters each in football, basketball at Wis-

Reid

consin; in East-West Shrine game 1932; coach for 1932 Winnipeg St. John's football team; threw what is believed longest pass in CFL history 1934, 68yds to Lynn Patrick who ran 10 more yds for a TD; five times all-Canadian; helped Winnipeg win first Grey Cup 1935; mem. Winnipeg Toiler basketball team 1933; coached HS, U of Wisconsin; mem. Canadian Football Hall of Fame; *res.* Portage, Wisc.

REED, George (football); *b.* 2 Oct 1939, Mississippi; *given name:* George Robert; *m.* Angelina; *children:* Keith, Vicky, Georgette; Washington State U, B.Ed.; sales promotion manager; established 44 CFL records; carried 3,245 times for all-pro record 16,115yds and all-pro 137 TDs; eleven 1,000-yd seasons for career avg. 4.97yds-per-carry; caught 300 passes for 2,772yds, three TDs; CFL all-star 11 times; Jeff Nicklin Memorial Trophy (WFC MVP) 1966; Canadian Schenley outstanding player award 1965, runner-up 1968, 1969; Tom Pate Memorial Trophy 1976; City of Regina, Province of Saskatchewan 'day' in his honor 1974; pres. Canadian Football League Players' Association; *res.* Regina, Sask.

REEVE, Ted (lacrosse, football); *b.* 6 Jan 1902, Toronto, Ont.; *given name:* Edward Henry; *m.* Alvern Florence Donaldson; *children:* Joseph, Susan; Kew Beach HS; sportswriter; nickname The Moaner; early football Toronto St. Aidan juniors, Argonauts; coach, player Toronto Beaches football club 1924-30; ORFU title 1927; Grey Cup victories 1927, 1930; four years lacrosse Brampton Excelsiors; won Mann Cup Brampton 1926, 1930, Oshawa 1928; coached Queen's U to three intercollegiate football titles 1933-38; Ontario, federal government

achievement awards; mem. Canadian Sports, Lacrosse, Football, Canadian News Halls of Fame; *res.* Toronto, Ont.

REID, Bobby (soccer, hockey, boxing); *b.* 13 Sep 1890, Hamilton, Scotland; *given name:* Robert John; soccer for Saskatoon Thistles 1914-15, 1919, twice city, league cups; 96th Highlanders boxing title; soccer for CNR Saskatoon 1920 winning Victory Cup; with Fifth Battalion soccer club 1921-26; joined NY Americans hockey organization, designed team jacket; returned to Saskatoon 1935, organized boxing training at YMCA and Navy barracks; coached-managed Ozzie Herlen to 1937 Saskatchewan lightweight, 1938 welterweight titles; secretary-treasurer Saskatoon Golden Gloves Boxing Club 1938-39; soccer with Theatricals club Saskatoon Mercantile League; coached, managed Saskatoon Thistles to 1936 provincial title losing Western title to Lethbridge 1-0; organized schoolboy soccer programs Mayfair, Westmount schools calling combined team Maymount and winning two titles 1937, runner-up to Saskatchewan Shield 1938; trainer Saskatoon Hearts soccer club early 40s; coach, trainer Legion soccer club 1947-48; coach, trainer Saskatoon Ahepa soccer club 1949-50 winning provincial title 1949, runner-up 1950; with Legion club which won Saskatchewan Shield by default 1951; trainer Gems' girls fastball team which won Western title, represented Canada 1954 Little World Series; trainer Saskatoon Commodores baseball team 1958-74; *res.* Saskatoon, Sask.

REID, Robert (golf); *b.* 10 Mar 1917, Swift Current, Sask.; *given name:* Robert Douglas; *m.* Eleanor Young; *children:* Bob, Gordon; U of Toronto; dentist; twice Canadian Intercollegiate golf title; five times Saskatchewan amateur champion; seven times mem. Willingdon Cup team; 1934 Sask. junior title, runner-up 1933; twice Sask. senior champion; pres. Sask. Golf Association 1955; pres. Sask. Seniors Golf Association 1976-77; *res.* Prince Albert, Sask.

REISER, Glenda (track); *b.* 16 Jun 1955, Ottawa, Ont.; U of Ottawa; student; Canadian native, open record 4:06.7 for 1500m 1972 Munich Olympics; three times Canadian champion 1500m; gold medal 1974 Commonwealth Games; *res.* Ottawa, Ont.

RENKEN, Brian (wrestling); *b.* 21 Jun 1955, Fort William, Ont.; Lakeview HS, U of Western Ontario; student; Canadian junior freestyle, Greco-Roman champion 74kg class (163lbs) 1974-75; mem. 1975 Canadian junior team world championships Bulgaria; mem. Canadian senior B team which toured Northern US 1974; Canada Winter Games freestyle champion 1975; Canadian Intercollegiate champion 1976; represented Canada in Greco-Roman at 1976 Montreal Olympics; UWO most valuable wrestler 1975-76; *res.* Thunder Bay, Ont.

RETI, Harvey (boxing); *b.* 1 Sep 1937, Paddock Wood, Sask.; *given name:* Harvey Neil; *m.* Mabel Martin; *children:* Douglas, Lawrence, Tyler, Debra Leigh; soldier; Canadian amateur welterweight title 1961; Canadian light welterweight title 1962-64; bronze medal 1962 Commonwealth Games; represented Canada 1964 Olympics; mem. Canadian Forces Sports Hall of Fame; *res.* Winnipeg, Man.

RICHARD, Henri (hockey); *b.* 29 Feb 1936, Montreal, Que.; *given name:* Joseph Henri; *m.* Lise Villiard; *children:* Michele, Gilles, Denis, France; sports columnist, club owner; scored 50 goals in single season as junior before joining Montreal Canadiens 1955 at 19; centred line with Maurice on right, Dickie Moore on left; with Habs 1955-75, retired holding club record for most seasons (20), most games (1,256); NHL record shows 1,256 games, 358 goals, 688 assists for 1,046 points, 928 penalty minutes, plus 180 playoff games, 49 goals, 80 assists for 129 points, 191 penalty minutes; on 11 Stanley Cup winners; once first team, three times second team all-star centre; scored first playoff hat-trick vs Toronto Maple Leafs 1967; tied playoff record for three assists one period vs Toronto Maple Leafs 1960; nickname Pocket Rocket; *res.* Montreal, Que.

RICHARD, Maurice (hockey); *b.* 4 Aug 1921, Montreal, Que.; *m.* Lucille; *children:* Huguette, Maurice Jr., Norman, Andre, Suzanne, Paul, Jean; fishing supply company owner; with Verdun juniors, Canadiens seniors; Canadiens (NHL) 1942-60; career total 544 goals in 978 games, plus 82 goals, 44 assists in 133 playoff contests; record 83 game-winning, 28 game-tieing goals; first to score 50 goals in 50 games 1944-45; record five goals, three assists Dec 1944; eight times first all-star team, six times second team; nickname Rocket; Hart Trophy (MVP) 1947; never won league scoring title; captain Canadiens several seasons, won eight Stanley Cups; suspension from playoffs for striking official triggered Montreal Forum riot; coached Quebec Nordiques WHA; CP poll male athlete of year three times; Lou Marsh Trophy 1957; mem. Hockey, Canadian Sports Hall of Fame; *res.* Montreal, Que.

RICHARDSON, Arnold (curling); *b.* 2 Oct 1928, Estevan, Sask.; *given name:* Arnold Wellington; *m.* Edna Shirley Fleming; *children:* Shelley Joanne, Kimbal Brian, Laurie

Susan, Nancy Anne; carpenter; played third on Richardson family rink with cousins Ernie, Garnet and Wes; best known foursome in Canadian curling history winning unprecedented four Briers, four world championships (Scotch Cup) 1959-63; mem. Sask. Sports, Canadian Curling, Canadian Sports Halls of Fame; *res.* Regina, Sask.

RICHARDSON, Blair (boxing); *b.* 1940, South Bar, N.S., *d.* 5 Mar 1971, Boston, Mass.; Canadian, British Empire middleweight titles, twice vs Gomeo Brennan of the Bahamas for the latter in 1965, lost the first and won the second; death from brain tumor; mem. Canadian Boxing Hall of Fame.

RICHARDSON, Ernie (curling); *b.* 4 Aug 1931, Stoughton, Sask.; *div.; children:* three; owner electrical wholesale-retail business; won five Saskatchewan titles, record four Briers and world championships; won CBC Cross Canada, Calgary Masters, numerous car, cash 'spiels; wrote several books on curling; mem. Canadian Curling, Sask., Canadian Sports Halls of Fame; *res.* Regina, Sask.

RICHARDSON, George (hockey); *b.* 1880s, Kingston, Ont., *d.* 9 Feb 1916, France; mem. Queen's U team which won 1909 CAHA senior title; OHA senior finals with 14th Regiment team 1906-07; won Allan Cup with Queen's 1909; killed in action in France; George Richardson Memorial Stadium is home of Queen's Golden Gaels Kingston; mem. Hockey Hall of Fame.

RICHMAN, Ruby (basketball); *b.* 22 Sep 1934, Toronto, Ont.; *given name:* Reuben; *m.* Eileen; *children:* Alana, Jacqueline; Vaughan Rd CI, U of Toronto, B.A., Osgoode Hall, LL.B.; lawyer; captain Toronto District

HS champions 1952; seven years mem. Varsity Blues basketball team, captain 1956-59, champion 1958; player-coach Canadian Maccabiah Games teams Tel Aviv 1961, 1965, 1969, 1973 (bronze medal), Sao Paulo Brazil 1966, Olympics 1964, 1968, 1972, Pan-Am Games 1967; player-coach Canadian senior men's champions 1963-64; mem. three Ontario junior softball titlists, two Toronto senior titlists, one Ontario junior baseball titlist, two Toronto junior champions; captain Ontario midget, juvenile, junior B hockey champions; pres. Basketball Ontario; outstanding all-around athlete U of T; W.A. Potter Trophy U of T Blues MVP 1958; executive-director Canadian Maccabiah Games Assoc., director CABA; *res.* Willowdale, Ont.

RIDD, Carl (basketball); *b.* 17 Aug 1929, Winnipeg, Man.; *m.* Beverley Tozer; *children:* Laurel, Brian, Karen; U of Manitoba, B.A., M.A., B.D., Ph.D.; university professor, United Church minister; on eight consecutive Manitoba champion basketball teams 1948-55, all-star 1950-55; on three Western Canada title teams (U of M Bisons 1950, Varsity Grads 1952, Winnipeg Paulins 1954); latter team won Canadian title; mem. 1952 Helsinki Olympic team; second all-star Canadian world tournament team Rio de Janeiro 1954; 1949-50 fourth highest college basketball scorer North America; *res.* Winnipeg, Man.

RIGNEY, Frank (football); *b.* 4 Sep 1936, East St. Louis, Ill.; *given name:* Frank Joseph; *div.; children:* Mitchell Frank, Lisa Karen, Kathy Dawn; U of Iowa, B.A.; investment broker, golf club distributor, TV commentator; played in North-South, Senior Bowl games, Rose Bowl 1957; third draft choice Philadelphia Eagles; joined Winnipeg

Blue Bombers 1958 playing in five Grey Cup finals, four winners; seven times all-pro; Beckett-DeMarco Trophy twice; Schenley defensive player of year 1961; since 1969 served as CBC TV football commentator; *res.* North Vancouver, B.C.

RILEY, Con (rowing); *b.* 1875, Ontario, *d.* 1950, Winnipeg, Man.; *given name:* Conrad Stephenson; *m.* Jean Isabel Culver; *children:* six sons, two daughters; director Hudson's Bay Co.; Winnipeg Rowing Club 1892-1929 as rower, coach, official; WRC pres. 1911, honorary pres. 1929; won 1910 Steward's Challenge Cup in fours as stroke of Winnipeg crew Royal Henley regatta; at Peoria Ill. 1912 led 14 WRC rowers to seven North American titles (eights, fours, senior, intermediate doubles, singles); last race at age 70; mem. Canadian Sports, Winnipeg Sports Halls of Fame.

RIZAK, Gene (basketball); *b.* 27 Aug 1938, Windsor, Ont.; *m.* Claire Anna Best; *children:* John, Ana, Joe, Susan, Samantha; Walkerville CI, Assumption College, B.A., McMaster U, B.P.E.; athletic director, basketball coach, assistant professor; all-star with Windsor HS champions 1957; with Assumption 1957-60, Ontario Intercollegiate title 1959, co-champions 1958; led league scorers, set record 44 points one game vs U of T, North American record 26 of 28 free throws; averaged 25 points per game, led league scorers McMaster 1960-61; with Tillsonburg Livingstons, later London Fredericksons, won Eastern Canadian title 1961-62; Montreal Yvon Coutu Huskies 1962-64 winning 1962 Eastern Canadian; UBC 1964-65; three Canadian titles 1965-67; Art Willoughby Trophy, Vancouver men's league rookie of year 1965; mem. Canadian national team 1967 Pan-Am

Games; Vancouver White Spots 1968 Canadian finalists; coached HS 1960-67, Simon Fraser 1968-70, Regina from 1970; varied administrative roles SABA; pitched two seasons London Senior Intercounty Baseball League; *res.* Regina, Sask.

ROBERTS, Gordon (hockey); *b.* 5 Sep 1891, Montreal, Que., *d.* 2 Sep 1966; McGill U, M.D.; physician; Ottawa Senators (NHA) 1910, Montreal Wanderers (NHA) 1911-16; Vancouver Millionaires 1917 setting PCHA record 43 goals in 23 games; Seattle Metropolitans (PCHA) 1918, sat out 1919, Vancouver 1920; scored 203 goals in 166 regular season games; twice scored six goals in single game, once scored five; mem. Hockey Hall of Fame.

ROBERTSON, Bruce (swimming); *b.* 27 Apr 1953, Vancouver, B.C.; *given name:* Bruce Richard; Prince of Wales HS, U of British Columbia; student; silver medal 100m butterfly (55.56), bronze 4x100 medley relay 1972 Munich Olympics; gold 100m butterfly (55.67), bronze 4x100 medley relay 1973 world championshps; gold 4x100 medley relay, 4x100 freestyle (FS) relay, silver 100m FS (53.67), 200m FS (1:57.22), bronze 100m butterfly (56.8) 1974 Commonwealth Games; bronze 4x200 FS relay, fourth 100m butterfly (56.31), 4x100 medley relay 1975 world championsips; silver 4x100 FS relay, 4x100 medley relay, 4x200 FS relay, bronze 100m butterfly (56.8), 100m FS (53.44) 1975 Pan-Am Games; mem. Canadian Sports Hall of Fame; mem. Canadian team 1976 Olympics; *res.* Vancouver, B.C.

ROBERTSON, Nancy (diving); *b.* 25 Dec 1949, Saskatoon, Sask.; *given name:* Nancy Jean; U of Manitoba; student; fourth 1967

Pan-Am Games 3m; eighth 10m, 13th 3m 1968 Mexico Olympics; silver 10m 1970 Commonwealth Games; gold 10m 1971 Pan-Am Games; seventh 10m 1972 Munich Olympics; *res.* Winnipeg, Man.

ROBERTSON, Sandy (all-around); *b.* 26 Feb 1923, Vancouver, B.C.; *given name:* Edward Alastair Sandy; *m.* Mary Patricia; *children:* Barbara Joyce, Bruce Richard, Carolyn Patricia; Kitsilano HS, U of British Columbia, B.Sc.; consulting engineer; baseball with Vancouver seniors 1939-46, Louisville Colonels, Durham Bulls 1946-47, Vancouver Capilanos 1947-53; basketball UBC Thunderbirds 1942-46, Canadian champion Vancouver Meralomas 1947, Vancouver Clover Leafs 1948-53, won four Canadian titles; soccer UBC 1946, Vancouver City, Pacific Coast League 1952; squash 1963-64 winning Vancouver City, B.C., Pacific Northwest titles; semifinalist Canadian senior doubles 1975-76; coach UBC, Pony, Babe Ruth, junior Pacific Coast baseball teams, Clover Leaf junior basketball; George Pringle Trophy, rookie of year UBC basketball 1943; MVP UBC basketball 1945; Vancouver athlete of year 1946; basketball MVP 1947-48; baseball MVP, all-star 1950; mem. Vancouver Baseball, B.C. Sports Halls of Fame; *res.* Vancouver, B.C.

ROBILLARD, Gene (football, tennis); *b.* 15 Jan 1929, Ottawa, Ont.; *given name:* Eugene Thomas; *m.* Virginia MacLean; *children:* Matthew Thomas, Timothy John; Ottawa Technical HS, McGill U, B.Sc.; HS teacher; represented Ottawa Tech in football, hockey, track and basketball during five-year period; 1947 Mayor of Ottawa Trophy as school's best athlete; Gerry Boucher Memorial Trophy as OHSAA best football player and Kinsmen Shield as OHSAA best hockey

player, only player to win both city awards; McGill quarterback intermediate football two years, senior football two years; three years varsity hockey; intermediate shot put champion 1950; intercollegiate all-star defensive back 1951; quarterbacked Ottawa Seconds in ORFU 1952 then turned pro with B.C. Lions during 1954 CFL season; twice Ottawa intermediate men's doubles tennis title, with Rick Marshall, Jacques Tamaro; intermediate men's singles title; Ottawa men's senior doubles with Murray Wiggins; Ottawa and Rideau Tennis club intermediate, senior singles, men's doubles and mixed doubles titles; *res.* Ottawa, Ont.

ROBINSON, Bill (football); *b.* 23 Apr 1951, Toronto, Ont.; *given name:* William Robert; *m.* Barbara-Jo MacNeil; Earl Haig HS, St. Mary's U, B.A., U of Western Ontario; executive-director Canadian Amateur Football Association; quarterbacked undefeated HS team 1968-69; runner-up Maritime Conference MVP 1970; Maritime MVP, conference titles 1971-73; won 1973 Canadian College Bowl vs McGill; all-star four consecutive years; at UWO won Western Bowl and College Bowl 1974; all-Canadian quarterback; George McCullah award as Western MVP; pro Ottawa Rough Riders 1975; mem. 1976 Grey Cup champions; *res.* Ottawa, Ont.

ROBINSON, Blondie (bowling); *b.* 3 Jan 1928, Kirkland Lake, Ont.; *given name:* Graydon Ormiston; *m.* Phyllis Jones; sheet metal mechanic; in five-pin led Intercounty League 1949-50 with 245; third in Canadian Bowling Association singles tournament 1946; with Ken Drury of Sarnia second in 1952 CBA doubles; averaged 265, rolled high triple of 1,066 (418) Regina 1953-54; in 10-pin 1962 rookie season avg. 189; seventh in first CPBA 10-pin tourney 1963; two 299 sanctioned games, three unsanctioned, two 290 sanctioned games, two unsanctioned; 745 sanctioned triple, 802 unsanctioned; rolled over 30 700s; Canadian all-events record for nine games with 1,941 1966; with Ray Mitchell mem. of team which set record 3,385 games; twice winner, three times runner-up provincial 700 tournament; three times winner Toronto 700 tourney; with Ray Mitchell winner Toronto scratch doubles; three times winner Toronto scratch all-events, twice city singles; winner Jim Brace Canadian all-stars tournament, runner-up twice; CPBA singles champion 1966; highlight of career 1969 when he topped a field of 25 to win world 10-pin title in Tokyo beating Thailand's Lenavat 379-373 in two game final; won Osaka Challenge tourney following Tokyo triumph but failed in world title defence at Copenhagen 1970; Toronto bowler of year; mem. Canadian Sports Hall of Fame; *res.* Weston, Ont.

ROBINSON, Bobby (track and field); *b.* 8 Apr 1888, Peterborough, Ont., *d.* 6 Jun 1974, Burlington, Ont.; *given name:* Melville Marks; *m.* Maribel Fair Hawkins; *children:* Edna Margaret; editor; organized first Empire (later Commonwealth) Games in Hamilton 1930; Canadian team manager 1934, 1938, Olympic team manager 1928, 1932; mem. AAU of C Hall of Fame.

ROBINSON, Larry (football); *b.* 18 Apr 1942, Calgary, Alta.; Mt. Royal College; quarterback Calgary Western Canada HS champions 1959; guided Mt. Royal Cougars to 1960 Western Canadian junior finals; Calgary Stampeders 1961-75, WFC rookie of year; twice won Dave Dryburgh Trophy as WFC scoring champion; three times WFC all-star; twice runner-up Schenley nominee;

CFL all-time scoring leader with nine TDs, 362 converts, 171 field goals, 101 singles for 1,030 points; fifty pass interceptions for 717yds, three TDs, returned fumble recoveries for 219yds; on one winner in three Grey Cup appearances.

ROBINSON, Tinker (track); *b.* 10 Oct 1956, Vancouver, B.C.; *given name:* Cynthia Gail; U of British Columbia; student; gold medal 200m, silver 100m 1973 Canada Summer Games; mem. Canadian junior team Bermuda, European tour 1974; Pan-Am Games 4x100m relay squad member 1975; *res.* Vancouver, B.C.

ROBITAILLE, Daniel (weightlifting); *b.* 11 Nov 1953, Val d'Or, Que.; *m.* Claudette Leblanc; U of Ottawa; student; Canadian junior featherweight title 1970; numerous Ontario junior, senior records; three bronze 1975 Mexico Pan-Am Games; Canadian 75kg class title 1977 with 282.5 overall lift; *res.* Ottawa, Ont.

ROBSON, Fred (speedskating); *b.* 1879, Toronto, Ont.; *d.* 1944, Toronto, Ont.; piano repairman; Toronto junior champion 1897; Ontario champion 1897-1902; at age 19 broke three world records; at 22 broke world marks in 220yd, 440yd hurdles, 60yd, 75yd sprints; at peak of career 1899-1916 held nine world records and shared mile mark of 2:41.2 with Philadelphia's Morris Wood; Canadian record for barrel jumping with 11 and running high jump of 4'2"; mem. Canadian Sports Hall of Fame.

ROCHON, Henri (tennis); *b.* 12 Mar 1924, Montreal, Que.; *given name:* Henri Denis; *m.* Yolande Belisle; *children:* Danielle, France; St. Viateur HS; insurance salesman; began playing tennis at six and entered first tournament at 11; won Quebec age-group titles, at 17 Quebec junior crown; won Canadian men's open singles 1949; mem. Canadian Davis Cup team 1946-53, 1955-56, captain 1956; with Dr. Breen Marian won Canadian senior men's doubles 1972; three years as teaching pro including year as resident pro Ville St. Laurent Indoor Tennis Club; *res.* Montreal, Que.

ROCK, Richard (track and field); *b.* 6 Nov 1957, Reading, Eng.; *given name:* Richard Oliver; Woburn CI, Southern Illinois U; student; won Scarborough SSAA, Toronto District IAA overall championships, set records four successive years; junior OFSSA 20m and long jump records, Canadian indoor midget long jump record; best personal performance 1976 10.4 for 100m, 25'10 ¾'' for long jump; Canadian junior long jump champion, fourth Canadian championships 1975; Olympic long jumper Montreal 1976; Missouri Valley Conference indoor long jump record 24'5'' 1976; *res.* Scarborough, Ont.

RODDEN, Mike (hockey, football); *b.* 24 Apr 1891, Mattawa, Ont.; *given name:* Michael James; *m.* Mildred Alice Wormith; *children:* William Bernard, Richard John; U of Ottawa HS, Queen's U, McGill U; retired sports editor; in football, hockey, soccer, lacrosse as player, coach, official, chronicler; HS football, four seasons Queen's, one McGill, all-star four times, each at a different position; 15 Tricolor letters, a record never equalled; hockey at Queen's, Haileybury, Toronto St. Pat's; coached Queen's football 1916; middle wing for Toronto Argos 1919 then coached Argos to 1920 Grey Cup final, lost to U of T; ORFU title 1921 coaching Parkdale Canoe Club, again 1922; guided Balmy Beach to 1924 Grey Cup final,

lost to Queen's; won Grey Cup 1928-29 as Hamilton coach; coached 42 football teams winning 27 league titles, two interscholastic titles, two of five Grey Cup appearances; coached Toronto de La Salle, St. Mary's, St. Pat's, U of T hockey; refereed 2,864 hockey games, 1,187 in NHL; mem. Canadian Football, Hockey Halls of Fame; *res.* Kingston, Ont.

ROGERS, Bruce (swimming); *b.* 4 Jun 1957, Toronto, Ont.; *given name:* Bruce Hibbert; U of Miami, U of Toronto; student; Canadian 200m butterfly title 1974-75 establishing Canadian records each time; competed 1973 Canada Games, 1974 Commonwealth Games, 1975 World Student Games, Pan-Am Games, 1976 Olympics; mem. touring swim team England 1975, Japan 1976; *res.* Mississauga, Ont.

ROGERS, Shotty (rowing); *b.* 1887, St. John's, Nfld., *d.* 1963, St. John's, Nfld.; *given name:* Levi; coxed more than 300 crews to victory; last victory 1962 at age 75; mem. Canadian Sports Hall of Fame.

ROLLICK, Bruce (badminton); *b.* 11 Apr 1943, Vancouver, B.C.; *given name:* Bruce Irwin Alexander; *m.* Judith Ellen Humber; *children:* Lisa Jane; U of British Columbia, B.Sc.; consulting actuary; began playing at 13 winning all age-group provincial junior honors; won Canadian men's open singles 1968, with wife Judi closed mixed doubles 1969, five times Canadian men's closed singles, with Rolf Patterson 1972 men's doubles, with Mimi Neilson 1977 mixed doubles; mem. four Thomas Cup teams, 1970 Commonwealth Games, 1972 China tour; coached junior players seven years; *res.* Vancouver, B.C.

ROLLICK, Judi (badminton); *b.* 17 Aug 1944, Seattle, Wash.; *given name:* Judith Ellen Humber; *m.* Bruce Rollick; *children:* Lisa Jane; Victoria HS; teacher; Canadian junior champion; won Canadian ladies' closed singles, mixed doubles once each and with Mimi Neilson ladies' closed doubles twice; twice mem. Uber Cup team; mem. China tour 1972; mem. Canadian Commonwealth Games teams three times; *res.* Vancouver, B.C.

ROOST, Ain (track and field); *b.* 5 Dec 1946, Upsala, Sweden; *m.* Dianne; *children:* Lindsey Melissa; U of Minnesota, Ph.D.; psychologist; fifth javelin 1966 Commonwealth Games; fourth discus 1974 Commonwealth Games; bronze discus 1971 Pan-Am Games; fifth discus 1975 Pan-Am Games; silver discus 1973 Pan-Pacific Games; competed 1972 Munich Olympics; Canadian discus title 1971-74; *res.* Evanston, Wyoming.

RORVIG, Ed (football); *b.* 24 May 1913, Binford, N.D.; *given name:* Edward Carlyl; *m.* Frances McQueen; *children:* Suzanne Caldarello, Paul Edward, Peter Gordon; U of North Dakota, B.Sc.; sales manager; turned pro Calgary Stampeders 1936; 1937 WFL all-star fullback, all-Canadian; *res.* Boonville, Mo.

ROSENFELD, Bobby (track); *b.* 28 Dec 1905, Russia, *d.* 14 Nov 1969, Toronto, Ont.; *given name:* Fanny; sportswriter; Canada's woman athlete of half century 1950 CP poll; silver medal 100m dash, gold 4x100 women's relay setting 1928 Amsterdam Olympics record 48.2; joint holder 11.00 100yd world record; broke world 220yd mark Toronto 1925 with 26.00 but not allowed when track found to be foot short; during 1925 Ontario ladies' T&F championships scored first in shot put, discus, running broad jump, 200yd dash, 100yd low hurdles and second in 100yd dash, javelin (all in one afternoon); 1924 Toronto grass courts tennis title; mem. Canadian Sports Hall of Fame.

ROSS, Art (hockey); *b.* 13 Jan 1886, Naughton, Ont., *d.* 5 Aug 1964, Boston, Mass.; *given name:* Arthur Howie; developed nets, pucks still in use in NHL; defenceman, played 14 years with Westmount (CAHL), Brandon (MHL), Kenora (MHL), Montreal Wanderers (ECAHA), Haileybury (NHA), Wanderers (NHA), Ottawa Senators (NHA); 85 goals in 167 games; best single season 1912 with 16 goals in 18 games; with Kenora 1907, Wanderers 1908 Stanley Cup winners; retired 1918 to referee; manager Hamilton Tigers then coach-manager Boston Bruins when they joined NHL 1924, won three Stanley Cups; Art Ross Trophy awarded to NHL scoring champion; mem. Hockey Hall of Fame.

ROSS, Earl (autosport); *b.* 4 Sep 1941, Charlottetown, P.E.I.; *given name:* Earl Seymour; *m.* Yvonne; *children:* three daughters; H.B. Beal Technical HS; auto mechanic, racing driver; raced stock cars as hobby at Delaware, Nilestown tracks; won 1972 Export A grand championship; competed in 21 NASCAR races 1974 and became first Canadian ever to win Grand National race, Old Dominion 500 at Martinsville Va.; second Michigan International Speedway Motor State 400, NASCAR Grand National rookie of year; Canadian Motorsport's man of year; *res.* Ailsa Craig, Ont.

ROSS, P.D. (rowing); *b.* 1 Jan 1858, Montreal, Que., *d.* 5 Jul 1949, Ottawa, Ont.; *given name:* Philip Dansken; *m.* Mary Littlejohn; McGill U; publisher; held Quebec single sculls title and twice stroked four-oared crews to Dominion championships; Stanley Cup trustee; mem. Hockey Hall of Fame.

ROUSSEAU, Bobby (hockey); *b.* 26 Jul 1940, Montreal, Que.; *given name:* Joseph Jean-Paul Robert; L'Ecole Casavant HS; played with St. Jean juniors at 15, later junior and senior with Hull-Ottawa; mem. 1960 Canadian Olympic silver medal team; in four junior seasons scored 150 goals; turned pro with Montreal, two games in Rochester (AHL) then joined Hull-Ottawa Canadians (EPHL) scoring 34 goals in 38 games; 12 goals in 14 playoff games; 1960-70 played right wing with Montreal Canadiens; became regular 1961-62, Calder Memorial Trophy as top rookie; with Minnesota 1970-71 and closed NHL career with NY Rangers 1971-75; one of first to use helmet; on four Stanley Cup winners; second team all-star 1966; twice scored 30 goals one season; in 15 NHL seasons played 942 games scoring 245 goals, 458 assists for 703 points, 359 penalty minutes, plus 128 playoff games scoring 27 goals, 57 assists for 84 points, 69 penalty minutes; five goals vs Detroit 1964; as baseball player, pitched no-hit game for St. Hyacinthe juniors; as golfer set Joliette Country Club competitive record 66; *res.* Montreal, Que.

ROWAN, Sheila (softball, curling); *b.* 22 Apr 1940, Young, Sask.; *given name:* Sheila Anne; stenographer; all-star with Saskatoon Imperials 1968 Canadian women's softball championships, won Canadian titles 1969-70; represented Canada world tournament Japan 1970; represented Sask. Canada Summer Games Halifax 1969; coach Saskatoon Baldwinettes two seasons, Canadian championships once; third with Vera Pezer rink winning consecutive Canadian curling

titles 1971-73; defeated 1972 Canadian men's champion Orest Meleschuk in televised match; mem. Canadian Curling Hall of Fame; *res.* Saskatoon, Sask.

ROWLAND, Gordie (football); *b.* 1 Sep 1930, Montreal, Que.; *m.* Joan Lloyd; *children:* Jill, Janet, Gary; William Pawson HS; salesman; football with Montreal Orfuns intermediates and soccer for Stelco seniors, Dominion champions 1954; Winnipeg Blue Bombers 1954-63; appeared in five Grey Cup games, four winners; five times WFC all-star defensive halfback; leading Canadian in WFC 1958, Schenley runner-up; returned career total 324 punts for 2,395yds, 7.8 avg.; returned 215 kickoffs for 9,546yds; intercepted 31 passes, four for TDs; on U of Manitoba coaching staff four years, guided Bisons to Vanier Cup 1970; *res.* Winnipeg, Man.

ROY, Aldo (weightlifting); *b.* 22 Mar 1942, Sudbury, Ont.; *given name:* Aldo Robert Joseph; Laurentian U, B.A., U of Ottawa, M.A.; HS history department head; 1960 Canadian senior title at 17, three Canadian senior and open records; represented Canada 1962 Commonwealth Games Perth Australia; eighth 1963 Pan-Am Games Brazil; second 1964 Olympic trials but not named to team; 13th Iran world championships 1965; fifth 1967 Pan-Am Games; broke all personal records, 15th in world 181lb class 1968 Olympics; turned to coaching 1972; TV colorcaster 1976 Olympics; *res.* Ottawa, Ont.

RUBENSTEIN, Louis (figure skating); *b.* 23 Sep 1861, Montreal, Que.; *d.* 3 Jan 1931, Montreal, Que.; partner, silverplaters and manufacturers; Montreal 1878 skating title at 17; Canadian title 1882, scored 45 of possible 48 points; US title 1885, 1888,

1889; world skating title 1890 St. Petersburg Russia; pres. International Skating Union of America 1907-09; monument to his memory Montreal 1939; mem. Canadian Sports Hall of Fame.

RUSSEL, Blair (hockey); *b.* 17 Sep 1880, Montreal, Que., *d.* 7 Dec 1961, Montreal, Que.; all-star with Montreal Victorias scoring 110 goals in 67 games; once seven goals in single game, also a six and five-goal game; mem. Hockey Hall of Fame.

RUSSELL, Ernest (hockey); *b.* 21 Oct 1883, Montreal, Que., *d.* 23 Feb 1963, Montreal, Que.; captain Sterling hockey juniors and Montreal AAA football juniors, Dominion title same year; senior hockey with Winged Wheelers 1905; Montreal Wanderers 1906-14; scored 180 goals in 98 games, three-goal hat-tricks in five successive games, 42 goals in nine games 1907; on four Stanley Cup winners; two league scoring titles, once scored in 10 consecutive games; mem. Hockey Hall of Fame.

RUSSELL, Ernestine (gymnastics); *b.* 10 Jun 1938, Windsor, Ont.; *div.* John Carter; *m.* Jim Weaver; *children:* Kelly; Kennedy CI, Michigan State U, B.S., Clarion State College; coach; Canadian women's gymnastics champion 1955-60; four times North American champion; represented Canada 1956, 1960 Olympics; five gold medals 1958 Pan-Am Games; competed 1959 world games; Velma Springstead Trophy (Canada's outstanding female athlete) 1955-57; wrote several gymnastics books; coach US women's gym team World University Games 1977; mem. AAU of C Hall of Fame; *res.* Shippenville, Pa.

RUTHOWSKY, Dave (softball); *b.* 10 May 1948, Kingston, Ont.; *given name:* David Carl; *m.* Wendy Lorraine Craig; *children:* Craig Steven; Kingston HS, Ontario Forest TS, Camosun College; carpenter; pitched Odessa Clippers to Ontario Amateur Softball Association juvenile A title 1966, Peterborough Heating to OASA junior A 1968-69, Victoria Bate to BSASA senior A titles 1972-75; latter co-holders 1975 world championships New Zealand; all-star 1973 Canadian finals Hull Que., 1974 Canadian finals Victoria, top pitcher 1974 B.C. championships; Peterborough junior athlete of year 1969; *res.* Victoria, B.C.

RUTTAN, Jack (hockey); *b.* 5 Apr 1889, Winnipeg, Man., *d.* 7 Jan 1973, Winnipeg, Man.; with Armstrong's Point team won Winnipeg juvenile title 1905-06; with Rustlers for another juvenile title; with St. John's College won 1907-08 Manitoba University HL title; Manitoba Varsity team won 1909-10 Winnipeg senior HL title; Winnipeg Hockey Club 1912-13, won league title, Allan Cup; coach Winnipeg seniors 1919-20, Manitoba U 1923; officiated Winnipeg Senior League 1920-22; mem. Hockey Hall of Fame.

RYAN, Joe (football); *b.* 1900, Starbuck, Man.; *given name:* Joseph Bernard; *m.* Helen Katherine Killeen; *children:* Mary Jo, Kathleen, James Timothy, Cynthia Ann; retired securities officer, football administrator; promoted rugby football in Winnipeg 1931-35; amalgamated Winnipeg Rugby, St. John's Club 1932; imported Carl Cronin from Notre Dame as player-coach and won 1933 title, Grey Cup (first for West) 1935; developed intercity league 1936-40; managed Winnipeg club seven of first 11 years of operation winning six league titles, three

Grey Cups; 14 years mem. CRU rules committee; with Lew Hayman, Eric Cradock, Leo Dandurand helped establish Montreal Alouettes; scouted talent like Frank Filchock, Joey Pal, Pete Thodos, Rod Pantages to help Als win 1949 Grey Cup; general manager Edmonton Eskimos five years; launched night football Winnipeg; hon. life mem. Winnipeg Football Club, Winnipeg FC Alumni Association; CRU plaque for service to football in Canada; mem. Canadian Football, Canadian Sports Halls of Fame; *res*. Victoria, B.C.

RYAN, Peter (autosport, skiing); *b*. 10 Jun 1940, Philadelphia, Pa., *d*. 2 Jul 1962, Paris, France; as teenager won major Quebec ski titles Taschereau, Ryan Cup, Quebec Kandahar; second to Buddy Werner in US Nationals; mem. national water-ski team, among top five two years; turned to auto racing, won Vanderbilt Cup, Canadian Grand Prix; while competing for Lotus factoy team at Reims France was injured, died in hospital.

RYAN, Tommy (bowling); *b*. 1882, Guelph, Ont., *d*. 19 Nov 1961, Toronto, Ont.; *m*. Ruth Robins; auctioneer, art gallery owner; invented five-pin bowling; opened Toronto's first bowling house 1905; founded Miss Toronto Beauty Contest; mem. Canadian Bowling, Sports Halls of Fame.

RYDER, Gus (swimming); *b*. 11 Jan 1899, Toronto, Ont.; *given name:* Augustus Joseph; *m*. Phyllis Hamilton; Parkdale CI; customs broker; junior hockey Auralee; football Exelsiors, Argos intermediates; rowed four years Argos; represented Canada four times internationally in handball; swam in several across-the-bay races Toronto; formed 700-mem. New Toronto (later Lakeshore) Swim Club; taught thousands of crippled children to swim; personally credited with 47 rescues from drowning; coached Marilyn Bell, Cliff Lumsdon; Canada's man of year 1955; US Presidental Sports Award 1975 from President Ford; many other honors; mem. Etobicoke, Toronto Playground, US Aquatic, Canadian Sports Halls of Fame; *res*. Toronto, Ont.

ST. GODARD, Emile (dogsledding); *b.* 1905, Quebec, *d.* 1948; dog breeder, trainer; gained fame in series of competitions vs Leonard Seppala; won 200-mile The Pas race 1925, 1926; beat Seppala Quebec City 1927; pair met annually at Quebec City over next six years with St. Godard winning four times, Seppala twice; pair also competed The Pas, Alaska, Minnesota, Laconia, North Conway with St. Godard winning majority of encounters; last meeting 1932 Lake Placid as Olympic demonstration sport following which Seppala, 54, conceded St. Godard's superiority; at peak 1925-35 St. Godard and team raced 1,500 miles per season; noted for kindness and concern for his dogs; when lead dog Toby was no longer up to rigors of racing, St. Godard retired from competition; mem. Canadian Sports Hall of Fame.

SALMOND, Gary (track and field); *b.* 28 Apr 1947, Vancouver, B.C.; *given name:* Garfield Donald; Burnaby South HS; Vancouver, District hammer championship in HS; Canadian record 67.30m (220'9½'') since broken by Murray Keating with 67.46; represented Canada 1967 Pan-Am Games,

1970 Commonwealth Games, 1969 Pacific Conference team; five years Canadian hammer champion; *res.* New Westminster, B.C.

SAMIS, John (badminton); *b.* 15 Nov 1918, Swift Current, Sask.; *m.* Grace Peggy; *children:* Page, Julie; investment dealer; seven times Vancouver City champion, provincial titlist; three times national singles champion; fourth in world; mem. Canada's first international Thomas Cup team; at 15 youngest to win Canadian senior singles title, a standing record; mem. B.C. Sports Hall of Fame; *res.* Vancouver, B.C.

SANDULO, Joey (boxing); *b.* 5 May 1931, Ottawa, Ont.; *given name:* Joseph Oleg; *m.* Mary Theresa Lewis; *children:* Patrick, Mary Jane, Kelly; Ottawa Technical HS; cartographer; began boxing 1946, won Ottawa Golden Gloves novice title; won 1947 Quebec Golden Gloves 106lb novice, Jack Dempsey Trophy; Ontario, Eastern Canadian, Canadian flyweight titles; youngest boxer to represent Canada in Olympics London 1948; 1949 Canadian Forces, B.C. bantam titles, represented Canada British Empire Games trials losing split decision in final to Lou Walters; with Gord Montagano operated boxing classes Ottawa 1950-53; started Ottawa RA fitness program 1959; launched Beaver Boxing Club 1974, pres. 1975; ring record shows five losses in 75 bouts; referee pro and amateur boxing bouts since 1953; candidate Ottawa ACT sportsman of year 1975; mem. Canadian Boxing Hall of Fame; *res.* Ottawa, Ont.

SANFORD, Aubrey (soccer); *b.* 4 Sep 1905, Nanaimo, B.C.; *m.* Muriel Audrey; *children:* Judith Ann, Anthony Albert; U of British Columbia; retired chartered accountant; in soccer 45 years from 1912; on three Dominion champions with Westminster Royals 1928, 1930, 1931; managed same club to national championships 1953, 1955; Canadian Soccer Association pres. 1969-72; runner-up Air Canada Amateur Sport Award 1972; mem. B.C. Sports Hall of Fame; *res.* Vancouver, B.C.

SAVAGE, Paul (curling); *b.* 25 Jun 1947, Toronto, Ont.; *given name:* Allin Paul; *m.* Barbara Lee; *children:* Bradley, Lisa; York Mills CI, Seneca College; publications manager; 1965 Schoolboy title; Ontario junior title 1966; four times Ontario Brier representative winning provincial Consols 1970, 1973, 1974, 1977; wrote *Canadian Curling, Hack to House* (1974); *res.* Agincourt, Ont.

SAWCHUK, Terry (hockey); *b.* 28 Dec 1929, Winnipeg, Man., *d.* 31 May 1970, New York, N.Y.; *given name:* Terrance Gordon; *div.* Pat; *children:* seven; Windsor Spitfires juniors to Omaha (USHL), rookie of year 1947-48; repeat Indianapolis (AHL) 1948-49, Detroit Red Wings (NHL) 1950-51; remained with Detroit through 1954-55 winning three Vezina Trophies; to Boston 1955-56, Detroit 1957-58, Toronto Maple Leafs 1964-65 sharing Vezina with Johnny Bower, Los Angeles 1967-68, Detroit 1968-69, NY Rangers 1969-70; in 971 regular season NHL games over 20 seasons; played 953 complete games allowing 2,401 goals for avg. 2.52; recorded 103 shutouts; 1952 led Detroit to Stanley Cup in eight straight games, posted four shutouts, allowed five goals; 106 Stanley Cup playoff games, yielded 267 goals for 2.64 avg., 12 shutouts; on three Stanley Cup champions with Detroit, one Toronto; NHL first team all-star three times, second team four times; died following altercation with teammate Ron Stewart (cleared of guilt); mem. Hockey Hall of Fame.

SAX, Joe (track); *b.* 5 Nov 1952, Toronto, Ont.; *given name:* Joseph Anton; Danforth Tech, U of Toronto, B.P.H.E., U of Western Ontario, B.Ed.; teacher; Canadian record 3000m steeplechase 1974 with 8:36.8; *res.* Toronto, Ont.

SAZIO, Ralph (football); *b.* 22 Jul 1922, South Orange, N.J.; *given name:* Ralph Joseph; *m.* Rose Louise Matthews; *children:* Mark, Peggy; College of William and Mary, B.Sc., Columbia U, M.A.; pres. Hamilton Tiger-Cats football club; captain William and Mary football team; turned pro Brooklyn Dodgers; joined Tiger-Cats as tackle, assistant coach 1950, head coach 1963; 59-25-1 five-year record making playoffs each year and guiding club to three victories in four Grey Cup appearances; general manager, director Ti-Cats 1968; club pres. 1973; CFL pres. 1975; *res.* Burlington, Ont.

SCHLEIMER, Joseph (wrestling); *b.* 31 May 1909, Austria; *m.* Margaret; *children:* Ewin; architectural draftsman, manufacturer wood products and construction; three times Canadian 164lb champion 1934-36; gold medal 1934 British Empire Games London Eng.; bronze 1936 Berlin Olympics; coach Canadian wrestling team 1959 Pan-Am Games Chicago, 1962 Commonwealth Games Perth Australia, 1962 world Toledo Ohio, 1963 Pan-Am Games Sao Paulo Brazil, 1964 Tokyo Olympics; chairman AAU of C wrestling committee 1960-64; pres. Ontario Amateur Wrestling Federation 1955-60; wrestling coach Broadview YMCA Toronto 1950-71; Ontario Achievement Award 1970-72, 1975 for service to sport; director Canadian AWA many years; mem. Canadian Amateur Athletic, Canadian Amateur Wrestling Halls of Fame; *res.* Toronto, Ont.

SCHMIDT, Milt (hockey); *b.* 5 Mar 1918, Kitchener, Ont.; *given name:* Milton Conrad; *m.* Marie Peterson; *children:* Milton Jr., Nancy; hockey executive, cement salesman; turned pro Providence 1936 moving to Boston midway through season; centred Kraut Line of Woody Dumart, Bobby Bauer; played until 1954-55, excluding three seasons with RCAF WW2 when he played for Allan Cup-winning Ottawa Hurricanes; in 16 NHL seasons scored 229 goals, 336 assists, plus 24 goals, 25 assists in 80 playoff games; NHL Art Ross Trophy (scoring) 1939-40; Hart Trophy (MVP) 1952; on two Stanley Cup winners; three times first team all-star, once second team; coached Bruins seven years, then general manager; general manager-coach Washington Capitals in NHL expansion program 1973; mem. Hockey, Canadian Sports Halls of Fame; *res.* Lynn, Mass.

SCHNEIDER, Bert (boxing); *b.* 1 Jul 1897, Cleveland, Ohio; *m.* Mary Ellen Henderson (*d.*); Montreal Commercial and Technical School; retired, US immigration service; with Montreal Swimming Club water polo team, skier, diver, swimmer and boxer; joined Montreal Casquette Club training under Eugene Brosseau; joined MAAA winning club welterweight title, city title once and Canadian title twice; in 1920 Olympics scored four wins in three days including gold medal; fought about 90 times as pro; mem. Canadian Boxing, Canadian Sports, AAU of C Halls of Fame; *res.* Stanwood, Wash.

SCHOLES, Louis (rowing); *b.* 1880, Toronto, Ont.; *d.* 1942, Toronto, Ont.; brother Jack held Canadian featherweight and lightweight titles, 1900-01 US amateur featherweight title; invited to US nationals 1901 Lou won intermediate singles at Philadelphia; won two major senior sculls events defeating US champion C.S. Titus at 1902 Harlem Regatta; with partner Frank Smith won both Canadian, US double sculls titles 1903 and took singles titles Dominion Day Regatta Toronto, Canadian Henley and NRA of US; first Canadian ever to win English Henley diamond sculls in record 8:23.2 1904; mem. Canadian Sports Hall of Fame.

SCHREIDER, Gary (football); *b.* 21 Apr 1934, Belleville, Ont.; *m.* Patricia; *children:* Gary Jr., Ronald, Thomas, Michael, Suzanne; Queen's U, U of Ottawa, LL.B.; lawyer; played with three Ontario Catholic Conference champions at Toronto St. Michael's; with intercollegiate champions Queen's 1953, 1955; nine CFL seasons 1956-64 with Ottawa, B.C., Hamilton; Canadian junior 60yd dash record of 6.3 in HS training under Lloyd Percival; first pres. CFL Players' Association 1963; three times CFL all-star; *res.* Ottawa, Ont.

SCHRIEWER, Tex (football); *b.* 30 Sep 1934, New Braunfels, Texas; *given name:* Menan; *m.* Sandra Jefferies; *children:* six; U of Texas (Austin), B.B.A.; insurance, real estate executive; all-South, Western Conference honors 1954-55, honorable mention all-American 1955; turned pro Toronto Argos 1956; led Argos in receptions with 43 for 691yds, one TD 1957; dealt to Sask. Roughriders for Cookie Gilchrist 1959; rejoined Argos 1960 remaining through 1962 before retiring; all-Eastern with Argos 1957; *res.* San Antonio, Tex.

SCHRINER, Sweeney (hockey); *b.* 30 Nov 1911, Calgary, Alta.; *given name:* David; Calgary minor hockey through PS, North Hill midget, Tigers juveniles, Canadians juniors to senior Bronks coached by Rosie Helmer; pro Syracuse 1933-34; NY Americans 1934-35 scoring 18 goals, Calder Memorial Trophy (NHL rookie of year); traded to Toronto Maple Leafs for five players 1938-39 and played balance of 11-year NHL career that team; scored 201 goals in NHL career; twice won Hart Trophy (scoring); on two Stanley Cup winners; first all-star team once, second team once; mem. Hockey Hall of Fame; *res.* Calgary, Alta.

SCHUETTE, Tom (football); *b.* 10 Jan 1945, East St. Louis, Ill.; *given name:* Thomas Paul; Indiana U, B.Sc.; football player, teacher; all-American coaches first team, *Sport Magazine* second team, honorable mention AP & UPI as offensive guard Indiana; all-Big 10 by AP & UPI; all-academic Big 10 1966; played in East-West Shrine all-star game San Francisco 1966; Balfour Award Indiana for athletic, academic excellence; turned pro Ottawa Rough Riders 1967 playing on four Grey Cup champions, two all-star games; twice topped East in CFL all-pro countdown series, finished second, third nationally; *res.* Ottawa, Ont.

SCHWENDE, Carl (fencing); *b.* 20 Feb 1920, Basel, Switzerland; *m.* Claire; *children:* Heidi, Maria; estimator-designer; began fencing under Master Roger Nigon at Basel 1933; competed for Audatia Basel until 1938 then F.C. Basel, Mulhausen France; 1945-47 competed for F.C. Basel; competed for Palestre Nationale in Montreal from 1949; coach Immaculate Conception 1956, Notre Dame Centre 1959; represented Canada 1954 British Empire Games Vancouver winning gold team sabre, silver team épée, individual épée and bronze team foil;

manager, coach, captain, competitor Canadian team 1958 British Empire Games Cardiff Wales winning silver team épée; silver team sabre, bronze team foil and épée 1962 British Empire Games Perth Australia; bronze team foil, sabre 1959 Pan-Am Games Chicago; mem. Canadian team 1960 Rome Olympics; frequent winner 1949-62 in provincial, national, international, individual, team épée, sabre, foil competitions; supervisor PQFA 1952-56; representative AAU of C mem. National Fencing Committee 1953-61; pres. PQFA 1956; coach McGill fencing team 1959, 1966-67; pres. Quebec Branch AAU of C 1962-67; *res.* Montreal, Que.

SCORRAR, Doug (track); *b.* 9 Sep 1948, Auckland, N.Z.; *given name:* Douglas Alfred; Perth DCI, Ohio State U, B.Sc., M.A.; civil servant; Canadian midget mile record 4:24.9 1964; Canadian HS two-mile record 9:16.6 1965, 9:12.3 1967; OFSSA two-mile title 1965-67, junior international (England, France, Canada) three-mile title 1967; won Big 10 conference cross-country 1968, three-mile runner-up 1970; Ohio State records two-mile indoor, one, two, three, six-mile outdoor and two, four-mile outdoor relay; mem. Canadian national team winning three-mile vs Norway, Sweden; Ontario team 10 000m, marathon 1974-76; Canadian national marathon runner-up 1975; *res.* Ottawa, Ont.

SCOTT, Alex (curling); *b.* 7 Mar 1940, Willowdale, Ont.; *given name:* Alex Victor Ferguson; *m.* Janet Isabel Ritchie; *children:* Sandy, Kathy, Jamie; Queen's U, M.D.; physician; Ontario Intercollegiate curling title at Queen's; 1969 won Ontario Governor-General's double rink title, Whitby Dunlop 'spiel; first Ontario representative in Edmonton carspiel; 1971 won first Ontario carspiel at Toronto Royal Canadians; frequent competitor in provincial Consols playdowns winning title as skip of rink with Ted Brown, Tom Miller, Mike Boyd 1975 Cambridge Ont.; 6-5 record Federicton Brier; *res.* Kingston, Ont.

SCOTT, Barbara Ann (figure skating); *b.* 9 May 1929, Ottawa, Ont.; *m.* Thomas V. King; began skating career with Minto Skating Club age six; at 10 years youngest to pass gold figures test; Canadian junior title 1940; Canadian senior champion 1944-48; North American Champion 1945-48; European champion 1947-48; world champion 1947-48; Olympic gold medal 1948; turned pro, starred with Hollywood Ice Review 1949-54; trains, shows horses, Tipper winner of numerous championships 1964-72; Lou Marsh Trophy (Canada's top athlete) 1945, 1947, 1948; mem. Canadian Sports Hall of Fame; *res.* Chicago, Ill.

SCOTT, Vince (football); *b.* 10 Jul 1925, Leroy, N.Y.; *m.* Wilton Lee Treadwell; *children:* Joseph, Robert, Vincent Jr., Gail; Leroy HS, Notre Dame U, B.Sc.; real estate salesman; nine athletic letters HS football, track, baseball; twice Western NY State football all-star; mem. 1943 Western NY State championship football team; NY State sectional shot put champion 1943, runner-up 1942; mem. 1946 national champions; Pitts all-opponents team 1945; mem. track team two years; turned pro Buffalo Bills 1947-48 playing in title game vs Cleveland Browns 1948; joined Hamilton Tiger-Cats 1949 remaining 13 seasons, Eastern all-star 10 times; Stuke's 1954 dream team; twice Ted Reeves' all-Canada team; 1955 coaches dream team; Jack Matheson's 1967 all-pro team chosen for US *All-Pro Magazine;*

Hamilton's Fabulous Fifty's all-star team; Eastern team of century; in four all-star games; twice honored by 'day' (with 1948 Buffalo Bills, by Hamilton quarterback Club); Batavia NY Notre Dame Booster Club outstanding athlete of decade; following retirement coached Oakville Black Knights (ORFU) three years, Hillfield College Hamilton three years; mem. six Grey Cup finalists, two winners; *res.* Hamilton, Ont.

SEIBERT, Earl (hockey); *b.* 7 Dec 1911, Kitchener, Ont.; *given name:* Earl Walter; NHL all-star teams 10 consecutive seasons, four times first team; scored 89 goals, 187 assists, plus 11 goals, eight assists in playoff action; turned pro 1929 with NY Rangers' Springfield farm club, Rangers 1931-32 season; to Chicago 1935-46, Detroit 1946; with father Oliver, first father-son combination Hockey's Hall of Fame; *res.* Agawam, Mass.

SEIBERT, Oliver (hockey); *b.* 18 Mar 1881, Berlin, Ont., *d.* 15 May 1944, Kitchener, Ont.; began hockey career as goaltender then forward line; at one time competed on team comprised solely of family members; six seasons with champion Berlin Rangers (WOHA) then turned pro Houghton Mich. 1907; played with London, Guelph in Ontario pro, Northwestern Mich. leagues; wearing old rocker skates once beat a trotter horse in one-mile match race on Grand River ice despite fact trotter set mile record 2:13; with son Earl first father-son combination Hockey's Hall of Fame.

SELLER, Peggy (synchronized swimming); *b.* 23 Jan, Edinburgh, Scotland; *given name:* Margaret Cameron Shearer; *m.* Dr. Reg Seller; *children:* Marna, Douglas, Donald; all Royal Life Saving Society awards 1923; won

Gale Trophy four years; three years captain national water polo team; three Canadian 3m diving records; won 1928 provincial titles 100yd dash, javelin, broad jump; wrote first rule book for CASA judges 1938; first secretary Federation Internationale de Natation Amateur 1948; wrote Federation's rules governing international competition 1952; attempting to get synchronized swimming on Olympic rolls since 1963; mem., honorary patron Pan-American Hall of Fame Winnipeg; mem. International Academy of Aquatic Art Florida, Canadian Sports Halls of Fame; *res.* Pointe Claire, Que.

SHANNON, Carver   (football); *b.* 28 Apr 1938, Corinth, Miss. *given name:* Carver Beauregard; *m.* Loraine; *children:* Michael; Southern Illinois U, B.S., UCLA, M.A.; aircraft co. manager; in four years with Southern Illinois set variety of school football records including scoring for one game, season and career, best rushing avg. game, season, career; set track record 9.4 for 100yd dash; led US major college scorers 1956; twice all-American; voted school's greatest athlete 1975; turned pro Winnipeg Blue Bombers 1959 playing on Grey Cup champion team that season; started 1961 season with Bombers, then to Hamilton playing in Grey Cup loss vs Winnipeg; Los Angeles Rams 1962; led Rams in yardage, best avg. single game on punt returns, most pass interceptions 1962; second in NFL kickoff returns, third punt returns 1963; World Team Tennis League umpire; *res.* Los Angeles, Calif.

SHARP, John   (track); *b.* 19 Nov 1952, Toronto, Ont.; *given name:* John Alexander; Victoria Park HS, Victoria College, U of Toronto, B.Comm.; chartered accountant; won Canadian junior cross-country 1971, OUAA individual cross-country 1974, team 1972-74, CIAU individual cross-country 1973-74, team 1972-74, OUAA 5000m setting record 1973, 1974 for which he received Hec Phillips trophy as outstanding performer; Canadian 5000m title 1974, fourth 1975; represented Canada 1975 Pan-Am Games Mexico; best personal times: 1500m 3:45.9, 3000m 8:01.6, 5000m 13:46.4, 10 000m 29:32.2; *res.* Toronto, Ont.

SHATTO, Cindy   (diving); *b.* 16 May 1957, Toronto, Ont.; student; daughter of Football Hall of Fame mem. Dick Shatto; national status 1971; gold medal 1972 winter nationals 1m, 15-16 national age-group 1m, 3m; silver 1973 summer nationals 1m; gold 1973 winter nationals 1m, bronze 3m; bronze 1974 summer nationals 3m; gold 1m, 3m 1974 age-group nationals; bronze 1975 winter nationals 3m; represented Canada 1973 world Yugoslavia, gold 1974 New Zealand Commonwealth Games 3m; 1976 Montreal Olympics; competed for Canada vs USSR, DDR, Sweden, US, Australia, Mexico, Cuba, three times in Canada Cup; coached by Don Webb; *res.* Toronto, Ont.

SHATTO, Dick   (football); *b.* 1934, Springfield, Ohio; *given name:* Richard Darrell; *m.* Lynne; *children:* Randy, Becky, Cindy, J, Kathy; U of Kentucky; football executive; quarterback, halfback and starred in track U of Kentucky; joined Argos 1954; played 12 years (1954-65) fullback, halfback, slotback, flanker; still holds 15 Argos offensive records: most points (career) 542, most TDs (career) 91, (game) four, most carries (career) 1,322, most yds gained rushing (career) 6,958, most 100-yd games (career) 16, most receptions (career) 466, most yds gained receiving (career) 6,584, most TDs rushing (career) 39, (game) three, most TDs receiving (career) 52, most kickoff returns (career) 83, (season) 25, most yds kickoff returns (career) 1,991, (season) 636; twice Jeff Russel Memorial Trophy winner; twice runner-up Schenley outstanding player award; six times EFC all-star, once all-Canadian; rejoined Argos 1974 as manager marketing, media and public relations; since 1976 Argos managing director; mem. Canadian Football Hall of Fame; *res.* North York, Ont.

SHAUGHNESSY, Frank Jr. (hockey, football, golf); *b.* 21 Jun 1911, Roanoke, Va.; Loyola U, B.A., McGill U; former director accreditation COJO, retired Bell Canada; son of Shag Shaughnessy; football all-star McGill 1934; with McGill intercollegiate hockey champions 1934-35; mem. Canadian Olympic hockey team 1936; played senior amateur hockey and various army teams; coach freshman football, hockey McGill; v.-pres. Laurentian Ski Zone 1952-55; technical chairman Quebec division CSA 1954-55; Canadian national ski team organization chairman 1954-55; Chef de Mission Canadian winter Olympic teams 1956, 1960, 1964, 1968, 1972; COA v.-pres. since 1957; director Quebec Golf Association 1958-64, pres. 1964; governor Royal Canadian Golf Association 1965-69; chairman RCGA 1967; pres. Montreal Sportsmen's Association 1968-72; chairman Air Canada amateur sport executive of year award committee 1968-72; mem. Loyola, Canadian Sports Halls of Fame; *res.* Montreal, Que.

SHAUGHNESSY, Shag (baseball); *b.* 8 Apr 1883, Amboy, Ill., *d.* 15 May 1969, Montreal, Que.; *given name:* Frank Joseph; *m.* Katherine Quinn; *children:* eight sons, one daughter; Notre Dame U; captain Notre Dame football, baseball team 1903-04; played pro baseball, managed Roanoke Va.,

Fort Wayne Ind.; coach football one year Clemson; McGill football coach 1912-28; managed Ottawa baseball team to three straight pennants; formed Canadian Pro Baseball League with teams from Ottawa, Brantford, Guelph, Kitchener and Peterborough; general manager Ottawa hockey club; managed Hamilton baseball club 1919, Syracuse 1921; coach, scout Detroit Tigers; rebuilt Montreal Royals and won first Montreal pennant of century 1935; instituted playoff system (adopted from hockey) initiating Little World Series; International League pres. 1936-60; broke baseball's color bar by signing Jackie Robinson to Montreal Royals; appointed by baseball commissioner Happy Chandler to recodify baseball rules 1949; mem. Baseball, Canadian Football Hall of Fame.

SHAW, Dan (football); *b.* 18 Dec 1933, Toronto, Ont.; *given name:* Dan Ross; *m.* Beverley; *children:* Stephen, Susan, Dani; Bloor CI; executive director Ontario Amateur Football Association; guard, tackle both ways Bloor CI 1947-51, Toronto all-star 1948-51; joined Toronto Balmy Beach senior ORFU 1952-53 winning league title latter year and losing to Winnipeg Blue Bombers Grey Cup semifinal; played with Toronto Argos 1954-57 finishing competitive career 1957 with Balmy Beach; since 1960 secretary-treasurer Argo Old Boys; convenor Ontario Junior Football Conference 1965-72; secretary Southwestern Ontario AFA 1965-70; pres. OAFA 1970-72, executive director since 1972; mem. founding committee Argo Playback Club 1967, director 1967-74; since 1975 v.-chairman Argo Double Blue Club; chairman founding committee Canadian Football Hall of Fame Club since 1976; Ontario Achievement Award 1972; *res.* Willowdale, Ont.

SHAW, Wayne (football); *b.* 24 Feb 1939, Bladworth, Sask. *m.* Joan; *children:* Kimberly; Notre Dame College, U of Saskatchewan; businessman; football 1956-58 Notre Dame College; junior football with Saskatoon Hilltops 1959-60, all-star middle linebacker 1959, offensive tackle 1960, Manitoba-Saskatchewan Junior League MVP 1960; won Western Canadian and national junior championship 1960; turned pro Sask. Roughriders 1961 playing as outside linebacker through 1972; five times WFC all-star, once all-Canadian; club's nominee for Schenley award once; played in four Grey Cup finals, won 1966; *res.* Winnipeg, Man.

SHEDD, Marjory (badminton); *b.* 17 Mar 1926, Toronto, Ont.; *given name:* Marjory Jean; lab technician, sport instructor; guard 1945 Canadian junior basketball champion Carltonettes; 1950 led Toronto Montgomery Maids to national senior title; switched from basketball to volleyball with U of T team winning five national titles; represented Canada 1967 Pan-Am Games volleyball team; finals national badminton singles 1951-52; won first of six Canadian singles titles 1953; five Canadian mixed, 14 Canadian ladies' doubles titles; mem. six Uber Cup teams, 1970 Commonwealth Games team; mem. Canadian Sports Hall of Fame; *res.* Toronto, Ont.

SHEPHERD, George (track); *b.* 23 Apr 1938, Port Colborne, Ont.; *m.* Sylvia Mary; *children:* Craig Andrew; U of Western Ontario, B.P.H.E.; HS teacher; Canadian 400m hurdles champion 1958-63 holding Canadian record 1958-65; mem. East York track club one-mile relay team 1960-68, won Canadian titles, set 3:08.6 record; represented Canada 1960 Olympics; pres. Olympic Club of Canada; *res.* Toronto, Ont.

SHERIDAN, Juan (football); *b.* 2 Feb 1925, Havana, Cuba, *d.* 7 Oct 1969, Ormstown, Que.; *m.* Elizabeth Hedrick; *children:* Martha, Gordon, Bob, Bruce, John; U of Toronto; sales representative; sports director HMCS Donnacona, mem. 1944 Grey Cup champions; played with Toronto Balmy Beach, Toronto Indians; joined Montreal Alouettes 1948, won 1949 Grey Cup; frequent all-star, all-Canadian centre; 11 CFL seasons, retired following 1959 campaign; nickname The Pear; coaching assistant to Frank Tindall at Queen's for a few seasons.

SHERRING, William (track); *b.* 1877, Hamilton, Ont.; *d.* 1964, Hamilton, Ont.; railway brakeman; at 16 won races at Ontario fairs; at 20 third Hamilton's around-the-bay race (about 19 miles); won same race 1899, 1903; second 1900 Boston Marathon; gold medal 1906 special Athens Olympics; took race lead after two and one-half hours, finished in record 2:51:23.6; accompanied over the line by Prince George of Greece; finished race weighing 98 lbs, a loss of 14 lbs during race; mem. Canadian Sports Hall of Fame.

SHERWOOD, Liv (yachting); *b.* 27 Nov 1923, Ottawa, Ont.; *given name:* Livius Anglin; *m.* Anne Galligan; *children:* Christopher, Mary; Loyola HS, St. Patrick's HS, U of Toronto, B.A., Osgoode Hall, LL.B; provincial court judge; international 14ft dinghy champion Britannia Yacht Club 1954-57, Dragon Class 1958-60, Shark Class 1964-67; North American Shark Class champion 1964-65; past pres. St. Lawrence Valley Yacht Racing Association; director Canadian Yachting Association since 1957; mem. rules committee CYA and International Yacht Racing Union; jury mem. International 14ft dinghy world team finals 1965,

Soling Class world championships 1971, 1975, Tornado Class 1973, America's Cup races 1974, Canadian Olympic training regatta Kingston 1969-71; director of sailing Canadian Olympic training program Kingston 1973-75, Olympic regatta 1976 Olympics; Ottawa citizen of year 1971; *res.* Ottawa, Ont.

SHIRK, Marshall (football); *b.* 3 Aug 1940, Pomona, Calif.; *given name:* Chester Marshall; *div.;* UCLA, B.A.; teacher; at UCLA all-Coast, all-Big Five, all-American, in 1962 Rose Bowl, Hula Bowl, all-American Bowl; turned pro with Minnesota Vikings where he was late cut in 1963 training camp; recruited by J. I. Albrecht for Ottawa Rough Riders; guard through 1971 appearing in three Grey Cup finals, two winners; Schenley nominee top lineman 1970, 1971; outstanding player nominee 1971; *res.* Manotick, Ont.

SHORE, Eddie (hockey); *b.* 25 Nov 1902, Ft. Qu'Appelle, Sask.; *given name:* Edward William; *m.* Katie McRae (*d.*); *children:* Ted; Manitoba Agricultural College; hockey executive; amateur hockey to Melville Millionaires 1923-24; turned pro Regina Caps (WCL) then shifted to Edmonton before joining NHL Boston Bruins 1926-27 season; in 13 seasons with Bruins on defence scored 105 goals, 179 assists; concluded NHL days with NY Americans 1939-40; Hart Trophy (MVP) four times; seven times first all-star team, once second; played on two Stanley Cup winners; owned, operated Springfield (AHL) franchise from 1940, excluding WW2 years as general manager, coach Buffalo Bisons; briefly operated New Haven franchise, owned Fort Worth (USHL), Oakland (PCHL) until sold to California Seals; past v.-pres. AHL; 1970 Lester Patrick Trophy for contribution to US hockey; mem. Hockey, Canadian Sports Halls of Fame; *res.* Springfield, Mass.

SHOULDICE, Hap (football); *b.* 12 Mar 1907, Ottawa, Ont.; *given name:* Hans; *m.* Lois McCulloch; *children:* Don, Doug, Drew; Glebe CI; retired chief administrator customer accounting, CFL director of officiating; organized, managed, coached Gowlings to 1927 Canadian juvenile basketball title; coach Rideau Aquatic Club senior ladies' canoe team; played juvenile lacrosse with Strathconas 1922-25; catcher Ottawa Hydro Mercantile softball league, Masonic League early 30s; paddled Rideau club 1925-35, five years war canoe captain, ladies' war canoe captain; represented Canada as paddler 1930 British Empire Games Hamilton; coach Shamrock Jr. hockey team 1927-29; coach, manager Rideau Jrs. 1930 Memorial Cup semifinals; began hockey, football officiating 1927; worked nine Canadian hockey finals, Memorial, Allan, Alexander Cups; appointed CFL official 1935 working eight Grey Cup finals before retiring 1958; EFC supervisor of officials 1958, same role for CFL 1972; organized first hockey, football officials associations in Canada; mem. Ottawa, Football Halls of Fame; *res.* Ottawa, Ont.

SIEBERT, Babe (hockey); *b.* 14 Jan 1904, Plattsville, Ont., *d.* 25 Aug, 1939, St. Joseph, Ont.; *given name:* Albert Charles; minor hockey Zurich Ont.; Kitchener OHA juniors 1922-23; Niagara Falls seniors 1924-25, NHL following season with Montreal Maroons; left wing five years on Big S line with Nels Stewart, Hooley Smith; dealt to NY Rangers 1932, Boston Bruins 1934, Montreal Canadiens 1936; retired following 1938-39 season; first team all-star defenceman three successive years; with Habs won

Hart Trophy as league MVP 1937; captain 1939 team, was to coach team following season but drowned during the summer; mem. Hockey Hall of Fame.

SILCOTT, Liz (basketball); *b.* 14 Dec 1950, Montreal, Que.; *given name:* Helen Elizabeth; U of British Columbia, Concordia U; student; mem. Canadian women's national basketball team 1972; competed internationally China, Italy; leading scorer UBC Canadian women's champions, all-conference guard 1972-73 season, repeat 1973-74, also all-Canadian; 1974-75 Canadian women's championships, led Concordia scorers, all-conference guard, set Canadian record points in two-game championship series with 77; in 1974 Canada-China tour, Italy, W. Germany, Bulgaria; Hungary, Yugoslavia, Czechoslovakia, China with 1975 Canadian team; in 1975 Pan-Am Games Mexico; Quebec athlete of year 1974, 1975; MVP 1974 Genoa Italy tournament; MVP 1975 Szombathely Hungary; *res.* Montreal, Que.

SIMPSON, Ben (football); *b.* 1878, Peterborough, Ont., *d.* 20 Oct 1964, Guelph, Ont.; Peterborough CI, Queen's U, M.A., Normal School; educator; began playing football at Queen's with intermediate team; joined Hamilton Tigers 1904 helping them win Ontario title; seven seasons with Tigers including Dominion title 1908, captain 1910; refereed three years in intercollegiate ranks, seven more in interprovincial league; mem. Tiger team which, with Ottawa, demonstrated Canadian game to US fans; mem. Canadian Football Hall of Fame.

SIMPSON, Bill (soccer); *b.* 13 Sep 1894, Paisley, Scotland, *d.* 1974, Toronto, Ont.; foreman; played for Fraserburg team Toronto, Toronto City in National Soccer League,

Davenport Albion, Toronto Scottish, won 1919 league title; 15 years secretary-treasurer Ontario Soccer Association, 14 years pres. Toronto District Soccer Association, four years pres. CSFA; credited with many innovations in Canadian soccer; first manager Canadian team to play USSR; launched Canada's soccer coaching schools; mem. Canadian Sports Hall of Fame.

SIMPSON, Bob (football); *b.* 20 Apr 1930, Windsor, Ont.; *div.* Cecile; *children:* Robert John, Gary Lee, Lynn Patricia, Mark Stanley, Mary Leigh; *m.* Mary Francis; Patterson CI, Assumption College; executive-director National Capital Regional Sports Council; forward with two Patterson provincial basketball championship teams; one year Windsor Rockets (ORFU); joined Ottawa Rough Riders 1950; caught 65 TD passes, record surpassed 1975 by Terry Evanshan; 386 lifetime points, 12 other defensive TDs, 274 receptions in nine recorded seasons, 6,034yds (22.0yds-per-catch avg. second only to Whit Tucker's 22.4); best single-game performance 258yds 1956; best single season 47 receptions 1956; six times EFC all-star, four times all-Canadian; outstanding player (Gordon Sturtridge Memorial Trophy) 1957 East-West Game; runner-up Schenley outstanding Canadian 1956; two Grey Cup winners 1951, 1960; Jersey No. 70 retired by Riders; coach Ashbury College football several years; PR director Ottawa Rough Riders; four years basketball with Tillsonburg Livingstons including 1952 Olympic team; several years Ottawa senior basketball league; mem. Canadian Football Hall of Fame; *res.* Ottawa, Ont.

SIMPSON, Bruce (track and field); *b.* 6 Mar 1950, Toronto, Ont.; *m.* Joanne Hakkabu; Agincourt CI, UCLA, U of Toronto,

U of Ottawa; student; Canadian pole vault title 1965 Saint John N.B. setting Canadian record 12'6½''; toured Norway, Sweden, England 1968, in top six world indoor vaulters; fifth 1970 Commonwealth Games; bronze medal 1971 Pan-Am Games; fifth 1972 Munich Olympics; silver medal 1975 World Student Games Italy; 10th in world 1974; failed to reach 1976 Olympic finals; Canadian indoor record 17''4¾''; *res.* Ottawa, Ont.

SIMPSON, Bullet Joe (hockey); *b.* 13 Aug 1893, Selkirk, Man., *d.* Dec 1973, Florida; *given name:* Harold Joseph; compensated for lightweight stature with speed to become great defenceman and earn nickname Bullet Joe; amateur hockey with Winnipeg Victorias 1914-15; joined Winnipeg 61st Battalion, won Allan Cup; 1919-20 season with Selkirk Fishermen; Edmonton Eskimos 1921-22 playing four seasons, won two Western Canada HL titles; NY Americans (NHL) 1925-31; managed Americans 1932-35; managed New Haven, Minneapolis clubs before retiring; mem. Hockey Hall of Fame.

SINCLAIR, Marjorie (curling); *b.* 25 Jan 1911, England.; *given name:* Marjorie Helen; *m.* Duncan S. Sinclair; *children:* Marjorie, John; 1936-46 competed regularly; secretary Western Canada Ladies' Curling Association 1949-50; delegate for Northern Alberta LCA on WCLCA 1950-52; WCLCA secretary 1954; pres. Eaton NALCA 1955-56; pres. NALCA 1957-58; pres. Edmonton LCC 1959-60; Western Canada delegate CLCA 1961-63; Sinclair Trophy presented annually to NALCA champions; pres. CLCA 1963-64; secretary NALCA 1961-68, also Alberta LCA twice during that period;

mem. first women's baseball team Calgary; mem. Canadian Curling Hall of Fame; *res.* Edmonton, Alta., Sun City, Ariz.

SINDEN, Harry (hockey); *b.* 14 Sep 1932, Collins Bay, Ont.; *given name:* Harry James; *m.* Eleanor; *children:* Nancy, Carol, Donna, Julia; hockey executive; coached five years senior OHA guiding Whitby Dunlops to 1958 world amateur championship; joined Boston organization 1961 as player-coach with Kingston (EPHL), Minneapolis, Oklahoma City (CPHL) for six years; led 1966 Oklahoma Blazers to second place in league, eight straight playoff games for Jack Adams Trophy; succeeded Milt Schmidt as Bruins' coach 1967, team into playoffs first time in nine years; led Bruins to 1970 Stanley Cup; Team Canada coach 1972, guided Canada to victory over USSR; rejoined Bruins as general manager 1972-73; through 1976-77 NHL coaching record 185 wins, 128 losses, 63 ties for .591 percentage, plus 28 wins, 16 losses for .636 percentage in playoffs; *res.* Winchester, Mass.

SITTLER, Darryl (hockey); *b.* 18 Sep 1950, St. Jacob's, Ont.; *given name:* Darryl Glen; *m.* Wendy; *children:* Ryan, Megan; Kitchener-Waterloo minor ranks to OHA junior A London Knights; first choice Toronto Maple Leafs, eighth overall 1970 amateur draft; TML as left-winger, broke wrist and missed 29 games in rookie season; restored to centre third NHL season; NHL record 10 points in game Feb 1976 vs Boston with six goals, four assists, six goals tied modern NHL mark shared by Syd Howe, Red Berenson; in playoffs vs Philadelphia same season scored five goals in single game, mem. Team Canada 1976; scored overtime winner vs Czechoslovakia which gave Canada title; TML captain 1975; through

1976-77 NHL record 503 regular season games scoring 207 goals, 274 assists, 481 points, 431 penalty minutes; *res.* Mississauga, Ont.

SKINNER, Larry (hockey, softball); *b.* 25 Jul 1930, Keyes, Man.; *m.* Marjorie Blair; *children:* Grant, David, Ruth, Larry, Shannon; John Oliver HS, U of Oregon; director marketing, communication Canadian Amateur Hockey Association; player, coach, manager in softball 30 years; in three world softball championships, six Canadian finals; five years Pacific Coast Soccer League; one Canadian soccer championship; executive-director Canadian Amateur Softball Association in Ottawa four years; *res.* Ottawa, Ont.

SLOAN, Susan (swimming); *b.* 5 Apr 1958, Stettler, Alta.; *given name:* Susan Estelle; Arizona State U; student; butterfly specialist, joined Deryk Snelling with Vancouver Dolphins Swim Club; competed in Canadian nationals since 1974; won 100m butterfly and Olympic trials with then personal best 1:02.41 June 1976; bronze 4x100m medley relay 1976 Montreal Olympics; Governor-General's silver medal 1976; Canadian record 100m butterfly 1:02.00 1977; *res.* Stettler, Alta.

SLOAN, Tod (hockey); *b.* 30 Nov 1927, Vinton, Que.; *given name:* Aloysius Martin; *m.* Jean Aird; *children:* Marilyn, Joanne, Donald; Falconbridge HS, St. Michael's College; salesman; minor hockey Falconbridge, two years junior A St. Mike's Majors; pro Toronto Maple Leafs 1947-58, Chicago Black Hawks 1958-61; once second team all-star centre; mem. four Stanley Cup winners; 13 NHL season record: 745 scheduled games, 220 goals, 262 assists, 482 points plus 47 playoff games, nine goals, 12 assists, 21

points; played in three all-star games; on retirement coached minor hockey several years; mem. Toronto Oldtimers hockey team; *res.* Jackson's Point, Ont.

SMITH, Alfred E. (hockey); *b.* 3 Jun 1873, Ottawa, Ont., *d.* 21 Aug 1953, Ottawa, Ont.; mem. first Ottawa team (Electrics) to compete in organized hockey 1890 OHA; joined Ottawa 1895 for three seasons, quit, returned age 30 to help Ottawa win two Stanley Cups; with Kenora 1907, Ottawa 1907-08, Pittsburgh in city pro league; retired to coach Renfrew, Ottawa, NY Americans, Moncton N.B., North Bay; player-coach Ottawa Cliffsides 1909 Allan Cup winners; starred with Bully's Acres lacrosse team 1889; coach Ottawa lacrosse club, 1922 Eastern Ontario title; quarterback Ottawa Rough Riders, 1903 Quebec titlists; with brother Tommy mem. Ottawa, Hockey Halls of Fame.

SMITH, Becky (swimming); *b.* 3 Jun 1959, Edmonton, Alta.; *given name:* Rebecca Gwendolyn; Strathcona HS; student; butterfly, individual medley (IM) specialist with national swim team since 1973; mem. Thunder Bay Thunderbolts coached by Don Talbot; silver medals 200m IM, 400m IM 1974 Commonwealth Games; eighth 200m butterfly, fifth 200m IM 1975 world; bronze 400m IM in personal best 4:50.48, 4x100 relay 1976 Montreal Olympics; personal bests: 100m freestyle (FS) 58.82, 200m FS 2:09.22, 200m butterfly 2:16.09, 400m IM 4:50.48; Edmonton amateur athlete of year 1974; Governor-General's silver medal 1976; *res.* Edmonton, Alta.

SMITH, Dallas (hockey); *b.* 10 Oct 1941, Hamiota, Man.; *given name:* Dallas Earl; *m.* Sharlene; *children:* two; Estevan Sask.

Smith

Bruins juniors to pro with Boston Bruins 1959-60; in minors with Hull-Ottawa (EPHL), Pittsburgh (AHL), Portland, San Francisco (WHL), Oklahoma City (CPHL) before staying with Bruins 1967-68; on two Stanley Cup winners; NHL record 803 regular season games, 52 goals, 228 assists, 280 points, 896 penalty minutes, plus 85 playoff games, three goals, 28 assists, 31 points and 128 penalty minutes; mem. Team Canada 1977; *res.* Crandall, Man.

SMITH, Glen (rowing); *b.* 5 Aug 1931, Grand Forks, B.C.; *given name:* Glen William; *m.* Jean McKerrow; *children:* JoAnne, Maureen, Gregory; U of British Columbia; physician; mem. 1954 British Empire Games gold medal eight-oared with cox; runner-up Grand Challenge Cup 1955 Royal Henley Regatta; mem. 1956 Olympic rowing team; mem. silver medal crew 1958 British Empire Games; mem. B.C. Sports Hall of Fame; *res.* Grand Forks, B.C.

SMITH, Graham (swimming); *b.* 9 May 1958, Edmonton, Alta.; *given name:* Donald Graham; Hillcrest HS; student; mem. Canadian swim team since 1973; at 16 youngest Canadian male swimmer to claim two titles one championship meet 1974, 100m breast stroke 1:08.04, 200m breast stroke 2:29.28; retained both titles since 1974; fastest times in world over 25m course in 100m breast stroke, 200m individual medley; through 1976 ranked third 100m, fourth 200m, ninth 200m IM, eighth 400m IM in world standings; silver medal 4x100m relay 1976 Olympics; set three Canadian records 100m breast stroke 1:03.92, 200m breast stroke 2:19.42, 400m IM 4:28.64; competed internationally Paris, London, Mexico, California, Cali Colombia; Governor-General's silver medal 1976; mem. Thunder Bay Thun-derbolts swim club under coach Don Talbot; *res.* Thunder Bay, Ont.

SMITH, Hooley (hockey); *b.* 7 Jan 1903, Toronto, Ont., *d.* 24 Aug 1963, Montreal, Que.; *given name:* Reginald Joseph; amateur hockey Toronto, mem. Granites team which won 1924 Olympic gold medal; turned pro Ottawa following season and helped Senators win 1927 Stanley Cup; to Montreal Maroons next season, in Stanley Cup final but lost; teamed with Nels Stewart, Babe Siebert to form famed Big S line five seasons; won 1935 Stanley Cup; captain team following season; once first team, once second team all-star; dealt to Boston Bruins 1936, NY Americans 1937; ended career 1941 with 200th goal; mem. Hockey Hall of Fame.

SMITH, Murray (hockey); *b.* 23 Oct 1945, Thunder Bay, Ont.; *given name:* Murray Edward; *m.* Sharon Wilson; *children:* Shannon Leigh; Lakehead U, B.A.; personnel manager; several seasons senior baseball Thunder Bay from Little League, Pony League; coach Little League baseball; all-time Lakehead hockey records in four-year college career: most career points 226, most single game points eight vs St. Cloud 1969, most career assists 134, most single game assists five 1969, most season assists 39 1969-70 shared with Rick Alexander 1973-74, most career hat-tricks six shared with Dwight Stirrett, most season hat-tricks three 1968-69 shared with Dave Vaillant 1971-72; led team scoring three seasons, team goals three seasons, team assists twice; twice league MVP; 1966-70 selected NAIA all-American; *res.* Sudbury, Ont.

SMITH, Shannon (swimming); *b.* 28 Sep 1961, Vancouver, B.C.; student; mem. Hyack Swim Club coached by Ron Jacks;

mem. national swim team since 1974; seventh 800m freestyle (FS), eighth 400m FS 1975 world; represented Canada 1976 Montreal Olympics, bronze 400m FS with personal best 4:14.60, sixth 800m FS; won 1977 Canada Cup title, four gold, four silver; Canadian record 800m FS 8:41.17 1977; B.C. junior athlete of year 1976; Governor-General's silver medal 1976; *res.* Vancouver, B.C.

SMITH, Sid (hockey); *b.* 11 Jul 1925, Toronto, Ont.; *given name:* Sidney James; *m.* June Millen; *children:* Scott, Blaine, Megan; Central Commerce HS; salesman; junior B de La Salle, junior A Oshawa Generals, Stafford seniors, Quebec Aces; pro 1946 Toronto Maple Leafs and after brief stint at Pittsburgh (AHL) farm club joined Leafs to stay through 1958; mem. three Stanley Cup winners; twice won Lady Byng trophy; once first team, twice second team all-star left wing; 12 NHL season record: 601 scheduled games, 186 goals, 183 assists for 369 points, plus 44 playoff games, 17 goals, 10 assists for 27 points; played in seven NHL all-star games; on retirement coached midget, junior C hockey briefly; mem. Toronto Oldtimers hockey team; *res.* Toronto, Ont.

SMITH, Tommy (hockey); *b.* 27 Sep 1885, Ottawa, Ont., *d.* 1 Aug 1966, Ottawa, Ont.; began playing with St. Patrick's Lyceum juniors; senior with Federal League Ottawa Victorias 1906, led scorers, scored six more in three games with Ottawa Senators end of season; joined Pittsburgh (IL) 1907 and led team with 23 goals in 22 games; as rover with Brantford led Ontario Pro HL scorers 1909, 33 goals in 13 games; with Galt led scorers, 1911 league title; lost vs Ottawa for Stanley Cup; joined Maritime pro league with Moncton 1912 winning league crown but again losing Cup vs Quebec Bulldogs (NHA); joined Quebec next season where he formed line with Joe Malone, Jack Marks; trailed Malone by four goals 39-43 in scoring race and won only Stanley Cup; nickname The Little Bulldog (5'4" 150 lbs); dealt to Canadiens 1917 and when NHA dissolved following season left hockey; returned for 10 games with Quebec 1919, scoreless, retired at 35; in 171 recorded games scored 239 goals plus 15 in 15 playoff games; five times led league scorers and during 1913 campaign scored in 14 consecutive games; twice scored nine goals in single game, one eight-goal game, four five-goal games, 10 four-goal games, 15 three-goal games; no records for International or Maritime League play; mem. Hockey Hall of Fame.

SMITH-JOHANNSEN, Herman (skiing); *b.* 15 Jun 1875, Olso, Norway; *m.* Alice Robinson; *children:* Alice Elizabeth, Robert, Ella Margaret; Norwegian Military Academy, U of Berlin; retired engineer; instrumental in introducing skiing as form of travel to North America; nicknamed Jackrabbit by Cree and Ojibway Indians; opened Maple Leaf Trail Labelle to Shawbridge 30s; since 1950 (age 75) confined skiing to cross-country; instrumental in setting trail for Lachute-Ottawa marathon, competes occasionally; at 99 honored by King Olav X of Norway with Medal of St. Olav, first time medal to non-resident; subject of CBC films "Jackrabbit" and "The Long Ski Trail" and book *Jackrabbit — his first 100 years;* Dubonnet skier of year 1975; Order of Canada 1972; *res.* Piedmont, Que.

SMYLIE, Rod (football); *b.* 25 Dec 1924, Toronto, Ont.; *given name:* Roderick; *m.* Helen Quebec; *children:* Catharine, Diane, Kristin, Rod; commercial traveller; nickname

Little Citation while playing 11 years in CFL with Argos 1945-46, 1948-55, Ottawa Trojans ORFU champions 1947; captain Argos 1951; mem. four Grey Cup champions; modern era (1945-73) Argo all-star team as slotback; *res.* Islington, Ont.

SMYTHE, Conn (hockey); *b.* 1 Feb 1895, Toronto, Ont.; *m.* Irene 1919; *children:* Hugh, Mariam, Stafford (*d.*), Patricia; U of Toronto; retired pres. sand and gravel co., hockey executive; captain Toronto Varsity 1915 Ontario champions; coached Varsity to 1927 Allan Cup, Varsity Grads to 1928 Olympic title; coach NY Rangers, released after assembling team that went on to win 1928 Stanley Cup; purchased Toronto Pats, changed name to Maple Leafs; involved in Maple Leaf Gardens construction 1931; managing director, later pres. of Gardens, retired 1961 after his team had won seven Stanley Cups; supervised construction of Hockey Hall of Fame, Toronto's CNE; his Winfield Farms racing stable produced Queen's Plate winners 1953, 1967; mem. Hockey, Canadian Sports Halls of Fame; *res.* Caledon, Ont., Palm Beach, Fla.

SNELLING, Charles (figure skating); *b.* 17 Sep 1937, Toronto, Ont.; *m.* Velma Green; *children:* Bradley, Lisa, Scott; U of Toronto, M.D.; plastic surgeon; Canadian junior men's title 1952; Canadian men's senior titles 1954-58, 1964; competed North American five times winning silver medal 1957; world championships seven times winning bronze 1957, fourth 1956; mem. Canadian Olympic teams 1956, 1964; *res.* Winnipeg, Man.

SNELLING, Deryk (swimming); *b.* 22 Jul 1933, Darwen, Lancashire, Eng.; pro swim coach; British national swimmer and English champion; coach Southampton Swim Club 1962, developed competitors Alan Kimber, Ray Terrell, Nigel Kemp, David Haller; head coach Dolphin Swim Club 1967, won Canadian team title each year during tenure with swimmers setting hundreds of records; protegées won gold, silver, bronze medals in Commonwealth, Pan-Am, Olympic, World Aquatic Games; placed 14 swimmers on 1972 Canadian Olympic team; coached Canadian national team 1971 Pan-Am Games, 1972, 1976 Olympics, 1973 World Aquatic championships, 1974 Commonwealth Games; Etobicoke swim coach 1977; wrote *All About Individual Medley* (1975); *res.* Toronto, Ont.

SOBRIAN, Jules (shooting); *b.* 22 Jan 1935, San Fernando, Trinidad; *m.* Frances; *children:* Camille, Glenn; St. Mary's College Trinidad, U of Toronto, M.D.; physician; since 1966 won frequent Canadian championships; silver medal free pistol, bronze rapid fire 1966 Commonwealth Games; bronze centrefire, silver team 1967 Pan-Am Games; bronze centrefire, silver team 1971 Pan-Am Games; silver rapid fire, gold free pistol 1973 Commonwealth Games; gold free pistol 1973 Western hemisphere championships; bronze free pistol, silver rapid fire 1975 Pan-Am Games; gold free pistol, rapid fire 1975 pre-Olympic international; represented Canada 1968, 1972, 1976 Olympics; *res.* Omeemee, Ont.

SOMERVILLE, Sandy (golf, cricket); *b.* 4 May 1903, London, Ont.; *given name:* Charles Ross; *m.* Eleanor Elizabeth Lyle; *children:* Philip, Kenneth; Ridley College, U of Toronto; retired life insurance executive; played in last international cricket match between Canada, US 1921; holds highest score for school cricket in Canada, 212 not out; mem. 12th Battery Ontario intermediate hockey champions 1926; won Canadian amateur six times between 1926-37, runner-up three times; 1926 won Manitoba amateur, first of four Ontario amateurs; first Canadian to win US amateur beating Johnny Goodman Baltimore 1932, CP poll Canadian male athlete of year; 1938 semifinalist British amateur; CP poll Canadian golfer of half century 1950; Canadian Seniors Golf Association title twice, shared title twice; pres. RCGA 1957, Canadian Seniors Golf Association 1969-70; mem. RCGA, Canadian Sports Halls of Fame; *res.* London, Ont.

SORENSEN, Ole (wrestling); *b.* 23 Apr 1948, Randers, Denmark; *given name:* Ole Toft; St. Catharines HS, U of Western Ontario, B.A., U of Alberta, B.P.E.; technical director Canadian Amateur Wrestling Association; letters, Ontario titles gymnastics, wrestling in HS; bronze W (most valuable wrestler), Claude Brown Memorial Cup (most valuable male athlete) UWO; block A most valuable wrestler at Alberta; Province of Alberta, Ontario Sports Achievement Awards, several aquatic awards; high jump, pole vault, wrestling titles in college; Alberta, Ontario, Western Canada Open, college and YMCA wrestling titles; represented Canada 1970 world, Commonwealth teams (bronze medal), 1972 Munich Olympics, Canadian U touring team, 1973 World Student Games Moscow; coached wrestling, gymnastics, aquatics; *res.* Ottawa, Ont.

SPENCER, Jim (soccer); *b.* 13 Feb 1915, North Vancouver, B.C.; *given name:* James Haggarty; *m.* Sheina Kathleen; *children:* Jesslen Helen; North Vancouver HS; retired fire chief; juvenile with North Shore Bluebirds winning all league titles plus several mainland, provincial cups; captained North Vancouver HS to bantam title; coach, manager four consecutive Vancouver all-star teams vs visiting Europeans; director, chairman B.C. Juvenile Soccer Association 1962-76; two Dominion soccer titles, finalist once; mem. every B.C. all-star team during first division career; played in California World's Fair for B.C. all-stars scoring seven goals in three games; mem. North Shore, B.C. Sports Halls of Fame; *res.* Vancouver, B.C.

SPIR, Peter (track); *b.* 6 Nov 1955, Manchester, Eng.; *given name:* Peter Charles; U of Oregon; student; 1974 set B.C. and Canadian junior mile record with 4:02.9; toured Europe with national team same year; set B.C. and Canadian 1500m junior record 1975 with 3:41.4 winning Canadian senior title; Canadian junior 800m title in 1:50.4, represented Canada World Student Games Rome; Canadian, B.C. junior 3000m steeplechase mark 8:53.4, B.C. senior 2000m 5:11.4 and B.C. junior 3000m 8:18 all in 1975; Pacific Eight Conference 1500m title in 3:42; B.C. indoor 1500m record in 3:46; personal bests in CASO competition placing second in 1500m 3:40.1, fourth 800m 1:49.7; represented Canada 1976 Montreal Olympics; *res.* Vancouver, B.C.

SPRAGUE, Dave (football); *b.* 11 Aug 1910, Dunkirk, N.Y. *d.* 20 Feb 1968, Ottawa, Ont.; *given name:* David Shafer; *m.* Catherine Anderson; *children:* David Jr., John, Judy, Peter, James; Delta HS; co. v.-pres; teamed with Huck Welch to lead Delta CI to Dominion championship; captain HS T&F team specializing in quarter-mile; football with Hamilton Tigers 1930; on two interprovincial, one Grey Cup winner; Ottawa Rough Riders 1933-41; twice captain Riders, helped win three Big Four titles, one

Grey Cup; all-Eastern, all-Canadian almost every year of 10-year career; mem. Ottawa, Canadian Football Hall of Fame.

SPRING, Doughy (lacrosse); *b.* 24 Jan 1888, Draper, Ont., *d.* 1974, New Westminster, B.C.; *given name:* Clifford; baker, mechanic; mem. New Westminster Salmonbellies 1905-36, five Minto Cup winners; prolific scorer judged by peers as outstanding player of his day; at 49 scored nine goals in single box lacrosse game; mem. Lacrosse Hall of Fame.

STACK, Frank (speedskating); *b.* 1 Jan 1906, Winnipeg, Man.; *m.* Edith Nixon; *children:* Bonnie, Diane; West Kildonan HS; retired salesman; competed regularly 1919-54 winning variety of honors; junior Western Canada titles 1919-23, senior 1924-29; Western Open indoor title 1929-32; North American senior men's indoor title Chicago 1931 setting world record five-mile standard 15:42.2; held title three years, runner-up four times; 1932 Olympics won bronze medal 10 000m, fourth 500m, 1500m for 10 points, highest by Canadian speedskater; six times Canadian champion, once runner-up; US outdoor title 1931; world indoor 500m record 47.0; won two events Norway 1934; represented Canada in six Olympics, three as competitor, others as official; only Canadian to win 10 000 Lakes championships also Silver Skate competition Minneapolis, set points record; age 60, after 12-year retirement, competed in Canadian indoor at Winnipeg taking three seconds, two thirds; lifetime mem. St. James Speedskating Club Winnipeg; Manitoba Centennial Committee 1970 speedskater of century; mem. Canadian Speedskating Association, Canadian Sports Halls of Fame; *res.* Winnipeg, Man.

STANLEY, Allan (hockey); *b.* 1 Mar 1926, Timmins, Ont.; *given name:* Allan Herbert; *m.* Barbara Bowie; hockey coach; began career with Holman Pluggers juvenile team twice winning Hepburn Trophy in OMHA; closed amateur career with Boston Olympics seniors; turned pro with Providence Reds (AHL); defence NY Rangers 1948-54; traded to Chicago 1954-56, Boston Bruins 1956-57, Toronto Maple Leafs 1958; on four Stanley Cup winners, eight all-star games; Philadelphia Flyers 1968-69, retired, rejected coaching offer Quebec Aces (AHL); operates successful hockey school; in 21 NHL seasons played in 1,244 games scoring 100 goals, 333 assists for 433 points, plus 110 playoff games scoring seven goals, 36 assists for 43 points; assistant coach Buffalo Sabres 1977; *res.* Fenelon Falls, Ont.

STANLEY, Barney (hockey); *b.* 1 Jun 1893, Paisley, Ont., *d.* 16 May 1971, Edmonton, Alta.; *given name:* Russell; junior hockey Paisley; amateur Edmonton Maritimers, Dominions and Albertas 1909-15 then joined Vancouver Millionaires 1915, won Stanley Cup; with Millionaires through 1918-19 season then played-coached amateur Edmonton Eskimos; rejoined pro ranks as player-coach Calgary Tigers 1920-22, Regina Capitals 1923-24, Edmonton Eskimos 1924-26, Winnipeg Maroons 1926-27; coach-manager Chicago Black Hawks 1927-28; next season with Minneapolis Millers then returned to coaching with Edmonton Pooler juniors for three years; during 15 years as pro played every position on the ice except goaler; in 216 games scored 144 goals; twice five goals in a game; mem. Hockey Hall of Fame.

STAPLETON, Pat (hockey); *b.* 4 Jul 1940, Sarnia, Ont.; *given name:* Patrick James; *m.* Jacqueline Prudence; *children:* Mary, Maureen, Tommy, Susan, Michael; hockey player; nickname Whitey; played junior B in Sarnia at 15, junior A with St. Catharines, all-star OHA defenceman and helped Teepees win Memorial Cup; turned pro with Sault Ste. Marie (EPHL) 1960-61; drafted by Boston and played parts of 1962-63 season with Bruins and Kingston (EPHL); two seasons with Portland (WHL), top defenceman first year, scored 29 goals second season; to Toronto in four-player deal then one day later drafted by Chicago 1965; remained with Black Hawks through 1973; player-coach WHA Chicago Cougars and with Ralph Backstrom, Dave Dryden, bought teams; became first person in major league hockey history to own team, manage, coach and play simultaneously; when Cougars collapsed joined Indianapolis Racers as player; mem. WHA Team Canada 1974 vs USSR; tied NHL playoff assists record with 13 in 1971 then set new standard of 15 in 1973 playoffs; Dennis Murphy Award as top WHA defenceman 1974; three times NHL second team, once WHA first team all-star; WHA record through 1976-77, 307 games, 22 goals, 167 assists for 189 points, 159 penalty minutes; in 10 NHL seasons played 635 games, 43 goals, 294 assists, 337 points, 353 penalty minutes; *res.* Indianapolis, Ind.

STEAD, Ron (baseball); *b.* 24 Sep 1936, London, Ont.; *m.* Betty; *children:* Ron, David, Heather, Jeff; Central Tech; training supervisor; began baseball career as batboy with Toronto International League 1945-54; launched pitching career in minor baseball Toronto, then London Senior Intercounty (IC) 1955; minor pro ball Toronto organization 1956-57; returned to Senior IC with Brantford 1958-66, Guelph 1967-72; 16-year IC record: 104-44 won-lost, 1,365 innings pitched, 1,231 strike outs, 262 walks, 119

complete games, 2.08 lifetime earned-run avg.; IC record lowest ERA one season, 0.35 in 77 innings Guelph 1967; four times first team all-star, twice second team; IC MVP 1960, 1963, 1965, 1967; mem. Ontario gold medal team 1969 Halifax Canada Summer Games; mem. Canadian Pan-Am Games team Winnipeg 1967; *res.* Chatham, Ont.

STEG, Ray (curling); *b.* 2 Feb 1938, Vita, Man.; *m.* Iris Kathleen Melnychuck; *children:* Shannon Donna Rae, Sean Colin; Emerson HS; RCMP staff sergeant; Canadian Branch Royal Caledonian Curling Club Royal Victoria Jubilee title 1967; three times winner Ontario Police title 1971, 1972, 1975, runner-up Canadian finals each time; represented Division Two OCA in Ontario Consols as third on John Winford's Navy Club rink 1971; mem. Ottawa RCMP, Lansdowne Curling Clubs; *res.* Ottawa, Ont.

STERNBERG, Gerry (football); *b.* 18 Mar 1943, Orsk, Russia; *given name:* Gerald; *div.; children:* Arlen; Bloor CI, U of Toronto, B.A., Osgoode Hall, LL.B.; barrister and solicitor; drafted by Edmonton 1965; Montreal Alouettes 1966-67; returned to Argos 1969-71; Hamilton Tiger-Cats 1971-72, Argos 1973; second to Jim Copeland in Argos records for punt returns with 151 for 861yds; *res.* Toronto, Ont.

STEVENS, Warren (football); *b.* 1905, Syracuse, N.Y., *m.* Charlotte "Chubby" Tickner; *children:* Jacqueline; Syracuse U, B.Sc.; retired U of Toronto athletic director; reputation as passing quarterback while leading Syracuse HS to city football title; all-American mention in university senior year; skilled baseball player; rejected pro offers from Philadelphia Athletics; lured to Canada by Shag Shaughnessy, Frank McGill, played for

MAAA Winged Wheelers and coached McGill backfield; made Canadian rugby-football history 1931 tossing first legal forward pass to end Frank Robinson; Wheelers went on to win Grey Cup that year and Stevens completed first Grey Cup 40-yd TD pass to Ken Grant; first to score convert on fake placement and run in Grey Cup; retired from competition and became first athletic director U of T 1932 remaining until 1970 retirement; as head football, basketball coach (roles he yielded 1941) claimed three Intercollegiate football and basketball championships; *res.* Toronto, Ont.

STEVENSON, Art (football); *b.* 30 May 1916, Gothenburg, Neb.; *given name:* Arthur Clement; *m.* Dorothy Bowden; *children:* Sally, Curtis, Gary; Hastings College; obstetrician, gynecologist; Little all-American, national honorable mention in basketball; Little all-American in football 1936 and conference discus championship; turned pro Winnipeg Blue Bombers 1937-41; after WW2 coached Bomber backfield; best all-around athlete ever at Hastings College; mem. Canadian Football Hall of Fame; *res.* Phoenix, Ariz.

STEVENSON, Roy (football); *b.* 21 Oct 1930, Drumbo, Ont.; *given name:* Douglas Roy; *m.* Barbara Jean St. Pierre; *children:* Chrystal Ann, Roderick Michael (*d.*), Tevy Joan, Reme Marie, Wendy May; U of Toronto, U of Alberta, M.Sc.; hydrogeologist; mem. U of T boxing team 1951-52; football with Kitchener-Waterloo Dutchmen 1953-54 winning ORFU title 1954 then losing Little Grey Cup game to Edmonton Eskimos; with Eskimos 1955-62; mem. Grey Cup champions 1955, 1956, finalists 1960; line coach U of Alberta Golden Bears 1964-70 winning Canadian college title 1967, runner-up 1965; *res.* Edmonton, Alta.

STEWART, Black Jack (hockey); *b.* 6 May 1917, Pilot Mound, Man.; *given name:* John Sherratt; race track judge; played two years junior Portage La Prairie; pro 1938 with Detroit Red Wings but spent all but 33 games with Pittsburgh (AHL); Detroit regular following season through 1949-50, Chicago Black Hawks 1950-52; twice mem. Stanley Cup winner; three times first team, twice second team all-star defenceman; Detroit MVP 1942-43; following retirement coached Chatham Maroons, senior OHA teams in Windsor, Kitchener and Pittsburgh (AHL); in 503 NHL games scored 30 goals, 79 assists; mem. Hockey Hall of Fame; *res.* Troy, Mich.

STEWART, Gordon (track and field); *b.* 6 Sep 1948, Toronto, Ont.; *given name:* Gordon William; *m.* Sandra Maynard; Simon Fraser U, B.A., M.Sc.; fitness director occupational health; five years minor hockey TMHL; city all-star basketball 1967; North Toronto CI athlete of year 1966-67; set Toronto junior pole vault, triple jump records 1962-67; Canadian midget triple jump 1964 with 43' 9¼"; competed in first pentathlon 1967, first decathlon 1968 setting Canadian junior record while winning title with 6,150 points; won Canada Games decathlon Halifax 1969; sixth decathlon Edinburgh Commonwealth Games 1970, eighth Cali Colombia Pan-Am Games 1971; Canadian decathlon record 7,438 points 1972; 16th World Student Games Moscow 1973; Canadian decathlon title 7,129 points 1974; third 181lb weightlifting class Pacific Northwest meet 1974, fifth B.C. Festival of Sport; first 1976 Canadian Olympic trials decathlon with 7,026 points but was not selected to team as effort below Olympic standard; *res.* Victoria, B.C.

STEWART, Mary (swimming); *b*. 8 Dec 1945, Vancouver, B.C.; *m*. R.H. McIlwaine; U of British Columbia, B.E.; teacher; coached by Howard Firby; age 13 represented Canada 1959 Pan-Am Games, second 4x100 freestyle (FS) relay, sixth 100m butterfly; 1960 Olympics eighth 100m FS; 1962 Commonwealth Games first 100yd butterfly, third 110yd FS; 1963 Pan-Am Games second 100m butterfly, FS; 1964 Olympics eighth 100m butterfly, sixth 4x100m medley relay; British, American, Canadian national titles in butterfly, FS, backstroke; Canadian female athlete of year (Velma Springstead Trophy) 1961-62; outstanding female swimmer 1961-62; exhibition tours New Zealand 1962, Rhodesia 1964; mem. Pan-Am Games headquarters committee 1975 Mexico City; B.C. Lions football team mascot 1958-63; *res*. Vancouver, B.C.

STEWART, Nels (hockey); *b*. 29 Dec 1900, Montreal, Que., *d*. 21 Aug 1957, Wasaga Beach, Ont.; *given name:* Nelson Robert; brewery rep; joined Montreal Maroons 1925-26 scoring 34 goals in rookie season and 39 the following season to earn nickname Old Poison; with Babe Siebert, Hooley Smith formed S Line; scored 134 goals, 56 assists during five years on Line; first NHL player to score more than 300 goals (324 goals, 191 assists in 653 league games), record stood many years; traded to Boston Bruins 1932 for three seasons then moved to NY Americans until 1939-40; twice won Hart Trophy; mem. one Stanley Cup winner; coach Port Colborne Seniors after retirement; mem. Hockey Hall of Fame.

STEWART, Ron (football); *b*. 25 Sep 1934, Toronto, Ont.; *m*. Wendy Thomas; Riverdale CI, Queen's U, B.A., B.P.H.E., U of Ottawa, LL.B.; lawyer, sports administrator; with Queen's 1955-56 Yates Cup winners, league MVP 1957, Webster scholarship 1958; pro football Ottawa Rough Riders 1958-70, Grey Cup winners 1960, 1968, 1969, finalists 1966; Jeff Russel Memorial Trophy 1960, 1967; Schenley top Canadian 1960; CP poll Canadian male athlete of year 1960; Walker Trophy (Ottawa football club MVP) 1960, 1967; Eastern Conference all-star 1960, 1964; Ottawa Jaycees young man of year, Ontario Achievement Award 1970; sweater No. 11 retired by Rough Riders; CFL record most yds gained single game (287 at Montreal Oct 1960); 13-season record 983 carries, 5690yds, 5.8yds-per-carry avg., 41 TDs; *res*. Edelweiss Valley, Wakefield, Que.

STEWART, Ron (hockey); *b*. 11 Jul 1932, Calgary, Alta.; *given name:* Ronald George; *m*. Barbara Christie; hockey executive; minor hockey ranks to junior Toronto Marlboros, Windsor Spitfires, Barrie Flyers, Guelph Biltmores all in one season helping latter win Memorial Cup 1952; to Toronto Maple Leafs for 13 seasons; to Boston, St. Louis, NY Rangers, Vancouver, NY Islanders during last eight years of NHL career; in 21 seasons played in 1,353 games scoring 276 goals, 253 assists for 529 points, 560 penalty minutes, plus 119 playoff games, 14 goals, 21 assists for 35 points, 60 penalty minutes; coached 1973-74 Portland (WHL) team from last place to playoff final, 1974-75 Springfield Kings to AHL championship; NY Ranger coach 1975-76; player personnel director 1977; on three Stanley Cup winners; *res*. Barrie, Ont.

STIMPSON, Earl (golf); *b*. 22 May 1914, Ottawa, Ont.; *m*. Cecile O'Hara; *children:* Beverley Anne, Colleen; Glebe CI; golf pro; CPGA mem. 1934, now life mem.; for 17 years owned and operated Ottawa region's largest driving range; 1966 taught game to United Nations troops in Egypt; 28 years operated winter golf school for YM-YWCA in Ottawa; first pres., only lifetime mem. Manderley Golf Club; trophy bearing name awarded annually top pro Ottawa Valley; *res.* Ottawa, Ont., Pinella Park, Fla.

STINSON, Wally (administration); *b.* 2 Jun 1918, Austin, Man.; *given name:* Edgar Wallace; *sep.; children:* Donna, Allan, Ronald; U of Manitoba, B.A., U of Saskatchewan, B.Ed.; professor; secretary Saskatchewan branch AAU of C 1951-58, pres. 1959; pres. AAU of C 1963; mem. National Council on Physical Fitness 1948-53, National Advisory Council 1961; since 1965 v.-pres. Commonwealth Games Association of Canada; director Sports Federation of Canada, Canadian Track and Field Association; chairman technical advisory board Canada Winter Games Saskatoon 1971; assistant manager Canadian Commonwealth Games team Edinburgh; general manager Canadian Commonwealth Games team Christchurch N.Z. 1974; track referee Winnipeg Pan-Am Games 1967, Canada Summer Games Halifax; CAHPER award of honor 1972; mem. Sask. Sports Hall of Fame; *res.* Saskatoon, Sask.

STIRLING, Bummer (football); *b.* 23 Oct 1907, London, Ont.; *given name:* Hugh; *m.* Jean; *children:* Heather, Susan; St. Thomas CI; director employee relations; on 1928 Dominion junior football champions, Sarnia Imperials (ORFU) 1929; starred with Imperials through 1937, all-star 1932-37, all-Eastern 1934-36, ORFU MVP 1936; CP poll Canadian male athlete of year 1938; mem. Canadian Football, Sports Halls of Fame; *res.* Calgary, Alta.

STOCKTON, Donald (wrestling); *b.* 22 Feb 1904, Montreal, Que.; *given name:* Donald Parker; *m.* Margaret Connolly; *children:* Alan, Barbara, Patricia, Eric; retired foreman; at 19 won Quebec 160lb wrestling title; represented Canada three Olympics, 1924, 1928, 1932, placed fourth 1924 158lb class, silver 1928 174lb class; 11 Quebec, six Canadian titles at varying weights 160-191lbs; aside from Olympics, lost only one major match in career, 1925 Canadian 174lb title to Arthur Coleman; defeated Coleman following night in 191lb title match; 1930 British Empire 174lb title; joined Verdun junior football team 1924; following year joined CNR Intermediates winning ORFU title over Sarnia; joined Montreal Winged Wheelers 1927-29; in mid-20s played with Verdun AC lacrosse team; coached several seasons minor football in Montreal winning one juvenile city and district, minor league city and district intermediate championships; chief referee, chief judge, supervisor of referees and judges for Quebec; mem. AAU of C, Canadian Amateur Wrestling Halls of Fame; *res.* La Salle, Que.

STOREY, Fred (curling); *b.* 3 Mar 1932, Empress, Alta.; *given name:* Frederick Lewis; *m.* Paulette Pronovost; *children:* Debbie, Wayne, Sandie, Cheryl, Ron, James; Mount Royal College; accounting supervisor; second for Alberta team in 1951 Canadian Schoolboy championships; lead for seven Alberta title rinks, appeared in seven Briers winning three titles and world championship as lead for Ron Northcott; as lead for H. Brown won 1961 Edmonton Tournament of Champions; with Northcott took CBC Cross Canada curling title Winnipeg 1964, Canadian Open Carspiel Edmonton 1965, Vancouver Evergreen Tournament of Champions 1971, repeat as lead for George Fink 1973; Calgary Masters title 1972; Brier all-star lead; since 1969 honorary life mem. Calgary Curling Club, pres. 1974-75; Canadian Curling Hall of Fame; *res.* Calgary, Alta.

STOREY, Red (football, hockey); *b.* 5 Mar 1918, Barrie, Ont.; *given name:* Roy Alvin; *m.* Helen Saint Pierre; *children:* Bob, Doug; Barrie CI; public relations; played football with Toronto Argos 1936-41 leading team to Grey Cup victories 1937-38; scored record three TDs in final quarter 1938 Grey Cup; received offers from NY Giants, Chicago Bears in NFL; officiated 14 years Quebec Football League, 12 years Intercollegiate League, 12 years CFL; hockey with Barrie juniors, RCAF Camp Borden, Atlantic City (EHL), Sault Ste. Marie (Michigan League), Montreal Royals (Quebec senior); refereed seven years Quebec junior, provincial, senior leagues, nine years AHL, nine years NHL; eight years lacrosse with Orillia, Hamilton Tigers, Lachine, Montreal Canadiens; once scored 12 goals in single game; refereed 10 years Quebec senior league; with son Bob (Hamilton 1967, Montreal 1970) only father-son combination Grey Cup history to play on two title winners each; mem. Hockey Hall of Fame; *res.* Montreal, Que.

STREIT, Marlene Stewart (golf); *b.* 9 Mar 1934, Cereal, Alta.; *m.* J. Douglas Streit; *children:* two; Rollins College; 1951 won first of nine Canadian ladies' Closed and 11 Canadian Opens; 1953 won British women's amateur, first of four US national mixed foursomes; 1956 won US women's amateur, US North-South (also 1974), US Intercollegiate, Jasper Totem Pole, Canadian Open and Closed, Rochester Invitational; won 34 consecutive matches, a feat unequalled; won nine Ontario ladies', three Helen Lee Doher-ty tourneys; only woman to win Canadian, British, Australian and US national amateur titles; 1956 Shell Wonderful World of Golf title beating pro Marilyn Smith in Oslo Norway, 1957 runner-up to Mickey Wright; 1961 low amateur in US Open; represented Ontario on numerous provincial teams and Canada in frequent international events; mem. Canadian Golf, Canadian Sports Halls of Fame; Lou Marsh Trophy 1951, 1956; Order of Canada; *res.* Streetsville, Ont.

STRIDE, Bryan (track); *b.* 9 Feb 1951, Guelph, Ont.; *given name:* Bryan Alexander; *m.* Margaret MacGowan; John F. Ross CVI, Brock U, B.P.E.; teacher; middle distance, cross-country specialist; fourth 3000m steeplechase (9:24) Pan-Am Games 1975, second 3000m steeplechase (8:45) Canadian national Sudbury 1975; winner OUAA cross-country Guelph 1975; second Canadian indoor 3000m (8:15) Edmonton 1976; third 3000m (8:22) Canada vs Great Britain 1976; times: 800m (1:52), 1500m (3:48), 3000m steeplechase (8:45); *res.* St. Catharines, Ont.

STRIDE, Margaret (track); *b.* 21 Sep 1954, Waterford, Ont.; *given name:* Margaret Eleanor MacGowan; *m.* Bryan Stride; Waterford DHS, Brock U; teacher; represented Canada 1974 Commonwealth Games, team bronze 4x400 relay; team gold 4x400 relay, individual sixth 400m final 1975 Pan-Am Games Mexico; won 400m 1975 Canadian national; third 400m 1975 pre-Olympics Montreal; led 1976 Olympics qualifiers 400m (53.9), third 200m (23.5); finalist 4x400 relay 1976 Montreal Olympics; best personal times: 100m (11.4), 200m (23.4), 400m (52.8); *res.* St. Catharines, Ont.

STRIKE, Hilda (track); *b.* 1 Sep 1910, Montreal, Que.; *m.* Fred Sisson; *children:* Barbara; Canadian Commercial College; stenographer; spotted 1929 by Olympic gold medalist Myrtle Cook while playing softball, joined Canadian Ladies' AC in Montreal; by 1932 won Quebec, Canadian sprint championships; finalist 1930 British Empire Games Hamilton; silver 100m sprint 1932 Olympics Los Angeles; equalled 1928 Olympic 100m record of 12.2 in Quebec championships 1932; anchored silver medal relay team 1932 Olympics; helped Murray's AC team win Montreal Ladies' Softball title as shortstop; with Myrtle Cook formed Murray's AC, Mercury Track Club and became coach; represented Canada 1934 British Empire Games, silver medals 100yd, 4x110 relay; Canadian female athlete of year, Montreal's most popular female athlete 1932; mem. AAU of C, Canadian Sports Halls of Fame; *res.* Montreal, Que.

STRONG, Lawrence (tennis); *b.* 17 May 1940, London, Eng.; *given name:* Lawrence Franklin; *m.* Vivienne Russel Cox; *children:* Nicole, Danielle, Suzette; U of London, B.Sc.; general management; in Great Britain won Schoolboy title, English International honors; with wife took Canadian mixed doubles title 1968, mixed doubles gold medal 1969 Canada Games; captain Canadian Davis Cup team 1970-71; won many Ontario men's, mixed doubles honors; pres. OLTA 1970-72, v.-pres. CLTA 1974-75, pres. CLTA 1976; *res.* Willowdale, Ont.

STUART, Bruce (hockey); *b.* 30 Nov 1881, Ottawa, Ont., *d.* 28 Oct 1961, Ottawa, Ont.; *m.* Irene; shoe store owner; joined Ottawa Senators 1898-99 as rover, left wing two seasons scoring 12 goals in six games; Quebec Bulldogs one season, rejoined Ottawa 1901-02 then moved to International pro league with Pittsburgh, Houghton Mich., Portage Lakes; helped Montreal Wanderers win 1908 Stanley Cup; returned to Ottawa following season, captained club to 1911 Stanley Cup; in three Cup victories scored 17 goals in seven games; in 45 career scheduled games posted 63 goals including six in single game vs Quebec; two five-goal games; mem. Ottawa, Hockey Halls of Fame.

STUART, Hod (hockey); *b.* 1879, Ottawa, Ont., *d.* 23 Jun 1907, Belleville, Ont.; *given name:* William Hodgson; public school hockey to Ironsides, Ottawa Senators, Quebec, Pittsburgh Victorias; managed Calumet Mich. two seasons before rejoining Pittsburgh, captain 1906; joined Montreal Wanderers and helped them win 1907 Stanley Cup; 16 goals in 33-game career; flying wing eight years with Ottawa Rough Riders; mem. Greater Ottawa Sports, Hockey Halls of Fame.

STUBBS, Lorraine (equestrian); *b.* 9 Jun 1950, Toronto, Ont.; *given name:* Constance Lorraine; York U, B.A., M.A.; dressage specialist; began riding 1952 with Eglinton Equestrian Club; mem. Canadian Equestrian team since 1971 competing in Cali Colombia Pan-Am Games that year; mem. sixth place 1972 Munich Olympics team; silver medal 1975 Mexico Pan-Am Games; third Aachen W. Germany international horse show 1974; fifth St. George's Rotterdam 1974; sixth intermediate Rotterdam 1974; 15th St. George's Copenhagen world 1974; seventh Aachen Grand Prix 1975; 12th in ride-off, fourth Vienna Grand Prix 1975; sixth Vienna intermediate 1975; second Nörten-Hardenburg Germany 1975; won Grand Prix, Special, Ontario dressage championships; mem. Canadian team 1976 Olympics; *res.* Willowdale, Ont.

STUKUS, Annis (football); *b.* 25 Oct 1914, Toronto, Ont.; *given name:* Annis Paul; *m.* Doris Louise Shannon; *children:* Suzanne, Sally, Mary Louise; Parkdale HS, Central Tech; sportscaster; played with junior Argos, then senior club 1935-41; Oakwood Indians 1942, Balmy Beach 1943, Toronto Navy 1944, Toronto Indians 1945-46; organized Edmonton Eskimos 1949, coach three seasons; coached B.C. Lions through formative stages; general manager Vancouver Canucks 1967; trophy in his honor awarded to CFL coach of year; mem. Canadian Football Hall of Fame; *res.* Vancouver, B.C.

STUKUS, Bill (football); *b.* 18 May 1916, Toronto, Ont.; *given name:* William Joseph; St. Frances, Parkdale CI, St. Michael's College; bookkeeper; Toronto Argos 1936-41, then RCAF Hurricanes; Toronto Indians 1945-46, rejoined Argos 1947, sat out 1948, Edmonton 1949-51; on four Grey Cup winners; *res.* Toronto, Ont.

STUKUS, Frank (football); *b.* 7 Aug 1918, Toronto, Ont.; *m.* Anna Havery *(d.); children:* Frank Jr., Maureen Elizabeth; *m.* Pauline Audrey Woolings; Central Tech; retired resort, camp operator; Argos 1938-41, Toronto Indians 1942, Toronto Beaches 1943-44; purchased Toronto Indians 1945 and established first co-op football club; established first summer hockey camp 1961; coached one season intermediate football Oshawa; *res.* Toronto, Ont.

SUGARMAN, Ken (football); *b.* 16 Jun 1942, Portland, Ore.; *given name:* Kenneth Lee; *m.* Carolyn; *children:* Kenny, Trevor; Whitworth College, B.A., Simon Fraser U; apple rancher, warehouse operator; Little all-American at Whitworth 1963; seventh draft choice Baltimore Colts, last cut 1964;

B.C. Lions 1964, remained nine seasons; three all-star games; captain Lions 1969-72, player representative 1968-72; Lions' most popular player 1969; Lauri Neimi award as outstanding B.C. lineman 1972; *res.* Tiefon, Wash.

SULLIVAN, Joe (hockey); *b.* 8 Jan 1901, Toronto, Ont.; U of Toronto; surgeon, senator; goaler with U of T Grads hockey team which won 1928 Olympic gold medal; 1950 CP poll team of half century; won Intercollegiate golf title, Ontario amateur, runner-up 1924 Canadian amateur; *res.* Toronto, Ottawa, Ont.

SULLIVAN, Tommy (boxing); *b.* 29 Dec 1904, Dublin, Ireland; *m.* Claire Carroll; *children:* Sharon, Deirdre; retired; boxed as amateur 1921-31 winning 147lb Quebec provincial title 1931; Lions Newsboy title Toronto 1931; finalist US junior nationals Boston 1931; refereed boxing for Montreal Athletic Commission 1936-56; boxing coach RCAF St. Thomas, Trenton, Moncton 1939-45; Canadian Grenadier Guards Montreal 1948-56; Canadian Olympic boxing coach Helsinki 1952; national coach Canadian Amateur Boxing Association 1971-72; *res.* Chapeau, Que.

SUZUKI, Arthur (basketball); *b.* 29 Jul 1937, New Westminster, B.C.; *m.* Marlene Dubrick; *children:* Robert, William, Karen; London Central CI, U of Western Ontario; supervisor production, inventory control; in HS two London Ont. city titles football, one basketball; one year junior varsity league champions UWO; joined Tillsonburg Livingstons, Canadian finals 1958, Ontario title 1959; senior A basketball London Five B's 1965; Ontario intermediate A champion 3M 1966; Ontario senior A champion Sarnia

Drawbridge Inn 1967 winning Canada Winter Games gold medal; played London PUC recreational basketball six different teams 1960-75; with Ontario champion London Celtics senior A 1973; basketball official 1961-66; *res.* London Ont.

SWAN, Bob (skiing); *b.* 1946, Winnipeg, Man.; *given name:* Robert George; Hull HS, Carleton U, Notre Dame U, B.Sc.; pro skier, summer ski camp coach, construction worker; mem. Canadian alpine team 1963-69 competing in 1964, 1968 Olympics; mem. 1966 FIS team; second US slalom championships 1965, eighth twice 1967 North American World Cup giant slalom; seventh Franconia National slalom World Cup 1967; top Canadian, third, 1971 Canadian slalom championships; mem. Head pro team 1972-76; third K2 cup giant slalom Boyne Mountain Michigan 1972; peddled three-speed bicycle 2,500 miles Nelson to Ottawa 1968 in 19 days; *res.* Nelson, B.C.

SZTEHLO, Zoltan (equestrian); *b.* 27 Nov 1921, Budapest, Hungary; *m.* Rhonda; Royal Hungarian Military Academy, U of Debrecen, LL.D.; lawyer, sheriff; accredited dressage judge International Equestrian Federation; competed in Hungary 1930; former Hungarian junior sabre champion; mem. 1971 gold medal Pan-Am Games dressage team; Western Canadian dressage title 1972, 1974, 1975; gold 1975 Western Canada Summer Games Regina; competed 1968 Olympics Mexico; trainer-coach modern pentathlon team Alberta gold medalists Western Canada Summer Games 1975; on equestrian jury 1967 Pan-Am Games; trainer 1971 gold medal team Cali Colombia Pan-Am Games, 1972 Munich Olympic team; award winning course designer; *res.* Calgary, Alta.

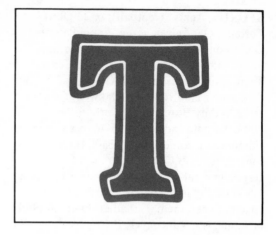

TAKACS, Ed (track); *b.* 12 Feb 1954, Brantford, Ont.; *given name:* Edward Donald; Brantford CIVS, Villanova U; student; winner OFSSA 800m (1:53) 1973; won Ontario senior 800m (1:51.1), Junior Olympics (1:51.1), Ontario Games (1:53) 1974; won Toronto Invitational 1500m (3:43.8), Metropolitan Games mile (4:03.8), IC4A 800m (1:46.9) 1975; *res.* Brantford, Ont.

TAKAHASHI, Allyn (judo); *b.* 20 May 1956, Montreal, Que.; *given name:* Masao Allyn; Merivale HS, Waterloo U; student; three times Ontario 120lb, once 127lb champion; 1969-76 winner 30, runner-up nine of 40 competitions entered in 120-139lb categories; bronze medal USJA nationals 1972; mem. Canadian youth team which toured Germany 1972; titles won include Eastern Canadian (three), Ontario HS (three), Kingston Y Asahi, Canadian junior Olympics, North East Regional trials (twice), CNE International (three), world junior Shiai; ACT (Ottawa) amateur sports award 1972-74, Merivale HS phys ed award 1972-73; Shodan black belt 1972; *res.* Ottawa, Ont.

TAKAHASHI, June (judo); *b.* 17 Jun 1933, Vancouver, B.C. *given name:* June Hayami; *m.* Masao; *children:* Allyn, Philip, Ray, Tina; first degree (Shodan) black belt 1968, second degree (Nidan) black belt 1975; assists husband Mas in operation of Japanese Martial Arts Centre; North East Region Canadian Judo Association secretary-treasurer, director of judo for women 1975-76; national councillor Judo Canada 1976-78; *res.* Ottawa, Ont.

TAKAHASHI, Masao (judo); *b.* 24 Jun 1929, Vancouver, B.C.; *m.* June Hayami; *children:* Allyn, Philip, Ray, Tina; judo instructor, operator Japanese Martial Arts Centre; holder of fifth degree black belt; numerous under-154lb class titles, holds three Canadian titles in unlimited weight category; mem. Canadian team 1961 Paris world championships; undefeated in Ontario Judo Masters championships; 1947 pitched Alberta Japanese evacuees (relocated from B.C.) to baseball league championship; medal winner in swimming and diving competitions while serving with RCAF at base Rockcliffe 1950; national councillor Judo Canada, v.-pres., councillor, regional director Judo Ontario, mem. grading committee; past referee-in-chief Judo Ontario; referee Pan-American Judo Federation; Centennial medal 1967; technical official for judo Montreal Olympics; *res.* Ottawa, Ont.

TAKAHASHI, Philip (judo); *b.* 12 Jun 1957, Toronto, Ont.; *given name:* Philip Masato; Bell HS, Algonquin College; student; Eastern Ontario Open title 80lb category 1969; 63 titles, six runner-up awards and five thirds in regional, provincial, national and international competitions including gold medals 58kg class Sonthofen Bavaria, Stuttgart Germany, Ontario Winter Games 1974, Canada Games 1975, Ontario Junior Olympics (twice), Canadian Youth Games, Ontario HS; first degree judo black belt 1973, second degree 1975; Detroit Mayor's Trophy for outstanding performance 1971-72; ACT (Ottawa) sports award for judo 1971, 1974, 1975; Ontario Sports Achievement Award 1970-75; *res.* Ottawa, Ont.

TAKAHASHI, Ray (judo, wrestling); *b.* 7 Aug 1958, Toronto, Ont.; *given name:* Raymond Hugh; Bell HS; student; competing at 55lbs won Ottawa Centennial tournament age eight; 38 gold medals, 12 silver, three bronze in regional, provincial, national, international judo competition; included are 1972, 1973 US junior nationals (gold, bronze), Ontario HS, Eastern Canadian, Ontario Opens and junior, Ontario Junior Olympics, Ontario Winter Games; freestyle wrestling gold medals in variety of Ontario meets, Michigan, Canadian junior, Ontario Winter Games, Canada Games, Ontario HS, Western Canadian Open; in 14 major wrestling competitions since 1973 has won 13 gold, one silver; represented Canada 1976 Olympics in 48kg (106lb) class winning one of three bouts; ACT (Ottawa) amateur sports award for wrestling, Ontario Sports Achievement Award 1975; *res.* Ottawa, Ont.

TAKAHASHI, Tina (judo); *b.* 13 Jan 1960, Toronto, Ont. *given name:* Alice Christina; Bell HS; student; judo honors Kingston 1968 in 60lb class; titles 48 times, runner-up once, third once, fourth once in major regional, provincial, national and international competitions; included are Ontario junior (five), Ontario Junior Olympics (three), Canadian Junior Olympics, USJA ladies, junior nationals, Eastern Canadian (twice), North

East Region (seven), Ontario Winter Games, Ontario HS (twice); first degree black belt 1976; *res*. Ottawa, Ont.

TALBOT, Jean Guy (hockey); *b*. 11 Jul 1932, Cap de la Madeleine, Que.; *m*. Pierrette Cormier; *children:* Carole, Danny, Michel; hockey coach; goaler for Dollard School midgets, then defence school, juvenile hockey Cap de la Madeleine; joined Trois-Rivières Reds; turned pro with Quebec Aces 1953-54, Shawinigan 1954-55, Montreal Canadiens through 1966-67; on seven Stanley Cup winners; Minnesota Jun 1967, Detroit for Bob McCord Oct 1967, St. Louis 1968, with Larry Keenan to Buffalo for Bobby Baun 1970; in 17 NHL campaigns played in 1,056 games scoring 43 goals, 242 assists for 285 points, 1,006 penalty minutes, plus 150 playoff games scoring four goals, 26 assists for 30 points, 142 penalty minutes; assistant coach NY Rangers from 1976; *res*. Montreal, Que.

TALLON, Dale (hockey, golf); *b*. 19 Oct 1950, Noranda, Que.; *given name:* Michael Dale Lee; Ryerson Polytechnical Inst.; Canadian junior golf championship 1969; missed Ontario title same year by single stroke; drafted out of midget hockey Noranda by Oshawa Generals of OHA, played one season then dealt to Toronto Marlboros for five players; first Vancouver choice, second overall in 1970 amateur draft; to Chicago Black Hawks 1973 for Jerry Korab, Gary Smith; seven games in Dallas (CHL) 1974-75, recalled to Chicago; through 1976-77 NHL record: 472 regular season games, 84 goals, 185 assists for 269 points, 459 penalty minutes, plus 25 playoff games, two goals, eight assists for 10 points, 41 penalty minutes; *res*. Vancouver, B.C.

TANNER, Elaine (swimming); *b*. 22 Feb 1951, Vancouver, B.C.; *m*. Ian Nahrgang; *children:* Scott; U of Alberta; operates sports store; 17 Canadian titles from 1965-68 including four successive years for 200m, 220yd backstroke and 100m, 110yd butterfly; title total includes 440yd freestyle (FS), sprint, backstroke, distance butterfly and both medleys; best times (in top three Canada all-time) FS 61.5 (100m), 2:14.8 (200m), 4:43.8 (400m), backstroke 66.7 (100m), 2:24.5 (200m), butterfly 65.4 (100m), 2:29.9 (200m), medley 2:31.8 (200m), 5:26.3 (400m); most successful woman swimmer 1966 Commonwealth Games at 15 with four gold, three silver, two world records; backstroke golds in world record times 1967 Pan-Am Games Winnipeg; Canadian, American, British butterfly sprint titles 1965; final competitive appearance 1968 Mexico Olympics, two silver, one bronze; Lou Marsh Trophy 1966, 1967; Canada's female athlete of year (Velma Springstead Trophy) 1966; Nickname Mighty Mouse; mem. Canadian Sports Hall of Fame; *res*. Prince George, B.C.

TATARCHUK, Hank (basketball); *b*. 2 Aug 1930, Vegreville, Alta.; *given name:* Waldman Erdi; *m*. Arlene Hauberg; *children:* Erik; U of Alberta, B.P.E., U of Ottawa, M.P.E.; major, Canadian Forces (RCAF); began athletic career playing hockey, baseball, softball, track, various championships in military 1951; phys ed specialist in training, fitness research sports programming; coach Royal Military College basketball 1963-67 with 62-32 won-lost record; assistant coach to Barry Michelson U of Alberta basketball 1967-68, Jack Lewis U of Manitoba 1968-71, Bob O'Billovich Carleton 1971-73, U of Ottawa 1973-76; director of basketball competition for COJO 1976

Olympics Montreal; National Association of Basketball Coaches of Canada merit award 1977; *res.* Ottawa, Ont.

TAYLOR, Betty (track); *b.* 22 Feb 1916, Ingersoll, Ont., *d.* 5 Feb 1977, Ottawa, Ont.; *m.* William Campbell; *children:* Margaret, David; McMaster U; competed in first hurdles event age 14, Canadian intermediate title 1930 in record time; competed Olympic Games 1932, 1936, British Empire Games 1934, women's world games London Eng.; won numerous Ontario races; final competitive event Berlin Olympics 1936 winning bronze when first four runners were given same time; CP poll Canadian female athlete of year 1936.

TAYLOR, Bobby (football, hockey); *b.* 5 Mar 1939, Barrow-in-Furness, Lancashire, Eng.; *div.; children:* Janet Lee, Bobby Jr.; hotel owner; played football Mount Royal College Cougars; pro 1961 Calgary Stampeders; remained in CFL 14 seasons playing wide receiver with Calgary (1961-65), Toronto Argos (1966-70, 1974), Hamilton Tiger-Cats (1971), Edmonton Eskimos (1971-73); career record 521 passes caught for 8,223yds, 15.8 avg. and 50 TDs; WFC record for Calgary 1963 with 74 receptions; twice led EFC receivers; all-Eastern 1969; played 10 years pro hockey in Toronto Maple Leafs, Philadelphia Flyers chains with Quebec City (AHL), Victoria, Seattle (WHL), Long Island, Cherry Hill N.J., Johnstown Pa. (EHL); *res.* Toronto, Ont.

TAYLOR, Cyclone (hockey); *b.* 23 Jun 1883, Tara, Ont.; *given name:* Fredrick; *m.* Thirza Cook; *children:* Fred Jr., John, Mary, Edward, Joan; retired, federal government; played in Listowel, Thessalon Ont., Portage La Prairie Man., before turning pro as defenceman with Houghton Mich. 1906; two years with both Ottawa, Renfrew, then Vancouver 1912-21; as rover, centre scored 194 goals in 186 league games, 15 more in 19 playoff games; five scoring titles; 32 goals in 18-game 1917-18 season, six in single game vs Victoria 1916-17; nickname Cyclone given him at Ottawa's CY Arena 1907 by Governor-General Earl Grey; on two Stanley Cup winners; Ottawa Capitals lacrosse team 1908-10 winning Mann Cup 1908; OBE; mem. Hockey, Lacrosse, Ottawa, B.C., Canadian Sports Halls of Fame; *res.* Vancouver, B.C.

TAYLOR, E.P. (horse racing); *b.* 29 Jan 1901, Ottawa, Ont.; *given name:* Edward Plunkett; *m.* Winnifred Thornton Duguid; *children:* one son, two daughters; Ashbury College, McGill U, B.Sc.; retired investment broker, brewer; owner of one of Canada's finest racing stables (Winfield Farms); Northern Dancer won Kentucky Derby 1964, Nijinsky II won Epson Derby 1970; pres. Ontario Jockey Club 1953-73; did much to revitalize and raise standard of racing in Ontario; nine Taylor horses have won Canadian horse of year, 15 won Queen's Plate; Thoroughbred Racing Association man of year 1973; mem. Canadian Sports Hall of Fame; *res.* Lyford Cay, W.I.

TERPENNING, Barbara (figure skating); *b.* 7 Sep 1956, Burnaby, B.C.; *given name:* Barbara Anne; Handsworth HS, Capilano College; pro skater; won B.C. ladies' senior sectionals, second Canadian junior, fourth Grand Prix International St. Gervais France 1972; won B.C. senior with special music, artistic award, sixth Canadian senior, third South African International Games, second Skate Canada International 1973; won

Western Canadian senior, second Canadian senior, sixth Skate Canada international, 13th world, fourth Prague Skate International 1974; third Canadian senior 1975, fourth 1976; turned pro with Ice Follies; *res.* North Vancouver, B.C.

TESSIER, Orv (hockey); *b.* 30 Jun 1933, Cornwall, Ont.; *given name:* Orval Ray; *m.* Charlotte Chouinard; *children:* Adele, Andre, Michael, Julie; Cornwall HS; hockey executive; through Cornwall minor hockey organization to pro 1953-54 with Montreal Royals (QHL); played with Montreal Canadiens, Boston Bruins, Hershey Bears, Springfield Indians, Kingston Frontenacs, Portland Buckaroos; reinstated as amateur joined Clinton (EHL), traded to Jersey Devils and retired at age 32; pro scoring record 1959-60 with Kingston (EPHL) 59 goals, 67 assists for 126 points; league scoring title 1961-62 as player-coach with Frontenacs scoring 54 goals, 60 assists for 114 points; league MVP, good conduct awards; coached Cornwall Royals to Memorial Cup 1972; full-time coach Quebec Ramparts 1972-73 taking club to Memorial Cup finals; rejoined Cornwall 1973-74, has guided Quebec junior league club since as coach-general manager; *res.* Cornwall, Ont.

THELEN, Dave (football); *b.* 2 Sep 1936, Canton, Ohio; *m.* Bonnie; *children:* David Jr., Dayna, Lana, John; Miami of Ohio, B.A.; partner electrical fixtures stores; lettered in football, baseball at college; played semipro baseball; 17th round draft choice Cleveland Browns; joined Ottawa Rough Riders 1958 playing nine CFL seasons, 1958-64 Ottawa, 1965-66 Toronto; 8,463yds in 1,530 carries for 5.5 avg., 47 TDs; best single game Sep 1960 Toronto at Ottawa with 209yds in 33 carries; mem. 1,000 carry club 1959-61 leading CFL with 1,407yds on 245 carries 1960; twice mem. 200 carry club; 1959 scored four TDs single game; rushed ball 87 consecutive games; *res.* Ottawa, Ont.

THIBODEAU, Nick (curling, shooting); *b.* 28 Apr 1885, Bathurst, N.B., *d.* 16 May 1959, Janeville, N.B.; *given name:* Nicholas Joseph; represented Canada and N.B. on 1914 Bisley rifle team; five times provincial curling champion, represented province in five Briers; 1931 skipped Bathurst CC rink to victory over champion Manitoba dealing Winnipeg rink lone loss; vs Montreal in same competition was victim of first end 'seven'; overall Brier record 16-26, best 1940 with third-place tie on 6-3 record; mem. N.B. Sports Hall of Fame.

THOM, Linda (shooting); *b.* 30 Dec 1943, Hamilton, Ont.; *given name:* Linda Mary Alice Malcolm; *m.* Donald Cullen Thom; *children:* Samantha; Lisgar CI, Ridgemont HS, Carleton U, B.J., Cordon Bleu School of Cooking, Paris; operator L'Academie de Cuisine; taught to shoot by father, a former Bisley competitor; second year in RA Rod and Gun club won title and President's Trophy; learned to shoot pistol 1967-68, won RA club title, unclassified bracket National Handgun Postal Matches sponsored by SFC; during next two years scored victories in variety of competitions throughout Canada setting personal and provincial women's records in Ontario, Quebec; won 1970 expert class .22 cal NRA style title Winnipeg setting national handgun mark for women; represented Canada Phoenix world championships placing seventh ladies' air pistol (.177 cal), 11th in both ladies' standard pistol, match pistol (.22 cal); Ontario open standard pistol title setting record 558 x 600; retained Canadian women's pistol title through 1975, mem. National Women's Handgun team, set variety of records; mem. l'Association de Tir de la Police of France attending shoots in France, Germany, Switzerland; at first Federation of the Americas Shooting championships in Mexico 1973 won ladies' air pistol (370x400) and match pistol (583x600); Canadian air pistol title with 376x400, fourth overall Canadian 1800, personal bests in national matches 1974; Thun Switzerland 1974 world championships seventh air pistol, 11th ladies' match; has held up to 16 Ontario records, two Canadian standards and two French marks as well as some US, North American and world standards unrecognized by officials; *res.* Ottawa, Ont.

THOMAS, Jim (football); *b.* 1940, Columbus, Miss.; Mississippi Industrial; nickname Long Gone; turned pro with Dallas (NFL) 1962 but was farmed to Louisville (US League), led team in scoring; joined Edmonton Eskimos 1963 as running back; played out option 1969 to seek berth with LA Rams; rejoined Eskimos 1970, retired following 1971 season; frequent WFC, all-Canadian all-star; twice Canada Packers Trophy as outstanding Eskimo player on fans' vote; joined 1,000yd rushing club with 1,006 in 172 carries 1967; in 10 CFL seasons carried 1,111 times for 6,060yds, 5.5 avg., 37 TDs; longest run 104yds from scrimmage.

THOMAS, Paul (basketball); *b.* 14 Apr 1926, Saint John, N.B.; *given name:* Paul Ernest; *m.* Barbara Diane Baker; *children:* Scott Paul, Misty Paige, Brett Arthur; U of Western Ontario, B.A., U of Toronto, teacher's certificate, U of Michigan, M.S., U of Southern California, Ph.D.; university professor, basketball coach; played baseball at all levels in Niagara Falls Minor Baseball Association winning several provincial titles and individual honors; several basketball titles, individual awards Niagara Falls CVI, including Pooch Hillisheim Trophy, MVP Greater Niagara Falls Basketball Association, set scoring records; at 17 signed pro baseball contract with Chicago Cubs, spent one and one-half years in minors before returning to school and basketball; played UWO basketball, all-star guard four years, team captain senior year as team won four CIAU titles; played Senior Intercounty baseball briefly with London Majors and summer basketball in Catskill Mountains; at U of T played for Toronto Tri-Bells Eastern Canadian senior men's titlists 1951; player-coach Tillsonburg Livingstons' 1952 Canadian champions and Helsinki Olympic representatives; not allowed to participate as player due to pro baseball background; coach Tri-Bells 1953-54, Canadian and Eastern titles; coached baseball all levels up to college in California, Windsor Little League, tennis at San Fernando Valley State College, basketball Niagara Falls, Toronto, Tillsonburg, Windsor, four years at U of Sask., 12 years San Fernando Valley; at 24 youngest Canadian national basketball team coach in Olympics; coach part of Canadian National Team 1972 China tour; coach Canadian team World University Games 1973 Moscow; pres. National Association of Basketball Coaches of Canada from 1974; *res.* Windsor, Ont.

THOMAS, Shirley (equestrian); *b.* 12 Jul 1936, Ottawa, Ont.; *given name:* Shirley Laura; *m.* Donald Prosser; *children:* Christopher, Laura, Ruth; Elmwood Ladies College, Millicent Hayes HS, Joan of Arc HS; first red ribbon in Toronto Pony Show at 12; at 18 1953 first female rider to claim international class honors at Madison Square Garden; invited to join 1952 Canadian team in Mexico but at 16 felt she was too young; first woman named to Canada's three-mem. international equestrian team 1953; same year at Toronto Royal Winter Fair shared top honors in puissance 5′ 10″ with Carol Durand of US; toured U.K. and Europe winning Ostende international ladies' jumping, Rotterdam ladies' championship; Government of Ireland Trophy; Ottawa ACT athlete of year; International Equestrian Association Cup; Montreal Press Association woman of year 1954; *res.* Alexander Bay, N.Y.

THOMPSON, George (lacrosse); *b.* 3 May 1910, Bowmanville, Ont.; *given name:* Walter George; *m.* Margaret McLaren; *children:* James, Gordon, Wayne, Barbara Jane; machine operator; mem. Brampton OLA junior champions 1930, Brampton Excelsiors Canadian senior Mann Cup winners 1930-31, Mimico-Brampton Combines Mann Cup winners 1942, finalist 1943; coached Brampton peewees to provincial title 1947, Brampton Minto Cup finalists 1956, Brampton Excelsiors juniors to successive Minto Cups 1957-59; pres. Lacrosse Old Timers 1969-70; since 1975 mem. Board of Governors Canadian Lacrosse Hall of Fame; mem. Canadian Lacrosse Hall of Fame; *res.* Brampton, Ont.

THOMPSON, Tiny (hockey); *b.* 31 May 1905, Sandon, B.C.; *given name:* Cecil; hockey scout; one of game's goaltending greats; early hockey Sandon then moved through amateur ranks with Calgary Monarchs juniors, Pacific Grain seniors, Bellvue Bulldogs, Duluth and Minneapolis; pro with Minneapolis then joined Boston Bruins (NHL) 1928-29 remaining 10 seasons, two more with Detroit; posted league game lifetime mark of 2.27 and 2.00 playoff percentage;

four times Vezina Trophy; twice named both first, second all-star teams; vs Toronto 1933 worked 104 minutes, 45 seconds of shutout hockey before being beaten 1-0 with shot at 104:46; chief Western Canadian scout for Chicago Black Hawks; mem. Hockey Hall of Fame; *res.* Calgary, Alta.

THOMSON, Earl (track); *b.* 15 Feb 1895, Birch Hills, Sask., *d.* 19 May 1971, Oceanside, Calif.; Long Beach HS, U of South Carolina, Dartmouth College, B.S.; as USC freshman set world record 14.8 for 110yd high hurdles; as mem. Royal Flying Corps took five firsts, one second, six cups, gold medal service track meet Toronto; 1919 world 110yd high hurdle mark of 14.4 IC4A meet Philadelphia, repeat 1920-21, low hurdles title 1921; Olympic gold high hurdles setting 14.8 Olympic mark; coach track U of West Virginia one year then assistant coach Yale to 1927; coach US Navy Academy track teams for more than 25 years; mem. Canadian, Saskatchewan Sports Halls of Fame.

THOMSON, Mabel (golf); *b.* 28 Sep 1874, Saint John, N.B., *d.* 13 Aug 1950, Saint John, N.B.; *given name:* Mabel Gordon; Canada's top woman golfer turn of century; national Open, amateur titles 1902, 1905-08; winner numerous regional, provincial competitions; mem. N.B. Sports Hall of Fame.

THORBURN, Cliff (snooker); *b.* 16 Jan 1948, Victoria, B.C.; *given name:* Clifford Charles Devlin; *div.;* pro snooker player; plays to a six handicap in golf; played six seasons, led scorers minor lacrosse; pitched two no-hitters leading team to B.C. Little League baseball title; played nine years minor soccer; 1970 Toronto snooker title; 1971 North American title with two perfect

147 games, second youngest in history; 1973 scored three perfect games in eight days, toured England on invitation, lost North American title to fellow Canadian Bill Werbeniuk; 1974 Canadian snooker title beating Julien St. Denis Hull Que. in marathon final; 1975 scored three more perfect games to total nine, reached world quarterfinals; first Canadian ever seeded in world play; retained Canadian championship beating Werbeniuk in final; won 1976 Canadian; finalist world 1977; set world tourney record 13 straight black balls, tied record of two century breaks in row 1977; *res.* Toronto, Ont.

THORNTON, Bernie (football); *b.* 18 Jul 1912, Hamilton, Ont.; *given name:* Bernard David; *m.* June; *children:* Carr Alison, Bernard Joseph; Delta CI, Queen's U; retired salesman; joined Hamilton Tiger-Cats 1932 in time to help them win Grey Cup vs Regina; Toronto Argos 1938 as end, Canadian all-star 1938-39, won 1938 Grey Cup vs Winnipeg; Big Four all-star outside 1938-40; with Winnipeg 1941 Grey Cup win vs Ottawa Rough Riders; while attending Queen's won Intercollegiate football title 1937 vs U of T; end with all-Argo (1921-41) team; *res.* Toronto, Ont.

THURLOW, Jim (shooting); *b.* 20 May 1948, Bridgewater, N.S.; *m.* Deborah Egan; *children:* Christopher, Karen; Ashbury College, Queen's U; auto mechanic; competed with success in Ontario, Quebec, NY shoots, Canadian pistol championships 1967-68, 1973-75; won National Rifle Association Canadian championship 1974; holds several provincial records; specializes in standard pistol, centrefire competitions; represented Canada internationally in Benito Juarez Games Mexico 1973, Federation of Ameri-

cas shoot Mexico 1973 winning standard pistol silver, team gold standard pistol, team silver centrefire world 1974; Ottawa RA Gun Club shooting award, NDHQ club championship award, Ottawa Valley League top gun award; *res.* Ottawa, Ont.

TIMMIS, Brian (football); *b.* 5 Dec 1899, Winnipeg, Man., *d.* 22 Aug 1971, Hamilton, Ont.; *m.* Ada Clements; *children:* Brian Jr; Lisgar CI; representative distiller's corp.; halfback, fullback Hamilton Tiger-Cats, won Grey Cup 1928, 1929, 1932; never played with helmet and suffered many injuries; coached Hamilton to 1943 Grey Cup triumph over Winnipeg; mem. Canadian Football Hall of Fame.

TINDALL, Frank (football); *b.* 16 Oct 1908, Syracuse, N.Y.; *m.* Mary; *children:* Frank Jr., Charles; Syracuse U, B.A., B.P.H.E.; professor phys ed, football, basketball coach; 1932 all-Eastern guard, honorable mention all-America, Syracuse U MVP; 1933 all-star lineman Toronto Argos, Grey Cup champions; all-time all-star tackle with Argos 1921-41 era; 1939 became football coach Queen's Golden Gaels; 1948-75 coached football, basketball at Queen's; teams won eight Intercollegiate football titles one national championship 1968, OUAA co-champions basketball 1956-57; 29-year coaching record college football 112 wins, 84 losses, two ties; trophy in his honor given annually by CIAU to best player in Central Bowl; *res.* Kingston, Ont.

TINDLE, Janice (tennis); *b.* 3 Jul 1950, Vancouver, B.C.; *given name:* Janice Lee; McGee HS, U of British Columbia, U of Arizona; tennis pro; numerous provincial, regional tennis titles; won Canadian girls-16 singles 1966, girls-18 singles 1967, with

Tinline

Michelle Carey girls-18 doubles 1968, Junior Federation Cup singles 1968, Canadian women's Closed 1972; three times Federation Cup team mem.; Pepsi-Cola Sportsmanship Trophy 1966; competed briefly as pro; coached Delta Airport Inn and with Tony Bardsley has conducted numerous teaching clinics; *res.* Alta Lake, B.C.

TINLINE, Dorothy (badminton); *b.* 25 Dec 1921, Scot, Sask.; *given name:* Dorothy Carol; Brandon College, U of Toronto; HS phys ed teacher; in tennis won 1965 Canadian ladies' senior doubles; three times mem. Canadian Uber Cup badminton team; four times Canadian Open doubles and ladies' doubles champion; Canadian Open mixed doubles champion 1962; Canada Winter Games silver team medal 1967; won Canadian ladies' senior singles three times, ladies' senior doubles twice, senior mixed doubles twice; won Canadian ladies' Master singles 1975; Ontario recognition awards in badminton 1968, tennis 1970; Ontario Achievement Award for badminton three times, special Fitness and Amateur Sport Achievement Award 1974; H.I. Evans Memorial Award 1971; chairman Canadian Badminton Umpires' Association 1967; first Canadian to umpire at all-England 1973-74; provincial badminton coach; head of badminton staff for York seminar 1975-76; CBA director since 1960; pres. Toronto and District Badminton Association 1964-65, 1973-76; pres. Ontario Badminton Association 1969-70; chairman Canadian Uber Cup program 1969; chairman Canadian Devlin Cup since 1968; *res.* Toronto, Ont.

TINSLEY, Buddy (football); *b.* 16 Aug 1924, Damon, Tex.; *given name:* Robert Porter Jr.; *m.* Hazel George Stevens; *children:* Cynthia Diane, Jack Steven; Baylor U,

B.P.E.; sales manager; turned pro as tackle with Los Angeles Dons 1949; joined Winnipeg Blue Bombers 1950-60, all-star seven times; coached St. James Rams to Western Canadian senior football title twice, national championship once; wife Hazel founded Winnipeg Bomberettes 1952; *res.* Winnipeg, Man.

TIPPETT, Karen (canoeing); *b.* 7 Apr 1955, Winnipeg, Man.; *given name:* Karen Mary; Brookfield HS, Carleton U; student; as mem. Rideau Canoe Club under coach John Bales won 1973 K2, K4 senior titles, second junior K1; with Sue Holloway placed fifth junior European K2 500m, third K2, second K4 in North American, ninth K2 500m in world championships; repeated Canadian senior title wins 1974-76; seventh kayak tandem world 1974-75; won North American K2, second K4, sixth K4 500m 1974; represented Canada 1976 Montreal Olympics; *res.* Ottawa, Ont.

TKACZUK, Walt (hockey); *b.* 29 Sep 1947, Emsdetten, Germany; *given name:* Walter Robert; hockey player; played centre with Kitchener Rangers OHA juniors as team won two league titles, lost in playoffs; turned pro with Omaha for three playoff games 1966-67; two-game stint with NY Rangers 1967-68 before opening 1968-69 campaign with Buffalo (AHL); elevated to Rangers that season; through 1976-77 NHL season played 669 games scoring 168 goals, 337 assists for 505 points, 424 penalty minutes, plus 65 playoff games scoring 15 goals, 22 assists for 37 points, 107 penalty minutes; *res.* New York.

TOMMY, Andy Jr. (skiing); *b.* 1 Nov 1932, Ottawa, Ont.; *given name:* Andrew Bailie; *m.* Marion Dunning; *children:* Sarah Jane,

Randy, Lisa, Michael; ski resort manager; prominent alpine skier 40s, 50s; winner of most major competitions in Gatineau, Laurentian regions; mem. Canadian team world championships, Canadian alpine champion 1950; represented Canada 1956 Olympics; head coach, manager 1960 Canadian Olympic ski team; *res.* Edelweiss Valley, Que.

TOMMY, Andy Sr. (football); *b.* 24 Dec 1911, Hartland, N.B., *d.* 23 Apr 1972, Wakefield, Que.; *m.* Helen Bailie; *children:* Andrew B, Arthur, Frederick; agronomist, statistician; played in backfield with Ottawa Rangers 1931-32 then moved to Ottawa Rough Riders 1933-45 excluding two seasons with Toronto Argos during WW2; played in five Grey Cup games, two winners; Jeff Russel Memorial Trophy 1940 as Big Four MVP; Canadian all-star several times; held record for longest run in Canadian football; mem. New Brunswick, Ottawa, Canadian Football, Canadian Sports Halls of Fame.

TOMMY, Art (skiing); *b.* 15 Dec 1933, Ottawa, Ont.; *m.* Marilyn Thorpe; *children:* Natalie, Jedson, Lizbeth; Lisgar CI; merchant, entrepreneur; dominated Canadian alpine skiing 1952-60; won Canadian alpine, Canadian Arlberg Kandahar, Ottawa Ski Club, Gatineau Zone, New York State, Quebec Taschereau, Quebec provincial titles, 11th in world as mem. of Canadian FIS team at 1954 world championships; mem. Canadian National Ski team 1954-60; participated world's first pro ski race but broke ankle; coach Ottawa Ski Club, Gatineau Zone, national team; mem. International Competitions Committee; coach Gatineau Zone and Quebec teams through 1974; *res.* Ottawa, Ont.

TOMMY, Fred (skiing); *b.* 24 Sep 1941, Ottawa, Ont.; *sep.* Christine Plouffe; *children:* Alexandre Frederic; U of Ottawa, B.Comm.; chartered accountant, director, v.-pres. of finance, realty firm; mem. Canadian FIS team 1958 world championships; represented Canada 1960 winter Olympics; *res.* Montreal, Que.

TOMSETT, Arthur (shooting); *b.* 19 Feb 1928, Vancouver, B.C.; *m.* Shirley; *children:* Terry, Danny, Kevin, Richard, Susan; Vancouver Institute of Engineering; engineer; mem. gold medal team first Canadian Games 1957; won B.C. indoor, outdoor championships 1973, Vancouver Island titles 1973-74; mem. national handgun team, free pistol, centrefire, standard pistol since 1973; mem. Canadian team Benito Juarez Games Mexico since 1973; competed in world championships Switzerland 1974, Pan-Am Games 1975; mem. bronze medal centrefire team 1975 Benito Juarez Games; *res.* Sidney, B.C.

TOOGOOD, Ted (football); *b.* 27 Aug 1924, Toronto, Ont.; *given name:* Alex Edgar; *m.* Joan Davidson; *children:* Sharon, Sandra, Sylvia, Shirley, Sonya, Glen; U of Toronto, B.A., B.P.H.E., U of West Virginia, M.Sc.; teacher; college football with Varsity Blues led to Canadian pro career with Toronto Argos 1950-54, played on two Grey Cup winners, captain 1952; established Argos, CFL record for TDs scored on punt returns in single game with two vs Hamilton in Toronto 1950; single-game punt return yardage mark with 155 on dashes of 90 and 65yds for majors; Eastern all-star 1953; *res.* Islington, Ont.

TOSH, Wayne (football); *b.* 7 Apr 1947, Kitchener, Ont.; *given name:* Wayne Kenneth; *m.* Marlene Grubbs; Sarnia HS, U of Richmond, B.Sc.; pro football player, civil servant; athlete of year Sarnia HS 1967; lettered for four years in football U of Richmond; turned pro 1971 with Ottawa Rough Riders; led EFC in interceptions 1975 with nine; EFC all-star 1975; mem. Grey Cup winners 1973, 1976; mem. Athletes in Action; *res.* Orleans, Ont.

TOTZKE, Bob (bowling); *b.* 6 Nov 1917, Kitchener, Ont.; *m.* Martha; *children:* Marilyn, John, Steve; bowling proprietor; one of organizers K-W five-pin bowling association with late Orv Bauman, June Gregg; hosted Canadian five-pin finals, BPAO convention; several years chairman Canadian finals, Molson's Sportsman's Show Toronto; for 15 years Zone C pres. BPAO; coach championship teams in Vancouver, Calgary, St. Catharines tournaments; chairman, treasurer 32-team Golden Horseshoe Intercity League 24 years; averaged 255 in 1970; mem. two Ontario title teams, has rolled 21 400-plus singles; Builders of Bowling Industry Award 1976; mem. Waterloo senior baseball executive 1948-54; junior, intermediate, senior ORFU football; has scored two holes-in-one; *res.* Kitchener-Waterloo, Ont.

TOTZKE, Carl (football, basketball); *b.* 25 May 1926, Waterloo, Ont.; *given name:* Carl Andrew; *m.* Lois Joan Pfeiffer; *children:* Sarah, Paul, Susan; Waterloo College, B.A., McGill U; director of athletics; competed in football, basketball, hockey, track at Waterloo College 1944-49, football at McGill 1949-50, football with K-W Dutchman of ORFU winning titles 1953-55; mem. YMCA national intermediate basketball champions 1951-52; coach U of Waterloo football 1954-67; FISU delegate World Student Games Moscow 1973, Rome 1975; CIAU pres. 1971-72, CAUAD pres. 1969-70; *res.* Waterloo, Ont.

TOWNSEND, Stephanie (skiing); *b.* 21 Mar 1948, Calgary, Alta.; *given name:* Stephanie Margaret; *m.* Dexter Williams; Notre Dame U, B.A.; owner-manager ski shop; Alberta juvenile champion 1960-61, junior 1962-64; named to Canadian national team 1965; competed with Canadian FIS team world finals Chile 1966; competed in Europe, North America International, World Cup races 1967-69; won slalom, second giant slalom, won combined Lowell Thomas Classic Utah 1968; 20th Val Gardena Italy downhill 1969, 13th Vail Colo. downhill 1969; instructor Aspen Colo. ski club 1969-70; Rotary Sportsman's Award 1963, Alberta Sportswomen's Association Award 1967; *res.* Aspen, Colo.

TRELLE, Herman (track and field, wrestling); *b.* 8 Dec 1894, Kendrick, Idaho, *d.* 4 Sep 1947, Fontana, Calif.; *m.* Bernice Irene Burdick; *children:* one son, one daughter; Blairmore, Alberta College, U of Alberta; grain grower; two Canadian field records, won Alberta heavyweight wrestling title.

TRIFUNOV, James (wrestling); *b.* 18 Jul 1903, Yugoslavia; *m.* Mary; *children:* Donald; promotion manager; won 10 Canadian titles (nine bantamweight, one featherweight) 1923-32; represented Canada 1924, 1928, 1932 Olympics, bronze medal 1928; gold medal 1930 British Empire Games Hamilton; coached YMCA juniors, U of Winnipeg, Canadian Olympic teams 1952-60; manager Canadian teams 1954, 1970 British Empire, Commonwealth Games, 1966, 1970 world; pres. Manitoba Amateur Wrestling Association; v.-pres. CAWA; secretary-founding director Manitoba Sports Federation; FILA medal for 1967 Pan-Am Games organizational work; finalist Air Canada amateur sports executive of year

1974; mem. Sask., AAU of C, Canadian AWA, Canadian Sports Halls of Fame; *res.* Winnipeg, Man.

TRIHEY, Harry (hockey); *b.* 25 Dec 1877, Montreal, Que., *d.* 9 Dec 1942, Montreal, Que.; *given name:* Henry Judah; McGill U; first man to utilize three-man line leaving rover to roam free and encouraged defence-man to carry the puck; starred in hockey with McGill, Montreal Shamrocks; played rover, captain Shamrocks when they won Stanley Cup 1899, 1900; retired 1901 with record of 46 goals in 30 games and 16 in eight playoff games; secretary-treasurer, later pres. CAHL leading league through disputes with Federal League 1904-05 then became advisor to Wanderers; refereed many league, Stanley Cup playoff games; pre-NHL record of 10 goals in single game during regular season; mem. Hockey Hall of Fame.

TRIPUCKA, Frank (football); *b.* 8 Dec 1927, Bloomfield, N.J.; *given name:* Francis Joseph; *m.* Randy; *children:* Heather, Tracy, Mark, Todd, T.K., Kelly, Chris; Notre Dame U, B.A.; pres. distributing co.; turned pro Detroit Lions 1949; later played with Chicago Cardinals, Dallas Texans (NFL); joined Saskatchewan Roughriders 1953, all-conference quarterback 1954; set record 216 completions 1956 (since topped by Ron Lancaster), 3,274yds passing; completed 158 of 257 passes for .615 percentage 1955; had 29 intercepted 1957; completed eight-year CFL career with Ottawa Rough Riders; CFL career record 15,506yds gained on 1,930 pass attempts of which 1,090 were completed for .565 avg. (fifth best in CFL recorded history), 136 intercepted; second to Lancaster in TD passes with 83; *res.* Bloomfield, N.J.

TUBMAN, Joe (football); *b.* 18 Aug 1897, Ottawa, Ont., *d.* 29 Nov 1975, Ottawa, Ont.; *given name:* Robert Elmer; *m.* Madge Whyte (*d.*); *children:* Mary; railway employee; starred in junior city league football and hockey; senior city league 1919 then Big Four team after one game; played with Ottawa Rough Riders through 1929 as kicking halfback, captain 1925-26 Grey Cup winners; refereed and umpired interprovincial and ORFU 15 years, retired end of 1944 season; as canoeist won Eastern tandem and Canadian war canoe titles for New Edinburgh club; played city league lacrosse, cricket, golf, lawn bowling; mem. Canadian Football, Ottawa, Canadian Sports Halls of Fame.

TUCKER, Whitman (football); *b.* 15 Nov 1940, Windsor, Ont.; *m.* Heather McCuaig; *children:* Ken, Kelly, Diane, Wendy; Forster CI, U of Western Ontario, B.A.; branch manager, investment consultants firm; starred football, basketball winning all-city Windsor 1958-59; Ontario scholastic long jump record (23'4½") 1958; Royal Arcanum Trophy as Windsor's outstanding HS athlete 1959; football, track, basketball UWO, Intercollegiate all-star football 1961; second draft choice Ottawa Rough Riders 1962 winning Gruen Award as Canadian rookie of year in Big Four; nine CFL seasons with Ottawa, all-star twice; three Grey Cup finals, won 1968-69; total 272 pass receptions for 6,092yds, 52 TDs; avg. gain 22.5 per-catch best in CFL; runner-up outstanding Canadian award 1968; *res.* Ottawa, Ont.

TUDIN, Conny (hockey); *b.* 21 Sep 1917, Ottawa, Ont.; *given name:* Cornell; *m.* Lois Darlene Sinnett; *children:* Terry, Rick; Ottawa Technical HS, St. Patrick's College; supervisor HS technical training; with Rideau juniors won Eastern Canadian title 1936-37, Arnprior Greenshirts Ottawa Valley League 1937-38, Harringay Greyhounds English League champions 1938-39; turned pro Montreal Canadiens' organization 1939-40 playing defence and all forward positions with Lachine Rapides, Washington Lyons, New Haven Eagles and Canadiens; mem. RCAF Flyers 1942-46 reaching Eastern Canadian Allan Cup finals; with Hull Volants 1946-47 then joined Ottawa Senators for four seasons reaching Allan Cup finals 1948, beat Regina Capitals 1949 for Allan Cup; to Smiths Falls Rideaus 1950-52 reaching Eastern Canadian finals; 1952-53 with Brockville Magedomas taking St. Lawrence League title; organized Ottawa Riverside Park minor hockey league 1961 coaching mosquito, peewee, midget teams; coach Glebe midgets Ottawa Cradle League, St. Jean's junior city league, St. James U.C. midgets; won scoring titles with Rideau Juniors, Lachine Rapides, RCAF Flyers; mem. Ottawa Old Timers Hockey committee since 1971; *res.* Ottawa, Ont.

TUPPER, Stephen (yachting); *b.* 6 Feb 1941, Vancouver, B.C.; *given name:* Stephen McGirr; *m.* Anne; *children:* Peter, Paul; U of British Columbia, B.Ed.; national team coach Canadian Yachting Association; three times Canadian Dragon Class champion; twice third North American Dragon championships; fourth 1968 Olympics Dragon Class; mem. Canadian team One Ton crew New Zealand 1971; mem. Canadian Onion Patch crew Bermuda 1974, second place; mem. Canadian Admiral's crew 1975; coach Canadian Pan-Am Games sailing team 1975; *res.* Vancouver, B.C.

TURCOTTE, Ron (horse racing); *b.* 22 Jul 1941, Drummond, N.B.; *m.* Gaetane; *children:* four daughters; Academie Notre Dame; jockey; to Toronto 1960, worked at race track as hot walker, groom, exercise boy; rode first race 1961 placing fifth; recorded first win 1962 and went on to become top Canadian jockey that year, repeat 1963; twice winner Kentucky Derby, Preakness, Belmont; first jockey in 70 years to ride Derby winners consecutive years with Riva Ridge, Secretariat; first Canadian, first jockey since Eddie Arcaro 1948 to win triple crown with Secretariat 1973; won Manitoba Centennial Derby 1970; twice winner Canadian International Stakes; other major stakes wins include Wood Memorial, Coaching Club American Oaks; in 15 years of riding has scored over 2,700 victories with purses totalling $24 million; Order of Canada 1973; N.B. Sports Hall of Fame; *res.* Valley Stream, N.Y.

TURNBULL, Barbara (golf); *b.* 6 Apr 1933, Saskatoon, Sask.; *given name:* Barbara Lois Stone; *m.* William Turnbull *(d.);* first of 18 Saskatoon Riverside Club championships 1957: since 1958 19 times mem. provincial amateur team; seven times Saskatchewan champion, six times runner-up; runner-up Canadian women's amateur 1969; mem. Sask. team which tied B.C. for 1967 interprovincial title; captain Canadian Women's World Games team Spain 1970; mem. 1973 international matches team Australia; nine times Saskatoon city champion; low amateur Winnipeg Glendale pro-amateur; Saskatoon sportswoman of year 1967; mem. Sask. Sports Hall of Fame; *res.* Saskatoon, Sask.

TURNER, Dave (soccer); *b.* 11 Oct 1903, Edinburgh, Scotland; *given name:* David Binnie; *m.* Margaret; *children:* Sandra Jean, David Robert; U of British Columbia, B.S.A., B.A., M.A., honorary Ph.D. Cornwall 1946; retired deputy minister; played with St. Andrews 1923, moved to Cumberland United; vs Canadian champion Nanaimo kicked five goals in two-game series; helped Cumberland win B.C. title and Connaught Cup semifinals; rejoined St. Andrews two seasons; one year pro in US then joined Toronto Ulster United; rejected 1924 offer to join Canadian all-stars on Australian tour but accepted 1927 invitation for New Zealand tour; joined New Westminster Royals nine seasons helping them claim Canadian titles 1928, 1930, 1931, 1936; mem. B.C., Canadian Sports Halls of Fame; *res.* Vancouver, B.C.

TURNER, John (track); *b.* 7 Jun 1929, Richmond, Surrey, Eng.; *given name;* John Napier; *m.* Geills McCrae Kilgour; *children:* Elizabeth, Michael, David, Andrew; St. Patrick's College, U of British Columbia, B.A., Oxford U, B.A., B.C.L., M.A., U of Paris; lawyer (QC), politician; Canadian junior 100, 220yd sprint champion 1947; mem. English track and field team 1950-51; Lib. MP 1962-76; cabinet minister various portfolios 1965-76; *res.* Toronto, Ont.

TWA, Don (curling); *b.* 2 Nov 1935, Coronation, Alta.; *given name:* Donald Ross; *m.* Kathleen Ellen McGinnis; *children:* Sherry Liegh, Kelly Ross, Ronald Terrence, Donald Wade, Mark Jeffery; hotelman, journeyman plumber, pipefitter; four times Northern Alberta zone men's champion, once mixed; eight times Yukon zone men's, three times mixed champion; became first skip of Northwest Territories-Yukon entry in Brier Fredericton 1975 posting 8-3 record; in 1977 Brier was 5-6; all-star Brier skip 1975; *res.* Whitehorse, Yukon.

UDVARI, Frank (hockey); *b.* 2 Jan 1924, Miltec, Yugoslavia; *m.* Colette Reinhardt; *children:* Martin, Jane; Guelph CI; supervisor NHL officials; officiated in Ontario Minor Hockey Association two years, OHA four years; turned pro 1951 refereeing 718 regular season, 70 NHL playoff games, 229 AHL, seven WHL, 15 EHL, seven CHL games; several seasons as AHL referee-in-chief; conducted numerous hockey schools across Canada and the US, two in Germany for the Canadian army; mem. Hockey Hall of Fame; *res.* Waterloo, Ont.

ULLMAN, Norm (hockey); *b.* 26 Dec 1935, Provost, Alta.; *given name:* Norman Victor Alexander; *m.* Bibiane Goueffic; *children:* Gordon, Linda; hockey player; mem. two provincial bantam championship teams, leading scorer; mem. provincial midget, juvenile title teams and with Edmonton Junior Oil Kings reached Memorial Cup finals; turned pro with Edmonton Flyers; 13 years with Detroit Red Wings before being traded with Paul Henderson, Floyd Smith to Toronto Maple Leafs 1968 for Frank Mahovlich, Garry Unger, Pete Stemkowski, Carl Brewer; defensive centre; past pres. NHL Players' Association; seventh player in NHL history to score 400 goals Dec 1970; after eight seasons with Leafs moved to WHA with Edmonton Oilers; first, second team NHL all-star centre once each; through 1976-77 played in 1,554 major league games scoring 537 goals, 822 assists for 1,359 points, 767 penalty minutes, plus 106 playoff games scoring 30 goals, 53 assists for 83 points, 67 penalty minutes; as junior set league record 55 goals, 46 assists for 101 points in 36-game schedule; *res.* Edmonton, Alta.

UNDERHILL, Eileen (badminton); *b.* 1 Apr 1899, Moosomin, Sask.; *given name:* Margaret Eileen Stuart George; *m.* John Edward Underhill *(d.); children:* John Gerald, Charles Stuart; B.C. singles title 12 times, shared B.C. ladies' doubles 11 times, B.C. mixed doubles five times; Canadian singles champion 1927, shared doubles four times and national mixed doubles with husband John four times; first husband-wife team elected to B.C. Sports Hall of Fame; *res.* Vancouver, B.C.

UNDERHILL, John (badminton); *b.* 3 Sep 1902, Vancouver, B.C., *d.* 1932 Vancouver, B.C.; *given name:* John Edward; *m.* Margaret Eileen Stuart George; *children:* John Gerald, Charles Stuart; five times B.C. singles champion, twice Canadian titlist; won B.C. men's doubles five times, each time with different partner; with wife Eileen won four Canadian mixed doubles titles; first husband-wife team elected to B.C. Sports Hall of Fame.

UNGER, Garry (hockey); *b.* 7 Dec 1947, Edmonton, Alta.; *given name:* Garry Douglas; hockey player; North Edmonton minor hockey league, South Calgary Community League; began junior play with Calgary in Western Canadian Junior League then was shifted by Toronto Maple Leafs to London Nationals; turned pro 1966-67 with Tulsa (CPHL) and Rochester (AHL); joined Toronto Maple Leafs for 15 games 1967-68; traded with Frank Mahovlich, Pete Stemkowski and rights to Carl Brewer to Detroit for Norm Ullman, Paul Henderson, Floyd Smith 1968; traded to St. Louis with Wayne Connelly for Red Berenson, Tim Ecclestone 1971; through 1976-77 NHL seasons played 733 games, scored 315 goals, 306 assists for 621 points, 803 penalty minutes, plus 35 playoff games with 11 goals, 15 assists for 26 points, 78 penalty minutes; *res.* St. Louis, Mo.

UNGERMAN, Irv (boxing); *b.* 1 Feb 1923, Toronto, Ont.; *given name:* Irving; *m.* Sylvia Rothstein; *children:* Shelley, Howard, Temmi; poultry processor, real estate agent, boxing promoter; active soccer, hockey player, boxer at YMCA; fought for Toronto 105lb title 1939; during three years RCAF service fought at 135lb, also served as phys ed officer; turned to managing, promoting careers of numerous fighters including Canadian heavyweight champion George Chuvalo, Canadian and Commonwealth welterweight champion Clyde Gray; awarded all-Canada Sports and City TV Trophy 1973; Jack Allen Trophy for contribution to world boxing 1965-66; mem. Canadian Boxing Hall of Fame; *res.* Toronto, Ont.

UPPER, Wray (baseball); *b.* 18 May 1931, Port Colborne, Ont.; *m.* Helen Bartok; *children:* Cindy, Shawn, Lisa; Welland HS; supervisor; played NY Giants organization 1951-52; joined Galt Senior Intercounty League 1953-55, Kitchener 1956, Galt 1957-72, Brantford 1973-74; in 23 Intercounty seasons compiled .289 lifetime batting avg.; led league hitters 1958 with .413; twice led league in hits, triples, once in runs scored; managed Galt 1962-67, 1970-72, 113-157 record; first team all-star third base six times, manager once, second team third base five times; mem. Ontario team 1969 Canada Games Halifax; *res.* Cambridge, Ont.

URBAN, Faye (tennis); *b.* 28 Oct 1945, Windsor, Ont.; *m.* William Mlacak; Walkerville CI, Windsor Teacher's College; bank employee; 1958 won Canadian 13 junior women's singles; 1960 won 15 doubles with Brenda Nunns; with same partner took 18 doubles 1961-62 and singles title; 1965 won women's doubles with Nunns, mixed doubles with David Body; with Vicki Berner won women's doubles 1966-69; took closed singles 1968-69, open singles 1969; 1966-70 competed for Canada on Federation Cup team, captain 1968; *res.* Toronto, Ont.

URNESS, Ted (football); *b.* 23 Jun 1937, Regina, Sask.; *given name:* Harold; *m.* Jacquelyn Joy; *children:* Mark, Dee Anne, Daniel; U of Arizona, B.S.; pres. auto equipment sales co.; Governor's Trophy as U of Arizona MVP 1960; with Saskatchewan Roughriders 1961-70; all-Canadian centre 1965-70; runner-up Schenley CFL lineman of year 1968; appeared in three Grey Cup finals, won 1966 vs Ottawa; *res.* Saskatoon, Sask.

URSULIAK, Wally (curling); *b.* 30 Jun 1929, Edmonton, Alta.; *m.* Kathleen VanKleek; *children:* Ken, Robin, Kelly; pro curling instructor, freelance broadcaster; attended Pittsburgh Pirates baseball training camp 1951; began curling 1949; played lead for Hec Gervais in 1961-62 Briers; won Brier,

world championship 1961; won Canadian Open, Edmonton Masters, Tournament of Champions 1965; coached European curlers including world champions Otto Danieli of Switzerland, Kjell Oscarius of Sweden; also coached 1975 Canadian Lassies champion Lee Tobin of Quebec; *res.* Edmonton, Alta.

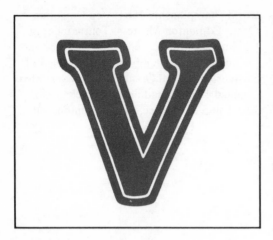

VACHON, Rogie (hockey); *b*. 8 Sep 1945, Palmarolle, Que.; *given name:* Rogatien Rosaire; hockey player; Rouyn-Noranda league to junior ranks with Thetford Mines; turned pro 1965-66 with Quebec (AHL); played with Houston (CPHL) 1966-67; to Montreal Canadiens late in 1966-67 for Stanley Cup playoffs, remained until 1971 when he was traded to Los Angeles for Denis DeJordy, Dale Hoganson, Noel Price and Doug Robinson; shared 1967-68 Vezina Trophy with Worsley; once second team all-star; with Team Canada 1976 in Canada Cup international series; in 10 NHL campaigns appeared in 457 games, played 26,564 minutes, allowed 1,232 goals, post 33 shutouts for 2.78 avg., plus 33 playoff games, 2,052 minutes, 69 goals, two shutouts and 2.02 avg.; *res*. Los Angeles, Calif.

VAILLANCOURT, Michel (equestrian); *b*. 26 Jul 1954, St. Felix de Valois, Que.; student; began riding at 11 and became mem. Canadian junior international equestrian team; with Robespierre Stables since 1971; winner Ottawa Winter Fair puissance 1972; in 1974 won Hornby, Aurora, Cobourg hunter titles, champion jumper Horseman-ship Club, St. Bruno, La Peinière horse shows, Hornby Reserve intermediate title, Hudson grand prix, champion green hunter Horsemanship Club, Man and His World horse shows; 1975 Ocala Fla. title and only Canadian to place (third) in Lake Placid Grand Prix; rode Branch County, a converted race horse, placed high in variety of Rothman's Grand Prix competitions; 1976 Montreal Olympics silver medal; mem. 1975 bronze medal Canadian jumping team Mexico Pan-Am Games; *res*. Hudson, Que.

VALAITIS, Donna (track); *b*. 26 Aug 1954, London, Ont.; *given name:* Donna Anne; U of Guelph; student; Ontario HS titles in 800m and 1500m events 1973, Ontario 800m title same year; joined Toronto Olympic Club, trained under Paul Poce; 1974 placed third in Canadian 800m finals and earned Canadian track team rating as C carded athlete with 2:04.7 in 800m; trained with Canadian team in Phoenix Christmas 1974, toured Europe summer 1975; ran 4:16.7 for 1500m in Stockholm placing second to Francie Larieu of US; trained with Canadian team in California spring of 1976, second in both Olympic trials for 1500 but best time 4:16.4 failed to achieve Olympic standard of 4:15; won Olympic rehearsal meet in Montreal 1976 but again fell short of standard; best personal times 1500m (4:16.4), 800m (2:04.7); *res*. Mt. Brydges, Ont.

VALENTAN, Walter (bowling); *b*. 23 Jun 1929, Graz, Austria; *given name:* Walter John; *m*. Connie West; *children:* Monica, Anita; tool engineer, bowling administrator; involved in five-pin bowling 1955; pres. Kitchener Bowlers' Association 1968; director Ontario Bowlers' Congress 1970; director public relations OBC 1972; administrator Bowling Proprietors Association of Ontario; *res*. West Hill, Ont.

VAN KIEKEBELT, Debbie (track and field); *b.* 1 Mar 1954, Kitchener, Ont.; Clarkson HS, York U, Ryerson Polytechnical Inst.; TV sports director; mem. Scarborough Lions Track Club; Canadian records midget high jump (5'10''), long jump (19'5½'') 1970; fifth high jump 1970 Commonwealth Games, second both high and long jump Canada vs Norway-Sweden; Canadian native and North American women's pentathlon record with 5,052 points 1971 Toronto; gold medal 1971 Pan-Am Games pentathlon with 4,290; represented Canada 1972 Munich Olympics; shared Canadian female athlete of year 1971 with Debbie Brill; *res.* Sudbury, Ont.

VARALEAU, Jack (weightlifting); *b.* 22 May 1922, Eastview (Vanier), Ont.; *given name:* James Patrick; recreation director, retired RCAF; represented Canada 1948 London Olympics, placed sixth and broke Olympic press record; same year won British Empire weightlifting title; retained British Empire title winning gold medal British Empire Games Aukland N.Z.; represented Canada 1952 Helsinki Olympics; assistant manager-coach for 1960 Rome Olympics weightlifting team; Gil O. Julien trophy as French Canadian athlete of year 1950; Ontario Sports Achievement Award; mem. Canadian Forces Sports Hall of Fame; *res.* Vancouver, B.C.

VAUGHAN, Kaye (football); *b.* 30 Jun 1931, Concordia, Kansas; *given name:* Charles Kaye; *m.* Lucile Wheeler; *children:* Myrle, Jake; Tulsa U, B.A., U of Kansas, M.S., McGill U; school administrator; lineman with Tulsa 1950-53; turned pro as tackle with Ottawa Rough Riders 1953-64; Schenley lineman of year 1956, repeat 1957, runner-up 1960; frequent all-star; played on 1960 Grey Cup winner; *res.* Knowlton, Que.

VEZINA, Georges (hockey); *b.* 7 Jan 1888, Chicoutimi, Que., *d.* 24 Mar 1926, Chicoutimi, Que.; nickname Chicoutimi Cucumber; never missed a league or playoff game in 15 years NHL; amateur ranks in Chicoutimi, turned pro with Montreal 1910 and played 328 consecutive league, 39 playoff games allowing 1,267 goals; on five title teams, two Stanley Cup champions; trophy in his memory awarded annually to NHL goaler with best goals-against avg.; mem. Hockey Hall of Fame.

VILLENEUVE, Gilles (autosport); *b.* 18 Jan 1952, St. Jean, Que.; *m.* Joan; *children:* Melanie, Jacques; racing driver; began competitive racing career with snowmobiles winning Canadian championships 1973, 1975, world championship 1974; won Quebec Formula Ford title 1973; world class status 1976 winning Canadian driving crown with four wins in five events; US Formula Atlantic championship winning four consecutive events; Molson Grand Prix Trois-Rivières beating graded world class drivers James Hunt, Allan Jones; mem. Marlboro McLaren Formula 1 auto racing team 1977; shared Que. athlete of year honors with Guy LaFleur 1975; *res.* Berthierville, Que.

VOYLES, Carl (football); *b.* 11 Aug 1898, McLowd, Okla.; *m.* Gertrude M. Hall (*d.*); *children:* Carl Jr., Robert; *m.* Dorothy Belknap; Oklahoma State U, B.S.; retired coach, realtor; captain college football team senior year, basketball team three years; coach basketball team Altus Okla. HS which won Southern Conference title; coach Southwestern State College three years, guided football team to 22 wins, five losses, three ties and basketball team to national championship tournament level twice; freshman coach Illinois U 1925, head scout for coach Bob

Wade

Zuppke; joined Wallace Wade at Duke U 1931 serving six years as assistant athletic director, assistant football coach, team competed in 1938 Rose Bowl; head coach, athletic director College of William and Mary 1939, won Southern Conference title and post-season match over Oklahoma, joined Auburn U as athletic director, head football coach 1944 remaining there four seasons; joined pro ranks as coach, general manager Brooklyn Dodgers (all-American Conference) 1947; coach, general manager with newly combined Hamilton Tiger-Cats in CFL 1950; won 1953 Grey Cup; *res.* Fort Myers, Fla.

WADE, Harry (basketball); *b.* 12 Mar 1928, Windsor, Ont.; *m.* Helen Lucas; *children:* Paul, William; Patterson CI, U of Western Ontario; business executive; mem. all-Ontario HS basketball champions 1947-48; on three Canadian Intercollegiate title basketball teams Western 1949-51; played two years football Western, 1949 league champions; with Canadian senior basketball champions Tillsonburg Livingstons 1951, 1952; Canadian Olympic basketball team Helsinki 1952; *res.* Tillsonburg, Ont.

WAGNER, Bill (curling); *b.* 19 Dec 1919, Wimborne, Alta.; *m.* Elaine Flynn; *children:* Darce, Kirk, Wendy, Heather, Douglas; U of British Columbia, B.S.A.; civil servant; played hockey Nanaimo Clippers 1940 Western Canada intermediate finalists, 1944 North-west Air Command RCAF champions, Alberta, UBC champions; softball with B.C. senior titlists 1941; represented Ottawa district 1965 Consols playdowns; won Ontario senior curling title 1975; *res.* Ottawa, Ont.

WAITE, Jim (curling, golf); *b.* 17 Feb 1941, St. Thomas, Ont.; *given name:* James Frederick; *m.* Sue Richardson; *children:*

Wallingford

Chris, David; McMaster U, U of Western Ontario, B.A.; teacher, PS principal; first of eight Ontario Consols bids as lead 1966, 1968 Ontario title winner; twice winner Ontario Challenge Round; with skip Stan Curtis won Ontario Governor-General's double rink competition 1970; with Dr. Don Gilbert as other skip won Ontario Silver Tankard 1973, 1975; senior coach Curl Canada; one-handicap golfer, mem. St. Thomas Golf and Country Club, five times club titlist; winner St. Thomas Early Bird twice vs field including Nick Weslock, Gary Cowan; winner several Ontario Invitational tournaments; 1973 winner Father and Three Sons championship; *res.* St. Thomas, Ont.

WALKER, Bill (football); *b.* 11 May 1933, Pittsburgh, Pa.; *m.* Nancy Jean Antrim; *children:* William, Richard, John; Munhall HS, U of Maryland, B.A.; auto dealer; with Maryland all-American in junior year; turned pro with Edmonton Eskimos 1956-58 as receiver and punter; played for 1956 Grey Cup champions; *res.* Doylestown, Pa.

WALKER, Jack (hockey); *b.* 28 Nov 1888, Silver Mountain, Ont., *d.* 16 Feb 1950, Seattle, Wash.; *given name:* John Phillip; from 1906 played on four consecutive Port Arthur city championship teams; joined Moncton (Maritime League) 1912-13, Toronto Arenas 1913-14 remaining two years and helping club win Stanley Cup; helped Seattle win 1916-17 Stanley Cup; with Victoria Cougars' 1925 Stanley Cup winner; Detroit (NHL) 1926-28 then Edmonton Eskimos; player-manager Hollywood Stars 1931-32 then retired to manage, coach, referee in PCL; originator of hook check; noted for ability to teach young players; PCL MVP awards twice, NHL MVP twice; mem. Hockey Hall of Fame.

WALKER, Louise (track and field); *b.* 21 Mar 1951, Toronto, Ont.; *given name:* Marilyn Louise Hanna; *m.* James Douglas Walker; Richview CI, U of Toronto, B.Sc.; high jump specialist; 1970 Canadian junior champion 1.68m; 1971 third Canadian nationals; won Canadian Olympic trials 1972, Pacific Conference Games, Canada vs Russia indoor meet 1973; won Canadian nationals 1.78m 1973; silver medal 1974 Commonwealth Games Christchurch N.Z. 1.82m; third Canadian nationals and European tour mem. same year; silver 1975 Pan-Am Games Mexico 1.86m; silver pre-Olympic meet Montreal 1.87m (Canadian record); won Canadian nationals 1.85m; won Canada vs E. Germany 1.86m; *res.* Toronto, Ont.

WALKER, Peahead (football); *b.* 1899, Birmingham, Ala., *d.* 16 Jul 1970, Charlotte, N.C.; *given name:* Douglas Clyde; *m.* Flonnie; *children:* Gwen; football executive; head coach 14 years (1937-50) Wake Forest compiling 79-47 won-lost record; assistant to Herman Hickman at Yale two seasons; head coach Montreal Alouettes 1952-59 guiding team to three consecutive Grey Cup finals only to lose each time to Pop Ivy's Edmonton Eskimos; after leaving Montreal became N Y Giants (NFL) scout.

WALLINGFORD, Ron (track); *b.* 13 Sep 1933, Ottawa, Ont.; *given name:* Ronald Roy; *m.* Heather June Magwood; *children:* Randy Roy, Anthony Alexander, Roxanne Rae, Cassandra Carmen, Darcy Dale; U of Michigan, B.Sc., McMaster U, B.P.E., U of Buffalo, M.A., Ph.D.; technical coordinator CTFA; distance runner, steeplechase specialist; Canadian junior three-mile record 1952; Canadian records in indoor mile, 3000m steeplechase, 5000m and marathon; mem. Canadian medley relay which held Canadian distance mark; third 1964 Boston Marathon, ninth 1971; sixth 1966 Commonwealth Games marathon; sixth Pan-Am Games 10 000m 1967, Pan-Am Games marathon 1971; represented Canada world masters marathon France 1974, set Canadian team record; represented Canada in Cuba, Mexico, South Korea, Holland, Puerto Rico road races; chairman Ontario Coaches Association 1971-73; senior evaluator Ontario coaches since 1970; marathon manager 1976 Montreal Olympics; director Ontario T&F Association 1971-73; competed in Olympic trials 1952-72 placing third 5000m 1952; won 5000m setting Canadian record, second 1500m 1956; won 3000m steeplechase in Canadian record time 1960; second marathon 1964, 1968 and 12th marathon 1972; *res.* Ottawa, Ont.

WALSH, Billy Jr. (curling); *b.* 8 Oct 1948, Winnipeg, Man.; *given name:* William Joseph; *m.* Tannys Aspevig; *children:* Casey; Churchill HS, U of Manitoba; chartered accountant; in 1974 representing Fort Rouge Curling Club skipped Manitoba bonspiel grand aggregate winner; wife Tannys three times Manitoba ladies golf champion and winner of several junior and senior Winnipeg area tournaments; *res.* Winnipeg, Man.

WALSH, Billy Sr. (curling); *b.* 20 Jan 1917, Haileybury, Ont., *d.* 7 Oct 1971, Winnipeg, Man.; *given name:* William James; *m.* Madeline Mary Metcalfe; *children:* William Joseph; Lord Roberts, Kelvin HS; provincial government auditor; guided Fort Rouge Curling Club to 1952 Manitoba Consols and Brier title, 10-0 record; unprecedented 17 consecutive Brier playdown victories while representing Manitoba in 1956 Brier; won 1956 Brier vs Ontario's Alf Phillips Sr. at Moncton N.B.; mem. Curling Hall of Fame.

WALSH, Brenda (track); *b.* 31 Dec 1952, Edmonton, Alta.; *given name:* Brenda Constance; McNally CHS, U of Alberta, B.P.E.; teacher; Canadian junior 400m title 1970 with 56.8; represented Canada vs Norway-Sweden 1970; Canadian, North American indoor 300m mark of 39.6, Canadian open indoor 400m 55.8, third Pan-Am Games trials 200m 1970; represented Canada 1971 Pan-Am Games, 1973 World Student Games, 1974 Commonwealth Games and on European tours 1971, 1974, 1975; Edmonton athlete of year 1973; *res.* Edmonton, Alta.

WALSH, Marty (hockey); *b.* 1883, Kingston, Ont., *d.* 1915, Gravenhurst, Ont.; *given name:* Martin; Queen's U, B.A.; initial impact on Canadian hockey scene with Queen's in OHA; in 1906 challenge match loss to Ottawa Silver Seven; Ottawa sought his services as replacement for centre Frank McGee but he elected to go to International Pro League where he broke his leg; joined Ottawa 1908; in five seasons with Ottawa scored 135 goals in 59 games, 26 goals in eight playoff games; mem. two Stanley Cup winners; three times NHA scoring champion; 10 goals vs Port Arthur Mar 1911, seven vs Montreal Mar 1908, six vs Galt Jan 1910, Renfrew Jan 1911, five vs Wanderers Jan 1908, Shamrocks Jan 1910; mem. Hockey Hall of Fame.

WALTERS, Angus (yachting); *b.* 1882, Lunenberg, N.S., *d.* 12 Aug 1968, Lunenburg, N.S.; sailor, dairy farmer; from 1921-42 managing owner of schooner Bluenose in which he won five international races; took Bluenose to Chicago 1933 to represent Canada at Century of Progress exhibition; sailed to England 1937 to compete in Silver Jubilee of King George V and Queen Mary; mem. Canadian Sports Hall of Fame.

WALTON, Dorothy (badminton); *b.* 7 Aug 1909, Swift Current, Sask.; *given name:* Dorothy Louise McKenzie; *m.* W.R. Walton Jr.; *children:* one son; U of Saskatchewan, B.A., M.A.; for several years holder of Canadian amateur badminton singles title; 1939-47 world badminton titlist; 1940 CP poll Canadian female athlete of year; 1950 CP poll one of six outstanding Canadian female athletes of half century; mem. Canadian Sports Hall of Fame; *res.* Scarborough, Ont.

WALTON, Mike (hockey); *b.* 3 Jan 1945, Kirkland Lake, Ont.; *given name:* Michael Robert; *m.* Candy Hoult; hockey player; helped Toronto Junior Marlboros win Memorial Cup and picked up father's nickname Shaky; turned pro with Tulsa (CPHL), scored 40 goals, rookie of year 1964-65; in AHL with Rochester following season earned Dudley 'Red' Garrett Memorial Trophy as rookie of year; Toronto Maple Leaf regular 1966-71; traded to Boston Bruins via Philadelphia 1970-71 and remained with that club until moving to WHA Minnesota Fighting Saints 1973; returned to NHL with Vancouver Canucks 1975; Bill Hunter Trophy as league scoring leader 1974 with 57 goals, 60 assists for 117 points; WHA second team all-star once; played with WHA Team Canada 1974 vs USSR; through 1976-77 major league seasons played 672 games scoring 291 goals, 339 assists for 630 points, 465 penalty minutes, plus 66 playoff games scoring 33 goals, 25 assists for 58 points, 71 penalty minutes; partner with Bobby Orr in hockey school; *res.* Toronto, Ont.

WAPLES, Keith (harness racing); *b.* 12 Aug 1923, Victoria Harbour Ont.; *m.* Eileen; *children:* Barbara, Donna, Karen, Gordon; Coldwater HS; harness racer, trainer, breeder; began driving career age 12 winning three heats with father's Grey Ghost at Sundridge Ont.; 1959 on one-half mile Richelieu Park track drove Mighty Dudley to Canada's first sub 2:00 mile 1:59.3; 1967 established record 246 wins on Canadian tracks; 1972 drove Strike Out at Blue Bonnets for first $100,000 race win in Canada (standard or thoroughbred); won Little Brown Jug, Adios Pace, Prix d'Ete, Tattersalls Pace (also 1973), all with Strike Out; topped Canadian dash winners 1967, 1968; career win record 2,785; 25 sub 2:00 minute miles; mem. Canadian Sports Hall of Fame; *res.* Durham, Ont.

WARD, Clint (water-skiing); *b.* 11 Jun 1932, Saskatoon, Sask.; *div.; children:* Rande, Kim, Clint Jr.; Saskatoon HS, U of Saskatchewan; captain Air Canada; Canadian titles in various age categories 1961-74; coach-manager Canadian national team 1965-71; organizing chairman 10th world water-ski championships 1967; pres. Canadian Water-Ski Association 1968-70; pres. Group One World Water-Ski Union 1971-75, Group One secretary since 1976; executive v.-pres. Sports Federation of Canada 1973-74; mem. Canada Games Council 1973-74; Director Sports Administration Centre 1974-76; COA administration staff mem. for 1976 Winter Olympics team; CBC water-ski commentator; with George Athans Jr. wrote *Water Skiing;* Air Canada sport merit award 1974; *res.* Montreal, Que.

WARREN, Harry (field hockey, track, cricket); *b.* 27 Aug 1904, Anacortes, Wash.; *given name:* Harry Verney; *m.* Margaret

Bessie Tidsall; *children:* Charlotte Louisa Verney, Victor Henry Verney; U of British Columbia, B.A.; B.A.Sc., Oxford U, B.Sc., Ph.D.; retired geology professor, consulting geological engineer; at Victor Ludorum-Victoria prep school won 100yd, high jump, long jump, half-mile cycle races, second quarter-mile, third three-mile run at 14, also captain cricket and football teams; at UBC starred in cricket, track, rugby and organized the school's first men's field hockey team; at Oxford played field hockey, cricket, rugby, track winning numerous team and individual awards; named to Canadian 1928 Amsterdam Olympic team as track alternate; set Irish record on grass winning 100m in Tailteann Games, set two intervarsity relay records in Oxford-Cambridge meet 1928; captain Queen's College Athletic Club 1928-29; 1929-32 introduced badminton, cricket, rugby, men's field hockey to Cal Tech, U of Utah and founded California Wanderers' hockey club to which he was elected honorary life mem.; father of Canadian field hockey with organization of UBC club 1923 at 19; represented Vancouver mainland vs Victoria in Allen Cup play 1938; organized Canadian Women's Field Hockey Association; honorary pres. Vancouver WFHA 1959, CWFHA 1963; helped establish, became first pres. CFHA 1962 and was instrumental in sending Canada's first field hockey entry to Olympic competition Tokyo 1964; CFHA pres. 1961-64, later director; twice recipient Big Block for rugby, track UBC; Achilles, Greyhound Blue, and Colors for track, rugby at Oxford; honored by University Hill's Men's Forum for contribution to amateur sport 1965; UBC playing field named in his honor 1970; B.C. Cricket Cap 1923; mem. B.C., AAU of C, Canadian Sports Halls of Fame; *res.* Vancouver, B.C.

WATSON, Harry (hockey); *b.* 6 May 1923, Saskatoon, Sask.; *given name:* Harry Percival; *m.* Lillian Thomson; *children:* Barry, Ron, Dale; Saskatoon THS; salesman; Saskatoon Junior Quakers to pro 1941 Brooklyn Americans; Detroit Red Wings 1942-43, 1945-46; Toronto Maple Leafs 1946-55; Chicago Black Hawks 1955-57; mem. three Stanley Cup winners; left wing on line of Syl Apps Sr., Bill Ezinicki with Leafs; 14 NHL season record: 809 games, 236 goals, 207 assists, 443 points, plus 62 playoff games, 16 goals, nine assists, 25 points; played in seven NHL all-star games scoring one goal, four assists; manager 12 years Tam O'Shanter hockey school; mem. Toronto Oldtimers hockey team; *res.* Markham, Ont.

WATSON, Ken (curling); *b.* 12 Aug 1904, Minnedosa, Man.; *m.* Marcella Dowdall; St. John's Tech, U of Manitoba, B.A.; retired insurance executive, teacher; entered first Manitoba bonspiel as lead 1923, won first of 32 major trophies in that 'spiel 1926; won MCA grand aggregate seven times including unprecedented six in succession 1942-47; four times Manitoba Consols winner claiming Brier championship 1936, 1942, 1949; promoted and helped organize first competitive international curling championship (Scotch Cup) 1959; organized and founded first Manitoba provincial HS 'spiel 1940; mem. 1960 Canadian team which toured Scotland; wrote four books on curling, *Ken Watson on Curling, Ken Watson, Curling to Win, Curling with Ken Watson, Curling Today, with Ken Watson;* honorary life mem. Strathcona CC, Manitoba, Canadian Curling Associations; mem. Canadian Sports, Canadian Curling Halls of Fame; *res.* Winnipeg, Man., Hawaii.

WATSON, Moose (hockey); *b.* 14 Jul 1898, St. John's, Nfld., *d.* 11 Sep 1957, Toronto, Ont.; *given name:* Harry; St. Andrew's College; played for St. Andrew's College, Aura Lee juniors; Toronto Dentals 1919; with Toronto Granites 1920, won two Allan Cups, 1924 Olympic championship; scored 13 of 30 goals by Canada vs Czechoslovakia in Olympics; player-coach Toronto National Sea Fleas winning Allan Cup 1931; mem. Hockey Hall of Fame.

WATSON, Sandy (hockey); *b.* 28 Mar 1918, Scotland; *given name:* Alexander Gardner; *m.* Patricia Brown; *children:* John, Alexander; U of St. Andrews, Harvard U, Cambridge U, Columbia-Presbyterian U; eye surgeon, university professor of ophthalmology; managed RCAF Flyers to 1948 Eastern Canada League title, world, Olympic championship honors; managed team in International Hockey Federation; governor Hockey Canada; *res.* Ottawa, Ont.

WATSON, Whipper Billy (wrestling); *b.* 25 Jun 1917, Toronto, Ont.; *given name:* William Potts; *sep.; children:* one daughter, two sons; pitched, played second base for Legion softball team; defence in hockey; football with Eastside, Balmy Beach juniors; as marathon swimmer competed in CNE, across Hamilton Bay, down Humber River swims; after four years in England returned to North America during WW2 as European light heavyweight champion; twice held world title, beat Wild Bill Longson 1947, lost to Lou Thesz 1948, reclaimed from Thesz 1956, lost in rematch; in 31 years of wrestling fought over 7,400 bouts in Europe and North America; mem. Order of Canada; *res.* Keswick, Ont.

WATT, David (track and field); *b.* 24 Feb 1952, Barrie, Ont.; U of Toronto, B.A., M.A.; student; Canadian juvenile triple jump title 1970, Canadian title with 14.88m 1971; Canadian junior title 1972; mem. Canadian national team 1974 European tour; Canadian triple jump title 1975 with Canadian record 16.05; represented Canada 1975 Pan-Am Games Mexico, World Student Games Rome; played varsity basketball U of T 1971-73, OUAA all-star 1973; U of T outstanding athlete 1974; *res.* Scarborough, Ont.

WATT, Laird (tennis); *b.* 21 May 1913, Montreal, Que.; *m.* Anne M. Fraser; *children:* Nancy, Linda, Sherrill; McGill U, B.Comm.; retired chartered accountant; playing mem. Canadian Davis Cup team 1934, 1938, 1946, non-playing captain several other occasions; number one in Canada 1938-39; with father claimed US national father-son title three times; Canadian Intercollegiate singles, doubles titles twice each; Canadian indoor men's doubles champion twice; Maryland State men's doubles champion once; Quebec singles title three times, men's doubles five times; Ontario singles, doubles champion once each; past pres. CLTA 1962-63, Quebec LTA 1951-52, International LTC of Canada 1965-69; hon. treasurer Commonwealth Games Assoc. of Canada 1953-59, v.-pres. 1959-63; Centennial medal 1967; *res.* Montreal, Que.

WATT, Robert (tennis); *b.* 11 Oct 1885, Tara, Ont., *d.* 4 Jul 1971, Montreal, Que.; *m.* Marguerita V. Vittie; *children:* Laird, Robert Jr. (*d.*); business executive; with son Laird won US national father-son doubles titles 1933, 1934, 1937; Canadian Lawn Tennis Association pres. 1937-45; only Canadian pres. International Lawn Tennis Federation 1957.

WATT, Tom (hockey); *b.* 17 Jun 1935, Toronto, Ont.; *m.* Mabs MacPherson; *children:* Kelly, Ruth Anne, Robert; U of Toronto, B.P.H.E., M.Ed.; hockey coach; played hockey and football at U of T; coached Toronto Jarvis CI 1959-64, Monarch Park HS 1964-65; assistant football coach U of T 1965-73 and since 1965 has been head hockey coach U of T guiding Varsity Blues to nine conference titles and eight national Intercollegiate championships; wrote *How to Play Hockey;* 1971 Canadian college hockey coach of year; TV color commentator 1977 world hockey tournament Prague; *res.* Toronto, Ont.

WEATHERALL, Jim (football); *b.* 26 Oct 1929, Texas; *m.* Ruth Williams; *children:* Tracy, Clay, Jamie; U of Oklahoma, B.B.A.; insurance, securities broker; with Oklahoma Sooners all-American 1950-51, Outland award 1951, in 1951 East-West Shrine Game, 1952 Senior Bowl and College all-star games; played all Navy and Marine games 1952-53; turned pro with Edmonton Eskimos 1954 helping them win Grey Cup; joined Philadelphia Eagles (NFL) 1955-57 playing in 1957 Pro Bowl; with Washington Redskins 1958-59, Detroit Lions 1960-62; mem. Panhandle of Texas, US College Football, Big Eight Football Conference Halls of Fame; *res.* Moore, Oklahoma.

WEBB, Don (diving); *b.* 22 Jul 1933, Toronto, Ont.; *m.* Mary Ann Parsons; *children:* Michaele, Kelly; Western Tech and Commercial HS; diving coach; represented HS in diving, gymnastics; pro diver at 15 competing in almost every major water show in world; world pro high diving title 1963; coached Canadian athletes to Olympic action 1964, 1968, 1972, 1976, Pan-Am Games 1971, Commonwealth Games 1974, world championships 1973, 1975 plus numerous international tours since 1964; trainees have won world-wide honors and Bev Boys twice was chosen Canada's female athlete of year; *res.* Pointe Claire, Que.

WEILAND, Cooney (hockey); *b.* 5 Nov 1904, Seaforth, Ont.; *given name:* Ralph; minor hockey Seaforth, junior with Owen Sound 1923 winning Memorial Cup 1924; played with Minneapolis 1925-28, NHL for 11 seasons with Boston, Detroit, Ottawa Senators; on Boston's Dynamite Line with Dit Clapper, Dutch Gainor; on two Stanley Cup winners 1929, 1939; scored 173 goals in 509 NHL games with best season 1929-30 when he scored 43 goals in 44-game schedule; second team all-star 1934-35; coach Harvard until 1971 retirement; mem. Hockey Hall of Fame; *res.* Wayland, Mass.

WEILER, Willie (gymnastics); *b.* 1 Mar 1936, Rastatt, Germany; *given name:* Wilhelm Friedrich; *m.* Fay Joy; *children:* Rick, Kimberley; soldier, tool and die maker; 1956 junior all-around German gymnastics title; Canadian gymnastics title 1957, 1958, 1960, 1962, 1966 working without coach; first in North America to perform Yamashita vault in competition; 1960 US vaulting title; first in North America to perform piked back somersault dismount off horizontal bar; 1963 Pan-Am Games Sao Paulo Brazil won three gold, four silver, one bronze; represented Canada 1964 Tokyo, 1968 Mexico Olympics; team manager Pan-Am Games Cali Colombia; competed world Dortmund W. Germany 1966; mem. AAU of C, Canadian Armed Forces Sports Halls of Fame; mem. Order of Canada; *res.* Lahr, W. Germany.

WELCH, Barbara (badminton); *b.* 28 Feb 1948, Toronto, Ont.; *given name:* Barbara Hood; *m.* Garry Welch; secretary; winner numerous Ontario, Toronto district championships since 1965; five times Canadian ladies' doubles champion; won Canadian mixed doubles 1973; three times mem. Canadian Uber Cup team; represented Canada 1974 Commonwealth Games; mem. Canadian team on tour of People's Republic of China 1972; won Canadian junior ladies' doubles, finalist Danish Open mixed doubles 1971; winner both Canadian Open ladies', mixed doubles 1974; *res.* Toronto, Ont.

WELCH, Huck (football); *b.* 12 Dec 1907, Toronto, Ont.; *given name:* Hawley; *m.* Helen (*d.*); *children:* Sandra, Patricia, Douglas, Robert; Collingwood HS, Hamilton Delta CI; sales manager florist shop; launched football career in Collingwood, twice topped scorers while helping Delta to three Canadian interscholastic titles; joined Hamilton Tigers 1928 helping club to interprovincial titles, Grey Cup 1928-29; with Montreal Winged Wheelers Grey Cup winners 1931; Jeff Russel Memorial Trophy 1933; frequent Big Four, all-Canadian all-star; rejoined Hamilton Tigers 1935-37; twice interprovincial scoring champion, twice runner-up; coach Delta CI seniors, Eastwood CI juniors; first post-war pres. Hamilton Tigers 1946; coach Kelvin CI, Winnipeg 1948-50, Regina juniors 1953; Hamilton representative of CFL commissioner 1959; mem. Collingwood, Canadian Football, Canadian Sports Halls of Fame; *res.* Hamilton, Ont.

WELSH, Alex (curling); *b.* 12 Oct 1907, Edinburgh, Scotland, *d.* 4 Jan 1971, Winnipeg, Man.; *m.* Edna Howard; *children:* Judy, Heather, Alexander Jr.; St. James HS; manager insurance co.; three times Manitoba Consols champion, third for John Douglas 1933 Brier, third for brother Jim 1947 Brier winner, again 1954; twice Manitoba Curling Association grand aggregate champion.

WELSH, Jim (curling); *b.* 18 Feb 1910, Leith, Scotland; *m.* Kathleen Lloyd; *children:* Kathleen, Patricia; St. James HS; retired; four times Manitoba Consols champion; second for John Douglas 1933 Brier, skipped 1937 Brier runner-up, 1947 Brier champion (9-0 records), 1954 Brier entry; mem. Deer Lodge Curling Club; pres. Manitoba Curling Association 1964-65; MCA bonspiel grand aggregate champion three times; *res.* Winnipeg, Man.

WELTON, John (football); *b.* 9 Dec 1929, Ottawa, Ont.; *m.* Joan King; *children:* John Jr., Dan, Caroline; Wake Forest U, B.B.A., Stanford U, M.B.A.; pres. development co.; trial with Montreal Alouettes 1950; joined Ottawa Rough Riders 1952-54, top rookie 1952; with Toronto Argos 1955-58, Eastern all-star 1957; senior city basketball in Ottawa 1952-54; *res.* Mississauga, Ont.

WENZEL, Joan (track); *b.* 24 Dec 1953, Hamilton, Ont.; *given name:* Joan Evelyn Eddy; *m.* Timothy Wenzel; U of Waterloo, B.A.; 24.1 for 200m as a juvenile; in 400m 1971 Pan-Am Games Cali Colombia; represented Canada as junior team mem. in Portugal, set junior Canadian mark of 53.6 for 400m; competed 1973 Canadian championships, 1974 Commonwealth Games, 1975 European tour; seventh 2:02.07 in 1975 pre-Olympic meet; bronze medal 800m 1975 Pan-Am Games Mexico, lost it because she took a cold remedy containing a prohibited drug; represented Canada 800m 1976 Olympics; *res.* Calgary, Alta.

WERENICH, Ed (curling); *b.* 23 Jun 1947, Benito, Man.; *given name:* Edrick; *m.* Linda Louise Goulsbra; Benito HS, Ryerson Polytechnical Inst.; fireman; with Paul Savage rink as third won three Ontario Consols titles, appeared in three Briers; twice winner Royal Canadian Classic, Thunder Bay Grand Prix; skipped own rink to three Ontario Firefighters titles, three national championship appearances; *res.* Scarborough, Ont.

WERTHNER, Penny (track); *b.* 5 Jul 1951, Ottawa, Ont.; *given name:* Penny Christine; Nepean HS, McMaster U, B.A., Carleton U, U of Waterloo; student; Canadian midget record :58.2, third 440yd at Junior Tri-Country meet Ottawa 1967; Canadian juvenile mark of 2:11.8 in 1968 while placing fourth in Canadian Olympic trial 880yd; ran 2:11.3 for 800m during 1968 Toronto international meet, top female athlete; 1969 best indoor 880yd with 2:13.4, followed with Canadian junior and juvenile record 2:14.3 in 91st Highlanders indoor meet Toronto; hampered by foot injury, competed in Pan-Pacific Games trials Victoria, placed second, established Canadian juvenile record for 1500m with 4:31 but failed to make team; mem. 1970 Commonwealth Games team Edinburgh placing fourth 1500m, sixth 800m; bronze medal 800m 1971 Pan-Am Games then toured Italy with Canadian track team; world 1000m record Vancouver with 2:45.9 1972; 1976 won 800m bronze medal in California meet, won Olympic trials Quebec City in 1500m; mem. 1976 Canadian Olympic team; personal bests: 2:05.4 for 800m 1976, 4:10.4 for 1500m; *res.* Ottawa, Ont.

WESLOCK, Nick (golf); *b.* 13 Dec 1917, Winnipeg, Man.; *given name:* Nick Wisnock; *m.* Elsie; *children:* Sheri-lee; owner steel engineering consulting and supply co.; first tourney win with Southern Ontario amateur using borrowed clubs at Roseland Golf Club

1939; won four Canadian amateurs, runner-up once, eight Ontario amateurs, runner-up seven times, seven Ontario Opens, runner-up once, one Ontario best-ball, runner-up four times, five Ontario seniors, two Canadian seniors (Rankin Trophy); 22 times mem. Ontario Willingdon Cup team; seven times mem. Canada's Americas Cup team; five times mem. Canadian Commonwealth team; four times mem. Canadian world amateur team; 1970 mem. Canadian team in Humberto Almeida Cup tourney Sao Paulo Brazil; 15 times low amateur in Canadian Open; four times invited to US Masters; mem. RCGA, Canadian Sports Halls of Fame; *res.* Burlington, Ont.

WEST, Art (football); *b.* 29 Jul 1918, Newport, Wales; *given name:* Arthur Philip; *m.* Veronica Ferriman; *children:* one son; Maumee Ohio HS, Michigan State U; distilling industry; won five HS athletic letters; centrefielder with Maher Shoes Toronto Senior Baseball League, guard with Broadview Rascals, Simpson Grads Toronto Senior Basketball League; halfback Toronto Argos 1936-40, 1945-46 playing on four Grey Cup champions; played on 1942 RCAF Hurricanes winning fifth Grey Cup; retired following 1947 season as end with Montreal Alouettes; captain 1940 Argos; led league in TDs 1937-38; all-star on Lionel Conacher's all-Canadian team 1937, Ted Reeve's all-Canadian team 1938; halfback on all-Argo dream team 1921-41 era; nickname Whippet; coach Junior Argos 1948-49, Parkdale Lions Intermediates 1950, Balmy Beach ORFU 1951, Cobourg Galloping Ghosts 1952, all reached playoffs; v.-pres. in charge of coaches, playing personnel Kitchener-Waterloo Dutchmen ORFU 1964; *res.* Toronto, Ont.

WESTLING, Gunnar (shooting); *b*. 25 Dec 1907, Trandstrand, Sweden; *m*. Gertrude; *children:* Kenneth; retired welder; since 1948 mem. DCRA national team specializing in fullbore, smallbore rifles and pistols; qualified seven times for Canadian Bisley team competing on six occasions; Duke of Gloucester prize 1960, Clocktower award 1972; Bisley aggregate winner 1966, same year silver cross as Canadian champion; represented Canada six times in NRA prize meetings; helped Canada win overseas team match 1970, 1972, Kalapore team match 1972; Queen's prize at Bisley to become one of seven Canadians in over 100 years of shooting to turn trick; winner frequent provincial titles; only marksman to win B.C. title in grand-slam style; five times B.C. target rifle champion, four times runner-up; four times Lt. Governor's match titlist; has won every match, aggregate and team event at least once at BCRA annual prize meet; provincial handgun champion 1956, centrefire titlist twice, smallbore titlist 1947; mem. B.C. Sports Hall of Fame; *res*. Vancouver, B.C.

WESTWICK, Harry (hockey); *b*. 23 Apr 1876, Ottawa, Ont., *d*. 3 Apr 1957, Ottawa, Ont.; *m*. Ruby Duval; *children:* Bill, Thomas, Barberry, Elaine, Ula, Beatrice; civil servant; began hockey as goaler Ottawa Seconds, switched to rover; played for city league Aberdeens; at 17 on Ottawa's 1892-93 title winners; joined Capitals (Silver Seven) 1895 remaining with club through 1908 except 1898 when he sat out season and 1899 when he was with Waterloo in Ontario Big Four; captained Ottawa 1903 to first of three successive Stanley Cups; best season 1904-05, scored 24 goals in 13 games; 1906 named to first senior all-star team in Canadian hockey; nickname Rat; on retirement refereed in NHA; starred 1896-1904 Ottawa Capitals lacrosse team which won three world titles; 1902 National Lacrosse Union all-star; football Ottawa Rough Riders; mem. Ottawa, Hockey Halls of Fame.

WHEELER, Lucile (skiing); *b*. 14 Jan 1935, Montreal, Que.; *m*. Kaye Vaughan; *children:* Myrle, Jake; Ste. Agathe HS, White Mountain School; ski coach; entered first downhill at 10 Mt. Tremblant placing seventh in field of 21; at 12 won Canadian junior; at 14 mem. Canadian national team; under master coach Pepi Salvenmoser launched five-year rigid training program 1952 in Europe; sixth place in giant slalom, first Canadian to claim Olympic skiing medal with bronze in downhill 1956 at Cortina; in 1957 won downhill, combined Hahenkammen, Kitzbuhel Austria; first North American to win world ski championship claiming gold in downhill, giant slalom and silver in combined 1958 world Badgastein Austria; Canadian athlete of year (Lou Marsh Trophy), Perry medal Ski Club of Great Britain 1958; mem. Canadian Sports, US National Ski Halls of Fame: *res*. Knowlton, Que.

WHITCROFT, Frederick (hockey); *b*. 1883, Port Perry, Ont., *d*. 1931, Vancouver, B.C.; played with Peterborough Colts 1901 winning OHA junior championship; rover in seven-man hockey days; played 1905 Midland Ont., returned to Peterborough where he captained intermediate club to OHA title; moved west for one season then returned to Ontario and Kenora Thistles when they won 1907 Stanley Cup; moved to Edmonton and captained senior team; scored 49 goals that season, Edmonton challenged Ottawa for Stanley Cup only to lose in two straight games; when Edmonton eliminated from

Stanley Cup action joined Renfrew Millionaires in 1909-10 season; mem. Hockey Hall of Fame.

WHITE, Betty (track); *b.* 14 May 1915, Niagara Falls, Ont.; *given name:* Elizabeth McCallum; *m.* Frank Lewington; *children:* Nancy, Bill; Thorold HS; sales clerk; won 100yd dash Canada vs US meet CNE 1932; second 100m, 200m 1933 Canadian championships, set Canadian 200m record, outstanding female athlete; competed in 1934 Canadian championships which served as British Empire Games trials, second 60m, third 100m; as mem. 1934 Canadian 660yd relay team won British Empire Games gold medal London Eng.; *res.* Hamilton, Ont.

WHITE, Bill (hockey); *b.* 26 Aug 1939, Toronto, Ont.; *given name:* William Earl; *m.* Gail; *children:* Kimberly, Karrie, Kristen; hockey player, executive; played in Toronto Maple Leaf organization from peewee, to bantam, midget, and junior where he played three seasons with Toronto Marlboros; turned pro by Leafs and farmed to Rochester (AHL) 1959-62, except for Sudbury (EPHL) 1960-61; sold to Springfield (AHL) 1962-63, Los Angeles 1967-68; traded to Chicago with Bryan Campbell, Gerry Desjardins for Gilles Marotte, Jim Stanfield, Denis DeJordy 1970; three times second team all-star; mem. Team Canada 1972 vs USSR; through 1976-77 NHL record: 604 games played, 50 goals, 215 assists, 265 points, 495 penalty minutes, plus 91 playoff games, seven goals, 32 assists for 39 points, 76 penalty minutes; coach Chicago Black Hawks 1976; *res.* Toronto, Ont.

WHITE, Dalt (coaching); *b.* 6 Jul 1917, Brampton, Ont.; *given name:* Alexander Dalton; *m.* Margaret; *children:* Peter, Ted, Laurie-Anne, Geoffrey, Brian, Douglas, Janet; U of Toronto, B.A., B.Ed., M.Ed., OCE; educator; mem. Orillia junior Canadian lacrosse champions 1932; played lacrosse with Toronto Marlboros, Hamilton Tigers, Brampton Excelsiors, U of T; senior basketball several years with Toronto West End Y; coached Port Colborne HS team to Central Ontario HS football title 1940; coached football, basketball, track at Toronto Western Tech four years winning city, provincial basketball titles; assistant football coach U of T 1951-55, head coach 1956-65, on Yates Cup twice; athletic director U of T since 1971; Thomas R. Loudon award for U of T athletic contributions 1976; *res.* Toronto, Ont.

WHITE, Dennis (boxing); *b.* 4 Dec 1898, Waterloo, Que.; retired railway employee; AAU of C boxing supervisor 1928, national chairman 1937-63; manager Canadian boxing team 1930 British Empire Games Hamilton; coach 1932 Canadian Olympic team; manager Olympic boxing teams 1948, 1952, 1960; elected to AIBA 1971, on executive committee through 1974; mem. AAU of C, Canadian Boxing Halls of Fame; *res.* St. Laurent, Que.

WHITE, Julie (track and field); *b.* 1 Jun 1960, Bancroft, Ont.; *given name:* Julie Margaret; Centennial HS; student; high jump specialist; world age-class (14) record of 1.80m Winnipeg 1974; second Canadian senior championships 1974; Canadian junior record 1.85m 1975, 1.86m 1976; US indoor title with 1.85m 1976; led Canadian Olympic qualifiers with 1.85m 1976, fourth place finish and personal best of 1.87m 1976 Olympics; *res.* Brampton, Ont.

WHITE, Tommy (baseball); *b.* 19 Apr 1922, Regina, Sask.; *given name:* Thomas Towersey; *m.* Sally Anne Jones; *children:* Thomas Barry, James Joseph; Sandwich CI, Assumption College; sporting goods store manager, HS phys ed teacher; pitched Windsor senior OBA 1939, Welland OBA 1940; pitching attracted pro scouts, played Cleveland farm system Appleton, Wausau Wisc. 1941-42, London Ont. army team 1943, London Majors Senior Intercounty 1944-53, St. Thomas Elgins Senior Intercounty player-manager 1953-60; twice led league won-lost percentage, in 18 Intercounty seasons 108-57 record, 25-1 record 1947; three victories in seven-game World Sandlot series triumph by London Majors over Fort Wayne 1948; frequent Intercounty all-star, MVP 1949; *res.* St. Thomas, Ont.

WHITEHOUSE, Reg (football); *b.* 8 Oct 1933, Montreal, Que.; *given name:* Reginald Alfred; *m.* Joanne Lee; *children:* Timber, Lee; self employed, electrical co.; with Notre Dame de Grace won 1951 Quebec Jr. grid title; joined Saskatchewan Roughriders 1952, played first string 15 years as offensive guard, defensive tackle, linebacker and placement kicker; during CFL career kicked 167 converts, 59 field goals; in 1956 all-star game Vancouver, kicked five converts; Tibbits trophy as Saskatchewan team MVP, WFC record for field goal completion percentage 76.4, fourth in league scoring race 1956; in 1957 Montreal all-star game; organized Saskatchewan players' association 1964; in 1966 Grey Cup winner; coached Verdun Invictus to Quebec junior football title 1971; *res.* Cranbrook, B.C.

WHITTALL, Beth (swimming); *b.* 26 May 1936, Montreal, Que.; *div.; children:* Lyne, Helene, Marc Couvrette; Purdue U, B.Sc.; sales representative; silver medal 400m freestyle (FS) relay, finalist 400m FS 1954 British Empire Games Vancouver; gold medal 100m butterfly, 400m FS, silver medal 400m medley relay, 400m FS relay 1955 Pan-Am Games Mexico; seventh 100m butterfly 1956 Melbourne Olympics; Lou Marsh Trophy Canada's top athlete 1955; mem. Aquatic Hall of Fame of Canada, AAU of C Hall of Fame; *res.* St. Laurent, Que.

WIEDEL, Gerry (fencing); *b.* 1 May 1933, Germany; *m.* Pacita Dumenieux; contractor; Canadian épée champion 1965, foil 1965, 1969, 1970; several times Ontario, Eastern Canadian titlist; winner numerous international competitions; represented Canada 1967 Pan-Am Games (fourth team foil), 1970 Commonwealth Games (bronze team foil), 1968, 1972 Olympics; *res.* Toronto, Ont.

WIEDEL, Pacita (fencing); *b.* 31 Mar 1933, Spain; *given name:* Pacita Dumenieux; *m.* Gerry Wiedel; Canadian women's foil title 1959-64, 1966, runner-up 1967-68, 1971; topped rankings 1970-71; nine times Ontario titlist; winner numerous tournaments 1959-71 in Canada, US; fifth US championships Los Angeles 1965, second US team championships 1964; represented Canada 1964 Olympics; sixth 1963 Pan-Am Games; bronze individual and team foil 1967 Pan-Am Games; bronze team 1970 Commonwealth Games; *res.* Toronto, Ont.

WIETZES, Eppie (autosport); *b.* 28 May 1938, Groningen, Holland; *m.* Dianne Louise Holland; *children:* Michael, Douglas, Marlain; Ontario Trade School; class A mechanic, owner auto dealership; drove Comstock Mustang, GT40 1965-67; with Ford team in several rallies including Winter Rally, Shell 4000; drove Formula One Lotus 1967 Canadian Grand Prix; Canadian Road Racing title with Lola T142, in four races SCCA Continental series 1969; sponsored by Formula Racing, drove McLaren M10B in Canadian, US Formula A competition repeating Canadian triumph; never placed lower than sixth in Canadian driving title series 1970-75; *res*. Thornhill, Ont.

WIGSTON, Fran (volleyball); *b*. 28 May 1935, North Bay, Ont.; *given name:* Frances Anne; U of Western Ontario, B.A., university professor; mem. Canadian volleyball championship teams 1966-68, Canadian basketball team 1967-68; coach-player London Grads basketball team 1969-74; competed in 1967 Canada Winter Games winning basketball silver, 1971 basketball gold; coached UWO women's volleyball team to Ontario titles three times, Canadian title once, runner-up twice; coached UWO women's T&F team 1969-71, team mem. 1964-74; coached London Junos volleyball team 1971-75 winning Ontario senior women's title 1973-74, Canadian finals 1974; coached senior men's London Kineldiego volleyball team 1973-75; coached Canadian women's volleyball team World Student Games Moscow 1973; coached London Lions Olympic T&F Club 1964-68; since 1976 mem. National Advisory Council on Fitness and Amateur Sport; *res*. London, Ont.

WILKES, Jimmy (baseball); *b*. 1 Oct 1925, Philadelphia, Pa.; *given name:* James Eugene; *div.; children:* two sons, two daughters; John Bartram HS; joined Negro American League 1945 teaming with Larry Doby, Monte Irvin, Don Newcombe, same league as Jackie Robinson, Josh Gibson, Willie Mays, Satchel Paige, Bob Thurman; signed

with Dodger organization 1950 playing two seasons in Eastern League at Elmira N.Y., Trois-Rivières and Lancaster Pa. in Interstate league; played 1952 season as Hank Aaron teammate with Indianapolis Clowns; began Intercounty career with Brantford 1953 and in 10 years amassed .294 lifetime avg., frequent all-star centrefielder; best season 1956, batted .344, led league in hits, doubles, times at bat, walks and was only player to appear in all league and playoff games; manager Brantford team 1958; played with three pennant winners, five playoff champions; turned to umpiring in Brantford city league 1964, Senior Intercounty 1965; *res*. Brantford, Ont.

WILKINS, Bruce (shooting); *b*. 29 May 1933, Hamilton, Ont.; *given name:* Bruce Gray; *m*. Bertha Stewart; *children:* Sandie, Janet; Westdale, Central HS, Mohawk College; electronics draftsman; National Open Sporting rifle champion 1966; seven times Ontario champion 1967-74; mem. Canadian champion Inter-Cities teams 1963-75; mem. National Rifle team 1970-72; competed in world championships Phoenix 1970, Pan-Am Games Cali Colombia 1971; National, Ontario Rifle coaching chairman since 1973; coach 1976 Olympic rifle team; rifle shooting chairman 1976 Olympiad for physically disabled; *res*. Ancaster, Ont.

WILKINSON, Tom (football); *b*. 4 Jan 1943, Greybull, Wyo.; *given name:* Thomas Edward; *m*. Anna Louise; *children:* Sherry, Tom Jr., Jodi; U of Wyoming; football player, salesman; turned pro with Toronto Rifles in Continental Football League; moved to Toronto Argos 1967-70, spent season with B.C. Lions, since 1972 mem. of Edmonton Eskimos; led CFL in pass completions avg. 1972; quarterbacked Edmonton to

Grey Cup final three times, one winner; in 10 CFL seasons has thrown 1,602 passes completing 987 for 13,800yds, .616 percentage, 88 TDs, 82 interceptions; Edmonton athlete of year 1974; Jackie Parker Trophy, Canada Packers Award 1972, 1974; Schenley outstanding player award 1974; *res.* Edmonton, Alta.

WILLIAMS, Jerry (football); *b.* 1 Nov 1923, Spokane, Wash.; *m.* Marian Munroe; *children:* Jerry Bill, Rebecca Sue, Todd David, Julie Ann, Tyler Laurie; Washington State U, B.S., Temple U; rancher, investor, football coach; competed in East-West Shrine Game, Chicago College all-star game; turned pro Los Angeles Rams 1949-52, world champions 1951; traded to Philadelphia Eagles 1953-54; head coach U of Montana 1955-57; defensive coach Philadelphia Eagles 1958-63; assistant coach Calgary Stampeders 1964, head coach 1965-68 guiding team to Grey Cup final 1968, WFC pennant 1965; head coach Philadelphia Eagles 1969-71, Hamilton Tiger-Cats 1972-75; guided 1972 team to single season team won-lost record 11-3 and Grey Cup victory; CFL coach of year 1967; fourth best won-lost record of any coach in CFL history; Dan Reeves' all-time Ram team; *res.* Kirkland, Ariz.

WILLIAMS, Percy (track); *b.* 19 May 1908, Vancouver, B.C.; insurance executive; gold in 100m (10.8), 200m (21.8) 1928 Olympics; tied world standard for 100m (10.6) on grass track 1925, tied world mark for 100yds (9.6); thigh injury ended racing career at 22; *res.* Vancouver, B.C.

WILLSEY, Ray (football); *b.* 30 Sep 1929, Griffin, Sask.; *m.* Barbara Bigelow; *children:* Lee Ann, Janet, Louise; U of California,

B.S.; football coach; turned pro Edmonton Eskimos 1953-55, all-Western defensive back rookie season; currently on staff of NFL St. Louis Cardinals; *res.* Baldwin, Mo.

WILLSIE, Harry (shooting); *b.* 20 Dec 1928, Jacksonville, Mo.; *div.; children:* Billie, Alan, Carol Dean, Debora; U of Missouri, B.A.; real estate owner, manager; pres. Canadian Skeet Shooting Association; director Shooting Federation of Canada; director QSSF; director COJO Tir Mission 1976; director QTSA 1959-67; director Amateur Trap Shooting Association of America 1959-68; pres. Canadian TSA 1963-67; gold medal, set record 1974 Commonwealth Games; mem. Canadian team Tokyo, Mexico Olympics, Pan-Am Games teams Winnipeg, Cali, Mexico; Canadian champion trap and/or skeet six times, winner several American style skeet titles; only Canadian to score perfect 100x100 in American trap doubles; *res.* Montreal, Que.

WILSON, Ben (football); *b.* 12 Jul 1926, London, Ont.; *given name:* Benson Andrus; *m.* Charlotte Henry Harrington; *children:* Benson Andrus, Meredith Jane; U of Western Ontario, B.Sc., Oxford U, B.Sc.; assistant deputy minister, Ministry of Colleges and Universities; outstanding lineman UWO Mustangs 1944-47; 1948-50 played for Oxford basketball team, captain 1949-50; University College Oxford rugger team reaching Inter-College Cup semifinals 1949-50; coach football, basketball Ridley College St. Catharines 1950-51; *res.* Toronto, Ont.

WILSON, Doug Jr. (hockey); *b.* 5 Jul 1957, Ottawa, Ont.; *given name:* Douglas Frederick; Laurentian HS, Westwood CI; minor hockey Ottawa; began junior play Winnipeg, joined Ottawa 67's 1974-75; OHA all-star defenceman; Memorial Cup finalist 1977; Memorial Cup tournament all-star defenceman 1977; two handicap golfer; Cedarhill Club champion 1976; won Toronto Thunderbird Invitational 1976; *res.* Ottawa, Ont.

WILSON, Doug Sr. (track, hockey); *b.* 24 Oct 1929, Toronto, Ont.; *given name:* Douglas Frederick; *m.* Verna Myers; *children:* Murray, Victoria, Patricia, Douglas Jr.; U of Western Ontario, B.A.; retired Canadian Forces; competed for UWO track team during 50s winning some intercollegiate honors; involved with Ottawa 67's hockey organization from inception working with minor league development program; v.-pres. Manitoba Track and Field Association; mem. national selection committee; since 1974 chief scout Ottawa 67's hockey club; *res.* Ottawa, Ont.

WILSON, Jean (speedskating); *b.* 1910, Glasgow, Scotland, *d.* 1933, Toronto, Ont.; Toronto indoor champion 1931, North American title in Ottawa same year; represented Canada 1932 Olympic demonstration event Lake Placid, won 500m in record 58:00, broke world record for 1500m (2:54.2); died at 23 from progressive muscular disease; *Toronto Telegram* donated Jean Wilson Trophy in her memory to fastest indoor woman skater in 1934; mem. Canadian Sports Hall of Fame.

WILSON, Murray (hockey); *b.* 3 Aug 1951, Toronto, Ont.; *given name:* Murray Charles; *m.* Cathy Lewis; Laurentian HS, Carleton U; hockey player; junior A Ottawa 67's; third Montreal choice, 11th overall 1971 amateur draft; one season Nova Scotia Voyageurs (AHL) before joining Canadiens 1972-73 season as left winger; mem. two Stanley Cup winners; through 1976-77 season NHL record: 316 scheduled games, 83 goals, 79 assists, 162 points, 148 penalty minutes; held Canadian juvenile discus record; Ottawa HS discus record 51.86m 1970; *res.* Montreal, St. Pierre de Wakefield, Que.

WILSON, Patti (track and field); *b.* 25 Apr 1954, Ottawa, Ont.; *given name:* Patricia Ann; U of Manitoba, B.A.; teacher; during seven-year T&F career, in which high jumping was a specialty, established numerous Ottawa HS records as junior, senior; also hurdler; with Debbie Brill shared national women's high jump record; mem. Canadian team 1971 Cali Pan-Am Games, Italian tour; *res.* Ottawa, Ont.

WILSON, Peter (ski jumping); *b.* 22 Oct 1952, Ottawa, Ont.; laborer; mem. Canadian National Ski team 1970 placing third as junior in Iron Mt. Mich. competition, Canada Games Saskatoon; as oarsman with Ottawa Rowing Club mem. Canadian junior and senior cox fours 1971, senior fours 1972; competed in Europe, US, Canada, Japan 1971-72; placed second North American ski jumping finals, 22nd of 60 in first world ski flying championships Planica Yugoslavia and represented Canada 1972 Sapporo Olympic 70m, 90m jumps; with national team 1972-73 took fifths St. Moritz Switzerland, Sapporo Japan, second in Canadian finals, 10th world ski flying Oberstdorf Germany; 32nd Falun Sweden world championships 1973-74; 36th of 54 in 70m, 45th of 55 in 90m 1976 Innsbruck Olympics; *res.* Ottawa, Ont.

WILSON, Phat (hockey); *b.* 29 Dec 1895, Port Arthur, Ont., *d.* Aug 1970, Port Arthur, Ont.; *given name:* Gordon Allan; remained amateur throughout career as player, coach; played defence for Port Arthur War

Veterans seniors 1918-20; moved to Iroquois Falls of Northern Ontario Hockey Association, won league title; returned to Port Arthur Bearcats taking Allan Cup 1926, 1927, 1929 and Western Canadian title 1930; coach Bearcats 1938, 1940; mem. Hockey Hall of Fame.

WILSON, Robert (rowing); *b.* 14 Oct 1935, Kamloops, B.C.; *given name:* Robert Andrew; *m.* Barbara Evon Andrews; *children:* Sharon Marie, Douglas James; Kamloops HS, U of British Columbia, B.Sc.; mem. eight-oared crew which won gold medal British Empire and Commonwealth Games 1954, 1958; silver medal 1956 Melbourne Olympics; mem. B.C. Sports Hall of Fame; *res.* Vancouver, B.C.

WILSON, Ruth (tennis, golf, basketball); *b.* 27 Apr 1919, Calgary, Alta.; *given name:* Ruth Plant; U of British Columbia, B.A., Western Washington State College, M.Ed.; teacher, counsellor; in basketball played on five national championship teams; coached three national senior A titlists (Eilers 1950-51, Buzz Bombs 1973), 1967 bronze medal Pan-Am Games team, university teams UBC, Simon Fraser, WWSC; manager 1959 Pan-Am Games team; in softball played in two women's world series, coached a third; in golf mem. eight B.C. interprovincial teams, won Canadian title four times; mem. one Canadian international team; runner-up Canadian Closed championship 1961; in tennis winner B.C. junior doubles, mixed doubles, Pacific Northwest doubles, mixed doubles; Whistle Award for basketball contributions by B.C. referees; mem. B.C. Sports Hall of Fame; *res.* Vancouver, B.C.

WINDEYER, Walter (yachting); *b.* 1900, Toronto, Ont., *d.* 1964, Toronto, Ont.; as mem. Royal Canadian Yacht Club won

Townsend Cup for International 14ft dinghies four times and Canada's first International Dragon Class world championship 1959; at 19 won Douglas Cup; three consecutive years in late 20s won Wilton Morse Trophy; mem. Canadian team which won Currie Cup in International 14ft class Lowestaft Eng. 1936; skipper Invader II in 1932 Canada's Cup challenge; 1958 O'Keefe Trophy with Corte on Great Lakes; 1959 Dragon Gold Cup in Europe; recorded wins in O'Keefe Trophy, Telegram Trophy and Olympic trials; Duke of Edinburgh Trophy Lake Ontario 1961; permanent possession O'Keefe Trophy with third victory; mem. Canadian Sports Hall of Fame.

WONG, Lester (fencing); *b.* 28 Aug 1944, China; *m.* Donna; U of Alberta, B.Sc.; production manager; individual silver medal épée, team bronze 1970 Edinburgh Commonwealth Games; Canadian épée title 1971, represented Canada in Cali Colombia Pan-Am Games in épée, foil same year; competed in épée, foil Munich Olympics 1972; Canadian foil title and represented Canada in same Mexico Pan-Am Games 1975; mem. Canadian Olympic team 1976; *res.* Caledon, Ont.

WOO, Wes (weightlifting); *b.* 11 Sep 1939, Vancouver, B.C.; *given name:* Westley; *m.* Joyce; U of British Columbia, B.S.P.; pharmacist; Canadian teenage middleweight lifting title 1956; B.C. junior champion, record holder 1960; UBC record holder; pres. B.C. Weightlifting Association 1966-70; since 1971 mem. Canadian Senior Coaches Association, chairman since 1974; coached Canadian weightlifting teams 1968, 1976 Olympics, 1971, 1975 Pan-Am Games, 1974 world championships, 1975 pre-Olympics; coached B.C. teams Canadian championships nine times since 1966, Canada Winter Games

Wood

Saskatoon 1971; formed Spartak Weightlifting Club 1968, has coached Canadian champions Keith Adams, Wayne Wilson, Doug Robertson, Brian Marsden, Paul Bjarnason, Christopher Dariotis; runner-up Air Canada coach of year 1975; *res.* Vancouver, B.C.

WOOD, Bryan (curling); *b.* 10 Mar 1944, Brandon, Man.; *given name:* Bryan David; *m.* Thelma Davis; *children:* Kevin, Robbie; Elton HS; real estate, farming; played for skips Don Duguid, Barry Fry, Rod Hunter as well as two seasons skipping own rink; mem. CBC televised series winners 1970, 1971, runner-up 1976; won Heather carspiel 1970, International Crystal Trophy, Switzerland 1970; runner-up with Bob Pickering Toronto Grey Cup 'spiel 1974; with Duguid's 1970, 1971 Manitoba Consols, Brier, Silver Broom champions; mem. Canadian Curling Hall of Fame; *res.* Winnipeg, Man.

WOOD, Howie (curling); *b.* 8 Jul 1918, Winnipeg, Man.; *given name:* Howard Francis Jr.; *m.* Christine Romano; *children:* Larry, Victor, Betty, Bob, Howie, Bruce, Ken, Dave; Kelvin HS; division manager Investors' Syndicate; at 11 in semifinals Manitoba 21-and-under championships; at 16 teamed with father to win Winnipeg city title beating Gordon Hudson in final; with father won first carspiel held 1947 at Nipawin, repeat 1953 with brother Lionel; second for father 1940 Brier winner with 9-0 record; skipped 1957 Manitoba Brier entry comprising Bill Sharpe, Don and Lorne Duguid, tied for third; skipped 1954 Manitoba Bonspiel winner; won Manitoba seniors 1970, third in Canadian; pres. Manitoba Junior Curling Association at 16; *res.* Winnipeg, Man.

WOOD, John (canoeing); *b.* 7 Jun 1950, Toronto, Ont.; *given name:* John Joseph; U of Toronto, B.A.; instructor fitness institute;

represented Canada Mexico 1968, Munich 1972, Montreal 1976 Olympics, silver medal in C1 (solo canoe) 1000m; won Canadian championships C1, C2 500m and 1000m 1975; won 1974 North American C1, C2 1000m, seventh 1970 world championships, fifth 1973, 1975, sixth 1974; *res.* Mississauga, Ont.

WOOD, Lionel (curling); *b.* 5 Dec 1924, Winnipeg, Man.; *given name:* Lionel Lawrence; *m.* Colleen Margaret Warner; *children:* Craig Wynn, Paul Daniel, Jayanne; U of Manitoba, LL.B.; owner-manager, office equipment; mem. 1938 Manitoba elementary school softball champions; 1939 soccer champions; won Manitoba Schoolboy curling title 1941; won Manitoba curling title 1945; mem. Manitoba-Lakehead lacrosse champions 1947; mem. Manitoba provincial HS football champions 1942; mem. 1946-47 Grey Cup finalist Winnipeg Blue Bombers; frequent Manitoba Bonspiel trophy winner including grand aggregate; *res.* Edmonton, Alta.

WOOD, Nora (curling); *b.* 19 Jan 1903, Arnprior, Ont.; *given name:* Nora Ward; *m.* Roy Wood; Arnprior HS; active curler since 1920; runner-up 1952 Tweedsmuir Trophy double rink competition using irons and winner 1954 Tweedsmuir using granites; pres. EOLCA 1961, 1970-72, Ontario Ladies' Curling Association 1970-71; *res.* Arnprior, Ont.

WOOD, Pappy (curling); *b.* 29 Aug 1888, Winnipeg, Man.; *given name:* Howard; *m.* Elizabeth Gillespie; *children:* Howard Jr., Lionel; business college; retired pres. contracting firm; as soccer player competed with Dominion champion Beavers 1915; joined Winnipeg-based team as one of two Canadians on all-Scottish team; began curling at 15 and is recognized in *Guiness Book of Records* for longevity by competing in 65 consecutive Manitoba bonspiels 1908-72; won MCA 'spiel grand aggregate four times; won original Macdonald Brier 1925 in conjunction with MCA 'spiel; skipped Brier winners 1930, 1940, played third on Jim Congalton's 1932 title winner; with son Howie captured first Nipawin carspiel 1947; mem. Canadian Curling, Canadian Sports Halls of Fame; *res.* Winnipeg, Man.

WOODS, Bob (curling); *b.* 2 Sep 1933, Carman, Man.; *m.* Ulla; *children:* Rolf, Keith; pres. importing firm; skipped Swedish champions to second place 1967 world championships Scotland; returning to Canada led Royal Canadians rink from Toronto to frequent provincial playdowns and major competitions; Ontario mixed champion 1977; *res.* Toronto, Ont.

WOODS, Doug (autosport); *b.* 31 Oct 1947, Ottawa, Ont.; Hillcrest HS, Carleton U, B.A.; competitions manager auto firm; with Walter Boyce won Canadian rally titles 1970-74, 'Press On Regardless' rally in Michigan 1973; rally master world class rally Rideau Lakes 1974; *res.* Ottawa, Ont.

WOODS, Maggie (track and field); *b.* 9 Jan 1960, Weston, Ont.; *given name:* Margaret Ann; Loretto Abbey HS; student; midget OFSSA 1975 high jump title (1.70m), long jump (5.25m), 1976 senior OFSSA high jump (1.76), long jump (5.60); best for 100m hurdles 14.8; second Canadian senior indoor high jump 1976 with 1.73m; won 1976 midget Ontario and Ontario Legion high jump, long jump; winner OFSSA individual senior girls trophy; *res.* Weston, Ont.

WOODWARD, Rod (football); *b.* 22 Sep 1944, Vancouver, B.C.; *given name:* Rodney William; *m.* Kay Whitacre; *children:* Tod William Brian, Carilena Mae; U of Idaho, B.Sc.; teacher, fitness director; at Everett Junior College 1963-64 earned all-conference honors as defensive halfback, honorable mention as offensive half; pro rights traded by B.C. Lions to Montreal where he played 1967-69, then traded with John Kruspe to Ottawa Rough Riders for Gene Gaines, Terry Black; through 1976 CFL record of 38 interceptions; CFL record for interceptions in seven consecutive games; all-Eastern Conference honors three times, all-Canadian once; Ottawa nominee defensive back of year 1975; mem. Athletes in Action; *res.* Ottawa, Ont.

WOOLF, George (horse racing); *b.* 1910, Cardston, Alta., *d.* 4 Jan 1946, Santa Anita, Calif.; nickname The Iceman; won 1936 Preakness on Bolt Venture, 1938 Pimlico Special on Seabiscuit; won American Derby, Hollywood Gold Cup three consecutive years; won 1945 Santa Anita Derby on Bymeabond; killed while riding Please Me at Santa Anita 1946; in 19-year racing career 721 wins, 589 seconds and 468 thirds; George Woolf Memorial award for most sportsmanlike jockey in his honor; mem. Canadian Sports, American Jockey Halls of Fame.

WORRALL, Jim (track and field); *b.* 23 Jun 1914, Bury, Lancashire, Eng., *m.* Aileen McGuire (*d.*); *children:* Anna Jane, Brian, Brenda; *div.* Lisbet Svensen; *children:* Ingrid; McGill U, B.Sc., Osgoode Hall, LL.B.; lawyer; Rector's Trophy as all-around athlete Montreal HS; held several Canadian Intercollegiate records for track at McGill; represented Canada British Empire Games

1934, won silver medal; mem. Canadian team 1936 Berlin Olympics; pres. two years Ontario T&F committee of AAU of C; eight years v.-pres. COA, pres. until 1968; first pres. Canadian Sports Advisory Council; mem. National Advisory Council on Fitness, Amateur Sport 1961-66, chairman two years; first Canadian on IOC executive board; mem. AAU of C Hall of Fame; *res.* Don Mills, Ont.

WORSLEY, Gump (hockey); *b.* 14 May 1929, Montreal, Que.; *given name:* Lorne John; *m.* Doreen; *children:* Lorne Jr, Dean, Drew, Lianne; graduated from NY Senior Rovers (EHL) to New Haven (AHL) 1949-50 and later played in St. Paul (USHL), Saskatoon (PCHL, WHL), Vancouver (WHL); joined NY Rangers 1952-53, Calder Trophy as rookie of year; next 10 seasons with Rangers with occasional stints in Vancouver (WHL), Providence, Springfield (AHL); traded to Montreal with Dave Balon, Leon Rochefort, Len Ronson for Jacques Plante, Phil Goyette, Don Marshall 1963 and, except for two seasons with Quebec (AHL), remained with Habs until 1969-70; to Minnesota 1970-74; 21-year NHL record shows 860 games, playing 50,201 minutes, 2,432 goals allowed, 43 shutouts, 2.91 avg., plus 70 playoffs, 4,080 minutes, 192 goals allowed, five shutouts, 2.82 avg.; named to first, second team all-stars once each; played on four Stanley Cup winners; USHL rookie of year Charles Gardiner Memorial Trophy; WHL MVP; WHL leading goaler; two Vezina Trophies (1966 with Charlie Hodge, 1968 with Rogie Vachon); *res.* Montreal, Que.

WORTERS, Roy (hockey); *b.* 19 Oct 1900, Toronto, Ont., *d.* 7 Nov 1957, Toronto, Ont.; nickname The Shrimp; pro hockey Pitts-burgh Yellowjackets (USAHA); Pittsburgh Pirates 1926-28, NY Americans 1928-29, Montreal Canadiens 1930, NY Americans 1930-37; averaged 2.36 goals-against in 488 league games, Vezina Trophy 1931 with 1.68 avg.; twice second team all-star; first goaler to win Hart Trophy (MVP) 1928-29 season; first goaler to use back of gloves to direct pucks to the corners; mem. Hockey Hall of Fame.

WRIGHT, Harold (track, administration); *b.* 10 Dec 1908, Winnipeg, Man.; *m.* Edna May Robinson; *children:* Linda Catherine, Lee Madison, James Kirkland; U of Alberta, Utah U, B.Sc., M.S., U of British Columbia, M.A.; engineer; represented Canada as sprinter 1932 Los Angeles Olympics and British Empire vs US meet San Francisco 1932; since 1957 director Vancouver Olympic Club, life mem. since 1969; pres. Canadian Field Hockey Association 1965-69; director COA 1966-68, pres. 1969-77; director 1973 Canada Summer Games; director organizing committee COJO 1976 Montreal Olympics; B.C. Sports Federation 1975 special achievement award; *res.* Vancouver, B.C.

WRIGHT, Joseph Jr. (rowing); *b.* 28 Mar 1906, Toronto, Ont.; *m.* Dorothy; *children:* Dianne; Parkdale CI; retired pres. coal co.; centre, guard Toronto Argonauts 1924-36; on 1933 Grey Cup champions; as rower stroked both junior, senior Argos Eights to Canadian Henley titles; rowed for Penn AC crew 1925 winning Middle States regatta; won three US national sculling titles in record times Wyandote Mich. 1927; nine Canadian titles; won diamond sculls Royal Henley England 1928; second 1929 defence of diamond sculls; silver, bronze medals 1928 Amsterdam Olympics; two bronze 1932 Los

Angeles Olympics; pres. Eastern Football Conference; mem. Canadian AAU, Sports Halls of Fame; *res.* Islington, Ont.

WRIGHT, Joseph Sr. (all-around); *b.* 14 Jan 1864, Villanova, Ont., *d.* 18 Oct 1950, Toronto, Ont.; *m.* Alethea Ainley Spink; *children:* George, Jessie, Nancy, Margaret, Joseph Jr.; U of Toronto; rowing coach; in boxing Canadian amateur heavyweight at 35; in T&F one of first Canadians to run 100yds in 10:00, set Canadian shot put, hammer throw records; in football played 18 years with Toronto Argos, 1911 Grey Cup match with son George; in wrestling Canadian amateur titlist; in billiards Canadian champion; stroked first Canadian eight-oared crew to win US national title 1901; first Canadian to win heat in British Henley diamond sculls; won Bedford Cup, English amateur singles title 1895 (first ever by Canadian); US junior singles 1891, intermediate singles 1892; honored by King of Sweden 1912 Olympics; coached eights who won Canadian Henley, US nationals 1905, 1907, 1911; intermediate eights did same 1905-06, 1909-11; coach U of Penn. 1916-26; Canadian oarsman of half century 1950 CP poll; mem. Canadian Sports Hall of Fame.

WRIGHT, Lee (field hockey); *b.* 28 Aug 1944, Vancouver, B.C.; *given name:* Lee Madison; *m.* Thelma Fynn; U of British Columbia, B.P.E., U of Southern California, M.A.; phys ed teacher; represented Canada in 1964, 1976 Olympics, 1963, 1971, 1976 pre-Olympics; competed in over 60 international matches for Canada including 1967, 1971, 1975 Pan-Am Games, bronze medal 1971, silver 1975; captain Canadian team on 1973 tour of England and Wales; both he and wife Thelma, a 1500m runner, won

silver medals at 1975 Mexico Pan-Am Games; *res.* West Vancouver, B.C.

WRIGHT, Thelma (track and field); *b.* 9 Oct 1951, Eastbourne, Eng.; *given name:* Thelma Sonia Fynn; *m.* Lee Madison Wright; U of British Columbia, B.P.E., teacher's certificate; teacher; Canadian T&F team mem. since 1969 specializing in middle distances 800-3000m; silver medal 1975 World Student Games Rome (3000m 8:54.9), 1975 Mexico Pan-Am Games (1500m 4:22.3); bronze medals 1970 Edinburgh Commonwealth Games (1500m 4:19.1), International cross-country, 1973 Pan-Pacific Games Toronto (1500m 4:18), 1974 New Zealand Commonwealth Games (1500m 4:12.3), 1975 New Zealand Games (1500m 4:19); four times Canadian 1500m champion, twice runner-up; once Canadian 3000m champion; once Canadian 800m runner-up; three times Canadian cross-country champion two and one-half miles, twice runner-up; bronze medal 1970 US cross-country; won 1974 road races Springbank four miles, Puerto Rico six and one-quarter miles; personal bests: 800m 2:05.1 1974, 1500m 4:10.5 1974, 3000m 8:54.9 1975; Canadian open 3000m record 1973-75, several age-class records; mem. Canadian 1972, 1976 Olympic teams; *res.* Vancouver, B.C.

WURTELE, Rhoda (skiing); *b.* 21 Jan 1922, Montreal, Que.; *given name:* Rhoda Isabella; *m.* Arnold Eaves; *children:* David Wurtele, John Ironside, Bruce Arnold; Trafalgar School for Girls, Notre Dame Secretarial School; ski club director; represented Canada 1948, 1952 Olympics; won US National downhill, combined Ogden Utah 1947, Canadian downhill, slalom, combined Mt. Tremblant 1951, Norwegian National Holmenkollen Vos slalom, giant slalom, combined 1952, Quebec Kandahar, Far West Kandahar, Harriman Cup Sun Valley, Roch Cup Aspen 1957, North American combined Aspen 1957; third Arleberg Kandahar downhill Chamonix France 1948; with twin sister won Canadian female athlete of year 1944, runner-up to Joe Krol as Canadian athlete of year 1945; mem. US National Ski, AAU of C Halls of Fame; *res.* Montreal, Que.

WURTELE, Rhona (skiing, swimming); *b.* 21 Jan 1922; *div.* Gene Alan Gillis; *children:* Christopher Wurtele, Margaret Rose, Nancy Joanne, Jere Alan; Trafalgar School for Girls, Mother House secretarial school, Sir George Williams U, U of Oregon; ski club director; won Quebec, Canadian swimming titles in 50, 100yd freestyle, set provincial records in both; Idaho State 1m diving title; with twin sister won Canadian female athlete of year 1944, runner-up to Joe Krol as Canadian athlete of year 1945, Canadian, US national titles in slalom, downhill, giant slalom and major races in US and Canada; mem. US FIS team 1950; mem. Canadian Olympic team 1948 St. Moritz; mem. 1973 Quebec ladies' interprovincial golf team, Summerlea club champion; mem. US National Ski, AAU of C Halls of Fame; *res.* Montreal, Que.

WYDARENY, John (football); *b.* 15 Feb 1941, Hearst, Ont.; *m.* Janet Elizabeth Gowans; *children:* John Christopher; U of Western Ontario, B.A., U of Toronto, B.Ed.; teacher; Ontario 440yd championship 1955-57; with Johnny Metras' Western Mustangs OQAA all-star as backfielder; turned pro Toronto Argos 1963-65, *Globe and Mail* all-star each year as defensive backfielder; dealt to Edmonton Eskimos with Ron Brewer for Al Ecuyer and Barry Mitchelson 1966-72; three times WFC all-star, twice all-Canadian; Jackie Parker Trophy as Eskimos' MVP 1969; in 10 CFL seasons 52 interceptions for 747yds; gained 208yds on interceptions 1967, 127yds in Edmonton at Calgary game 1967; both 1969, 1970 recorded 11 interceptions to lead WFC and CFL; *res.* St. Albert, Alta.

WYNNE, Ivor (coaching); *b.* 2 Nov 1918, Wales, *d.* 1 Nov 1970, Hamilton, Ont.; *given name:* Ifor; *m.* Frances; *children:* Bob, John; Central HS, McMaster U, B.A., Syracuse U, M.A., OCE; educator; nickname The Driver; played two seasons with Canadian champion Cloverleafs basketball team including tour of Philippines; appointed athletic director McMaster 1948; pres. CIAU, governor O-QAA; 16 years color commentator for pro, intercollegiate football games on radio, TV with sportscaster Norm Marshall; Hamilton Civic Stadium renamed in his honor.

YETMAN, Wayne (track); *b.* 8 Oct 1946, Toronto, Ont.; *given name:* Wayne Douglas; U of Western Ontario, B.A., U of Toronto; park planner; won 1968 Detroit marathon; 10th Antwerp, 13th Puerto Rico, 19th Boston marathons 1969; 10th 1970 Boston Marathon and member of championship Toronto Olympic team; won 1975 Toronto Police Games marathon; second Skylon (Buffalo to Niagara Falls) 1975; won Canadian Olympic trials, top honors in 1976 Ottawa National Capital marathon in 2:16.32; 36th 1976 Olympic marathon in 2:24; *res.* Toronto, Ont.

YORK, Teri (diving); *b.* 11 Nov 1955, Winnipeg, Man.; *given name:* Theresa Kathleen; Simon Fraser U; student; Canadian junior 3m, 1m diving champion 1969-72; mem. 1972, 1976 Olympic diving teams; 1974 third Swedish Cup 3m, second Finnish championships 10m, won Czechoslovakian 3m, won US national 10m; won Canadian national 3m, tower 1973-75; third Commonwealth Games Christchurch N.Z. 1974; sixth 10m, seventh 3m world championships Cali Colombia 1975; *res.* Simon Fraser campus, B.C.

YOST, Ken (coaching); *b.* 24 Sep 1905, Winnipeg, Man.; *given name:* Elmer Kenneth; *m.* Leona Pearl Tetrault (*d.*); *children:* Raymond, Carolyn, Richard; *m.* Christina Jackson; business college; retired railroad employee; coach 1948 Olympics Canadian T&F team, manager 1952 British Empire Games Canadian team; past pres. Winnipeg AA, Greater Winnipeg Girls' Senior Softball League, Manitoba Softball Association, Western Canada Softball Association, Canadian Softball Association; treasurer, later secretary AAU of C; convenor Winnipeg Senior Hockey League; mem. AAU of C Hall of Fame; *res.* Winnipeg, Man., Florida.

YOUNG, George (swimming); *b.* 1910, Toronto, Ont., *d.* 1972, Niagara Falls, Ont.; parks commission employee; won Toronto across-the-bay swim four times, Montreal bridge-to-bridge swim three times; held Canadian 220yd championship; swam Catalina channel in 15:45 1927; nickname Catalina Kid; staged own Lake Ontario marathon 1928 but pulled from water after only five miles; failed to finish three more CNE swims, won 1931; mem. Canadian Sports Hall of Fame.

YOUNG, Jim (football); *b.* 6 Jun 1943, Hamilton, Ont.; *given name:* James Norman; *div.; children:* Jamie, Sean, Cory; Queen's U, B.A.; pro football player; at Queen's won Omega Trophy 1964 as OUAA MVP; two years with Minnesota Vikings (NFL) before joining CFL and B.C. Lions; through 1976 season caught 455 passes for 8,182yds, 17.9 avg, 58 TDs and rushed 170 times for 849yds, 4.9 avg., 3 TDs; holds club records for receptions, yds receiving, TDs on passes; fifth all-time CFL receivers; all-Canadian 1972, twice WFC all-star; Schenley outstanding Canadian award 1970, 1972, runner-up 1969; represented B.C. in Countdown, Superstars competitions; subject of book *Dirty 30* by Jim Taylor; *res.* Vancouver, B.C.

YOUNG, Joe (track and field); *b.* 4 May 1920, Hamilton, Ont.; *given name:* Joseph Riley; *m.* Mary; *children:* Joseph, Jennifer, Martha; McMaster U, B.A., B.P.E., OCE; supervisor phys ed Hamilton Board of Education; won Ontario intermediate 440yd championship 1936, Canadian junior 440yd 1938, mem. Canadian senior mile relay champions 1938; coached HS teams in T&F, basketball, football 1946-66 in Woodstock, Ottawa, Hamilton; since 1960 registered Canadian T&F official; chief starter 1976 Montreal Olympics; *res.* Ancaster, Ont.

YOUNGBERG, Jane (badminton); *b.* 25 Dec 1948, Alysbury, Eng.; *given name:* Jane Marie Dubord; *m.* Edward Youngberg; Kelvin HS, U of British Columbia, B.Ed.; teacher; with Sue Latournier won 1965 junior doubles age 15; with Barbara Nash won Canadian ladies' junior doubles 1967-68; Canadian ladies' Open and Closed singles titles, with Barb Welch Open and Closed doubles 1974; repeat doubles victory 1975; mem. Canadian Uber Cup team Jakarta Indonesia 1972, 1975 beating former world champion Etsuko Takenaka of Japan 1975; competed in 1974 Christchurch Commonwealth Games, Devlin Cup Matches vs US; with Sherry Boyce Canadian women's doubles 1976, quarterfinals all-England singles; won 1977 Canadian women's singles, with Barb Welch Canadian women's doubles; World Cup semifinals with Wendy Clarkson; *res.* Surrey, B.C.

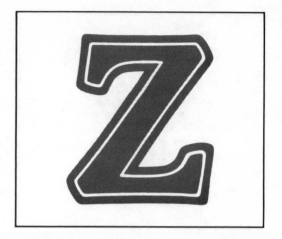

ZUGER, Joe (football); *b.* 25 Feb 1940, Homestead, Pa.; *given name:* Joseph Mark; *m.* Eleanor Townsend; *children:* Beth, Joe Jr., Amy; Arizona State U; sales rep.; led all US colleges in punting, passing; Arizona State MVP 1961; pro Hamilton Tiger-Cats 1962 as defensive back until injury to Bernie Faloney provided opportunity to quarterback team; CFL record 1962-71: threw 1,618 passes, 814 completions for 12,676yds, 95 interceptions, 76 TDs, 1,075 punts for 48,930yds, 68 singles, record 45.5 avg.; managed Hamilton Wentworth Curling Club; coached Mount Hamilton peewee hockey teams to two league titles; closed football career with Detroit Lions 1972; *res.* Hamilton, Ont.

Index

Autosport

BECK, Gary
BOYCE, Walter
BRACK, Bill
CARTER, Moe
EMERSON, Eddie
HEIMRATH, Ludwig
HILL, Craig
KROLL, Horst
RATHGEB, Chuck
ROSS, Earl
RYAN, Peter
VILLENEUVE, Gilles
WIETZES, Eppie
WOODS, Doug

Backpacking

PIOTROWSKI, Irene

Badminton

BARNES, Rolph
CARNWATH, Jim
CLARKSON, Wendy
FABRIS, Lucio
HARRIS, Lesley
KEMP, Sally
KIRKCONNELL, Herb
LYLE, Dulcie
MACDONNELL, Wayne
NASH, Jack
PAULSON, Jamie
PURCELL, Jack
ROLLICK, Bruce
ROLLICK, Judi
SAMIS, John
SHEDD, Marjory
TINLINE, Dorothy
UNDERHILL, Eileen
UNDERHILL, John
WALTON, Dorothy
WELCH, Barbara
YOUNGBERG, Jane

Ballooning

RATHGEB, Chuck

Baseball

ADAMS, Dick
ANDERSON, Gabby
BENSON, Lorne
BERTOIA, Reno
BLAKE, Toe
BONIFACE, George
BOX, Ab
BRIGHT, Johnny
CHAPMAN, Art
COLMAN, Frank
CONACHER, Lionel
CONGALTON, William
COSENTINO, Frank
CREIGHTON, Dale
DALTON, Chuck
EDWARDS, Jake
ELIOWITZ, Abe
ELLIOTT, Bob
EVON, Russ
FARMER, Jim
FINNAMORE, Arthur
GIARDINO, Wayne
GIBSON, George
GORMAN, T. P.
HARVEY, Doug
HAYES, George
HILLER, John
JACKSON, Russ
JENKINS, Ferguson
KARCZ, Zeno
LAPTHORNE, Whitey
LOGAN, Tip
MABEY, Hap
MALCOLM, Andrew
MARCHILDON, Phil
MASTERS, Wally
MCKAY, Roy
MCKENZIE, Tom
MCKILLOP, Bob
MILES, Rollie
MILNE, Howie
MORRIS, Jim
O'BRIEN, John
O'NEILL, Tip
ORR, Bobby
PARRY, Jack

PEARSON, Mike
PEDEN, Doug
PERRY, Gordon
PYZER, Doug
ROBERTSON, Sandy
ROUSSEAU, Bobby
SHAUGHNESSY, Shag
SMITH, Murray
STEAD, Ron
TAKAHASHI, Masao
THOMAS, Paul
THORBURN, Cliff
UPPER, Wray
WHITE, Tommy
WILKES, Jimmy

Basketball

AGER, Barry
AITCHISON, Gordon
ALDRIDGE, Dick
ALLISON, Ian
ANDREWS, Porky
BAKER, Norm
BRIGHT, Johnny
BRUNO, Al
BURNHAM, Faye
CAMPBELL, Woody
CHAPMAN, Art
CHAPMAN, Chuck
COOKE, Jack Kent
COULTHARD, Bill
COURTRIGHT, Jim
CREIGHTON, Dale
CZAJA, Mitch
DALTON, Chuck
DONOHUE, Jack
DOUTHWRIGHT, Joyce
DUFRESNE, Coleen
ELLIOTT, Bob
EVON, Russ
FARMER, Jim
FERRARO, John
FRASER, Bud
GARROW, Alex
GLOAG, Norm
GOLAB, Tony
GRANT, Bud

GURNEY, Jack
HEANEY, Brian
HENDRICKSON, Lefty
HEVENOR, George
HOWSON, Barry
KAUFMANIS, Eric
KEMP, Sally
LOGAN, Tip
MACDONALD, Noel
MACFARLANE, Gus
MACPHERSON, Kitch
MALCOLM, Andrew
MCDONALD, Vern
MCKIBBON, John
METRAS, John
MONNOT, Ray
MORRIS, Jim
MULLINS, Peter
NAISMITH, James
O'BILLOVICH, Bob
O'CONNOR, Zeke
OSBORNE, Bob
PAGE, Percy
PATAKY, Bill
PATRICK, Lynn
PATRICK, Muzz
PEDEN, Doug
PETTINGER, Glen
PHIBBS, Bob
PICKELL, Bob
PYZER, Doug
RAE, Al
RICHMAN, Ruby
RIDD, Carl
RIZAK, Gene
ROBERTSON, Sandy
SHEDD, Marjory
SHOULDICE, Hap
SILCOTT, Liz
SIMPSON, Bob
STEVENSON, Art
SUZUKI, Art
TATARCHUK, Hank
THOMAS, Paul
TINDALL, Frank
TOTZKE, Carl
VOYLES, Carl
WADE, Harry

WHITE, Dalt
WIGSTON, Fran
WILSON, Ben
WILSON, Ruth
WYNNE, Ivor

Billiards

CHENIER, Georges
EMERSON, Eddie
MILLER, Doug Jr.
THORBURN, Cliff
WRIGHT, Joe Sr.

Bobsledding

ANAKIN, Doug
EMERY, John
EMERY, Vic
KIRBY, Peter
RATHGEB, Chuck

Bowling

BALLANTINE, Bonny
EDGE, Ken
ELFORD, Gear
EVON, Russ
HOHL, Elmer
MARTEL, Marty
MARTIN, John
MILLER, Doug Jr.
MILLER, Russ
MITCHELL, Ray
ROBINSON, Blondie
RYAN, Tommy
TOTZKE, Bob
VALENTAN, Walter

Boxing

ANDERSEN, Dale
BATH, Doc
BELANGER, Frenchy
BENSON, Lorne
BROSSEAU, Eugene
BROUILLARD, Lou
BURNS, Tommy
CALLURA, Jackie
CHUVALO, George

CONACHER, Lionel
CONNELL, Charlie
CONNOLLY, Edward
COTTON, Harry
DELANEY, Jack
DIXON, George
DUBOIS, Theo
DURELLE, Yvon
FAUL, Adam
FEAR, Cap
GRAHAM, Charles
GWYNNE, Lefty
HERLEN, Ossie
HUNT, Ted
KERWIN, Gale
LABLANCHE, George
LANGFORD, Sam
LUFTSPRING, Sammy
MCLARNIN, Jimmy
MCWHIRTER, Cliff
PATRICK, Muzz
PEARCE, Bobby
PELKEY, Arthur
PERCIVAL, Lloyd
PULFORD, Harvey
REID, Bobby
RETI, Harvey
RICHARDSON, Blair
SANDULO, Joey
SCHNEIDER, Bert
SULLIVAN, Tommy
UNGERMAN, Irv
WHITE, Dennis
WRIGHT, Joe Sr.

Broomball

HAYES, John

Builder

ANDERSON, George
BERGER, Sam
BISHOP, Jim
CAMPBELL, Clarence
CAMPBELL, R. D.
CAPOZZI, Herb
COOKE, Jack Kent
DARWIN, Howard

DAVIES, Jack
ELLIOTT, Bob
GORMAN, T. P.
HAMILTON, Jack
HAMMOND, Gord
HANSEN, Ina
HANSEN, Warren
HUME, Fred
KELLS, Morley
LALLY, Joe
LAVIOLETTE, Jack
MARTIN, John
MCKENZIE, Tait
NAISMITH, James
O'BRIEN, J. Ambrose
PATRICK, Frank
PATRICK, Lester
PERCIVAL, Lloyd
RATHGEB, Chuck
ROBINSON, Bobby
ROSS, Art
ROSS, P. D.
RYAN, Joe
RYAN, Tommy
SMYTHE, Conn
TAYLOR, E. P.
TRIHEY, Harry
WARREN, Harry

Canoeing

AMYOT, Frank
BALES, John
EMERY, John
GERARD, Eddie
GREENSHIELDS, Harry
HEVENOR, George
HOLLOWAY, Sue
HOMER-DIXON, Marjorie
HUNT, Claudia
PULFORD, Harvey
SHOULDICE, Hap
TIPPETT, Karen
TUBMAN, Joe
WOOD, John

Coaching

ABEL, Sid
ADAMS, Jack
ADAMS, Robert
ALDRIDGE, Dick
ALLISON, Ian
ANDERSON, Verne
ANDREWS, Porky
APSIMON, John
ARBOUR, Al
ARMSTRONG, George
BATSTONE, Harry
BAUER, David
BEDECKI, Tom
BLAIR, Wren
BLAKE, Toe
BOESE, Kurt
BOUCHER, Bob
BOUCHER, Frank
BOUCHER, George
BOWMAN, Scotty
BRABENEC, Hana
BRABENEC, Josef
BRANCATO, George
BREEN, Joe
BRODA, Turk
BROWN, Dick
BRUNO, Al
BURNHAM, Faye
CAHILL, Leo
CAMPBELL, Hugh
CAMPBELL, R. D.
CLAIR, Frank
CLANCY, King
CLAPPER, Dit
COSENTINO, Frank
COULTER, Bruce
CURTIS, Ulysses
CUSTIS, Bernie
DAIGNEAULT, Doug
DAVIS, Pat
DAWSON, Bob
DAY, Hap
DELAHEY, Wally
DELVECCHIO, Alex
DOJACK, Paul
DONOHUE, Jack

ELIOWITZ, Abe
ELLIOTT, Bob
EON, Suzanne
EYNON, Bob
FILCHOCK, Frank
FITZGERALD, Billy
FOOT, Fred
FRACAS, Gino
FREDRICKSON, Frank
FRITZ, Bob
GADSBY, Bill
GARVIE, Gord
GILBERT, Don
GORDON, Jack
GORMAN, T. P. Tommy
GOTTA, Jack
GRANT, Bud
GRIFFING, Dean
GRIFFITH, Harry
HALDER, Wally
HARTLEY, Errol
HAYES, John
HAYMAN, Lew
HEANEY, Brian
HENDERSON, Paul
HENDERSON, Scott
HENLEY, Garney
HENRY, Camille
HILDEBRAND, Ike
HILL, Harvey
HINDMARCH, Bob
HOWELL, Harry
IMLACH, Punch
IRVIN, Dick Sr.
IVAN, Tommy
JACKSON, Russ
JACOBS, Dave
JACOBS, Jack
JANZEN, Henry
JAUCH, Ray
KELLS, Morley
KELLY, Red
KEMP, Sally
KEYS, Eagle
KILREA, Brian
KNOX, Walter
LACH, Elmer
LASHUK, Mike

LEAR, Les
LEMHENYI, Dezso
LEYSHON, Glynn
LINDLEY, Earl
LINDSAY, Ted
LONEY, Don
LONG, Bill
MANNING, Peter
MASTERS, Wally
MCCANCE, Ches
MCDONALD, Vern
MCKENNA, Ann
MCKINNON, Archie
MEEKER, Howie
METRAS, John
MILLER, Doug Jr.
MOORE, George
MORRIS, Teddy
MULLINS, Peter
MURPHY, Ron
NAKAMURA, Hiroshi
NEVILLE, Bill
NEWMAN, Bernie
NEWTON, Jack
OBECK, Vic
O'BILLOVICH, Bob
O'MALLEY, Terry
PAGE, Percy
PARKER, Jackie
PATRICK, Lester
PATRICK, Lynn
PEARSON, Mike
PERCIVAL, Lloyd
POCE, Paul
PRIMEAU, Joe
PUGH, Bob
PUGH, Lionel
PULFORD, Bob
REAY, Billy
REBHOLZ, Russ
REEVE, Ted
REID, Bobby
RICHMAN, Ruby
RODDEN, Mike
ROSS, Art
RYDER, Gus
SANDULO, Joey
SAZIO, Ralph

SCHLEIMER, Joseph
SHORE, Eddie
SHOULDICE, Hap
SINDEN, Harry
SNELLING, Deryk
SPENCER, Jim
STANLEY, Barney
STEVENS, Warren
STEWART, Ron
STUKUS, Annis
SULLIVAN, Tommy
SZTEHLO, Zoltan
TESSIER, Orv
THOMAS, Paul
THOMPSON, George
THOMSON, Earl
TIMMIS, Brian
TINDALL, Frank
TOTZKE, Carl
VOYLES, Carl
WALKER, Peahead
WATT, Tom
WELLAND, Cooney
WEST, Art
WHITE, Dalt
WIGSTON, Fran
WILLIAMS, Jerry
WOO, Wes
WRIGHT, Joseph Sr.
WYNNE, Ivor
YOST, Ken

Cricket

FLETCHER, Doug
LYON, George S.
PERCIVAL, Lloyd
RATHGEB, Chuck
SOMERVILLE, Sandy
WARREN, Harry

Curling

ADAMS, Harry
ANDERSON, Don
AVERY, Frank
BALDWIN, Matt
BEGIN, Terry
BENSON, Lorne

BRAUNSTEIN, Terry
BRAZEAU, Howard
BROWN, Gord
BROWN, Ted
BUCHAN, Ken
CALLES, Ada
CAMPBELL, Clarence
CAMPBELL, Colin
CAMPBELL, Garnet
COLE, Betty
CONGALTON, Jim
COOMBE, Eldon
CREBER, Bill
CZAJA, Mitch
DEWITTE, Marcel
DUGRE, Lou
DUGUID, Don
EDWARDS, Jake
ELLIOTT, Bob
FEDORUK, Sylvia
FERGUSON, Reid
FORGUES, Keith
GERVAIS, Hec
GILBERT, Bob
GILBERT, Don
GILBERT, Gord
GILBERT, Peter
GREEN, Ron
GUROWKA, Joe
HANSEN, Ina
HANSEN, Warren
HUDSON, Bruce
HUDSON, Gordon
HUNTER, Rod
LAMB, Joe
LANGLOIS, Al
LEACH, Al
LEWIS, Bill
LEWIS, Elinor
LOGAN, Tip
MABEY, Hap
MANAHAN, Cliff
MANN, Avard
MANN, Bob
MARTIN, Flora
MCCANCE, Ches
MCKEE, Joyce
MCMILLAN, Roy

MCMURRAY, Mary
MCTAVISH, Boyd
MELESCHUK, Orest
MILLER, Russ
MORRISON, Lee
NASH, Jack
NORTHCOTT, Ron
PERRY, Gordon
PETTAPIECE, Jim
PEZER, Vera
PHILLIPS, Alf Jr.
PHILLIPS, Alf Sr.
PHILLIPS, Dave
PHILLIPS, Peter
PIASKOSKI, Jim
PICKERING, Bob
PORTER, Muriel
PROULX, Rita
PROVOST, Barry
RICHARDSON, Arnold
RICHARDSON, Ernie
ROWAN, Sheila
SAVAGE, Paul
SCOTT, Alex
SINCLAIR, Marjorie
STEG, Ray
STOREY, Fred
THIBODEAU, Nick
TWA, Don
URSULIAK, Wally
WAGNER, Bill
WAITE, Jim
WALSH, Billy Jr.
WALSH, Billy Sr.
WATSON, Ken
WELSH, Jim
WERENICH, Ed
WOOD, Bryan
WOOD, Howie
WOOD, Lionel
WOOD, Nora
WOOD, Pappy
WOODS, Bob

Cycling

BURKA, Sylvia
CASSAN, Gerry

DAVIES, Jim
DUBOIS, Theo
LOVELL, Jocelyn
MCLAUGHLIN, Sam
MCRAE, Ed
MURPHY, Pat
PEDEN, Doug
PEDEN, Torchy
WARREN, Harry

Darts

MILLER, Russ

Diving

ARMSTRONG, Ken
ATHENS, George Sr.
BOYS, Bev
CARRUTHERS, Liz
CRANHAM, Scott
FRIESEN, Ron
GROUT, Glen
KIEFER, Eniko
MACDONALD, Irene
MACLEOD, Tammy
MCKINNON, Archie
MEISSNER, Ernie
NUTTER, Janet
PHILLIPS, Alf Sr.
PHOENIX, Skip
ROBERTSON, Nancy
SELLER, Peggy
SHATTO, Cindy
WEBB, Don
YORK, Teri

Dogsledding

NANSEN, Elizabeth
ST. GODARD, Emile

Entrepreneur

COOKE, Jack Kent
DARWIN, Howard
GORMAN, T. P.

Equestrian

BOYLEN, Christilot
DAY, Jim
DUNLAP, Moffat
ELDER, Jim
GAYFORD, Tom
HAHN, Robin
HALL-HOLLAND, Kelly
IRVING, Wendy
MCLAUGHLIN, Sam
MILLAR, Ian
SCOTT, Barbara Ann
STUBBS, Lorraine
SZTEHLO, Zoltan
THOMAS, Shirley
VAILLANCOURT, Michel

Fencing

ANDRU, John
APSIMON, John
CONYD, Magdy
FOXCROFT, Bob
HENNYEY, Donna
HENNYEY, Imre
LAVOIE, Marc
SCHWENDE, Carl
SZTEHLO, Zoltan
WIEDEL, Gerry
WIEDEL, Pacita
WONG, Lester

Field Hockey

BURNHAM, Faye
DOUTHWRIGHT, Joyce
HARTLEY, Errol
HOBKIRK, Alan
KEMP, Sally
MCKENNA, Ann
PLUMMER, Reg
WARREN, Harry
WRIGHT, Lee

Figure Skating

ALLETSON, Kim
BAIN, Dan
BARRON, Andy

SMITH, Alfred
SMYLIE, Rod
SPRAGUE, Dave
STERNBERG, Gerry
STEVENS, Warren
STEVENSON, Art
STEVENSON, Roy
STEWART, Ron
STIRLING, Bummer
STOCKTON, Don
STOREY, Red
STUKUS, Annis
STUKUS, Bill
STUKUS, Frank
SUGERMAN, Ken
TAYLOR, Bobby
THELEN, Dave
THOMAS, Jim
THORNTON, Bernie
TIMMIS, Brian
TINDALL, Frank
TINSLEY, Buddy
TOMMY, Andy Sr.
TOOGOOD, Ted
TOSH, Wayne
TOTZKE, Carl
TPIPUCKA, Frank
TUBMAN, Joe
TUCKER, Whit
URNESS, Ted
VAUGHAN, Kaye
VOYLES, Carl
WADE, Harry
WALKER, Bill
WALKER, Peahead
WEATHERALL, Jim
WELCH, Huck
WELTON, John
WEST, Art
WESTWICK, Harry
WHITE, Dalt
WHITEHOUSE, Reg
WILKINSON, Tom
WILLIAMS, Jerry
WILLSEY, Ray
WILSON, Ben
WOOD, Lionel
WOODWARD, Rod

WRIGHT, Joe Jr.
WRIGHT, Joe Sr.
WYDARENY, John
YOUNG, Jim
ZUGER, Joe

Golf

ANDERSON, Don
ANDREWS, Porky
BALDING, Al
BOURASSA, Jocelyne
BRYDSON, Gordie
COLE, Betty
COOKE, Graham
COWAN, Gary
DARLING, Dora
DARLING, Judy
EDWARDS, Jake
ERVASTI, Ed
FARLEY, Phil
FLETCHER, Doug
FLETCHER, Pat
FRASER, Alexa Stirling
GAY, Mary
GETLIFFE, Ray
HEVENOR, George
HOLTSCHEITER, Herb
HOMENUIK, Wilf
JACKSON, Robbie
JENSEN, Al
JOHNSTON, John
KAUFMANIS, Eric
KERN, Ben
KNUDSON, George
KOLAR, Stan
LAMB, Joe
LAMB, Willie
LEDDY, Jack
LEONARD, Stan
LYLE, Dulcie
LYON, George S.
MACKENZIE, Ada
MOORE, Gail Harvey
NASH, Jack
NEZAN, Andy
NORMAN, Moe
PALMER, Marilyn

PANASIUK, Bob
PEZER, Vera
POST, Sandra
REID, Robert
ROUSSEAU, Bobby
SHAUGHNESSY, Frank Jr.
SOMERVILLE, Sandy
STIMPSON, Earl
STREIT, Marlene Stewart
SULLIVAN, Joe
TALLON, Dale
THOMPSON, Mabel
TURNBULL, Barbara
WAITE, Jim
WESLOCK, Nick
WILSON, Doug Jr.
WILSON, Ruth

Gymnastics

CARRUTHERS, Liz
DIACHUN, Jennifer
GAGNIER, Ed
KIHN, Richard
MITRUK, Steve
NEWMAN, Bernie
NOONEY, John
RUSSELL, Ernestine
WEILER, Willie

Handball

DUMELIE, Larry
KULAI, Dan
LAVOIE, Marc
RYDER, Gus

Harness Racing

BALDWIN, Ralph
CHAPMAN, John
FEAGAN, Ron
FILION, Herve
FINDLEY, John
GILMOUR, Buddy
GORMAN, T. P.
HODGINS, Clint
MACKINNON, Dan
WAPLES, Keith

Hockey

ABEL, Sid
ADAMS, Jack
AHEARN, Frank
APPS, Syl Sr.
ARBOUR, Al
ARMSTRONG, George
BACKSTROM, Ralph
BAIN, Dan
BARRY, Martin
BATH, Doc
BATHGATE, Andy
BAUER, Bobby
BAUER, David
BAUN, Bobby
BEDARD, Bob
BEDECKI, Tom
BELIVEAU, Jean
BENEDICT, Clint
BENSON, Lorne
BENTLEY, Doug
BENTLEY, Max
BERENSON, Red
BISHOP, Jim
BLAIR, Wren
BLAKE, Toe
BOON, Dickie
BOUCHER, Bill
BOUCHER, Bob
BOUCHER, Frank
BOUCHER, George
BOWER, Johnny
BOWIE, Russell
BOWMAN, Scotty
BREWER, Carl
BROADBENT, Punch
BRODA, Turk
BRUNETEAU, Mud
BRYDSON, Gordie
BUCYK, John
BURCH, Billy
CAMERON, Harry
CAMPBELL, Clarence
CHABOT, Lorne
CHEEVERS, Gerry
CLANCY, King
CLAPPER, Dit

CLARKE, Bobby
CLEGHORN, Odie
CLEGHORN, Sprague
COLVILLE, Neil
CONACHER, Charlie
CONACHER, Lionel
CONNELL, Alec
COOK, Bill
COOKE, Jack Kent
COPP, Bobby
COULTER, Art
COURNOYER, Yvan
COWLEY, Bill
CRAWFORD, Rusty
DARRAGH, Jack
DARWIN, Howard
DAVIDSON, Scotty
DAY, Hap
DELVECCHIO, Alex
DENNENY, Cy
DIONNE, Marcel
DRILLON, Gordie
DRINKWATER, Graham
DRYDEN, Ken
DUFF, Dick
DUNDERDALE, Tommy
DUNLAP, Frank
DURNAN, Bill
DYE, Babe
EAGLESON, Alan
EBBELS, Bill
ELLIOTT, Chaucer
ESPOSITO, Phil
EVON, Russ
FARMER, Ken
FERGUSON, John
FLETCHER, Doug
FORHAN, Bob
FOYSTON, Frank
FREDRICKSON, Frank
GADSBY, Bill
GARDINER, Chuck
GARDINER, Herb
GEOFFRION, Bernie
GERARD, Eddie
GETLIFFE, Ray
GILBERT, Rod
GILMOUR, Billy

GOODFELLOW, Ebbie
GORDON, Jack
GORMAN, T. P.
GRANT, Mike
GREEN, Shorty
GRIFFIS, Si
HAINSWORTH, George
HALDER, Wally
HALL, Glenn
HALL, Joe
HAMILTON, Jack
HAMMOND, Alvin
HARVEY, Doug
HAY, George
HAYES, George
HEBENTON, Andy
HENRY, Camille
HERN, Riley
HEXTALL, Bryan Sr.
HIBBERD, Ted
HILDEBRAND, Ike
HILLMAN, Larry
HINDMARCH, Bob
HOLMES, Derek
HOLMES, Hap
HOOPER, Tom
HORNER, Red
HORTON, Tim
HOWE, Gordie
HOWE, Syd
HOWELL, Harry
HOWELL, Ron
HULL, Bobby
HUME, Fred
HUTTON, Bouse
HYLAND, Harry
IMLACH, Punch
IRVIN, Dick Sr.
ION, Mickey
IVAN, Tommy
JACKSON, Busher
JAMES, Gerry
JOHNSON, Ching
JOHNSON, Moose
JOHNSON, Tom
JOLIAT, Aurel
JUCKES, Gordon
KEATS, Duke

KOVITS, Herman
LEACH, Al
MABEY, Hap
MARTIN, Flora
MORRISON, Lee
PEZER, Vera
PUGH, Bob
PYZER, Doug
ROWAN, Sheila
RUTHOWSKY, Dave
SHOULDICE, Hap
SIMPSON, Bill
SKINNER, Larry
STRIKE, Hilda
WAGNER, Bill
WILSON, Ruth
YOST, Ken

Speedboat Racing

HAYWARD, Bob
LOMBARDO, Guy

Speedskating

BAPTIE, Norval
BARRON, Andrew
BROOKS, Lela
BURKA, Sylvia
CASSAN, Gerry
GORMAN, Charles
HURDIS, John
KELLY, Con
MACKAY, Craig
MCCULLOCH, Jack
PRIESTNER, Cathy
ROBSON, Fred
STACK, Frank
WILSON, Jean

Squash

ADAIR, Colin
BRUCE, Ian
EBBELS, Bill
HENDERSON, Paul
LYLE, Dulcie
MACKEN, Brendan
MACKEN, Jim

PULFORD, Harvey
ROBERTSON, Sandy

Swimming

AMUNDRUD, Gail
ARUSOO, Toomas
BAKER, Joann
BARBER, Sara
BARRON, Andy
BELL, Marilyn
BOURNE, Munroe
CAMPBELL, Shirley
CHENARD, Line
CLARK, Barbara
CLIFF, Leslie
COOK, Wendy
CORSIGLIA, Robin
COUGHLAN, Angela
DEWAR, Phyllis
DOCKERILL, Sylvia
EMERY, John
EVANS, Clay
EVON, Russ
EYNON, Bob
FARMER, Jim
FOWLIE, Jim
GARAPICK, Nancy
GIBSON, Cheryl
GRIFFIN, Audrey
GROUT, Cameron
GURR, Donna-Marie
HARTZELL, Irene
HAUCH, Paul
HAYES, Cheryl
HODGSON, George
HUNT, Helen
HUTTON, Ralph
JARDIN, Anne
KASTING, Robert
KENNEDY, Bill
KENNEDY, Louise
KER, Michael
LAY, Marion
LOARING, John
LOCKHART, Gene
LUMSDON, Cliff
LUMSDON, Kim

LYLE, Dulcie
MACDONALD, Gary
MAHONY, Bill
MCGILL, Frank
MCKINNON, Archie
NICHOLAS, Cindy
PATRICK, Muzz
PEDEN, Doug
PICKELL, Stephen
POUND, Richard
PRIESTLEY, Gladys
QUIRK, Wendy
ROBERTSON, Bruce
ROGERS, Bruce
RYDER, Gus
SLOAN, Susan
SMITH, Becky
SMITH, Graham
SMITH, Shannon
STEWART, Mary
TANNER, Elaine
WATSON, Whipper Billy
WHITTALL, Beth
YOUNG, George

Synchronized Swimming

EON, Suzanne
HARTZELL, Irene
SELLER, Peggy

Table Tennis

ATHWAL, Nimi
CAETANO, Errol
DOMONKOS, Mariann
FORGO, Christine
HEAP, Alan
HSU, Gloria
NESUKAITIS, Violetta

Tennis

BABBITT, Ethel
BABBITT, John
BEDARD, Bob
BELKIN, Mike
BLACKWOOD, Marjorie